Deliberate Force

A Case Study in Effective Air Campaigning

Final Report of the Air University Balkans Air Campaign Study

Edited by
Col Robert C. Owen, USAF

Air University Press
Maxwell Air Force Base, Alabama

January 2000

Library of Congress Cataloging-in-Publication Data

Deliberate force a case study in effective air campaigning : final report of the Air University Balkans air campaign study / edited by Robert C. Owen.
    p. cm.
  Includes bibliographical references and index.
  ISBN 1-58566-076-0
    1. Yugoslav War, 1991–1995—Aerial operations. 2. Yugoslav War, 1991–1995—Campaigns—Bosnia and Hercegovina. 3. Yugoslav War, 1991–1995—Foreign participation. 4. Peacekeeping forces—Bosnia and Hercegovina. 5. North Atlantic Treaty Organization—Armed Forces—Aviation. 6. Bosnia and Hercegovina—History, Military. I. Owen, Robert C., 1951–

DR1313.7.A47 D45 2000
949.703—dc21
                                                               99-087096

Disclaimer

Contents

Illustrations

Tables

Foreword

Every airman or person interested in the art and science of air and space warfare should read this book. True to the direction of Gen James Jamerson, former deputy commander in chief of US European Command, and me, the Air University Balkans Air Campaign Study (BACS) has emerged as a balanced and wide-ranging discussion of the Deliberate Force air campaign, which occurred during the fall of 1995. Exploiting the sources and resources available to them, the BACS team members have laid out a mile-wide and foot-deep exploration of the context, theoretical foundations, planning, execution, leadership, and effects of this milestone event. In so doing, they have contributed significantly to our knowledge about the political, military, technical, and human elements that shape air campaigns and influence their outcomes. Moreover, the BACS offers insights into persistent questions of military planners, such as the relationship of diplomacy and war; the synergy of land power, space power, and airpower; and the role of chance and "fog" in the conduct and outcome of air and space warfare. Finally, because the BACS team from the start wrote this report for immediate declassification, virtually the entire report and all of its substantive elements are available here as an open source, only four years after the event. Given its scope, this book should contain material of interest to all aerospace-warfare practitioners and/or thinkers, regardless of their area of expertise.

The following are core implications of the BACS:

- Deliberate Force was *a* decisive element in shaping the outcome of the allied intervention into the Bosnian conflict, but its full effect must be understood in the context of the other political and military developments also under way at the time.
- The characteristics and weaponry of air and space warfare gave the diplomats and soldiers of the intervention a *usable*

tool of great power and flexibility with which to influence events in the Balkans region.

- For all of the capabilities of modern information technology, the scale, pace, human factors (such as leadership, culture, and conceptualization), and other nontechnical elements of Deliberate Force ensured that Clausewitz's trilogy of fog, friction, and chance remained important in shaping its ultimate outcome.
- If Deliberate Force is considered a new form of interventionism on behalf of peace, then the experience gained from that operation suggests the need for a review of our conceptions about the nature of military and diplomatic leadership in such circumstances.
- If it is to be useful, doctrine—as formalized advice on what military leaders should do when faced by certain kinds of problems—must be read and understood. But it also must be understood as a guide for *thinking* through problems ahead of time, rather than a recipe for their solution after the fact.

The study makes other important points, of course, and any given reader likely will find things with which to agree and disagree. However, these core implications of the BACS serve to illustrate its value, both as a historical document and as a spark for debate and thought—its real purpose.

I would be remiss if I did not commend the dedication and persistence of all the members of the BACS team. When they volunteered to participate in this study, we all understood that it would be a focused effort to capture the most important political and operational events of Deliberate Force and to start an archive of related materials to support further research. As they pursued their research, however, the team members soon realized that they had a hold on the tail of a much bigger "elephant" than anyone at Air University originally had expected. Deliberate Force turns out to have been a very complex event, composed of layered political, military, and human elements that all bore some level of examination. Despite its growing scale and complexity, every team member elected to stay with the study, even though it definitely was a "voluntary society" and even though their work on it was in

SEGMENT

addition to their assigned duties as faculty and staff at Air University. After most of the BACS team members dispersed to new assignments as far away as Germany and Hawaii, they continued to work the project and to meet all of the deadlines imposed on them by the editorial and declassification processes. The result of their dedication is this fine report, one that certainly benefited from the wide-ranging experiences and intellectual capabilities of the people who wrote it.

JAY W. KELLEY
Lieutenant General, USAF, Retired
Colorado Springs, Colorado
June 1999

About the
Editor

Col Robert C. Owen is chief of the Policy and Doctrine Division, Air Mobility Command, Scott AFB, Illinois. In that position he supervises the development and articulation of air-mobility concepts and doctrine and special projects, such as the command's involvement in the Expeditionary Air Force and Future Total Force Unit. At the time he directed the Balkans Air Campaign Study, Colonel Owen was dean of the School of Advanced Airpower Studies at Maxwell AFB, Alabama. While he served as chief of the Joint Doctrine Branch of the Doctrine Division at Headquarters United States Air Force, he wrote the *Chronology* volume of the *Gulf War Air Power Survey*. He also has published a number of journal articles and has a book, *The Rise of Global Airlift in the USAF*, in final editorial review. A command pilot with over three thousand hours of operational flying in the C-130 and T-41 aircraft, Colonel Owen holds an MA in African studies from UCLA and a PhD in military history from Duke University.

Preface

Operation Deliberate Force was the North Atlantic Treaty Organization (NATO) air campaign conducted between 30 August and 20 September 1995 to advance the cause of peace in the Balkans region. Lt Gen Jay W. Kelley, commander of Air University, Maxwell Air Force Base, Alabama, and Gen James L. Jamerson, deputy commander in chief of United States European Command, Stuttgart, Germany, jointly chartered the Balkans Air Campaign Study (BACS) in October 1995. They directed the BACS team to "capture" the planning and operational experience of Deliberate Force on behalf of Air University students preparing for future responsibilities as air-warfare planners and leaders, and on behalf of the broader community of air-warfare thinkers. Their specific direction entailed (1) writing a "mile-wide-and-foot-deep" report laying out the salient events, causal relationships, and implications of this important air campaign and (2) assembling a comprehensive archive of relevant oral and documentary evidence to support future research into the planning, execution, and diplomatic exploitation of Deliberate Force.[1]

To highlight this study's focus on the planning and execution of an air campaign, the BACS team adopted the following as its core research question: How and with what considerations did the planners and executors of Deliberate Force link military operations with the strategic, political, and diplomatic goals they were charged to attain? To make the report useful to a potentially broad audience, team members set out to answer this question through a wide-ranging examination of the geopolitical, sociological, diplomatic, technological, and operational factors that shaped the characteristics and outcome of this particular air campaign. Thus, the chapters of this report deal broadly with (1) the political and institutional context of Deliberate Force planning, (2) the actual planning of the campaign, (3) the execution of the campaign, and (4) the implications of those experiences. An important initial subtheme of the study was an effort to determine to what extent the planners and executors of Deliberate Force were cognizant of and/or wielded influence over factors that most significantly shaped the operation and determined its outcome. In other words, to what extent were they in charge of events and to what extent were events in charge of them? The team expected that the answer to those and other questions raised by the study would carry significant implications for theories and doctrines of airpower strategy and planning.

Assembling a comprehensive database on Deliberate Force proved more challenging than the campaign's relatively compact dimensions of scale and time first suggested. In contrast to their counterparts during the Persian Gulf War of 1990–91, the non-US coalition partners in Deliberate Force played a more independent and nearly coequal political and, to a lesser extent, military role with their American counterparts in the planning and conduct of the campaign. This level and consequence of non-US participation obliged BACS researchers to look far afield for data and perspectives on Deliberate Force. Their search was complicated by the return of many non-US midlevel planners and flying personnel involved in Deliberate Force to their home countries shortly after the campaign ended. Diplomatic circumstances further obliged the team to cast a wide net for data. Conducted as a step in a long effort to maintain peace in or at least contain the violence of the Balkans region, Deliberate Force was shaped and exploited by the often conflicting interests of numerous regional and global actors, including the United Nations (UN), NATO political and military agencies, diplomatic and military agencies of numerous European states, and, of course, the warring regional groups themselves. To the extent that barriers of secrecy, national sensitivities, and the limits of its charter allowed, the BACS team at least *asked* many of these sources for information and comments—with limited results.

Given the breadth of available sources and the constraints of time and resources, the BACS team focused on analyzing and describing Deliberate Force as a distinct military campaign. The team members did this in full awareness that the operation was a complex event—one that could be understood only in its full political and military context. The team also remained cognizant of the reluctance within some US military circles to use the word *campaign* to label the activities of a specific military component of a multiservice (joint) or multinational (combined) command. This reluctance is buttressed by fundamental US joint doctrine, which reserves the planning of campaigns for joint force commanders (JFC) and which relegates their component commanders to planning "operations" or annexes to the JFC's campaign plan.[2]

Nevertheless, describing Deliberate Force as a campaign makes good analytical sense. As a consciously connected series of air actions aimed at coercing the Bosnian Serbs to make military and political concessions, what happened over the skies of Bosnia in August and September 1995 essentially coincides with the US joint doctrinal definition of a campaign as "a series of related military operations aimed at accomplishing a strategic or operational objective within a given time and space."[3] Moreover, labeling Deliberate Force as a campaign fits authoritative usage by senior US defense leaders such as Secretary of Defense William Perry, who described it as a "massive air campaign" that "stunned" the Serbs with its "power and effectiveness."[4] Still, given the importance of definitions in the development and articulation of doctrine, the choice of *campaign* in this case will carry uncomfortable policy and budgetary implications for some readers. But that discomfort should not block an open-minded reading of this report.

For similar reasons of focus and conciseness, most members of the BACS team did not set out on their research in the expectation that Deliberate Force would fit neatly into some niche of the so-called continuum of war articulated in US doctrine.[5] As a method of articulating the types of conflict and war that might exist between the extremes of absolute peace and absolute war, the continuum-of-war concept usefully predicts the broad causes and political objectives of various kinds of conflict and, by implication, the sacrifices combatants will make. But the concept is not particularly useful as a predictor of the likely intensity, tactics, strategies, political ramifications, or many other specific details of such conflicts and wars. For example, for the United States and most UN member states, Deliberate Force was a campaign of limited importance to tangible vital interests. For the Balkan states, however, its outcome carried grave importance for their foreseeable political, social, and cultural destinies. Similarly, at the strategic level, Deliberate Force was a constrained exercise in power and risk management. At the tactical level, though, NATO airmen experienced the campaign as a microcosm of the operating tempos, tactics, weapons, and threats they would have expected to face in a high-intensity conflict in central Europe had the cold war gone hot.

Deliberate Force also does not fit neatly into the military operations other than war (MOOTW) subcategory of the continuum of war. Perhaps the campaign fit the MOOTW category politically since the UN and NATO launched it as a "peace operation," without any formal declarations of war. However, even in secondary research materials available to the team at the beginning of the study, Deliberate Force clearly had a split personality in terms of where it fit into the MOOTW concept. To the extent that NATO initiated the bombing to help the UN force Bosnian Serb military forces to cease shelling the UN-declared technical exclusion zones or "safe areas" around several large Bosnian cities, Deliberate Force was an exercise in "peacemaking." But to the extent that the bombing also underpinned ongoing efforts by the UN and the five-nation Contact Group to force the Serbs to enter into serious peace negotiations, the operation involved "peace enforcement." The operational complexity of Deliberate Force reinforced the sense that the real-world boundaries of this campaign would not conform to the theoretical boundaries delineated in MOOTW theory. Deliberate Force may have been a restrained peace operation strategically, but tactically it was an energetic operation characterized by the employment of technologically cutting-edge air forces.

As a consequence of these definitional ambiguities, the BACS report was never intended to fix Deliberate Force's place in an existing conflict taxonomy. Instead, as director of the report, I wanted it to describe the event as accurately and in as much detail as practical at the time. Even at the beginning, it was obvious to most—probably all—BACS team members that this particular air campaign had distinctive characteristics, the description of which would in itself justify the report. Several of these features stood out already, in outline at least, in the fall of 1995. First, Deliberate Force was strategically more of a match than might have first appeared. The countervailing commitments and objectives of the combatants tended to reduce the advantage of NATO's overwhelming military power. Second, the air campaign was tactically one-sided. The deployed land- and sea-based air forces of the NATO partners dwarfed the "air force" and ground-based air defenses of the Bosnian Serbs. Third, Deliberate Force was not a politically or militarily isolated event. It was, after all, conducted in support of—or at least in the context of—the political activities of several organizations and nations intervening in the Bosnian conflict. For that reason, by the fall of 1995, the air commanders had already stated their belief that, in the politically charged circumstances of the campaign, every tactical event of the operation potentially carried significant and immediate strategic political importance. Also, at the time of the air campaign, Croatia and the Bosnian Federation were conducting a coordinated ground offensive that successfully pushed Croatian Serb and Bosnian Serb military forces out of areas they had conquered previously. The BACS team understood that any useful assessment of the shape and influence of Deliberate Force eventually would have to consider the simultaneous impact of the ground campaign.

Given these salient elements, Deliberate Force's theoretical "survey mark," upon which most aspects of this study are oriented, is its unique identity as an air campaign conducted against an airpower-weak opponent, under conditions of political subtlety and limited time, in which every tactical event had great potential importance. This description of the characteristics and context of Operation Deliberate Force facilitates the effort of placing it in the existing body of theory and doctrine. As propositions, respectively, of how things work and of what actions will most likely produce desired results under anticipated circumstances, theories and doctrines are contextually dependent in their meaning and application. One must present any theoretical proposition about the forces of human affairs, cause-and-effect relationships, and so on, in the context of an accurate description of the circumstances under which such observed events and processes happened. Likewise, effective doctrine must reflect both a solid foundation of relevant theories, based on experience, and a carefully constructed description of the circumstances under which one expects an anticipated action to produce desired results. To become credible, an air planner's implicitly doctrinal statement that a new strike plan should incorporate an element of surprise, for example, must meet two criteria:

1. It must be related, even if only subconsciously in the minds of the people involved, to a theoretical understanding that a direct rlationship may exist between surprise and mission success.
2. It also must show—again, even if only subliminally—that a direct relationship exists between the circumstances of the action proposed and those underpinning the general theory relating surprise and success.

Likewise, future air commanders and their advisors can extract the wisdom of the Deliberate Force commander's decision to make all weapon aim-point selections himself, only if they have a clear understanding of the theoretical rationale for the decision, the criteria under which it was made, and the relation of these two things to the circumstances in which they contemplate making similar decisions themselves.

The ultimate goal of this study—to identify the implications of the Deliberate Force experience for the future—thus called for a precise description of the event against the backdrop of the theoretical and doctrinal expectations of the participants for the planning and execution of air campaigns, particularly under circumstances similar to those surrounding the actual event. This requirement, in turn, raised two research questions corollary to the core one about the matching of means and ends:

1. To what extent did the planning, execution, and outcome of Deliberate Force reflect the expectations of the existing body of airpower theory and doctrine?
2. Given the outcome of Deliberate Force and the relationship of theory and practice in its planning, execution, and effect, what are its implications for the body of future airpower theory, doctrine, and policy?

Team members believed that the answers to these and the core research question would extract a great deal of benefit from the BACS for its intended "audiences." They expected that those answers would be loaded with theoretical and doctrinal implications for future air-warfare thinkers, planners, and leaders. They were not disappointed.

ROBERT C. OWEN, Colonel, USAF
Scott Air Force Base, Illinois
June 1999

Notes

1. This archive, held at the Air Force Historical Research Agency at Maxwell AFB, Ala., consists of over 10,000 pages of documents, about one hundred hours of oral interviews on audiotape, and a number of computer disc files.

2. Joint Publication (Pub) 3-0, *Doctrine for Joint Operations*, 1 February 1995, chap. 3, throughout.

3. Joint Pub 1-02, *Department of Defense Dictionary of Military and Associated Terms*, 1994, 60.

4. William H. Perry, remarks to Adjutant General Association of the United States, National Guard Association Building, Washington, D.C., 7 February 1996.

5. Joint Pub 3-0, I-2 and I-3.

Chapter 1

The Demise of Yugoslavia and the Destruction of Bosnia: Strategic Causes, Effects, and Responses

Dr. Karl Mueller

To understand United States and Western policy in Bosnia-Herzegovina and the surrounding states in general, and Operation Deliberate Force in particular, one must place these policies in strategic context. The sequence of events that led to the North Atlantic Treaty Organization (NATO) air campaign of August and September 1995 did not really begin in the fourteenth century, as some writers have suggested, but it does predate the breakup of Yugoslavia and the civil war in Bosnia that began in 1992.

This chapter lays the groundwork for those that follow by describing the actors, relationships, and conditions at the strategic level that not only caused but shaped and constrained Western actions in and around Bosnia in 1992–95. Most of the chapter is in narrative form, with occasional analytical interruptions, but it does not purport to be a history of its subject. It can provide no more than a superficial account of Yugoslavian and Bosnian history, and the reader who seeks a reasonably complete understanding of these complex matters would be well advised to consult some of the excellent accounts and analyses cited in the notes.[1]

The Yugoslavian Prologue

The state of Yugoslavia was constructed after the First World War from the ruins of the Austro-Hungarian Empire and the independent Allied states of Serbia and Montenegro, themselves calved off the disintegrating Ottoman Empire in the late nineteenth century. The Great War had been triggered by the July Crisis of 1914, which began when a member of a

Serbian-supported Bosnian separatist organization assassinated Archduke Franz Ferdinand, heir to the Austro-Hungarian throne, and his consort during a visit to the Bosnian provincial capital of Sarajevo. Encouraged by Germany, Austria blamed Serbia for the killing, leading to a confrontation with Russia, Serbia's Pan-Slavic great-power ally, and eventually to a general European conflagration.[2] In redrawing the map of central and eastern Europe after the war, the victorious Allies broke up the Austrian empire, combining its South Slavic provinces with the ethnically related Serbian and Montenegrin states to form Yugoslavia.[3]

The Allies intended the creation of Yugoslavia and the other post-Versailles multinational states of Eastern Europe (Czechoslovakia, Poland, and an expanded Romania) to help stabilize the continent. France in particular strove during the 1920s to create a network of alliances with these states against the possibility of expansionism by the defeated central powers.[4] The most successful aspect of this effort was the establishment of an alliance between Czechoslovakia, Yugoslavia, and Romania directed mainly against Hungary, which became known as "the Little Entente." Although it deteriorated in the 1930s as its members' security concerns began to diverge, during the early years of the League of Nations, some statesmen optimistically viewed the Little Entente as the functional equivalent of a sixth major European power, at least in the diplomatic sphere.[5]

On the domestic political plane, Yugoslavia was dominated by Serbs, who were not only on the winning side in the war but were the most numerous of its ethnic groups, comprising about 38 percent of the population; the Serbian king and capital became those of the new Yugoslavian state. Interwar Yugoslavia was never a paragon of political stability, and its troubled democracy was replaced by a troubled dictatorship in 1928. Belgrade's various efforts to overcome the country's ethnic divisions and forge a politically united state during the interwar years met with considerably less success than did those of the postwar Yugoslavian government.[6]

As the power of Fascist Italy and Nazi Germany grew in the 1930s, Belgrade's ties to France weakened, and it sought increasingly to appease the looming Italian threat. Finally, in

2

April 1941, while the Italian invasion of Greece was flounder-
ing, the Yugoslavian government's efforts to reach a modus
vivendi with the Axis—like the one Sweden was developing
with Germany—led to a pro-Allied military coup. Germany and
its allies responded by invading Yugoslavia, conquering the
country in short order before going on to defeat Greece and
then to invade the Soviet Union.[7] Under brutal Axis control,
parts of Yugoslavia were annexed by Germany, Italy, Hungary,
and Bulgaria, and the rest was divided into German and Italian zones of occupation and a nominally independent Croatian fascist state (including part of present-day Croatia and all
of Bosnia-Herzegovina), which was in practice an Italo-Ger-
man condominium.[8] The Fascist Ustasas, who ran wartime
Croatia, set out to kill a third of their state's Serb population
and expel another third, prior to converting the remainder to
Catholicism.[9]

Yugoslavia was one of the few Axis-occupied countries that
saw significant resistance-fighting during the war. This fighting involved two main guerrilla groups: the royalist Chetniks
and the communist partisans led by the Croat-Slovene leader
of the Yugoslav Communist Party, Josip Broz, known by the
pseudonym *Tito*.[10] The resistance forces fought a grisly war
against the Axis occupiers and their Croatian allies and, more
often, against each other. The Chetniks grew increasingly col-
laborationist under German pressure, and their campaign of
violence against Croats and Muslims prevented the Yugoslavian government-in-exile in London from gaining substantial
support from non-Serbs. Tito's partisans received Soviet support (although Tito rejected Moscow's instructions to cooperate with the Chetniks and other anticommunist forces), and,
ultimately, the Western Allies decided to back Tito as well.
They did so since he seemed far more willing than the Chetniks to prosecute the war against the Axis in spite of horrific
German reprisals against the civilian populace. Over a million
Yugoslavs died at the hands of their various domestic and
foreign enemies during the Second World War; this number
represented more than 6 percent of the country's prewar
population—a greater proportional loss than was suffered by
any other state in the war except for Germany, Poland, and
the Soviet Union.

Tito became premier and later president of postwar Yugoslavia, as well as Communist Party general secretary. He established a political system based on a strong federal government but with significant powers and perquisites reserved for each of the six Yugoslav republics and protections for the various official ethnic groups.[11] This system underwent several rounds of revision over the years, most notably in 1971, when Muslims received full recognition as an ethnic nation, and in the 1974 constitution, which increased federal decentralization and gave virtual republic status to the autonomous Serbian regions of Kosovo and Vojvodina.

Yugoslavia emerged from the war as a leading member of the communist movement in Eastern Europe, but Tito and his Soviet allies soon parted ways; Yugoslavia was expelled from the Cominform in 1948 for its disobediently militant foreign policies and for Tito's criticism of Stalin, although Yugoslavian relations with Moscow improved somewhat following Stalin's death.[12] The United States provided arms to Yugoslavia under the Mutual Assistance Pact during the 1950s, along with large amounts of other foreign aid, and for a while Yugoslavia even appeared to be a potential candidate for eventual NATO membership. In the 1960s relations between Belgrade and Moscow improved, and Yugoslavia became one of the solidly neutral states of Europe, enjoying the attentions of both East and West as the superpowers vied for influence over it.[13]

Together with neutral Austria—and Albania after its break with Moscow—Yugoslavia was a buffer between the southern flanks of NATO and the Warsaw Pact during most of the cold war, largely insulating Italy from external military threat.[14] Yugoslavia based its defensive strategy upon a national army (the JNA) supported by territorial defense forces organized in each republic.[15] In the event of invasion (most likely from the Soviet Union), the JNA would delay the aggressor long enough for the mobilization of territorial forces, after which national defense would increasingly fall back upon a strategy of guerrilla warfare, especially in the mountainous regions of Bosnia-Herzegovina (where Belgrade concentrated Yugoslavia's developing defense industries), Montenegro, and Kosovo. The prospect of fighting a long and bloody guerrilla war in the Yugoslavian mountains would likely deter any prospective conqueror of the country. The leadership of the JNA included disproportionate numbers of Serbian officers—especially Bosnian Serbs—due to factors relating to historical tradition and to the limited economic opportunities available in rural Bosnia. The multinational army, however, was probably the Yugoslavian institution that contributed the most to federal unity.[16]

On the international political scene, Yugoslavia rose to additional prominence in the 1960s and 1970s as a principal leader of the nonaligned nations movement. The post-Stalinist Yugoslav experiment of an economic middle course between capitalism and Soviet communism seemed to be, if not a roaring success, at least a modest one, especially compared to some of its neighbors. However, during the 1970s, speculation abounded about the likely results of Tito's presumably impending death. An impression widely held in the West was that Yugoslavia had an intrinsic tendency towards disintegration and interethnic conflict held off only by Tito's personal prestige and power. Yet, after Tito did finally die in 1980, his political creation survived. Defying many expectations, Yugoslavia seemed to continue inertially along its decentralized socialist path between East and West more or less as before. Other leaders peacefully succeeded Tito, although without his leadership, making any new changes in the federal system would prove difficult. The 1984 Winter Olympics showcased the apparent success of the Yugoslav experiment; they were held in Sarajevo, where, as Olympic television viewers were reminded almost nightly, the spark that ignited the First World War had been struck 70 years earlier.

Beneath the superficial level, however, the Yugoslavian system came under acute economic pressure in the 1980s.[17] As Yugoslavia's political system ossified, its economic fortunes declined due to a variety of factors, including rising energy prices. Both the state and the republics increasingly turned to foreign borrowing to sustain themselves. In the 1980s, the International Monetary Fund required Belgrade to institute increasingly stringent austerity measures as a condition for further loans. Despite efforts to reduce them, income disparities between the richest and poorest republics continued to grow. The evaporation of the cold war reduced the superpowers' interest in buying Yugoslavia's friendship, and Western investment heading east found more and more alternative places to land. These forces combined to undermine Tito's elaborate spoils-distribution system among the republics and regions, thus weakening the adhesive that held the country together. Between 1982 and 1989, the Yugoslavian standard of living fell by 40 percent.[18] When newly elected Yugoslav prime minister Ante Markovic launched an economic and political reform program in 1989, little interest or support was forthcoming from a US government that was preoccupied with developments in the Soviet Union and the Warsaw Pact.[19] As economic conditions grew more difficult, support for the federal structure eroded, especially in the wealthiest republics, so that when domestic revolution and international realignment swept Eastern Europe in 1989, the stage was set for the breakup of Yugoslavia.

The Dissolution of Yugoslavia

It is not unusual to hear Western observers characterize the explosive decompression of Yugoslavia as the inevitable result of ancient and enduring hatreds among the country's constituent ethnic groups. They suggest that only Tito's program of repression was able to keep the state together during the cold war, and after his death no one else could hold back the mighty centrifugal forces of age-old interethnic animosity. Implicit, and occasionally explicit, in this argument is a suggestion that the Yugoslavian populace is primitive and even savage in a way that full-fledged, civilized Westerners are not.[20] Although Americans manage to live in relative peace in multiethnic communities,[21] Serbs and Croats (like Rwandans, Cypriots, and Kashmiris) cannot forget the wrongs their ancestors did to each other. Therefore, we should not have been surprised by Yugoslavia's breakup, and we should not feel guilty about it.[22]

This explanation for the catastrophe is attractively simple, but it is too ad hoc to be satisfying—and it is at odds with the facts. Many peoples recall ancient (and twentieth-century) wrongs done by their traditional enemies but live peacefully with each other anyway. Moreover, although Tito did use an

6

iron fist to repress antifederal nationalism, progress towards the creation of a pan-Yugoslav identity proceeded by many means, only some of them coercive.[23] Forces similar to those that lay behind classical social revolutions caused the revolutionary changes in Yugoslavia:[24] demand for political change from below, triggered in this case primarily by economic hardship, combined with the weakening of the state's capacity to resist these pressures—attributable here not only to Tito's death but also to the collapse of the bipolar European order and the wave of revolutions sweeping Eastern Europe in 1989–91. As these revolutionary forces strengthened, leaders (and national media) who recognized the potential power of ethnic and religious pride and hatred eagerly kindled those emotions, as wartime and warmongering leaders have often done before.[25] In short, ethnic relationships in Yugoslavia did not simply burst into flames; rather, incendiary ethnic fuel was thrown onto the fires of regional and class conflict.[26]

Nevertheless, Yugoslavia was unusually fertile ground for the growth of ethnic conflict. Serbs did recall the Battle of Kosovo Polje in 1389, in which Serbia's army was gloriously defeated by Ottoman forces, and considered it relevant to themselves five hundred years later. It was much more important that memories of the Second World War were far from distant and even farther from pleasant, especially since conflict between Serbs and Croats was in fact quite unusual before the twentieth century.[27] Such factors did a great deal to make the slope towards warfare and atrocity in Yugoslavia much steeper and more slippery than it otherwise would have been. To describe postwar Yugoslavia as a powder keg or a house of cards implies far too much determinism, but it was certainly a complex system with many serious instabilities. It did not simply fail; it tore itself apart—as a result of being vandalized.

The first major cracks in the Yugoslavian federation began in Kosovo following Tito's death. Local Serbs, who were becoming an ever smaller minority in the region known as the historical heart of Yugoslavia,[28] began to complain of persecution and injury by the poorer Albanian majority in Kosovo—accounts widely reported and believed elsewhere in Serbia. In 1987, as a popular groundswell of Serb resentment against the Kosovan Albanians grew, Slobodan Milosevic, the ambitious president of the Serbian League of Communists, capitalized upon the potential power base and established himself as leader of a new nationalist Serbian political movement.[29] Milosevic's party rebuked him for his deviation from its federalist principles, but in the ensuing power struggle, Milosevic gained an overwhelming victory and expelled his key opponents from the party. He then set out to build his and Serbia's power within Yugoslavia: in rapid succession, he and his supporters took control of communist parties in Vojvodina, Montenegro, and then Kosovo, installing pro-Milosevic presidents in each region or republic.[30] When the Albanian majority in Kosovo objected, Milosevic used the threat of Serbian mob violence in Belgrade to coerce the federal government into granting him emergency powers to use the JNA against them and declared that this showed that Serbia had regained its former power.[31]

Kosovans' resistance to Belgrade's recision of their regional autonomy found widespread support from Slovenia, the wealthiest and most Westernized of the Yugoslav republics. Relaxation of Slovenian press controls in recent years had resulted in the prominent display of antifederal and anti-Milosevic opinion there; Serbia's apparent bid for hegemony in Yugoslavia increased this sentiment. Belgrade's efforts to suppress this dissent further fanned the flames of resentment, and when Milosevic responded by calling an extraordinary Yugoslav Party Congress in which the Serbian bloc consistently defeated reforms proposed by Slovenia, the Slovenian delegation walked out. Faced with the possibility of a potentially catastrophic split in the federation, Milosevic tried to persuade the Croatian delegation not to follow suit, but the Croatians departed after deciding they could not accept a federated Yugoslavia that excluded the Slovenes. Later, Milosevic would blame Slovenia for causing the breakup of Yugoslavia and all that followed.[32]

Milosevic's nationalism contributed substantially to the election of Franjo Tudjman as president of Croatia in April 1990.[33] Tudjman's nationalism and his invocation of symbols from Croatia's brief heyday of independent Fascism in turn caused fear and alarm among Croatian Serbs, who made up local majorities in parts of the impoverished, so-called Croatian Krajina and of Eastern Slavonia, regions along the republic's borders with Bosnia and Serbia. Croatian Serb resistance to the election of Tudjman and his nationalists was centered in the town of Knin, where local authorities refused to accept the authority of the new government in Zagreb. They asked for support from Belgrade and received Serbian encouragement and advice for their budding rebellion. Croatian leaders were keen to move against the Serbs, especially since key transport routes to the Dalmatian coast passed through the Knin area, but they feared that this might trigger intervention by the JNA. When the confrontation escalated and Zagreb sent several helicopters carrying special forces to Knin, they were intercepted and turned back by MiG fighters of the Yugoslav air force. The Croatian government began secretly to import arms for use against the Serbs and potentially the JNA.[34] Croatia approached the United States as a potential arms supplier, but the US government rebuffed the inquiries, still hoping to keep Yugoslavia united and thereby minimize instability in the Balkans. Croatia found other vendors, however.

Milosevic favored sending the JNA against the Croats, but this required a majority vote within the Yugoslav State Council. On 12 March 1991, State Council chairman Borisav Jovic of Serbia called a meeting of the council to consider a proposal by the minister of defense to establish a national state of emergency to stop the civil war that he accused the Croats of planning. The Croats and Macedonians opposed the plan, and the Slovenian delegation was absent, fearing arrest by the Serbs. With the Serbian, Vojvodinan, Kosovan, and Montenegrin representatives supporting martial law, Bosnia-Herzegovina held the deciding vote. Although Bosnia seemed to have the most to lose in an intra-Yugoslavian civil war, the Bosnian representative surprised Milosevic by opposing the motion. In response, Milosevic announced that Serbia and its allies would withdraw from the State Council, calculating that with civilian authority over the JNA eliminated, the army would be free to act on its own against those who threatened the federation.

The United States ambassador warned Belgrade not to use force against Croatia, causing considerable concern among the Serbian leadership. Therefore, the minister of defense secretly traveled to Moscow to meet Soviet defense officials and asked for a promise of Soviet assistance in the event of Western intervention in Yugoslavia.[35] The Soviets provided him with intelligence information indicating that the United States would not intervene, and Milosevic concluded that the way now lay clear for federal forces to reassert Belgrade's control over Croatia. However, Milosevic's plan ultimately foundered because the commander of the JNA could not bring himself to establish military rule in Yugoslavia.

In May 1991 Croatians overwhelmingly voted to declare their republic's independence effective in late June, coordinating with the date a similar Slovene independence declaration was already set to take effect. Slovene and Croat representatives lobbied the European Community (EC), which they aspired to join, to recognize their independence, but the EC had no desire to see Yugoslavia break up. Instead, the West set about exerting pressure on Slovenia and Croatia to remain within Yugoslavia, culminating in a visit to Belgrade by James Baker, US secretary of state. Baker declared that the United States would not recognize Croatia and Slovenia under any circumstances, which all sides took as a signal that Washington would not object to the use of force to hold the federation together.[36]

The two republics decided to press ahead anyway, and when the independence date came on 25 June, Slovenia expelled Yugoslavian customs officials from their posts on the Italian and Austrian frontiers. Slovene president Milan Kucan and his government resolved to fight the JNA if necessary. When the JNA sent some two thousand predominantly conscript troops to retake the various border posts, expecting no serious resistance, these units soon found themselves surrounded by 35,000 Slovene militia forces who used the territorial-defense tactics designed to defend Yugoslavia against Soviet invasion. Slovene troops blocked all major roads in the republic, trapping unprepared and stunned JNA forces in their barracks. JNA efforts to break through the barricades and resupply their besieged bases by air met with fire from the Slovene militia, and the first of a number of its helicopters was shot down. Croatia was not so eager as Slovenia to break away from the federation but was more reluctant yet to remain behind without Slovenia in a Serbian-dominated state.

The European Community sent envoys to Zagreb to encourage Slovenia and Croatia to de-escalate the crisis in return for eventual political recognition by the EC. Although the Slovenes agreed to a cease-fire and negotiations, fighting continued in Slovenia, with the Slovene militia continuing to fare better then its opponents. In Belgrade, the federal Ministry of Defense proposed a massive military attack against Slovenia, predicting high casualties on both sides, but Milosevic surprised the State Council by opposing the scheme. Slovenia contained virtually none of the Serbs whom Milosevic wanted to include in his Yugoslavia. He calculated that after Slovenia's secession, Serbia would have a sufficient preponderance of power to do as it liked about—or to—Croatia. Serbia agreed to withdraw the JNA from Slovenia, and the war in the republic ended after 10 days of fighting and some 62 deaths.

A much larger war would soon begin in Croatia.[37] Tudjman's ruling party became increasingly assertive and nationalistic, and the Krajina Serbs grew increasingly threatened and defiant, asking for and receiving arms from Belgrade. The local chief of the Croatian national police, who tried to de-escalate the conflict instead of moving to crush the Serbs, was assassinated by members of Tudjman's inner circle, who also launched a rocket attack against a Serb suburb of Vukovar.[38] Each killing, sensationalized by either the Serbian or the Croatian media, escalated the crisis; as the violence intensified, JNA forces under Col Ratko Mladic went to the Krajina as "peacekeepers" to protect the Serbs and seized many Croat towns.

Because widespread desertions, not limited to its Slovene and Croatian troops, weakened the JNA, the forces sent to Croatia were bolstered by Serbian paramilitary units ranging from ultranationalist extremist groups to criminal gangs. These units soon began a pattern of massacres and other terrorism designed to drive Croats out of areas they conquered, and *ethnic cleansing,* also practiced on a smaller scale by their enemies, entered the international lexicon.[39] Serb shelling of the medieval Dalmatian city of Dubrovnik also stimulated Western concern with the conflict, and the EC called representatives of the six Yugoslav republics to the Hague to meet with mediator Lord Peter Carrington.

Milosevic agreed to a proposal by Carrington that Croatia be allowed to secede from Yugoslavia, provided the rights of the Serb minority were protected. However, he subsequently rejected the formal plan that Carrington proposed, which expanded this principle to allow the independence of all six Yugoslav republics with similar guarantees. The Croatian, Bosnian, and Macedonian presidents all agreed to the Carrington plan, as did Montenegrin president Momir Bulatovic, who did not entirely share Milosevic's zeal for building a Greater Serbia. Shocked and chagrined by this betrayal by his protégé, Milosevic walked out of the negotiations and finally forced Bulatovic to retract his agreement to the plan, thus killing it.[40]

In Croatia the JNA had gained control over all of the territory it sought—approximately one-third of the republic—except for the city of Vukovar, which it besieged. With Vukovar's fall an obvious inevitability, Germany granted diplomatic recognition to Croatia and Slovenia, and the rest of the European Community followed suit, effective 15 January 1992. Britain, the least inclined of the major EC members to become entangled in Yugoslavia, felt very much dragged along by a degree of German political assertiveness not seen before in the postwar era. The Croatian fighting ended in January 1992, and in March the United Nations Protection Force (UNPROFOR) began deploying as peacekeepers in the Serb-held areas of Croatia, which had declared themselves the independent Republic of Serbian Krajina (RSK).

The Bosnian Civil War

Analyses of the nature of the war that began in Bosnia-Herzegovina in 1992 tend to lean towards one of two major schools of thought, although many intermediate perspectives lie between the two polar extremes. One school sees the Bosnian war as primarily the result of Serbian aggression and expansionism, and its proponents point out the close and active ties between the Belgrade and Bosnian Serbs. The US government has generally adopted something close to this perspective, often associated with support for outside military intervention or aid to assist the Bosnian government against the Serbs. (A variant of this view would add Croatia to the list of external aggressors and fomenters of conflict, although this refinement is not typical of official US views.) The opposite school holds that the Bosnian war is essentially internal in nature, in spite of the involvement of outside states, and that no side in the conflict is an innocent victim. This civil-war perspective has been associated in particular with the British government (and to a lesser extent the French), and it is usually held by people who argue that any external intervention in the conflict ought to be based on an impartial peacekeeping or peace-enforcement approach. As described in the following sections, the truth lies somewhere between these two characterizations, and this multifaceted nature of the war in Bosnia was one of the major obstacles to Western efforts to deal with the crisis.

As the fighting wound down in Croatia, Bosnia-Herzegovina headed towards the most catastrophic post-Yugoslav war to date.[41] Within Yugoslavia, Bosnia-Herzegovina had been the most multiethnic of all the republics, both in aggregate and to a considerable extent on the local level, although the Bosnian Serb population was relatively rural while the Bosnian Muslims tended to live in and around Sarajevo and other relatively affluent urban areas. As the Yugoslav federation disintegrated, the non-Serb populations of Bosnia-Herzegovina feared domination by Serbia, while the large Bosnian Serb minority feared domination by the more numerous Bosnian Muslims, should the republic become independent. The leaderships of both the Bosnian government and the Bosnian Serbs considered their two positions irreconcilable.

The European Community's decision in December 1991 to recognize Slovenia and Croatia in January 1992 included establishment of a panel to consider applications for recognition, which other Yugoslav republics might submit by 20 January. This placed considerable pressure on Bosnia-Herzegovina and Macedonia to move quickly towards independence, and both made their applications to the EC by the deadline. The EC panel approved the Macedonian application and rejected one from Kosovar Albanians, but in Bosnia the panel decided that a referendum on independence should be held.

Bosnian Serbs led by Montenegrin psychiatrist Dr. Radovan Karadzic declared their independence from Bosnia in January 1992, calling themselves the *"Republika Srpska"* and establishing their capital at Pale, near Sarajevo. At the end of February, Bosnian president Alija Izetbegovic held a republicwide plebiscite on whether Bosnia-Herzegovina should declare its independence from Yugoslavia. Muslims and Croats voted almost unanimously in favor of independence, while most Serbs boycotted the referendum. Interethnic violence escalated during March, and large-scale fighting began on 2 April. The United States had not initially joined the Europeans in recognizing Croatia and Slovenia, still seeing their secession as destabilizing, but did recognize them on 6 April, simultaneously joining the EC in recognizing the independence of Bosnia-Herzegovina.[42] The West's rather forlorn hope that recognition might help stop the violence in Bosnia went unfulfilled.

Milosevic and Tudjman, each with plans for enlargement of his country to include its extraterritorial ethnic brethren, had already met secretly to discuss carving up Bosnia between them, leaving little if any territory for the Bosnian Muslims. Izetbegovic had made few preparations for a war that seemed too horrible to contemplate;[43] however, Belgrade had prepared for Bosnian secession by posting Bosnian Serbs to JNA units in Bosnia-Herzegovina. There they would be in place to join Karadzic's fight against the Bosnian government without requiring the JNA to mount an overt invasion, with all the international criticism that would generate, and Serbia arranged to bankroll the Bosnian Serbs. Once the war was under way, Milosevic also sent Serbian paramilitary groups, often armed by the Serbian secret police, to assist in the fight. These forces included political extremist groups, profit-seeking criminals, and eventually even young Serbians looking for fun and plunder, who would spend their weekends fighting or pillaging in Bosnia and then return home. These groups took a leading role in the campaign of civilian massacres, rape, and other atrocities that soon horrified the West.

Enjoying the advantage of ex-JNA military equipment and other forms of assistance from Belgrade, the Bosnian Serbs made rapid gains in the April fighting and soon held some two-thirds of Bosnia. Artillery units in Serbia shelled defenders of the Bosnian border city of Zornik; when it fell, two thousand Muslims were executed or sent to concentration camps, and all others were expelled. By May 1992, the Bosnian Serbs were able to mount a major offensive against Sarajevo along multiple axes, almost overwhelming the government defenders until the Serb armor was knocked out in street-to-street fighting. A Bosnian army (BiH) counterattack established a local stalemate that would endure for three years, and the Serb siege and bombardment of the city continued.[44] The EC, which had just recognized Bosnia's sovereignty, now sent Lord Carrington to Bosnia with a plan for the partition of the republic into separate ethnic provinces, which Izetbegovic rejected. The JNA sent Ratko Mladic to Bosnia to become the new commander of the Bosnian Serb army (BSA).

In spring 1993, Mladic launched a major offensive against the eastern Bosnian city of Srebrenica, which had filled with Muslim refugees from surrounding areas already conquered and cleansed by the Serbs. Under pressure from the defenders (who would not let him leave after a visit to Srebrenica), Gen Philippe Morillon, UNPROFOR commander, promised that the UN would protect them, alarming the UN leadership in New York. In the General Assembly, a large bloc of nonaligned states proposed the establishment of UN-protected safe havens in eastern Bosnia. Although the UN military staff strongly criticized this proposal as unworkable,[45] the Security Council adopted it on 16 April, after the European powers succeeded in watering it down to a designation of six cities (Sarajevo, Srebrenica, Gorazde, Tuzla, Zepa, and Bihac) as "safe areas" that both sides would be asked to respect. UNPROFOR's mandate was expanded to include deterring but not defending against attacks on the safe areas, and Mladic agreed to leave Srebrenica alone only on the condition that the defenders disarm. This they did, making it possible for the Serbs to take the city whenever they chose to do so.

The war in Bosnia resembled the 1941–45 war in Yugoslavia not only in its brutality but also in its complexity. The Bosnian Croats were nominal allies of the Bosnian government early in the war, but at various times, each of the three sides made war against the other, sometimes fighting an enemy at one location while simultaneously cooperating with that army's forces against the third side in another.[46] This tendency towards chaos was further exacerbated by the fact that each army had only a limited ability to control the actions of many of its component units, especially—but not only—those consisting of paramilitary thugs. As a result, forces in the field often ignored cease-fire or safe-passage agreements made by senior commanders, and although many atrocities were carried out with the approval or knowledge of central authorities, many others probably were not.[47]

While the Bosnian Serb spring offensive of 1993 was under way in the east, Bosnian Croat (HVO) forces under Mate Boban turned against their nominal Bosnian government allies in the southwest and began carving out their own state within Bosnia (which they named "Herceg-Bosna"). Boban had previously been seen in Austria holding meetings with Karadzic about possible partitions of Bosnia. Now Tudjman sent substantial numbers of Croatian regular forces into Bosnia to support Boban's troops as they began rounding up their former Muslim comrades and placing them in concentration camps, and Bosnian government forces fought to contain the Croat offensive.

On the diplomatic front, a new peace plan had been proposed in January 1993. The [Cyrus] Vance-[Lord David] Owen plan called for a federated Bosnia divided into ethnic provinces that would have considerable local autonomy but would be distributed so that the Serbs could not easily secede and join a greater Serbia. As in previous peace plans, the Bosnian Serbs would have to withdraw from much of the territory they had conquered; however, Milosevic, under pressure from Western economic sanctions against Serbia, agreed to support the plan and tried to persuade Karadzic to sign on. Karadzic proved extremely reluctant to do so. Although Milosevic argued that the Vance-Owen plan could not work and therefore would not endanger the Bosnian Serbs, Karadzic was loathe to give up the required territory and feared that several thousand NATO troops on the ground in Bosnia could cripple his logistics and make future operations by the BSA impossible. Finally, Karadzic signed the agreement, pending its ratification by the Bosnian Serbs, and the West became cautiously optimistic. But in a referendum held in May, 96 percent of Bosnian Serb voters rejected the plan, killing it.

Western Reactions

The course of Western military responses to the conflicts in the ruins of Yugoslavia was one of gradual but inconstant escalation. A definite lack of consensus existed within the ranks of the Western powers regarding ultimate strategic objectives in the region, due in part to differing analyses of the nature of the wars, especially in Bosnia. Moreover, different NATO allies were differently disposed towards the various parties in the conflict,[48] the most visible examples of which were the amity of Germany towards Croatia, of Greece towards Serbia, and of Turkey towards the Bosnian Muslims. This led to policies directed towards achieving those objectives on which existed a reasonable amount of agreement, complicated by all of the major NATO powers' desires to do something—or at least to be seen to be doing something—about the problems without suffering substantial losses in the defense of interests less than vital to them. In general, among NATO's leading nations, the United States was usually the most "hawkish" regarding the use of force in Bosnia, while the United Kingdom was the least inclined to take actions that seemed to represent a departure from the path of impartial peacekeeping.[49] French views tended to correspond with those of the British, although this was not always true, and when it was, it was not always for the same reasons. Germany consistently supported the United States in discussions of intervention policy, but since it did not contribute forces either to UNPROFOR or to Operation Deny Flight (discussed below), its opinions carried less weight than those of the three alliance leaders.

The possibility of Western military intervention was of special concern to Izetbegovic and the Bosnian Muslims, who were eager for the West to step in and stop their enemies. At times the Bosnian government pursued this goal by having its forces stage attacks against its own civilian population in order to outrage the Western press and turn popular opinion against the Serbs, although the Bosnian Serbs and the Croatian government were not above doing the same thing. As the war in Bosnia continued, Western negotiators found themselves alternately—even simultaneously—trying to convince the Serbs that the West might intervene in the conflict if no progress occurred in the peace negotiations, and trying to persuade the Bosnian government that the West would not intervene and save it in the absence of such progress.

Aside from humanitarian aid to the region, sent almost from the outset of the fighting,[50] the incremental process of intervention may be said to have begun with the July 1992 deployment of naval forces under NATO and Western European Union auspices to the Adriatic Sea to monitor shipping to the former Yugoslav republics. This began after the UN imposed an embargo against arms shipments to all states in the former Yugoslavia in September 1991, followed by imposition of an economic blockade on Serbia and Montenegro in May 1992.[51] In November 1992, these forces were empowered not only to monitor shipping but actually to enforce the embargo and sanctions.[52] As the conflicts progressed, the arms embargo quickly fell into disrepute since it worked to the advantage of the Serbs, who had inherited most of the JNA's arsenal. Britain and France consistently opposed lifting the arms embargo for Croatia and Bosnia, however, fearing the effects of any escalation of the conflict upon their peacekeeping troops. Eventually, the embargo lost some of its effectiveness as the Bosnians, Croats, and foreign supporters became more skilled at evading it. In contrast, economic sanctions against Serbia slowly grew more effective as some of the many obstacles to enforcing them were addressed.

United Nations peace-enforcement efforts in the region began with the deployment of UNPROFOR to Croatia in spring 1992. With its headquarters imprudently placed in Sarajevo (over the objections of the force's commanders), it was inevitable that UNPROFOR would find itself entangled in the Bosnian war, and a decision made in September 1992 called for dramatic expansion of UNPROFOR's presence in Bosnia in order to protect shipments of humanitarian aid under the auspices of the UN High Commissioner for Refugees.[53] As described above, UNPROFOR rapidly became a key player in the Bosnian conflict, and all sides consistently damned it for allegedly favoring their enemies.

NATO began patrolling the skies over Bosnia on 16 October 1992 in Operation Sky Monitor, following a UN resolution banning flights by any aircraft without approval from UNPROFOR. On 12 April 1993, this operation was renamed Deny Flight after UN Security Council Resolution (UNSCR) 816 granted it authority to intercept and, if necessary, shoot down aircraft violating the prohibition.[54] Its mandate was further expanded from 22 July to include providing close air support (CAS) as necessary to protect UN peacekeepers. NATO's 5th Allied Tactical Air Force (5 ATAF) controlled the operation, and a combined air operations center near Vicenza, Italy, managed it.[55] The United States, United Kingdom, France, Italy, the Netherlands, Spain, Turkey, and the multinational NATO airborne early warning force eventually provided aircraft for Deny Flight. Most were based in Italy or on US, British, and French aircraft carriers in the Adriatic, although some tankers, airborne-warning and other support aircraft operated directly from bases in Germany, France, and the United Kingdom.

Although UN resolutions prohibited all flights over Bosnia, a decision made at Allied Forces Southern Europe (AFSOUTH) and approved at higher levels limited Deny Flight to intercepting fixed-wing aircraft. All sides in the conflict continued to use helicopters in a variety of roles, often painting red crosses on helicopters actually being used for tactical resupply and other missions. Although US and NATO officials claimed rather implausibly that the helicopter flights were not militarily significant, they were allowed to continue because of the very plausible fear that if one were shot down, its owners would rapidly fabricate evidence that it had been on a humanitarian mission loaded with noncombatants, potentially causing a public-relations disaster for NATO.

In August 1993 the Deny Flight mandate further expanded to include the possibility of launching non-CAS air strikes to deter or retaliate for attacks against peacekeeping forces in Bosnia. Following a meeting of NATO leaders in London, on 8 August the North Atlantic Council (NAC), NATO's governing body, approved a contingency plan for air strikes in Bosnia, which laid out three general options for targeting.[56] The first and most limited involved attacking only forces that posed a direct and immediate threat to friendly forces. The second expanded the target set to include potentially, but not immediately, threatening forces and assets. The third—and most expansive—added to the set a wide range of targets that would contribute to the adversary's ability to pose such threats over the long term. This strategic blueprint for NATO air strikes would ultimately form the basis for Operation Deliberate Force two years later.

Starting in late 1993, the US government began to take an increasingly active role in the Bosnian crisis, driven by the rising domestic political costs of appearing to be doing nothing to stop it, and by the growing realization that the Europeans did not appear to be making progress towards a solution.[57] The first order of business for the United States was a project to end the fighting between the Bosnian Croats and the Bosnian government, which would simplify the Bosnian situation considerably and do much to even the local balance of power. The United States pressured Zagreb by pointing out that Croatia would have little chance of ever regaining its Serb-held territories without American support. On 18 March 1994, the BiH-HVO alliance was restored with the announcement of a new federation between the Bosnian government and the Bosnian Croats, marking a key turning point in the conflict.

Within NATO, the United States advocated more forceful action against the Bosnian Serbs. Following a mortar shell explosion in a Sarajevo marketplace on 4 February 1994 that killed 68 Bosnian civilians, the United States proposed retaliatory air strikes against the Bosnian Serbs. London and Paris continued to oppose exacerbating the conflict between the BSA and the West, especially (though not solely) because the British and French had thousands of peacekeeping troops in harm's way on the ground in Bosnia. However, in an 8 February meeting of the British cabinet, Foreign Minister Douglas Hurd argued to his colleagues that the future not just of Bosnia but also of NATO was at stake, and that the survival of the alliance needed to be their foremost concern. The following day, the NAC demanded that the BSA withdraw its heavy weapons from a 20-kilometer-wide exclusion zone around

Sarajevo within 10 days or NATO would bomb them. The Bosnian Serbs refused to comply.

The NATO ultimatum met with strong opposition from the Russian government. Serbia had been an important ally of pan-Slavist Russia in the early years of the century, and the Russian nationalist right, led by Vladimir Zhirinovsky, argued that it was time for Russia to stand up against NATO in defense of its traditional interests. Russian envoy Vitaly Churkin traveled to Serbia to meet Karadzic and brokered a deal under which BSA artillery would withdraw from the exclusion zone and Russian peacekeepers would deploy there to prevent the Serbs' enemies from taking advantage of the withdrawal to attack them. The presence of Russian peacekeepers would also prevent NATO from easily launching air attacks at targets in the exclusion zone.

NATO's Deny Flight aircraft soon drew first blood (and the alliance's first ever) on 28 February 1994, when two pairs of US Air Force F-16 fighters intercepted six Yugoslav air force Super Galeb light attack aircraft on a bombing mission against Bosnian government forces and shot down four of them. This was followed on 12 March by the first launch of a CAS mission to support UN peacekeepers, although no attacks actually occurred. The first CAS strikes took place on 10 and 11 April, when UN troops came under fire during a Bosnian Serb offensive against the newly designated safe area of Gorazde, in response to which the Serbs took 150 UN peacekeepers hostage to deter further air attacks.[58] During subsequent missions over Gorazde, ground fire damaged a French navy Etendard IVP on 15 April, and the following day a British Sea Harrier was shot down. The pilot ejected, and UN forces rescued him.

The BSA offensive against Gorazde led the United States to advocate punitive air strikes against the Bosnian Serbs, whom President Bill Clinton declared to be the "complete aggressors" in the action. On 22 April, the United States persuaded the NAC to demand that the BSA withdraw its heavy weapons from the front line around Gorazde and to threaten that strikes would also be launched against any heavy weapons that might be used to attack the other safe areas. Seeking to avert this escalation of the fighting, UN envoy Yasushi Akashi negotiated a new cease-fire.

On 20 July 1994, the Bosnian Serb Assembly considered yet another partition plan for Bosnia that required significant territorial concessions from them. Even though it received support from Slobodan Milosevic, whose country had by this time been suffering from two years of UN economic sanctions, the assembly rejected it. Milosevic reacted by announcing in August that he was breaking Serbia's ties with the Bosnian Serbs and closing their common border. The UN responded with an easing of the sanctions against Serbia in September. Meanwhile, on 5 August, BSA forces broke into a UN weapons-collection site near Sarajevo and removed several armored vehicles and artillery pieces they had previously turned over to UN custody. In response, several US A-10s strafed and destroyed a BSA 1945-vintage M18 tank destroyer, and the Serbs returned the other weapons they had seized. NATO aircraft struck again on 22 September, when another A-10 and two Royal Air Force (RAF) Jaguars attacked a tank near Sarajevo that had fired on an armored vehicle belonging to French UNPROFOR forces and wounded one of its crew.

Starting in late October, the Bosnian government–Croat federation launched its largest offensive so far in the war in western Bosnia, defeating the antigovernment Muslim forces of Fikret Abdic near Bihac. During the heavy fighting in this region, the BSA received air support from aircraft based in the Serb-held Krajina region of Croatia, which NATO could not intercept due to the short flight time between their bases and the battlefield, and the UN Security Council expanded the Deny Flight mandate to permit attacks against territory in Croatia to prevent such flights. On 21 November, some 30 NATO aircraft from four countries attacked the airfield at Udbina, cratering the runway but sparing the aircraft based there at the request of the UN.[59] Two days later, US jets launched high-speed antiradiation missile attacks against BSA surface-to-air missile (SAM) batteries in western Bosnia that had fired on two British aircraft the day before. A massive poststrike reconnaissance-in-force mission against these sites was planned but canceled at the demand of the British and French governments, which wanted to prevent further escalation.[60] The year ended with negotiation efforts by former US president Jimmy Carter producing a four-month cease-fire between the BSA and the Bosnian-Croat federation forces, effective 31 December.

Final Approach to Intervention

By the end of the cease-fire in April 1995,[61] significant changes had occurred in the balance of power in and around Bosnia, although they were widely recognized only in retrospect. The Bosnian army had continued to grow in strength, through reorganization and an increased flow of arms and equipment, much of which came from Muslim states in the Middle and Far East.[62] Croatia had steadily rearmed, in part by keeping a portion of the arms shipments to Bosnia that it allowed to cross its territory after they penetrated the rather leaky international blockade. Organizational advice for the Croatian military had come from a team of former US military officers in the nongovernmental guise of Military Professional Resources, Incorporated. The BSA and the RSK army remained in a powerful strategic position in spite of receiving reduced material support from Serbia, but the local balance of power was shifting in favor of their opponents. Perhaps as significant, as would soon be revealed, years of war and deprivation had apparently begun to take a toll on the Serb armies' morale and political cohesion.[63]

Dramatic signs of this weakness came when the Croatian army launched an invasion of Serb-held Western Slavonia (*Sector West* in UNPROFOR parlance) on 1 May 1995. Called Operation Flash, the Croatian offensive conquered the territory in less than two days, surprising most observers—including Western officials—who had expected the RSK forces to resist any Croatian attack with far greater determination and effectiveness.[64] Elsewhere in the Krajina, planning began for a military reorganization, and a new commander was appointed for the RSK army.

However, a key weakness of the Western powers soon emerged as well. In response to renewed shelling of safe areas and the continued presence of Serb artillery in the exclusion

23

zone around Sarajevo, the UN requested punitive air strikes against the Bosnian Serbs. On 25 and 26 May, NATO aircraft attacked ammunition storage sites in Pale, the Bosnian Serb capital.[65] The Serbs responded as they had to previous air strikes, by taking 370 UN peacekeepers hostage, and placed many of them at strategic locations as human shields to deter further NATO air strikes. The bombing ceased, and by 18 June the Serbs had released all of the hostages. UNPROFOR redeployed the rest of its outlying units to protect them from capture by the BSA in similar circumstances in the future.

Shortly after the Pale raids, American domestic attention focused on Bosnia as never before, when a Bosnian Serb SA-6 Kub SAM shot down a US Air Force F-16 near Banja Luka in western Bosnia on 2 June. The pilot ejected safely, and his fate became the subject of intense speculation until a US Marine Corps combat search-and-rescue mission rescued him six days later. Popular American concern about Bosnia quickly subsided to its original level of relative indifference, and even at the height of Operation Deliberate Force, Bosnia received less US media attention than it did during this incident.[66] In the wake of the loss, Deny Flight operations were adjusted to keep patrolling aircraft farther out of harm's way, over the Adriatic, in spite of British and French insistence that occasional casualties were to be expected in such an operation. The allies argued that Deny Flight aircraft should continue to patrol the skies over Bosnia, at least until it became clear that the F-16 shootdown was not a fluke. However, AFSOUTH commanders maintained that since relatively few airplanes were violating the no-flight zone and since NATO would not allow the preemptive destruction of the BSA integrated air defense system (IADS),[67] the risks involved in further overflights were not worthwhile.[68]

In July the BSA seized the long-isolated Muslim enclave of Srebrenica after several days of heavy fighting, during which US Navy and Dutch air force fighters flew CAS missions to support Dutch UNPROFOR peacekeepers when they came under attack. After occupying the city on 11 July, the BSA expelled its Muslim population and bused them to Tuzla, except for some seven thousand men who remain unaccounted for. Almost immediately, the BSA began shelling and then launching ground attacks against Zepa and threatened to attack Gorazde. Galvanized by the seizure of Srebrenica and facing growing domestic pressure to act, especially in Europe, Western leaders increasingly advocated major military action. French president Jacques Chirac called for Western intervention on 14 July, and although the British government urged caution, British, French, and American defense officials met in London, and preparations were made to deploy a Rapid Reaction Force (RRF) of French, British, and Dutch combat troops, including heavy artillery, to Sarajevo. American officials, led by Secretary of Defense William Perry, advocated widespread air strikes against the BSA.

On 21 July, as RRF artillery units arrived in Sarajevo and prepared to deploy on Mount Igman, overlooking Sarajevo, officials from all the NATO allies held a summit meeting in London and agreed to launch large-scale air strikes if the BSA either attacked Gorazde or concentrated forces or weapons that posed a direct threat to it.[69] Although this was a dramatic political action, on a strategic level the decision was not conceived as a departure from past policy so much as a continuation of it, since the members had agreed on the possibility of such a course of action two years earlier. At NATO the campaign that became known as Deliberate Force was seen simply as a further phase of Deny Flight, and AFSOUTH's name for the air campaign came into use in Brussels only after the fact. However, the London conference did add several noteworthy aspects to the air strike plan of 1993. First was the establishment of two "zones of action" in Bosnia—one covering the southeast, including Sarajevo and Gorazde, and the other the northwest, including Bihac. Instead of AFSOUTH aircraft being limited to striking targets in the close vicinity of whichever safe area(s) came under attack, the entire zone of action containing the safe area(s) in question would be subject to air attack. Second, at least in theory, once a campaign began, only mutual agreement between NATO and UNPROFOR would stop it. As one official characterized the arrangement, both of the dual keys were required to turn off the bombing, instead of just one.[70]

The North Atlantic Council approved the air strike plan on 25 July, the same day that Zepa fell to the BSA and the same day that the UN War Crimes Tribunal at the Hague indicted

Radovan Karadzic and Ratko Mladic. One week later, the NAC extended the deterrent threats to cover attacks against the other remaining safe areas (Sarajevo, Tuzla, and Bihac) as well, while the US Congress sent a resolution to President Clinton calling for the lifting of the UN arms embargo against the Bosnian government.[71]

Immediately after the London conference, a delegation of NATO air force generals traveled to Serbia to deliver the alliance's ultimatum to General Mladic in person and to warn him further about the consequences that would follow from a BSA violation of the remaining safe areas. Delegation leader Air Chief Marshal Sir William Wratten reported that Mladic seemed not to have expected the ultimatum. Mladic did not question NATO's ability to strike, as promised, when and where it chose, but he rejected NATO's demands following what Western diplomats had by then discovered to be a typical, lengthy soliloquy on injustices the Serbs had suffered through history.[72] Soon NATO and UNPROFOR officers were working out coordination arrangements to prevent RRF artillery fire from endangering aircraft in the event of air strikes around Sarajevo, and Lt Gen Bernard Janvier, UNPROFOR commander, agreed with NATO air campaign planners on a joint target list for a possible air campaign.

If the military strategy for Operation Deliberate Force was principally laid out in the London conference of August 1993, the London meeting of July 1995 was its pivotal moment in political terms. The sacking of Srebrenica in spite of its UN protection and the ensuing carnage catalyzed Western determination to do something decisive about the war in Bosnia. Moreover, this occurred at the same time that the British government was reaching the conclusion that the peacekeeping approach to the problem embodied in UNPROFOR had accomplished as much as it was likely to do. This belief may have been encouraged by AFSOUTH's decision to stop Deny Flight patrols over Bosnia in the absence of permission for preemptive suppression of enemy air defenses.[73] The French were also growing tired of the unremitting crisis, and the election of President Chirac may have contributed significantly to French movement towards the American position regarding intervention. Finally, the Europeans widely viewed airpower as an option of last resort, and few European leaders were confident that it could be used both with decisive effect and at low physical and political cost in Bosnia until after the very limited air strikes launched in 1994 and 1995 had produced some equally limited results.[74] Overall, it is reasonable to say that US leadership was a necessary but not a sufficient condition for NATO to decide to intervene in Bosnia with extensive air strikes in 1995.

In western Bosnia, intense fighting had developed in the Bihac pocket in late July. Ten thousand Croatian army (HV) troops crossed the Bosnian border to assist BiH and HVO forces in their offensive against BSA forces in the Livno valley, while Croatian air force (HRZ) fighters and helicopters provided air support. Then on 3 August, the HV and HRZ launched Operation Storm, a massive offensive against the Krajina Serbs, who collapsed or fled before the onslaught with a speed that shocked observers, including US and British government officials.[75] The skill with which the operation was organized led to speculation that nongovernmental American advisors had been actively involved in its planning.[76] Knin fell to the Croatian forces on 5 August, and by the end of the next day, virtually all of the Serb-held Krajina had been taken and HV forces had linked up with the BiH at Bihac.[77] Twenty thousand RSK troops fled their imploding political entity to join BSA forces around Bihac, while over two hundred thousand Serb civilian refugees ultimately took to the roads to the east. At the time, many analysts believed that the influx of troops from the Krajina would bolster the Serb forces in western Bosnia; later it would appear that these bitterly demoralized military refugees had actually helped to weaken the BSA.[78] Fighting continued in western and southern Bosnia, and the situations of the BiH, HVO, and HV forces gradually improved. Karadzic declared that Milosevic was a traitor for allowing the collapse of the Krajina, while Milosevic responded that Karadzic was a warmonger for refusing to accept the West's peace proposals.

On 17 August Slobodan Milosevic reiterated his 1994 agreement to the Contact Group peace plan for Bosnia presented to him by US assistant secretary of state Richard Holbrooke, which Presidents Tudjman and Izetbegovic had already approved. The

Richard Holbrooke

Bosnian Serbs remained defiant, however. Holbrooke turned up the heat further on 27 August when he appeared on the television news program *Meet the Press* and threatened a six- to 12-month campaign of air strikes against the Bosnian Serbs to "level the playing field" in the conflict.[79] He further prophesied that "if the Bosnian Serbs don't want to negotiate, then the game will basically just be to wait for the trigger for air strikes."[80]

The objectives of leveling the playing field or of bombing the Bosnian Serbs to the bargaining table were not ones upon which NATO had agreed, and the overt goal of Operation Deliberate Force always remained securing the safe areas from Bosnian Serb attacks. However, US policy, at least since late 1993, appears to have been oriented consistently towards shifting the regional balance of power in favor of Croatia and the Bosnian government. Perhaps the most obvious indication of this is that blatant Croatian intervention in the war in Bosnia was never criticized by Washington in the way that Serbian involvement in the war was, let alone seen as a reason to use airpower against Croatian forces.[81] Somewhat ironically, it is at least conceivable that the US-engineered federation between the Bosnian Croats and the Bosnian government, the improvement in Croatian and BiH military power, and the success of economic sanctions and other international pressures in persuading Milosevic to withdraw his support from the Bosnian Serbs had finally combined by mid-1995 to make a Croatian-Bosnian victory over the BSA possible, even without direct involvement by NATO.[82] It is noteworthy that the developing capabilities and possible actions of the Croatian and BiH forces did not figure prominently in US and NATO campaign planning, as some of the following chapters discuss.[83]

The trigger for NATO air strikes that Holbrooke had foretold was provided the very next day when two mortar shells fell in a Sarajevo marketplace, killing 37 people and wounding 85. The Bosnian government threatened to withdraw from the on-going Paris peace talks if the Serbs were not punished, while Karadzic accused the BiH of launching the attack itself. On 29 August, UNPROFOR announced that it had confirmed "beyond all reasonable doubt" that the shells had been fired from a Serb-held area. In spite of the Bosnian Serb parliament's announcement that it now accepted the Western peace plan in principle (and a Russian statement that NATO should not retaliate for the shelling, even if the Serbs were responsible for it), NATO decided to execute its air campaign plan against the BSA.[84] On 30 August, US, British, Spanish, and French aircraft began launching air strikes against Bosnian Serb targets in the southeast zone of action, while French and British gunners on Mount Igman shelled BSA targets around Sarajevo, as Operation Deliberate Force began.

Notes

1. Among the recent accounts of Yugoslavia's disintegration and its consequences, perhaps the best and most accessible is Christopher Bennett, *Yugoslavia's Bloody Collapse* (New York: New York University Press, 1995). Also worthy of examination, among others, are Susan L. Woodward, *Balkan Tragedy* (Washington, D.C.: Brookings Institution, 1995); Laura Silber and Allan Little, *Yugoslavia: Death of a Nation* (New York: TV Books/Penguin USA, 1996); Miron Rezun, *Europe and War in the Balkans* (Westport, Conn.: Praeger, 1995); Lenard J. Cohen, *Broken Bonds: Yugoslavia's Disintegration and Balkan Politics in Transition,* 2d ed. (Boulder, Colo.: Westview, 1995); James Gow, *Legitimacy and the Military: The Yugoslav Crisis* (London: Pinter, 1991); Misha Glenny, *The Fall of Yugoslavia* (New York: Penguin, 1992); Branka Magas, *The Destruction of Yugoslavia* (London: Verno, 1993); and Mihailo Crnobrnja, *The Yugoslav Drama* (Montreal: McGill-Queen's University Press, 1994). Focusing on Bosnia-Herzegovina in particular are Noel Malcolm, *Bosnia: A Short History* (New York: New York University Press, 1994); and Robert J. Donia and John V. A. Fine, *Bosnia and Hercegovina: A Tradition Betrayed* (London: Hurst, 1994). Many of these works also provide useful summaries of earlier (and pre-) Yugoslav history.

2. On the July Crisis see, among many others, L. C. F. Turner, *Origins of the First World War* (New York: Norton, 1970), which also describes the preceding Balkan Wars; and James Joll, *The Origins of the First World War,* 2d ed. (New York: Longman, 1992).

3. Bulgaria was the only South Slavic nation not included in Yugoslavia, which means "Land of the South Slavs" in Serbo-Croatian. General histories of Yugoslavia that predate the 1980s include Stephen Clissold, ed., *A Short*

History of Yugoslavia (Cambridge: Cambridge University Press, 1968); and Stevan Pavlowitch, *Yugoslavia* (London: Ernest Benn, 1971). On the formation of Yugoslavia in particular, see Dimitrije Djordjevic, ed., *The Creation of Yugoslavia, 1914–1918* (Santa Barbara, Calif.: Clio, 1980); and Ivo Banac, *The National Question in Yugoslavia* (Ithaca, N.Y.: Cornell University Press, 1984).

4. See Piotr S. Wandycz, *France and Her Eastern Allies, 1919–1925* (Minneapolis: University of Minnesota Press, 1962); and *The Twilight of the French Eastern Alliances, 1926–1936* (Princeton, N.J.: Princeton University Press, 1988).

5. Robert Rothstein, *Alliances and Small Powers* (New York: Columbia University Press, 1968), 128–70.

6. On interwar and wartime Yugoslavia, see Bennett, chap. 3; J. B. Hoptner, *Yugoslavia in Crisis, 1934–1941* (New York: Columbia University Press, 1962); Aleksa Djilas, *The Contested Country: Yugoslav Unity and Communist Revolution, 1919–1953* (Cambridge, Mass.: Harvard University Press, 1991); and Donald Cameron Watt, *How War Came* (New York: Pantheon, 1989), chap. 17.

7. On the invasion and occupation of Yugoslavia, see also Iliva Jukic, *The Fall of Yugoslavia* (New York: Harcourt Brace Jovanovich, 1974); Jozo Tomasevich, *War and Revolution in Yugoslavia: The Chetniks* (Stanford: Stanford University Press, 1975); Elizabeth Wiskemann, "The Subjugation of South-Eastern Europe," in *Survey of International Affairs, 1939–1946: The Initial Triumph of the Axis*, ed. Arnold Toynbee and Veronica M. Toynbee (London: Oxford University Press, 1958), 319–63; and idem, "Partitioned Yugoslavia," in Toynbee and Toynbee, 648–73.

8. For geographic details of the Axis partition, see *The Times Atlas of the Second World War*, ed. John Keegan (Avenel, N.J.: Crescent Books, 1995).

9. Bennett, 43–46.

10. Among many biographical studies of Tito, see especially Stevan Pavlowitch, *Yugoslavia's Great Dictator: Tito, a Reassessment* (London: Hurst, 1992).

11. See Bennett, chap. 4; and Woodward, chap. 2. On postwar Yugoslavia's economic system, see also Dennison Rusinow, *The Yugoslav Experiment, 1948–1974* (London: Hurst, 1977).

12. Although the West welcomed Tito's withdrawal from the Soviet bloc, until (and in some cases even after) the Sino-Soviet split in the 1960s, many American policy makers (in spite of the contrary advice of George Kennan) continued to view the communist world as a united monolith and argued that the West would waste its efforts by trying to foment further splits in the international communist movement.

13. On Yugoslavia's foreign relations during the cold war, see also David L. Larson, *United States Foreign Policy toward Yugoslavia, 1943–1963* (Washington, D.C.: University Press of America, 1979).

14. On the other hand, Italian domestic politics were a long-standing hotbed of East-West competition, with the United States and the USSR

providing extensive covert assistance to Italian political parties on the right and left.

15. See Adam Roberts, *Nations in Arms: The Theory and Practice of Territorial Defense,* 2d ed. (New York: Saint Martin's, 1986), chaps. 5–6; and Douglas A. Fraze, "The Yugoslav All-People's Defense System: A Pessimistic Appraisal" (master's thesis, Naval Postgraduate School, June 1981).

16. See Woodward, chap. 2.

17. See ibid., chaps. 3–4; and Bennett, chap. 5.

18. Bennett, 69.

19. Warren Zimmerman, *Origins of a Catastrophe: Yugoslavia and Its Destroyers—America's Last Ambassador Tells What Happened and Why* (New York: Times Books, 1996), 42–48.

20. Presumably Slovaks, Ukrainians, Quebecois, and other relatively peaceful secessionists would occupy some intermediate rung on this hypothesized civilizational ladder.

21. It may or may not be significant that, as some observers have noted, during most of the Bosnian civil war, Sarajevans have faced a lower risk of violent death than do residents of some cities and towns in the United States.

22. And, usually most important in such arguments, therefore we should not get involved. Of course, the same noninterventionist policy prescription could also follow from a number of very different analyses of the problem. For an elegantly scathing critique of one prominent example of this perspective (Robert D. Kaplan's *Balkan Ghosts: A Journey through History* [New York: Saint Martin's, 1993]), see Noel Malcolm, "Seeing Ghosts," *The National Interest,* Summer 1993, 83–88.

23. One indicator of this trend was the rising number of people identifying themselves in censuses as ethnic Yugoslavs rather than as members of one of the subnational ethnic groups. Not the least of the factors working to erode traditional ethnic boundaries (and to create most of the self-identified Yugoslavs) was the substantial and rising number of marriages between members of different ethnic groups.

24. See Theda Skocpol, *States and Social Revolutions* (Cambridge: Cambridge University Press, 1979).

25. See V. P. Gagnon Jr., "Ethnic Nationalism and International Conflict," *International Security* 19, no. 3 (Winter 1994–95): 130–66.

26. Many scholars and observers have argued that this trend is effectively irreversible, at least for the foreseeable future, and that memories of the latest wave of internal wars in Yugoslavia, especially in Bosnia, now leave no alternative to ethnic partition. See, for example, John J. Mearsheimer and Stephen Van Evera, "When Peace Means War," *The New Republic,* 18 December 1995, 16–21.

27. See, among others, Bennett, chap. 2.

28. Kosovo is also the spiritual home of the Serbian Orthodox church. See ibid., 86–87.

29. On Milosevic's rise to power, see V. P. Gagnon Jr., "Serbia's Road to War," *Journal of Democracy* 5, no. 2 (April 1994): 117–31.

30. Although comparing lesser dictators to Adolf Hitler has become a troublingly popular cottage industry in recent years, Christopher Bennett, in *Yugoslavia's Bloody Collapse,* offers the following, unusually worthwhile, example of the art form: "Contemporary Yugoslav commentators were immediately struck by the similarities [with] . . . the tactics Adolph Hitler had employed . . . during the 1930s. Hitler's remilitarization of the Rhineland and the failure of the international community to react in 1936 corresponded to Milosevic's assault against Serbia's autonomous provinces and the inertia of Yugoslavia's federal authorities in 1988 and 1989. *Anschluss* with Austria in 1937 was akin to the Milosevic *coup d'état* in Montenegro. Similarly the Serb communities of Croatia and Bosnia-Hercegovina served the same purpose as the German minorities in Czechoslovakia and Poland" (page 116).

31. Milosevic himself was finally elected president of Serbia in December 1990, following a campaign in which he enjoyed complete control over the media and was able to finance his effort by having the main Serbian bank print the $1.7 billion he deemed necessary to ensure his election (ibid., 121–22).

32. Television documentary *Discovery Journal,* "Yugoslavia: The Death of a Nation," episode 2 (1995).

33. His election also benefited from campaign financing from expatriate Croats abroad (Bennett, 124). For detailed discussion of elections in Yugoslavia, see Cohen.

34. Unlike the Croatian government, the Slovenian government had foreknowledge of the JNA's plan to disarm the two republics' territorial defense forces in late 1990 and thus was able to retain control of a significant portion of its arms (Bennett, 144).

35. "Yugoslavia: The Death of a Nation," episode 2.

36. Bennett, 154–56.

37. For a detailed analysis, see Norman Cigar, "The Serbo-Croatian War, 1991: Political and Military Dimensions," *Journal of Strategic Studies* 16, no. 3 (September 1993): 297–338.

38. "Yugoslavia: The Death of a Nation," episode 3.

39. See Norman Cigar, *Genocide in Bosnia: The Policy of "Ethnic Cleansing"* (College Station, Tex.: Texas A&M University Press, 1995).

40. Milosevic threatened to destroy Bulatovic by revealing that the Italian government had offered him an attractive package of foreign aid and personal enrichment in return for acceptance of the EC plan.

41. In addition to the broader accounts of Yugoslavia's breakup and the resulting wars, see Edward O'Ballance, *Civil War in Bosnia, 1992–94* (New York: Saint Martin's, 1995).

42. The sixth of April was also the anniversary of the German terror bombing of Belgrade and invasion of Yugoslavia in 1941.

43. Bennett, 184–85.

44. As O'Ballance repeatedly observes, the siege of Sarajevo was never quite as impermeable as the Bosnian government and many journalists portrayed it to be—and sometimes was much less so (ibid.).

45. Senior UN official, interviewed by author, spring 1996.

46. Moreover, not only were the Bosnian government's forces not exclusively Muslim, in western Bosnia the Muslim militia force led by Fikret Abdic was an important ally of the Bosnian Serbs in the Bihac area.

47. The incendiary question of which side(s) committed the most atrocities in Bosnia cannot be addressed adequately here—nor need it be. As a first approximation, all but the most partisan analysts generally agree that in the wars in Croatia and Bosnia, all sides committed ethnic cleansing and even more vile acts, and that in both conflicts, Serbs committed by far the most.

48. Vice Adm Norman W. Ray and United Kingdom delegation, Headquarters NATO, interviewed by author, 9 February 1996.

49. Headquarters NATO, various interviews by author, 7–9 February 1996. One US diplomat suggested it was relevant that in 1995 the British military was finalizing official doctrine regarding peace operations, which held that peacekeeping and peace enforcement ("Chapter VI" and "Chapter VII" operations in UN parlance) are fundamentally different from each other and ought to be kept separate.

50. Of course, humanitarian aid was far from irrelevant to the military dimension of the conflict since shipments of food and other supplies often played a key role in sustaining the various belligerent forces. For details of various humanitarian aid efforts, see O'Ballance.

51. In UN Security Council Resolutions 713 and 757, respectively.

52. With the granting of enforcement powers on 22 November, the Western European Union's Operation Sharp Vigilance and NATO's Operation Maritime Monitor were renamed Sharp Fence and Maritime Guard, respectively. They were consolidated into a combined operation called Sharp Guard in June 1993.

53. A vivid and disturbing account of UNPROFOR's deployment and early days in Sarajevo and of what peacekeeping is like more generally appears in the memoirs of Lt Gen Lewis MacKenzie, a Canadian who originally commanded the UN force in Sarajevo. See *Peacekeeper: The Road to Sarajevo* (Vancouver: Douglas and McIntyre, 1993).

54. Four hundred sixty-five flights over Bosnia had been monitored by the time the Security Council adopted UNSCR 816.

55. Senior military command of Deny Flight lay with US admiral Leighton Smith, the commander of Allied Forces Southern Europe, and below him, day-to-day operational command resided with US Air Force lieutenant general Michael Ryan, commander of Allied Air Forces Southern Europe.

56. Memorandum for the NATO secretary-general, NAC Decision Statement, MCM-KAD-084-93, subject: Operational Options for Air Strikes in Bosnia-Herzegovina, 8 August 1993.

57. Some segments of the US administration, such as the National Security Council staff, had long favored strong Western intervention in the Bosnian crisis but had been outweighed by those who argued that intervention would produce little gain but involve potentially high political costs.

58. Air Force F-16s and Marine Corps F/A-18s flew the April CAS strikes. The UN hostages were subsequently released.

59. The NAC had anticipated a far more substantial air attack when it approved the strike against Udbina (US Mission officials, Headquarters NATO, interviewed by author, 8 February 1996).

60. Various interviews at Headquarters NATO, 8–9 February 1996.

61. The cease-fire did not actually last out its fourth month, as BiH forces launched a number of successful local offensives during April.

62. *Jane's Sentinel: The Balkans Newsletter* 1, no. 10 (October 1994): 2; and vol. 2, no. 7 (n.d.): 1–3. On the growth of the HZS and apparent German involvement therein, see Georg Mader, "Hrvatske Zrance Snage: Croatia's Embargoed Air Force," *World Air Power Journal* 24 (Spring 1996): 140–47.

63. Strains in the Bosnian Serb leadership between President Karadzic and General Mladic would soon become apparent as well. See Robert Block, "The Madness of General Mladic," *The New York Review*, 5 October 1995, 7–9.

64. US mission and British delegation officials, Headquarters NATO, interviewed by author, 8–9 February 1996.

65. NATO identified the attacking forces as including four US Air Force F-16s and one Dutch F-16, two US and two Spanish F-18s, and one French Mirage, in addition to tanker, electronic warfare, and search-and-rescue aircraft.

66. According to Vanderbilt University Television News Archive statistics, the three major US television networks together devoted a total of almost 45 minutes of coverage to stories about Bosnia on 2 and 3 June 1995, compared to just over 33 minutes on 30 and 31 August, the first two days of bombing in Operation Deliberate Force. One should note that on the first day of Deliberate Force, a Bosnian Serb SA-16 shot down a French Mirage 2000D, and the fate of its two-man non-American crew remained unknown for several weeks.

67. The United States had long been lobbying for such permission from NATO, even to the point of revealing previously unshared intelligence information about the Bosnian Serb IADS with its allies, but differences between American and European attitudes towards proportionality and definitions of hostile intent led the NAC consistently to reject these requests. AFSOUTH did not have sufficient defense-suppression aircraft available to provide routine protection from SAMs for Deny Flight patrols over Bosnia (Ray interview).

68. The same difference of opinion between the United States and its European allies about the tolerability of friendly losses also characterized some aspects of the planning and execution of NATO air strikes in Septem-

ber 1995 (Group Capt Trevor Murray and British UN delegation officials, RAF Uxbridge and Headquarters NATO, interviewed by author, 6–9 February 1996).

69. During this time, one of the stranger incidents of the conflict occurred when it was widely reported that an explosion heard in Pale on 22 July had been a unilateral French bombing attack against the home of a relative of Radovan Karadzic in retaliation for the killing of two French peacekeepers the day before. The French Defense Ministry denied this, and subsequently it appeared that the noise had actually been a sonic boom (*Jane's Sentinel: The Balkans Newsletter* 2, no. 7 [n.d.]: 6). However, the mystery has been fueled by a comment from French defense minister Millon that if such an attack had been launched, "it would obviously be part of an appropriate response to the logic of war chosen by the Serbs," and by a comment from President Chirac that he had ordered unspecified retaliation for the deaths of the peacekeepers ("French Revenge Strike in Bosnia?" *World Air Power Journal* 24 [Spring 1996]: 5).

70. US and British delegation, Headquarters NATO, interviewed by author, 7–8 February 1996. In practice, either of the key holders would probably have been able to halt the bombing unilaterally if sufficiently set on doing so (Ray interview).

71. President Clinton vetoed this resolution on 11 August.

72. Air Chief Marshal William Wratten, RAF High Wycombe, interviewed by author, 5 February 1996. In addition to Air Chief Marshal Wratten, commander in chief of RAF Strike Command, the NATO delegation included Air Force general James Jamerson, deputy commander in chief of US European Command, and an *Armée de l'Air* major general. Wratten ended the visit when a heated argument began between Mladic and the French general.

73. Several diplomats in the US NATO mission retrospectively assessed the military decision to discontinue routine overflights after the loss of the F-16 in June as having been a powerful political lever to encourage the British to support new measures in Bosnia (interviews, 8 February 1996).

74. Various interviews by author, 7–9 February 1996.

75. Ibid. For details of the offensive, see Tim Ripley and Paul Beaver, "Analysis: Operation Storm," *Jane's Sentinel: The Balkans Newsletter* 2, no. 8 (n.d.): 2–3.

76. Ripley and Beaver, 2.

77. During the fighting, US Navy EA-6Bs and F/A-18s fired high-speed antiradiation missiles at Serb SAM sites near Knin and Udbina that had locked on to them.

78. On 13 August, RSK troops who had fled to Yugoslavia were ordered to return to Bosnia; soon Belgrade began sending Krajina Serb refugees to find new homes in Kosovo, leading to rising ethnic tensions there (*Jane's Sentinel: The Balkans Newsletter* 2, no. 8 [n.d.]: 3).

79. Steven Greenhouse, "U.S. Officials Say Bosnian Serbs Face NATO Attacks If Talks Stall," *New York Times*, 28 August 1995, A1, A6.

80. Ibid., A6.

81. On 4 August 1995, NATO aircraft were in fact sent to provide a deterrent overhead presence for Canadian UNPROFOR peacekeepers who were under fire from HV forces during Operation Storm. However, RSK forces illuminated the flight with their radars, and the aircraft responded by firing antiradiation missiles, which seemed likely to have emboldened rather than deterred the Croatian forces (Capt Chip Pringle, Ramstein Air Base, interviewed by Lt Col Chris Campbell, 14 February 1996).

82. This study cannot—and will not try to—answer the question of what might have happened if Operation Deliberate Force had not been launched, but the question deserves further study and consideration. In light of the rapid successes that Croatia scored against the RSK in mid-1995 and the slower progress made against the BSA in late August, it must fall to those who argue that NATO bombing not only accelerated but determined the outcome of the war in Bosnia to prove their case.

83. Given the splendid synergy between the air campaign and HV/HVO/BiH operations, it is not surprising that there has been widespread speculation about whether this was the result of accident or design. The US government has consistently maintained that no strategic coordination existed between Washington and the belligerents, pointing to the fact that US diplomats in Zagreb tried unsuccessfully to persuade the Croatian government not to launch its major offensives in 1995. Ambassador Richard Holbrooke, interviewed by author, 24 May 1996.

If any such collaboration occurred—and for that matter, if the United States were even aware of the extent to which Croatia and the BiH had improved their capabilities relative to the RSK army and the BSA—it remains a closely held secret.

84. The day after the air strikes began, Russia switched to blaming the Bosnian Serbs for provoking NATO.

Chapter 2

The Planning Background

Lt Col Bradley S. Davis

In the aftermath of the deadly mortar attack on the crowded Mrkale marketplace in Sarajevo in August 1995, Adm Leighton W. Smith, commander in chief of Allied Forces Southern Europe (CINCSOUTH), called British lieutenant general Rupert Smith, commander of the United Nations Protection Force (UNPROFOR) in the former Yugoslavia,[1] to tell him that if the Bosnian Serbs were responsible, he would recommend retaliatory air strikes by the North Atlantic Treaty Organization (NATO). At 2300 (local time) that same night, Admiral Smith and General Smith agreed to "turn the key" (the prevailing metaphor for strike authority), thus setting in motion NATO's intense offensive air action—Operation Deliberate Force, the culmination of events and related planning efforts by the UN and NATO over a long period of time. Although by the standards of modern warfare, Deliberate Force was a modest operation, it nonetheless served as a significant example of the efficient use of military force in pursuit of international stability in the post-cold-war era.

In this unique operation, NATO military forces fulfilled United Nations Security Council resolutions (UNSCR) and NATO political mandates by assisting UN political and military efforts to bring peace to the region of the former Yugoslavia. Parallel UN and NATO command and control (C^2) structures used for the previous two years provided less than optimum political and military coordination and guidance during Deliberate Force. As one might expect, tensions existed between UN and NATO commanders, and the system occasionally proved less than timely in applying NATO airpower in response to UN requests; nonetheless, it seems to have worked. This chapter describes the UN and NATO political and military structures and their unusual interrelationships, and discusses the anticipated flow of planning they provided for Deliberate Force.

Adm Leighton W. Smith holds a poster of alleged war criminals.

Following chapters address the planning process as it actually occurred and the execution of the operation.

United Nations and NATO Political Structures

The UN has been politically and militarily involved in the former Yugoslavia since the civil war spread to Bosnia in 1992. One can trace the UN's political and military intervention activities to the UN Charter and the Security Council resolutions concerning civil strife in the former Yugoslavia. The UN evoked the Charter to provide the basis of its actions and to meet its primary responsibility of maintaining international peace and security. Chapter 7, Article 39 of the Charter allows the Security Council to survey the world for any threat to the peace, breach of the peace, or act of aggression; make recommendations for action in accordance with Articles 39, 41, and 42 of chapter seven; and then maintain or restore international peace and security. These three articles specifically allow the UN to employ military forces volunteered by member nations to intervene within the sovereign territory of another member nation to maintain or restore the peace.[2] Article 48 allows member states to carry out Security Council decisions directly and through appropriate international agencies of which they are members.

Based on recommendations and resolutions of the UN Security Council, Secretary-General Boutros Boutros-Ghali directed the UN's political efforts and military forces in the war-ravaged former Yugoslavia throughout the Bosnian crisis prior to mid-1995. Yasushi Akashi, the secretary-general's special representative for that country, headed the political and military forces, UNPROFOR, there for the period leading up to and including Operation Deliberate Force. UNPROFOR, headquartered in Zagreb, Croatia, included military, civil affairs, civilian police, public information, and administrative components. Akashi was directly responsible to Boutros-Ghali for coordination of political initiatives with the warring parties, UN humanitarian relief efforts, and in-theater civilian control of UN military peacekeeping forces.

UN Security Council resolutions 781, 816, and 836 had a direct and far-reaching impact upon the ultimate planning structure for Deliberate Force. Through UNSCR 781 (1992), the UN requested member states to assist UNPROFOR in monitoring the UN ban on any military flights over Bosnia-Herzegovina. NATO military forces began their monitoring activities in support of this resolution in October 1992.[3] On 31 March 1993, UNSCR 816 (1993) extended the ban to cover all flights not authorized by UNPROFOR and directed member states to take all necessary measures to ensure compliance with the ban.[4] The North Atlantic Council (NAC, the day-to-day political arm of NATO)[5] approved NATO's plans for the enforcement of this extended ban on 8 April 1993 and then notified the UN of NATO's willingness to undertake the operation. NATO's Operation Deny Flight began at noon Greenwich mean time on Monday, 12 April 1993, with aircraft from the air forces of France, the Netherlands, the United Kingdom, and the United States flying what would eventually become a 24-hour, around-the-clock air patrol over the skies of Bosnia-Herzegovina. (For a succinct review of the applicable UNSCRs and NAC decisions that led to Operation Deliberate Force, see fig. 2.1.)

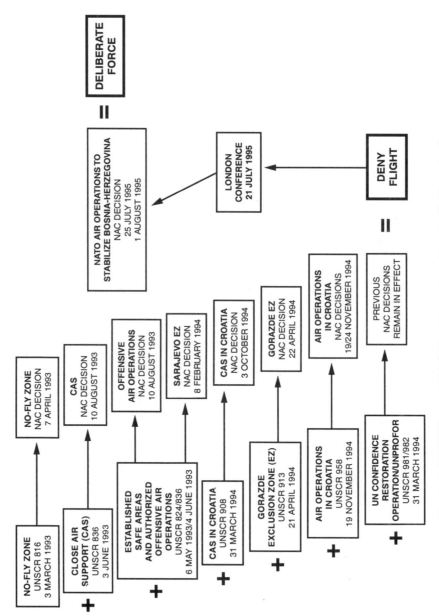

Fig. 2.1. UNSCRs and NAC Decisions Leading to Deliberate Force

Paragraph 10 of UNSCR 836 (1993) had the greatest impact on the planning for Operation Deliberate Force. It stated that "member states, acting nationally or through regional organizations or arrangements, may take, under the authority of the Security Council and subject to close coordination with the Secretary-General and UNPROFOR, all necessary measures, through the use of air power, in and around the safe areas in the Republic of Bosnia and Herzegovina, to support UNPRO-FOR in the performance of its mandate set out in paragraphs 5 and 9."[6] In response to this resolution, NATO foreign ministers agreed on 10 June 1993 that NATO would provide protective airpower in case of attacks against UNPROFOR in Bosnia-Herzegovina. The alliance's aircraft began this coverage on 22 July 1993.

The Bosnian Serb army's (BSA) shelling of the same Mrkale marketplace in Sarajevo in February 1994 precipitated the enforcement of UNSCR 836. In accordance with that resolution, the UN secretary-general requested preparations for air strikes to deter further attacks. He also informed the Security Council that he had requested Willy Claes, secretary-general of NATO, to obtain "a decision by the North Atlantic Council to authorize the Commander in Chief of NATO's Southern Command to launch air strikes, at the request of the United Nations, against BSA artillery or mortar positions in and around Sarajevo which are determined by UNPROFOR to be responsible for attacks against civilian targets in that city."[7]

The NAC accepted Boutros-Ghali's request and authorized CINCSOUTH to launch air strikes in close coordination with the secretary-general on behalf of UNPROFOR. Boutros-Ghali then instructed Akashi to finalize detailed procedures for the initiation, conduct, and termination of requested air strikes with CINCSOUTH. He also delegated to Akashi the specific authority to approve a request from the force commander of UNPROFOR for close air support in defense of UN personnel anywhere in Bosnia-Herzegovina. Prior to this delegation, only the UN secretary-general approved UNPROFOR's requests for NATO air support—a time-consuming, inefficient process. Even with Akashi's newly delegated authority, delays still occurred. For example, in March 1994, a request to attack a 40-millimeter gun firing on UN forces in the Bihac area took over six hours for approval. Ironically, two AC-130 gunships over the area had the offending gun in their sights, but by the time they received clearance, the gun had moved back under camouflage and escaped.[8]

Earlier, at a meeting of the NAC in Oslo, Norway, in June 1992, NATO foreign ministers announced their readiness to support the UN in Bosnia-Herzegovina by making available NATO resources and expertise for peacekeeping operations on a case-by-case basis; thus they laid the political foundation for NATO's role in the former Yugoslavia. In December 1992, the NAC reiterated its readiness to support peacekeeping operations under authority of the UN Security Council, which has primary responsibility for international peace and security. The foreign ministers reviewed peacekeeping and sanctions-enforcement measures already undertaken by NATO countries, individually and as an alliance, to support the implementation of Security Council resolutions relating to the conflict. Upon the recommendations of the Defense Planning Committee (DPC),[9] the foreign ministers indicated that NATO stood ready to respond favorably to further initiatives that the UN secretary-general might take in seeking alliance assistance in this endeavor (fig. 2.2).

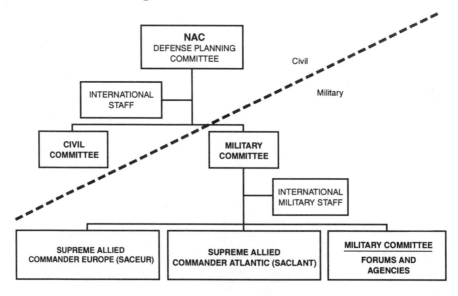

Fig. 2.2. NATO Organization

The first military engagement undertaken by the alliance since the inception of the organization[10] occurred on 28 February 1994, when NATO aircraft shot down four warplanes violating the UN-mandated no-fly zone over Bosnia-Herzegovina. One finds the next evolutionary step in the cooperative efforts between UN and NATO military forces in the NAC's announcement on 22 April 1994 of far stricter protection of the safe areas during Deny Flight. The council asserted that if any BSA heavy-weapons attacks occurred on the UN-designated safe areas of Gorazde, Bihac, Srebrenica, Tuzla, and Zepa, these weapons and other BSA military assets, as well as their direct and essential military-support facilities such as fuel installations and munitions sites, would be subject to NATO air strikes in accordance with the procedural arrangements worked out between NATO and UNPROFOR.[11]

Specifically, the NAC declared that, consistent with its decisions of 2 and 9 August 1993, any violation of the provisions of those decisions would constitute grounds for the NATO military command to begin air attacks on targets preapproved by UN/NATO without further approval by the council. These targets included any military assets directly related to the violation and located in the vicinity of the area concerned. Under all circumstances, NATO forces would carry out such attacks in close coordination with UNPROFOR. Based upon its view of the violation, the NATO military command could recommend additional air attacks in coordination with UNPROFOR. However, such recommendations required conveyance to the NATO secretary-general through the NATO chain of command for NAC approval. These attacks could continue until the NATO military command judged the mission accomplished. The NAC also reaffirmed its earlier decision of February 1994 that authorized the NATO military command to initiate air attacks to suppress BSA air defenses representing a direct threat to NATO aircraft operating under the agreed UN/NATO coordination procedures, and to take all necessary and appropriate action for their self-defense. The final NAC direction instructed US Army general George A. Joulwan, Supreme Allied Commander Europe (SACEUR), to delegate to CINCSOUTH the necessary authority to implement the council's decisions, coordinating with UNPROFOR in accordance with the relevant operations plan.

Over the next 17 months, the political and military situation slowly worsened in Bosnia-Herzegovina. Following the international meeting on Bosnia-Herzegovina held in London in July 1995, the NAC authorized NATO commanders to deter a BSA attack on the safe area of Gorazde and to ensure the timely and effective use of NATO airpower if this area were threatened or attacked.[12] On 1 August the council announced similar decisions regarding the use of NATO airpower aimed at deterring attacks on the safe areas of Sarajevo, Bihac, and Tuzla. The NAC decisions following the London conference of July 1995 specified that NATO meet further Bosnian Serb offensive action with a firm and rapid response designed to deter attacks on the safe areas and authorized the timely and effective use of airpower, if necessary. Through both the UN and the NATO political apparatus, the coordination of military actions by both CINCSOUTH and the force commander of UN Peace Forces (UNPF)[13] was always a strategic and operational necessity.

United Nations and NATO Military Structures

Before discussing the UN and NATO military structures in the former Yugoslavia, one should note the strategic political objectives of Operation Deliberate Force as agreed upon by the UN and NATO communities in the summer of 1995: (1) reduce the threat to the Sarajevo safe area and deter further attacks there or on any other safe area, (2) force the withdrawal of Bosnian Serb heavy weapons from the 20-kilometer total-exclusion zone around Sarajevo, (3) ensure complete freedom of movement for UN forces and personnel as well as nongovernmental organizations, and (4) ensure unrestricted use of the Sarajevo airport.[14]

The UN originally established its military forces—UNPROFOR—in the former Yugoslavia in February 1992 and redesignated them UNPF in the spring of 1995, the latter organization commanded by a senior military officer from one of the UN's member states. From 1 March 1995 until after Operation Deliberate Force, Lt Gen Bernard Janvier of France, headquartered in

Zagreb with Yasushi Akashi, commanded UNPF, which included three subordinate commands: the UN Confidence Restoration Operation in Croatia, also headquartered in Zagreb; UNPROFOR Bosnia-Herzegovina, headquartered in Sarajevo; and UN Preventive Deployment Forces in the former Yugoslav Republic of Macedonia, headquartered in Skopje. The three commanders reported to the force commander of UNPF, who, together with the civilian diplomatic and humanitarian relief components, acted under the overall direction of Special Representative Akashi.[15] As of September 1995, about 35,000 UN military personnel were deployed in-theater. Combined with civilian police and civilian personnel, UNPF totaled nearly 50,000 people.[16]

The initial mandate for UNPROFOR called for ensuring the demilitarization of the UN-protected areas by withdrawing or disbanding all armed forces in them, as well as protecting all persons residing in them from attack. Outside these areas, UNPROFOR military observers were to verify the withdrawal of all Yugoslav national army and irregular forces from Croatia. Finally, UNPROFOR was to facilitate the safe, secure return of displaced civilians to their homes within the protected areas. In May and June 1993, the Security Council adopted resolutions 824 and 836, respectively, the former expanding UNPROFOR's mandate to protect the safe areas of Sarajevo, Tuzla, Zepa, Gorazde, and Bihac. This included deterring attacks against them, monitoring cease-fire arrangements, promoting the withdrawal of military or paramilitary units other than those of the Bosnian government, and occupying key points. Resolution 836 authorized the use of airpower in and around the declared safe areas to support UNPROFOR.[17]

In an attempt to convey the delicate interrelationship of the UNPROFOR and NATO missions in Bosnia-Herzegovina, Akashi sent a letter in December 1994 to Dr. Radovan Karadzic, leader of the Bosnian Serbs, explaining the role assigned by the UN Security Council to NATO in support of UNPROFOR's mandate. He described the four missions of NATO in the airspace over Bosnia and how/why NATO would be employed, placing special emphasis on the restraint of using NATO airpower and the impartiality of UNPROFOR and NATO:

45

> Except for self-defense, NATO aircraft will not conduct air-to-ground operations without advance authorization from the Special Representative of the Secretary-General. If the armed forces in conflict respect the terms of the Security Council resolutions and the NAC decisions, do not attack UNPROFOR, and do not threaten NATO aircraft, they will have nothing to fear from NATO. In conclusion, I wish to reiterate that NATO operates over Bosnia only in support of the United Nations mission. Its aircraft provide essential support to UNPROFOR in the impartial and effective discharge of its Security Council mandates, and are neither the enemy nor the ally of any combatant.[18]

The issuance of UNSCR 836 made it necessary to allow then-UNPROFOR forces in Bosnia-Herzegovina to request both NATO airpower within their area of responsibility and the means to coordinate it. This led the UN to create the air operations control center (AOCC) at Kiseljak in July 1993. The center requested and coordinated NATO air assets on behalf of the UNPROFOR ground commander. As a UN organization, the AOCC had no controlling authority over NATO air assets. In addition to AOCC staff, UNPROFOR member nations provided tactical air control parties (TACP) for terminal guidance of aircraft.

British, Canadian, Dutch, French, and Spanish forces provided more than 20 TACPs in Bosnia-Herzegovina. Often located in the areas of greatest tension, solitary, and without support, they were tasked by the AOCC but remained under the command of their country's parent battalion. If deployed by the local battalion to an area of fighting, the TACP, in close consultation with the ground-incident commander, would make a request for air support to the AOCC, which initiated action to request that aircraft be scrambled by NATO; it also started the air-request assessment for the UN secretary-general. The request proceeded through the UN's C^2 chain to the Security Council or, subsequently, the special representative for approval or refusal. If the request was approved, the AOCC simultaneously coordinated aircraft through NATO's airborne battlefield command and control center aircraft and the combined air operations center (CAOC) of NATO's 5th Allied Tactical Air Force (5 ATAF) at Vicenza, Italy. The AOCC then issued necessary clearances to the battalion and TACP for attack. At times, UN forces would request air support despite knowing that clearance would not be forthcoming, simply because they realized NATO aircraft would be overhead quickly. This established a presence that often suppressed the BSA's offensive activities without the need for actually using direct attacks from the air.[19]

The separation of the UN/NATO C^2 structures required close liaison between the operational arms of both elements, best achieved not only by having NATO and UN liaison officers assigned to each organization's command posts but also by establishing a close relationship between the AOCC staff and the staff at 5 ATAF's CAOC. This enabled the direct and focused passage of tactical information without the attenuation

Gen Michael E. Ryan

or amplification associated with additional layers of unneeded bureaucracy. Such close cooperation was vital for the successful attainment of political and military objectives.

The Military Committee (MC), the supreme military authority in NATO, falls under the political authority of the NAC and the Defense Planning Committee. It provides for maximum consultation and cooperation between member nations on military matters and serves as the primary source of military advice on alliance matters to the secretary-general, NAC, and DPC. Its members include the chiefs of staff of member nations—except France, which maintains contact through its military mission at NATO, and Iceland, which has civilian-observer status only. The MC also gives military guidance to the major NATO commanders, the NAC, and DPC as required and acts as the critical pivot between the political and military bodies of NATO.

The MC provided instructions to SACEUR, by direction of the NAC and DPC, to delegate authority and operational control for the development, coordination, and implementation of Operation Deliberate Force to Adm Leighton Smith, CINCSOUTH, headquartered in Naples, Italy. Admiral Smith, in turn, delegated control of air operations to the Air Force's Michael E. Ryan, then a lieutenant general and commander of Allied Air

Forces Southern Europe (COMAIRSOUTH), also headquartered in Naples.[20] Italian air force lieutenant general Andrea Fornasiero, commander of 5 ATAF at Dal Molin Air Base, Vicenza, Italy, had responsibility for the day-to-day mission tasking and operational control of all NATO air assets over the former Yugoslavia.

The original mission of 5 ATAF was the coordination and control of peacetime and combat air defense of NATO's Southern Region for COMAIRSOUTH. Since it was not able to adequately command and control the added responsibility for Operation Deny Flight, this fell to the CAOC, specifically established for such a mission. Technically a multinational organization assigned to 5 ATAF under the command of General Fornasiero, in reality the CAOC worked directly for COMAIRSOUTH.

An exchange of representatives between 5 ATAF and UNPF headquarters in Zagreb and UNPROFOR Bosnia-Herzegovina headquarters in Sarajevo provided coordination between NATO and the UN. These liaison officers ensured a continuous exchange of information between NATO and UNPF (fig. 2.3). The headquarters of General Janvier and Lt Gen Rupert Smith, as well as the UN AOCC, housed the NATO liaison officers, while CINCSOUTH's headquarters and the CAOC included the UNPF liaison officers. These officers proved essential to the detailed coordination of airpower requests, approval, mission planning, force application, and bomb damage assessment. Although Admiral Smith and Mr. Akashi (and, later, General Janvier) approved the use of airpower, the liaison officers, in close cooperation with the in-place UN and NATO air staffs, got the aircraft to their targets. The separate UN and NATO military organizations did not represent the first tenet of warfare—unity of command—but their coordination from the top down, including the liaison officers, did eventually facilitate a rudimentary unity of effort.

The CAOC was the focal point of all NATO air activity in the former Yugoslavia. Located at Vicenza since the spring of 1993, when NATO air forces embarked upon Operation Deny Flight, the CAOC was to be a six-month temporary operation and was not originated for Operation Deliberate Force.[21] Directed by the US Air Force's Hal M. Hornburg, then a major general, the CAOC included personnel drawn from all the countries participating in Deny Flight, but most of them were Americans. The CAOC followed a conventional air-staff structure, with a NATO

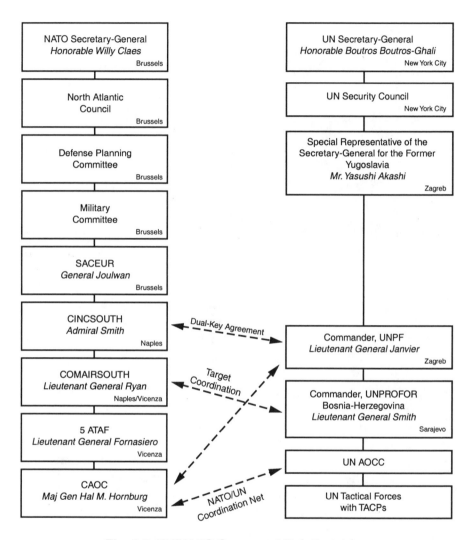

Fig. 2.3. UN/NATO Command Relationships

flavor for personnel, intelligence, operations, logistics, plans, and communications branches. Also based at Vicenza were senior national representatives from the United Kingdom, France, Germany, the Netherlands, Spain, and Turkey—countries that had assigned aircraft to Deny Flight. The UN, US Navy, and NATO's airborne early warning force also maintained liaison cells at the CAOC. The center maintained close links with the Italian Ministry of Defense.

Lt Gen Hal M. Hornburg

The CAOC ensured safe deconfliction of airspace usage over the theater of operations. The daily production of air tasking messages (ATM), which translated the intention of NATO commanders into orders, achieved these objectives. ATMs, which included routes, call signs, weapons loads, and other information, provided aircrews with the taskings and coordinating instructions they needed to carry out their daily missions. Although members of the NAC had to unanimously approve all rules of engagement, the CAOC served as the sole command element for issuing these rules to aircraft flying in the area of operation. A satellite-communications network, centered on Vicenza, allowed the CAOC operations staff to maintain strict control over all aircraft in the area of operation.

The ATM was a time-phased management of air resources, and its production cycle accounted for all the factors necessary to conduct a high-intensity air campaign. Although the ATM provided information on mission type, times, and configuration to assigned units, the units themselves accomplished specific mission planning. The process (just prior to Operation Deliberate Force) began with the NAC's decisions, which were transmitted through SACEUR, along with Admiral Smith's and General Ryan's guidance, to the CAOC (fig. 2.4). A spreadsheet dubbed the "Gucci," which projected events six weeks into the future, considered all the various taskings. Each senior national representative received the Gucci every Monday, and unit representatives received it at their daily meeting. The latter representatives then scoured the Gucci to ensure that their unit's aircraft could meet the tasking requirements. This process fostered long-term planning, and by the time the plan came to the week-in-progress, those requirements were well defined. The ATM then rolled into a 72-hour cycle before the current operations day.

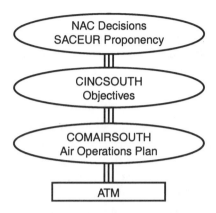

Fig. 2.4. Air Strategy to Execution

Each day, unit representatives received 72-hour, 48-hour, and 24-hour flows showing what their aircraft needed to do over the upcoming days. These flows—graphic illustrations of what the Gucci indicated—described aircraft, type, and country and might differ from the Gucci since aircraft broke, pilots got sick, or units were simply unable to perform a mission. The last stage in the process involved presenting the finalized ATM for the next 24 hours to the CAOC's director. If he authorized the ATM, the full 12- to 16-page document was published by early afternoon, and the taskings took effect at 0300 the following morning.

When a crisis developed, planners quickly broke into their ATM cycle and provided the required forces. If UNPF called at 0900 saying it was going to request NATO air strikes against some location not currently in the 24-hour flow, the CAOC incorporated that request into the ATM cycle. If the request for airpower support occurred after publication of the ATM, the CAOC's current-operations cell manipulated the schedule to meet the request, or, if that did not prove feasible, the cell published a change message. At times, COMAIRSOUTH or the CAOC director rejected the ATM, and the CAOC team started over again. The entire ATM cycle was normally 18 hours from start to finish but was known to take less time.[22]

Development of the ATM was not just a problem of air-traffic scheduling. Planners matched aircraft weapons loads to likely threats and targets; they also considered the ground situation.

General Hornburg, all the cell chiefs, and the senior national representatives received two intelligence briefs a day. Based on this information, General Hornburg could heighten the readiness posture of NATO air forces in the planning cycle, putting extra aircraft on ground-alert lines or more aircraft in the air. CAOC planners also provided contingency plans to respond to new missions or requirements, such as air supply to besieged enclaves or air cover for any UN withdrawal. During the summer of 1995, the CAOC developed a concept of operations to provide air support for the new UN Rapid Reaction Force.

From the CAOC, the ATM and orders to execute air operations went to the various tactical units of the combined NATO air forces spread across the European continent (table 2.1 and fig. 2.5). Aviano Air Base, Italy, home of the American 31st Fighter Wing and other deployed NATO and US units, exemplified the manner in which the ATM was transmitted. The CAOC sent the ATM by multiple, secure-communication systems to the Deny Flight/Deliberate Force operations center at Aviano. The center then passed it along to the wing mission-planning cell for weaponeering and issuance of "frag" orders. The various flying units stationed at Aviano used the ATM's guidance to plan the mission from takeoff to recovery back at Aviano and then finally carried through with the actual missions.

As a result of the increasing number of units tasked to fly missions over Bosnia-Herzegovina, C^2 of these forces became increasingly difficult. On 1 July 1995, Headquarters United States Air Forces Europe (USAFE), established the 7490th Wing (Provisional)[23] at Aviano to exercise operational and administrative control of the Deny Flight forces assigned to that base. These forces, consisting of both home-station and deployed personnel, represented not only the active duty US Air Force but also elements of the Air Force Reserve, US Navy, Marine Corps, and two NATO member nations—Spain and the United Kingdom.[24] The commander and operations group commander of the 31st Fighter Wing assumed the same positions in the new wing. One of the most important aspects of this organizational readjustment was that the increased personnel it brought to Aviano allowed around-the-clock manning of the provisional wing's operations center. This permitted Aviano forces to be more responsive to late-breaking or changing

Table 2.1

NATO Aircraft for Deliberate Force

Nation	Number	Aircraft Type	Location
France	8	Mirage F-1	Istrana
	8	Jaguar	Istrana
	18	Mirage 2000	Cervia
	6	Super Etendard	*Foch**
	1	E-3	Avord
	1	C-135	Istres
	8	Puma	Brindisi
Germany	14	Tornado	Piacenza
Italy	8	Tornado	Ghedi
	6	AMX	Istrana
	1	KC-135	Pisa
	1	C-130	Pisa
	4	G-222	Pisa
NATO	4	E-3A	Geilenkirchen
	4	E-3A	Trapani
	4	E-3A	Preveza
Netherlands	18	F-16	Villafranca
Spain	1	CASA C-212	Dal Molin
	8	EF-18	Aviano
	2	KC-130	Aviano
Turkey	16	F-16	Ghedi
United Kingdom	6	Tornado	Gioia del Colle
	17	Harrier	Gioia del Colle
	6	Sea Harrier	HMS *Invincible**
	2	K-1 Tristar L-1011	Palermo
	2	E-3D	Aviano
United States	20	F-16	Aviano
	12	O/A-10	Aviano
	7	EC-130	Aviano
	4	AC-130	Aviano
	6	EF-111A	Aviano
	12	KC-135	Pisa
	12	KC-135	Istres
	10	EA-6B	Aviano
	24	FA-18	USS *America**
	5	KC-10	Genoa
	8	E-3A	Geilenkirchen, Trapani, Preveza

*When the aircraft carrier is in the Adriatic Sea

53

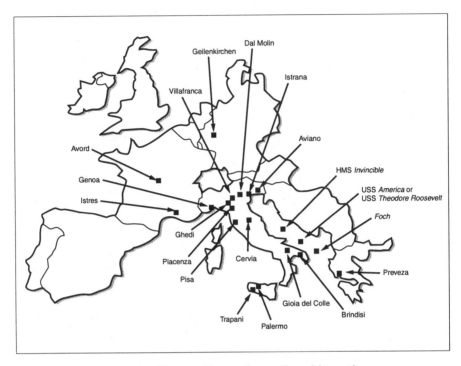

Fig. 2.5. Deliberate Force Operational Locations

ATMs during sustained operations. Along with the Deny Flight operations center, created in conjunction with the 7490th and fully operational only days before Deliberate Force, the military planning structure was now in place from the highest political echelons of both the UN and NATO down to each of the tactical military units.

The Planning Process: The Shakedown

Up to the early part of 1995, NATO had accomplished small "tit-for-tat" air operations. Anticipating a greatly expanded role for NATO airpower, given the deteriorating situation in Bosnia-Herzegovina, General Ryan decided to collocate his Sixteenth Air Force staff with that of the CAOC. Most of his strategic planning staff assigned to Headquarters AIRSOUTH stayed in Naples under the direction of Col Daniel Zoerb, while the operational

54

and tactical experts of Sixteenth Air Force moved with General Ryan to the CAOC. There, the general realized that Operations Plan 40101, which governed AIRSOUTH air operations over Bosnia, had not been updated to cover a full-scale operation over Bosnia-Herzegovina.[25] Thus, in April 1995 he initiated a planning process—without direct UN/NATO political guidance—to develop a plan of action outlining some strategic and operational assumptions, a framework, and a concept of operations. During the early phases of its development, he kept this new plan on close hold but did brief the chairman of Joint Chiefs of Staff (JCS) on his conceptual plan. The JCS's intelligence directorate and the Air Staff's Checkmate division (AF/XOOC) evaluated the plan.[26]

In late May 1995, COMAIRSOUTH's strategy cell, headed by Colonel Zoerb at Headquarters AIRSOUTH in Naples, nominated target lists covering broad categories of targets for two zones of action in Bosnia-Herzegovina (one northwest and one southeast) to General Ryan. At the same time, General Ryan requested assistance for air campaign planning from the deputy chief of staff for plans and operations at Headquarters USAF, who in turn tasked Checkmate to provide any requested help. A Checkmate planner sent to Vicenza in early June provided invaluable insights for the initial feasibility assessment and campaign phasing. General Ryan, General Hornburg, and the tactical-unit representatives completed the feasibility assessment in late May/early June and identified the nominal forces to be tasked in the yet-unnamed operational plan. General Ryan forwarded this plan to Admiral Smith for his recommendations and coordination.[27]

While Admiral Smith reviewed the plan, the CAOC underwent a renaissance. Col John R. Baker from Headquarters USAF, Director of Operations, led a US joint-service assessment team to the CAOC on 24–31 July 1995. Specifically, COMAIRSOUTH wanted the Baker team to identify improvements and capabilities needed for the CAOC to perform current Deny Flight/5 ATAF missions and to develop a fused intelligence-operations organization able to plan and execute a robust, sustained air campaign of two simultaneous air operations in support of the safe areas. Colonel Baker investigated manning, stability, and equipment to determine what assets the CAOC needed to improve the short-term and long-term planning process.[28] The team strongly recommended that additional manpower and equipment immediately be sent to the CAOC, and the JCS and NATO took these recommendations seriously. Consequently, beginning in mid-August, additional hardware/software capabilities such as the Air Campaign Planning Tool (now known as the JFACC [Joint Force Air Component Commander] Planning Tool), the Joint Situational Awareness System, and the Contingency Theater Air Planning System, along with increased manpower (planners from USAFE's 32d Air Operations Group) arrived daily to augment the operation. On the negative side, Colonel Baker's report stepped on the toes of a few of our NATO partners. That is, most of the NATO contingent thought that the report and subsequent large-scale infusion of US military personnel and equipment further isolated them from the operation. This reinforced their underlying feeling that this operation was going to be an American show.[29]

On 10 August 1995, Admiral Smith and General Janvier signed a memorandum of understanding that contained the joint UN/NATO arrangements for implementing the actions specified in the NAC and UN Security Council decisions. These arrangements aimed to deter attacks or threats of attack against the safe areas and, should deterrence fail, to prepare to conduct operations to eliminate the threat or defeat any force engaged in an attack on a safe area. The memorandum described the authority each man possessed (euphemistically called "dual-key" authority) to launch broad retaliatory counterattacks in Bosnia. In an earlier letter to NATO secretary-general Claes, UN secretary-general Boutros-Ghali agreed that this was a prudent decision: "I have decided to delegate the necessary authority in this respect to the UN military commanders in the field. I have accordingly delegated authority in respect of air strikes, which I had hitherto retained, to General Janvier, the Commander of United Nations Peace Forces, with immediate effect. As regards close air support, my Special Representative, Mr. Akashi, has today delegated the necessary authority to General Janvier, who is authorized to delegate it further to the UNPROFOR Force Commander when operational circumstances so require."[30] Both men (Admiral Smith and General Janvier or Lt Gen Rupert Smith) had to agree to turn their "keys" to approve air strikes before the first bomb could fall.[31]

Consistent with the memorandum of understanding, Admiral Smith took General Ryan's plan to the NATO/UNPF Joint Targeting Board on 14 August 1995 for coordination and initiation of the process for United Nations approval.[32] He obtained agreement, in principle, from the force commander of UNPF for both the operation and associated targets. The plan moved through UN political and military structures at the same time it moved through the NATO approval process. Admiral Smith presented the plan to Secretary-General Claes and General Joulwan, who in turn took it to the NATO Military Committee. Both the UN and NATO political structures approved the plan, accepting a broad set of three target categories or options. They delegated final approval for target-list selections to General Ryan, overseen by the Military Committee, General Joulwan, and Admiral Smith.

With this tentative approval, General Ryan again tasked his strategy cell to perform target selection and prioritization, keeping in mind and harmonizing the political objectives outlined by UNSCRs and NAC decisions—a strategy-to-task process. General Hornburg ensured that the CAOC planners also closely followed this construct and monitored the process so that each mission matched and was linked directly to the strategy and objectives.[33] General Ryan wanted targets that would influence the behavior of the Bosnian Serbs—their centers of gravity.[34]

These various requirements led General Ryan to develop a unique blend of strategy and operational concepts for the forthcoming campaign. In this situation he considered himself the air campaign planner.[35] As far as he was concerned, he could not and would not delegate target-selection responsibility to anyone else because of the political implications: "If we had committed one atrocity from the air, NATO would forever be blamed for crimes, and the military threat would be lessened. Henceforth, the air commander will be—must be—applying the overarching air strategy at the tactical level. You cannot delegate the selection. The commander must ask all of the detailed questions. There will be no time in the future when he will have the option to say, 'I delegated that responsibility.' The commander must be accountable for all actions taken by his forces."[36] General Ryan's personal perspective for the campaign on how best to meet the objectives set forth by the political leadership was to take away what the Bosnians Serbs held dear and drive them to parity with the Bosnian Croats and Muslims. He also believed it vital that the Bosnian Serbs understand and know what was happening to their forces and how the balance of power was ebbing away from them. If they wanted this surgical reduction from the air halted, they had to comply with the objectives outlined to them by the UN.

General Ryan further instructed his AIRSOUTH strategy cell and the CAOC operational planners to limit collateral damage as much as possible (no civilian casualties or undue military casualties) and to ensure the protection of NATO forces to the highest degree. He strongly believed, as did Admiral Smith and General Janvier, that any NATO air operation of this size must ensure that attacks in Bosnia-Herzegovina struck only military targets and inflicted only the absolute minimum of military casualties. The UN and NATO were not trying to destroy the BSA but strongly move it toward the UN/NATO objectives. Civilian casualties would have precluded this end state. The use of NATO military power in support of the UN mandates was a critical issue in all of the participating NATO countries. General Ryan correctly understood the political ramifications in those countries if NATO casualties sustained during the operation became excessive. Thus, his second restriction—ensuring force protection—permeated the entire planning process.

The strategy cell briefed General Ryan on suggested target categories: integrated air defense systems; command, control, and communications; lines of communication; and ammunition storage sites. After General Ryan approved this targeting plan, General Hornburg—together with the unit and senior NATO representatives—began the target-sequencing and force-packaging process. On 22 August 1995, at the end of a grueling four-to-five-month planning process, the tactical units received the first ATM of what would eventually become Operation Deliberate Force. No one could have guessed that it would be implemented almost without major change only one week later.

On the morning of 30 August 1995, NATO secretary-general Willy Claes stated that

NATO aircraft commenced attacks on Bosnian Serb military targets in Bosnia. The air operations were initiated after the UN military commanders concluded, beyond reasonable doubt, that Monday's brutal mortar attack in Sarajevo came from Bosnian Serb positions. The operations were jointly decided by the Commander in Chief, Allied Forces Southern Europe and the Force Commander, UN Peace Forces under UN Security Council Resolution 836 and in accordance with the North Atlantic Council's decisions of 25 July and 1 August, which were endorsed by the UN Secretary-General. Our objective is to reduce the threat to the Sarajevo safe area and to deter further attacks there or on any other safe area. We hope that this operation will also demonstrate to the Bosnian Serbs the futility of further military actions and convince all parties of the determination of the Alliance to implement its decisions. NATO remains strongly committed to the continued efforts of the international community to bring peace to the former Yugoslavia through the diplomatic process. It is my fervent hope that our decisive response to Monday's mortar attack will contribute to attaining a peaceful settlement.[37]

Conclusions

The unusual, parallel NATO and UN C² structures were fertile ground for problems, especially in the planning and coordination functions. Differing NATO and UN C² systems with Band-Aid connections would not have lasted forever; neither were they necessarily time sensitive to the needs of all concerned—especially the on-scene tactical forces. However, a great deal of determination by the men and women of both organizations and the ceaseless efforts of key people in senior positions of authority as well as those in the UN and NATO tactical units made the process work. Nonetheless, despite the obvious success of Deliberate Force, the operational effectiveness of the planning process was lower than it could have been.

Some people have called into question the concept of the dual-key command-authorization system uneasily developed between the UN and NATO. Undoubtedly, this process violated the principle of unity of command, especially in cases of tactical-level close air support operations that demand a suitable structure to relay near-real-time information and command decisions. Ambassador Richard Holbrooke flatly stated that "the dual key system was an unmitigated disaster. It did great damage to both the UN and NATO."[38] Because of the differences between the two organizations and their mandates, he believed that NATO and the UN never should have been related in this fashion. Ultimately, though, a modified version of this process could have—perhaps should have—been devised.

The authorized air strikes of Deliberate Force to relieve the strangulation of Sarajevo and other threatened safe areas constituted a series of decisive military actions by NATO in support of the UN mission in the former Yugoslavia. Together with a determined diplomatic effort, the surgical application of NATO's airpower stopped the Bosnian Serb army's siege of Sarajevo and strongly encouraged the negotiated solution to the conflict in the fall of 1995.

The UN and NATO had developed a cooperation, at times tenuous, that when forcibly applied during Deliberate Force, highlighted the ability of separate political and military organizations to work together. In hindsight, critics can declare that the arrangements could have been much better, and to some extent that viewpoint has validity. However, the bottom line is that cooperation in military planning between the UN and NATO worked and successfully fulfilled political and military objectives.

This experience shows that NATO can adapt its military forces and policies to the European requirements of the post-cold-war world and continue to provide collective security and defense for all allies. It offers tangible proof that, in addition to carrying out the core functions of defending the alliance, NATO can use its military forces outside their normal area of responsibility (e.g., in operations under the authority of the UN Security Council and with political objectives that define the required military tasks). NATO's military capabilities and its adaptability to include forces of non-NATO countries are decisive factors in the alliance's role in implementing the Dayton Peace Agreement. Deliberate Force marked the successful end to a less-than-successful peacekeeping operation and allowed UNPROFOR to withdraw in favor of a force unified in both mission and command.

Notes

1. Admiral Smith first attempted to contact Lt Gen Bernard Janvier, force commander of United Nations Peace Forces and General Smith's commanding officer. General Janvier was on leave in France at the time.

2. Charter of the United Nations; on-line, Internet, 18 December 1998, available from http://www.tamilnation.org/humanrights/uncharter/contents.html.

3. UN Security Council Resolution 781, 9 October 1992, adopted by the Security Council at its 3122d meeting on 9 October 1992.

4. UN Security Council Resolution 816, 3 March 1993, adopted by the Security Council at its 3191st meeting on 3 March 1993.

5. The NAC, consisting of permanent representatives of the 16 member countries and chaired by the NATO secretary-general (the council's principal spokesperson), meets twice a year at the ministerial level and weekly at the ambassador level. It has effective political authority and powers of decision over the daily operations of NATO and is the only body within NATO to derive its authority explicitly from the North Atlantic Treaty. The council provides a unique forum for wide-ranging consultation between member governments on all issues affecting their security and is the most important decision-making body in the alliance. All other committees in NATO derive their authority from NAC. Decisions reflect the collective will of member governments arrived at by common consent and must be unanimous.

6. UN Security Council Resolution 836, 4 June 1993, adopted by the Security Council at its 3228th meeting on 4 June 1993.

7. Boutros Boutros-Ghali, UN secretary-general, to the president of the UN Security Council, letter, subject: Air Strikes against the BSA, 6 February 1994, United States Air Force Historical Research Agency (AFHRA), Maxwell AFB, Ala.

8. Lt Col Lowell R. Boyd Jr., AIRSOUTH Plans, Headquarters AIRSOUTH, Naples, Italy, interviewed by Lt Col Rob Owen, 6 December 1995, AFHRA.

9. Composed of representatives from all NATO member states except France, the DPC focuses on collective defense planning and provides guidance to NATO's military authorities. Within the area of its responsibilities and competence, it has the same functions, attributes, and authority as the NAC. Although France withdrew from the NATO integrated military structure in 1966, it still interacts with the DPC and other NATO military organizations through its military mission to the alliance.

10. NATO Basic Fact Sheet no. 4, March 1997; on-line, Internet, 18 December 1998, available from http://www.nato.int/docu/facts/fs4.htm.

11. Headquarters NATO, press release, "Decision on the Protection of the Safe Areas Taken at the Meeting of the NAC on 22 April 1994."

12. General Ryan, commander of Allied Air Forces Southern Europe, believed that the UN Security Council would be unwilling to approve offensive military operations because of the expected opposition of Russia. He further believed that the London Conference of NATO Defense Ministers

(basically from the same countries on the Security Council, minus Russia) in July 1995 was a political expedient to allow military operations under the guise of NATO. Gen Michael Ryan, interviewed by authors of the Air University Balkans Air Campaign Study at Air Command and Staff College, Maxwell AFB, Ala., 7 February 1996, AFHRA.

13. The UN military command structure was reorganized in the spring of 1995. The previous command structure remained in place but now had new names and a modified mandate. UN Protection Force, the overall command organization in the former Yugoslavia, was redesignated UN Peace Forces. Subordinate command maintained the designation of UNPROFOR in Bosnia-Herzegovina.

14. NATO Basic Fact Sheet no. 4.

15. The following countries currently provide military and/or civilian police personnel for UNPROFOR: Argentina, Bangladesh, Belgium, Brazil, Canada, Colombia, Czech Republic, Denmark, Egypt, Finland, France, Ghana, Indonesia, Ireland, Jordan, Kenya, Malaysia, Nepal, Netherlands, New Zealand, Nigeria, Norway, Pakistan, Poland, Portugal, Russian Federation, Slovak Republic, Spain, Sweden, Switzerland, Tunisia, Ukraine, United Kingdom, United States, and Venezuela. During its existence, UNPROFOR/UNPF has incurred sixteen hundred casualties, including 198 fatalities.

16. UN Peace Forces Fact Sheet, UN Peace Forces Division of Information, September 1995.

17. UN Security Council Resolution 824, 6 May 1993, adopted by the Security Council at its 3208th meeting on 6 May 1993; and UN Security Council Resolution 836.

18. Yasushi Akashi, special representative of the UN secretary-general for the former Yugoslavia, to Dr. Radovan Karadzic, letter, subject: NATO Airpower in Bosnia, 10 December 1994, AFHRA.

19. Boyd interview.

20. General Ryan has dual responsibility as commander of Sixteenth Air Force, headquartered at Aviano Air Base, Italy (Sixteenth Air Force is a subordinate command to United States Air Forces Europe [USAFE], headquartered at Ramstein Air Base, Germany), and as COMAIRSOUTH. As such, he simultaneously wears the hats of a NATO and US Air Force commander.

21. Maj Gen Hal M. Hornburg, interviewed by Dr. Wayne Thompson and Maj Tim Reagan, 16 October 1995, AFHRA.

22. Col Steve Teske, director for plans, CAOC, Headquarters USAFE, interviewed by author, 14 February 1996, AFHRA.

23. Headquarters USAFE Special Order GD-19, Activation of the 7490th Wing (Provisional) at Aviano Air Base, Italy, 30 June 1995, AFHRA.

24. Briefing, 7490th Wing (Provisional), subject: Deny Flight Support—"Aircraft Status Snapshot Slide," 24 August 1995, AFHRA.

25. Briefing, Major General Hornburg to Joint Doctrine Air Campaign Course, class 96D, Maxwell AFB, Ala., subject: Deliberate Force, 14 March

1996, AFHRA. Planning had actually begun in February 1995 for Deadeye, the suppression of enemy air defenses portion of what was to become Operation Deliberate Force.

26. Lt Gen Michael Ryan, interviewed by Dr. Wayne Thompson and Maj Tim Reagan, 18 October 1995, AFHRA.

27. Ibid.

28. Briefing slides (unclassified), Col John R. Baker to General Ryan, subject: CAOC Assessment, 30 July 1995, AFHRA.

29. Ibid.

30. Boutros Boutros-Ghali, UN secretary-general, to Willy Claes, NATO secretary-general, letter, subject: Delegation of Authority, 25 July 1995, AFHRA.

31. Under intense pressure from NATO and US officials, who believed that military commanders should determine when Serb transgressions warranted reprisals, UN secretary-general Boutros Boutros-Ghali took the key from Mr. Akashi and gave it to General Janvier on 25 July 1995. But NATO hoped to push it even further down the UN chain of command to General Smith, known to be more inclined to martial action than the cautious Janvier. The secretary-general declined and, supported by France, kept the key with Janvier. Ironically, General Janvier was on vacation when Admiral Smith called on 28 August, and General Smith actually had the key. After consultation with Janvier, General Smith and Admiral Smith made the initial decision to launch the attacks. General Janvier returned before the attacks commenced, reclaimed the key from General Smith, and reaffirmed the decision to attack the Bosnian Serbs.

32. The NATO/UNPF Joint Targeting Board was a high-level coordinating body established by the UN and NATO to jointly validate targets and link them to mandated UN/NATO mission objectives. The board included CINC-SOUTH and the force commander of UNPF.

33. Hornburg briefing.

34. Ryan interview, 18 October 1995.

35. Ryan interview, 7 February 1996. General Ryan was convinced that the Serbs knew when NATO was flying and even who was flying—right down to knowing that Capt Scott O'Grady was the pilot of Basher 52, the F-16 shot down in the summer of 1995.

36. Ibid.

37. Press statement (95)73 by NATO secretary-general Willy Claes, 30 August 1995.

38. Ambassador Richard Holbrooke, New York City, interviewed by Maj Mark McLaughlin and Dr. Karl Mueller, 24 May 1996, AFHRA.

Chapter 3

US and NATO Doctrine
for Campaign Planning

Col Maris McCrabb

Operation Deny Flight/Deliberate Force provided a unique challenge for campaign planners, especially those reared in the North Atlantic Treaty Organization (NATO) environment. Since the founding of the alliance, it had focused on large-scale, conventional war. But Deny Flight possessed characteristics best described as operations other than war (OOTW), such as the pivotal role of the United Nations (UN) and the lack of clear-cut, militarily achievable objectives. Furthermore, this action in the former Yugoslavia constituted an out-of-area operation for NATO, something prohibited under the Washington Treaty of 1949. Because of these differences, NATO air doctrine offered planners limited guidance on planning and executing an air operation in Bosnia.

Likewise, although US joint doctrine offers considerably more guidance on OOTW, that guidance generally focuses on US-only operations, and it relegates multilateral and coalition considerations to separate sections in the applicable publications.[1] Thus, NATO possesses air-planning doctrine that focuses on coalition considerations but remains largely silent on OOTW, while US joint doctrine features greater emphasis on the unique aspects of OOTW but does not fully consider coalition considerations. An additional issue that bedevils both sets of doctrine is the role of airpower in either OOTW or conventional war.

Since the first use of airpower[2] in a military campaign, commanders have struggled with the question of how best to employ this capability. Was airpower just another means of fire support planned into land operations, much like artillery, to strike at an enemy army's most important "operational centers," those targets most affecting its ability to resist the advance of friendly surface forces? Or was airpower somehow

65

unique in that it could operate well beyond the range of surface battles and strike an enemy nation's "vital" or "strategic centers," those that most affected its ability and will to continue fighting? Although the latter provided a strategic option previously denied to operational commanders, it also introduced a unique tension in airpower strategy: the choice of striking either of two distinct target sets, each with distinctly different relationships to surface-combat operations and with different physical and temporal effects on the will and ability of an enemy nation to continue resisting the political will of its opponent. Choosing the best or most remunerative targets for air attack became a critical decision for air planners, one requiring new categories of military intelligence to locate them and assess their absolute and relative importance to an enemy's will and ability to continue fighting.

Given all these relationships and tensions associated with airpower campaign planning,[3] the essence of air strategy is captured in an aphorism: "airpower is targeting, targeting is intelligence, and intelligence is analyzing the effects of air operations on chosen strategic and operational centers."[4] This formula, however, omits two important questions: (1) What constitutes a vital center? (2) Since scarce resources prevent one from attacking all centers at once, what are the priorities?[5] A related question deals with who makes the choices, but airpower theorists almost dogmatically insist that airmen not only choose the relevant targets, using the overall commander's intent as their guide, but also command all airpower resources available to the operation.[6]

This essay examines US joint and NATO doctrine for planning and conducting air operations with an emphasis on OOTW considerations, as well as strategy development from the national or alliance level down to the operational level. Further, it explores, in some detail, the process of air-operations planning and addresses guidance offered when this process involves other players, such as the UN. It does all this with the aim of determining whether an adequate body of written doctrine was available to the planners of Deliberate Force to guide their efforts to set objectives, develop strategies, and assign tasks appropriate to the objectives of higher political and military leaders.

US Doctrine

US doctrine outlines a very specific process for making strategy that ties national political strategy down to every target struck in a campaign. National security strategy[7] lays out broad political guidance, while national military strategy[8] provides general guidance for the military instrument of power. The Joint Strategic Capabilities Plan provides classified guidance to the commanders in chief of joint unified commands for developing plans to meet potential threats.[9] For both contingencies and crises, the commanders in chief develop theater campaign plans largely composed of operations plans (OPLAN) from the various components—land, sea, air, and special operations. The joint air operations plan (JAOP) provides the foundation to build the daily air tasking order (ATO). As this flow implies, the entire process ideally progresses from the top down through levels of increasing but logically connected levels of refinement and specificity. The ATO, therefore, is *not* a stand-alone document. Rather, it is a small slice (normally delimited by time—usually 24 hours) of a chain of guidance and planning documents that extends from the level of national strategy right down to the level of tactical operations. Therefore, an "ATO-only" focus is too narrow a view for any useful explication of the body of theories and doctrines available to guide the planners of Deliberate Force. Likewise, a focus only on an air "campaign" is too narrow a view for analyzing a theater campaign.

Together, these documents provide important guidance to campaign planners. First, although the US armed forces must prepare for a wide variety of contingencies, the most important are the two postulated major regional contingencies. Second, the United States will use force decisively and with clear objectives. Third, the United States might fight unilaterally, but for the most part it will fight as part of a coalition. Fourth, the United States must retain the capability to project power overseas. Finally, US forces must train and prepare to fight in both combined and joint environments, with clear vision regarding the use of land, maritime, air, space, and special forces.[10]

This formal US strategy process also produces so-called strategic-concept documents at the national and theater level, and concept of operations (CONOPS) documents at the component level.[11] Working in concert with other components, theater-level air component commanders develop CONOPS as basic expressions of their air strategies—the foundations of their JAOPs. The latter, in turn, provide daily guidance—refined as conditions warrant—for master air attack plans that guide development of the ATO in the final step of strategic and operational planning.

The primary duties and responsibilities of joint force commanders (JFC) entail exercising command and control over assigned forces in the accomplishment of missions assigned to them by higher command authorities. Fundamentally, JFCs must understand their missions and assigned objectives, as well as the intent and "end state" or outcome envisioned by their commander. Joint Publication (Pub) 3-0, *Doctrine for Joint Operations*, lists eight ways in which commanders exercise their command responsibilities: (1) assigning missions, (2) designating priorities of effort, (3) designating and allocating priorities for resources, (4) assessing risks, (5) deciding when adjustments need to be made, (6) committing reserves, (7) understanding the needs of senior and subordinate commanders, and (8) guiding and motivating the organization toward the desired end.[12] These command prerogatives are inherent in JFC campaign plans that provide the bases for subordinate component plans.

At their heart, these component plans epitomize the operational art, defined by US joint doctrine as "the employment of military forces to attain strategic and/or operational objectives through the design, organization, integration, and conduct of strategies, campaigns, major operations, and battles. Operational art translates the joint force commander's strategy into operational design, and, ultimately, tactical action, by integrating key activities at all levels of war."[13] Further, it "determines when, where, and why the joint force will be employed" and "provides a framework for the efficient use of resources to achieve objectives and a means for planning campaigns and major operations."[14] Some of the more important facets of operational art include synergy, simultaneity and depth, and anticipation. Synergy prompts the JFC to consider the complementary capabilities of the various parts of the joint force.

Simultaneity and depth deny the enemy sanctuary or respite by imposing competing and simultaneous demands on enemy commanders. And anticipation makes the JFC alert to the unexpected and to opportunities for exploiting rapidly chang-ing situations.[15]

In US Air Force doctrine, operational art consists of four tasks. The first involves creating a concept for aerospace op-erations to determine "when, where, or even if air and surface engagements should be sought, based on how they might con-tribute to the combatant commander's intent." The second task entails orchestrating aerospace forces "so they can help provide advantages (e.g., concentration, position, and sur-prise) to aerospace and surface forces that will give those forces the best chance of tactical success."[16] Third, the air commander must make adjustments based on mission results and/or changes in the JFC's operational intent. Finally, the air commander must be able to exploit fleeting opportunities. Air Force basic doctrine emphasizes the key role airpower can play in directly attacking the enemy's sources of power: "One way a commander can exercise operational art is through a strategic air campaign that directly attacks an enemy's cen-ters of gravity [COG]. . . . If a strategic air campaign is not feasible, achieving a campaign's objective can depend on com-bining aerospace and surface operations in a way that creates powerful synergies."[17]

Joint doctrine offers a conceptual model for planners to develop JAOPs in a war or OOTW situations.[18] According to joint doctrine, "though missions vary widely across the range of military operations from war to [OOTW], the framework and processes for [command and control] of joint air operations are consistent."[19] However, "the key difference . . . is that in opera-tions other than war, other US Government agencies and host nations have a preeminent role and the military contribution to the strategic objective is likely to be indirect. . . . Therefore, the major challenge is joint, combined, and interagency con-sensus building."[20] Furthermore, "settlement, not victory" may be the ultimate measure of success.[21]

The model of joint planning so far described is iterative, not linear. Each phase occurs simultaneously, and no one phase is ever complete because each is influenced by unfolding developments in the other phases. Still, in practice, the planning process should begin with the articulation of the JFC's objectives. As the process continues, however, even fundamental objectives may be altered by developments in other phases of planning. Feedback mechanisms imbedded in the planning process may require changes in earlier ideas. For example, detailed analysis of COGs may reveal that the original strategy is inadequate and that the change in strategy may require a modification of the objective. As outlined in Joint Pub 3-56.1, *Command and Control for Joint Air Operations*, this planning model has five phases.

Phase One: Operational-Environment Research

During this phase, one gains information about "friendly and adversary capabilities and intentions, doctrine, and the environment in which the operations will take place."[22] Answering the key question of this planning phase—what is the nature of the war or conflict?[23]—entails incorporation and synthesis of information taken from sources as diverse as newspaper articles, novels, and satellite imagery. Order-of-battle data alone decidedly will not provide the answer. Likewise, this phase of planning must synthesize inputs from individuals and agencies with expertise in such areas as intelligence, operations, national strategy, economics, anthropology, and a host of other specialties.

This question of conflict identity is particularly crucial and generally more difficult to answer for OOTW situations than for more conventional conflicts. Limitations in US intelligence, coupled with a current focus on major regional threats in specific global areas, increase the difficulty by limiting intelligence coverage of other areas. For military leaders, OOTW also requires a somewhat unconventional strategic outlook whereby enemy military forces may prove less a concern to planners than political, economic, or sociocultural factors. Finally, OOTW usually includes non–Department of Defense government agencies, nongovernmental organizations, or international organizations.

Phase Two: Objective Determination

This is the crucial planning phase because it results in an articulation of the end state that leaders want from military action. Often, however, higher-level guidance (e.g., from national leaders to theater commanders) can be imprecise. In that case, subordinate planners must determine their own objectives, based on whatever sources are available, and then pass them to the next higher level of authority for approval.[24] Just as importantly, the end state sought (the ultimate military objective) represents only the set of conditions necessary to resolve the immediate crisis and move from the predominant use of military force to the predominant use of other instruments of national power (e.g., diplomacy or economics). In OOTW, however, military terms cannot solely define these conditions. In many cases, "conditions which need to be created can only occur with emphasis on political/diplomatic, economic, or social activities."[25] This does not mean they do not exist. As joint doctrine warns, "an essential consideration . . . is an understanding, regardless of the nature and extent of military involvement, of the parameters which spell success, failure, or conflict termination."[26] Finally, multiple objectives—often not prioritized—may conflict. Of most importance, however, is that "the objectives of each level must support the objectives of the higher level to ensure unity of effort."[27]

Other considerations in objective determination include constraints, restraints, and rules of engagement. Constraints are items planners must do; restraints are things they must not do. The latter may include prohibited targets, restrictions on the use of certain weapons or tactics, or buffer zones between enemy territory and neutral countries. Rules of engagement—based on international law, operational requirements, capabilities of the force, host-nation law and agreements, the threat, and US policy[28]—are directives issued by competent authorities that delineate the circumstances and limitations on the use of force.

Phase Three: Strategy Identification

US joint doctrine defines strategy as "the art and science of developing and using political, psychological, and military forces as necessary during peace and war, to afford the maximum support to policies, in order to increase the probabilities and favorable consequences of victory and to lessen the chances of defeat."[29] Thus, in practice, separating strategy from objectives can prove difficult in some ways. The objective sought implies some notion of how one can achieve it. One rule of thumb is that higher-level strategies become the objectives of the next lower level. If a JFC, for instance, promulgates a strategic objective of "undermining the military power of the palace guard," then theater component commanders must develop strategies for their forces that will undermine the palace guard in some way. The advantage of subordinates linking their strategies to the objectives of their superiors is that it allows the more senior commanders to pick the strategy most likely to produce the desired result. In a more relevant example to the issue at hand, "the joint air operations plan is how the JFACC [joint force air component commander] communicates, promulgates, and articulates strategy," in support of the JFC's objectives.[30]

As in the case of other planning phases, several items complicate strategy making in OOTW, compared to strategy making in war. First, as noted in phase two, OOTW objectives are generally less clear cut than those for war, especially in terms of desired end states. Second, OOTW lends itself more toward a preventive strategy than a positive strategy.[31] In other words, the goals of OOTW are more likely to involve stopping things from occurring, such as keeping safe areas in Bosnia from being overrun, rather than making something happen, such as militarily defeating the Bosnian Serb army.

Phase Four: Identification of Centers of Gravity

US doctrine defines COGs as "those characteristics, capabilities, or localities from which a military force derives its freedom of action, physical strength, or will to fight."[32] The need to identify the COGs correctly is clear: they are the "things" or concepts that strategy "targets" to accomplish its positive or negative objectives. As Joint Pub 3-0 states, "The essence of operational art lies in being able to mass effects against the enemy's sources of power in order to destroy or neutralize them. In theory, *destruction or neutralization of enemy centers of gravity is the most direct path to victory*" (emphasis in original).[33]

Again, identifying COGs in an OOTW situation can prove extremely challenging, given their ephemeral nature as compared to those in war. For example, a friendly COG (one to protect) may be the legitimacy of the supported host nation's government, while the enemy's COG may be ideology. In this case, directly attacking or influencing the enemy's COG in OOTW could prove difficult. US doctrine stresses decisive points in indirectly attacking COGs. But these points generally are geographic in nature and, although in themselves not COGs, "they are the keys to attacking protected centers of gravity."[34]

Phase Five: Development of Joint Air Operations

This phase is the most difficult part of air campaign planning. One method of organizing JAOP development calls for categorizing operations by function or task (e.g., by air superiority). Another involves categorizing operations by time or event (e.g., by phase or by operations occurring after a particular event). Particularly for OOTW, with its many intangible strategic issues, event-based planning offers important advantages over function-based planning. The former forces planners to outline a desired operational sequence from the starting set of conditions down to the final conditions that define the end state. This technique focuses intelligence-collection assets and sharply identifies key decision points in anticipated operations and strategies. These, in turn, help other planning functions, such as logistics, to ascertain support requirements. Event-based planning also describes the priorities of effort and resources. For example, air superiority—the prerequisite for the success of further operations—is usually the JFC's first priority. The JFACC is the supported commander for air superiority operations. An event-oriented approach, therefore, describes the series of related unified or joint operations that lead to air superiority, and it should describe the amount of air superiority needed to open subsequent operational phases.

Identifying planning branches and sequels is especially critical in putting the JAOP together. Branches are options that anticipate situations that could change the basic plan, while "sequels are subsequent operations based on the possible outcomes of the current operation."[35] Together, they form the phases, sequenced together, that lead from the starting condition down to the desired end state. Thus, branches and sequels build flexibility into plans and preserve freedom of action under rapidly changing conditions.

For each phase of the JAOP, including its branches and sequels, planners must develop measures of merit to assist in determining how well the plan achieves its goals. These measures must not limit themselves to mere sortie counting or accounting of physical damage done to enemy materiel but should focus on effects achieved in terms of the JAOP and its branches and sequels, and in relation to the effects planned. Naturally, too, the planning ambiguities of OOTW increase the difficulty of this part of JAOP development.

The center of JAOP development in the joint air operations center (JAOC) is the strategy cell. Although some current JAOCs formally establish this cell within their Combat Plans divisions, all have functional strategy cells somewhere in their organization. Fundamentally, the strategy cell is responsible for translating JFC and JFACC guidance into an air strategy. Strategy-cell planners, in conjunction with other component planners, determine the best use of the JFC's airpower assets to achieve operational objectives. Based on their determination, these planners then propose air CONOPS to their JFACCs that underpin the advice of these air commanders to their JFCs.[36]

The other sections of the JAOC produce and execute the daily ATO. All components (i.e., land, sea, air, and special operations) nominate targets to accomplish their assigned mission on any specific ATO. The joint guidance, apportionment, and targeting (JGAT) cell, composed of representatives from these components, prioritizes those requests into a joint, integrated, prioritized target list for force application. The driving principle is guidance provided by the JFC/JFACC, found in the JFACC's CONOPS. The most common model used is strategy-to-tasks because it connects each supported objective to an individual target.[37] From this process also comes the apportionment recommendation—the determination and assignment of the total expected air effort by percentage, priority, or weight of effort devoted to counterair, strategic attack, interdiction, or close air support.

Emerging joint doctrine rightly emphasizes that "forwarding desired effects rather than strict target nominations gives those responsible for conducting joint interdiction maximum flexibility to exploit their capabilities." Further, "supported commanders should provide supporting commanders as much latitude as possible in planning and executing their operations. . . . Supported commanders should clearly state how they envision interdiction enabling or enhancing their maneuver operations and what they want to accomplish with interdiction (as well as those actions they want to avoid)."[38] This target list goes to the JFC for approval.

The joint, integrated, prioritized target list forms the basis of the master air attack plan, which—using the Contingency Theater Automated Planning System (CTAPS)—matches targets, along with weaponeering data, weather information, intelligence, and so forth, to available resources, according to the principle of economy of force. The master air attack plan turns into the ATO and goes to the appropriate units, normally 12 hours before execution.

Although commanders want to know how well the executed missions have accomplished the desired effects, combat assessment remains an often-overlooked aspect of JAOP planning. Traditional battle damage assessment can provide both quick looks and detailed examination of the damage done. Weapons effects determine the correctness of the weaponeering and establish data on the performance of munitions. Further, based upon the objective sought, overall mission effectiveness recommends whether or not to restrike the target.

NATO Doctrine

As with US doctrine, the key to understanding how NATO plans air operations starts with an understanding of how the alliance develops strategic guidance. This process has its roots in the origins of the alliance and in its fundamental principles

(over)

75

of policy making: defensive orientation, consensus, cohesion, and an initial prohibition on out-of-area operations. Since the end of the cold war and the demise of NATO's raison d'être—the Warsaw Pact—NATO reaffirmed some of these principles and modified others. At the Rome Summit of 1991, NATO put forth a new strategic concept that softened the Washington Treaty's prohibition on out-of-area operations. According to this concept, NATO must be capable of responding to instability arising from "the serious economic, social and political difficulties, including ethnic rivalries and territorial disputes, which are faced by many countries in Central and Eastern Europe."[39] In 1994 NATO affirmed this expanded orientation when it declared its "offer to support, on a case by case basis in accordance with our own procedures, peacekeeping and other operations under the authority of the UN Security Council . . . including making available Alliance resources and expertise."[40]

Structurally, NATO's grand-strategy process starts with the North Atlantic Council (NAC) and its military arm, the Military Committee (MC). The NAC includes all the heads of state and government from the 16 member states, represented in the council's day-to-day business by permanent ambassadorial-level ministers. The secretary-general chairs the NAC, and the International Staff supports it. The MC, composed of the chiefs of staff of the member nations or their military representatives, reports to the council on the military affairs of the alliance. An elected chair heads the MC, and the International Military Staff supports it. This staff, which has no independent intelligence-gathering function but only collates and distributes intelligence provided by the nations, receives scant attention in most discussions of NATO operations. Nevertheless, it can play an important role. The plans and policy division and the operations division provide independent advice to the MC on proposed policy matters, including plans put forth by the operational commands.

The NATO strategy process continues from the NAC and MC down through the alliance's integrated command structure, which is divided at the top into two major NATO commands: (1) Supreme Allied Commander, Atlantic (not addressed here) and (2) Supreme Allied Commander, Europe. The latter commands three major subordinate commands: Allied Forces Northwest

Europe, Allied Forces Central Europe, and Allied Forces Southern Europe (AFSOUTH), which had responsibility for the Balkans area during Deliberate Force. Allied Air Forces Southern Europe (AIRSOUTH), one of AFSOUTH's six principal subordinate commands, is collocated with AFSOUTH in Naples, Italy.[41] According to NATO doctrine, AIRSOUTH's principal planning organization is the combined air operations center (CAOC) located at Vicenza, Italy, with the 5th Allied Tactical Air Force (5 ATAF).

Two operational-level issues also influenced the NATO strategy process at the time of Deliberate Force. First, in the post-cold-war era, NATO significantly strengthened its Rapid Reaction Forces (RRF) by dividing them into immediate reaction forces, consisting of land, air, and maritime components, and an RRF consisting of the Allied Command Europe Rapid Reaction Corps and supporting air and maritime components. On the one hand, this enhancement of NATO's reaction forces gave the alliance greater flexibility in dealing with problems like the Bosnian conflict; on the other hand, these reaction forces operated under an important limitation: NATO does not task member nations for forces. Each nation assigns "operational command or operational control, as distinct from full command over all aspects of the operations and administration of those forces."[42] In effect, each nation determines what forces it will provide and the conditions under which those forces may be employed. Thus, NATO commanders had to make their plans for land and air operations with the understanding that, if any participating state disagreed with them, it had the option of withdrawing its forces at any time.

Second, although emerging NATO doctrine emphasizes the need for interoperability between forces and the overarching need to have a common doctrine for joint planning and execution,[43] NATO tactical doctrine actually provides only scant guidance concerning air operations planning. For example, Allied Tactical Publication (ATP)-33(B), *NATO Tactical Air Doctrine*,[44] the functional equivalent of Joint Pub 3-56.1, does not offer a model for campaign planning, as is found in US doctrine. It does, however, offer some brief guidance on how an air commander should allot, apportion, and allocate air resources.[45] The first factor is the objective to be achieved, followed

77

by the nature of the conflict, strategy employed, operational capabilities of the forces assigned, terrain, weather, logistics support available, and political restraints in effect.[46] Another limitation on NATO tactical air doctrine is the absence of any detailed discussion of OOTW, which reflects the fact that most of NATO doctrine still predates the end of the cold war. Thus, at least to the extent that they looked to NATO's air doctrine to guide planning for Deliberate Force, AFSOUTH planners largely were on their own.

Although not directly relevant to this essay, one might note (since it in part reflects the experiences of Deny Flight and Deliberate Force) that Allied Joint Publication (AJP)-1(A), "Allied Joint Operations Doctrine" (draft), addresses peace-support operations. This doctrinal guidance foresees events starting with requests from the UN Security Council for assistance from NATO. The draft publication emphasizes NATO military involvement in planning activities from the earliest stages. Once the NAC authorizes peace-support operations, the major NATO command develops "appropriate contingency plans to include the recommended size, composition, operational concept and command structure of the Alliance contribution, the tasks for the Force Commander/COMAJF [Commander, Allied Joint Force], and anticipated timelines for mission execution."[47] Importantly, this publication gives explicit guidance on interposition force operations, which seek to keep opposing military forces apart following a cease-fire agreement through placing an impartial force between the belligerents and establishing a buffer zone with continuous monitoring. However, this draft NATO doctrine still offers no guidance on the use of force to facilitate achieving an agreement between opposing forces.

Three ATPs provided procedural guidance to Deliberate Force planners, although they dealt primarily with tactical employment and included little discussion about how one should develop overall air strategy or CONOPS. ATP-40 and ATP-42, neither of which are discussed here, dealt with airspace control procedures and counterair operations, respectively.[48] Presently, no ATP deals exclusively with interdiction or strategic attack, although ATP-33(B) discusses the former and AJP-1(A) mentions the latter.[49] In NATO parlance, air support to land operations consists of counterair, air interdiction, tactical air transport, and offensive air support (OAS), the last category consisting of tactical air reconnaissance, battlefield air interdiction (no longer a recognized air mission in US doctrine),[50] and close air support. OAS is specifically tied to the land battle, in that it involves "doctrine and procedures [that] permit air forces to assist directly in achieving the immediate and short-term objectives of land forces."[51]

Despite the paucity of detailed air-planning guidance in NATO doctrine manuals, some NATO plans do address an ends-ways-means formula that has some similarity to US doctrine. For example, the Deny Flight OPLAN of the commander in chief of Allied Forces Southern Europe (CINCSOUTH) starts with the mission assigned to a particular phase of an operation.[52] Within that mission, one finds two measures: one deals with the deployment of forces, listing timing of the deployment, objectives sought, and required actions; the other deals with employment operations during the phase, starting with the objectives, actions, and results expected from the actions. Missing from this formula, and from the US ends-ways-means formula, is any discussion of how actions taken produce expected results—in other words, the *mechanism*, which outlines the "why" part. That is, "if the *strategy* occurs, then the *end* likely occurs because of a certain mechanism." It specifies the theoretical foundation for the strategy. For example, the mechanism for Operation Deliberate Force may have taken the following form: "If force is applied to critical communications facilities of the Bosnian Serbs, then they will accede to UN demands because the *loss of those communication facilities will result in a loss of central control over their forces.*"

ATO air doctrine emphasizes that planning must be joint at all levels of command. For OAS operations, the land-force commander establishes target priorities based on the JFC's daily apportionment decision. Army request nets forward preplanned OAS missions to the air force headquarters responsible for the allocation of air resources, normally an ATAF. The joint command operations center, normally collocated with a CAOC, allocates resources to meet the requests. Land-force channels let the requesting units know whether their requests have been accepted or rejected. An air support operations center (ASOC), subordinate to the CAOC and normally with the highest land-force formation deployed (e.g., a corps), may have tasking authority for OAS. Any combat unit may send requests for immediate OAS missions directly over dedicated communication links to the ASOC. Any intermediate army command may disapprove a request. If not, the ASOC attempts to fill the request out of available assets. If none are available, based upon the ASOC's delegated authority, it may divert lower-priority missions to fill the immediate request.[53]

NATO doctrine for the organization and planning processes of the CAOC parallels US doctrine for a JAOC. For example, the CAOC under 5 ATAF at Vicenza, Italy, has a plans element charged with utilizing guidance from higher headquarters, along with the commander's intent and unit inputs, to develop the plan for the daily air tasking message (ATM). Plan development may cover up to 30 days, 48 to 72 hours, or 24 hours. Along with the ATM, affected units also receive special instructions and an airspace control order. An operations element in 5 ATAF executes the published ATM and exercises command and control through regional operations centers and their subordinate sector operations centers. The CAOC's airborne elements may include airborne warning and control system as well as airborne command, control, and communication aircraft. As in US doctrine, liaison elements play a crucial role. In the multinational environment of NATO, national representatives to the CAOC are especially important.

Conclusion

US and NATO doctrines share many characteristics. They both emphasize that planning—at all levels—must include inputs from every relevant participant. Further, these doctrines point out that although flexibility is one of airpower's greatest assets, it can also be its worst dilemma since every combat arm seeks as much airpower support as it can get, generally exceeding the amount available.

Because airpower is best employed in mass, these competing demands may inadvertently lead to "penny packeting" among several forces, to the detriment of the total force. Therefore, both NATO and US doctrines argue for centralized control of all assets under an airman charged with the responsibility to plan and conduct air operations in support of the JFC's objectives. Finally, since US national security strategy states that the purpose of armed forces is to win wars, each body of doctrine tends to emphasize conventional state-versus-state conflict rather than OOTW. However, to the extent that peace-support operations become more the norm than the exception, doctrinal guidance needs expanding.

Despite their similarities, the differences between the two sets of doctrine remain substantial. Most importantly, NATO doctrine provides little guidance on how to develop an air operations strategy. Beyond a brief discussion of the principles of war in ATP-33(B) and a single page in AJP-1(A), the other manuals focus exclusively on tactical events. US doctrine, both joint and service, pays a great deal of attention to operational art and the making of operational strategy. Likewise, Joint Pub 3-56.1 offers an excellent model to guide air operation planners through a process of turning strategic-level guidance into an ATO. NATO air doctrine is disturbingly mute. OOTWs or peace-support operations present the most difficult problem to military planners because the very nature of the task—preventing conflict—is almost the exact opposite from the traditional military role of concluding conflict on terms favorable to the political leadership. Therefore, for the planners of Operation Deliberate Force, NATO doctrine provided virtually no guidance for building conventional air strategy, and it proved even less useful—if such were possible—as a guide for developing strategy for the OOTWs with which they were concerned. The question, therefore, of whether these planners consulted the existing body of doctrine or just "winged it" is largely moot—they had almost nothing to which they could refer.

Notes

1. For example, in Joint Publication (Pub) 3-0, *Doctrine for Joint Operations*, 1 February 1995—the keystone document of joint doctrine—"Multinational Operations" is a separate chapter. Nevertheless, this chapter does provide useful guidance on several key considerations that planners must bear in mind when planning and conducting multinational operations.

2. As used in this essay, *airpower* means the ability to do something in or through the air—the definition used by William "Billy" Mitchell, an airpower pioneer, in *Winged Defense: The Development and Possibilities of Modern Air Power—Economic and Military* (1925; reprint, New York: Dover Publications, 1988), 3–4.

3. For most of its history, air operations conducted against the enemy, whether or not in direct support of surface operations, were called *campaigns*. Examples included "air superiority" or "counterair" campaigns, "air interdiction" campaigns, and the like. In the 1990s, the term *air operations* has replaced *air campaign* in the US armed forces' joint doctrine, emphasizing the existence of a single theater campaign consisting of supporting operations. This essay follows that convention.

4. See Col Phillip S. Meilinger, *10 Propositions Regarding Air Power* (Washington, D.C.: Air Force History and Museums Program, 1995), 20–27. Meilinger writes that "selecting objectives to strike or influence is the essence of air strategy. Virtually all the air theorists recognized this; unfortunately, they were frustratingly vague on the subject" (page 21).

5. The classic air theorist Giulio Douhet wrote that "objectives vary considerably in war, and the choice of them depends chiefly upon the aim sought, whether the command of the air, paralyzing the enemy's army and navy, or shattering the morale of civilians behind the lines." Such variance led him to conclude that "no hard and fast rules can be laid down on this aspect of aerial warfare. It is impossible even to outline general standards, because the choice of enemy targets will depend upon a number of circumstances, material, moral, and psychological, the importance of which, though real, is not easily estimated." See his *The Command of the Air,* trans. Dino Ferrari (1942; new imprint, Washington, D.C.: Office of Air Force History, 1983), 50, 59–60. Operation Desert Storm is often touted as an example of "parallel" or "simultaneous" warfare, which involves striking every key target at once, made possible by advances in precision attack and stealth aircraft. Leaving aside the question of whether US and allied forces will always have the overwhelming numbers of aircraft they had in that war, even then they did not strike every target the very first night. Therefore, some prioritization occurred. For a discussion of parallel attack, see Col John A. Warden III, "Air Theory for the Twenty-first Century," in *Challenge and Response: Anticipating US Military Security Concerns,* ed. Karl P. Magyar (Maxwell AFB, Ala.: Air University Press, August 1994), 311–32.

6. Meilinger, 49–55.

7. See William J. Clinton, *A National Security Strategy of Engagement and Enlargement* (Washington, D.C.: The White House, February 1995).

8. See Joint Chiefs of Staff, *National Military Strategy of the United States of America 1995: A Strategy of Flexible and Selective Engagement* (Washington, D.C.: [Joint Chiefs of Staff,] 1995).

9. For a discussion of the Joint Strategic Capabilities Plan, see Joint Pub 5-0, *Doctrine for Planning Joint Operations,* 13 April 1995, II-10–12.

10. *National Military Strategy,* 14–15.

11. These are *"statements of intent as to what, where, and how operations are to be conducted in broad, flexible terms."* They provide for unity of effort and achieve strategic advantage that is the *"favorable overall power relationship* that enables one group of nations to effectively control the course of politico-military events to ensure the accomplishment of objectives through national, international, and theater efforts" (emphasis in original). See Joint Pub 3-0, III-4. A concept of operations is "a verbal or graphic statement, in broad outline, of a commander's assumptions or intent in regard to an operation or series of operations." See Joint Pub 1-02, *Department of Defense Dictionary of Military and Associated Terms,* March 1994.

12. Joint Pub 3-0, II-16–17.

13. Joint Pub 1-02.

14. Joint Pub 5-00.1, "Joint Tactics, Techniques, and Procedures for Campaign Planning," 2d draft, 18 May 1995, II-1.

15. Joint Pub 3-0, III-9–13.

16. Air Force Manual (AFM) 1-1, *Basic Aerospace Doctrine of the United States Air Force,* vol. 2, March 1992, 129.

17. Ibid.

18. For a complete discussion of this model, see the author's "Air Campaign Planning," *Airpower Journal* 7, no. 2 (Summer 1993): 11–22.

19. Joint Pub 3-56.1, *Command and Control for Joint Air Operations,* 14 November 1994, I-2.

20. Joint Pub 3-07, "Joint Doctrine for Military Operations other than War," final draft, April 1993, VII-2–3.

21. Joint Warfighting Center, *Joint Task Force Commander's Handbook for Peace Operations* (Fort Monroe, Va.: Joint Warfighting Center, 28 February 1995), 6. The Joint Warfighting Center issued this handbook as a resource tool for commanders even though it is not US joint doctrine.

22. Joint Pub 3-56.1, III-4.

23. See Carl von Clausewitz, *On War,* ed. and trans. Michael Howard and Peter Paret (Princeton, N.J.: Princeton University Press, 1976), 88.

24. *Handbook for Peace Operations,* 11.

25. Joint Pub 3-07, VII-3.

26. Ibid., I-7. However, the doctrine goes on to say that "the paradox . . . is that . . . policy is often developmental and contingent on the results of preceding actions. As such, planning for [OOTW] should be an open-ended and interactive process adaptive to the political and policy drivers of the US Government and its foreign policy at any stage of the process."

27. Joint Pub 3-56.1, III-4.

28. *Handbook for Peace Operations,* 74–75.

29. Joint Pub 1-02.

30. Joint Pub 3-56.1, III-5.

31. Joint Pub 3-07, I-10.

32. Joint Pub 1-02.

33. Joint Pub 3-0, III-20.

34. Ibid., III-21.

35. Ibid., III-20.

36. For a recommended JAOP format, see *JFACC Primer,* 2d ed. (Washington, D.C.: US Air Force Deputy Chief of Staff, Plans and Operations, February 1994), 46–50.

37. David E. Thaler, *Strategies-to-Tasks: A Framework for Linking Means and Ends* (Santa Monica, Calif.: RAND, 1993).

38. Joint Pub 3-03, "Doctrine for Joint Interdiction Operations," draft, n.d., II-13–14.

39. "The Alliance's Strategic Concept," in *NATO Handbook* (Brussels: NATO Office of Information and Press, 1995), 237.

40. "Declaration of the Heads of State and Government Participating in the Meeting of the North Atlantic Council Held at NATO Headquarters, Brussels, on 10–11 January 1994," in *NATO Handbook,* 271.

41. The others include Allied Land Forces Southern Europe, Allied Land Forces South Central Europe (not activated), Allied Land Forces Southeastern Europe, Allied Naval Forces Southern Europe, and Naval Striking and Support Forces Southern Europe. AFSOUTH has six principal subordinate commands as opposed to the three found in Allied Forces Central Europe and Allied Forces Northwestern Europe because of the continuing animosity between Greece (host to Allied Land Forces South Central Europe and 7 ATAF, when they are activated) and Turkey (home of Allied Land Forces Southeastern Europe and 6 ATAF).

42. *NATO Handbook,* 167.

43. Allied Joint Publication (AJP)-1(A), "Allied Joint Operations Doctrine," draft, 1995. Also noteworthy in this publication is the discussion of operational art. It generally follows US doctrine but with a clear examination of the military conditions required to achieve the strategic objectives, the events that will likely produce those conditions, the way military resources should be applied to accomplish those events, and the risks involved. See chap. 2, sec. 3, par. 0206.

44. ATP-33(B), *NATO Tactical Air Doctrine,* November 1986.

45. NATO defines allotment as the temporary change of assignment of tactical air forces between subordinate commands. Apportionment is the determination and assignment of the total expected air effort devoted to various air operations, normally by percentage and/or priority. Allocation is the translation of apportionment into numbers of sorties by aircraft type. Ibid., 3-5.

46. Ibid., 3-6.

47. AJP-1(A), par. 2231.

48. ATP-40, *Doctrine and Procedures for Airspace Control in the Combat Zone,* January 1977; and ATP-42, *Counter Air Operations,* March 1981.

49. See ATP-33(B), chap. 5, sec. 2; and AJP-1(A), chap. 18, sec. 2.

50. For an extended discussion of the origin of battlefield air interdiction in NATO, see David J. Stern, *The Development of NATO Tactical Air Doctrine, 1970–1985* (Santa Monica, Calif.: RAND, December 1987).

51. ATP-27(B), *Offensive Air Support Operations,* May 1980, 1-3.

52. Headquarters Allied Forces Southern Europe, CINCSOUTH OPLAN 40101, "Deny Flight," 3 May 1995. (NATO Confidential) Information extracted is unclassified.

53. Ibid., chaps. 5 and 6. (NATO Confidential) Information extracted is unclassified.

Chapter 4

The Deliberate Force Air Campaign Plan

Col Christopher M. Campbell

The first bomb impact of Operation Deliberate Force, at 0012Z on the morning of 30 August 1995, did not occur by happenstance or without considerable deliberation and soul-searching on the part of many individuals. NATO's first true "air campaign," Deliberate Force was in fact the product of years of planning. The alliance's focus on an expected Warsaw Pact adversary preceded that planning effort by decades, and the doctrine that developed as a result of that focus shaped those plans.

Many people planned and executed Deliberate Force to achieve narrowly defined military objectives that emanated from the North Atlantic Council (NAC) and the United Nations (UN) Security Council. These objectives underwent revision over more than three years of military operations in the Balkans and finally became militarily viable. Simply put, the declared Deliberate Force air objective was to "execute a robust NATO air operation that adversely alters the BSA's [Bosnian Serb army's] advantage in conducting successful military operations against the BiH [Bosnian army]." This objective reflected a desired end state which envisaged that the Bosnian Serbs would "sue for cessation of military operations, comply with UN mandates, and negotiate."[1] A tactical objective of "leveling the playing field" bolstered this overt objective. Such leveling ensured that the Bosnian government forces could adequately defend themselves. Implied objectives included the minimizing of casualties, collateral damage, and political and military costs. The combined force air component commander (CFACC) adopted these objectives, both for humanitarian reasons and to ensure that NATO conducted the air campaign in a manner politically acceptable to the intervening countries. The requirement to achieve consensus on all alliance decisions was critically important to maintain in the background of all operational decisions.

Given the generally recognized success of Deliberate Force, one should seek to understand the planning of this air campaign and compare it to available doctrine and procedure. To be effective, a body of doctrine must be relevant, accepted, and used. Maj Gen I. B. Holley Jr., US Air Force Reserve (USAFR), Retired, defines doctrine as "officially approved prescriptions of the best way to do a job. Doctrine is, or should be, the product of experience. Doctrine is what experience has shown usually works best."[2]

The success of Deliberate Force should drive us to discover important insights that might assist air campaign planners. Toward that end, this essay addresses several questions. First, it seeks to determine whether the success of the operation was premeditated or serendipitous. Just as plans often go awry because of unforeseen developments of war, so can they go better than expected. Second, did the planning and outcome of Deliberate Force reflect the provisions of existing doctrines? If not, did air campaign planners deviate from doctrinal norms due to the inadequacy or inappropriateness of the existing doctrine or because they did not refer to that doctrine in the heat of events? Or was a deviation inspired by some combination of reasons?

Answering those questions depends on the answers to at least three corollary questions. First, how did the planners and leaders of this campaign actually go about developing such a successful plan? Of concern here are the institutional and physical environments under which these planners worked, the factors they considered, and the way they deliberated and "processed" the plan. Second, what constituted the actual Deliberate Force air campaign plan, and how did NATO ensure that it would work at the time of execution? Of particular interest is the linkage that existed between the objectives pursued and the strategies employed—the so-called ends versus means as the plan changed over time before the operation began. If one accepts the truth of the adage that "no plan survives first contact with the enemy," the third corollary question becomes understanding how the executors of the Deliberate Force plan altered it to reflect unfolding events and what success they enjoyed. Finally, the essay examines the relationship of the planning and outcome of the operation to doctrinal planning norms. Chapter 3 demonstrated the limitations of the existing body of doctrine. These observations should have broad future implications for future air campaign planners. Thus, this chapter sets out to examine the development process of the air campaign plan for Deliberate Force; show the key components of the plan itself, emphasizing how it was modified over time; compare the "starting" plan to the conduct of the operation and describe adaptations to the plan in the heat of battle; and compare the Deliberate Force experience to doctrinal air campaign planning norms.

The Planning Effort

During the more than two and one-half years of air operations leading to Deliberate Force, a wide array of political and military factors influenced NATO air action in the Balkans. Competing interests constrained air campaign planning and decision making into forms that did not always coincide with current airpower doctrine. This section examines some of those factors as they related to the planning process that culminated in Deliberate Force.

NATO and UN Institutional Factors

A review of NATO's historical planning process leading up to Deliberate Force helps one understand what NATO planned and executed—and why. Deliberate Force did not fit NATO's traditional planning focus, historically oriented on a defensive strategy. That strategy accepted the premise that the enemy (i.e., the Warsaw Pact) would attack first. NATO, bloodied but not bowed, would withstand the initial onslaught, regain whatever territory it might have lost, and at least restore the borders of NATO member nations. That strategy envisioned no requirement to project force beyond the territory of member nations, except to reestablish alliance borders. Thus, involvement in Deny Flight and Deliberate Force—both of which were out-of-area, proactive operations—compelled NATO to rethink its historical planning focus.

For its part, the UN had never been involved in an operation on the scale of Deny Flight or in one with the projected mission of Deliberate Force. Because the UN has no standing military department and relies on troop-contributing nations to provide forces to conduct its operations, very little corporate memory exists within the institution other than for quite limited missions.

A disparity existed between UN and NATO institutional perceptions of the capabilities and limitations of airpower. That disparity stemmed from de facto differences in their historic roles in conflict resolution in general and in Bosnia-Herzegovina in particular. On the one hand, the UN—focused on humanitarian relief and peacekeeping—emphasized strict neutrality and impartiality, no matter the provocation. NATO, on the other hand, sought to protect UN troops and others under the UN umbrella, eventually arraying the alliance against the Bosnian Serbs. These institutional differences in viewpoint created a dilemma for NATO air campaign planners. Their accumulated military experience and wisdom argued for aggressive, robust operations to coerce an adversary to accede to NATO's will (i.e., to "win the war"). The UN's logic of peacekeeping, however, spoke for careful, measured, minimalist operations to preserve the dialogue—not to militarily "defeat" one group or the other.

Throughout the years of NATO's involvement in Bosnia, UN leaders—both military and civilian—had proven much more reluctant than NATO leaders to authorize employment of significant force against the region's combatants. Despite numerous atrocities perpetrated against one or the other factions and despite countless provocations committed against UN and NATO forces, the UN leadership steadfastly refused to authorize air strikes for other than retaliatory demonstration events.

Key Players

Although individuals and organizations from many nations influenced the planning and execution of Deliberate Force, the pronounced "US" hue of its core planning and command functions was a fact of life. Ironically, the fact that virtually all senior commanders and many of the key planning-staff directors involved in the Deliberate Force chain of command were American was largely a quirk of fate. Since NATO's founding, its members have sought to ensure that leadership throughout the military command structure closely mirrors the force contribution of the member states. The national identity of commanders positioned throughout the alliance is a carefully crafted political decision, usually requiring years of dialogue and negotiation to change. Lt Gen Mike Ryan, US Air Force (USAF), was commander of Allied Air Forces Southern Europe (COMAIRSOUTH) and was designated the CFACC. Lt Gen Andrea Fornasiero, Italian air force, was commander of the 5th Allied Tactical Air Force (5 ATAF) at Dal Molin Air Base (AB), Vicenza, Italy. Maj Gen Hal Hornburg, USAF, director of the 5 ATAF combined air operations center (CAOC) at Vicenza, Italy, worked directly for General Ryan. Brig Gen David A. Sawyer, USAF, was both deputy commander of 5 ATAF and deputy director of the CAOC. Most of the senior leadership in the CAOC consisted of USAF colonels. The collegial relationship between the AIRSOUTH and CAOC staffs eased General Ryan's task of planning and executing the Deny Flight—and, later, Deliberate Force—air operations.

Recognizing the lack of sensitivity and undesirability of an all-US chain of command for Operation Deny Flight, Generals Ryan and Hornburg asked all participating NATO nations to provide senior staff members for the CAOC—with limited success.[3] Although each nation (except the United States) had a senior national representative at the CAOC, US officers provided the bulk of air operations planning and leadership there.[4]

Adm Leighton W. Smith, US Navy, commander in chief of Allied Forces Southern Europe (CINCSOUTH)—the combined force commander in the region—ensured that a direct line of communications existed between his headquarters and that of his air component commander, General Ryan. The two commanders could thus share an understanding of the Bosnia situation. Admiral Smith provided General Ryan appropriate guidance and direction, ensuring that he had the forces to accomplish the mission. Admiral Smith saw to it that the air operations plan was in harmony with the strategic direction forthcoming from his boss, Gen George Joulwan, US Army, Supreme Allied Commander Europe (SACEUR). Thus, a de facto all-American chain of NATO air command existed for Bosnia operations—clearly anomalous to the international nature of NATO.

NATO commanders (and, by extension, their staffs) coordinated their actions at several levels with their opposite numbers in the UN hierarchy. Admiral Smith worked closely with Lt Gen Bernard Janvier, French army, force commander (FC) of the United Nations Peace Forces (UNPF, previously known as United Nations Protection Force [UNPROFOR]), headquartered in Zagreb, Croatia.[5] Subordinate to General Janvier was Lt Gen Rupert Smith, British army, commander of UNPROFOR in Bosnia, headquartered in Sarajevo. General Smith and General Ryan coordinated their tactical and operational decisions directly, just as General Janvier and Admiral Smith did at the strategic levels.

Both the NATO and UN military commands were responsive to their respective civilian political masters. The NAC, the highest civilian body of the alliance, and Willy Claes, NATO secretary-general, exercised command authority over NATO military forces through General Joulwan. The UN Security Council exercised its authority through Boutros Boutros-Ghali, UN secretary-general. Yasushi Akashi, special representative to the UN secretary-general, exercised day-to-day civilian authority over the UN-assigned forces through General Janvier.

The "Contact Group" of nations and its negotiating team, led by US ambassador Richard Holbrooke, also served as key players prior to and during Deliberate Force. Although not formally in the chain of command of either the UN or NATO, the Contact Group exercised considerable sway over the military actions taken. The focus of concern for Ambassador Holbrooke and his team was the political negotiations in which they were involved. However, they were quite familiar with the air operation as it unfolded and were in the best place to witness firsthand its impact on the leadership of the warring factions. As time wore on and the start of Deliberate Force approached, this negotiating team became much less responsive to the Contact Group and much more directed from the US leadership.

Despite the heavy American flavor of the NATO command structure, international concerns and relationships helped shape the planning for Deny Flight and, later, Deliberate

Force. Because many of the individuals wearing UN blue berets on the UNPF/UNPROFOR staffs and in the units were from NATO member nations, they were quite familiar with NATO tactical and operational planning methods and procedures. However, they operated within a political system very different than that of NATO—one, as mentioned above, that did not have the same depth of experience or knowledge of military capabilities and limitations. Thus, although most political leaders of the NATO nations were familiar with military air operations on the scale being contemplated for Bosnia-Herzegovina, UN leadership had little experience in planning a coercive operation on this scale. But because of the increasing importance of "offensive" air operations in Deny Flight/Deliberate Force planning, considerable debate resulted within both the UN and the NATO nations.

The Planning Trail Begins

The roots of what would become Deliberate Force stem from late 1992. The Serbs (of the Federal Republic of Yugoslavia) and Bosnian Serbs were flying combat missions in support of ground operations in the newly recognized Bosnia-Herzegovina. Deciding to monitor the situation in an effort to carry out its mandate, the UN Security Council in October 1992 asked NATO to provide air surveillance in support of UNPROFOR. Consequently, NATO began Operation Sky Monitor later that month. In December 1992, as the United States prepared to support humanitarian airdrop and airlift operations into Bosnia-Herzegovina, Gen Robert C. Oaks, then commander in chief of US Air Forces Europe (CINCUSAFE),[6] appointed Maj Gen James E. Chambers (then commander of Seventeenth Air Force) joint force air component commander (JFACC) for US Joint Task Force Provide Promise. The joint task force commander at that time was Adm Jeremy M. Boorda, US Navy, Admiral Smith's predecessor as CINCSOUTH and (as was Admiral Smith) commander in chief of US Naval Forces Europe. General Chambers operated for the first four months from Ramstein AB, Germany, building his staff and conducting operations in coordination with the UN on a bilateral basis.

In March 1993 the UN Security Council voted to establish a no-fly zone over Bosnia, and NATO began enforcement of that exclusionary zone in April. NATO activated the CAOC, and General Oaks dispatched General Chambers to form its core. The established command relationships placed the CAOC technically under command of General Fornasiero yet also subordinate to COMAIRSOUTH; General Chambers became the director of the CAOC. Lt Gen Joseph W. Ashy, then COM-AIRSOUTH, assumed duties as the CFACC. The CAOC remained responsive to the commander of 5 ATAF yet became the de facto command post for COMAIRSOUTH as the CFACC. From the start of Deny Flight in April 1993, Generals Ashy and Chambers worked closely, their two staffs essentially becoming the long-range planning and operations elements of a single organization.

From the beginning of the no-fly-zone enforcement in the spring of 1993 through the completion of Deliberate Force, military commanders and their staffs on both sides of the Adriatic developed close working relationships that resulted in unity of effort, if not unity of command and control (C^2). The primary tool used by NATO to effect this coordination and to lay out its plan for support of the political decisions was CINC-SOUTH Operations Plan (OPLAN) 40101 "Deny Flight." Although the plan was NATO's theater plan and thus bore the logo of Allied Forces Southern Europe (AFSOUTH), AIRSOUTH contributed considerable time and talent to its development. Indeed, the UNPROFOR staff in Zagreb also played a role in formulating the plan to ensure that it truly supported the UN forces and achievement of their mandate.[7] This plan became the "off-the-shelf" plan for implementation or revision as necessary and later formed the backbone for Deliberate Force.

OPLAN 40101 had its political roots in UN Security Council resolutions (UNSCR) and decisions of the NAC. The developing plan incorporated the constraints and restraints imposed by the political authorities. During the summer of 1993, adoption of UNSCR 836 initiated the planning for and deployment of forces to support the first-ever provision of offensive air support to a UN effort.[8] Admiral Boorda and General Ashy oversaw the planning process although the respective staffs had responsibility for day-to-day refinement of the plan. General

Ashy formed a small core of air planners—the Deny Flight air operations center (AOC) at COMAIRSOUTH's Naples headquarters—charging them to think more broadly than the AIRSOUTH staff did. This cell served as a strategy-development team upon which General Ashy and, later, General Ryan depended to develop the air operations plans to pursue NATO objectives in the Balkans. This strategy cell functioned similarly to the "Black Hole" of Operation Desert Storm notoriety. Even during the early stages of Deny Flight, it became apparent to General Ashy that much more might be required in the end. As a result he took steps to ensure the identification of significant targets and the maintenance of target folders that would support a more involved mission than the one envisioned early on. Col Daniel "Doc" Zoerb assumed leadership of this strategy cell in early 1994.

The operational environment within which the AIRSOUTH and CAOC planners had to operate differed in many aspects from any they had previously experienced. The political complexities, even the difficulty in identifying the "enemy," guaranteed that NATO's first large-scale operation would be very different from America's last large-scale operation—Desert Storm. Bosnia contains extremes of geography and weather not found in Southwest Asia; mountainous and heavily foliaged terrain render the gathering of target intelligence and the precise delivery of weapons more problematic than over flat, open deserts. Dug-in troops and dispersed field equipment would prove relatively difficult to locate and accurately target. The presence of friendlies (not to mention the press and nongovernmental organizations) in the vicinity of targets posed another concern not faced to the same extent in Desert Storm. The airspace was constrained both in shape and size, comprising a virtual triangle of 150 nautical miles on a side. The presence of "neutral" countries on two sides and extensive civil air traffic transiting all sides of the triangle greatly complicated the airspace-control problem. The rules of engagement (ROE), therefore, were crafted very carefully to render mistakes in employment a very remote possibility.

From its inception in 1993, OPLAN 40101 contained provisions to go beyond the strict enforcement of a no-fly zone over Bosnia-Herzegovina. Following the issuance of UNSCR 836 in

June 1993, NATO revised the draft of OPLAN 40101 to include provisions for taking offensive action in support of UN objectives, if and when that should ever be approved.

Each provocation of the UN or new attack on a safe area prompted a response—always political or occasionally military (see chaps. 2 and 3 for a detailed treatment of the background to the actual operation). The large number of provocations indicated that the offending party ignored the political responses. Suffice it to say that in response to the changing situation in Bosnia and to the world community's reaction to it, the plan underwent continuous revision from early 1993 onward—most recently in May 1995, only four months before Deliberate Force began. The core of OPLAN 40101, the concept of operations (CONOPS), established five phases for the air operation, extending from initial planning through final redeployment upon mission completion (table 4.1). Construction of the phases was closely linked to the ROE that were established and continuously modified (see chap. 14 for a detailed discussion of ROE).

Within phases three and four, steps and measures further delineated specific actions that the commander could take to respond to a changing operational environment. These steps and measures allowed NATO and the UN to gradually increase the level of force applied to any warring faction in response to noncompliance with terms of the UNSCRs. This planned gradualism served to place checkpoints (some would say roadblocks)

Table 4.1

OPLAN 40101 "Deny Flight" Phases and Objectives

Phase	Objective(s)
1	Compliance
2	Show Presence
3	Air-to-Air Enforcement and Close Air Support (CAS) Operations
4	Offensive Air Operations
5	Termination and Redeployment

Source: Condensed from Headquarters Allied Forces Southern Europe, CINCSOUTH OPLAN 40101, "Deny Flight," change 4, 3 May 1993.

to unrestrained escalation by the NATO commanders. The NAC required those checkpoints to account for the very complex political influences weighing on the military commanders. Until the initiation of Deliberate Force, the air-to-air and CAS steps of phase three were authorized only in direct support of UN forces. Additionally, the UN on occasion had authorized the offensive air operations of phase four—the so-called first-strike option one. These strikes were derisively known as "pinpricks," an accurate description of the level of damage inflicted on the target. Other than these, the UN had authorized no subsequent air operations. Any further actions would require both UN and NATO commanders' approval for any air attacks, which became known as the "dual-key" mechanism (see chap. 2).

Facilities and Processes

NATO C^2 facilities are not known for being state-of-the-art or, in some cases, even for being adequate to the task at hand. Historically, NATO's Southern Region has received system and facility upgrades only after the other regions received theirs. Therefore, 5 ATAF and AFSOUTH/AIRSOUTH had long existed with less-than-optimal facilities and equipment. Communications and computers constituted obvious weaknesses, and the lack of adequate office or command-center space proved problematic. Thus, in the summer of 1995, as events in Bosnia heated up—sparked specifically by vulnerabilities identified after the downing of a US Air Force F-16 that June—the United States took unilateral action. At General Ryan's request, a Headquarters USAF team conducted the so-called Baker Study in late July, which sparked numerous improvements to operational conditions at the CAOC and put in motion many personnel and equipment enhancements. The US 32d Air Operations Group from Ramstein AB, Germany, among others, provided direct support to planning and tasking in the form of computers, communications, and personnel.

Although the United States initiated the Baker Study and resultant C^2 systems improvements, NATO should have purchased the improvements to its systems under normal conditions. However, the question of who would pay the bills remained a nonissue set aside for settlement at a later date. As the US national force provider for the NATO European theater, Gen Richard E. Hawley, then CINCUSAFE, did not concern himself with the idea that NATO planning and procurement processes were being usurped. He was more interested in getting the job done. When General Ryan identified a requirement, therefore, USAFE (or even Headquarters USAF) provided it as completely and quickly as possible. In fact by the time Deliberate Force began, the opposite problem occurred, with equipment virtually flooding the CAOC.[9]

During July 1995, in an effort to improve the air campaign planning process, the CAOC invited Col Dave Deptula, one of the architects of the Desert Storm air campaign, to assist the CAOC and the AOC planners in thinking through the development of their air operations plan.[10] Checkmate planners at Headquarters USAF/XOCC provided more help—in terms of both intellect and equipment. The assistance provided by these and other individuals markedly improved the planning process itself, helping the staff focus on the essentials of the plan.

This effort to improve the processes and products of the CAOC became quite intense by late August 1995, as NATO and the UN made the necessary political decisions to authorize the employment of airpower. Not only would the impending action be NATO's first sustained employment of aircraft in the air-to-ground mission, but also it would be the UN's first use of offensive airpower to coerce belligerent parties to resolve a conflict. The precedent-setting importance of that fact was not lost on the CFACC or his planning staff.

The Air Campaign Plan

The Deliberate Force air campaign plan eventually reflected several elements of OPLAN 40101 but also differed from it in many ways. To fully understand the plan as NATO eventually executed it, as well as the rationale for it, one needs to examine the progression of the various related and supporting plans that resulted in the first weapon delivery on 30 August 1995. This involves examining the framework established by OPLAN 40101 as described above and then moving through several key events in the development of the Deliberate Force air campaign plan. The metamorphosis of the military objectives and the strategies employed to achieve them are of particular importance.

Early Plan Development

Antecedents of the initial planning for what would become Deliberate Force date from the decisions made by the NAC in August 1993. In response to UNSCR 836, which authorized the use of force to protect UNPROFOR and the safe areas, NATO planners developed the so-called operational options for air strikes in Bosnia-Herzegovina.[11] Those options looked very much like the skeleton of a CONOPS for an air campaign plan and did, in fact, become the touchstone for all future plans. The document essentially established options or progressive phases that NATO could implement to support varying levels of need from the UN:

Option One: First-Strike Phase
- limited in scope and duration
- aimed against militarily significant targets that impede or prevent implementation of UNSCRs
- low chance of collateral damage, high chance of success
- attack conducted by more than one nation—ideally as many as possible
- example: artillery batteries participating in the siege of Sarajevo

Option Two: Initial Follow-on Phase
- limited to immediate environs of safe area
- relief of siege; later expanded to support of UNPROFOR
- examples: artillery and heavy weapons; supply points and munitions sites; C^2 facilities; early warning (EW) radar and surface-to-air missile (SAM) sites

Option Three: Expanded Operations Phase
- expanded outside immediate area under siege
- reattacks approved against previous targets as necessary
- required additional political approval

- examples: same as option two plus military-related petroleum, oil, and lubricants; counterair threats; and CAS

The two main differences between options two and three were geographic linkage and infrastructure. Whereas option two was closely tied to particular safe areas and targets immediately affecting the warring factions there, option three permitted more robust attack without specific linkage to a safe area and could affect the infrastructure of the belligerent. The differentiation between option-two and -three targets was muddled, however, in that option-three strikes might well result in increased collateral damage and were seen as a huge political step to take.

In conjunction with this skeleton planning effort, in the fall of 1993 NATO and the UN began to coordinate lists of poten- tial targets that might be struck in the event the UN requested "air support." Although planners did considerable work on the target lists over the intervening two years, few people outside the AOC at AIRSOUTH in Naples seem to have considered the targets part of a theaterwide campaign plan. From time to time, in response to some sort of provocation, the UN would request—and NATO would fly—limited strikes against selected targets. One such strike took place in early 1994 against the Bosnian Serb airfield at Udbina in the Krajina region of Croa- tia. NATO hit the airfield in response to flagrant violations of the no-fly zone, yet without having a clear operational objec- tive. The UN prevented NATO from destroying significant tar- gets and putting the airfield out of business, intending the attack merely as a signal of the "resolve" of the world commu- nity to enforce the provisions of UNSCRs to end the fighting. Such pinprick attacks—disconnected events with no real link- age to one another—accomplished little in the end.

Throughout 1994 NATO military and civilian leaders contin- ued to encourage their counterparts in the UN to take a broader view of the potential impact of an air campaign and such a campaign's ability to achieve theater objectives. Detailed coor- dination of a list of targets began in earnest. More impor- tantly, the military objectives and, specifically, the air objec- tives began to come into much better focus. This increasingly clear direction allowed planners at the AOC and the CAOC in Vicenza to plan the prosecution of target sets systematically with the intent of affecting the BSA's center of gravity (COG). The list of targets became more than simply an à la carte menu from which to choose one or two items.

Following a series of incidents in late 1994 involving the targeting of NATO aircraft by the Bosnian Serb integrated air defense system (IADS), and with UN Security Council concurrence, the NAC approved the planning and conduct of suppression of enemy air defenses (SEAD) apart from the CAS or other targeting of option two. In response to this broadened planning authorization, the CAOC developed a plan to systematically attack EW, SAM, and C^2 sites that posed a threat within Bosnia-Herzegovina. Most of the potential targets existed in Bosnian Serb–held territory. The plan later became known as Operation Deadeye. Throughout the spring of 1995, the CAOC conducted extensive nodal analysis and completed initial work on the plan.[12] It focused on force protection through the elimination, or at least degradation, of the Bosnian Serb army's IADS (fig. 4.1). For political reasons, this operation was later split into two halves, Deadeye Southeast and Deadeye Northwest.

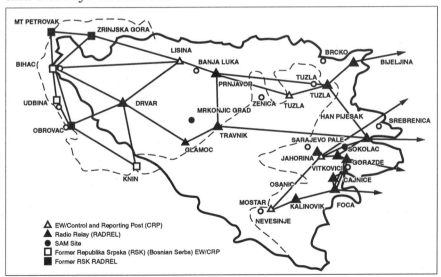

Figure 4.1. Operation Deadeye Key Nodes (Extracted from briefing, Lt Gen Michael Ryan, COMAIRSOUTH and commander, Sixteenth Air Force, to US Air Force Corona Conference, subject: Operation Deliberate Force, February 1996. [Secret] Information extracted is unclassified)

Summer 1995: The Situation Intensifies

NATO aircraft attacked the Pale ammunition depot on 24–25 May 1995 in response to escalating Bosnian Serb threats to the eastern safe areas. In response, the Bosnian Serbs took UN personnel hostage, a situation that persisted for weeks and spurred development of yet another plan which finally began to draw together the disparate elements of previous planning efforts. This plan, "NATO Air Operations in Bosnia-Herzegovina," existed in the form of briefing slides and memos only and was the immediate precursor to Deliberate Force. A two-step and time-sequenced campaign plan, it provided for escalatory measures should the UN and NATO commanders agree that they were not meeting earlier objectives. The CAOC requested and received assistance from Checkmate in reviewing the plan; this helped further refine the objectives and associated tasks and measures of merit for achieving each objective.[13] Planning for Deadeye, which had not yet been implemented, continued to percolate on a separate but parallel track.

On 2 June 1995, Basher 52, a US F-16 flying a Deny Flight mission, was shot down near the Bosnian Serb stronghold of Banja Luka. Consequently, COMAIRSOUTH briefed Operation Deadeye for the first time and spurred intensified work on its provisions.[14] The objective of Deadeye was to provide support to ongoing Deny Flight operations and ensure freedom of movement throughout Bosnia-Herzegovina by NATO aircraft enforcing the no-fly zone. With the shootdown of Basher 52, the Deny Flight operational concept was revised and refocused with a stronger emphasis on force protection. The revised CONOPS, therefore, sought to reduce friendly force exposure yet continued to support UN mandates.[15] Interestingly, planners made no formal modifications to OPLAN 40101 at this time but revised the guidance and direction to account for the change in policy.

During late June and July, events in-theater escalated the pace of work at a number of locations. At national, NATO, and UN headquarters, officials formulated plans to respond to the changing nature of the conflict. The UN safe areas of Zepa and Srebrenica fell, and Gorazde came under increased threat. Although NATO employed CAS around Srebrenica in an attempt to forestall its being overrun, a broad application of force on a wider scale that would noticeably affect the Bosnian Serbs was lacking. Escalating violence and threats of violence against the remaining safe areas made it appear likely that NATO would have to use sustained offensive military force.

AIRSOUTH and CAOC planners had already begun developing a plan to provide CAS or battlefield air interdiction to prevent Gorazde from being overrun. Although of a scale larger than that previously employed, the plan would fall short of an air "campaign" plan. Shortly after the July summit in London and the subsequent NAC decision to get tough, planners developed similar documents for the defense of Sarajevo, Tuzla, and Bihac. The plans existed principally in the form of briefing slides with little supporting material. All of them were safe-area-specific and not part of an operational-level theater air campaign.

The Deliberate Force Plan Takes Shape

Each of the safe-area-specific plans focused on militarily significant targets in the immediate vicinity of that safe area. Concentrations of forces, heavy weapons, and lines of communications constituted typical target sets. These plans sought to defend their respective populations from Bosnian Serb attack. Deadeye Southeast and Northwest would provide SEAD for any of those area plans.

The chance of the UN's approving sustained, large-scale air strikes had seemed quite remote before, but the decisions taken at the London summit solidified NATO resolve and emboldened the UN.[16] The earlier CONOPS, "NATO Air Operations to Stabilize Bosnia-Herzegovina," again underwent revision.

A key modification to the plan, resulting from activity among warring factions in July, was the UN's adoption of the NATO view of wider zones of action (ZOA), which entailed an increase in radius of the total-exclusion zone around each safe area from 20 kilometers (km) to 25 km. The ZOAs proposed by AIRSOUTH, however, coincided with the subdivision of the Deadeye plan, partitioning Bosnia-Herzegovina into southeast and northwest ZOAs. An area of overlap existed in the northeast corner of Bosnia-Herzegovina in the vicinity of the Posavina

Corridor (fig. 4.2). The southeast ZOA contained the safe areas of Sarajevo and Gorazde, while Bihac lay in the northwest ZOA. The Tuzla safe area was in both ZOAs. The UN ultimately accepted this ZOA subdivision of Bosnia and the implication that targets well away from the safe areas could be attacked. This change in UN thinking was important to the eventual approval of the relatively wide-scale Deliberate Force.

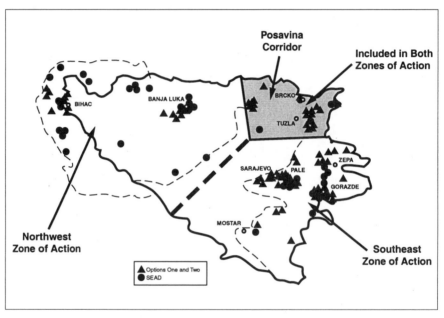

Figure 4.2. Zones of Action (Extracted from briefing, Lt Gen Michael Ryan, COMAIRSOUTH and commander, Sixteenth Air Force, to US Air Force Corona Conference, subject: Operation Deliberate Force, February 1996. [Secret] Information extracted is unclassified)

Adoption of the wider ZOAs permitted the application of systematic air-to-ground targeting to effect the desired outcome in the safe areas. Although the ZOA concept did not allow unfettered application of airpower by NATO throughout Bosnia-Herzegovina, the concept was a significant step in the direction of a "strategic" air campaign. The UN finally understood that activities occurring outside the safe areas by the warring factions had a significant impact on more than one safe area—indeed, on the entire country.

Planning for Deliberate Force continued simultaneously with planning for the protection of individual safe areas and for the conduct of Deadeye throughout July and August. Another intermediate plan developed by AIRSOUTH and CAOC planners was for Operation Vulcan, designed to bring together the constituent parts of other area plans' elements into a cohesive air operation in the southeast ZOA—especially the Sarajevo area. This plan consisted of a master attack plan (MAP),[17] which existed in the form of briefing slides. The Vulcan plan primarily targeted radio relays (RADREL), SAMs, ammunition depots, and military repair facilities.

At about the same time as the development of Vulcan and the updates to the other individual safe-area plans, another AFSOUTH plan/briefing entitled "Graduated Air Operations"[18] showed the connectedness of targets in the various safe-area zones and ways they might be attacked in a progressive and systematic manner. The plan suggested expanding operations into neighboring safe areas or across the entire country, if necessary. As a precursor, the plan assumed freedom of action of NATO air forces, and its assurance remained a key element of all planning efforts.

Even as these several plans evolved, the NATO Military Committee provided guidance and direction for the application of a "graduated" strategy "to assess possible reactions of the parties in conflict" following its meeting of 31 July 1995: "First, the objective of deterrence and, thereafter the two objectives of providing CAS to defend Friendly Forces . . . and the wider application [of] airpower in a wider context. . . . Finally, if approved, the application of airpower on a greater scale."[19]

Following that guidance, AIRSOUTH planners devised a sequence of operations to represent the "building block" nature of planned operations and phased an escalation of attacks on targets near the safe areas. Implementation of the phases depended upon the response by the Bosnian Serbs to the previous phase. The planners also proposed other so-called nonphased targets, but these largely fell into the option-three category (OPLAN 40101 was still operative during this time).[20] The London summit had authorized incorporation of only option-one and option-two targets into air-strike operational plans.

escalation 105

Also in August a key memorandum of understanding known as the Air/Land Operations Coordination Document emerged. That memorandum established the basis for coordination between AIRSOUTH (and by extension, the CAOC) and the UN Rapid Reaction Forces (RRF) operating under UNPROFOR, in the event that offensive air-strike operations began. The resultant draft plan[21] called for close cooperation between the air and land components of the overall operation (AIRSOUTH and RRF, respectively) although they technically served different masters. This plan foresaw the need to coordinate CAS and battlefield air interdiction missions with RRF artillery fires. More than that, coordination mechanisms evolved to minimize the chance of fratricide, limit collateral damage, and give the RRF maximum opportunity to jointly effect the desired outcome. In addition, one should note that the fourth and most violent phase carried the descriptor *air/land operations* rather than *air operations*, as used in the CINCSOUTH/FC UNPF memorandum. This seemingly minor modification reflects the nature of the document's dominant land-operations theme.

By mid August, therefore, NATO had developed a patchwork of air operations plans to deal with a variety of contingencies and taskings.[22] The plans themselves existed in the form of briefing slides only, not as formal written documents like OPLAN 40101. Each briefing—therefore each plan—was refined to greater fidelity with each presentation and as the situation in the area of responsibility changed. The name *Deliberate Force* surfaced about this time as a label for the collection of plans. Deliberate Force brought several common characteristics to these plans: common understanding of events that could trigger NATO action, planning assumptions, objective (or end state), and summary of the phased sequences of attack:

Triggers
- killing of UN hostages
- attack on UN forces
- concentration of forces or heavy weapons deemed to be a direct threat to a safe area
- shelling of civilian population areas or safe areas

- opposition to UN withdrawal (preemptive or reactive response contemplated)

Air Campaign Plan Assumptions
- international recognition of Bosnian Serbs as the aggressors
- necessary mandates provided by UN and NATO
- no opposition by Croatia to necessary air strikes on Krajina
- neutrality of Serbia
- availability of assets from NATO contributing nations
- agreement of basing nations to operations from their territories
- Bosnian Serb COG: historic fear of domination
- Bosnian Serb military advantage with respect to BiH: ability to swing more capable but less numerous forces equipped with heavy weapons to places of their need or choosing
- attacking Bosnian Serb advantages leads to changing the balance of power to their disadvantage
- Bosnian Serb realization of a shift in advantage eventuates in their suing for termination of hostilities
- only robust attack leads Bosnian Serbs to that realization

Military [Air] Objective
- a robust NATO air campaign that adversely alters the BSA's advantage in conducting successful military operations against the BiH; desired end state: Bosnian Serbs sue for cessation of military operations, comply with UN mandates, and negotiate

Phased Sequence of Attack
- isolate leadership and attack concentrated, time-sensitive targets
- isolate fielded forces and attack supply/logistics base
- attack fielded forces and selected infrastructure
- maintain nonphased sensitive target options[23]

Deliberate Force: The Plan

As a result of the UN/NATO Joint Targeting Board[24] of 14 August 1995, COMAIRSOUTH distilled the approved list of 151 targets to 87 mission-specific targets for inclusion in the

Deliberate Force plan. These targets were of the option-one and -two variety—and Bosnian Serb only.[25] The few targets grouped in the "demonstration" category consisted of only option-one targets and were subsumed within the broader plan. Option-two targets fell into the "air operations" category. The "IADS" target set was not originally part of the Deliberate Force concept but constituted the Deadeye piece of the overall operation (fig. 4.3).[26]

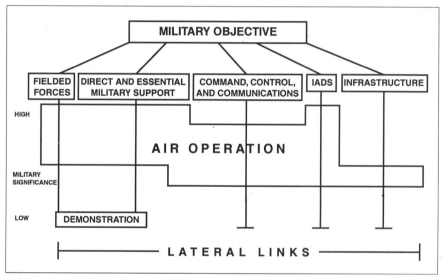

Figure 4.3. Deliberate Force Air Strike Concept (Extracted from briefing, Lt Gen Michael Ryan, COMAIRSOUTH and commander, Sixteenth Air Force, to US Air Force Corona Conference, subject: Operation Deliberate Force, February 1996. [Secret] Information extracted is unclassified. Although this depiction is substantially the same as the Deliberate Force briefings of August 1995, those earlier briefings had divided communications into a separate category from C²/Leadership, and "IADS" was called "EW/AIR DEF." See AIRSOUTH briefing, subject: NATO Operations in Bosnia-Herzegovina—Deliberate Force, c. August 1995 [NATO Secret], US Air Force Historical Research Agency, Maxwell AFB, Ala.)

Fielded forces consisted mainly of heavy weapons rather than the personnel who manned them. Direct and essential targets included munitions depots and storage facilities as well as supply depots and storage facilities. Command, control, and communications (C³) consisted largely of RADRELs, other communications nodes, and a few select command facilities. The IADS targets consisted of EW and SAM sites primarily, initially in the southeast and then into the northwest as necessary. Targets in the infrastructure category actually looked more like lines of communications: transportation choke points, bridges, and tunnels. Most true infrastructure targets were contained in option three. Planners closely examined the linkage of all targets in an attempt to achieve paralysis of the BSA with minimal effort and loss of life on both sides.

Obviously, one doesn't drop bombs on target sets or COGs but on things—hopefully those things the adversary considers valuable. CAOC intelligence personnel had aggressively sought to identify as many potential targets as possible. They evaluated targets within the categories as to their potential military value and the possibility for collateral damage associated with each desired mean point of impact (DMPI). Intelligence specialists then devised a target matrix to aid the CFACC and planners in selecting targets for attack (table 4.2).

Table 4.2

Example Target Matrix

Target Category	Demonstration Value	Moderate Value	High Value
Air Defense	EW Site Radar	East SAM Storage Facility, DMPI: I-3	Electricity Plant
C^3	Station	Military C^3 RADREL Bunker	Military C^3 RADREL Bunker, DMPI: I-6
Leadership	Brigade Headquarters	Division Headquarters	Ground-Forces Headquarters
Direct and Essential Military Facilities	Explosives Storage Facility DMPI: 12, 15	Vehicle Storage Depot	Military Repair Depot
Lines of Communications	Highway Bridge	Highway Bridge	Highway Tunnel
Infrastructure	Petroleum Storage	Ammo, Metal Parts Plant DMPI: 8, 11, 12	Military Plant

Source: Extracted from briefing, Lt Gen Michael Ryan, COMAIRSOUTH and commander, Sixteenth Air Force, to US Air Force Corona Conference, subject: Operation Deliberate Force, February 1996. (Secret) Information extracted is unclassified.

As one may accurately surmise from the foregoing discussion of planning efforts that preceded the actual start of airstrike operations, no single plan contained all component pieces of an air campaign plan. Because the safe areas were under constant and increasing threat from the Bosnian Serb faction and because of shifting strategic guidance from both UN and higher NATO commands, the CAOC and AIRSOUTH planners were prepared to implement any one of the series of air operations plans. As it happened, an exercise of the Vulcan operation plan was scheduled for 29 August to 1 September 1995. The C^2 capabilities of the NATO forces and coordination arrangements with the UN were set for evaluation. The impact of a Bosnian Serb mortar round in Sarajevo, however, would change those plans.

The Deliberate Force Plan in Action

With the completion of the various contingency plans for protection of the safe areas and the formation of the overarching Deliberate Force plan, the implementation of any of them now awaited two events that had to occur before air strikes could begin. One of the warring factions had to pull one of the so-called triggers, and NATO and the UN had to turn the keys. Before the latter event could occur, the UNPF commander decided that he had to completely redeploy his forces within Bosnia-Herzegovina in order to minimize the possibility of a repeat of the earlier hostage taking of UN peacekeepers (following the May attack on Pale). UNPROFOR completed its redeployment, and General Janvier, UNPF force commander, was prepared to turn his key after 25 August.[27] The marketplace mortaring on 28 August served to pull the required trigger. Admiral Smith turned the NATO key immediately, and Lt Gen Rupert Smith—commander of UNPROFOR in Bosnia-Herzegovina and General Janvier's subordinate—turned the UN key[28] on 29 August. NATO aircraft flew their first missions at the end of that tasking day.[29]

At 0600Z on 29 August, COMAIRSOUTH and his staff from Naples arrived at the CAOC. Colonel Zoerb, AOC director, and Col Steve Teske, CAOC Plans director, jointly oversaw the planning, tasking, and targeteering process from that point on. Involved in these processes were several special-purpose cells, each with its own area of expertise or responsibility and staffed mostly by US Air Force personnel on temporary duty.

The first day's planned operations derived mostly from Operations Vulcan and Deadeye Southeast. Initial SEAD and air strikes targeted Bosnian Serb IADS, C^2, and fielded forces. Five additional waves of strikes were planned against targets in the southeast ZOA. Pre- and poststrike reconnaissance, tanker, airborne early warning, electronic intelligence, airborne battlefield command and control, and combat air patrol were integrated to provide 24-hour coverage. This heavy reliance on support assets continued for the duration of the operation. The actual sortie rate was nearly double that anticipated prior to Deliberate Force, requiring the rapid deployment of additional SEAD, tanker, and other support assets to the theater, most from the United States.[30] The F-16CJ with the high-speed antiradiation missile targeting system, for instance, was in great demand, as was the airborne battlefield command and control center aircraft. The latter provided not only critical radio linkage between the CAOC and air forces that flew "feet dry" (i.e., over land) but also much-needed C^2 capability. The high demand for such supporting players was a lesson learned for air planners at all levels.

Because COMAIRSOUTH was extremely concerned with the possibility of fratricide and collateral damage resulting from the bombing, he personally selected each target and DMPI that the aircrews used throughout Deliberate Force. His direct involvement, however, introduced another element of delay into the air tasking message (ATM) process. For example, rapid retargeting of "shooter" missions required revision of the tanker flow plan. Each time a change was introduced into the ATM cycle, the planning-time clock would reset, which meant that planners were constantly trying to respond to new command guidance and bomb damage assessment or otherwise be responsive to the UN.

According to doctrine and practice prior to Deliberate Force, the MAP was a single-source targeteering, weaponeering, and strike-package construction tool that should have contributed to production of the ATM. The latter should have been produced by 1600Z of the day preceding the start of tasking (i.e., 11 hours before the start of the tasked day). During the course of Deliberate Force, however, the MAP evolved from a working-level tool to a vital input to the ATM during the first week or so. By the second week of operations, the MAP nearly took on a life of its own and was issued, along with its often numerous daily changes, as the concise authority on taskings. The ATM was essentially relegated to the status of a "cookie-cutter" style of planning document subject to any number of changes implemented by MAP alterations or other real-time taskings from CAOC current operations.

The crisis action team produced the MAP after receipt of commander's guidance, newly approved targets, and DMPIs, as well as any other specific guidance as to types of aircraft or ordnance to use. Although pre–Deliberate Force planning procedures generally approximated those of Joint Publication (Pub) 3-56.1, *Command and Control for Joint Air Operations*, actual procedures after the first couple of days did not. Using cookie-cutter ATMs and tanker plans, faxing the MAP and its numerous changes to units in lieu of adhering strictly to a planning cycle, and employing similar work-arounds were devised to account for the dynamic and politically sensitive nature of the operation.

Given the abundance of forces available and the rather limited target set, someone outside the operation might be tempted to ask why it was so difficult to adhere to a tasking cycle with a minimal number of changes and turbulence. An example may serve to show the pressures on COMAIRSOUTH and the CAOC staff. During the first week of the operation, planners targeted an ammunition-storage depot, wrote that attack into the ATM, and tasked a mission of eight strike aircraft plus all the necessary support to destroy the depot. Shortly before mission takeoff, the CAOC received word that a company of French peacekeepers was close to the target. Rather than canceling the mission outright, planners retasked it within the same planning cycle for a different target. That change then rippled into the tanker-flow plan as well as into the tasking for all other assets planned to support the strike mission. These types of mission changes were relatively commonplace and affected the entire day's schedule.

The reason for canceling the original mission in the above example is fairly straightforward: to avoid the potential for fratricide in the mission area. The rationale for dynamically retasking the mission, rather than rolling the target into the next ATM cycle, is more complex. An undercurrent of apprehension existed within the CAOC senior leadership that the political leadership of the UN and NATO might halt the operation before the military deemed the job accomplished and objectives achieved. Thus, the CAOC felt pressure to prosecute all potential targets as rapidly as possible just in case that occurred.

Constantly changing the tasking for so many of the CFACC's assets had the effect of substantially compressing the original 24-hour planning/tasking cycle. The ATM and MAP underwent major modifications, but because of communications deficiencies, the CAOC had to fax the changes to units; the latter often did not have the latest message. This compression of the cycle was also evident in a subcycle called the reconnaissance attack cycle (RAC). During the RAC, planners identify reconnaissance requirements and assign aircraft, based on the ground commander's needs. Those aircraft then attack the targets and (if necessary) fly poststrike reconnaissance. Having to respond to the UNPROFOR commander's stated needs and those of the RRF commander at one point compressed the RAC to six hours.[31]

As should be apparent, the theater strategy to achieve NATO and UN objectives in the Balkans was essentially an air strategy. Since the objective was to coerce an enemy into a particular pattern of behavior rather than destroy or defeat him, commanders maintained a very short leash on employment measures in order to stop the operation rapidly at any time.

The ability to measure the effectiveness of an air campaign is often elusive. Moreover, in an operation in which one cannot quantify the success or lack thereof in traditional terms (e.g., body counts, enemy-unit combat-effectiveness ratings, aircraft shot down, etc.), establishing measures of merit proves particularly difficult. In addition, subdivision of the campaign into phases allowed prosecution of the various established target sets to be measured. Although not explicitly defined by beginning and end points, the phases corresponded to the target sets that supported the identified Bosnian Serb

COG. Analysts measured the overall progress of the air campaign primarily against the desired end state.

The air campaign began with an intense pounding of the Bosnian Serb IADS on 30 August. Targets were selected throughout southeast Bosnia to ensure freedom of movement for NATO aircraft operating there. Strike targets included key communications nodes and large ammunition-storage facilities. On 1 September the UN requested that NATO "pause" the operation.

The turning off of the UN "key" had been anticipated but was not warmly greeted. The pause permitted intensified diplomatic efforts by both the UN and Ambassador Holbrooke's team. During the pause the UN and NATO spelled out terms the Bosnian Serbs would have to meet in order to forestall resumption of the Deliberate Force campaign. Poor weather hampered NATO monitoring of compliance, but by the morning of 5 September, it was obvious that the Bosnian Serbs were not meeting the UN-NATO demands, so Deliberate Force resumed. The very fact that NATO restarted the air operation was in all likelihood the single most important decision made during the entire course of Deliberate Force.[32] Ambassador Holbrooke observed that the resumption of the operation was the "most critical moment of the bombing" and that "if the bombing had not resumed that day, the negotiations would have been very adversely affected."[33]

When the campaign resumed on 5 September, COMAIRSOUTH was determined to intensify the pace as much as practical. Although the target list was not long, very poor weather diminished the success of many missions or forced them to abort. The ROE required positive identification of the assigned DMPI before dropping bombs, and that was not always possible because of bad weather. Despite the problems encountered, the operation proceeded so smoothly that by 7 September CINCSOUTH apprised SACEUR of substantial progress:

a. Attack of the IADS in the southeastern ZOA had been largely successful. Its robustness and redundancy, however, made continued suppression necessary.

b. Responsive CAS and RRF artillery continued to pound targets in and around the Sarajevo area. The synergism of this coordinated air-land response had proven very successful in suppressing Bosnian Serb shelling of Sarajevo.

c. A systematic attack of fielded forces continued, including C^3 as well as direct and essential military support.

d. Targeting of multiple choke points and bridges had begun. NATO closely coordinated with UNPROFOR to achieve the desired effect yet preserve routes that could sustain resupply and humanitarian relief of Sarajevo.[34]

At the same time, COMAIRSOUTH realized that he was quickly facing a targeting dilemma. Even with the forced slow-down in operations due to poor weather, the approved target list from the 14 August Joint Targeting Board was almost exhausted. On the one hand, General Ryan wanted to prosecute the targets as rapidly as possible in case of another halt. On the other hand, he became very concerned about reaching the end of the approved option-two targets before achieving the end state.

Some of the temporary personnel that had arrived to augment the CAOC came equipped with both a good ability to think "outside the box" (using a fresh approach to the same problem) and a computer system called the JFACC Planning Tool.[35] At about this time, using the JFACC Planning Tool and working apart from the ongoing Deliberate Force planning process, a small team developed options for attacking targets in the option-three category. Although the likelihood of ever receiving clearance to prosecute those targets was remote because of the likelihood of collateral damage, planning for that contingency continued nonetheless. COMAIRSOUTH had already identified his targeting predicament to CINCSOUTH; fortunately, the team never had to pursue option three. As a consequence, AIRSOUTH became even more selective about the targets it would strike. The planners hoped to wear down the Bosnian Serbs by continuing to strike those few remaining targets to ensure their total destruction.

On 14 September Admiral Smith and General Janvier agreed that NATO had substantially achieved the military objectives and that they needed another pause to determine the actual compliance of the Bosnian Serbs with their agreements.[36] At that time only eight targets of the original 56 had escaped destruction. Following an extension of the original 72-hour pause for another 72 hours, the two commanders issued a joint statement on 20 September, declaring success of the operation and achievement of the end state.

Conformity to and Deviation from Planning Doctrine and Practice

Many similarities existed between planning doctrine and the practical experience of Deliberate Force due to the credibility and influence of existing US (Air Force and joint) doctrine. Experience diverged from doctrine, however, as a result of conflicts between the underlying assumptions of existing doctrine and those that framed Deliberate Force.

Of particular importance to the commander fighting the battle is clarity of the objective. Without a clearly defined objective for operations and a desired end state, the military commander may flounder in uncertainty. Numerous periods of uncertainty about strategic objectives existed throughout the two and one-half years of NATO involvement in the Balkans leading up to Deliberate Force. The CINCSOUTH/FC UNPF memorandum of understanding of 14 August 1995 clearly established conditions for the initiation of hostilities and strategic objectives. However, the evolution of operational objectives during the weeks preceding the operation does indicate significant changes in the desired end state. For example, compelling the Bosnian Serbs to negotiate was added to those objectives.[37]

Another similarity between Deliberate Force experience and US doctrine is the asymmetric nature of the strategy that NATO employed. Without effective air opposition from the BSA, NATO established air superiority quickly and was threatened only by ground-based air-defense systems. Having characteristics sharply asymmetric from those of the faction under attack, the NATO air armada remained free to strike at targets of its choosing. For example, although the BSA enjoyed significant advantages in (ground-based) heavy weapons over the federation forces, those weapons were of little use against NATO airpower. Although attacking individual artillery tubes proved too difficult for NATO to conduct economically, indirectly attacking those weapons through strikes on ammunition-storage, repair, and weapon-storage facilities largely negated

the BSA advantage. The supremacy of space and information capabilities on NATO's part likewise overwhelmed the Bosnian Serbs, denying them any security of operations or information about their enemy.

The selection of target sets by AIRSOUTH planners indicated a clear understanding of direct- and indirect-targeting strategies. Few option-one and -two targets directly affected the Bosnian Serb COG, thus requiring an indirect strategy. For example, AIRSOUTH had assessed that the BSA's advantage in heavy weapons hinged on its ability to shift a small number of highly trained personnel from one battle to another, using equipment stored in dispersed locations. With devastating air attacks on the means of C^2 of those personnel rather than direct attacks on the equipment or personnel, the BSA could no longer effectively command and control them and respond to rapid changes on the battlefield. Thus, indirectly attacking that strength by attacking the supporting C^2 nodes greatly reduced its effectiveness.

The topography and weather in the mission area militated against successfully attacking individual artillery pieces or tanks. Moreover, it made little sense to attack the tubes that the UN demanded the Serbs remove from the total-exclusion zones. The Serbs could have claimed, with some justification, that they were being prohibited from withdrawing their artillery by NATO air strikes. This example of asymmetric and indirect attack served to neutralize the strength of the BSA.

Although Deliberate Force incorporated many of the doctrinal concepts found in US joint doctrine and NATO procedures (such as they were), the operation diverged in significant areas as well. Of special concern was the "friendly" C^2 arrangement. Although the military forces assigned to NATO and the UN had worked together for nearly three years, there was never a single commander over all air and land forces. Yet, even after the UN turned its key and Deliberate Force began, CINCSOUTH had to coordinate with the force commander of UNPF (as a de facto "land component commander") and RRF and respond to their concerns. The initial 24-hour "pause" on 1 September that stretched into four days is a prime example of the fragility of that C^2 arrangement. The pause had emanated from outside CINCSOUTH's change of command and required intensive coordination to ensure that no operational military problems developed. Yet another example of fragile C² occurred between the CAOC and RRF. They essentially revalidated the targets each night during the planning process.[38] Although the August Joint Targeting Board had given explicit approval to prosecute the option-two targets, the UN reviewed and approved them anew each day.

Even within the NATO command structure, significant challenges existed. For instance, a simple yet telling change had to be made in terminology and procedure. For years, the United States and NATO have issued to flying units an air tasking order, the directive coordinating all flying activities of the command. One of the coalition partners, however, refused to accept "orders" from NATO, thus necessitating a name change to "air tasking message." Although not significant at first glance, the distinction highlights a potential area for exploitation by a future adversary. Of more significance, however, is the seeming lack of adequate authority, planning, and integration of search-and-rescue assets of the member nations. When a French Mirage 2000 (call sign Ebro 33) was shot down (the only NATO aircraft lost during Deliberate Force), NATO made rather faltering attempts to locate and rescue the aircrew. Both US Joint Special Operations Task Force (JSOTF) forces and Navy rescue teams participated but not in coordination.[39]

Another doctrinal area from which Deliberate Force significantly deviated had to do with the concept of synergy—a key tenet of aerospace power. Although AIRSOUTH achieved certain internal synergies at the tactical level, it realized little planned external synergy. Internal synergy, through use of composite force packages that contained all elements necessary to accomplish the strike mission, ensured force security by utilizing the full range of capabilities of airpower platforms. On the other hand, although the Air/Land Operations Coordination Document set forth operating procedures for land and air forces, it merely provided deconfliction of operations. The primary purpose of the agreement was to avoid collocating an artillery round and an aircraft in the same piece of sky. It neither established nor fostered synergistic effects of the RRF and NATO air forces.

Airpower, however, did achieve one unintended synergy with land forces. Because of the simultaneous nature of Deliberate Force and the BiH/Croatian Defense Council (HVO) federation ground offensive, both operations seem to have benefited from the battlefield successes of the other. COMAIRSOUTH took great pains to avoid even the appearance that NATO had somehow coordinated operations with the federation. The fact remained, however, that the BSA was severely pressed from the western offensive, was being hurt by the bombing, and was unable to exercise effective C^2 over its forces as a result. NATO determined that it had been so successful in this regard that at one point General Hornburg suggested providing Gen Ratko Mladic (the BSA commander) with a cellular phone and some satellite photos, thinking that Mladic did not have a clue as to what was happening to his forces.[40] Thus, ground and air forces achieved de facto synergies with each other's operations that undoubtedly propelled both toward achievement of their respective objectives.

Whereas political and military strategic objectives during the cold war focused on the war-winning nature of military operations, planners and commanders have experienced something of a vacuum when it comes to clear strategic guidance in operations other than war (OOTW). Even the definition of OOTW and the differentiation between it and "war" have proven difficult to establish. To strategic-level planners and decision makers (e.g., at NATO headquarters and the UN in New York), Deliberate Force was an OOTW. But to aircrews dropping bombs and dodging SAMs over Bosnia-Herzegovina, the operation looked every bit like a war. Not having a clear, warlike focus from strategic decision makers placed operational- and tactical-level warriors in a tenuous position. The pressure to implement warlike air actions while receiving OOTW-like political and military guidance seemed to culminate at the CAOC. As our nation's history has shown, military and political pressures often compete during US unilateral action. The problems can (and likely will) be exacerbated in a coalition endeavor such as Deliberate Force in which member nations have different agendas to advance and in which national military doctrine and practice may not coincide. A number of factors, such as lack of coalition consensus, active involvement of the UN, or diffused influence of other bodies (e.g., the Contact Group) can further complicate the effective employment of airpower.

Clearly, existing NATO military doctrine—specifically, airpower doctrine—is woefully inadequate to give proper guidance to NATO military commanders engaged in UN-sponsored NATO missions. Because of NATO's historic focus on self-defense rather than any out-of-area employment, little in the way of useful doctrine has arisen to support such "new world order" activities. Each member nation's citizenry and leadership must wrestle with the question of whether or not NATO should involve itself in out-of-area activities. The question remains important for military leaders because of the potential uncertainty it can lend to their impending mission and the political will supporting it. Although several member nations, including the United States, have brought recent operational experience to the alliance, the NATO bureaucracy still seems mired in a historical rut.

Grasping the differences in the relative sophistication of US and NATO planning processes and mechanisms is key to understanding why Deliberate Force looked so much like a US effort. Due in large measure to its relatively large military force structure, the United States was best suited for the leadership role in the operation. Many allies had taken part in US training of one sort or another, giving them a basic understanding of the US method of planning, tasking, and—in some cases—campaign planning.[41] Yet, even with that very significant cross-flow of information and expertise, COMAIRSOUTH found himself with a limited number of planners in whom he had confidence to conduct the important planning for Deliberate Force. General Ryan also knew that he had the option at any time of asking higher US headquarters for support if he needed it—and he exercised that option. Although Deny Flight/Deliberate Force most definitely remained a NATO effort, no one hesitated to request unilateral assistance from the United States—which did not hesitate to provide it.

Even with its long history of peacekeeping involvement around the world, the UN has no doctrine of airpower employment. Until Deny Flight enforcement actions began in April 1993, the UN had not had any significant air force at its disposal—certainly not one with a "shooter" capability. Correspondingly, prior UN operations typically had been commanded and controlled by land-force commanders, some with little experience or familiarity with airpower theory and doctrine. The resulting lack of detailed understanding of airpower missions and capabilities, therefore, is not surprising. Throughout the early days of peacekeeping operations in the former Yugoslavia, small cells of air force personnel at the in-theater headquarters managed to bring some "air sense" to the UN operation. But because the UN secretary-general, his special representative, and the UNPF force commander made most of the critical decisions driving the UN operation, their collective lack of understanding of airpower often resulted in constraints that effectively hobbled its potential impact.

During the height of the cold war, SACEUR's General Defense Plan sought to defend NATO against attack into the alliance's territory, meet force with force, reestablish the borders, and force the Warsaw Pact to desist in its military operations. Such war planning engendered an attitude of steadiness—a sense that nothing would ever change and that the correlation of forces contributed stability to the European continent. In the past, what people have considered NATO "doctrine" has actually been little more than procedure. In the Jominian tradition, the defense of Central Europe would be rather mechanistic—from both the ground and air perspectives. Decision processes could afford to be slow and measured. However, the inherent instability and requirement for rapid responsiveness in OOTW put stress on the NATO civilian and military bureaucracy, forcing it to shift its operational focus toward a much more fluid "maneuver warfare" strategy. Further, competing national interests of NATO member nations can sometimes negatively affect the achievement of alliance goals. No longer can member nations focus on defeating a common enemy; now they must strive to achieve somewhat less defined objectives against less clearly identified adversaries.

Due to the lack of solid NATO, UN, or other coalition doctrine for the operational environment of the Balkans, commanders and planners had to fall back on their national doctrine and personal experience. Yet, even that doctrine was incomplete, so they had to deviate from it when the situation demanded. The unique circumstances of the theater required

CAOC and AIRSOUTH planners to exercise considerable original thinking in devising a workable and acceptable strategy for implementation.

Of first priority in Air Force doctrine is control of the air.[42] Some modern airpower advocates, such as Col Phillip Meilinger, have gone so far as to equate air superiority with victory.[43] Colonel Meilinger calls into question the usefulness of air superiority, however, if the enemy believes that his opponent will not exploit it or if there is nothing that air superiority can effectively exploit. NATO unequivocally achieved air superiority almost immediately on 30 August, yet overall success remained in question even after the final bomb fell on 14 September. The nature of the operation did not lend itself to final solution through the application of airpower although such application absolutely facilitated success. Perhaps a redefinition of *victory* in the OOTW context would be appropriate for the future.

In contrast, prior to Deliberate Force some people maintained that airpower could not be decisive. In an interview, Ambassador Holbrooke pointed this out, saying that many people believed, "almost as a Mantra, that you cannot use airpower unless it's backed up by ground troops."[44] He believed that an ambivalence existed concerning the capability of airpower to achieve the objective without the introduction of significant ground forces. Airpower, however, overcame that skepticism in the end.

Although the impact of existing doctrine was substantial, deviations from it ensured success in this nontextbook operation. Because doctrine has evolved over the decades to enable air forces to contribute to war winning, it is less than optimally suited for OOTWs. But if one views doctrine as guidance rather than as "Holy Writ," the tenets of flexibility and versatility can extend beyond the machines themselves to the Air Force planners and commanders who direct their employment.

As described in the previous chapter, US joint-doctrine publications have sought to lay common foundations upon which the individual services can build their doctrine. Such commonality has advantages but can drive inappropriate decisions if one follows it too rigidly. For example, Joint Pub 1-02, *Department of Defense Dictionary of Military and Associated Terms,* associates a COG with a "military force." That is certainly true in most scenarios, but in Bosnia-Herzegovina the COG was the Bosnian Serbs' mental attitude—their fear of domination. That attitude extended well beyond the force to the populace and civilian leadership.

Although AIRSOUTH determined that the "historic Bosnian Serb fear of domination" was the COG to attack, it was equally important to defend the Bosnian-government COG—the city of Sarajevo. More than any other location in Bosnia-Herzegovina, that city symbolizes the core issue for Bosnian Muslims. Loss of Sarajevo would have led to the fall of the federation and the end of Bosnia-Herzegovina as a unitary, sovereign nation. Thus, protection of the "friendly" COG was every bit as important to the overall success of the operation as was attack of the "enemy" COG. Current doctrine is virtually silent about the issue of defending friendly COGs.

On a more practical level, the "standard" 24-hour tasking cycle has given military planners a schedule tied to the sun and their circadian rhythms. However, rigid adherence to such a cycle may detract from the very flexibility that airpower affords the commander. The need to respond rapidly to changing situations required massive daily changes to current operations tasked by the CAOC. More responsive systems, both hardware and management, would contribute to breaking that reliance on a 24-hour cycle and getting inside an adversary's observe-orient-decide-act loop[45] or his tasking cycle.

Joint Pub 3-56.1 provides joint air campaign planners an excellent tool to help them organize an air operations plan. AIRSOUTH and the CAOC planners used elements of the five-phase air campaign planning process described in section three of that publication (and chap. 3 of this book) prior to and during Deliberate Force. That process, not linear but iterative in nature, has excellent applicability across the spectrum of war and OOTW. The first phase, "Operational Environment Research," which was conducted continuously, affected the other four phases. The tool, having no fixed length, can be customized for the contingency; it is also results-oriented and responsive to the fog and friction of warfare (or of OOTW). Too few planners in the CAOC and AIRSOUTH were familiar with either this doctrinal tool or the training available in its application.[46]

The physical and organizational layout of the CAOC, as previously described, did not adequately support planning requirements for a dynamic operation such as Deliberate Force. The CAOC lacked a central command facility, and a sense of unit cohesion did not exist because of the short-duration, temporary-duty assignments of personnel. Further, it lacked adequate communications means, and competing national and parochial service interests were abundant.

For example, because the physical layout of the CAOC buildings and lack of office space prevented collocation of the command's various cells, they had to work very hard to coordinate their work. The JSOTF, headquartered at San Vito dei Normanni AB, Italy (the joint US Special Operations Forces [SOF] contingent), had posted liaison officers in three separate locations at the CAOC: the combined rescue coordination center, the CAS cell, and intelligence (C-2). These liaison officers had different reporting chains for their SOF specialty area. A special-operations liaison element did not exist in the CAOC, thus ensuring a piecemeal approach to the provision of US SOF to the CFACC. JSOTF did not have a strong advocate for its capabilities and, therefore, was underutilized—or, in at least one instance, utilized incorrectly. The CAOC's strategic plans were formulated at "Fort Apache," nickname for the temporary facility outside the main building. Most decisions about tasking were worked between Fort Apache and the commander's office. Thus, inadequate facilities and competing priorities resulted in less-than-optimal SOF employment.

In at least one instance, the use of AC-130 gunships in a purely reconnaissance role nearly resulted in the loss of 15 aircrew members.[47] During the first week of the campaign, gunships were tasked to conduct reconnaissance of roads around Sarajevo, looking for movements of Bosnian Serb heavy weapons. The gunships were retasked and flew five successive nights following the same general flight profile. On the fifth night, the aircraft came under antiaircraft artillery (AAA) and SAM fire. After the AAA exploded above the aircraft and flares defeated the SAMs, the AC-130 recovered without further incident. Although gunships have an armed-reconnaissance role, the CAOC decided time and again to use the AC-130 in a purely reconnaissance role, rather than employ other special-operations assets tailored to the tasking. This highlights the lack of a viable special-operations advocate on the CAOC planning and operations staff. Because SOF representatives, such as a special-operations liaison element, were not involved in initial targeting decisions, very scarce and high-value assets suffered from less-than-optimal employment.

The practical outgrowth of the planning process—the Deliberate Force air campaign plan—and the way in which it was executed at the operational level dramatically altered the tactical conduct of the operation. In most wars and OOTWs, the reaction of the enemy will dictate changes to operations, but three major external factors influenced the conduct of Deliberate Force even more profoundly. First, force protection was of paramount importance to COMAIRSOUTH, CINCSOUTH, and the UN commanders. On the NATO side of the Adriatic, the opinion that not a single target was worth the life of one aircrew member typified the concern for force protection. As for the UN, it was unwilling to turn its key until all UN forces redeployed to more defensible cantonments. After Deliberate Force started, any UN movement usually affected NATO targeting and often resulted in mission cancellations or changes. The second major external factor, the avoidance of fratricide, proved nearly as important as force protection. Planners made every effort to prevent striking targets in proximity to known UN or other friendly personnel. Third, because of NATO's extreme concern for collateral damage, planners viewed the selection of each DMPI through the filter of potential collateral damage. Commanders were extremely concerned that even one stray bomb might kill innocent civilians and thereby undermine world support for the operation. Rather than extending to the politicians and Contact Group negotiators, this concern for collateral damage appears to have been a constraint self-imposed by NATO.[48]

Conclusion

As we have seen, the Deliberate Force air campaign was carefully planned and executed to achieve both explicit and implicit objectives that emanated from the NAC and the UN

Security Council over the course of years of involvement in the Balkans. The air objective established by COMAIRSOUTH for his command would cause the Bosnian Serbs, as noted above, to "sue for cessation of military operations, comply with UN mandates, and negotiate."

This chapter has endeavored to examine the nature of Deliberate Force's remarkable success, which was largely unpremeditated and resulted from the unforeseen impact of the stopping and restarting of the air campaign. The restart of 5 September shocked the Bosnian Serb leadership and for the first time convinced General Mladic of NATO's resolve. The chapter also examined the relationship of airpower doctrine to the planning and conduct of Deliberate Force. Clearly, the operation both deviated from established airpower doctrine in certain key areas and adhered to it in others. A vacuum exists in the area of good doctrine for OOTW in US joint and service doctrine.

When Admiral Smith and General Janvier issued their joint statement from Zagreb on 20 September 1995 declaring achievement of the end state, Deliberate Force ended.[49] The operation realized all theater and air objectives and established preconditions for the eventual Dayton Peace Accord talks. Although airpower had not operated in isolation from other components, it was decisive. Perhaps future contingencies will feature naval or land forces more prominently than air forces. As Gen Ronald Fogleman, former chief of staff of the US Air Force observed, "Joint warfighting is not necessarily an equal opportunity enterprise."[50] Airpower doctrine and planning must support the full range of aerospace operations as well as support and complement the capabilities of other components. But such doctrine and planning must enable the strategic and independent employment of airpower.

Notes

1. Extracted from briefing, Lt Gen Michael Ryan, COMAIRSOUTH and commander, Sixteenth Air Force, to US Air Force Corona Conference, subject: Operation Deliberate Force, February 1996. [Secret] Information extracted is unclassified.

2. Maj Gen I. B. Holley Jr., USAFR, Retired, "Of Saber Charges, Escort Fighters, and Spacecraft," *Air University Review*, September 1983, 4.

3. Briefing, Maj Gen Hal Hornburg, director, 5 ATAF CAOC, Vicenza, Italy, to study team, Maxwell AFB, Ala., subject: Operation Deliberate Force, 14 March 1996.

4. The senior national representative maintained an understandably "national" view of the operation. This representative would conduct liaison with his nation, and any objections to the operation would come through him. Nations would get information directly from those representatives for their own decision-making bodies to act on. Curiously, the United States did not have such a representative. Although it might seem obvious that the United States did not need a senior national representative since the operation used US commanders, the Joint Chiefs of Staff and others felt that other nations sometimes had better information than they did. For the purposes of Deliberate Force and with only limited exceptions, the commanders diligently maintained their identification as NATO commanders rather than US commanders.

5. UNPROFOR reorganized in the spring of 1995, which changed the overall body to UN Peace Forces in the former Yugoslavia; the former Bosnia-Herzegovina Command changed to UNPROFOR.

6. CINCUSAFE also serves as the NATO commander of Allied Air Forces Central Europe (COMAIRCENT). Thus, he has the unique ability to cross over between national and NATO responsibilities—and often does so. Gen Richard Hawley replaced General Oaks prior to Deliberate Force.

7. Author's experience as commander of UNPROFOR's Monitoring and Close Air Support Coordination Center, Zagreb, Croatia, May–October 1993.

8. Within two weeks of passage of UNSCR 836 in June 1993, the position of force commander of UNPROFOR changed hands to Lt Gen Jean Cot of the French army. Speculation at the time linked those two events.

9. Gen Richard Hawley, CINCUSAFE and COMAIRCENT, interviewed by author, Ramstein AB, Germany, 12 February 1996.

10. Col Steve Teske, executive to Headquarters AIRCENT/Deputy Chief of Staff for Plans and Policy, and CAOC Plans (served on temporary duty), interviewed by author, Ramstein AB, Germany, 14 February 1996.

11. North Atlantic Council, memorandum to the secretary-general, North Atlantic Treaty Organization, subject: NAC Decision Statement MCM-KAD-084-93, Operational Options for Air Strikes in Bosnia-Herzegovina, 8 August 1993.

12. Allied Air Forces Southern Europe, "Deliberate Force Factual Review," draft, 14 November 1995, 2-2. (NATO Secret) Information extracted is unclassified.

13. Deputy chief, Checkmate Division, Headquarters USAF/XOOC, memorandum to director, CAOC Plans, 28 May 1995.

14. Ibid., 2-3.

15. Briefing, Gen George Joulwan, SACEUR, to the NAC, 21 June 1995.

16. Notice C-N (95) 65, "Decisions Taken at the Meeting of the [North Atlantic] Council on Tuesday, 25th July 1995 at 2:30 p.m."

17. As used here, the MAP is roughly equivalent to the master air attack plan (MAAP) as specified in Joint Publication 3-56.1, *Command and Control for Joint Air Operations*, 14 November 1994.

18. The term *graduated air operations* may sound vaguely familiar and unpleasant. The policy of gradual escalation during Operation Rolling Thunder of 1965–68 sought to achieve success through the sending of "signals" to the North Vietnamese and Vietcong. Political restraints placed on the operation and many other factors mitigated against success. Deliberate Force had quite different goals and perhaps even more sensitive political ramifications.

19. Military Committee, memorandum to the secretary-general, NAC, MCM-KAD-057-95, 31 July 1995. (NATO Confidential) Information extracted is unclassified.

20. In his letter to the UN secretary-general to convey C-N (95) 65, "Decisions Taken at the Meeting of the [North Atlantic] Council on Tuesday, 25th July 1995 at 2:30 p.m.," NATO secretary-general Willy Claes states the NAC's willingness to authorize option three or elements thereof. In response, Boutros Boutros-Ghali "notes" that the option-three question remains open, but he is obviously unenthusiastic about prosecuting a belligerent that severely.

21. "Air/Land Operations Coordination Document," draft, Rapid Reaction Forces (RRFOS) 1000-12, August 1995.

22. The US Air Force Historical Research Agency at Maxwell AFB, Ala., maintains electronic and paper copies of these plans.

23. AIRSOUTH briefing, subject: NATO Air Operations in Bosnia-Herzegovina—Deliberate Force, c. 1 August 1995, US Air Force Historical Research Agency, Maxwell AFB, Ala. (NATO Secret) Information extracted is unclassified.

24. The Joint Targeting Board, whose key members included CINCSOUTH and the force commander of UNPROFOR/UNPF, was the high-level coordination body that reviewed the target listing.

25. "Deliberate Force Factual Review," 2-6. (NATO Secret) Information extracted is unclassified.

26. Naming of the separate safe-area air-strike operations and determining where one ended and another began are difficult tasks. Operations Vulcan and Deadeye were separate but closely linked, in that the first would not happen without the second. During the conduct of the operation, COMAIRSOUTH directed that the overall operation be named Deliberate Force, a convention used throughout the remainder of the discussion.

27. Lt Gen Bernard Janvier, deputy commander, Implementation Force (earlier, the force commander of UNPF), interviewed by author, Sarajevo, Bosnia-Herzegovina, 9 February 1996.

28. Although the authority for key turning had been delegated to General Janvier, he was out of the country on leave this day and had delegated "key control" to General Smith. According to his own account, Janvier learned about the situation and agreed fully with Smith's decision. He

immediately returned to his headquarters in Zagreb prior to initiation of the air campaign on the 29th/30th.

29. The 24-hour tasking day extended, for example, from 0300 29 August to 0259 30 August. Dispatch of the air tasking message (ATM)—the planning/tasking document—was planned to (theoretically) allow adequate time for executing units to receive the ATM, complete mission planning and coordination, and complete mission-crew briefings.

30. After reevaluation of the Deny Flight mission earlier in the summer of 1995, many aircraft redeployed to their home bases with the understanding that they were on a relatively short "string" for recall in the event they were needed in-theater.

31. Hornburg briefing.

32. Diplomatic channels indicated that General Janvier fully intended to make the pause a halt. Yugoslav president Milosevic was truly shocked when the bombing resumed. Ambassador Richard Holbrooke, interviewed by Maj Mark McLaughlin and Dr. Karl Mueller, New York, N.Y., 24 May 1996.

33. Ibid.

34. Message, 070800Z SEP 95, CINCSOUTH to SACEUR, 7 September 1995. (NATO Secret) Information extracted is unclassified.

35. Headquarters USAF/XOOC (Checkmate) sent Maj John Riggins along with the JFACC Planning Tool. Checkmate had maintained a presence in the CAOC for many months and was well acquainted with the situation. The "home office" had also provided much help.

36. Exchange of letters between Admiral Smith (CINCSOUTH) and General Janvier (FC UNPF), 14 September 1995.

37. Briefing slides, CAOC, Vicenza, Italy, subject: Deliberate Force, c. early August 1995.

38. Brig Gen David Sawyer, deputy director, 5 ATAF CAOC, interviewed by Maj Tim Reagan, Vicenza, Italy, 16 October 1995.

39. Lt Col Randy P. Durham, chief, Strategy and Doctrine Branch, Air Force Special Operations Command (AFSOC), Hurlburt Field, Fla., "Trip Report, JSOTF2, San Vito dei Normanni AB, IT, 5 Aug–11 Oct 95." Colonel Durham served as the JSOTF2/J-3 (Operations) during Deliberate Force.

40. Hornburg briefing.

41. Headquarters AIRCENT at Ramstein AB, Germany, has recently developed an air campaign planning course for presentation to NATO campaign planners. The course is patterned closely after the USAF's Joint Doctrine Air Campaign Course taught at Maxwell AFB, Ala. (see also note 44). The AIRCENT course is the only one of its kind in NATO and has recently moved to the NATO School (Supreme Headquarters Allied Powers Europe [SHAPE]) at Oberammergau, Germany.

42. Air Force Manual (AFM) 1-1, *Basic Aerospace Doctrine of the United States Air Force,* vol. 1, March 1992, 10.

43. Col Phillip S. Meilinger, *10 Propositions Regarding Air Power* (Washington, D.C.: Air Force History and Museums Program, 1995), 6.

44. Holbrooke interview.

45. Col John R. Boyd, "A Discourse on Winning and Losing," briefing slides, August 1987, available at Air University Library, Maxwell AFB, Ala.

46. Air University's College of Aerospace Doctrine Research and Education at Maxwell AFB, Ala., conducts a course appropriately named the Joint Doctrine Air Campaign Course.

47. Durham, trip report.

48. Ambassador Christopher Hill, US State Department deputy chief negotiator, interviewed by Lt Col Rob Owen, Washington, D.C., 27 February 1996.

49. Joint Statement by Adm Leighton W. Smith, CINCSOUTH, and Lt Gen Bernard Janvier, FC UNPF, Zagreb, Croatia, 20 September 1995.

50. Gen Ronald R. Fogleman, US Air Force chief of staff, speech to the Air and Space Doctrine Symposium, Maxwell AFB, Ala., 30 April 1996.

Chapter 5

Executing Deliberate Force,
30 August–14 September 1995

Lt Col Mark J. Conversino

News of the mortar attack on the Mrkale marketplace in Sarajevo on 28 August 1995 finally moved the West to act. Since French general Bernard Janvier, United Nations Protection Force (UNPROFOR) commander, was on vacation in France to attend his son's wedding, Adm Leighton W. Smith, commander in chief of Allied Forces Southern Europe (CINC-SOUTH), contacted British lieutenant general Rupert Smith, the acting UN commander. Admiral Smith confirmed in a letter to General Smith that, in their "common judgment," the Mrkale shelling represented an attack against a safe area and that air strikes would commence as soon as United States Air Force (USAF) lieutenant general Michael E. Ryan, commander of Allied Air Forces Southern Europe (COMAIRSOUTH), deemed the conditions suitable. Admiral Smith also wrote that Ryan would delay the start of his air campaign until midnight, 29 August, to allow UN forces on the ground to withdraw from their more isolated outposts and thus preclude another embarrassing rash of hostage taking by the Serbs, as had occurred during the North Atlantic Treaty Organization's (NATO) bombing of Pale the preceding May. Nevertheless, the UN and NATO had turned their "keys," and the most intense military operation in the history of NATO was about to get under way.[1]

Indeed, Admiral Smith had already taken several actions to ready his forces. Specifically, he had allowed units belonging to participating NATO countries under the alliance's operational control to return home on an "on-call" status and requested additional aircraft, including F-16C/Ds and F-4G "Wild Weasels" armed with high-speed antiradiation missiles (HARM), to counter the Serb integrated air defense system (IADS). Upon issuing the order to initiate Deliberate Force, Admiral Smith also recalled his on-call tactical forces, including three Mirage F1-CTs, one Mirage F1-CR, two Jaguars, four Mirage 2000Cs, and six Mirage 2000D/Ks from France; four F-16As and two F-16Rs (reconnaissance) from the Netherlands; 10 F-16C/Ds from Turkey; four GR-7 Harriers from the United Kingdom; and six F-4G Wild Weasels, four EA-6Bs, five KC-10s, two C-21s, two MC/HC-130s, two airborne command and control center (ABCCC) EC-130Es, and two EC-130H Compass Call electronic-warfare (EW) aircraft from the United States. As a result of the initial success of the operation, CINCSOUTH would cancel the requests for the F-4Gs, the two EC-130Hs, and one of the EC-130Es.[2]

The sudden intensification and expansion of air operations actually required few substantive organizational changes from those already established for the ongoing Deny Flight operation, of which Deliberate Force actually constituted a particularly intense phase. As he had for Deny Flight, US general George Joulwan, Supreme Allied Commander Europe (SACEUR), delegated operational control of the impending Deliberate Force activity to Admiral Smith, who in turn delegated operational control for all theater-level air forces to General Ryan. Lt Gen Andrea Fornasiero of the Italian air force, commander of the 5th Allied Tactical Air Force (5 ATAF), would exercise command and control (C²) of Deliberate Force operations through the combined air operations center (CAOC) at Dal Molin Air Base (AB), Vicenza, Italy. US Air Force major general Hal Hornburg, director of the CAOC, oversaw both the center's day-to-day operations and—through US Air Force colonel Douglas J. Richardson, his chief of current operations (C-3)—those of Deliberate Force as well. As the CAOC director, General Hornburg used the call sign Chariot to identify himself to NATO aircrews. Since both Deliberate Force and Deny Flight were coalition efforts, representatives from the NATO nations were also assigned to the CAOC.[3]

As was the case with Deny Flight, NATO's Deliberate Force operations and command structure remained wedded to the UN's. As the commander of UNPROFOR, General Janvier served as Admiral Smith's counterpart. General Smith also would work closely with General Ryan. The course eventually taken by Deliberate Force resulted from the coordination and planning among these men in particular. Liaison officers from

NATO and 5 ATAF served with the UN headquarters in Zagreb, Croatia. Further, a NATO liaison officer was attached to UN-PROFOR's air operations control center (AOCC) in Kiseljak (near Sarajevo) as well as to the Rapid Reaction Force (RRF).[4]

In the meantime, upon hearing of the Serb attack, General Janvier hurried back to his post in Zagreb, taking the key from General Smith's hands and settling final strategy with Admiral Smith, who pressed for an "indirect" use of his air-power to take out the "anthill" of Serbian logistics and C[2] facilities, rather than the "ants" of the offending artillery and other heavy weapons themselves. UN intelligence estimated that the 240-square-mile zone around Sarajevo contained some 250 Serb heavy weapons. Finding and destroying these targets with any consistency would be well-nigh impossible. General Janvier agreed that the Serbs should be punished, but he was anxious to keep Deliberate Force on a short leash—he wanted to "inflict pain but not death." After some tense haggling, the American admiral and the French general came to an agreement by 2130 on 29 August. Deliberate Force would start with the Operation Deadeye target list, which included 25 air-to-ground targets and 15 others on Mount Igman outside Sarajevo designated for shelling by guns of the Anglo-French-Dutch RRF. The attack would begin in roughly five hours—at 0200 on 30 August. In the waning moments of calm, UN peacekeepers blew up their bunkers and slipped away to safety.[5]

The air fleet at General Ryan's disposal represented a formidable collection of NATO air assets. At the outset of Deliberate Force, he would have available more than 280 aircraft from the United States (Air Force, Marine Corps, and Navy), France, Britain, Turkey, the Netherlands, Italy, Spain, and Germany. NATO also provided eight E-3A airborne warning and control system (AWACS) aircraft. With the arrival of on-call aircraft and the inclusion of additional non-NATO assets, COMAIR-SOUTH would ultimately have nearly 350 aircraft at his disposal. Although most of the units flew from bases in Italy, Deliberate Force sorties also launched from bases as far away as Britain, Germany, and France.[6]

By far, the single largest concentration of allied aircraft was at Aviano AB, north of Venice, Italy. To accommodate the influx of people and aircraft as tensions rose over the summer, Col Charles F. Wald, the newly arrived commander of Aviano's 31st Fighter Wing, assumed command of a new provisional outfit—the 7490th Wing. On an installation designed for 42 F-16s and 16 CH-47 helicopters, Wald's staff eventually had to bed down a total of 140 aircraft, including 52 F-16s, 16 CH-47s, 12 US Marine Corps F/A-18s, 12 A-10s, three British E-3Ds, 10 Spanish EF-18s, 10 F-15Es, 10 EA-6Bs from the carrier USS *Roosevelt*, nine C-130s of various types, and six EF-111s. Of these, 114 were in place when Deliberate Force opened on the night of 29–30 August. Nevertheless, as commander of the 7490th Wing (Provisional), Wald did not exercise command authority over the non-USAF units.[7]

Overseeing this varied array of air assets was the Deny Flight operations center, which stood up in conjunction with the provisional wing and superseded a sparsely manned Deny Flight coordination cell already operated by the 31st Wing. Becoming fully operational just days before the initiation of Deliberate Force, the center served as Aviano's primary C^2 center for the impending aerial activity. Manned by aviators on temporary duty to Aviano and combined with the 31st Fighter Wing's logistics and munitions personnel in the logistics control center, the operations center worked directly with the CAOC in Vicenza. Despite sporadic lines of communications between Vicenza and Aviano, senior officers at Aviano believed that their air operations center was instrumental in the wing's ability to meet its taskings.[8]

Against NATO airpower, the Bosnian Serbs could count on an efficient and well-developed IADS. The Bosnia Serb army (BSA) also possessed a small air force, estimated at a couple of dozen combat aircraft of limited military capability. Bosnian Serb aircraft had flown against Croatian forces earlier in August in a desperate attempt to halt Zagreb's spectacular five-day campaign to reclaim the Serb-held Krajina region of Croatia. Using cluster munitions, five Serb aircraft killed four civilians and wounded 14 in Slavonia. During the attack, the Serbs lost two aircraft to Croat air defenses and did nothing more than further enrage the Croatians.[9]

The real threat to NATO airpower lay in the BSA's inventory of surface-to-air missiles (SAM) and antiaircraft artillery (AAA).

NATO air planners estimated that in late August the BSA possessed seven SA-2, six SA-6, and 12 SA-9 SAM batteries, unknown numbers of man-portable missiles, and nearly eleven hundred pieces of AAA ranging in caliber from 20 millimeters (mm) to 76 mm. Air planners also considered the possibility that the Bosnian Serbs could count on information from the Republic of Yugoslavia's air defense network, the main target of the Deadeye portion of the Deliberate Force plan. In the region of Sarajevo, the area of most immediate concern to General Ryan and his staff, the BSA mustered three corps—the Romanja, Drina, and Herzegovina—numbering some 15–20,000 personnel backed by an estimated 250 heavy weapons, including more than 50 tanks. As mentioned previously, however, Deliberate Force would not seek to engage and destroy these weapons unless necessary.[10]

Bosnian Serb leaders made crude attempts to counter the perceptibly growing international outrage at the mortar attack on Sarajevo. Radovan Karadzic, for example, blamed the Muslim government of Bosnia for the attack, stating that he hoped the "international community would no longer buy that kind of story," and called for an international investigation. Likely, he was heartened by Moscow's open skepticism regarding Serb culpability for the attack. Momcilo Krajisnik, chairman of the Serb Republic Assembly, personally condemned the attack, stating that "it means no good for Serbs, Muslims, or Croats, and it is not good for the continuation of the peace process either."[11] Yet, the cries of "foul" by the Serb leadership fell on deaf ears—at least outside of Russia. Armed with the earlier UN assessment of Serb responsibility for the Mrkale attack and convinced of the need to back NATO's threats with force, the Western alliance finally moved toward decisive action.

A warning order of 29 August defined the combined land/air operation and set the CAOC into motion. NATO planners and commanders had no idea how long the NATO and UN authorization keys, particularly the UN's, would remain turned on and thus planned to hit as many targets as possible, as quickly as possible. As a preparatory step, General Hornburg canceled most of the preplanned Deny Flight missions scheduled after 1400 central European time (CET). The air tasking message (ATM) for the remainder of that day, as well as for the next, was changed to implement the air-strike plan, initially code-named Vulcan but soon changed to Deliberate Force. As planned, the initial attack included Deadeye targets and those around Sarajevo included in *Bouton D'or*—an earlier plan. On the morning of 29 August, General Ryan arrived at Vicenza to take a more direct role in the execution of the impending operation. Particularly concerned that even a single incident of collateral damage could undermine or even halt the air campaign and convinced that commanders were ultimately responsible for all the actions of their forces, Ryan intended to personally select all targets and desired mean points of impact (DMPI) (i.e., aiming points) for attack. If anything went wrong, he wanted to accept the blame.[12]

Still, even for many NATO personnel, the notion that something big was about to happen did not strike home until very late. Indeed, upon landing at Aviano late in the evening of 29 August, US Navy captain Ken Calise, a CAOC staff officer, found Col Jim Turner, commander of the 31st Operations Group, incredulous that Deliberate Force was really about to begin. Moreover, many of the people at the CAOC envisioned Deliberate Force lasting no more than 48 to 72 hours. The doubts of some of his subordinates aside, at 0140 CET General Hornburg cleared the first strike package into Bosnia-Herzegovina from the Adriatic. The first NATO bombs struck their targets roughly half an hour later.[13]

Bombs Away: Deliberate Force Begins

The first aircraft bound for Bosnia launched from Aviano and the carrier *Roosevelt* shortly before midnight. Once cleared by Chariot, 43 strike aircraft escorted by 14 aircraft performing suppression of enemy air defenses (SEAD) struck targets on the Deadeye Southeast list. Four F-16Cs of Aviano's 510th Fighter Squadron, each carrying two GBU-10 two-thousand-pound laser-guided bombs, struck the Han Pijesak radio-relay station near the Bosnian Serb "capital" of Pale, a key communications node in the region, all weapons hitting their targets.[14] Other aircraft struck at the Jahorina communications complex near Pale, an SA-6 site at Sokolac, and targets as far away as the Tuzla region in the north-central part of the country. Five strike packages, Alpha through Echo, hammered at targets in the Sarajevo region throughout the day. More SEAD packages, as well as day-and-night close air support (CAS) missions rounded out the day's activity. The CAOC coordinated all aerial sorties to allow the RRF a firing window early on the morning of 30 August. Numerous reconnaissance missions flown by both manned aircraft and Predator unmanned aerial vehicles augmented pilot mission reports and weapons film for bomb damage assessment (BDA).[15] By the end of ATM Day Two, 0259 31 August, Deliberate Force had logged 364 sorties, including support missions such as aerial refueling, airborne early warning (AEW), and C[2].[16]

Despite a great deal of success during this critical first day, not all went well. A US Air Force U-2R reconnaissance aircraft tasked to support Deliberate Force crashed on takeoff from its base in the United Kingdom. The pilot ejected but died several hours later in the hospital from his injuries.[17] Over Bosnia itself a Serb man-portable missile brought down a French Mirage 2000K. Although observers on the ground reported two good chutes, attempts to establish radio contact with the downed airmen proved unsuccessful. The loss of the Mirage, call sign Ebro 33, was a sobering reminder of the dangers to all allied airmen. Indeed, Serb gunners and SAMs engaged other aircraft, including US A-10s, Dutch NF-16s, and British Tornadoes, but did not inflict additional friendly losses.[18]

Ebro 33's shootdown launched a series of ad hoc and preorganized combat search and rescue (CSAR) activities. Upon hearing of the shootdown, an EF-111—Nikon 24—volunteered to stay on station to continue suppressing Serb radar. AWACS controllers retasked an F-15E whose target was obscured by clouds to serve as the on-scene commander for the initial recovery effort. Again, aircraft overhead could not establish contact with the French pilots. In an effort to reach the crew of Ebro 33 before the Serbs did, the CAOC ordered a CSAR package of two MH-53 Pave Low helicopters and one HC-130 put on airborne alert off the coast of Croatia. So as to enhance the CSAR activity, the CAOC redirected a scheduled flight of fighters to hit targets in the rescue area that bad weather had obscured earlier in the day. Despite these efforts, rescuers could not locate the French pilots.[19]

The third ATM day of Deliberate Force began at 0300 on 31 August with three strike packages hitting targets in the Sarajevo area. As on the day before, the CAOC scheduled CAS and SEAD sorties to provide more or less continuous coverage. Aviano-based aircraft struck Bosnian Serb ammunition-storage facilities as well as depots near Sarajevo—some for the second time. Poor weather delayed two additional packages that were added to the schedule later in the day, but both still managed to strike at depots, storage sites, and command posts with varying degrees of success. Indeed, on this day numerous missions were canceled or rated noneffective due to the characteristically adverse weather conditions in the region at that time of the year.[20]

While bombs fell across the Bosnian Serb Republic, UN and NATO representatives mounted a diplomatic blitz to keep the onus of responsibility for the air attacks on the Serbs. Karadzic remained defiant, calling the air operation "blackmail" and insisting that Serbs could not be "bribed with money" or "frightened by bombs." He warned darkly that Deliberate Force was setting a precedent for Western meddling in other civil conflicts in both China and Russia. Undeterred by such talk, UN envoy Yasushi Akashi announced that a decision to end the bombing depended on "the attitudes and policies of the Bosnian Serb party." NATO secretary-general Willy Claes called on the Serbs to stop "provoking" the West and to observe the "most basic rules of civilized society."[21]

Nevertheless, Serb efforts to halt the bombing by offering to talk were not completely in vain. Yugoslav president Slobodan Milosevic contacted Akashi in Zagreb on the afternoon of 30 August. Earlier, General Janvier had sent a fax to Gen Ratko Mladic, Bosnian Serb commander, informing him that the air strikes would continue until Janvier was convinced that the BSA no longer posed a threat to the safe areas. Milosevic now told Akashi that if General Janvier would send Mladic another letter outlining his conditions for a cessation of the bombing, the Bosnian Serb general was likely to give in. Akashi and General Janvier wrote such a letter in which they demanded an end to BSA attacks, the withdrawal of heavy weapons from around Sarajevo, and an immediate and complete end to hostilities throughout Bosnia. The letter went out at 1600. Realizing that the last demand might prove unattainable without the assent of the Croatians and Bosnian Muslims, both the UN and NATO backed away from it. Still, contacts continued between Pale and Zagreb throughout 31 August. Shortly after midnight on 1 September, the CAOC in Vicenza received a copy of a message from General Smith's headquarters that suspended all air strikes for the next 24 hours, effective 0200 Greenwich mean time (GMT), pending negotiations with the Serbs. The UNPROFOR commander did promise to allow attacks to counter any BSA offensive and to permit attacks on heavy weapons moving into or manned in the Sarajevo sector. The general emphasized that this was only a pause and that NATO should prepare to resume air strikes no later than 0200 GMT on 2 September. All ATM Day Three missions were off their targets before the suspension took effect. Roughly 48 hours into the operation, Deliberate Force was on hold.[22]

Key leaders differed over the utility of the operational pause. Richard C. Holbrooke, the US assistant secretary of state tasked with finding a diplomatic solution to the Balkan mess, initially endorsed the idea of a bombing pause. General Janvier seemed ready for a break as well. In contrast, both NATO secretary-general Claes and General Joulwan were not convinced of the Serbs' sincerity and thought that the alliance would forfeit whatever initiative it had only recently gained. Nevertheless, Janvier and Mladic met for nearly 14 hours in a hotel in the town of Mali Zvornik, attempting to reach an understanding. Mladic, however, showed no signs of acceding to the earlier UN ultimatum. When he produced a letter outlining his own conditions for a cease-fire, Joulwan was outraged. Sensing Serb intransigence, Admiral Smith, who had also initially agreed to the bombing pause, sought guarantees from General Janvier that if the operation resumed, it would do so in a significant fashion.[23] While Claes wondered if NATO's unity and credibility would survive and while US Air Force officers entertained visions of the ill-fated, on-again-off-again Rolling Thunder campaign of the Vietnam War, US and NATO air units used the pause to assess their own situations.

At Aviano AB, senior officers of the 31st Fighter Wing viewed the bombing halt as a mixed blessing. Anxious to get on with the operation, they realized that with their human and material resources stretched taut by increases in the tempo of operations, the pause would allow people to get a much-needed rest. As the first true combat test of an Air Force wing organized according to the "objective wing" concept, Deliberate Force uncovered the consequences of the personnel reductions entailed in the concept. Reductions in authorized field-grade positions forced many supervisors to work extended hours. Aircrews often flew missions and then proceeded to work 12-hour shifts afterwards. Compounding the problem, units that had deployed to Aviano usually had not brought along adequate supervisory "overhead." Thus, the burden for overseeing a vastly expanded combat wing fell on the shoulders of permanent-party personnel.[24]

A critical part of the objective-wing reorganization involved placing organizational—flight-line—maintenance under the commander of the operations group. Colonel Turner, commander of both the 31st Operations Group and the 7490th Operations Group (Provisional), after the first night, found it physically impossible to oversee both flying and flight-line maintenance operations. Thus, after the first night of Deliberate Force, Col David Stringer, commander of the 31st Logistics Group, took control of flight-line maintenance and weapons loading—an arrangement reminiscent of the "trideputative" wing concept recently replaced by the newer concept.[25]

Members of Aviano's logistics group had indeed planned for an increase in operations, but no amount of planning in the summer of 1995 could remedy some of the problems that lay ahead. Colonel Stringer and his staff, for example, planned for a sortie rate at Aviano of 175 per day. At that rate, the demand for fuel would top nearly 388,000 gallons every 24 hours. By working with their Italian hosts, Stringer's staff was able to ensure a daily flow of four hundred thousand gallons. With the actual peak sortie rate at Aviano at just over 120 sorties and roughly three hundred thousand gallons in fuel, the advanced planning paid off; an inadequate supply of fuel at the outset likely would have resulted in lost sorties.[26]

Other problems, however, were not so easily overcome. Aviano consists of a main operational area, including the runway, key service facilities, and several support areas, all separated from one another by farmland or small settlements and villages. Moving munitions from the storage area to the flight line required coordination with the local Italian *carabinieri* to get weapons convoys across a major local highway. The Italians cooperated closely with US security personnel, but the arrangement made a munitions stockpile on the flight line mandatory if sorties were to be turned in an adequate amount of time. Munitions were first built up and then moved to a flight-line holding area—Aviano's normal "hot-cargo" pad. Because the wing did not have sufficient security police available to guard this new bomb dump and maintain adequate protection of the air fleet now crammed onto every available square foot of pavement, it used maintenance and munitions personnel to safeguard weapons thus stored. By the second day, base civil engineers constructed from concrete slabs a 30,000-square-foot revetted pad within the storage area to help handle the increase in munitions buildup. Without such measures, Aviano's sortie-generation capabilities would have been greatly diminished.[27]

Yet, finding adequate weapons storage was only part of Aviano's challenge. With so many aircraft on the base, maintaining safe intermagazine distances between aircraft proved virtually impossible. This situation put added stress on supervisors and further highlighted the dangers of both chronic and acute fatigue for all personnel involved in handling weapons. Using commonsense safety and coordinating closely with the Spanish and marines (each of whom maintained their own weapons account at the base), the wing prevented a potentially dangerous situation from arising. Still, the use of the hot-cargo pad as a storage site increased hazards in other ways. Transport aircraft actually delivering hot cargo (mainly munitions) to the base had to do so in alternate and less-than-optimal locations. The need to maintain safe clearances at these alternate locations forced numerous support agencies periodically to cease operating and evacuate their areas.[28]

Two potential "showstoppers" emerged both at the outset of Deliberate Force and as the operation expanded. In the words of Colonel Stringer, the depots at Warner Robins, Georgia, and Ogden, Utah, "didn't know there was a war on." The Air Force's "lean logistics" philosophy precludes large stockpiles of parts and equipment at operating bases, making resupply from stateside air-logistics centers vital. The first weekend of the campaign coincided with the three-day Labor Day holiday, so the depots were closed. Stringer's staff contacted managers at both centers who then reacted quickly, recalling workers and moving orders out as soon as possible. Unfortunately, that represented only half the battle. Unaware that parts could be sent via Federal Express directly to Aviano, Defense Logistics Agency personnel shipped items by this means only to Dover Air Force Base (AFB), Delaware, where the shipments then sat, awaiting airlift through the standard military channel. Even from Dover the parts would then travel to Ramstein AB, Germany—not Aviano. The 86th Airlift Wing offered intratheater airlift to Aviano as a means of expediting the delivery of parts. Unfortunately, members of the staff at Aviano, not anticipating a slowdown in the movement of supplies, turned down the offer.[29]

The second potential showstopper for Aviano was rather mundane. On the typical flight line, nothing gets done without MB-4 and "Bobtail" tow vehicles to move aircraft and their supporting heavy aerospace ground equipment. Despite the rapid influx of aircraft, Aviano's Bobtail inventory remained unchanged, and the wing found itself short 47 Bobtails and 25 MB-4s relative to the number of aircraft it had to support. Moreover, usage of the available tow vehicles increased dramatically. Bobtails—small, odd-looking vehicles that look like truck cabs with a tow (or "pintle") hook attached—have an extremely tight turning radius that allows drivers to safely position or remove equipment close to aircraft. These tight turns wear tires quickly—a problem increased at Aviano by the accelerated use of its Bobtail fleet. The logistics group commander, although able to procure additional tires through Air Force sources in both Europe and stateside and thus allow the wing to maintain its accelerated sortie-generation rate, must have pondered some version of the addage that "for want of a nail. . . ."[30]

Aviano's leadership faced another challenge as well. As one post–Deliberate Force report noted, not since the use of American bombers stationed on Guam during the Vietnam War did a "peacetime" base community of airmen and their families face extended combat operations together. Although the jargon surrounding Deliberate Force labeled it a peacemaking or peace-enforcement operation, the fact of the matter remained that airmen kissed their spouses and children good-bye, left their homes, and headed off to fly over a hostile and potentially deadly theater. Several officers expressed concern that their families might fall prey to terrorists. Others commented on the stressful effects created by the sudden change from a peacetime environment to combat.[31] Lt Col Steve Hoog, commander of the 555th Fighter Squadron, believed that if Deliberate Force had gone on much longer or entered an indefinite period of operations, spouses and families should have been moved out of the area to eliminate a potential distraction for his crews and better ensure the safety of families. As events unfolded, however, such action proved unnecessary.[32]

But many officers at Aviano appreciated having their families with them to provide support. Spouses provided meals in the squadrons every evening as a way of supporting the unit and providing comfort to one another. Lt Col Gary West, commander of the 510th Fighter Squadron, noted that although he and his wife parted each day with a bit of apprehension, she was better able to follow events at Aviano than during his combat flying in Operation Desert Storm.[33]

Thus, Aviano made a rapid transition from peacetime to combat operations in a relatively short period of time. The wing went to war with the manning, facilities, and equipment allotted it under normal conditions. The base served as a deployed location for numerous units but retained all the baggage of a fully functioning peacetime wing. Swamped by an influx of people and aircraft and still required to see to the needs of the wing's dependent population, Colonel Wald and his staff orchestrated with aplomb and determination the activities of what became the world's largest composite wing. Aviano's experience, however, should prompt a review of the capabilities and limitations of the objective wing in combat.

143

Who should determine the requirements of units deploying to such locations to carry on extended, high-tempo operations? The Air Force commands task units to deploy people and equipment based on preplanned packages known as unit type codes (UTC). Units have the option to tailor UTCs in certain situations. If Deliberate Force is a harbinger of future operations, arriving packages may augment existing organizations that must consider maintaining day-to-day taskings as well as provide the backbone for contingency activities. Is an altogether separate UTC appropriate for this kind of deployment? Certainly, a review of manning—particularly field-grade levels, facilities, and equipment—is in order for those wings that might find themselves the hub of radically expanded activities.

Assessing the First Strikes

By the end of ATM Day Three, 0259 on 1 September, the CAOC recorded 635 sorties of all types flown. Of that total, 318 were strike sorties—CAS or battlefield air interdiction (BAI). At the request of UNPROFOR, NATO actually flew 16 CAS missions, the first of Deliberate Force, on 30 August, largely against artillery and mortar positions. Despite the general difficulty of finding heavy weapons in the rugged terrain of Bosnia-Herzegovina, the CAS missions carried out against clearly defined targets that day were largely successful and caused little, if any, collateral damage. As the operation progressed, though, bad weather often precluded additional CAS missions, as did a simple lack of requests for such strikes by UNPROFOR.[34]

In the first two days of operations, NATO air strikes, in COMAIRSOUTH's estimation, eliminated 48 DMPIs, leaving nearly three hundred on the target list. Of the targets (not DMPIs) tasked in the ATMs and attacked through the early hours of 1 September, CAOC intelligence considered 10 nonoperational, three probably nonoperational, two capable of minimal operations, and six probably-to-fully operational. For example, by dawn on 1 September, the Cajnice and Tuzla Mountain radio-relay targets remained operational, while most of the other IADS and communications targets—together with several significant ammunition depots—were out of business or damaged to varying degrees.[35]

National imagery and signals intelligence painted a picture of mixed success for the first few days of Deliberate Force. Initial BDA showed the BSA communications network severely damaged; however, further analysis revealed the BSA's communications capability degraded but still functioning.[36]

Damage to major BSA air defense sites also left the Bosnian Serbs with a degraded but effective system. Important targets such as the Sokolac SA-6 site had sustained considerable damage, and the BSA IADS was not as integrated as it was on 29 August. But Deliberate Force's opening blows had not rendered it impotent.[37]

Nevertheless, Ryan's staff determined that initial attacks against direct and essential support facilities had severely degraded the BSA's ability to manufacture, store, and distribute ammunition. In particular, the Vogosca ammunition depot, a major source of production of large-caliber munitions for the Serbs, had been hit hard. Although analysts still deemed the facility operational, the strikes had severely reduced its production of ammunition.[38]

Still, intelligence analysts at Aviano were not totally impressed with the first days' results against the BSA. They also determined that strikes against the BSA's IADS had only a minimal "blinding" effect. Additionally, the Serbs were well aware of US capabilities and often refused to turn on their target-acquisition radars and thereby invite HARM strikes. Although this action degraded their effectiveness tremendously, it also meant that much of the Serbs' air defense network remained capable of fighting back and would require reattack for continued suppression. The Serbs had also relocated and dispersed much of their stock of ammunition to temporary sites.[39]

Despite the halt in air strikes, NATO air units were hardly idle. Planners in the CAOC and the field units continued to develop notional strike packages and to assign backup targets and DMPIs to aircraft on CAS alert. Reconnaissance missions blanketed the country to determine Serb compliance with the UN ultimatum to withdraw heavy weapons from the 20-kilometer total-exclusion zone around Sarajevo. C-130 ABCCC aircraft continued to direct aircraft from refueling tracks over the Adriatic through the area of responsibility (AOR) and to receive immediate in-flight reports of any hostile activity. German aircraft flew reconnaissance sorties in support of the RRF. Importantly, although no bombs fell during the pause, RRF artillery continued to fire on BSA positions. Continuous daylight CAS, area SEAD, combat air patrols (CAP), and various other support missions rounded out these daily activities.[40]

As the diplomats attempted to find a solution to the conflict, planners in the CAOC fine-tuned operations during the bombing pause. During ATM Day Five, 2 September, planners developed BAI packages and placed them in a "floating-alert" status when the suspension was extended. Uncertainty over the status of the air campaign drove the CAOC to update and change the packages continuously, causing some frustration and confusion at Aviano. The following day, planners reverted to packages tasked via the ATM as BAI packages that were on alert for specific periods. Thus, changes to one package did not drive changes to the others. The size of the packages varied from eight to 12 aircraft on ATM Day Six to four to 32 on ATM Day Seven. In the meantime, CAS assets assisted the RRF by locating and relaying information on BSA firing positions. NATO aircraft flew roughly 180 sorties each day of the suspension. To no one's surprise, weather continued to adversely affect all sorties, especially reconnaissance flights and attempts to locate the crew of Ebro 33.[41]

As the bombing pause stretched through 2 September, some crews reported Serb movement on the ground, possibly away from the safe areas. Still, NATO and UN officials became increasingly convinced that General Mladic was playing a shell game with his heavy weapons to give only the appearance of compliance with UN and NATO demands. Stormy talks between General Janvier and Mladic had threatened to break down repeatedly in the face of Serb intransigence. Early on Sunday, 3 September, NATO secretary-general Claes gave Mladic until 2300 the following day to halt all attacks on Sarajevo and the other three safe areas, withdraw his heavy weapons from the Sarajevo total-exclusion zone, and guarantee freedom of movement for the UN. General Janvier sent a letter to Mladic incorporating these terms. The Serb general responded with a five-page harangue of his own.[42]

Aerial reconnaissance continued to paint a confusing picture of Serb activity. Monday's deadline passed with no firm indication from the Serbs that they had agreed to General Janvier's conditions. In the absence of an extension of the pause, Admiral Smith did not want to risk an immediate resumption of air strikes in the middle of the night that might result in attacks on Serb units actually withdrawing from the safe areas. Shortly after dawn on 5 September, when unmanned aerial vehicles confirmed Admiral Smith's suspicions that the Serbs were not pulling back, he told Janvier that "there's no intent being demonstrated. Let's get on with it."[43] At 1000 CET on 5 September, Admiral Smith directed General Ryan to recommence air strikes with a time on target no earlier than 1300 CET. That afternoon, Secretary-General Claes announced to the world that, because of the BSA's failure to comply with UN demands, NATO had resumed Deliberate Force. Shortly after 1300 CET, the bombs began falling again.[44]

Resumption

The operation resumed with a major effort in the air. Initially, planners had scheduled 191 operational sorties, but with the resumption of air strikes, they added 84. Four packages struck with mixed success throughout the afternoon. In the first strike package, F-16s from the 555th Fighter Squadron struck at Jahorina and the Hadzici ammunition depot. A second package hit military command, control, and communications bunkers at Han Pijesak. The third package—F-15Es of the 494th Fighter Squadron, carrying four GBU-12s each—made a highly successful strike on DMPIs within the Han Pijesak storage facility. As the day progressed, the fourth package of Marine F/A-18Ds of VMFA 533, F-16Cs of the 510th Fighter Squadron, and F-15Es hit communications targets with varying degrees of success.[45]

In order to cope with the rapidly changing situation on the ground, CAOC planners abandoned efforts to produce a full ATM each day and resorted to a novel "cookie-cutter" approach to scheduling strike packages. The cookie-cutter specified times-on-target windows into which packages would be inserted using available aircraft. Planners then published this rough ATM with the intent that change messages would reflect the latest master-attack-plan target/DMPI assignments. General Ryan and his staff wanted to ensure that the unfolding air campaign remained sufficiently flexible to hit targets whose destruction or degradation would hurt the BSA in a way that would speed up political developments in NATO's direction. This extreme Clausewitzian approach of using military force to foster political ends was correct in theory.[46]

Implementing cookie-cutter ATMs had its problems. On more than a few occasions, the CAOC did not release approved targets and DMPIs (crews were constantly reminded to strike only these) until late in the day, sometimes less than an hour before the beginning of a new ATM cycle. Even then, DMPIs might change right up to takeoff and thereafter. At times, this technique of executing the campaign led to less-than-optimum missions, crew frustration, and confusion. For example, one day's ATM tasked pilots of four F-16s from the 510th Fighter Squadron to hit DMPIs within the Hadzici ammunition-depot target area, only to have the CAOC change their assigned DMPIs shortly after they arrived at their aircraft. Moreover, information contained in the target folder misidentified one DMPI for one already hit and destroyed; the other DMPI was "not found." Pilots described yet another DMPI as "a crater," evidently one previously destroyed. Fighters missed the remaining DMPI, the bombs impacting one hundred meters east of it. Technically, then, all ordnance expended for this mission was "off target."[47]

Searching for Ebro 33

As the flow of strike packages going into Bosnia continued on 6 September, efforts to locate the crew of Ebro 33 intensified. On the day before, German reconnaissance aircraft reported visual signals in the region of the downed aircraft, and the USS *Roosevelt* launched a CSAR mission that aborted because of bad weather in the region. Responding to continued intercepts of weak beacon signals, the CAOC ordered another CSAR package of four MH-53s and four HC-130s launched on 7 September from Brindisi, in southern Italy. Although it penetrated to the objective area, ground fog prevented this package from conducting a search.[48]

A third CSAR package mounted out of Brindisi on 8 September. This time, the weather was good, and the aircraft conducted a thorough search of the area. Bosnian Serb troops in the area fired on the helicopters with heavy machine guns, wounding two crew members and damaging one of the aircraft. Escort aircraft, including two A-10s from the 104th Fighter Group, returned fire, destroying one of five Serb vehicles observed on a road below. The failure of this mission marked the last active CSAR effort to locate the Ebro 33 crew, although passive efforts to locate the French crewmen continued while CSAR forces stood by on alert. Not until 27 September did the Serbs confirm to the rest of the world that they had indeed captured and were holding the two French pilots.[49]

Choke Points

Meanwhile, the evolving nature of the overall situation in Bosnia-Herzegovina began to influence Deliberate Force targeting. As previously agreed, General Ryan worked closely with General Smith to ensure that aircraft hit the proper targets. Initially, AIRSOUTH planners were reluctant to target bridges for fear of inflicting civilian losses. General Smith, however, suspected that the Serbs would begin reinforcing units around Sarajevo and wanted bridges in the southeast zone of action (ZOA) attacked to preclude such a move. As time went on, General Smith also wanted to channel the movements of the Serbs' heavy weapons so that his men could count them more easily.

As in previous wars, the bridges in Bosnia proved difficult targets. From its long axis, a bridge presents a narrow target, and, from its lateral axis, a small target—with a great deal of empty space beneath for guided or unguided bombs to pass through harmlessly. Thus, bridges are hard to hit, and even a near miss usually has little effect on strongly built structures.

Consequently, the campaign against bridges was only partially successful. Of the 12 bridges attacked, five remained standing at the end of the operation, albeit with varying degrees of damage.[50]

The bridges in Bosnia also heightened concerns in the minds of General Ryan and others that attacks against them would produce collateral damage. Indeed, responding to an instance of collateral damage during a bridge attack, General Ryan mandated on 11 September that pilots not release their weapons on the first pass over the target. After several complaints from commanders in the field, the general lifted the restriction the next day. However, he still restricted aircrews to dropping a single weapon on the first "hot" pass in an ongoing effort to reduce collateral damage. Regardless, aircrews could mount subsequent attacks if necessary.[51]

Widening the Attack: Deadeye Northwest

During the pause in operations, COMAIRSOUTH contemplated strikes in the northwest ZOA, should the Serbs fail to meet UN and NATO demands. The Serb IADS in that sector of the country had remained untouched thus far, posing a threat to NATO aircraft striking targets in the southeast ZOA. From the outset—and in accordance with agreements between NATO planners and UN representatives—COMAIRSOUTH's plans for Deliberate Force did not link IADS to either of the ZOAs. Thus, since it appeared likely that air operations would have to continue, COMAIRSOUTH had to address the IADS in the northwest part of Bosnia. Refinement of plans for Deadeye Northwest got under way.[52]

Believing that the Serbs had redeployed their entire SAM system into the northwest zone, air planners expected the region to pose formidable risks to NATO aircraft. On 5 September, General Ryan requested the use of Tomahawk land attack missiles (TLAM) against IADS targets near the Serb stronghold of Banja Luka. Because the general and his staff recognized the danger that Serb air defenses posed to NATO aircraft in this area, he wanted to soften the area before sending in manned aircraft in large numbers. The reliability and accuracy of TLAMs also meshed well with the operation's emphasis on minimal collateral damage. Furthermore, use of TLAMs and stealth, in General Ryan's opinion, would reduce the risk to crews substantially.[53]

General Ryan broached the topic of expanding the campaign to Admiral Smith on 7 September. In the general's plan, Deadeye Northwest would unfold in three parts over the course of several days. The various parts would involve an intricate combination of SEAD assets, TLAMs, and F-117A stealth fighters against the BSA IADS. Through Admiral Smith, COMAIRSOUTH immediately requested the deployment of six F-117s, which, along with crews and support personnel, would bed down at Aviano. General Ryan expected to keep them there for approximately two weeks.[54]

In its military essentials, the planning for Deadeye Northwest was sound. No authoritative individual in the US or NATO command structure argued against the use of high-value assets such as F-117s and TLAMs against such a hard target as the Banja Luka IADS. Accordingly, on 9 September William J. Perry, the US secretary of defense, approved SACEUR's request to bring six F-117s to Aviano, stipulating their return to national control no later than 30 October—well beyond the period during which Ryan envisioned using them. On the same day of Secretary Perry's approval, an advanced echelon of nearly 190 people of the 49th Fighter Wing's 9th Fighter Squadron deployed to Aviano from Holloman AFB, New Mexico. Apparently, the US Air Force's most advanced operational aircraft was about to enter the fray.[55]

Ryan's plan did run into political obstacles, however, mainly because the government of Italy was not yet on board with it. On 9 September the US Embassy in Rome reported that the Italian government was upset at being excluded from the multinational Contact Group formed to deal with problems in the former Yugoslavia. Although the request for the aircraft had been made through NATO channels and they were urgently needed, the Italian Foreign Ministry remained unmoved. Apparently, the Italian prime minister had informed Ambassador Holbrooke that they would review further requests for support of operations in Bosnia beyond those currently approved at "political levels in terms of the responsiveness of others to

Italy's participation in the Contact Group." The Italians were "tired of always saying yes to others while others always say no to Italy." That afternoon the US Embassy informed Ryan of this state of affairs.[56]

While the diplomats attempted to find a settlement to this latest tangle, Ryan's staff forged ahead with Deadeye Northwest. COMAIRSOUTH delayed the start of the operation, initially scheduled to start in the early hours of 8 September, by 24 hours in order to better align the required assets. He also wanted to validate targets along the active front and minimize the impact of the weather. Part One thus began early on 9 September with a package of 30 SEAD aircraft, which fired 33 HARMs at seven SAM sites, including those at Majikici, Donji Vakuf, Sipovo, and Kolonija, with less than optimal results.[57]

The following night, Deadeye Northwest Part Two struck at targets on Lisina Mountain. Delayed three hours because of bad weather, this package, consisting of 42 aircraft, enjoyed only moderate success. For the first time, F-15Es launched three GBU-15s, one of which struck the Prnjavor radio-relay site. In another first combat use of a weapon, Navy F-18s launched standoff land attack missiles (SLAM). Still, analysts at the CAOC deemed the overall results disappointing, particularly of this second Deadeye package.[58]

TLAM strikes proposed for the night of 10–11 September promised to strengthen the attacks on the Banja Luka IADS but not before planners overcame some substantial barriers. Planners from the Navy's Sixth Fleet initially expressed concerns about the suitability of their weapons against COMAIRSOUTH's requested targets: the Lisina Mountain military radio-relay station and the Lisina EW site. Eventually, imagery for the Lisina targets became available on the afternoon of 7 September, which permitted Navy targeteers to complete the full mission plans required. Some confusion also arose between the Sixth Fleet and the CAOC over the availability of existing target coordinates. The CAOC had a set of coordinates for both Lisina targets. Nevertheless, the two staffs worked together to overcome the previous "fog," and the TLAMs hit the Lisina targets.[59]

COMAIRSOUTH pressed ahead with the third strike of Deadeye Northwest, undeterred by the absence of the F-117s.

Viewing this package as a variation of Deadeye Two, planners scheduled 30 SEAD aircraft, 18 strike aircraft, and 13 TLAMs to hit not only Lisina but also sites at Mrkonjic and Glamoc, as well as the Prnjavor radio-relay station at Mount Svinjar. The aircraft assigned to the latter target struck before midnight during the evening of 10 September. Four F-15Es carrying GBU-15s scored hits on three of four assigned DMPIs. Unfortunately, F/A-18Cs armed with SLAMs did not enjoy the same success as their Air Force brethren. Seven SLAMs fired at the radio-relay site at Glamoc as well as both Lisina Mountain targets suffered weapons-datalink-control anomalies, resulting in poor target acquisition and the inability of the pilots to transmit commands to the weapons. Because of these technical problems, intelligence analysts reviewing poststrike data deemed all SLAMs to have missed their targets.[60]

The TLAMs, however, proved remarkably accurate. Launched from the USS *Normandy*, seven TLAMs hit the Lisina EW site while others struck the radio-relay station. Poststrike reconnaissance showed the latter completely destroyed, with debris scattered throughout the site. The operations building and bunkers at the Lisina EW site also suffered direct hits. The impact of three missiles south of the site's radar position rendered it nonoperational. Tactically successful, the use of TLAMs demonstrated to the Serbs that the Americans in particular were willing to use some of their most advanced weapons.[61]

Overall, this heretofore most significant Deadeye strike was relatively successful. In addition to the damage noted above, images provided by unmanned aerial vehicles showed heavy damage to the Prnjavor military radio-relay site. Only at the Lisina Mountain radio-relay and TV transmitter site—one of the SLAM targets—did reconnaissance show no apparent damage.[62]

But Deadeye was not over. Another strike planned for the night of 11–12 September, Deadeye Part Three, was to have included the long-awaited F-117s. Unfortunately, on 11 September the Italian government officially disapproved the beddown of these aircraft at Aviano. Nevertheless, targets and DMPIs remained, and General Ryan wanted them attacked with the best means available. With the F-117s out of the picture, planners moved the upcoming mission to the daytime, thus reducing the opening blow of Deadeye Part Three to a

SEAD package and two F-15Es carrying GBU-15s, one of which hit its target at the Mrkonjic radio-relay station.[63]

Still, General Ryan pressed the attack on the Serb IADS forward. On 13 September planners added a Deadeye Part Three strike for targets at the Lisina EW site and the Lisina radio-relay/TV transmitter. Two SLAMs found their targets on this occasion, scoring hits on the Lisina targets. Analysts said that damage to these targets ranged from "severe" to "destroyed." This turned out to be the last Deadeye strike since another package scheduled for 14 September failed to fly because of bad weather.[64] As a result of Deadeye Northwest and Deadeye Southeast operations, the SEAD campaign achieved the goal of degrading and neutralizing the Serb IADS throughout the country.[65]

Closing Out Option Two

In addition to Deadeye, NATO aircraft continued to hammer the rapidly diminishing number of targets and DMPIs still available under option two (see chap. 4) of Deliberate Force. The CAOC staff sought to maximize the effectiveness of all available assets. For example, at the outset of the operation, Brig Gen David Sawyer, deputy director of the CAOC, ordered CAS aircraft held over water until a tactical air control party (TACP) requested support. In the absence of such requests since 30 August, however, CAOC planners assigned CAS sorties "hip-pocket" (alternate) targets in an effort to make use of otherwise wasted assets.[66] The CAOC battle-staff director assigned all secondary targets from a preapproved target list. As before, CAS sorties required Chariot's approval both to go over land and to release their weapons against BAI hip-pocket targets because the military situation in Bosnia remained fluid.[67]

Close coordination among the NATO and UN units in and over Bosnia was indeed crucial. In theory, CAOC staff officers notified the AOCC in Kiseljak of any impending strikes against target complexes in proximity so as to give the UN soldiers time to take shelter in their bunkers. Only after the AOCC confirmed that the peacekeepers were out of harm's way was an aircraft to drop ordnance.[68]

Still, the rapid pace of air operations and the fog of war often conspired to upset carefully laid plans. During the early afternoon of 8 September, CAOC staff officers learned that a British GR-7, properly reroled from reconnaissance to BAI and cleared to drop its weapons, nevertheless struck a DMPI close to Russian peacekeepers, seemingly without warning. Upon investigating the matter, the CAOC staff discovered other GR-7s added to an upcoming strike with a time on target of 1630 CET. The CAS desk officer, battle-staff director, and controller aboard the ABCCC had no information, including assigned targets, for these sorties. Working quickly, battle-staff personnel assigned the aircraft proper targets, precluding further surprises for UN troops on the ground.[69]

Problems within C^2 were amenable to swift and competent fixes, but poor weather remained the greatest obstacle to NATO air strikes. On 9 September, for example, the first two of five strike packages were unable to expend their ordnance due to deteriorating weather conditions in the target area. The remaining three packages had to delay their times by two to three hours although they did fly. Foul weather limited ATM Day 16, 13–14 September, to 140 sorties, and only 20 sorties flew on ATM Day 17.[70]

Nevertheless, the list of targets and DMPIs became appreciably shorter with each passing day, and diplomatic talks held in Geneva on 8 September did nothing to slow the air campaign. As planned, strikes continued against support facilities, bridges, and communications targets.

The situation on the ground remained volatile despite allied air activity. On 10 September NATO aircraft flew CAS missions for only the second time in the operation. In response to the shelling of the Tuzla airport, which wounded a UN soldier, the CAOC tasked a flight of F/A-18Ds to contact the Tuzla TACP—Hamlet 02. The F/A-18s dropped one GBU-16 each, while other aircraft—including GR-7s—joined in the fray. The air strikes destroyed two bunkers at the top of a nearby hill and a large-caliber artillery piece. Additional flights maintained an air presence in the area for the following two and one-half hours until the ground commander determined that the situation had stabilized.[71]

As a result of the shelling of Tuzla airport, UNPROFOR requested that NATO planners develop BAI boxes, similar to the "kill boxes" used during the Gulf War. CAOC planners designated one box each for Sarajevo, Tuzla, and Gorazde. The CAOC would employ the box system whenever UN commanders requested CAS but could not provide a TACP. In turn, the ground commander would accept full responsibility for control of air activity within the boxes. Over the next few days, the plans began to take more definite shape as CAS/forward air controller–A assets reconnoitered the areas. Deliberate Force would end, however, before NATO air units employed the system.[72]

Despite myriad challenges, Deliberate Force operations made rapid progress. By 10 September only nine targets and 33 DMPIs remained on the Deadeye list, with 16 targets and 128 DMPIs left in the southeast zone. Still, with the possibility of a political settlement nearing, the execution of Deliberate Force operations took on added significance. On 11 September General Ryan and his staff conducted a careful review of the status of remaining option-two targets and DMPIs to ensure that air strikes maintained sufficient pressure on the Serbs to meet both military and political objectives.[73]

In the absence of a political settlement, NATO pressed forward with the air campaign. In order to strike targets precluded by bad weather over the last few days, the CAOC added a strike package of 44 aircraft and 12 targets to the day's five other scheduled packages on 11 September. Strike packages hit ammunition depots and storage facilities at Hadzici, Ustikolina, and Sarajevo on several occasions throughout the day. The Vogosca ammunition-loading plant, already heavily damaged, received additional attention. On 12 September strike aircraft attacked ammunition depots and supply facilities around Doboj, near the Tuzla safe area.[74]

As the number of approved option-two targets and DMPIs dwindled, the CAOC began to reduce the number of actual sorties. Planners placed BAI packages on an alert posture on 12 September. The Current Operations Division at the CAOC then tasked four of the packages real-time against targets in the Doboj area. By the end of the day, however, a lack of suitable targets for the weapons loaded on the tasked aircraft resulted in a cancellation of the last package. The only other notable event for the day was midday reports of fixed-wing aircraft operating out of Banja Luka. With designated CAP sorties in the midst of refueling from tankers over the Adriatic, the CAOC battle staff simply reroled CAS aircraft to fly CAP over Tuzla and provide both visual and radar coverage of Banja Luka. This ad hoc CAP encountered no hostile aircraft.[75]

Concurrent with the reduction of available targets, weather in the region deteriorated rapidly. On 13 September the day's first strike package failed to engage half its assigned DMPIs because of conditions in the target area. The second package canceled, and the third, a Deadeye mission, was delayed until midafternoon. The fourth package, containing eight aircraft tasked against the Sarajevo armor-training area and ammunition-storage facility, flew as planned late in the afternoon. It achieved only mixed success, again due to inclement weather. By early evening the only assets over land included SEAD packages and an AC-130 that was searching for signs of the crew of Ebro 33. Forty percent of the day's scheduled sorties did not fly.[76]

The bad weather, however, may have been a blessing in disguise. By 13 September only two approved targets with 13 DMPIs remained on the Deadeye list. Seven targets and 43 DMPIs were still available in the southeast ZOA. As a result of that day's activity, these numbers dropped to 1/11 and 7/32, respectively. On 14 September poor weather caused the cancellation of all but airborne-early-warning, U-2, and air-refueling sorties. The CAOC placed all other packages on hold pending better weather.[77]

Meanwhile, Croat and Bosnian army (BiH) units continued to advance against the faltering BSA. Donji Vakuf fell into the hands of the Muslim-led government, and the Croats took Jajce. BiH and Croat advances in the west-central part of the country posed a menace to Banja Luka itself. Perhaps the perceived collapse of their field army and the punishment it had endured from the sky drove the Bosnian Serb leaders to signal their acceptance on 14 September of UN and NATO demands. Admiral Smith agreed to institute another bombing pause, this one of 72 hours, beginning at 2200 CET on 14 September. The NATO chain of command authorized him to agree in principle with General Janvier's assessment that General Mladic's willingness to halt all attacks on safe areas, allow the UN freedom of movement and the use of the Sarajevo airport, and withdraw his heavy weapons from around Sarajevo constituted compliance with Janvier's letter of 3 September. Thus, Deliberate Force went on hold once again. However, Admiral Smith asked Janvier to inform Mladic that NATO would continue to fly normal Deny Flight missions, including tactical reconnaissance, CAS, CAP, SEAD, and—if required— CSAR. NATO intended to exercise full freedom of action over all of Bosnia-Herzegovina. These flights, the admiral wrote, would be nonprovocative in nature, but aircrews would respond, within existing rules of engagement, "to any hostile act or hostile intent."[78]

The pause came at an opportune moment for General Ryan and his staff. NATO planners realized that if Deliberate Force continued, they would be hard-pressed to find additional suitable targets without going into option three, a move most officers in the CAOC felt would not receive political approval. Nevertheless, after combing the list of option-two targets, COM-AIRSOUTH forwarded to Admiral Smith a list of nine to 12 additional targets: equipment-storage facilities, communications targets, and a handful of bridges, tunnels, and choke points in the southeast ZOA.

Fortunately for NATO and COMAIRSOUTH, the need to restart what was sure to be a brief and politically charged third wave of attacks never arose. Initial BSA compliance with General Janvier's demands led to a 72-hour extension of the bombing pause. NATO convoys began moving, with air presence, on 15 September. A French C-130 landed at the Sarajevo airport that afternoon. By the following day, NATO aircraft reported BSA tanks and vehicles moving away from Sarajevo. On 20 September both Admiral Smith and General Janvier agreed that Deliberate Force had indeed met its objectives. They agreed to inform the world that, as of 20 September, "the resumption of air strikes is currently not necessary." Fighting between Bosnian and Croat units and those of the BSA would continue for some weeks. The creation of a lasting peace in Bosnia now rested in the hands of the statesmen and diplomats, and Deliberate Force passed into history.[79]

Deliberate Force: Effective But Not Efficient?

One of the oldest clichés regarding military operations is that no plan survives first contact with the enemy. This notion applies with some qualification to Deliberate Force as well. With the exception of the politically driven bombing pause from 1 to 5 September, NATO air units executed the operation in a fashion that closely mirrored the planning. There were no sudden shifts in targeting, rules of engagement, or priorities. COMAIRSOUTH and his staff factored in political constraints during the planning process, designing a campaign capable of gradual escalation that nevertheless sought to destroy things rather than kill people. To that end, the execution of Deliberate Force clearly reflected the intentions of its planners. Still, as with any large and complex operation, problems existed. The leadership provided at all levels to the units employed in the operation, as well as the discipline of the crews involved, prevented these problems from thwarting the successful execution of the campaign.

Collateral Damage and the Targeting Process

General Ryan's desire to limit collateral damage and Serb casualties to the lowest possible level reflected the political realities of the Balkans. Should NATO be responsible for the killing and maiming of even relatively limited numbers of Serb military personnel and civilians, Pale, Belgrade, and, indeed, Moscow might view (on Cable News Network) the allies as belligerents fighting on the side of the Croats and Bosnian Muslims. Adding yet another level of grievances to those already existing in the Balkans would have been counterproductive to the peace process that NATO and the UN intended Deliberate Force to help move forward.[80]

This desire to avoid collateral damage, together with the rapidly changing ground and political situation, drove the CAOC to tightly manage the conduct of the air campaign. For example, special instructions (SPINS) issued by the CAOC directed pilots to attack only their assigned DMPI, even if that meant dropping a weapon in a crater. This requirement proved particularly frustrating to a number of airmen.[81]

Officers at Aviano and with American naval units involved in Deliberate Force also expressed dissatisfaction with the CAOC's apparent involvement in tactics. Although a detailed discussion of tactics is treated elsewhere in this study (see chap. 11), one should note here that by dictating things such as the number of passes and weapons-release pulses, General Ryan and his staff sought to minimize the likelihood of collateral damage. Crews recognized this imperative, but many of them agreed with one Aviano pilot that a low tolerance for misses and mistakes also seemed to take "the judgment out of the cockpit." Repeated passes over a target increased the crews' exposure to enemy fire. Coupled with their inability to strike alternate targets or DMPIs, some aviators believed that COMAIRSOUTH's intolerance for collateral damage often placed them in harm's way with little to gain.

Although this view might be somewhat overblown, unit-level planners and weaponeers seemed to share it as well. For example, members of the 7490th viewed the standard configuration loads specified in the daily ATMs as gospel, therefore limiting the unit's ability to determine the most appropriate munitions for the assigned target. But the CAOC did not always dictate weapon loads; often the ATM simply referred to the "best available." As an example, General Ryan pointed to an Aviano-based unit making its own interpretation of this term by using two CBU-87 cluster munitions. Fortunately, the weapons were expended on a SAM site and evidently did not cause any collateral damage. These munitions were the only ordnance of this type employed throughout the campaign. If anything, such an incident reinforced the importance of a tightly executed campaign in Bosnia.[82]

The compressed ATM cycle also rankled many people outside the CAOC. General Ryan's tight control over BDA data placed him in the position of determining whether a target required a second strike. The fluid political situation and the ongoing Croat/BiH offensive often resulted in the CAOC's adding strikes against previously withheld targets while removing others from the approved list. Thus, as noted above, the CAOC resorted to cookie-cutter ATMs that simply specified times on target. From the perspective of the 7490th, however, the accelerated planning cycle also drove a maddening number of changes, right up to takeoff. In one instance, officers at Aviano protested to the CAOC that they could not meet the time on target and rolled it back by one hour.[83]

But the CAOC staff had a clear understanding of the situation driving the ATM cycle, derived in part from their proximity to Generals Ryan and Hornburg. Colonel Richardson, CAOC chief of current operations during Deliberate Force, realized that the ATM process had to address emerging targets as well as put airpower against the targets most critical to achieving a political settlement in the least amount of time. Navy captain Calise, deputy chief of plans, agreed that planning inside the ATM cycle, together with hardware problems associated with disseminating the final product, presented a challenge to everyone involved. Nevertheless, he could see no other way to react to the commander's guidance and believed that if the operation were to resume, ATM production would continue in this fashion.[84]

Changes to the ATM, however, did interfere with mission-planning efficiency in the field. As mission or flight leaders attempted to coordinate with other units involved in a strike package, they sometimes found that each was working from a different version of the ATM.[85]

Despite the ever-present potential for confusion, given the existing state of affairs, proactive leadership at Aviano and in the CAOC—together with disciplined crews—ensured that packages struck only approved targets. Collateral damage was indeed minimal; Serbian leader Milosevic admitted to Ambassador Holbrooke that only 25 Serbs died as a result of the campaign.[86] Although the Bosnian Serbs made a few crude attempts at portraying widespread collateral damage, Deliberate Force's heavy reliance on precision munitions and tightly controlled execution probably made it the cleanest military operation ever.

Tactical Command and Control

Chariot and his CAOC staff had several means at their disposal to ensure that subordinate units executed each day's ATM in a manner that conformed to the commander's intent. ABCCC Compass Call aircraft served as a conduit of information to the

CAOC from units entering, flying in, and exiting the AOR. Aviano-based NATO E-3 AWACS aircraft also flew tracks over the Adriatic while other NATO assets orbited over Hungary. Navy air-control units, ground-based controllers, and the AOCC in Kiseljak—call sign Longbow—rounded out the constellation of C² assets linking all elements of Deliberate Force.

Although the assets listed above allowed the CAOC battle staff to retain control over the course of events in the skies above Bosnia, problems inevitably developed. On the very first night of Deliberate Force, a mechanical malfunction forced the on-station ABCCC aircraft, call sign Bookshelf, to return to base. At 2317 CET, as aircraft began arriving on station, the CAOC decided to proceed without Bookshelf. The E-3, call sign Magic, advised all aircraft of the problem, and Chariot cleared the first package over land at 2340. Half an hour later, Bookshelf arrived on station—not an auspicious beginning, but the existing SPINS had considered this possibility. The redundancy and flexibility of NATO C² assets proved instrumental in ensuring that the CAOC maintained control over the operation.[87]

What Clausewitz aptly termed the "fog and friction" of war, however, would still bedevil Deliberate Force despite advanced communications technology. At times, confusion reigned over proper backup targets, and on several occasions NATO airborne early warning (NAEW) controllers were sometimes not abreast of certain situations. On 30 August, for example, the SEAD commander, Nikon-23, detected threat emissions and made the appropriate call. Neither the E-3 on station nor HARM assets acknowledged the call. Apparently, the last HARM shooters had failed to check out with either the SEAD commander or the E-3. Neither ABCCC nor NAEW could determine when any HARM assets would return to the AOR. With the SEAD window closing, mass confusion set in as multiple packages began calling for vectors to their tankers from ground controllers. At least one element returned to base due to lack of fuel.[88]

Problems maintaining "the big picture" were not limited to airborne control centers. On several occasions confusion among CAOC staff members resulted in near pandemonium in the sky. At approximately 2000 on 1 September, the CAOC, via Bookshelf, ordered three aircraft to go over land. Ten minutes later,

ABCCC ordered them to return over water. Fifteen minutes after that, Bookshelf told them to go over land, again on orders from the CAOC. When controllers aboard Magic sought confirmation for the counterorder, the CAOC informed them that it had issued no such orders. The aircraft held over water. An hour later the CAOC ordered another sortie, Sleepy 11, to return to base. Ten minutes later, the CAOC apparently ordered Sleepy 11 over land. It turned out that CAS cell officers were coordinating directly with Bookshelf rather than going through the senior operations officer on the battle staff, who also evidently issued contradictory instructions. Such confusing incidents diminished as personnel gained experience.[89]

Technical problems and poor radio discipline also dogged the NATO C[2] network. Extraneous chatter as well as mission-related transmissions crowded the various radio frequencies. Other aircraft entering the area sometimes failed to contact Magic or Bookshelf, confusing an already difficult air picture.[90]

As regards force protection, the SPINS of August 1995 prohibited aircraft from operating over land without SEAD coverage. Given a limited number of available SEAD assets at any one time, planners scheduled SEAD packages to provide windows during which time other aircraft could enter the area and carry out their missions. In theory the SEAD mission commander informed NAEW of his estimated time of arrival at the ingress corridor. NAEW, in turn, transmitted the window-open time over all relevant frequencies. Ten minutes prior to departure, the SEAD commander again advised NAEW of his estimated arrival time at the egress corridor so that controllers could announce the time the window would close.[91]

As in any conflict, the fog and friction of war, including human error, confusion, conflicting orders, and poor weather often led to the breakdown of even the most meticulously planned mission. SEAD packages were just as vulnerable to such factors, thereby complicating C[2] during Deliberate Force. The apparent lack of coordination between penetrating sorties and SEAD packages proved frustrating to many aircrews and, in turn, led to a fair amount of wasted effort.

Clearly, with the safety of NATO crews paramount, one cannot overstate the importance of SEAD assets. Furthermore, CAOC intelligence analysts knew that Serb SAMs had gone into hiding, as General Ryan pointed out to Admiral Smith in his letter of 16 September outlining his plan to resume air strikes if so directed. With a very real threat still present and Serb tactics blunting the efficacy of HARMs, the proper management and control of SEAD packages became vital. Fortunately, the incidents related above represent only a portion of the total picture, albeit a portion most crews will tend to remember. Of greater importance, however, is what these scenes of confusion can teach. For the foreseeable future, human failings will continue to serve as the limiting factors behind our increasingly complex and sophisticated technology. A shortage of critical assets, regardless of the overall strength and numbers of an entire force, can thwart or at least slow the tempo of any air campaign. When the fog of war exacerbates this shortage, missions are wasted and lives potentially placed in danger. Fortunately, Ebro 33 remained Deliberate Force's first and only loss—a tribute to the ultimately successful suppression and neutralization of the Serbs' IADS.

Coalition Effort or American Show?

From the beginning, Deliberate Force was a NATO operation. The air campaign involved US Air Force, Navy, and Marine Corps aircraft together with units from Great Britain, France, Spain, the Netherlands, Italy, Turkey, and Germany. The United States flew approximately two-thirds of all sorties—not surprising considering that roughly two-thirds of the aircraft employed were American. US aircraft dropped 622 of the 708 precision munitions employed but only 12 of 318 nonprecision weapons. French, Spanish, and British units expended the remaining precision weapons.[92]

Outwardly, Deliberate Force gave the appearance of a true coalition effort. Indeed, although journalist Rick Atkinson noted "bickering allies" as one of General Ryan's challenges, he described the operation as a "coming of age party for a Western alliance that in more than four decades had fired few shots in anger and had never fought an extended campaign."[93] Still, perceptions of just how much Deliberate Force was a coalition effort varied among the NATO allies.

For example, several senior officers at the CAOC saw the operation as a means of forging closer ties between the United States and its allies. In particular, Colonel Richardson believed that Italian general Andrea Fornasiero, commander of 5 ATAF, was largely responsible for the many positive changes and improvements in CAOC facilities and capabilities. The American leadership, in turn, realized that the CAOC was subordinate to Fornasiero. Evidently, however, Fornasiero recognized the dominant role played by the Americans in Deliberate Force.[94]

Both Colonel Richardson and Navy captain Calise also recognized the personal nature of allied relations forged at the CAOC. Richardson believed that the face-to-face interaction between American and allied officers laid a foundation for future cooperation and increased levels of trust among the NATO allies. Calise, as deputy of plans, was particularly sensitive to international feelings. On more than a few occasions, he worked quickly to smooth over any misunderstandings and was responsible for keeping national representatives at the CAOC in the planning loop.[95]

Even in the absence of open enmity between NATO participants, views of the combined nature of Deliberate Force varied considerably among America's allies. Many non-US NATO officers complained that the operation was little more than an American-run air campaign and that they were just along for the ride. General Ryan's decision to move from Naples to Vicenza served to reinforce that perception. Wing Commander Andy Batchelor, a Royal Air Force officer working in the BDA cell at the CAOC, noted that the absence of non-American officers in key positions on General Hornburg's staff created the impression that the Americans had taken over the entire operation. Others remarked that only the United States lacked a national representative at the CAOC, relying instead on liaison officers from individual units.[96]

The Americans took a far different view than their allies as to why US personnel occupied so many key positions. General Hornburg, for example, stated that he had offered to fill key positions with allied officers but that no one had stepped forward to accept the offer. The CAOC director also cited a difference in work habits among the various allied air forces that seemed to cause them to shun the day-to-day operations of the CAOC but then demand the option to become more involved when something important was about to happen. Indeed, American officers shared the belief that allied officers were only selectively involved in the air campaign. Thus, although the CAOC was technically under General Fornasiero, General Sawyer—Hornburg's deputy—was a US Air Force officer, as were the directors of operations, plans, intelligence, communications, and personnel. A handful of US Navy officers filled a few other key positions. The director of logistics, an Italian colonel, was the only non-US officer to hold a critical position.[97]

Still, American officers operating at lower levels of planning and execution saw the allied coalition as functioning smoothly. Maj Keith Kiger, a key member of the team that built the plans for Deliberate Force, did not detect any allied resentment at his level toward US leadership. Working with a British officer as they built the target list, Kiger also felt that members from other NATO countries were deeply involved in the planning process.[98]

Technical capabilities rather than national prejudices often drove the air role played by each member of the alliance. Other than those from the United States, only British, French, and Spanish units possessed the equipment to deliver precision-guided munitions. The Dutch and Italians did not have such capabilities, and, as previously mentioned, both the Turkish and German contingents were limited in their participation for various reasons. Still, only the United States expended an overwhelming percentage of precision munitions. The French dropped 73 nonprecision weapons, more than five times the number of precision weapons they employed. Likewise, the British dropped 47 Mk-83 nonprecision bombs but expended only 48 laser-guided munitions. Considering NATO's desire to limit collateral damage, most coalition officers thus recognized that their ability to employ precision-guided weaponry relative to that of American units dictated their place in the campaign.[99]

Nevertheless, allied cooperation proved absolutely essential to the success of Deliberate Force. On the ground inside Bosnia, for example, an international UN force—composed to a significant degree of units from NATO countries—worked closely with COMAIRSOUTH and his staff. The RRF, made up of British, French, and Dutch units, coordinated its activity with that of Ryan's air units. UNPROFOR could—and did—request CAS when necessary. NATO and 5 ATAF liaison officers served with all critical UN C² elements. Of those, possibly the most important to the CAOC was the UNPROFOR/NATO partnership represented in the AOCC at Kiseljak. NATO officers working there passed on vital weather and ground information and, as noted above, ensured that NATO bombs did not catch UN peacekeepers unaware and in the open. On the one hand, officers of the CAOC's CAS cell worked closely with the AOCC to deconflict the RRF's artillery fire with planned sorties; on the other hand, the RRF's guns often fired on suspected Serb positions in an effort to drive them to the ground and reduce the threat to aircraft from hostile fire.[100]

The Exception or the Rule?

Whatever else may be said about it, Deliberate Force marked a turning point for NATO and the course of events in Bosnia. As a coalition effort, the air campaign had its problems. American air planners assumed that basing nations would agree to operations from their territories. By and large they did—with the notable exception of Italy, which refused to allow the beddown of the F-117s. Still, America's NATO allies came to realize that without US participation in the form of military muscle and diplomatic influence, a meaningful solution to the Bosnian crisis would come only in the form of a victor's peace of the worst kind. Although some people doubted the efficiency of Deliberate Force, few could overlook its effectiveness. Planners of the air campaign sought to end the threat from the Bosnian Serb army to government safe areas, bring about the cessation of military operations, and force Serbian compliance with UN mandates. In meeting these goals, they were generally successful. To what extent Deliberate Force proved responsible for the accords reached in November 1995 in Dayton, Ohio, however, is beyond the scope of this chapter.

the mantra

Although problems abounded, Deliberate Force demonstrated the inherent flexibility of airpower in the most circumscribed of settings. NATO air units flew 3,535 sorties and dropped more than eleven hundred bombs, losing only a single aircraft. As intended, collateral damage was minimal—Serb deaths numbered slightly more than two dozen.[101] Precision munitions accounted for nearly three-quarters of those expended. General Ryan's air campaign, carefully planned and tightly executed, benefited from the discipline of NATO aircrews and their high state of training, as well as the availability of superior weaponry. Crafted to respond to a potentially explosive and complex situation, Deliberate Force may not be the template for all future operations. Considering the goals sought and the restrictions present, however, the employment of airpower over Bosnia from 30 August to 14 September 1995 achieved much more than most people thought possible just a few short months before.

Notes

1. Adm Leighton W. Smith, US Navy, to Lt Gen Rupert Smith, commander, UN Protection Force, Sarajevo, Bosnia-Herzegovina, letter, 28 August 1995, Deliberate Force Collection, Air Force Historical Research Agency (AFHRA), Maxwell AFB, Ala., NPL-15; and briefing slides (U), Lt Gen Michael E. Ryan, subject: NATO Air Operations in Bosnia-Herzegovina: Deliberate Force, 29 August–14 September 1995, AFHRA, NPL-16.

2. Allied Air Forces Southern Europe, "Operation Deliberate Force, 29 Sep 95–14 Oct 95 [sic] Factual Review," 14 November 1995, 2-7 through 2-8. (NATO Secret) Information extracted is unclassified.

3. Ibid., 1-5, 3-1 (NATO Secret) Information extracted is unclassified; and briefing, Lt Gen Michael Ryan, subject: Command Relationships.

4. "Operation Deliberate Force, 29 Sep 95–14 Oct 95 [sic] Factual Review," 1-5, 3-1; and Ryan briefing, subject: Command Relationships.

5. Rick Atkinson, "Air Assault Sets Stage for Broader Role," *Washington Post,* 15 November 1995.

6. Briefing, Lt Gen Michael Ryan, subject: Deliberate Force Structure; and fact sheet (U), "Deliberate Force," CAOC/Historian (HO), n.d., AFHRA, CAOC-13.

7. Message (U), 061402Z JUL 95, commander, US Air Forces Europe, to commander, Third Air Force et al., subject: Activation of the 7490th Wing (Provisional), 6 July 1995; briefing (U), Col Jim Turner, commander, 31st Operations Group and 7490th Operations Group (Provisional), and Col David Stringer, commander, 31st Logistics Group, subject: Deliberate Force

Lessons Learned: The Objective Wing in Combat, to members of the USAFE staff, 5 October 1995; and Col David Stringer, commander, 31st Logistics Group, interviewed by the author and Maj Ronald M. Reed, Aviano AB, Italy, 18 January 1996.

8. Turner/Stringer briefing; Stringer interview; and SMSgt Richard R. Morris, 31st Fighter Wing/HO, "Operation Deliberate Force," n.d., AFHRA, AVI-02-01. (NATO Secret) Information extracted is unclassified.

9. Roderick de Normann, "Operation Storm: Attack on the Krajina," *Jane's Intelligence Review,* November 1995, 495–98.

10. Briefing, Lt Gen Michael Ryan, subject: Air Defense Threat, Sarajevo Fielded Forces.

11. "Karadzic, Krajisnik Comment on Sarajevo 'Massacre,'" Banja Luka Srpski Radio Network, 1700 GMT, 28 August 1995, in Foreign Broadcast Information Service [FBIS], Eastern Europe, "Bosnia-Herzegovina," FBIS-EEU-95-168, 30 August 1995, 27; and Atkinson.

12. Briefing (U), Lt Gen Michael D. Ryan, to students of the School of Advanced Airpower Studies (SAAS), Maxwell AFB, Ala., subject: Deliberate Force, 7 February 1996.

13. Capt Ken Calise, US Navy, CAOC battle-staff director, interviewed by the author and Maj Ronald M. Reed, Dal Molin AB, Vicenza, Italy, 16 January 1996 (Secret) Information extracted is unclassified; Col Jim Turner, 31st Fighter Wing/Operations Group et al., interviewed by the author and Maj Ronald M. Reed, Aviano AB, Italy, 19 January 1996 (Secret) Information extracted is unclassified; and fact sheet, "Deliberate Force."

14. "Deliberate Force: Summary of Daily Status, 29 Oct [sic]–14 Sep 95," package flow, 29–30 August 1995 (NATO Secret) Information extracted is unclassified, AFHRA, NPL-15; target folder/graphics, target no. D093, Han Pijesak military radio-relay station, n.d. (NATO Secret) Information extracted is unclassified, AFHRA, AVI-43; and 7490th Wing (Provisional) mission results, 14 September 1995 (NATO Secret) Information extracted is unclassified, AFHRA, AVI-40-01, 1.

15. "Operation Deliberate Force . . . Factual Review," 4-1 through 4-2 (NATO Secret) Information extracted is unclassified; and "Deliberate Force: Summary of Daily Status." (NATO Secret) Information extracted is unclassified.

16. Deny Flight, commander's daily report, 290300Z–300259Z and 300300Z–310259Z, August 1995 (NATO Secret) Information extracted is unclassified; CAOC daily mission summary from 300300Z to 310259Z August 1995 (NATO Secret) Information extracted is unclassified, AFHRA, CAOC-15; and "Operation Deliberate Force . . . Factual Review," 4-2 (NATO Secret) Information extracted is unclassified.

17. Commander's daily report, 290300Z–300259Z August 1995 (NATO Secret) Information extracted is unclassified; and "U-2 Crashes in England," *Aviation Week and Space Technology* 143 (4 September 1995): 24.

18. Commander's daily report, 300300Z–310259Z August 1995. (NATO Secret) Information extracted is unclassified.

19. "Operation Deliberate Force . . . Factual Review," 4-1 through 4-2 (NATO Secret) Information extracted is unclassified; and message, mission report from 494th Fighter Squadron/deployed to commander, 5 ATAF/CAOC/Intelligence (INT), mission no. 5C3099, 30 August 1995 (Confidential) Information extracted is unclassified, AFHRA, AVI-46.

20. "Operation Deliberate Force . . . Factual Review," 4-2. (NATO Secret) Information extracted is unclassified.

21. "Karadzic Defiant Following NATO Air Attacks," *Belgrade SNRA*, 1438 GMT, 30 August 1995, in FBIS-EEU-95-168, 30 August 1995, 26; "Akashi: Halt in Air Operations Depends on Serbs," *Paris AFP*, 0857 GMT, 31 August 1995, and "Claes Warns Serbs to Stop 'Provoking Us,'" *Brussels La Une Radio Network*, 1600 GMT, 30 August 1995, both in FBIS-EEU-169, 31 August 1995, 2.

22. Atkinson; message (U), 010001B SEP 95, Office of the Commander, UNPROFOR, to Rapid Reaction Force Operations Staff (RRFOS) et al., subject: Warning Order—Suspension of Air Strikes, 1 September 1995, AFHRA, NPL-15; and "Operation Deliberate Force . . . Factual Review," 4-2 (NATO Secret) Information extracted is unclassified.

23. Rick Atkinson, "Put to the Test, NATO Shows Its Mettle," *International Herald Tribune*, 20 November 1995; and Bruce W. Nelan, "More Talking, More Bombing," *Time*, 18 September 1995, 76–77.

24. 31st Fighter Wing/CVR, memorandum for record (U), subject: Deliberate Force Lessons Learned, 11 October 1995, AFHRA, AVI-35; and Stringer interview.

25. Turner/Stringer briefing; and Stringer interview.

26. Turner/Stringer briefing; and Stringer interview.

27. 31st Fighter Wing/CVR, memorandum for record, attachment 2-2; Turner/Stringer briefing; and Stringer interview.

28. 31st Fighter Wing/CVR, memorandum for record, attachment 2-2; Turner/Stringer briefing; and Stringer interview.

29. 31st Fighter Wing/CVR, memorandum for record, attachment 2-2; Turner/Stringer briefing; and Stringer interview.

30. 31st Fighter Wing/CVR, memorandum for record, attachment 2-2; Turner/Stringer briefing; and Stringer interview.

31. Capt Todd Gentry, 510th Fighter Squadron, interviewed by Lt Col Brad Davis and Maj Chris Orndorff, Aviano AB, Italy, 20 February 1996.

32. Ibid.; and Turner interview. Colonel Hoog took part in a group discussion about Deliberate Force chaired by Colonel Turner.

33. Dr. Wayne Thompson and Maj Tim Reagan, "Deliberate Force: A Distinctive Campaign," Washington, D.C., December 1995, 17–18 (Secret) Information extracted is unclassified; and Lt Col Gary West, commander, 510th Fighter Squadron, interviewed by Lt Col Brad Davis and Maj Chris Orndorff, Aviano AB, Italy, 20 February 1996.

34. "Operation Deliberate Force . . . Factual Review," 5-2 through 5-3 (NATO Secret) Information extracted is unclassified; AOCC/Ops/1, to Lt Gen Michael Ryan, memorandum, subject: Effectiveness of CAS, 12 Sep-

tember 1995 (NATO Confidential) Information extracted is unclassified, AF-HRA, NPL-18.

35. BDA summary spreadsheet, 9 April 1995 (NATO Secret), in "Excerpt, Close Air Support Cell Daily Log," Combined Air Operations Center, Vicenza, Italy, 29 August–16 September 1995. (Secret) Information extracted is unclassified.

36. Briefing, Joint Chiefs of Staff (JCS), Intelligence Directorate, to vice chairman, JCS, subject: Impact of Air Strikes on BSA Communications, copy faxed from Headquarters European Command (EUCOM) to General Ryan and General Hornburg, n.d. (NATO Secret) Information extracted is unclassified, AFHRA, CAOC-19.

37. Ibid. (NATO Secret) Information extracted is unclassified.

38. Ibid. (NATO Secret) Information extracted is unclassified.

39. Message, 070800Z SEP 95, CINCSOUTH, to SACEUR, subject: Operation Deliberate Force, 7 September 1995 (NATO Secret) Information extracted is unclassified, AFHRA, NPL-15.

40. "Operation Deliberate Force . . . Factual Review," 4-2 through 4-3 (NATO Secret) Information extracted is unclassified; message, 031600Z SEP 95, Headquarters 5 ATAF, subject: Air Task, reference message, commander, 5 ATAF, 3 September 1995 (NATO Secret) Information extracted is unclassified, AFHRA, CAOC-18; and "BSA Weapons Withdraw Recce" (U), n.d., AFHRA, CAOC-18.

41. "Operation Deliberate Force . . . Factual Review," 4-2 through 4-4 (NATO Secret) Information extracted is unclassified; and "Deliberate Force: Summary of Daily Status," package flows, 1 through 5 September 1995. (NATO Secret) Information extracted is unclassified.

42. Atkinson, "Put to the Test"; and Lt Gen Bernard Janvier, Headquarters, United Nations Peace Forces, to Gen Ratko Mladic, letter (U), 3 September 1995, AFHRA, NPL-15.

43. Adm Leighton Smith, quoted in Atkinson, "Put to the Test"; and transcript of press conference, Adm Leighton W. Smith, commander in chief, Allied Forces Southern Europe, "NATO Recommences Air Strikes against Bosnian Serbs," NATO Club, Headquarters AFSOUTH, Naples, Italy, 6 September 1995.

44. Message, 050800Z SEP 95, CINCSOUTH, to COMAIRSOUTH, subject: Air Strike Execution, 5 September 1995 (NATO Confidential) Information extracted is unclassified, AFHRA, NPL-15; and statement by the NATO secretary-general, press release (95)79, 5 September 1995.

45. "Deliberate Force: Summary of Daily Status," package flow, 5 September 1995 and 5–6 September 1995; and 7490th Wing (Provisional) mission results, 5 September 1995.

46. "Operation Deliberate Force . . . Factual Review," 3-2 through 3-3 (NATO Secret) Information extracted is unclassified.

47. Mission report, 5C0654/Seagull 11, 062332Z SEP 95, 6 September 1995 (Secret) Information extracted is unclassified, AFHRA, AVI-57; and

"Operation Deliberate Force . . . Factual Review," 3-4 (NATO Secret) Information extracted is unclassified.

48. Commander's daily report, 060300Z–070259Z September 1995 (NATO Secret) Information extracted is unclassified; Deliberate Force fact sheet, 6 and 7 September 1995; "Operation Deliberate Force . . . Factual Review," 4-5 (NATO Secret) Information extracted is unclassified; and briefing, Lt Gen Michael Ryan, subject: CSAR Time Line.

49. "Operation Deliberate Force . . . Factual Review," 4-5 (NATO Secret) Information extracted is unclassified; commander's daily report, 070300Z–080259Z September 1995 (NATO Secret) Information extracted is unclassified; and mission report, MRP1, 8 September 1995, from 104th Fighter Group, deployed to commander, 5 ATAF/CAOC/INT (Secret) Information extracted is unclassified.

50. Thompson and Reagan, 9; and Deliberate Force BDA tracking sheet, 31 OSS/OST, 19 September 1995, 11 (Secret) Information extracted is unclassified, AFHRA, AVI-40-01.

51. Maj Gen Hal Hornburg, CAOC director, interviewed by Lt Col Robert Owen et al., Air Force Wargaming Institute, Maxwell AFB, Ala., 14 March 1996; 7490th Wing (Provisional) results; ATM, 110300Z to 120259Z September 1995, 1 (Secret) Information extracted is unclassified, AFHRA, C-!a3; and ATM, 130300Z to 140259Z September 1995, 4 (Secret) Information extracted is unclassified, AFHRA, C-!a3.

52. Ryan briefing, 7 February 1996; and message, 070001Z SEP 95, COMAIRSOUTH, to CINCSOUTH, subject: Operation Deliberate Force, 7 September 1995 (NATO Secret) Information extracted is unclassified, AFHRA, NPL-15-01.

53. Message, 051100Z SEP 95, COMAIRSOUTH, to commander in chief, European Command (USCINCEUR), subject: Tomahawk Operations, 5 September 1995 (Secret) Information extracted is unclassified, AFHRA, NPL-15; and Hornburg interview.

54. Message, 081100Z SEP 95, CINCSOUTH, to SACEUR, subject: IADS West, 8 September 1995 (NATO Secret) Information extracted is unclassified, AFHRA, NPL-17.

55. Message, 091053Z SEP 95, from USCINCEUR, to Supreme Headquarters Allied Powers Europe et al., subject: Change to ACEORBAT TOA-Air, 9 September 1995 (NATO Confidential) Information extracted is unclassified, AFHRA, NPL-15.

56. Message, American Embassy, Rome, to US secretary of state et al., subject: Government of Italy's Delay in Approving NATO F-117A Deployments to Italy, 9 September 1995 (Secret) Information extracted is unclassified, AFHRA, NPL-16.

57. Commander's daily report, 080300Z–090259Z September 1995 (NATO Secret) Information extracted is unclassified, AFHRA, CAOC-15; "Operation Deliberate Force . . . Factual Review," 4-5 (NATO Secret) Information extracted is unclassified; and briefing, Gen Michael Ryan, subject: Deadeye Results.

58. "Operation Deliberate Force . . . Factual Review," 4-6 (NATO Secret) Information extracted is unclassified; and commander's daily report, 090300Z–100259Z September 1995 (NATO Secret) Information extracted is unclassified.

59. Calise interview; commander, Sixth Fleet, "Tomahawk Operations in Support of Operation Deliberate Force," 5 September 1995 (Secret) Information extracted is unclassified, AFHRA, NPL-16; and Captain Hlavka, memorandum to General Ryan via General Hornburg, subject: TLAM Update, 7 September 1995, AFHRA, NPL-15-01.

60. Report, "CAOC C-2 Assessment of Operation DEADEYE Part III—10/11 Sep 95" (NATO Secret) Information extracted is unclassified, AFHRA, EUCOM-14.

61. Ibid.; Hornburg interview; and Calise interview.

62. "CAOC C-2 Assessment."

63. "Operation Deliberate Force . . . Factual Review," 4-7 (NATO Secret) Information extracted is unclassified; message, 111125Z SEP 95, Ministry of Defense, Italy, to AIRSOUTH plans cell, subject: Beddown Request for F-117A Aircraft, 11 September 1995 (NATO Confidential) Information extracted is unclassified, AFHRA, NPL-16; 7490th Wing (Provisional) mission results; and "Deliberate Force: Summary of Daily Status," package flow, 11–12 September 1995.

64. "Operation Deliberate Force . . . Factual Review," 4-8 through 4-9 (NATO Secret) Information extracted is unclassified; and Deliberate Force BDA tracking sheet, 19 September 1995.

65. "CAOC C-2 Assessment."

66. "Close Air Support Cell Daily Log," 7 September 1995.

67. Ibid., 8 September 1995; and "Operation Deliberate Force . . . Factual Review," 4-6 (NATO Secret) Information extracted is unclassified.

68. "Close Air Support Cell Daily Log," 6–9 September 1995.

69. Ibid., 11 September 1995.

70. Commander's daily report, 130300Z–140259Z September 1995 and 140300Z–150259Z September 1995; and "Operation Deliberate Force . . . Factual Review," 4-8 through 4-9 (NATO Secret) Information extracted is unclassified.

71. Commander's daily report, 100300Z–110259Z September 1995; "Close Air Support Cell Daily Log," 10 September 1995; AOCC/Ops/1 memorandum; and "Operation Deliberate Force . . . Factual Review," 4-7 (NATO Secret) Information extracted is unclassified.

72. Ibid., 4-8 through 4-9; "Close Air Support Cell Daily Log," 11–12 September 1995; and Calise interview.

73. Ambassador Christopher Hill, interviewed by Lt Col Rob Owen, Washington, D.C., 27 February 1996; Ryan briefing, 7 February 1996; and "Operation Deliberate Force . . . Factual Review," 4-7 (NATO Secret) Information extracted is unclassified.

74. "Deliberate Force: Summary of Daily Status," package flow, 11–13 September 1995; target folder no. C005, Vogosca ammunition-loading plant

(NATO Secret) Information extracted is unclassified, AFHRA, AVI-43; and target folder no. C026, Doboj ordnance depot, (NATO Secret) Information extracted is unclassified, AFHRA, AVI-43.

75. "Close Air Support Cell Daily Log," 12 September 1995; and "Operation Deliberate Force . . . Factual Review," 4-8 (NATO Secret) Information extracted is unclassified.

76. Commander's daily report, 130300Z–130259Z September 1995 (NATO Secret) Information extracted is unclassified; "Operation Deliberate Force . . . Factual Review," 4-9 (NATO Secret) Information extracted is unclassified; and "Deliberate Force: Summary of Daily Status," package flow, 12–13 September 1995.

77. Briefing, Lt Gen Michael Ryan, subject: Deliberate Force, Air Operation: Targets Remaining, DMPIs Remaining; and commander's daily report, 140300Z–150259Z September 1995 (NATO Secret) Information extracted is unclassified.

78. Janvier letter to Mladic; and Adm Leighton W. Smith, commander in chief, Allied Forces Southern Europe, to Lt Gen Bernard Janvier, letter (U), 14 September 1995, AFHRA, NPL-15.

79. "Close Air Support Cell Daily Log," 14–15 September 1995.

80. Ryan briefing, 7 February 1996; Calise interview; and Col Douglas J. Richardson, CAOC C-3 and chief of staff, interviewed by the author, Vicenza, Italy, 16 January 1996.

81. 31st Fighter Wing/CVR memorandum for record, 3.

82. Ibid., 4; Capt Scott MacQueen, 510th Fighter Squadron, interviewed by Lt Col Brad Davis and Maj Chris Orndorff, Aviano AB, Italy, 20 February 1996; and Ryan briefing, 7 February 1996.

83. Turner/Stringer briefing; and 31st Fighter Wing/CVR memorandum for record, 3.

84. Richardson interview; and Calise interview.

85. Richardson interview; and Calise interview.

86. Hill interview.

87. "Close Air Support Cell Daily Log," 29–30 August; and Deny Flight SPINS, commander, 5 ATAF CAOC SPINS/028, effective 260300 August 1995 (NATO Confidential) Information extracted is unclassified.

88. Mission report, Mission ID/05/7C3007, 429 ECS, 300858Z August 1995, AFHRA, AVI-46. (Secret) Information extracted is unclassified.

89. "Close Air Support Cell Daily Log," 3 September 1995.

90. Mission report, Mission ID I8M942, Magic 80, 9 September 1995 (Confidential) Information extracted is unclassified, AFHRA, AVI-52; and mission report, Mission ID/05/7C0842, 429 ECS, 081602Z September 1995 (Secret) Information extracted is unclassified, AFHRA, AVI-51.

91. Deny Flight SPINS, 4; Ryan briefing, 7 February 1996; and Thompson and Reagan, 18.

92. Ryan briefing, 7 February 1996.

93. Atkinson, "Put to the Test."

94. Richardson interview; and Calise interview.

95. Calise interview.

96. Wing Commander Andy Batchelor, BDA cell, interviewed by Lt Col Brad Davis and Maj Chris Orndorff, Ramstein, Germany, 14 February 1996.

97. Hornburg interview; and Thompson and Reagan, 11.

98. Maj Keith Kiger, Sixteenth Air Force, interviewed by the author and Maj Ronald M. Reed, Aviano AB, Italy, 18 January 1996, and by Lt Col Brad Davis and Maj Chris Orndorff, Aviano AB, Italy, 21 February 1996; and Calise interview.

99. Calise interview; and Col Arjen Koopmans, Netherlands air force, interviewed by Lt Col Brad Davis and Maj Chris Orndorff, Vicenza, Italy, 21 February 1996.

100. Thompson and Reagan.

101. Hill interview.

Chapter 6

Combat Assessment:
A Commander's Responsibility

Maj Mark C. McLaughlin

This chapter examines the combat-assessment process in
Operation Deliberate Force, placing particular emphasis on
battle damage assessment (BDA). During combat assessment,
intelligence and operational communities analyze strike results and weapons effects to refine strategies, operational
plans, and target lists, as well as select weapons for subsequent strikes. Because of the multinational nature of the
planning, command, and execution of this air campaign and
as a result of decisions by senior leaders, combat assessment
experienced problems with the cohesion, completeness, and
distribution of battle-damage information. Although these
problems were obvious at the time and have been well docu-
mented since then, the issue for future air planners and commanders remains whether they were avoidable or somehow
inherent to air warfare. In other words, were these problems
the consequence of inappropriate doctrine and policies (which
one can change), or were they the consequence of the particular circumstances of Deliberate Force, which may or may not
be relevant to future air campaigns (and thereby probably
beyond the power of airmen to change)? Clearly, implications
of the assessment are important for the future planning and
execution of airpower.

Combat Assessment in Theory

From a US doctrinal standpoint, combat assessment includes
three elements: BDA, munitions effectiveness assessment
(MEA), and reattack recommendations.[1] BDA, "the subjective
estimate of damage to enemy forces resulting from the application of force to achieve operational and tactical objectives,"[2]

is based on the physical damage to a target, the effect on that target system's functional or operational capability, and the overall impact on the enemy's operational capability. Normally, the chief intelligence officers in US joint or coalition commands—J-2s or C-2s, respectively—are responsible for BDA. As chief of operations, the J-3 is responsible for MEA—the effectiveness of friendly weapons systems and munitions. A reattack recommendation—determining what needs to be done next—follows directly from BDA and MEA. The joint/combined force air component commander determines future courses of action based on inputs from the J-2/C-2 and J-3/C-3. As the sum of these elements, combat assessment "closes the loop" in the targeting process and seeks to determine if strategic objectives are being—or have been—met.

Combat assessment involves both science and art. Intelligence personnel begin by collecting information from all available sources—mainly from communications and electronic intercepts (i.e., signals intelligence), imagery, and human reporting. Analysts assess or "fuse" this information to estimate the direct physical and functional damage to a target or targets and to determine the overall impact of that damage to the functional and operational effectiveness of the target system. The integration of BDA and MEA underpins decisions of whether and how one should reattack the target(s) or add new targets. To the extent that the degree of an attack's destruction or disruption of a target determines physical and functional damage, measuring such damage is a science. But judging whether such attacks have met strategic and operational objectives remains more of an art, since this determination rests on factors that one cannot easily quantify. The latter include the enemy's psychological state or valuation of the targets under attack.

Effective combat assessment requires substantial investment in command attention and physical resources. According to US military doctrine, joint force commanders are responsible for providing guidance and adequate resources to conduct combat assessment in support of their operations. This guidance should include clear instructions on how subordinates should measure damage and convert those measurements into assessments of the effectiveness of attacks in terms of the command's operational and strategic objectives.[3] Joint force commanders should provide enough resources to establish an intelligence architecture capable of supporting information collection, conversion of that information into usable intelligence, and dissemination of appropriately detailed intelligence "products" (imagery, BDA reports, etc.) to valid users. The latter may range from tactical squadrons planning strikes to the National Command Authorities assessing the strategic progress of the campaign.

Similarly, in North Atlantic Treaty Organization (NATO) operations, senior commanders should ensure that a process and architecture exist to carry out combat assessment. An established doctrine accompanied by training is necessary for allied forces to know what combat assessment is and how to perform it. Operations and exercises allow personnel to practice combat assessment, gain proficiency, and refine the doctrine according to lessons learned. Thus, at the theoretical level at least, successful combat assessment includes adequate physical resources, properly trained providers and users of intelligence data, clear and rapid communication among all connected elements, and mutual trust among leaders and followers.

Combat Assessment in Reality

In the specific case of planning and executing Deliberate Force, the people responsible for establishing and running effective combat assessment faced daunting guidance and resource challenges from the start. Preparations for providing combat-assessment support to Deliberate Force resided in the combined air operations center (CAOC) at Headquarters 5th Allied Tactical Air Force (5 ATAF) just outside Vicenza, Italy. Following the Bosnian Serb attack on a Sarajevo market in February 1994 and the subsequent NATO ultimatum to the Bosnian Serb army to withdraw its heavy weapons outside the 20-kilometer total-exclusion zone around Sarajevo, CAOC planners, working with little formal guidance, began to set up BDA procedures to support possible air attacks on heavy weapons in the zone. No published NATO standard agreements on BDA or combat assessment existed, and the formal guidance available did little to make up for the shortfall in doctrinal guidance. For instance, Allied Air Forces Southern Europe (AIRSOUTH) Directive 80-50, vol. 2, *AIRSOUTH Reporting Directive,* established time lines for moving information from subordinate units to higher headquarters (which would prove unrealistically short)[4] but said or implied nothing about the actual art and science of using that information to make usable and timely assessments.

Lacking sufficient NATO guidance, US personnel used American doctrine from joint publications. CAOC targeteers produced a CAOC BDA guide[5] in March 1994 based on a Defense Intelligence Agency guide developed from the lessons of the 1990–91 Persian Gulf War. Moreover, MSgt Mark Sweat, a targeteer for 20 years who worked in the CAOC, pinpointed NATO's shortcomings: "There is no BDA career field. A targeteer does not make one a BDA expert. There is no school, and it [BDA] is never done the same way twice."[6] Maj Dave Minster, who helped write the CAOC's BDA guide, added that the NATO targeting school, which he attended, is only a basic course designed to convey the lowest common understanding of targeting and fails to address BDA at all.[7]

Throughout Operation Deny Flight, which involved the monitoring and subsequent enforcement of the no-fly zone over Bosnia-Herzegovina, the CAOC BDA cell stood up as offensive missions (e.g., attacks on the Krajina Serb airfield at Udbina, Croatia, in November 1994 and the Pale ammunition-storage facilities outside Sarajevo in May 1995) took place and then stood down as operations returned to normal levels. As the security situation in Bosnia deteriorated throughout the summer of 1995, the challenge increased for CAOC personnel to set up a NATO combat assessment capable of supporting a concerted air offensive. The shootdown of Capt Scott O'Grady by the Bosnian Serbs on 2 June 1995 provided additional impetus to bring the CAOC up to a level required to execute a robust air campaign.[8]

In order to do that as quickly as possible, the Joint Chiefs of Staff (JCS) and other agencies—mainly the Air Staff and US European Command—circumvented the slower funding process of Supreme Headquarters Allied Powers Europe (SHAPE) and provided additional money, people, and equipment to the CAOC.

Many of the high-tech systems were still in the final stages of test and evaluation, and NATO had not purchased most of them for coalition operations. Augmentees from the 32d Air Operations Group (AOG) at Ramstein Air Base, Germany; Headquarters AIRSOUTH at Naples; and elsewhere raised the BDA cell's manning from four people at the start of Deliberate Force to 10. More computers, printers, and other equipment used to process and communicate BDA data, such as Linked Operations-Intelligence Centers Europe (LOCE), arrived in-theater prior to the start of the operation, and more arrived as it progressed.

Despite these improvements in materiel, the multinational character of Deliberate Force infused combat assessment with problems of cohesion, completeness, and distribution of information. Combat assessment is a cumbersome and murky process in any operation, but several challenges made it particularly so in Deliberate Force. According to Maj Gen Hal Hornburg, the CAOC director, the policy of sending personnel on temporary duty to the CAOC for three to six months, sometimes less, meant that "approximately 90 percent of the positions are manned by temporary personnel [who] rotate at a rate of 25 percent or more a month."[9] This lack of fully trained personnel and continuity by an experienced staff undermined the smooth functioning of the BDA cell. Consequently, some CAOC BDA representatives, including some US personnel but particularly many of the European allies, needed training in computer software as well as in target-coordinate mensuration.[10] Training levels differed considerably among individuals from the various nations, especially in computer automation, as did their experience in actual BDA methodology. Thus, training posed a significant problem—at least in the campaign's early stages.

Another issue of cohesion concerned the releasability of intelligence to NATO allies, which caused some European officers to question whether Deliberate Force was a NATO operation or a "US and NATO" operation.[11] Adm Leighton Smith, commander in chief of Allied Forces Southern Europe, remarked that the biggest problem of combined operations was the "ability to share intelligence [with the allies]" but added that this was overcome when "we got national agencies to share intelligence."[12] This decision helped foster trust within the multinational CAOC.

In light of lessons learned in Operation Desert Storm, NATO assigned responsibility for BDA to the CAOC, although other organizations—mainly the joint analysis center at Royal Air Force Molesworth, United Kingdom, which provided theater-level intelligence support, and national-level intelligence agencies, such as JCS/J-2T (Targets), the Central Intelligence Agency, and the National Security Agency—provided battle-damage inputs to support the CAOC's deliberations. The CAOC BDA cell produced spreadsheets, among other things, to track target names; assigned basic-encyclopedic numbers to newly identified targets as a cross-reference to the target name; and identified and described desired mean points of impact (DMPI [aiming points for each target]) and tracked their status during the campaign.

The scope and scale of the air campaign during its first few days overwhelmed the CAOC BDA cell.[13] For several reasons, the BDA cycle of poststrike analysis took up to 48 hours to feed back into the air tasking message (ATM) cycle. The need to train so many personnel in computers and BDA methodology caused some delay, as did the slow arrival and poor quality of critical elements of information. As one CAOC member complained, "[mission reports] were slow to arrive, and the quality and resolution of gun camera imagery was too poor for BDA purposes."[14] Other delays resulted from the fact that different services and nations used a variety of video formats in their aircraft recorders and that LOCE, the main dissemination system, had limited bandwidth to transmit the large volumes of imagery data required for timely BDA. At the beginning of Deliberate Force, the target cell shared the LOCE terminal used by the collection, coordination, and intelligence-requirements management cell. It did not receive a dedicated LOCE until 17 September—after the air strikes had stopped. Poor weather over the targets also contributed to delays in the BDA cycle, although the intelligence community partly overcame this problem by using multiple sensors.

BDA improved during the operation as more equipment and support personnel arrived and as the latter received on-the-job training. Despite the hard work of well-intentioned and dedicated personnel, imperfect communication down the chain of command made combat assessment difficult. Michael Short, then a major general and AIRSOUTH chief of staff, noted that

"BDA success criteria and meth- odology were not conceptually determined before the cam- paign."[15] Within the first few days, however, Lt Gen Michael Ryan, commander of Allied Air Forces Southern Europe, who personally retained authority to add and re- move targets from the master at- tack plan, authorized removal of a target from this plan when it was "two-thirds destroyed."[16] At least, the proximity of the BDA special- ists and General Ryan eased the physical act of communicating BDA. The BDA team chief, Wing Comdr Andrew Batchelor, briefed

Lt Gen Michael C. Short

General Ryan and/or other CAOC leaders twice a day— sometimes more often—and General Ryan or his deputies regu- larly briefed Admiral Smith on BDA. The admiral, in turn, re- tained sole authority for releasing BDA to non-CAOC organiza- tions, including field units, national intelligence centers, SHAPE, and the US State Department.[17]

Although the CAOC BDA team knew the location of each DMPI and could determine physical damage to the targets, linking the apparent physical damage to functional damage and to the theater objective of compelling the Bosnian Serbs to withdraw equipment from the total-exclusion zone proved dif- ficult.[18] Given the limited training of the BDA personnel and the rapid pace of the air campaign, the 32d AOG, which aug- mented the CAOC, highlighted one aspect of the combat- assessment problem: "The CAOC . . . did not close the ATM loop (cycle) with a unified assessment of operational results. BDA focused on target status as a result of bomb damage. Partially attributable to a 'lack' of detailed campaign objectives, the BDA effort measured the 'lower teir' [sic] results of planned strikes to the exclusion of 'higher teir' [sic] task-achievement, objective-attainment, and strategy implementation."[19] As a re- sult, the group noted that "senior leaders and strategists per- formed their own analysis of operational results vis-à-vis the chosen strategy. . . . Leaders had to pull the information, analyze the data, and determine a course of action, without a fully supporting staff effort."[20]

General Ryan, however, exercised his prerogative by intentionally reserving for himself the responsibility for overall combat assessment. Consequently, the BDA cell briefed him on the physical damage inflicted on targets. As noted by Lt Col Robert Wallace, the CAOC's chief of targets, "No one was slated to perform functional or target system analysis because with air supremacy and the ability to perform what amounted to saturation bombing, albeit with smart bombs, it was easier to continue to hit known, approved targets than identify new targets that might function as backups for the destroyed targets."[21] General Ryan then discussed the results with his senior staff and Admiral Smith to assess overall progress and plan future attacks because, as Col Daniel Zoerb, director of the AIRSOUTH Deny Flight air-operations cell, pointed out, "Only commanders held accountable/responsible for execution (CINC & COMAIRSOUTH) were fully aware of all considerations and implications, and in proper position to judge the extent to which attacks achieved [the] desired result."[22]

However, the decision not to disseminate BDA outside the CAOC (except to Admiral Smith) was a contentious issue, particularly for aircrews flying the missions. Aviano pilots complained of the lateness and incompleteness of the BDA reaching them. Because planners often ordered restrikes without much explanation about BDA, many pilots suspected that, in some cases, they had restruck already-destroyed targets. Also tending to strengthen this suspicion was the CAOC's practice of sending down target photos showing all DMPIs associated with a target but not distinguishing between those already destroyed and those to be attacked.

Given the limitations of their prestrike information and rigid rules of engagement, pilots generally had to identify the assigned DMPI during an initial pass over the targets—a requirement that further increased their risks. Aviano's intelligence unit tried to mitigate this problem by coming up with its own BDA, using gun-camera footage, mission reports, and any imagery available.[23] In the final analysis, pilots flew a few redundant strikes in the first days of Deliberate Force, but as BDA caught up with the ATM cycle, the problem of redundant strikes seemed to disappear, although knowledge of bomb damage remained clouded in the field.

Colonel Zoerb acknowledged the frustration of the Aviano pilots over the imperfect communication of BDA to the units but stressed that the established BDA system served a broader agenda than simply telling field units how well they were doing. He later explained that "internal release of BDA information was restricted to prevent this information from being misrepresented (unintentionally) to NATO and the nations," while "external release [outside the CAOC] was restricted to avoid compromise and to avoid divulging strategic and tactical plans. Widespread release (media) would have given the warring factions insight into targeting strategy, increasing aircrew risk and making objective attainment more difficult."[24]

Conclusions

Combat assessment in Deliberate Force reflected the preferences of General Ryan and Admiral Smith. Overall, both men were pleased with the process.[25] Due to the relatively small number of targets (56) and DMPIs (346), General Ryan and his senior staff were able to gauge the progress in meeting theater and strategic objectives by examining the physical-damage assessments. However, had the operation been broader, longer, or without pauses, the burden on the senior staff would have been much greater. Moreover, the debate over the releasability of BDA outside the CAOC continues.

From a US perspective, BDA has improved since Desert Storm, and it worked relatively well during Deliberate Force. In general, the CAOC had the difficult task of transitioning from a small-scale operation in a largely benign environment (Deny Flight) to an offensive posture in a short amount of time. After the necessity for air strikes became more apparent, CAOC personnel adapted as best as they could to the changed circumstances, and resources poured into the CAOC. In terms of specific progress, the theater is now the focal point for BDA, with intelligence inputs from various systems and agencies. Furthermore, US systems are more interoperable, communications have improved between shipborne and land-based units, and personnel have acquired training through operations such as Deny Flight and Deliberate Force.

However, NATO as a whole remains relatively backward and unpracticed in combat assessment. It lacks sufficient doctrine on how to perform BDA, let alone combat assessment, and the NATO targeting school does not address even the first step of combat assessment—BDA. This lack of doctrine and the disparity in training and experience among member nations manifested itself during the rapid expansion of the CAOC BDA cell just prior to and during Deliberate Force. Successful combined operations require additional improvements since future operations likely will involve US forces operating as part of a coalition.

Although the United States and NATO differ in their institutional capabilities to practice BDA, both lack formal doctrinal guidance for the actual assessments phase of combat assessment, particularly for Deliberate Force, in which political indicators proved critical to assessing bombing effects. US doctrine provides some guidance for measuring and describing physical and functional damage. However, neither body of doctrine explains how to link physical and functional damage to desired political end states. Perhaps this deficiency is due to the uniqueness of each operation, but one can preview in doctrine a conceptual framework for measuring progress towards political goals so that commanders need not rely on their instincts alone. The small scale of Deliberate Force, its short duration, and the leadership of General Ryan and Admiral Smith mitigated the lack of specific doctrine to some degree, but these special circumstances may not always be present or relevant in future applications of airpower.

This is not to say that Deliberate Force had no general applications for the employment of airpower. Indeed, one can anticipate many of the campaign's features as elements of future campaigns, which likely will be characterized by a requirement for the rapid expansion of operational and intelligence capabilities, the blending of multinational personnel with differing levels of theoretical and practical training and experience, and a high pace of operations. In addition, the large number of targets hit in every air tasking order (ATO) cycle will require robust computer systems capable of transmitting high volumes of data from the continental United States and across a theater of operations, as well as timely assessments in support of subsequent ATO planning.

Thus, while combat-assessment practice and infrastructures always have room for improvement, the most compelling area for future resource investment lies in developing a body of doctrine that permits the efficient blending of multinational personnel and provides combined assessments and recommendations to air commanders on all aspects of combat assessment—from sensor-data interpretation to political advice. This doctrine can guide education and training, as well as provide ready-made staff manuals suitable for quick modification to reflect idiosyncratic circumstances. Airmen must push doctrine as far into the strategic levels of political-military connections as possible. This effort may require closer coordination with political advisors, both from within NATO—if appropriate—and from the US Department of State and/or appropriate foreign ministries. But we should welcome such connectivity, given the close and continual military and diplomatic interactions of operations such as Deliberate Force.

Notes

1. Joint Pub 2-01.1, "Joint Tactics, Techniques, and Procedures for Intelligence Support to Targeting," third draft, April 1995, III-23–III-32.

2. Ibid., III-26.

3. Ibid.

4. Lt Col Robert Wallace, JCS/J-2T, previously CAOC chief of targets and deputy C-2, telephone interview by the author, 6 March 1996.

5. "Battle Damage Assessment Guide," 5th ed., 5 ATAF CAOC, 1 October 1995, Air Force Historical Research Agency (AFHRA), Maxwell Air Force Base (AFB), Ala., NPL-03. (Confidential) Information extracted is unclassified.

6. MSgt Mark Sweat, CAOC, telephone interview by the author, 6 March 1996.

7. Maj Dave Minster, JCS/J-2T, telephone interview by the author, 6 March 1996.

8. Col John R. Baker, Headquarters USAF/XOO, interviewed by Lt Col Chris Campbell and the author, 11–12 December 1995, AFHRA, Misc-13.

9. "Quick Look at the CAOC Ops/Intel Architecture Needs," Headquarters USAF/XOO, n.d. (created 28 July 1995), 3, AFHRA, SAGC-01-05. (Secret) Information extracted is unclassified.

10. Wallace interview. Colonel Wallace had to train some Europeans in converting degrees, minutes, and seconds to degrees, minutes, and hundredths of minutes.

11. Wing Comdr Andrew Batchelor, Royal Air Force, interviewed by Maj Chris Orndorff, 14 February 1996, AFHRA, Misc-18.

12. Adm Leighton Smith, videotaped presentation to Air War College students, Maxwell AFB, Ala., 9 November 1995, AFHRA, Misc-19.

13. Batchelor interview.

14. History, 5 ATAF Combined Air Operations Center Organization and Function from April 1993, 18, AFHRA, SAGC-10. (NATO Secret) Information extracted is unclassified.

15. Maj Gen Michael Short, vice commander, AIRSOUTH, interviewed by Lt Col Robert C. Owen and Lt Col Richard L. Sargent, 4 December 1995.

16. Batchelor interview.

17. AIRSOUTH DE [sic] air operations center, memorandum to Lt Col Robert C. Owen, Air University, Maxwell AFB, Ala., subject: Deliberate Force BDA Process, 25 March 1996.

18. History, 5 ATAF Combined Air Operations Center. (NATO Secret) Information extracted is unclassified.

19. "32 Air Operations Group (AOG) After Action Report," Ramstein Air Base, Germany, n.d., 10.

20. Ibid., 11.

21. Wallace interview. Col Daniel Zoerb, director of the AIRSOUTH Deny Flight air-operations cell, contends that "AIRSOUTH/CAOC intelligence personnel and targeteers accomplished what analysis was possible given constraints of time, qualification and training, and made requests for analytical support to appropriate national agencies. Shortfalls in internal capability and lack of timeliness and coherence on the part of national support agencies were significant limitations in this regard." Faxed comments on 2d draft of Balkans Air Campaign Study to Col Robert C. Owen, Air Command and Staff College, Maxwell AFB, Ala., 16 July 1997.

22. AIRSOUTH DE [sic] air operations center memorandum.

23. Pilots who flew in Desert Storm also had difficulty getting BDA. See Thomas A. Keaney and Eliot A. Cohen, Gulf War Air Power Survey: Summary (Washington, D.C.: Department of the Air Force, 29 March 1993), 139.

24. AIRSOUTH DE [sic] air operations center memorandum.

25. Lt Gen Michael Ryan, "NATO Air Operations in Bosnia-Herzegovina: 'Deliberate Force,'" After Action Report, n.d. (NATO Secret), information extracted is unclassified, AFHRA, CAOC-13; and Smith presentation. Colonel Zoerb, another key participant in the combat-assessment process, pointed out that "the Combat Assessment process was made to work and accomplished basic objectives . . . but nobody was pleased with it. This is another traditional lesson that U.S. and NATO forces must take as a priority." Faxed comments.

Chapter 7

Assessing the Effectiveness of Deliberate Force: Harnessing the Political-Military Connection

Maj Mark C. McLaughlin

This chapter assesses whether and to what extent Operation Deliberate Force achieved its military and political objectives. No military operation ever takes place in isolation; consequently, any study of whether and how Deliberate Force achieved its goals must take into account not only the air strikes themselves but also other dynamic forces that may have influenced the Bosnian Serbs' eventual decision to meet NATO's demands. In addition, one must judge the operation's effectiveness from the perspective of the intended target—the Bosnian Serb political and military leadership. In this context, one should judge NATO air operations in light of their direct impact as well as the concurrent victories by Croatian and Muslim (federation) ground forces, American-sponsored diplomatic initiatives, and Serbia's political pressure on its Bosnian Serb cousins.

In Operation Desert Storm, the number of Iraqi divisions destroyed was a key measure of progress toward the objective of ejecting the Iraqis from Kuwait. During Deliberate Force, in addition to the tangible effects of the air attacks, nonquantifiable measures of progress emerged because US diplomats met face-to-face with the Serbs even as air strikes took place. These diplomats had the unique opportunity to judge firsthand the impact of the air strikes on the Serbian leaders' faces and by the political movement on the part of the Serbs. Moreover, the diplomats were ideally positioned to advise the military on the campaign's effectiveness.

189

Identifying the Objectives

Chapter 4 of this volume noted that Deliberate Force contained both overt, limited objectives as well as implicit, strategic objectives. From the beginning, Lt Gen Michael Ryan, commander of Allied Air Forces Southern Europe and the operational commander of the campaign, said the operation was "not intended to defeat the BSA [Bosnian Serb army] but to convince the BSA to stop attacking Sarajevo—to take away military capability, not lives."[1] The military objective entailed "execut[ing] a robust NATO air campaign that adversely alters the BSA's advantage in conducting successful military operations against the BIH [Federation forces]." The desired end state of the campaign for NATO commanders, therefore, called for the "Bosnian Serbs [to] sue for cessation of military operations, comply with UN [United Nations] mandates, and negotiate."[2] This articulation of the desired end state tied the military objectives of the operation to the UN's declared goal of securing the safe areas—particularly Sarajevo—and to US assistant secretary of state Richard Holbrooke's more circumspectly announced objective of "leveling the playing field" in order to bring the Bosnian Serbs to the negotiating table.[3] Nonetheless, Holbrooke emphasized that the "bombing was not planned as a part of the negotiating track. . . . It [the air campaign] was a result of the Bosnian Serbs' decision to mortar the [Sarajevo] marketplace."[4]

The Cycle of Strike, Pause, and Negotiation

Air operations began at 0200Z on 30 August 1995, and later that day Lt Gen Bernard Janvier, force commander of United Nations Peace Forces in the Balkans, sent a letter to Gen Ratko Mladic, BSA commander, setting the conditions for ending the air strikes. These included removing heavy weapons from inside Sarajevo's 20-kilometer (km) total-exclusion zone (TEZ), ceasing attacks against the other remaining safe areas, and accepting a cease-fire throughout all of Bosnia.[5]

Meanwhile, Ambassador Holbrooke, lead negotiator of the five-nation Contact Group representing the United States,

France, Britain, Germany, and Russia, shuttled between Belgrade and Zagreb from 30 August to 1 September and urged Serbian president Slobodan Milosevic and Croatian president Franjo Tudjman to accept a comprehensive peace plan. On 31 August, as NATO air strikes continued a second day, President Milosevic, representing the Bosnian Serbs, accepted the principle that would divide Bosnia in a 51/49 percent split between the Muslim-Croat federation and Bosnian Serbs.[6] Although representing the Bosnian Serbs politically, President Milosevic had not yet convinced General Mladic to accede to NATO's demands.

After two days of air strikes, NATO paused at 0200Z on 1 September. While NATO leaders assessed the effects of their bombing campaign, diplomatic contacts continued. General Janvier met General Mladic at the Serb border town of Mali Zvornik, where Mladic harangued Janvier and handed him a letter filled with conditions of his own. During this time, Ambassador Holbrooke's delegation was able to measure the political impact of the air strikes by observing the faces of the Serbs. Christopher Hill, who assisted Holbrooke, noted that President Milosevic welcomed the pause on 1 September because it would make restarting the campaign difficult.[7] According to Hill, the Serbian president finally realized the true power of the air campaign when, during a meeting with Ambassador Holbrooke later on 1 September, he tried to contact General Mladic, only to learn from an aide that NATO forces had severed the communications links between Pale—the Bosnian Serb headquarters in Bosnia-Herzegovina—and Belgrade. It dawned on Milosevic, to his chagrin, that the air strikes would, of course, target telecommunications systems.

The bombing pause gave UN and NATO leaders direct and indirect opportunities to tighten the screws on the Serbs. Responding to General Mladic's tirade of the day before, General Janvier sent him a letter on 3 September, informing him that his conditions were unacceptable and warning him that air strikes would resume if by 5 September the Serbs did not remove heavy weapons from Sarajevo's 20 km TEZ, cease attacks against the other safe areas, allow freedom of movement for humanitarian relief workers and the United Nations Protection Force (UNPROFOR), and allow unrestricted use of the

Sarajevo airport. Janvier hoped that the pause would allow Mladic to see just how damaging the air strikes had been. Maj Gen Hal Hornburg, the combined air operations center (CAOC) director, even wanted to send photos and a cellular phone to Mladic so he could see the extent of the damage and stay in better contact with UN and NATO leaders.[8]

However, the pause also allowed doubts to fester among some military leaders about the efficacy of resuming the bombing. During his shuttle diplomacy, Ambassador Holbrooke received reports of the existence of "great ambivalence in Washington about resumption of the bombing and about the bombing itself. . . . Senior American military personnel were sharply divided on whether to resume or not, whereas the diplomats were not." Holbrooke aptly summed up some military leaders' unease by noting that "the same people who had doubts about it ran it so brilliantly."[9]

When imagery from unmanned aerial vehicles indicated no withdrawal from the TEZ, NATO air strikes resumed on 5 September. In retrospect, Hill noted that resuming the air campaign had an unforeseen and perhaps even more stunning effect on the Serbian leaders than had the initial strikes.[10] The resumption of air strikes dashed President Milosevic's hopes that NATO once again had spent its political energy in a halfhearted air campaign and that the predictable pattern of protracted negotiations would follow.

While the NATO air strikes continued, diplomats made progress on 8 September when the foreign ministers of Bosnia, Croatia, and "Yugoslavia" (Serbia and Montenegro) agreed to abide by basic principles that would govern future peace negotiations. The agreement called for two entities—the existing Bosnian federation (of Croat and Muslim-controlled territory) and a Serb republic (Republika Srpska)—to form a federation of Bosnia-Herzegovina. Although Bosnia-Herzegovina would remain a single country, the accord called for two autonomous parts and a "central connecting structure."[11] The agreement also allowed the entities to "establish parallel special relations with neighboring countries," a concession that permitted links between Serbs in Bosnia and Serbia.[12]

On 14 September diplomatic and military pressure came to a climax. Hill did not need up-to-the-minute bomb damage assessments to tell him the effectiveness of the air campaign: he could see the impact on President Milosevic's face. Hill recalled that when the delegation met with Milosevic that day in Belgrade, the Serbian president looked "very worried."[13] Milosevic implored Ambassador Holbrooke to call a halt to the air strikes but without offering any assurances that the BSA would remove the weapons from around Sarajevo or comply with NATO's other demands. When Holbrooke responded that the BSA leadership knew what it must do to stop the bombing, President Milosevic asked if Holbrooke would talk directly with the BSA leaders. Holbrooke consented, and, to his astonishment, Milosevic had General Mladic and Bosnian Serb "president" Radovan Karadzic driven over from a nearby villa. Because Mladic reluctantly agreed to withdraw the heavy weapons and acceded to other demands, NATO suspended offensive air operations for 72 hours. At the end of that period, NATO suspended those operations another 72 hours, and on 20 September NATO and UNPROFOR announced that a "resumption of airstrikes is currently not necessary."[14]

A Propitious Convergence of Events

Hill remarked that on 14 September, when General Mladic reluctantly agreed to NATO's terms, "this was a guy who really looked like he'd been through a bombing campaign." He concluded that "the use of airpower and our ability to . . . sustain it for a couple of weeks was really the signal the Bosnian Serbs needed to get to understand that they had to reach a peace agreement. . . . They basically had to surrender some major war aims. I think the way it was done was with this air campaign."[15]

From a ground perspective, Hill concluded that the federation offensive in western Bosnia would not have been as successful without the air campaign.[16] Croatian and Muslim (federation) forces, which had begun operations against the BSA in western Bosnia by mid-August, capitalized on the BSA's difficulty in bringing its forces to bear when and where they were needed. By 13 September the military balance in Bosnia had tilted in the federation's favor against the Bosnian Serbs, just as it had tilted in Croatia's favor against the separatist

Krajina Serbs earlier, from May to August. Press reports indicated up to 50,000 Bosnian Serbs in western Bosnia fled to the Bosnian Serb stronghold of Banja Luka during the fighting. This number was in addition to the 160,000 Krajina Serbs who had fled to Banja Luka in the wake of Croatia's swift reconquest of Sector West in early May and Sectors North and South in early August. (See chap. 1 for more on Croatia's recapture of the Krajina, which Krajina Serbs had held for four years.) The rout in the west continued, and by 19 September the federation offensive had recaptured over three thousand square kilometers from the Bosnian Serbs, trimming the area they controlled from 70 percent to about 49 percent. This area matched what the Contact Group had offered them.

In assessing the air campaign's effectiveness, Adm Leighton Smith, commander in chief of Allied Forces Southern Europe, concluded that the federation ground offensive in the west "helped dramatically," although NATO air and federation ground operations did not integrate intentionally.[17] General Ryan also pointed out the value of the federation ground operations in western Bosnia by noting that "it took both—airpower nailed down the forces," hamstringing the BSA's ability to communicate and respond to the western offensive.[18] General Hornburg observed that "without the territorial loss, the air campaign would not have been as effective. . . . One without the other would not have been as effective."[19] Similarly, Holbrooke described the federation ground offensive as "extremely important" but concluded that the air campaign remained the "most important single factor" influencing the Serbs.[20]

From a political standpoint, Ambassador Holbrooke's diplomacy benefited from the bombings, which allowed him to maintain pressure on President Milosevic to convince the Bosnian Serbs to comply with NATO's ultimatum. He concluded that "never has airpower been so effective in terms of a political result."[21] For his part, Milosevic knew that the UN would not lift the ongoing sanctions against Serbia—in effect since the summer of 1992 due to Serbia's support of the BSA—until the factions reached a peace agreement on Bosnia. The economic sanctions had put the Serbian economy on its back. Moreover, because Milosevic realized the UN would not remove the sanctions without US approval, this gave Holbrooke additional leverage with the Serbian president. As a result, Milosevic had little choice other than agreeing to pressure the Bosnian Serb leadership to withdraw its weapons from around Sarajevo.

Conclusions

The BSA had to deal with foes fighting on the ground and attacking from the air. The overall military balance in the region had begun to shift with Croatia's recapture of three of the four UN sectors in Croatia from May to early August 1995. The tide in Bosnia began to shift in mid-August as Croatian, Bosnian Croat, and Muslim forces began an offensive to retake territory from the BSA in western Bosnia. The air campaign unintentionally aided that offensive. The federation's recapture of territory from the BSA tidied up the map, bringing proportional distribution of territory between the factions more into line with what the Contact Group offered the Bosnian Serbs. The territorial losses also meant that the Bosnian Serbs ceded at the negotiating table at Wright-Patterson Air Force Base (AFB) in Dayton, Ohio, only what had been taken from them on the battlefield. Nonetheless, the balance of power had shifted perceptibly from the BSA to the federation. If General Mladic continued to resist NATO's demands, he risked losing more territory and combat capability.

NATO air strikes, coupled with the federation offensive out west, confronted the BSA with a military challenge it had not experienced during the previous three-plus years of fighting. Moreover, Ambassador Holbrooke's just-in-time diplomacy—the prospect of getting economic sanctions against Serbia removed and the recognition of a Serb republic within Bosnia with "special links" to Serbia—provided President Milosevic with everything he needed to pressure the Bosnian Serbs.

By the end of Deliberate Force, the air strikes not only had achieved the objective of compelling the Bosnian Serbs to comply with NATO's demands but also, when combined with the federation ground offensive, had contributed to the shift in the military balance in the region. This military reality, in turn, helped influence the warring factions' decision to negotiate a final peace agreement at Dayton. Hill reported that the air campaign had a lingering effect at Dayton by "establishing a record of compliance."[22] Through Deliberate Force, NATO had proven its willingness to enforce an agreement.

In the end, the combination of military power and diplomacy made a difference in Bosnia. Ambassador Holbrooke's diplomatic initiatives capitalized on the federation offensive in the west and the NATO air strikes to pressure the Serbs and Bosnian Serbs. Diplomacy without military leverage would have proved insufficient to persuade the Bosnian Serbs—as previous attempts to bring peace to the Balkans had amply demonstrated—while military operations without diplomacy would have proved unsustainable.

Notes

1. Lt Gen Michael Ryan, interviewed by Maj Tim Reagan and Dr. Wayne Thompson, 18 October 1995, Air Force Historical Research Agency (AFHRA), Maxwell AFB, Ala., CAOC-30.

2. Briefing slides (U), Lt Gen Michael E. Ryan, subject: NATO Air Operations in Bosnia-Herzegovina: Deliberate Force, 29 August–14 September 1995, AFHRA, NPL-16.

3. Steven Greenhouse, "U.S. Officials Say Bosnian Serbs Face NATO Attack If Talks Stall," *New York Times,* 28 August 1995.

4. Richard Holbrooke, interviewed by Dr. Karl Mueller and the author, 24 May 1996.

5. Rick Atkinson, "The Anatomy of NATO's Decision to Bomb Bosnia," *International Herald Tribune,* 17 November 1995, 2.

6. Roger Cohen, "Serb Shift Opens Chance for Peace, a U.S. Envoy Says," *New York Times,* 1 September 1995.

7. Christopher Hill, director, Office of South Central European Affairs, Bureau of European and Canadian Affairs, US Department of State, interviewed by Lt Col Robert Owen and the author, 27 February 1996.

8. Maj Gen Hal M. Hornburg, presentation to Joint Doctrine Air Campaign Course students, College of Aerospace Doctrine Research and Education, Maxwell AFB, Ala., 14 March 1996.

9. Holbrooke interview.

10. Hill interview.

11. Chris Hedges, "Three Enemies Agree to Serbian State as Part of Bosnia," *New York Times,* 9 September 1995.

12. Ibid.

13. Hill interview.

14. "Joint Statement by Admiral Leighton W. Smith, Commander, Allied Forces Southern Command and Lt. Gen. Bernard Janvier, Force Com-

mander, United Nations Peace Forces," Headquarters, United Nations Peace Forces Zagreb, 20 September 1995, AFHRA, NPL-06-13.

15. Hill interview.

16. Ibid.

17. Adm Leighton Smith, "NATO Operations in Bosnia-Herzegovina: Deliberate Force, 29 August–14 September 1995," videotaped presentation to Air War College, Maxwell AFB, Ala., 9 November 1995, AFHRA, Misc-19.

18. Ryan interview.

19. Maj Gen Hal M. Hornburg, interviewed by the Air University Balkans Air Campaign Study Group, 12 March 1996, AFHRA, Misc-20.

20. Holbrooke interview.

21. Ibid.

22. Hill interview.

Chapter 8

Aircraft Used in Deliberate Force

Lt Col Richard L. Sargent

Operation Deliberate Force was a robust 17-day air campaign conducted by the North Atlantic Treaty Organization (NATO) to adversely alter the advantages of the Bosnian Serb army (BSA) in conducting successful military attacks against Sarajevo and other safe areas. By conducting active bombing operations between 29 August 1995 and 14 September 1995, NATO launched its first sustained air-strike operation, one that included several operations and weapons-employment highlights:

- first air campaign to predominantly employ precision-guided weapons (69 percent);
- first employment of Tomahawk missiles in the European Command theater—the Balkans area of responsibility (AOR);
- first sustained use by United States Air Force (USAF) F-16s of both 500 lb (GBU-12) and 2,000 lb (GBU-10) laser-guided bombs (LGB) in combat;
- first sustained use by USAF F-15Es of the 2,000 lb GBU-15 electro-optical guided bomb in combat;
- first use by USAF F-16s of the high-speed antiradiation missile (HARM) Targeting System (HTS) and first firing of the AGM-88 HARM in combat;
- first time in combat that strafing passes by USAF A-10s exceeded 15,000 feet+ slant range;
- first employment of the Predator unmanned aerial vehicle (UAV) in combat;
- first deployment of the German Luftwaffe into combat since World War II;
- first deployment of modern Spanish air force units into combat;
- first contribution by Italian air force units to NATO/Deny Flight operations; and

199

- first delivery by the French Mirage 2000D/K and Sepecat Jaguar of Matra 1,000 lb LGBs and US GBU-12s in combat.

This chapter and its four companion chapters (9–12) take a tactical-level look at the use, performance, and effectiveness of the individual weapon systems, support systems, and tactics employed against the BSA during Deliberate Force. Primarily, they deal with fundamental war-fighting elements (forces, weapons, targets, and tactics) and the way they interlink—from initial conception, to employment, to their effects on the BSA. Together, they translate air combat power into success in air-strike operations.

This chapter, together with chapters 9, 10, and 12, reviews the military "science" of Deliberate Force, its physical aspects (such as force structure, military hardware, and technological tools), and other quantifiable subjects.[1] Chapter 11 provides insight into the operational "art" of the campaign—the employment of platforms, weapons, and tools against the target array. Each chapter examines its subject in light of one basic question: What effect(s) did politico-military constraints and limitations (e.g., the rules of engagement and the tight, centralized control exercised by the combined force air component commander [CFACC]) have on the forces, weapons, targets, and tactics in pursuit of Deliberate Force's objectives?

Deliberate Force's multinational force composition included

- over five thousand personnel from 15 nations;
- over four hundred aircraft (including 222 fighters) available at any one time;
- approximately 260 land-based aircraft—40 percent based at Aviano Air Base (AB), Italy;
- 18 air bases in five countries across Europe; and
- up to three aircraft carriers in the Adriatic Sea.

What follows is an examination of NATO air platforms used during Deliberate Force, including fixed- and rotary-wing aircraft as well as UAVs. These platforms consist of both "shooters" (lethal-weapon platforms) and "supporters" (nonlethal, although some are capable of self-defense). Further, one can distinguish these platforms by a variety of operating characteristics and capabilities that give them unique flexibility and versatility to perform various roles and missions. Thus, for purposes of differentiation, this discussion matches the players with their primary role and mission even though some platforms are not limited to particular roles or missions.

The Players

After Deny Flight launched its first sorties in April 1993, the force structure grew proportionally to mission tasking. The pace of growth accelerated after 2 June 1995 with the shootdown of Basher 52, a USAF F-16 patrolling Bosnian airspace, by a Serbian SA-6 surface-to-air missile (SAM). Gen Michael Ryan, commander of NATO's Allied Air Forces Southern Europe (COMAIRSOUTH), began to augment his force structure with additional suppression of enemy air defenses (SEAD) assets over Bosnia-Herzegovina. COMAIRSOUTH's other requests included extension of the assignment of Spanish EF-18s to Aviano AB and a new request for an additional 12 "jammers" and 24 "HARM shooters."[2]

By mid-July two Compass Call EC-130Hs arrived at Aviano to support SEAD against the Bosnian Serb integrated air defense system (IADS). By the end of July, Adm Leighton Smith, commander in chief of Allied Forces Southern Europe (CINCSOUTH), requested additional forces for possible air strikes in Bosnia-Herzegovina. He also requested that F-16 HTS aircraft, F-4G Wild Weasels, and additional support aircraft be placed on alert for recall.[3]

On 13 August 1995, in response to activity in Iraq, the USS *Theodore Roosevelt* (CVN-71) departed the Adriatic Sea, creating a requirement to deploy electronic combat (EC) and HARM-capable aircraft previously placed on alert to fill the SEAD gaps. In addition CINCSOUTH requested an extension of the deployment of EF-111s already based at Aviano.[4]

By 18 August 1995, COMAIRSOUTH requested a recall posturing of Deny Flight assets: seven Mirage F-1s, eight Jaguars, and 17 Mirage 2000s from France; 18 NF-16s from the Netherlands; 18 TF-16s from Turkey; and 12 Jaguars and eight Tornados from the United Kingdom. At the same time, these aircraft received approval for deployment from their alert bases to their respective beddown bases in Italy.[5]

By the end of August, as tensions mounted, CINCSOUTH increased the alert posture of all "on call" aircraft. On 29 August, with the concurrence of Lt Gen Bernard Janvier, force commander of United Nations Peace Forces (FC UNPF), CINCSOUTH issued the order to initiate Operation Deliberate Force and recalled 61 aircraft to their respective beddown bases. These recalled air assets included three Mirage F1-CTs, one Mirage F1-CR, two Jaguars, four Mirage 2000Cs, and six Mirage 2000Ds/Ks from France; four NF-16As and two NF-16Rs from the Netherlands; four GR-7s from the United Kingdom; 10 TF-16Cs from Turkey; two AC-130Hs, two EC-130Es, five KC-10s, six F-4Gs, four EF-111As/EA-6Bs, two C-21s, two EC-130Hs, and two MC/HC-130s from the United States.[6]

Onset Force Structure

After the shootdown of Basher 52 in June, air assets assigned to Deny Flight grew nearly 20 percent. Of these, land-based aircraft increased nearly 30 percent, and aircraft assigned to the 7490th Composite Wing (Provisional) at Aviano nearly doubled to 114.[7] The largest gain came in the increase of overall air platforms available (assigned plus nonassigned) to 385, a 27 percent increase in assigned aircraft and a 22 percent increase in aircraft available to fly missions. This is an overall change of 57 percent from Deny Flight numbers (see table 8.1 and fig. 8.1). Additionally, 14 support assets not assigned to NATO were available day-to-day, and another 80 such assets—62 carrier aircraft and 18 aircraft based at Aviano—were available immediately if needed.

As a result of the initial success of Deliberate Force's first-day air strikes against the Serbian IADS and communications infrastructure, CINCSOUTH canceled the requirement for two Compass Calls, one airborne battlefield command and control center (ABCCC) aircraft, and six Wild Weasels. In addition the return of the *Theodore Roosevelt* to the Adriatic Sea and Aviano's dedication of a second squadron of 18 F-16Cs increased the number of platforms available to conduct NATO air strikes.[8] This initial force structure remained in place for the remainder of Deliberate Force. On the second day of operations, CINCSOUTH requested an additional three KC-135 tankers to

Table 8.1

Players Available at Onset

Category	Assigned	Available*	On Call
Shooters	193	166	15
Supporters	76	74	2
Total	269	240	17

*Assigned aircraft available to fly missions at the start of the air campaign.

support the increased tempo in the AOR until the KC-10 detachment became fully operational.[9]

By 5 September 1995, the SAM threat to NATO aircraft in Bosnia-Herzegovina remained high, and the need for precision-munitions-capable aircraft to attack radar sites and SAM launchers increased. As a result, CINCSOUTH requested two additional F-16 HTS aircraft and two additional F-15Es.[10] On the same day, Greece turned down Turkey's request to fly 10 recalled TF-16s through Greek airspace.[11] Nevertheless, the Turkish aircraft circumvented Greece and eventually arrived at their beddown base in Ghedi, Italy.

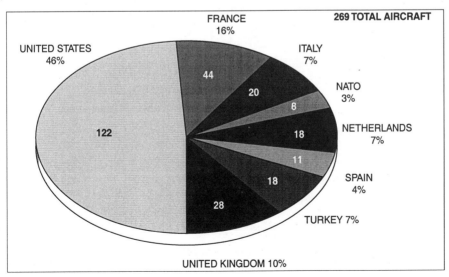

Figure 8.1. Assigned Aircraft by Nationality (30 August 1995)

On 8 September 1995, the continued increase in operations tempo resulted in CINCSOUTH's request to increase the tempo of tankers based in the United Kingdom to support the surge in refueling requirements.[12] In addition the robust sortie rate began to take its toll on aircraft availability, leading to a request for one additional Raven and one Compass Call aircraft. Before the EF-111 and EC-130H could be deployed, "the conditions which led to the requests for these aircraft were overcome by additional logistics support from the US and the request for these aircraft was canceled."[13] This day would see another force-structure change when CINCSOUTH requested six F-117A Stealth fighters, to be based at Aviano, to conduct air strikes against the high-threat air defenses around Banja Luka in support of Deadeye Northwest operations. Italian leaders, however, did not cooperate (discussed later in this chapter).[14]

End-State Force Structure

At the close of Deliberate Force on 14 September 1995, the forces available to conduct operations had reached 414 total aircraft (NATO assigned plus NATO nonassigned)—an 8.1 percent increase over the onset numbers (see fig. 8.2 and table 8.2). Remarkably, this includes a net gain of only 36 aircraft assigned to NATO—an increase of only 13.4 percent.

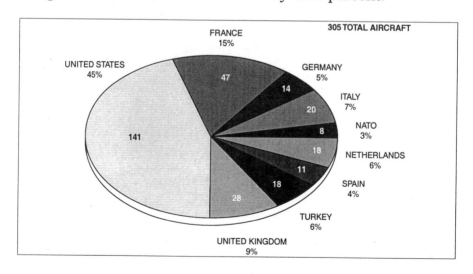

Figure 8.2. Assigned Forces by Nationality (14 September 1995)

204

Table 8.2

End-State Force Structure

(Assigned Aircraft Only)

MISSION / NATION	Offensive Air Operations	Offensive Counterair	SEAD	Air-to-Air Refueling	Airborne Early Warning	Reconnaissance	Combat Search and Rescue	OTHER	ON CALL	TOTAL	National %
France / CV	6 JAGA 4 M2000D 5 M2000K 6 Super Etendard	6 M2000C		1 C-135	1 E-3F	5 F-1CR	3 Puma		3 JAGA 3 M2000C 3 F-1CT 1 F-1CR	47	15.4
United Kingdom / CV	10 GR-7 6 FA-2	6 FMK-3		2 L-1011	2 E-3D	2 GR-7				28	09.2
Netherlands	7 NF-16A	6 NF-16A				5 NF-16R				18	05.9
Turkey		18 TU-16C								18	05.9
Spain		4 EF-18	4 EF-18	2 KC-130				1 CASA		11	03.6
United States / CV	12 A-10A 10 F-15E 4 AC-130H 6 F-18C	12 F-16C 12 F-18C	12 F/A-18D 10 EA-6B 6 EF-111A 10 F-16 HTS 6 EA-6B	5 KC-10 15 KC-135			6 MH-53J 4 HC-130	4 ABCCC 3 EC-130H 2 C-21	1 ABCCC 1 EC-130H	141	46.2
Italy	8 ITORN 6 AMX			1 IB-707				4 G-222 1 C-130		20	06.6
Germany			8 ECRT			6 GTORN				14	04.6
NATO					8 E-3A					8	02.6
Total	90	64	59	26	11	18	13	15	12	305	100.0
Mission %	29.5	21.0	18.4	08.5	03.6	05.9	04.3	04.9	03.9	100.0	

205

F-16s

The Shooters

As mentioned above, shooters comprise lethal air platforms—weapon systems capable of expending (shooting) munitions on air or ground targets to effect a kill. The primary roles of these aircraft are aerospace control and force application, the former typically including missions such as offensive counterair (OCA), defensive counterair (DCA), and SEAD, and the latter typically including missions such as air interdiction (AI), battlefield air interdiction (BAI), and close air support (CAS). During Deliberate Force, AI, BAI, and CAS were grouped into a catchall NATO mission category referred to as offensive air operations (OAS).[15]

Typically, air-to-air platforms perform OCA and DCA missions, primarily with a tasking to conduct air sweeps, air escort, and combat air patrol (CAP); however, OCA missions can involve air strikes against the enemy's air bases and aircraft on the ground. Air-to-ground players perform SEAD and OAS missions. During Deliberate Force, aircraft flew all of these missions in one form or another (see table 8.3).

Table 8.3

Shooter Missions

Mission	Sorties	% of Total Sorties	% of Shooter Sorties
CAP	294	08.3	12.1
SEAD	785	22.2	32.2
OAS	1,365	38.6	55.7
Total	2,444	69.1	100.0

Only a third of these sorties, which involved HARM shooters and OAS missions, actually dropped or fired ordnance during operations. The other two-thirds did not shoot for several reasons: (1) the CAP missions did not engage and shoot any aircraft, (2) the SEAD shooters did not always fire HARMs on every mission, and (3) not all of the shooters actually expended munitions on every target/sortie (e.g., some missions jettisoned ordnance in the Adriatic Sea due to bad weather).

Regardless of what constituted a "true" shooter, the various Deliberate Force shooter platforms could perform more than one mission and could use different tactics to perform a mission (e.g., the swing-capable F-15Es, F-16s, and F-18s). Given the shooters' roles and missions, the following review examines how and why these lethal platforms were actually used—as well as who used which ones.

Combat Air Patrol. Since the early days of enforcing the no-fly zones during Deny Flight, the skies over Bosnia-Herzegovina have been controlled and dominated by multinational forces. Prior to Deliberate Force, the only fixed-wing air-to-air challenge resulted in the "splashing" of four Galebs on 28 February 1994. However, identifying, intercepting, and controlling rotary-wing aircraft became such a confusing and difficult problem that the helicopters had to be written off by the rules of engagement. Rotary-wing aircraft were given a sanctuary at or below three thousand feet while Deny Flight aircraft were at four thousand feet and above to deconflict traffic, thereby not affecting Deliberate Force air operations as a whole. The bottom line is that Deny Flight operations established and maintained air supremacy, which continued throughout Deliberate Force.[16]

This aerospace control was a prerequisite to accomplishing Deliberate Force's roles and missions as well as a requirement for the effectiveness of the roles and missions of the United Nations Protection Force (UNPROFOR).

During Deliberate Force, France, the Netherlands, Turkey, and the United Kingdom provided the primary CAP shooters, with US aircraft filling in as required. Their missions included roving and barrier CAPs, the former providing enforcement of the no-fly zones and the latter providing DCA for high-value air assets. The following aircraft flew CAP during Deliberate Force:

Mirage 2000

- *Dassault Mirage 2000C (M2000C)*—a French single-seat, air-superiority aircraft capable of Mach 2, a ceiling of 59,000 feet, and a combat range of 920+ miles with drop tanks. It has a postulated "look-down/shoot-down" capability with a Doppler radar optimized for interception of low-altitude opposing aircraft. The M2000C has an air-to-air ordnance load of Matra Super 530D semiactive radar missiles, two Magic infrared missiles, and two 30 mm Defa 554 guns with 125 rounds per gun.[17] Six M2000Cs were assigned and deployed to Cervia, Italy, with another three on call. Cervia launched and recovered four M2000Cs a day, on the average, for a total of 60 sorties or 20 percent of all Deliberate Force CAP.[18]

- *Netherlands/General Dynamics NF-16A Fighting Falcon*—an American-export, single-seat, air combat, and multirole fighter capable of Mach 2+ and a combat ceiling of 50,000 feet. The NF-16A has a combat radius of 575+ miles with an air-to-air weapons load of Sidewinders and a 20 mm M61A1 Vulcan cannon.[19] Based at Villafranca, Italy, with six aircraft assigned, NF-16As launched and recovered, on the average, four sorties a day through the first 15 days but did not fly the last two days of the campaign for a total of 56 sorties—19 percent of the Deliberate Force CAP sorties.[20]

- *Turkey/General Dynamics TF-16C Fighting Falcon*—basically a standard USAF F-16C purchased by the Turkish government, which allowed its aircraft to fly only CAP and, if required, to support the NATO Rapid Reaction Force (RRF). Operating out of Ghedi, Italy, the 18 assigned TF-16Cs flew four to six sorties per day for a total of 70 sorties—24 percent of the Deliberate Force CAP sorties.[21]

- *British Aerospace (Hawker Siddeley) FMK-3 Harrier*—the Royal Air Force's (RAF) single-seat, vertical/short takeoff and landing (V/STOL) aircraft, with a maximum speed of 737 MPH at low altitude, a 55,000-foot ceiling, and a 414-mile combat radius with a basic fuel load.[22] Although the Harrier is primarily a CAS and reconnaissance (recce) platform, the RAF designated and assigned six air-to-air-dedicated FMK-3s to Gioia del Colle, Italy. Their weapons include four heat-seeking missiles ("heaters") and two 30 mm Aden guns. The FMK-3s launched and recovered anywhere from four to eight sorties per day for the first 15 days of the campaign for a total of 68 sorties—23 percent of the Deliberate Force CAP sorties.[23]

- *British Aerospace FRS.MK2 alias FA-2 Sea Harrier*—the Royal Navy's shipborne, single-seat, V/STOL, multirole aircraft. Like the other Harrier, it is primarily a tactical-strike and recce platform, but six of them flew 12 CAP sorties from HMS *Invincible* in the Adriatic Sea.[24] The Sea Harrier patrolled with a weapons load of four AIM-120 advanced medium-range air-to-air missiles (AMRAAM), two or four heaters, and two 30 mm Aden cannons.

- *Grumman F-14D Super Tomcat*—the US Navy's F-14A upgrade, including engines, fire control, and cockpit redesign to make a "more capable air machine." This Tomcat variant carries improved Phoenix air-to-air missiles (AAM),

F-14

four AIM-7 Sparrows, four AIM-9 Sidewinders, and an internal 20 mm gun.[25] The F-14D launched and recovered from the USS *Theodore Roosevelt*, located in the Adriatic Sea. The Super Tomcat flew CAP on only three days—the first night and 8–9 September—for a total of 16 sorties.

As for the remaining 12 CAP sorties, USAF F-16s based at Aviano flew eight, and US Navy F-18Cs based on the *Theodore Roosevelt* flew four. These multirole fighters primarily flew OAS missions.

Suppression of Enemy Air Defenses. SEAD assets neutralize, degrade, or destroy ground-based emitters such as early warning/ground controlled intercept; command, control, and communications (C^3) systems; and SAM/antiaircraft artillery (AAA) fire-control systems and their associated surface-to-air weapons. Aircraft accomplish the SEAD mission either by disruptive or destructive means.[26] Examples of electronic combat assets used for disruption include EF-111s and Compass Call aircraft. (Because these assets are non-HARM shooters, they are included in the discussion of supporters.) HARM shooters accomplish SEAD by destructive means. Deliberate Force used six different platforms as HARM shooters (four US and two NATO):

- *McDonnell Douglas F-18C Hornet*—the Navy's single-seat, carrierborne, multirole fighter, capable of Mach 1.8+ speed

F-18

at altitude with a ceiling of 50,000 feet and a combat radius of 662 miles. The Hornet's normal SEAD configuration includes two or four HARMs.[27] Launching and recovering from the USS *Roosevelt* (29 August–12 September 1995) and the USS *America* (13 September 1995), the Hornet took top billing by flying 210 SEAD sorties.[28]

- *Grumman EA-6B Prowler*—the Navy's land- or carrier-based electronic combat platform, capable of 530 knots at sea level, a combat ceiling of 38,000 feet, and an unrefueled combat range of 1,099 miles. Equipped with five ALQ-99 tactical jammer pods, the Prowler can detect, sort, classify, and deal with electronic threats across a broad spectrum of frequency bands. The E-6's SEAD weapons load consists of four to six HARMs.[29] The Prowler flew 183 SEAD sorties, 58 from the USS *Roosevelt* and 125 from Aviano AB. VAG (carrier air group) 141/209 "Tacelrons" flew land-based sorties from Aviano.[30]

- *General Dynamics F-16 HTS*—the USAF's new single-seat "Wild Weasel," incorporating an ASQ-213 HTS. The standard F-16 HTS configuration consists of two HARMs, two AIM-120 AMRAAMs, and two AIM-9 L/M infrared missiles.[31] The

211

EA-6B

F-16 HTS made its debut in Deliberate Force and fired HARMs for the first time in combat. The 23d Fighter Squadron from Spangdahlem AB, Germany, deployed 10 F-16 HTS aircraft to Aviano AB, Italy, where they flew a total of 176 SEAD sorties.

- *McDonnell Douglas F/A-18D Night Attack Hornet*—the US Marine Corps's two-seat, multirole fighter with night-attack and HARM capabilities. The aircraft is capable of a maximum speed of 1,000+ knots at 40,000 feet, a ceiling of 50,000 feet, and a combat radius of 635 miles.[32] A dozen F/A-18D Hornets (call sign "Hawks") from the 2d Wing, 31st Group, 533d Fighter Air Squadron, Beaufort, South Carolina, were assigned to the 7490th Composite Wing (Provisional) at Aviano and flew 66 SEAD sorties during Deliberate Force.[33]

- *McDonnell Douglas/Spain (España) EF-18A Hornet*—the Spanish single-seat, land-based, multirole fighter is a HARM-capable variant of the F/A-18A, with performance similar to that of the F/A-18D (above). Spain deployed eight Hornets from its 31st Group to the 7490th Composite Wing (Provisional) at Aviano; they flew 52 SEAD sorties in all.[34]

- *Panavia ECR-Tornado (ECRT)*—Germany's two-seat, tandem, electronic combat and reconnaissance (ECR) version

212

of the interceptor air defense and air strike (IDS) Tornado, capable of a maximum speed of Mach 2.2 and a ceiling of over 50,000 feet. The ECRT's normal combat load includes two AGM-88s, two AIM-9s, as well as an electronic countermeasures (ECM) pod, chaff/flares, and two drop tanks.[35] Germany based eight ECRTs at Piacenza, Italy; they flew 28 SEAD missions during Deliberate Force.[36]

The Navy's S-3B (described under electronic intelligence [ELINT] platforms, below) and the Air Force's EF-111A Raven (described under electronic support measures [ESM] platforms, below) both contributed SEAD missions to Deliberate Force. The S-3B flew two missions, and the Raven logged 68 dedicated SEAD missions.

The United States flew 89 percent of Deliberate Force's 785 SEAD sorties, with the remainder split between Spain (7 percent) and Germany (4 percent). Of the 705 US SEAD sorties, 56 percent (395) were the Navy's, 35 percent (244) were the Air Force's, and 9 percent (66) belonged to the Marines.[37]

Offensive Air Operations. As mentioned previously, during Deliberate Force, force-application or "striker" aircraft performed three basic missions: AI, BAI, and CAS. Rather than being linked to any particular types of aircraft, these mission categories were defined by the effects that General Ryan expected them to have on the Serbs.[38] Specifically, AI involves "air operations conducted to destroy, neutralize, or delay the enemy's military potential before it can be brought to bear effectively against friendly forces at such distance from friendly forces that detailed integration of each air mission with the fire and movement of friendly forces is not required."[39] BAI refers to "air operations conducted against enemy forces near enough to friendly forces to require coordination, though not necessarily integration, with the fire and maneuver of those friendly forces."[40] And CAS involves "air action by fixed- and rotary-wing aircraft against hostile targets which are in close proximity to friendly forces and which require detailed integration of each air mission with the fire and movement of those forces."[41] Deliberate Force air operations accomplished all of these types of missions while flying 1,365 OAS sorties utilizing 19 different strike platforms from eight different nations:

- *General Dynamics F-16 Fighting Falcon*—the USAF's single-seat, air combat, multirole fighter capable of a maximum speed of over Mach 2, a combat ceiling of 50,000+ feet, and a combat radius of over 575 nautical miles with in-flight refueling. The aircraft can carry over 20,000 pounds of ordnance, although a maximum of about 12,000 pounds is the normal limit for sorties requiring nine-G maneuvering.[42] During Deliberate Force an F-16C standard combat load consisted of two or four LGBs, two AIM-120 AMRAAMs, two AIM-9Ms, five hundred rounds of 20 mm for the M61A1 Vulcan nose cannon, an ALQ-131 ECM pod, ALE-40 or -47 chaff/flares, and the LANTIRN navigation and targeting pod. During Deliberate Force the 31st Fighter Wing/7490th Composite Wing (Provisional) at Aviano provided 12 F-16Cs rotating through day and night shifts between the 510th Fighter Squadron "Dimes" and the 555th Fighter Squadron "Triple Nickels." Both combined to fly 340 strike missions.[43]

- *Fairchild Republic OA/A-10A Thunderbolt II*—the USAF's single-seat CAS and BAI aircraft, capable of a maximum speed of 380 knots at sea level and a combat radius of 250 miles, which allows for a two-hour loiter over a target area with a full weapons load plus 750 rounds of nose-gun ammunition. The "Warthog" can carry up to 16,000 pounds of ordnance on 11 hard points, including conventional bombs, cluster bomb units (CBU), Rockeye, Maverick air-to-surface missiles (ASM), LGBs, and 750 to 1,350 rounds of 30 mm for its GAU 8/A cannon.[44] In support of Deliberate Force, the 104th Fighter Group's 131st Fighter Squadron, the "Death Vipers" from Barnes Air National Guard Base, Massachusetts, deployed 12 A-10s to the 7490th Composite Wing (Provisional) at Aviano AB, Italy. They flew 142 CAS/BAI missions.[45]

- *McDonnell Douglas F-15E Eagle*—the USAF's two-seat, dual-role fighter, capable of a maximum speed of Mach 2.5, a combat ceiling of 60,000 feet, and a maximum unrefueled range of 3,570 miles. The "Strike Eagle" is an adverse-weather and night deep-penetration strike aircraft equipped with a LANTIRN navigation/targeting pod,

A-10

F-15

which allows it to provide laser designation for its own guided bombs, including GBU-10s, -12s, and -24s. The aircraft's AXQ-14 data-link pod provides electro-optical guidance for the GBU-15 bomb. Normally, the aircraft also carries two AIM-7 F/M Sparrows, two or four AIM-9 L/M Sidewinder missiles, and a 20 mm M61A1 Vulcan six-barrel cannon.[46] During Deliberate Force, the 48th Fighter Wing's 494th Fighter Squadron deployed 10 F-15Es from Lakenheath, England, to Aviano AB. They flew 94 strike sorties against key targets, particularly bridges.[47]

AC-130

- *Lockheed AC-130H Spectre*—the USAF's multisensor ground-attack gunship capable of a maximum speed of over 330 knots and an endurance of over five hours. Armament includes a 105 mm howitzer, two 40 mm Bofors cannons, two 20 mm Vulcan cannons, and four 7.62 mm miniguns.[48] During Deliberate Force the 16th Special Operations Squadron of the 1st Special Operations Wing, Hurlburt Field, Florida, deployed four AC-130Hs to Brindisi, Italy, as part of the Joint Special Operations Task Force (JSOTF). The Spectre flew 32 missions, including BAI, CAS, recce, and combat search and rescue (CSAR).[49]

- *McDonnell Douglas F-18C Hornet*—the US Navy's carrier-based, single-seat, multirole fighter, with performance similar to that of the SEAD-configured aircraft. This aircraft flew 178 strike missions, providing additional LGB precision-weapon deliveries during Deliberate Force. In addition the sister variant F/A-18C Hornet (also a carrier-borne night-attack fighter) is an improved F/A-18A with data-bus-linked small computers; it is reconnaissance equipped and has AIM-120 AMRAAM and AGM-65F capability. During Deliberate Force the F/A-18C flew a total of 10 missions—four strike, four CAP, and two recce.[50]

- *Grumman Super Tomcat F-14D*—the US Navy's two-seat, multirole fighter capable of carrying 14,500 pounds of various ordnance loads of free-fall weapons.[51] (For other specifications see the discussion under CAP platforms.) These Super Tomcats flew 47 strike missions during Deliberate Force.[52]

- *McDonnell Douglas F/A-18D Hornet*—the US Marine Corps's night-attack, two-seat, multirole fighter (see description under SEAD platforms). The Hawks provided another 94 strike sorties for Deliberate Force, flying out of Aviano AB.[53]

- *Sepecat Jaguar A (JAGA)*—the French single-seat, CAS, tactical strike, tactical reconnaissance fighter/bomber, capable of a maximum airspeed of Mach 1.5, a combat ceiling of 40,000+ feet, and a combat radius of 357 miles on a low-altitude mission profile on internal fuel, or eight hundred+ miles on a medium-altitude mission profile with full internal and external fuel. Armament combinations include two 30 mm Defa cannons with 150 rounds per gun, air-to-air missiles, bombs, rocket-launcher pods, laser-guided air-to-ground missiles, and drop tanks on five external hard points.[54] In support of Deliberate Force, the French air force deployed six Jaguars to Istrana, Italy, from which they flew 63 strike missions.[55]

- *Dassault Mirage 2000D/K*—the French single-seat, delta-wing, CAS, tactical strike, and tactical reconnaissance fighter. (See the discussion of the M2000C, above, for performance characteristics). The strike Mirages in Deliberate

217

Force were night/laser capable and could carry nearly 14,000 pounds of external stores, including AAMs, ASMs, bombs, rockets, ECM and recce pods, and two drop tanks. Like the 2000Cs, they have two 30 mm Defa 554 cannons with 125 rounds per gun.[56] Operating out of Cervia, Italy, Mirage 2000Ds flew 10 strike missions, and M2000Ks flew 36 missions. One Mirage 2000K was lost to an infrared man-portable missile on the first day of operations, the only NATO aircraft lost during the campaign.[57]

- *Panavia GR.MK1/Italy Tornado IDS (ITORN)*—the Italian all-weather fighter, capable of a maximum speed of Mach 2.2, a service ceiling of 50,000 feet, and a combat radius of 865 miles with a heavy weapons load on a medium-to-low-altitude mission. The aircraft can carry nearly 20,000 pounds of ordnance on seven hard points, including Hunting JP 233 weapon packs, ALARM antiradiation missiles, AAMs, ASMs, free-fall and guided bombs, CBUs, ECM pods, and drop tanks. The aircraft also carries internally two 27 mm IWKA-Mauser cannons with 180 rounds per gun.[58] During Deliberate Force, the ITORNs flew 26 strike sorties out of Ghedi, Italy.[59] Unfortunately, during operations the Italian pilots' lack of proficiency in refueling from US KC-135 drogue tankers minimized the aircraft's surge capability, since they were restricted to using only the Italian air force's IB707 tanker.[60]

- *General Dynamics/Netherlands NF-16A*—the Netherlands' single-seat, multirole fighter (see CAP discussion for specifications). For strike operations, the NF-16A can carry 15,000 pounds of ordnance, including AAMs; ASMs; rockets; conventional bombs; smart-weapon kits, including laser-guidance systems; ECM pods; and external tanks. Flying out of Villafranca, Italy, Dutch F-16s flew 86 OAS sorties in support of Deliberate Force.[61]

- *McDonnell Douglas/Spain EF-18A*—the Spanish single-seat, multirole fighter (see SEAD discussion). EF-18s contributed 46 strike missions during Deliberate Force.

- *McDonnell Douglas/BAe GR-7 Harrier II*—the RAF's single-seat, V/STOL, CAS, tactical strike, and tactical reconnaissance aircraft. Capable of carrying up to nine thousand

218

pounds of ordnance, the GR-7 has a maximum speed of 575 knots at sea level and a combat ceiling of 50,000 feet. With a 6,000 lb payload, its combat radius is 172 miles. Its normal armament load consists of two 25 mm Aden 25 cannons with 125 rounds per gun, AAMs, ASMs, general-purpose and guided bombs, CBUs, rocket launchers, and an ECM pod carried on six external hard points.[62] Based at Gioia del Colle, Italy, the RAF's GR-7 Harrier II flew 126 strike sorties during Deliberate Force.[63]

- *British Aerospace FRS.MK2 (FA-2) Sea Harrier*—the Royal Navy's all-weather, single-seat, V/STOL, carrierborne, multirole (tactical strike, tactical reconnaissance, and antiship) aircraft. (See CAP discussion for specifications). In the strike mission, the FA-2 is equipped with two 30 mm Aden cannons plus eight thousand pounds of stores carried on five pylons.[64] In addition to the Sea Harrier's CAP support, the aircraft flew a total of 30 strike sorties from the HMS *Invincible* in the Adriatic Sea in support of Deliberate Force.[65]

- *Other*—the few remaining Deliberate Force strike missions were flown by German ECRTs (three), Turkish TF-16s (four), and US Navy EA-6Bs (four). (See previous discussions for specifications.)

The Supporters

The shooters could not perform their missions effectively and efficiently without support from aircraft that fulfilled various force-enhancement roles. Force enhancement, which multiplies the combat effectiveness of fighting forces and enables and improves operations, may be the major contribution air forces make to a campaign such as Deliberate Force.[66] Force supporters, better known as "force multipliers," contributed over 30 percent (1,091) of the sorties flown in Deliberate Force. Supporter missions include air-to-air refueling (AAR) and intelligence, surveillance, and reconnaissance (ISR). The latter includes ELINT, airborne early warning (AEW), recce, ABCCC, electronic warfare (EW)/ESM, and CSAR. Other support came from intratheater airlift provided by the Spanish CASA 212 (see table 8.4).

Table 8.4

Supporter-Mission Sorties

Mission	Sorties	% of Total Sorties	% of Supporter Sorties
AAR	383	10.8	35.1
Recce	312	08.8	28.6
ELINT	169	04.8	15.5
AEW	166	04.7	15.2
ABCCC	32	01.0	03.0
CSAR	19	00.5	01.7
Other	10	00.3	00.9
Total	**1,091**	30.9	100.0

Air-to-Air Refueling. For the 17 days of the campaign, tanker aircraft from several NATO member states provided aerial refueling support. Operating mainly from two stations over the Adriatic—"Speedy" and "Sonny"—these tankers flew 383 (35.1 percent) of all Deliberate Force support sorties. The United States provided the majority of the AAR platforms and 310 (80.9 percent) of the refueling sorties, with the United Kingdom providing 32 (8.4 percent), France 18 (4.7 percent), Spain 17 (4.4 percent), and Italy six (1.6 percent). These nations operated six different types of AAR aircraft.

- *US/Boeing KC-135R Stratotanker*—the USAF upgrade of the KC-135E with four large, high-bypass-ratio CFM F-108 turbofans, capable of a speed of 460 MPH and a mission radius of 2,875 miles. The KC-135R has a maximum takeoff weight of 322,500 pounds with a maximum fuel load of 203,288 pounds.[67] During Deliberate Force, 12 US Stratotankers (an even mix of KC-135Es and Rs) flew 265 (69.2 percent) of the AAR sorties and over 85 percent of the US tanker sorties from bases at Pisa, Italy; Sigonella, Sicily; Istres, France; and RAF Mildenhall, United Kingdom. To make up for an initial unavailability of larger KC-10 aircraft, the Stratotankers from Mildenhall flew 108 missions down to the Balkans area of operations.[68]

- *US/Douglas Aircraft Company KC-10A Extender*—the USAF's long-range, aerial tanker/transport, capable of a

KC-135

cruise speed of 520 MPH at a ceiling of 42,000 feet. The Extender can provide boom and drogue pod refueling and can transfer almost twice as much fuel as the KC-135—360,000 pounds.[69] KC-10As did not fly their first Deliberate

KC-10

Force missions until 2 September 1995. Based at Genoa, Italy, these Extenders flew 45 AAR missions.[70]

- *United Kingdom/Lockheed K.MK1 L-1011K Tri-Star*—the RAF's tanker, capable of a maximum speed of 520 knots at 35,000 feet, a service ceiling of 43,000 feet, and a range of 4,836 miles with a maximum payload.[71] In support of Deliberate Force, the RAF deployed two Tri-Stars to Palermo, Italy; from there they flew 32 AAR sorties.[72]

- *France/Boeing C-135FR Stratotanker*—the French air force's equivalent to the USAF KC-135R. Unlike the refueling boom of the USAF version of this aircraft, the French KC-135's ended in a drogue instead of a probe, which made it compatible with many NATO aircraft that the American version could not service without temporary modification.[73] The French deployed one of their C-135FRs to Istres, France, in support of Deliberate Force. The aircraft flew every day except on the first and last days, for a total of 18 sorties.[74]

- *Spain/Lockheed KC-130H Dumbo*—a rough-field, all-weather, tactical, in-flight-refueling tanker, capable of a refueling speed of 308 knots and an operating radius of one thousand miles to offload 31,000 pounds of fuel.[75] Spain deployed two KC-130Hs of the 31st Group, 12th Wing to Aviano; from there they launched and recovered 17 sorties.[76]

- *Italy/Boeing IB-707*—the Italian air force's modified Boeing 707 tanker with drogue-refueling capability. Operating out of Pisa, this aircraft flew six missions. Primarily it refueled Italian Tornados, whose pilots had not been trained to refuel from US tankers.[77]

Intelligence, Surveillance, and Reconnaissance. ISR aircraft are tasked primarily for combat-information support. When ISR assets are properly integrated, their synergism can produce results greater than the total of their individual efforts. The situational awareness provided by ISR enables the CFACC to exploit the capabilities of forces more fully by warning of enemy actions and threats.[78]

Many theater organic, service, Department of Defense, and national ground-, air-, sea-, and space-based sensor systems collect combat information. In turn, these sensors have various processing, analysis, and production centers and nodes, from theater field locations to national agencies and joint intelligence centers. Their "products" are usually disseminated to users at all levels via dedicated and common-use communications links and architectures, including ground-air-space systems and their relays, direct downlinks, and even "runners" or "shuttles" to other locations. Military and civilian satellite communications systems play a critical role in distributing combat information where and when it is needed.[79] Other ISR sources include pilots' postmission reports, theater-controlled U-2s, Rivet Joint, tactical recce aircraft, and satellite systems of the United States and other nations.

The recce priorities of NATO air commanders in relation to Bosnia-Herzegovina focused on heavy-weapons sites, SAMs, fixed targets, weapons-collection points, and the airfields at Udbina and Banja Luka. The general UN and NATO requirement to minimize both the risk to NATO aircrews and the risk of conflict escalation was best fulfilled by the use of pre-planned recce by strategic and national assets, including U-2 flights, tactical reconnaissance aircraft, and UAVs. U-2 missions were tasked primarily against heavy weapons, Udbina airfield, fixed targets, and weapons-collection points. Generally, national assets were tasked against SAM sites and Banja Luka airfield. Using these assets to gather information on those targets allowed NATO commanders to minimize the use of manned and unmanned theater platforms and thus reduce their exposure to enemy threats. Tactical reconnaissance assets, therefore, were used mainly for tactical, often short-notice, missions. AIRSOUTH kept them at various levels of alert to maintain their readiness for such scramble missions.[80] During Deliberate Force, five nations employed 13 different manned or unmanned recce platforms for purposes that included monitoring the movement of heavy weapons out of the Sarajevo total-exclusion zone (TEZ) towards the weapons-collection points, as well as making assessments of directed targets and battle damage.

- *French Dassault Mirage F-1CR*—the French air force's tactical and strategic all-weather reconnaissance aircraft assigned to the 33d Reconnaissance Squadron based at Strasboling, France. This aircraft is capable of a maximum speed of Mach 1.8 and a combat radius of 863 miles on a medium-altitude mission.[81] During Deliberate Force, five F-1CRs based in Istrana, Italy, were listed as ELINT assets but actually flew 66 tactical reconnaissance sorties.[82]

- *French Dassault Mirage M2000D*—the French air force's multirole fighter. This aircraft can fly reconnaissance when equipped with a recce pod. During Deliberate Force, M2000Ds flew 12 tactical reconnaissance sorties from Cervia, Italy, in support of the RRF.[83]

- *French Sepecat Jaguar A (JAGA)*—a French air force strike fighter. Jaguars operating from Istrana, Italy, also flew three recce missions in support of the RRF.[84]

- *German Panavia Tornado GR.Mk1(TORNR)/1a (GTORN)*—the German air force's tactical reconnaissance aircraft with variants from the Tornado IDS/ECR. Restricted to support of the RRF only, six TORNRs operating from Piacenza, Italy, flew 32 tactical reconnaissance sorties during Deliberate Force. Also operating from Piacenza, GTORN aircraft flew four recce sorties in support of the RRF in addition to performing their normal electronic combat and reconnaissance roles.[85]

- *Netherlands General Dynamics NF-16R "Recce Falcon"*—a modified F-16A recce aircraft. Five NF-16Rs, based at Villafranca, Italy, flew 52 tactical reconnaissance sorties during Deliberate Force.[86]

- *United Kingdom McDonnell Douglas/BAe GR.Mk7 Harrier II*—recce version of the RAF's close-support aircraft. Two of them flew 49 sorties during Deliberate Force.[87]

- *United Kingdom British Aerospace FRS.Mk2 (FA-2) Sea Harrier*—Royal Navy multirole aircraft. Flying from the *Invincible* and equipped with camera pods, these aircraft flew 12 tactical reconnaissance sorties during the air campaign.[88]

- *US Navy Grumman F-14A TARPS*—US Navy fleet defense fighters. Equipped with the tactical air reconnaissance pod system (TARPS), these aircraft flew 32 tactical reconnaissance sorties from the *Roosevelt* and the *America*.[89] The F-14As were capable of a maximum speed of Mach

2.37, a service ceiling of 56,000 feet, and a range of over two thousand miles. Reflecting their primary air combat role, TARPS F-14As also carried a war load of missiles and an internal cannon.[90]

U-2

- *USAF Lockheed U-2R Dragon Lady*—US high-altitude re-connaissance aircraft, capable of a cruising speed of 430 MPH, an operational ceiling of 90,000 feet, and a maxi-mum range of 6,250 miles.[91] U-2Rs have a variety of sensors for performing all ISR missions, including ELINT, surveillance, and recce. ELINT U-2s have large "farms" of gathering antennas or windows for optical sensors. Battlefield-surveillance U-2s have high-resolution radar such as the Hughes Advanced Synthetic Aperture Radar System Type 2. Also, the precision location strike system was developed for use with the Dragon Ladies to locate hostile radar emitters. Flying out of RAF Fairford or RAF Alconbury, U-2Rs attempted 44 launches in support of Deliberate Force. Fifteen recce and 10 ELINT sorties were successful, while 13 and five were ground or air aborted, respectively. On 29 August 1995, a U-2R crashed on takeoff at RAF Fairford, and the pilot died of injuries.[92]

- *US Army Schweizer RG-8 Lofty View and RG-8A Condor*—a single-engine, two-seat, fixed-wing reconnaissance air-craft. Lofty View has an endurance of at least four hours and a cruise speed of less than 80 knots. RG-8 Condors have two engines, three seats, an endurance of six hours, and a cruise speed of one hundred knots. During Deliberate Force, Lofty View and Condor aircraft based at Dezney, Turkey, flew nine sorties, logging more than 52 hours of recce and surveillance time.

Two aircraft previously mentioned flew weather reconnaissance missions. On two different weather days, a pair of F/A-18Cs and a pair of F-16Cs logged a total of four reconnaissance sorties as collateral missions.

By May 1994 the military commanders of Deny Flight were looking for ways to improve their ability to monitor the TEZs or safe areas established around certain Bosnian cities. By that time it was clear that UNPROFOR would not be able to fully monitor the safe areas, particularly if more were activated. Air recce offered a vital complement to ground-force capabilities in this area, but it too had limitations, mainly due to bad weather, roughness of the Bosnian terrain, camouflage skill of the Serbs, and limited availability and flexibility of manned aircraft available to do the mission. Unmanned aerial vehicles, therefore, became a third potential source of valuable information, both in relation to TEZ monitoring and to the situation in Bosnia in general.[93]

UAVs date back to World War I. Prior to Deliberate Force, they were employed in combat during the Persian Gulf War. These included the Pioneer, Pointer, and Exdrone, operated by the Army, Navy, and Marine Corps, respectively. In Operation Desert Storm, these UAVs showed that they could provide near-real-time battlefield surveillance and detection—ideal capabilities for Deny Flight's TEZ monitoring.[94] Moreover, UN commanders on the scene recognized that during Deny Flight, "if employed overtly, the RPV [remotely piloted vehicle] acts as yet another deterrent to potential violators of the TEZ rules. The system can track/follow weapon systems that violate the TEZ, whether during the day or at night."[95] Consequently, they believed that in the event of additional TEZ tasking, UAVs would enhance their surveillance resources at low risk. Two UAV systems subsequently deployed to the Balkans region:

- *General Atomics "Gnat" 750 (UAV-2)*—the US Army's modified RG-8A Condor with control and data relay, later named an interim medium-altitude endurance, surveillance, and reconnaissance drone. Prior to Deliberate Force, the Gnat had seen service during Deny Flight operations, unlike Predator. During Deliberate Force, the Gnat launched and recovered from Dezney, Turkey, and inside Croatia. In all, the Gnat 750 attempted 12 launches and flew seven successful flights.[96]

Predator UAV

- *General Atomics Predator (UAV-1)*—the USAF's medium-altitude-endurance UAV for surveillance, reconnaissance, and target acquisition. This air platform cruises at speeds less than 250 knots and carries electro-optical, infrared, and synthetic aperture radar sensors. Images captured by the sensors go from the aircraft to the ground-control cell and then by satellite to video units throughout the theater or even the world. NATO planners and peace-implementation force commanders at several levels used images from the Predator. These included UNPROFOR in Bosnia; the combined air operations center (CAOC) at Vicenza, Italy; the allied RRF; and the European Command Joint Analysis Center at RAF Molesworth, England. Commanders watching the video downlink screens see pictures less than two seconds old—what the military calls near real time. The ability to pull still photo images from the video is a popular feature, but the resolution still needs work.[97] During Deliberate Force a US Army unit launched and recovered Predator from Gjader, Albania. It launched 15 flights (17 were attempted), 12 of which were effective, logging over 150 hours of coverage over Bosnia-Herzegovina.[98] A prime demonstration of Predator's value occurred on 5 September 1995, as Admiral Smith and General Janvier pondered whether or not to resume bombing. Their decision hinged on whether the Serbs were withdrawing, or at least demonstrating an intention to withdraw, their heavy weapons from the Sarajevo safe area. Based on a Predator sortie launched just before dawn, Admiral Smith advised Janvier that "there were no intents being demonstrated; let's get on with it!"[99]

During Deny Flight the United States, Great Britain, and France routinely provided airborne signals intelligence (SIGINT) and electronic intelligence by using five different types of aircraft—Rivet Joints, U-2Rs, and EP-3s from the United States; Nimrods from Great Britain; and C-160s from France. Flying roughly 75 sorties per month and averaging seven to eight hours of coverage per day, these platforms added to the total information available to the CAOC. During Deliberate Force, airborne intelligence missions increased nearly fivefold. The same three nations added four more ELINT platforms to increase around-the-clock coverage of the area of operations with an average of 11 sorties per day.[100]

- *US Navy/Lockheed ES-3A/S-3B Viking*—the Navy's carrier-borne electronic warfare aircraft, capable of a maximum speed of 450 knots at 25,000 feet, a service ceiling of 35,000 feet, and a combat range of more than twenty-three hundred miles. The Viking's passive ELINT configuration wasn't known at the time of this writing. During Deliberate Force, Vikings launched and recovered from the USS *Theodore Roosevelt* or the USS *America* in the Adriatic Sea. ES-3As flew 38 ELINT sorties, and S-3Bs flew 33.[101]

228

S-3 Viking

- *US Navy/Lockheed EP-3E Orion*—a Navy ELINT platform. Also known as Aries II, this aircraft has a maximum cruise speed of 380 knots at 15,000 feet, a service ceiling of 28,000 feet, and a maximum mission radius of 2,532 miles. During Deliberate Force, four EP-3Es supported CAOC operations, normally patrolling off the coast of Bosnia "feet wet" over the Adriatic Sea in a northwest/southeast orbit. Based at Sigonella Naval Air Station, Sicily, the Orions flew 18 ELINT missions.[102]

- *USAF/Boeing RC-135W "Rivet Joint"*—the Air Force's electronic reconnaissance platform featuring a side-looking airborne radar capability. The aircraft's direct-threat warning system can provide a broadcast "heads-up" threat warning to friendly airborne aircraft. The RC-135W flies at a maximum speed of 535 knots at 25,000 feet, a service ceiling of 40,600 feet, and an operational radius of 2,675 miles. The aircraft has no armament and limited ECM.[103] During Deliberate Force, Rivet Joint aircraft "commuted" from RAF Mildenhall. They flew 21 ELINT

P-3 Orion

missions feet wet over the Adriatic Sea, orbiting northwest to southeast, like the Orion, but at a higher altitude.[104]

- *RAF/British Aerospace Nimrod R.Mk1*—the RAF's electronic intelligence platform, capable of a maximum speed of five hundred knots, a service ceiling of 42,000 feet, and a ferry range of 5,755 miles on internal fuel without in-flight refueling. The main visible sensors are three very large spiral-helix receiver domes—one facing ahead on the front of each wing and one facing aft on top of the vertical fin. It

RC-135

230

carries no armament.[105] During Deliberate Force, Nimrods flew seven ELINT missions—one mission on each of the first three days and one on each of the last four days, averaging six hours of coverage time. Like the other ELINT assets, it orbited northwest to southeast over the Adriatic Sea, just off the coast of Bosnia-Herzegovina.[106]

- *France/Transall C-160NG Gabriel*—a French medium-range SIGINT aircraft that flies at a maximum speed of 277 knots at 16,000 feet. It has a service ceiling of 27,000 feet, a typical range of 1,151 miles, and no armament.[107] Based at Avord, France, Gabriels flew four SIGINT missions in support of Deliberate Force—one mission on each the first two days and one on each the last two days.[108]

- *France/DC-8*—a SIGINT-modified DC-8. During Deliberate Force, these aircraft flew three ELINT support sorties.[109]

Electronic warfare/electronic support measures aircraft enhanced the effectiveness of Deliberate Force's penetrating aircraft when these EW/ESM systems operated in mutually supportive roles at opportune times and places within the AOR. These systems proved essential to the process of detecting, identifying, and fixing the exact locations of enemy air defense systems—the first steps in the process of deciding whether to avoid, degrade, or destroy particular systems. NATO conducted these EW operations in a combined environment.[110]

Because electronic combat assets have a broader field of influence than surface-based assets, the EC mission both increases the lethality of combined forces and improves their survivability. Throughout Deliberate Force the whole range of EC missions, including SEAD, EW, or ESM, coordinated with other missions to control the EC environment by denying its use to the BSA while preserving its use by the multinational force. During Deliberate Force the following nonlethal, force-enhancer EW/ESM platforms conducted EC missions against ground-based electromagnetic emitters such as C^3, early warning, and SAM/AAA fire-control systems, as well as their associated surface-to-air weapons:

- *USAF/Grumman (General Dynamics) EF-111A Raven*—the USAF's ESM tactical jammer. The Raven combines low-

EF-111

altitude, high-speed, night, all-weather capabilities with a modern, tactical, radar-jamming system. Capable of a maximum speed of 2.14 Mach at high altitude, a service ceiling of 45,000 feet, and an unrefueled endurance of more than four hours, the EF-111A has no armament.[111] The Raven has three operational modes: (1) standing off in its own airspace to screen the routes of attack aircraft, (2) escorting packages that are penetrating the enemy's defenses, and (3) neutralizing enemy radars in the force-protection role. The EF-111A's primary-role equipment is the Eaton Corporation's ALQ-99E tactical jamming subsystem (JSS), housed in the weapons bay; the sensitive JSS emission receiver system is in its fin-top fairing. System inputs activate the aircraft's 10 powerful jammers. The ALQ-99E JSS has proven to have sufficient power to allow the aircraft to penetrate the most concentrated electronic defenses.[112] During Deliberate Force, Ravens of the 429th Electronic Combat Squadron flew a total of 68 EC sorties in support of both SEAD and ESM missions.[113]

- *USAF/Lockheed EC-130H Compass Call*—a USAF aircraft featuring a computer-assisted, operator-controlled, selective jamming system. When supporting offensive operations, the EC-130H can become part of a SEAD effort. Capable of a maximum speed of 325 knots at 30,000 feet, a service ceiling of 33,000 feet, and a range of 2,356 miles, this specialized aircraft can also support ground, sea, amphibious, and special forces. It carries no armament. The 43d Electronic Combat Squadron flew four Compass Call aircraft for a total of 35 EW/ESM missions in support of Deliberate Force; these were logged as ELINT missions.[114]

In addition to flying its primary SEAD role, the US Navy's EA-6B Prowler performed ESM missions as well. This aircraft's jamming capability is similar to the EF-111's, but, unlike the Raven, the Prowler can also destroy enemy radars.

All-weather surveillance performed by space-based platforms and/or aircraft in the Balkans AOR provided NATO commanders information to plan and direct combat air operations. In addition, air surveillance platforms provided C³ to enhance the situational awareness of NATO units and commanders.

- *NATO/Boeing Aerospace E-3A/D/F Sentry*—an airborne warning and control system aircraft. The large rotodome on NATO's E-3A/D and France's E-3F Sentry aircraft houses a 24-foot-diameter antenna that permits surveillance from the Earth's surface up into the stratosphere, over land and water. The radar has a range of more than two hundred miles for low-flying targets and farther for air platforms flying at medium to high altitudes. As an air defense system, the E-3 can look down to detect, identify, and track enemy and friendly low-flying aircraft by eliminating ground-clutter returns that confuse other radar systems. In its tactical role, the Sentry can provide information needed for interdiction, reconnaissance, airlift, and CAS for NATO forces. This high-value air asset is capable of a maximum speed of 530 MPH at altitude, a service ceiling of 40,000 feet, and an endurance of six hours at a distance of one thousand miles from its homeplate. The Sentry has no armament.[115] During Deliberate

E-3 airborne warning and control system aircraft

Force, NATO Sentries flew a total of 99 AEW missions (74 by E-3As and 25 by E-3Ds). The French E-3Fs flew an additional five missions.[116]

- *US Navy/Grumman E-2C Hawkeye*—the US Navy's carrier-borne and land-based AEW and C³ aircraft. The Hawkeye is equipped with a General Electric APS-125 radar and a Litton L-304 general-purpose computer capable of automatically tracking 250 targets and controlling 30 intercepts simultaneously up to 250 miles away. Also, the aircraft's systems allow for an ABCCC role. Operationally, the Hawkeye has a maximum speed of 325 knots, a service ceiling of 30,800 feet, and a patrol endurance of up to six hours. During Deliberate Force, Hawkeyes launched and recovered 62 AEW sorties from the USS *Theodore Roosevelt* and USS *America* in the Adriatic Sea.[117]

By obtaining needed combat information, ISR platforms played a key role in the planning, execution, and combat assessment phases of Deliberate Force. Overall, NATO flew 647 ISR sorties during the operation, accounting for 59.3 percent of the support sorties and 18.3 percent of the total sorties flown.

Airborne Battlefield Command and Control Center. As an airborne battle staff's command post, the ABCCC functions

E-2 Hawkeye

as a direct extension of the CAOC. By flying near the scene of air operations, ABCCC aircraft and crews ensured continuous command and control over NATO aircraft by linking them and the CAOC by radio or by exercising some direct-control functions themselves.

- *USAF/Lockheed-Georgia EC-130E*—USAF C-130Es configured to accept a battlefield command and control center capsule in their cargo bays. They were the only dedicated ABCCC aircraft flying during Deliberate Force. With 16 battle-staff members in their capsule, these aircraft could communicate via UHF, VHF, HF, and FM radios; secure teletype and voice communications systems; and automatic radio relay. The aircraft have a maximum speed of 318 knots, an unrefueled range of twenty-three hundred miles, and long endurance through air-to-air refueling. USAF ABCCCs are unarmed.[118] During the operation, four EC-130Es flew 32 sorties from Aviano AB, each usually

235

involving a 12-hour shift on patrol station for 24-hour coverage. One sortie was aborted and then relaunched the first day of operations. The only other time ABCCC did not fly occurred on the last day of Deliberate Force because of extremely bad weather conditions at Aviano and within the Balkans AOR.[119]

Combat Search and Rescue. During Deliberate Force, special operations forces assigned to the JSOTF at Brindisi, Italy, had primary responsibility for CSAR operations. These forces plus three French air force Puma helicopters and several US Navy carrierborne sea-rescue assets remained on call for CSAR missions. On 30 August 1995, Ebro 33, a French Mirage 2000, was hit by a man-portable infrared SAM, and the aircrew ejected. With mission reports of "two good chutes" and various intermittent, unidentified radio transmissions, US JSOTF air assets attempted three different CSAR missions on three different days, totaling 19 sorties: three on 30 August, eight on 6 September, and eight on 7 September. Unfortunately, rescuers could not reach the downed Frenchmen before Bosnian Serb forces captured them.

- *USAF/Sikorsky MH-53J Pave Low III*—a heavy-duty, multirole helicopter equipped with a forward-looking infrared sensor; high-resolution, terrain-avoidance radar; an inertial navigation system; and a Global Positioning System for low-level flight and precision navigation in all weather conditions. The aircraft also has a radar warning system, dispensers for flares and chaff, and three .50-caliber machine guns for self-defense. The Pave Low III is air refuelable and has a maximum speed of 170 knots, a service ceiling of 18,500 feet, and an unrefueled range of 1,290 miles. During Deliberate Force, six assigned MH-53Js based at Brindisi, Italy, flew a total of 10 CSAR sorties. During the mission of 7 September to find the downed Ebro 33 crew, some Pave Low IIIs took battle damage, and some helicopter aircrews received wounds from ground fire in the vicinity of the crash site. The aircraft recovered safely.[120]

- *USAF/Lockheed HC-130P Hercules*—the USAF's fixed-wing, rescue-and-recovery aircraft equipped with outer wing pods

MH-53

for refueling helicopters in flight. The CSAR Hercules has a maximum speed of 325 knots, a service ceiling of 33,000 feet, and a range of 2,356 miles.[121] During Deliberate Force, four HC-130Ps flew nine CSAR sorties in concert with MH-53Js, searching for the Ebro 33 aircrew.[122]

Airlift. Prior to Deliberate Force, Deny Flight had already established routine, scheduled strategic and theater airlift to sustain its normal level of operations. Since the establishment of the 7490th Composite Wing (Provisional) at Aviano AB, Italy, and the force-structure changes following the shootdown of a US F-16 in early June 1995, the gradual tempo of needed airlift for force enhancement and support increased substantially. By the onset of Deliberate Force, C-5 Galaxies, C-17 Globemasters, and C-141 Starlifters were providing daily strategic airlift flights into air bases in and around Italy. A limited number of C-21s, C-130s, G-222s, and CASA C-212s provided intratheater airlift capability within the AOR to sustain operations.

C-17s

Two USAF C-21s from Capodichino Airport in Naples, Italy, made daily ferry flights of tactical-reconnaissance and cockpit videotapes in support of the battle damage assessment process. In addition they provided senior leadership with intratheater transportation, particularly between AIRSOUTH in Naples and the CAOC at Vicenza.[123] The Italian air force provided one C-130 and four Aeritalia G-222 general-purpose transport aircraft, which operated from Pisa, Italy.[124] Spain assigned one CASA C-212 Aviocar as a utility transport for CAOC use at Vicenza. The only theater-airlift aircraft to appear

C-21

on the daily mission summaries, the CASA C-212 logged 10 airlift missions during Deliberate Force.[125]

Throughout Deliberate Force, supporters fulfilled an important role in multiplying the combat effectiveness of the shooters. The force-supporter missions previously discussed enhanced the mobility, lethality, survivability, and/or accuracy of the land, sea, and air force missions during the operation. However, none of the missions within their respective roles—aerospace control, force application, or force enhancement—could be effectively performed without the surface activities of force support to sustain and maintain all the players.

Although a discussion of Deliberate Force logistics is beyond the scope of this chapter, all platforms performing their air roles depended on the availability of secure, functional bases to provide needed materiel and facilities to the entire force structure. In all, 18 bases across eight nations supported the air campaign. In particular, Aviano AB was a beehive of activity, supporting 40 percent of all Deliberate Force platforms and the majority of US platforms.

The Nonplayers

For all of the technological sophistication and power of the fleet of aircraft employed by NATO during Deliberate Force, the operation did not utilize every type of aircraft potentially useful and available to the participating air forces. The aircraft left out of Deliberate Force comprise an interesting issue because the reasons for their absence reveal much about the operational, logistical, and political forces that shaped and galvanized this particular air campaign. A brief examination of why certain systems did not participate in or were removed from the fight provides a window into the nature of this kind of warfare—one that complements the preceding discussion of systems that did fly in the skies over Bosnia. At the core of that examination is the question of whether commanders or governments withheld or withdrew systems as a result of military or political considerations. The answer to that question will indicate just how limited or expansive was the military challenge and political significance of Deliberate Force in the eyes of the governments contributing to it.

Absent from the Deliberate Force air order of battle were a number of US aircraft types whose inclusion one would have expected, given their important contributions to the coalition air effort during the Gulf War of 1990–91. These aircraft, all of which remained operational in the US inventory, included B-52s or other heavy bombers; fighter aircraft such as the F-4E, F-111, F-15C, F-117, A-6, and AV-8; and the RF-4C manned reconnaissance aircraft. The United States also did not bring in the MC-130 special-operations aircraft or the F-4G electronic-combat and defense-suppression aircraft. Each of these offered capabilities to Deliberate Force planners that would have or could have filled or mitigated important capability gaps or weaknesses in their order of battle.

For the most part, explanations for the absence of these aircraft from Deliberate Force are straightforward, dealing with the routine and prudent management of military force structure. NATO commanders likely did not bring in some aircraft, such as the F-111F, A-6E, and F-4G, because they were nearing retirement, logistically unique and costly to support, and functionally replicated to an adequate degree by other, newer aircraft. Others, like the US Marine Corps's AV-8

F-15C

vertical-takeoff aircraft, were in-theater but not assigned and simply did not participate in Deliberate Force. The operation did not require RF-4Cs since the French and other NATO air forces provided or could provide manned reconnaissance air-craft as needed. The absence of these aircraft, therefore, was the consequence of purely military calculations of mission re-quirements and logistics.

Military considerations also restrained NATO commanders from requesting deployment of the E-8C joint surveillance, target attack radar system (JSTARS) aircraft, capable of elec-tronically observing an area of the Earth's surface approxi-mately 180 kilometers wide and extending up to 160 kilome-ters beyond the forward line of troops under observation.[126] Appropriate to its designer's intentions, prototypes of the air-craft proved very successful during the Gulf War in locating Iraqi equipment, supply dumps, and field formations. JSTARS also cooperated with aircraft such as the F-15E in striking those targets. Given those capabilities, it was only natural for military commanders to examine the aircraft's utility for op-erations over Bosnia. As early as July 1994, US military lead-ers at the Pentagon examined the possibility of deploying JSTARS to English and German bases as well as one Euro-pean southern-tier base. They were particularly interested in deploying the aircraft to Aviano AB or elsewhere in Italy in support of a Bosnian flight and ground demonstration. But a Pentagon talking paper of 22 September concluded that "limited facilities, increased logistical problems, added costs/program impacts and increased risk combine to make a Joint STARS demonstration in NATO's Southern Tier undesirable."[127]

At that time, the tactical situation also did not lend itself to employing JSTARS in Bosnia. Unlike the desert terrain in the Gulf War, the mountainous local terrain would mask many ground-target movements. To find them would require flying E-8s directly over Bosnia—at unacceptably high political and military risk to these high-value aircraft.[128] In any event, E-8s did not enter the Balkans theater until after Deliberate Force, under military and political conditions vastly changed from those that prevailed before.

The absence of heavy bombers from Deliberate Force opera-tions reflected more of a mix of military practicality and political

B-52

calculation. Heavy bombers, particularly the B-52, had two distinct roles at the time of this operation. Either they could act as "bomb trucks," dropping massive patterns of unguided bombs against area targets, or as cruise-missile carriers, launching standoff attacks against point targets. Although NATO air planners might have seen opportunities to employ pattern bombing against some Deliberate Force targets such as ammunition dumps, political restraints on collateral damage absolutely precluded such attacks. Moreover, there was no getting around the fact that the shorter-range strike aircraft already available in-theater were capable of "servicing" all planned targets within all of the applicable constraints of time and precision. This was also true in relation to the B-52's precision-strike capabilities. Whatever the B-52's conventional air-launched cruise missiles could do in terms of performing precision strikes and minimizing risks from Serbian air defenses, other aircraft weapon-systems combinations and the US Navy's Tomahawk missiles could do also. Even had a significant military reason existed to bring heavy bombers into the fight, Deliberate Force commanders likely would have had second thoughts, given the big airplane's inherent political liability of signaling escalation. Because of the lack of compelling military reasons to bring heavy bombers into the fight, therefore, the potential political liabilities of the aircraft remained

F-117s

dominant in the calculations of NATO air commanders. As estimated by Maj Gen Hal Hornburg, director of the CAOC at Vicenza, employing heavy bombers would have meant "going beyond the psychological threshold" of the campaign and could have had an adverse effect on the Bosnian Serb peace process.[129]

The fate of NATO's effort to bring the Lockheed F-117A Nighthawk into Deliberate Force, mentioned previously, was more clearly the outcome of the background political forces at play during the air campaign. This single-seat fighter was designed to exploit low-observable stealth technology in order to penetrate high-threat enemy airspace under the cover of darkness and attack high-value targets from medium or high altitudes with pinpoint accuracy. These two attributes made the Nighthawk a particularly valuable weapon for the SEAD mission. Consequently, midway through the campaign, General Ryan requested six F-117As to employ against the Bosnian Serb IADS. Ryan based his request on information that the Serbs had relocated virtually their entire SAM system in a protective ring in and around Banja Luka, the logical focus of subsequent NATO air attacks. In Ryan's assessment the risk of going against this "formidable array of SAMs is very high" and therefore justified the use of stealth fighters to reduce the risks to aircrews.[130] Ryan's boss, Admiral Smith, supported his request, stating that "we should therefore pit our strengths against BSA weakness and that means [using the] F-117."[131] On the same day, Admiral Smith approved and forwarded his request to Gen George Joulwan, Supreme Allied Commander Europe (SACEUR), for immediate action.[132] Smith also sent a message that day to the Italian Ministry of Defense (MOD) requesting permission to bed down six F-117A aircraft at Aviano AB for at least a 30-day period.[133]

US secretary of defense William Perry approved the F-117 deployment at 0051Z on 9 September for a period not to exceed 60 days. The aircraft and their associated crews and support equipment were to deploy to Aviano immediately. The secretary further directed that General Joulwan, who was also commander in chief of US European Command (USCINCEUR), take the lead in obtaining diplomatic clearances for all deploying aircraft.[134] Given the potential diplomatic sensitivity of the pending deployment, General Joulwan sent a message to the commander in chief of US Atlantic Command, whose command would be releasing the F-117s to European Command (EUCOM), emphasizing the proper procedures for clearing the deployment with the appropriate governments: "HQ USEU-COM is the single-point facilitator for obtaining host nation approvals of all country clearances. Requests should be made [in accordance with] foreign clearance guide instructions. . . . No US personnel are authorized to enter any host nation until specifically cleared by the country team."[135]

On that same day—9 September—F-117 maintenance personnel and support equipment began arriving at Aviano to support the F-117 beddown. But the Italian government had yet to give formal approval for the deployment. In pressing the matter with the Italians, US ambassador Reginald Bartholomew discovered that the holdup apparently was due to Italian prime minister Lamberto Dini's absence from the country. This left the diplomatic initiative in the hands of Italian foreign minister Susanna Agnelli, whose communications on the issue had already impressed Bartholomew with their "vehemence." She evidently failed to see any sense of urgency about the matter that would require her to contact Dini about the request. Bartholomew also conveyed in his message that the prime minister had told him and US ambassador Richard Holbrooke on 7 September that "requests for support of Bosnia operations beyond the support currently approved would be reviewed at political levels in terms of the responsiveness of others to Italy's participation in the contact group."[136] Later, Foreign Minister Agnelli emphatically told Bartholomew that Italy was "tired of always saying yes to others while others always say no to Italy!"[137]

The US ambassador felt that the Italians were in a "high political spin" on the issue, mainly as a consequence of the slight they felt from not having been made a member of the Contact Group conducting negotiations with the Serbs, and from their relations with other members of the European Union. While acknowledging their concerns, Bartholomew told the Italians that there were limits on what the United States could do for them in these areas. Two days later, on 11 September 1995, the Italian MOD advised NATO that the F-117 deployment was "not authorized."[138]

Force Issues

Eight participating nations comprised the Deliberate Force multinational alliance: France, Germany, Italy, the Netherlands, Spain, Turkey, the United Kingdom, and the United States. Although the multinational effort successfully accomplished mission objectives, alliance relationships sometimes became strained and affected the forces.

For example, long-standing intra-NATO diplomatic tensions hampered the deployment of 10 Turkish TF-16s to participate in Deliberate Force, mentioned previously. On 30 August, at CINCSOUTH's request, Supreme Headquarters Allied Powers Europe—NATO's military headquarters—recalled the Turkish fighters in support of the operation. Turkey responded positively to the request and asked permission to overfly Greek airspace on the way to Italy.[139] Acting consistently with a long history of strained relations with Turkey and NATO on such issues, Greece rejected the Turkish request.[140] Despite the urgency of the situation, the Greek authorities stated that "the overflight request should have been made on a weekday and five days prior to the flight," the normal procedure for routine operations.[141] The TF-16s did deploy to Italy but arrived late after circumnavigating Greek national airspace.

Differing political assessments of the situation in Bosnia by the governments of the Netherlands, Germany, Turkey, and Italy, in part, led them to restrict the kinds of operations their air forces could perform. Dutch aircraft, for instance, flew only CAP, OAS, and recce missions, and the Germans' restrictions on NATO's use of their ECR and IDS Tornados became a significant limitation. Because Germany would not authorize missions in direct support of the RRF, the latter had to request support in order for the CAOC to schedule either of these types of aircraft. The CAOC met the RRF's recce requests by using German IDS recce escorted by ECRs. Also, the Turkish government limited its aircraft to CAP missions in protection of the UN ground forces. Lastly, political pressures within the Italian government and postconflict relationships with neighbors across the Adriatic Sea resulted in the Italian air force's coming into the fight about a week late, and its aircraft flew only OAS, aerial refueling, and airlift missions. The political background to these decisions to limit participation is complex and beyond the scope of this chapter. Nevertheless, the limitations had a direct effect on the planning and execution of the air campaign. Most importantly, they shifted the burden of flying most of the more dangerous strike sorties onto the air forces whose governments left them free to conduct offensive operations. Clearly, the domestic political dynamics of coalition partners is an important area of thought for future air leaders and planners.

In general the CFACC had adequate numbers and types of aircraft to perform missions and maintain the requisite operational tempo of Deliberate Force. Still, an examination of the mix of aircraft available to him and of the mission loads they carried indicates some force-structure imbalances (see table 8.5). Some mission areas enjoyed a relative abundance of aircraft and platforms, while others could have used some augmentation. For example, once operations were under way, tactical reconnaissance, early warning, ELINT, and other support units flew almost double the sortie rate originally anticipated for them by NATO air planners. This increased rate required the deployment of augmentation forces into the theater, mostly from the USAF.

One also notes a possible surplus of aircraft allocated to perform CAP. A little over one-fifth of the platforms flew less than 10 percent of the mission tasking. Perhaps the CFACC could have reassigned some of these aircraft to other mission categories without compromising the OCA mission. However, because some of the allies deployed with a predetermined mission, especially in the air-to-air role, General Ryan's flexibility was probably more restricted than it appears.

The SEAD allocation also bears closer examination. Although, in raw numbers, assets allocated to SEAD represented about one-fifth of the total aircraft employed in Deliberate Force, differential capabilities existed in the mix of assets provided. Of the 56 SEAD platforms available, 50 were capable of firing HARMs while 22 were jammers, and 16 could both jam and shoot HARMs. Because of this mixed capability, Deliberate Force planners resorted to creating SEAD "windows" over Bosnia, whereby jammers and shooters provided common-use support to a cluster of strike packages rather than remaining tied to a particular package.

Table 8.5

Allocation and Apportionment of Aircraft in Deliberate Force

Mission	Allocation		Apportionment	
	No. of Assets	%	No. of Sorties	%
CAP	64	22.3	294	08.3
SEAD	56	19.5	785	22.2
CAS/BAI	87	30.3	1,365	38.6
Recce	18	06.3	312	08.8
Support	62	21.6	779	22.1
Total	287	100.0	3,535	100.0

A subtle imbalance also existed in the structure of forces allocated to the CAS and AI missions. At one level the allocated mix of CAS and AI aircraft was adequate to accomplish the mission tasking of Deliberate Force. Indeed, informal interviews conducted by the Balkans Air Campaign Study team members with F-15E, F-16, F/A-18, and A-10 pilots indicated that some felt underutilized during the campaign. Still, from the start of operations, the demand for precision-weapons-capable aircraft pressed the capacity of the available fleet more than the number of available precision and nonprecision aircraft would indicate. The great pressure on NATO commanders to minimize casualties and collateral damage meant that precision weapons had to be used in the majority of all strikes. Fortunately for the intervention, the Spanish, French, British, and American air forces fielded enough precision-strike aircraft to do the job, and they likely would have deployed more into the fray had combat requirements increased. Thus, the real conclusion about precision strikers in Deliberate Force is that the political circumstances of the campaign created a greater demand for precision than for nonprecision strike aircraft. Given the availability of adequate types and numbers of precision weapons, the suitable uses of nonprecision weapons are decreasing.

The allocation of aircraft to on-call CAS during Deliberate Force also bears close examination. Tying air forces to directly supporting ground-component combat operations on a prolonged or routine basis reduces their flexibility. But under many circumstances, CAS is an extremely important mission, both militarily and emotionally, given its ability to underpin the success of ground operations and to reduce near-term casualties. Historically, CAS allocations have often been inflated, compared to the number of missions actually flown. As a case in point, over 30 percent of the sorties were tasked on Deliberate Force air tasking messages for CAS; just over 1 percent actually flew such missions. Under the circumstances, of course, plenty of aircraft were available to stand CAS alert. But under circumstances in which the requirements of the overall air campaign are more demanding in relation to the forces available, the practice of designating CAS alert missions demands review. This is particularly true, given the availability of other techniques of providing responsive CAS—such as maintaining ground-alert windows or redirecting interdiction missions to answer critical but sporadic calls for help.

In the main, the support aircraft available for Deliberate Force met mission requirements. Early or transient shortages did occur in a few areas, such as tanker support and the availability of ABCCC aircraft, but force transfers from outside the theater quickly rectified these incipient problems. Given the small scale and short duration of Deliberate Force, such augmentations did not challenge the capabilities of the US Air Force. But because worldwide shortages of some types of aircraft do exist, as is the case with tactical reconnaissance, SEAD, and ABCCC platforms, future air planners should look carefully at plans that depend on their ready availability.

Notes

1. See Air Force Manual (AFM) 1-1, *Basic Aerospace Doctrine of the United States Air Force*, vol. 2, March 1992, essay D, 27.

2. COMAIRSOUTH, Operation Deliberate Force "Factual Review," 14 October 1995 (Secret) Information extracted is unclassified, US Air Force Historical Research Agency (hereinafter AFHRA), Maxwell AFB, Ala., NPL-07.

3. Ibid. (Secret) Information extracted is unclassified.

4. Message, 131338Z Aug 95, commander in chief of US European Command (USCINCEUR) to CINCSOUTH, 13 August 1995 (Secret) Information extracted is unclassified, AFHRA, NPL-14-02.

5. Message, 180930Z Aug 95, Italian Ministry of Defense to CINCSOUTH, 18 August 1995 (Secret) Information extracted is unclassified, AFHRA, Balkans Air Campaign Study special collections archive.

6. Message, 281817Z Aug 95, CINCSOUTH to AIRSOUTH plans cell, 28 August 1995 (Secret) Information extracted is unclassified, AFHRA, Balkans Air Campaign Study special collections archive.

7. Deny Flight Logistics Report, 282100Z Aug 95 (Secret) Information extracted is unclassified, AFHRA, AVI-05/06.

8. Message, 301726Z Aug 95, CINCSOUTH to AIRSOUTH plans cell, 30 August 1995 (Secret) Information extracted is unclassified, AFHRA, Balkans Air Campaign Study special collections archive.

9. Message, 311914Z Aug 95, CINCSOUTH to AIRSOUTH plans cell, 31 August 1995 (Secret) Information extracted is unclassified, AFHRA, Balkans Air Campaign Study special collections archive.

10. Message, 051534Z Sep 95, CINCSOUTH to AIRSOUTH plans cell, 5 September 1995 (Secret) Information extracted is unclassified, AFHRA, Balkans Air Campaign Study special collections archive.

11. Message, 050815Z Sep 95, TGS [Turkish government sends] to AIR-SOUTH plans cell (information only), 5 September 1995 (Secret) Information extracted is unclassified, AFHRA, Balkans Air Campaign Study special collections archive.

12. Message, 081418Z Sep 95, CINCSOUTH to AIRSOUTH plans cell, 8 September 1995 (Confidential) Information extracted is unclassified, AFHRA, Balkans Air Campaign Study special collections archive.

13. "Factual Review," 2-8. (Secret) Information extracted is unclassified.

14. Message, 081639Z Sep 95, CINCSOUTH to AIRSOUTH plans cell, 8 September 1995. (Secret) Information extracted is unclassified.

15. The term *offensive air operations (OAS)* is derived from CINCSOUTH Operations Plan 40101 "Deny Flight" Concept of Operations, annex D, change 4, 3 May 1995.

16. In fact, none of the enemy MiGs ever challenged the coalition; thus, no air-to-air engagements and/or shootdowns occurred during Deliberate Force.

17. *The Encyclopedia of Modern Warplanes* (New York: Aerospace Publishing, Ltd., 1995), 104.

18. Extracted from CAOC daily mission summaries, 29 August–14 September 1995 (Confidential) Information extracted is unclassified, AFHRA, CAOC-15.

19. *Encyclopedia of Modern Warplanes,* 123.

20. Extracted from CAOC daily mission summaries, 29 August–14 September 1995 (Confidential) Information extracted is unclassified, AFHRA, CAOC-15.

21. Ibid. (Confidential) Information extracted is unclassified.

22. *Encyclopedia of Modern Warplanes,* 78.

23. Extracted from CAOC daily mission summaries, 29 August–14 September 1995 (Confidential) Information extracted is unclassified, AFHRA, CAOC-15.

24. Ibid. (Confidential) Information extracted is unclassified.

25. *Encyclopedia of Modern Warplanes,* 131.

26. Multi-Command Manual (MCM) 3-1, vol. 1, *Tactical Employment, General Planning & Employment Considerations,* attachment 6, *Guide to Aircraft Combat Capabilities,* 17 March 1995, 8-6. (Secret) Information extracted is unclassified.

27. *Encyclopedia of Modern Warplanes,* 179.

28. Extracted from CAOC daily mission summaries, 29 August–14 September 1995 (Confidential) Information extracted is unclassified, AFHRA, CAOC-15.

29. *Encyclopedia of Modern Warplanes,* 127.

30. Extracted from CAOC daily mission summaries, 29 August–14 September 1995; and unit mission logs (Confidential) Information extracted is unclassified, AFHRA, CAOC-15.

31. MCM 3-1, vol. 1, 8-14. (Secret) Information extracted is unclassified. See also *Encyclopedia of Modern Warplanes,* 123.

32. *Encyclopedia of Modern Warplanes,* 180.

33. Extracted from CAOC daily mission summaries, 29 August–14 September 1995; and unit mission logs (Confidential) Information extracted is unclassified, AFHRA, CAOC-15.

34. Ibid. (Confidential) Information extracted is unclassified.

35. *Encyclopedia of Modern Warplanes*, 225.

36. Extracted from CAOC daily mission summaries, 29 August–14 September 1995 (Confidential) Information extracted is unclassified, AFHRA, CAOC-15.

37. Ibid. (Confidential) Information extracted is unclassified.

38. AFM 1-1, vol. 2, 106.

39. Joint Publication (Pub) 1-02, *Department of Defense Dictionary of Military and Associated Terms;* on-line, Internet, 12 August 1999, available from http://131.84.1.34/doctrine/jel/doddict/data/a/00265.html. This is both the US and NATO definition.

40. No US joint definition exists for BAI. It remains, however, a NATO term covered in NATO Pub AAP-6 and is now termed "indirect air support" (NATO): "support given to land or sea forces by air action against objectives other than enemy forces engaged in tactical battle. It includes the gaining and maintaining of air superiority, interdiction, and harassing." Joint Pub 1-02; on-line, Internet, 12 August 1999, available from http://www.dtic.mil/doctrine/jel/doddict/natoterm/i/00403.html.

41. This is the US definition. The NATO definition is similar but would be included under the general definition of "close support." Joint Pub 1-02; on-line, Internet, 12 August 1999, available from http://131.84.1.34/doctrine/jel/doddict/data/c/01182.html.

42. *Encyclopedia of Modern Warplanes*, 123.

43. Extracted from CAOC daily mission summaries, 29 August–14 September 1995; and unit mission logs (Confidential) Information extracted is unclassified, AFHRA, CAOC-15.

44. *Encyclopedia of Modern Warplanes*, 119.

45. Extracted from CAOC daily mission summaries, 29 August–14 September 1995; and unit mission logs (Confidential) Information extracted is unclassified, AFHRA, CAOC-15.

46. *Encyclopedia of Modern Warplanes*, 178.

47. Extracted from CAOC daily mission summaries, 29 August–14 September 1995; and unit mission logs (Confidential) Information extracted is unclassified, AFHRA, CAOC-15.

48. *Encyclopedia of Modern Warplanes*, 154.

49. Extracted from CAOC daily mission summaries, 29 August–14 September 1995; and unit mission logs (Confidential) Information extracted is unclassified, AFHRA, CAOC-15.

50. Extracted from CAOC daily mission summaries, 29 August–14 September 1995 (Confidential) Information extracted is unclassified, AFHRA, CAOC-15.

51. *Encyclopedia of Modern Warplanes*, 131.

52. Extracted from CAOC daily mission summaries, 29 August–14 September 1995 (Confidential) Information extracted is unclassified, AFHRA, CAOC-15.

53. Ibid. (Confidential) Information extracted is unclassified.

54. *Encyclopedia of Modern Warplanes*, 242.

55. Extracted from CAOC daily mission summaries, 29 August–14 September 1995 (Confidential) Information extracted is unclassified, AFHRA, CAOC-15.

56. *Encyclopedia of Modern Warplanes*, 104.

57. Extracted from CAOC daily mission summaries, 29 August–14 September 1995 (Confidential) Information extracted is unclassified, AFHRA, CAOC-15.

58. *Encyclopedia of Modern Warplanes*, 223.

59. Extracted from CAOC daily mission summaries, 29 August–14 September 1995 (Confidential) Information extracted is unclassified, AFHRA, CAOC-15.

60. Colonel Paladini, ITAF/DO, memorandum to Col Daniel R. Zoerb, director of the AIRSOUTH Deny Flight operations cell, subject: Lack of Pilot Proficiency on Tankers, 7 September 1995, AFHRA, NPL-14-02.

61. Extracted from CAOC daily mission summaries, 29 August–14 September 1995 (Confidential) Information extracted is unclassified, AFHRA, CAOC-15.

62. *Encyclopedia of Modern Warplanes*, 182.

63. Extracted from CAOC daily mission summaries, 29 August–14 September 1995 (Confidential) Information extracted is unclassified, AFHRA, CAOC-15.

64. *Encyclopedia of Modern Warplanes*, 78.

65. Extracted from CAOC daily mission summaries, 29 August–14 September 1995 (Confidential) Information extracted is unclassified, AFHRA, CAOC-15.

66. AFM 1-1, vol. 1, p. 3-6.

67. *Encyclopedia of Modern Warplanes*, 62.

68. Extracted from CAOC daily mission summaries, 29 August–14 September 1995 (Confidential) Information extracted is unclassified, AFHRA, CAOC-15.

69. USAF fact sheet, no. 88-28, December 1988, Office of the Secretary of the Air Force/Public Affairs, Washington, D.C.

70. Extracted from CAOC daily mission summaries, 29 August–14 September 1995 (Confidential) Information extracted is unclassified, AFHRA, CAOC-15.

71. *Encyclopedia of Modern Warplanes*, 160.

72. Extracted from CAOC daily mission summaries, 29 August–14 September 1995 (Confidential) Information extracted is unclassified, AFHRA, CAOC-15.

73. *Encyclopedia of Modern Warplanes*, 62.

74. Extracted from CAOC daily mission summaries, 29 August–14 September 1995 (Confidential) Information extracted is unclassified, AFHRA, CAOC-15.

75. *Encyclopedia of Modern Warplanes*, 156.

76. Extracted from CAOC daily mission summaries, 29 August–14 September 1995; and unit mission logs (Confidential) Information extracted is unclassified, AFHRA, CAOC-15.

77. Unit mission logs. (Confidential) Information extracted is unclassified.

78. AFM 1-1, vol. 1, p. 14.

79. MCM 3-1, vol. 1, 7-24. (Secret) Information extracted is unclassified.

80. CMC (I,) AIRSOUTH, memorandum to CINCSOUTH chief of staff, subject: The Way Ahead with Air Recce, 5 June 1995, AFHRA, NPL-22-01.

81. *Encyclopedia of Modern Warplanes*, 102.

82. Extracted from CAOC daily mission summaries, 29 August–14 September 1995 (Confidential) Information extracted is unclassified, AFHRA, CAOC-15.

83. Ibid. (Confidential) Information extracted is unclassified.

84. Ibid. (Confidential) Information extracted is unclassified.

85. Ibid. (Confidential) Information extracted is unclassified.

86. Ibid. (Confidential) Information extracted is unclassified.

87. Ibid. (Confidential) Information extracted is unclassified.

88. Ibid. (Confidential) Information extracted is unclassified.

89. Ibid. (Confidential) Information extracted is unclassified.

90. *Encyclopedia of Modern Warplanes*, 130.

91. Ibid., 169.

92. Extracted from CAOC daily mission summaries, 29 August–14 September 1995 (Confidential) Information extracted is unclassified, AFHRA, CAOC-15.

93. In the evolution of unmanned aircraft platforms, earlier schools referred to them as *remotely piloted vehicles*. Presently, the term applied to these aircraft is *unmanned aerial vehicles*. Regardless of the semantics, they are both unmanned, remotely controlled, data-linked airframes.

94. Thomas A. Keaney and Eliot A. Cohen, *Gulf War Air Power Survey*, vol. 2, *Operations and Effects and Effectiveness* (Washington, D.C.: Government Printing Office, 1993), pt. 1, 231.

95. Facsimile, "TEZ Monitoring with RPV," routine correspondence from Headquarters Bosnia-Herzegovina Command to Headquarters UNPROFOR, 5 May 1994, AFHRA, NPL-23-05.

96. Extracted from CAOC daily mission summaries, 29 August–14 September 1995 (Confidential) Information extracted is unclassified, AFHRA, CAOC-15.

97. MSgt Dale Warman, "Air Force Squadron Takes Over Predator Operations," United States Air Forces in Europe/Public Affairs, Air Force News Service, 5 September 1996.

98. Extracted from CAOC daily mission summaries, 29 August–14 September 1995 (Confidential) Information extracted is unclassified, AFHRA,

CAOC-15; and Corona briefing slides, Lt Gen Michael Ryan, 5 December 1995, AFHRA, CAOC-13.

99. Message, CINCSOUTH to COMUNPROFOR, subject: BSA Noncompliance and Resumption of Air Strikes, 6 September 1995 (Confidential) Information extracted is unclassified, AFHRA, NPL-15-01.

100. See the previous discussion about recce platforms for information about the U-2R's contribution of 10 sorties to the ELINT mission. EC-130Hs flew 35 ELINT missions, but that platform is described in the electronic-combat section of this chapter.

101. Extracted from CAOC daily mission summaries, 29 August–14 September 1995 (Confidential) Information extracted is unclassified, AFHRA, CAOC-15.

102. Ibid. (Confidential) Information extracted is unclassified.

103. *Encyclopedia of Modern Warplanes*, 63.

104. Extracted from CAOC daily mission summaries, 29 August–14 September 1995 (Confidential) Information extracted is unclassified, AFHRA, CAOC-15.

105. *Encyclopedia of Modern Warplanes*, 75.

106. Extracted from CAOC daily mission summaries, 29 August–14 September 1995 (Confidential) Information extracted is unclassified, AFHRA, CAOC-15.

107. *Encyclopedia of Modern Warplanes*, 269.

108. Extracted from CAOC daily mission summaries, 29 August–14 September 1995 (Confidential) Information extracted is unclassified, AFHRA, CAOC-15.

109. Ibid. (Confidential) Information extracted is unclassified.

110. MCM 3-1, vol. 1, 8-6. (Secret) Information extracted is unclassified.

111. *Encyclopedia of Modern Warplanes*, 129.

112. MCM 3-1, vol. 1, 8-7. (Secret) Information extracted is unclassified.

113. Extracted from CAOC daily mission summaries, 29 August–14 September 1995 (Confidential) Information extracted is unclassified, AFHRA, CAOC-15.

114. Ibid. (Confidential) Information extracted is unclassified. Note that the 35 Compass Call missions were logged as ELINT missions and not as electronic-combat or electronic-support missions.

115. Christopher Chant, ed., *The Presidio Concise Guide to Military Aircraft of the World* (Novato, Calif.: Presidio Press, 1981), 36–38.

116. Extracted from CAOC daily mission summaries, 29 August–14 September 1995 (Confidential) Information extracted is unclassified, AFHRA, CAOC-15.

117. Ibid. (Confidential) Information extracted is unclassified.

118. *Encyclopedia of Modern Warplanes*, 157.

119. Extracted from CAOC daily mission summaries, 29 August–14 September 1995 (Confidential) Information extracted is unclassified, AFHRA, CAOC-15.

120. Ibid. (Confidential) Information extracted is unclassified.

121. *Encyclopedia of Modern Warplanes*, 155.

122. Extracted from CAOC daily mission summaries, 29 August–14 September 1995 (Confidential) Information extracted is unclassified, AFHRA, CAOC-15.

123. CAOC records indicate that the aircraft flew, but the flights were not logged. Because one cannot determine the total number of sorties flown, they are not included in support-sortie totals.

124. Ibid.

125. Extracted from CAOC daily mission summaries, 29 August–14 September 1995 (Confidential) Information extracted is unclassified, AFHRA, CAOC-15.

126. MCM 3-1, vol. 1, attachment 6, A6-33, through -34. (Secret) Information extracted is unclassified.

127. Major Rincon, "Talking Paper on Joint STARS Demonstration in NATO's Southern Tier," Office of the Secretary of the Air Force/IASW, 22 September 1994, AFHRA, NPL-23-06.

128. Ibid.

129. Gen Hal Hornburg, CAOC director, videotaped interview by members of the Balkans Air Campaign Study, Maxwell AFB, Ala., 14 March 1996 (Confidential) Information extracted is unclassified, AFHRA, Misc-20.

130. Message, 081100Z Sep 95, CINCSOUTH to SACEUR, subject: IADS West, 8 September 1995 (Secret) Information extracted is unclassified, AFHRA, NPL-15-01.

131. Ibid. (Secret) Information extracted is unclassified.

132. Ibid. (Secret) Information extracted is unclassified. See also message, 081639Z Sep 95, CINCSOUTH to Supreme Headquarters Allied Powers Europe, subject: Request for Aircraft, 8 September 1995, AFHRA, NPL-15-01.

133. Message, 081706Z Sep 95, CINCSOUTH to RIFD/Italian Ministry of Defense, DGS, subject: Beddown Request for F-117A Aircraft, 8 September 1995 (Secret) Information extracted is unclassified, AFHRA, NPL-15-01.

134. Message, 090051Z Sep 95, chairman of the Joint Chiefs of Staff, Washington, D.C., to USCINCEUR, subject: Deployment of Fighter Aircraft for Deny Flight, 9 September 1995. (Secret) Information extracted is unclassified, AFHRA, NPL-15-01.

135. Message, 090935Z Sep 95, USCINCEUR to CINCUSACOM, subject: Command Relationships, 9 September 1995 (Secret) Information extracted is unclassified, AFHRA, NPL-15-01.

136. Message, ambassador, United States Embassy, Rome, to CINCSOUTH, subject: Government of Italy's Delay in Approving NATO F-117A Deployments to Italy, 9 September 1995 (Confidential) Information extracted is unclassified, AFHRA, NPL-15-01.

137. Ibid. (Confidential) Information extracted is unclassified.

138. Message, 111125Z Sep 95, Italian Ministry of Defense, Rome, to CINCSOUTH, subject: Beddown Request for F-117A Aircraft, 11 September 1995 (Confidential) Information extracted is unclassified, AFHRA, NPL-15-01.

139. Message, 050815Z Sep 95, TGS (Turkey) to Supreme Headquarters Allied Powers Europe, subject: Greek Rejection of Turkish Overflight Request, 5 September 1995 (NATO Confidential) Information extracted is unclassified, AFHRA, NPL-15-01.

140. Ibid. (NATO Confidential) Information extracted is unclassified.

141. Ibid. (NATO Confidential) Information extracted is unclassified.

Chapter 9

Weapons Used in Deliberate Force

Lt Col Richard L. Sargent

With respect to combat airpower, "weapons should be selected based on their ability to influence an adversary's capability and will."[1] With regard to Deliberate Force's mission-execution issues, the constraints on force application entailed avoiding collateral effects and unintended consequences that would be counterproductive to the political peace process. This effort to avoid collateral and unintended damage extended not only to the surrounding physical targets but also to concerns about fratricide, refugees, and noncombatant civilian casualties.[2] The need for precision offensive air operations (OAS) platforms and weapons to limit collateral damage while accomplishing mission objectives became an overriding concern during the Balkans air campaign. Thus, precision-guided munitions (PGM) became the overwhelming weapons of choice during air strike operations. Indeed, Deliberate Force became the first air campaign in history to employ more precision-guided bombs and missiles than unguided ones.

Described as "revolutionary" in Operation Desert Storm, PGMs came to fruition during Deliberate Force. The multinational effort expended 1,026 bombs and missiles (excluding cannon shells, rockets, and high-speed antiradiation missiles [HARM]), of which 708 (69 percent) were precision guided by laser, electro-optical (EO), or infrared (IR) sensors.[3] Although the total bomb tonnage amounted to fewer than five hundred tons—less than 1 percent of the 70,000 tons dropped in Desert Storm,[4]—the proportion of precision-guided ordnance employed in Deliberate Force was more than eight times greater than the percentage of PGMs used in the Gulf War air campaign (8 percent).[5]

This chapter discusses the abundance of air-to-surface weapons, both precision and nonprecision, available to North Atlantic Treaty Organization (NATO) forces during Deliberate Force. It also notes some precision weapons not used by the combined forces and concludes by addressing weapons issues that arose as a result of the air campaign.

Precision-Guided Munitions

With respect to force and weapons capabilities, "weapons selection comprises one of the highest-leverage means of tailoring forces to accomplish missions."[6] Precision capability drove the OAS mission roles of coalition platforms; only the United States, United Kingdom, France, and Spain had fighter-bombers capable of employing PGMs. Of the 708 PGMs dropped or fired during Deliberate Force, the United States expended 622 (87.8 percent), followed by the United Kingdom with 48 (6.8 percent), Spain with 24 (3.4 percent), and France with 14 (2 percent) (table 9.1). Given their visual-attack capability, Dutch, German,

Table 9.1

Deliberate Force's Precision Munitions

	France	Germany	Italy	Netherlands	Spain	United Kingdom	United States	Total
Laser-Guided:								
GBU-10							303	303
GBU-12	10						115	125
GBU-16					24	48	143	215
GBU-24							6	6
AS-30L	4							4
Totals	14	0	0	0	24	48	567	653
EO/IR:								
SLAM							10	10
GBU-15							9	9
AGM-65							23	23
Totals	0	0	0	0	0	0	42	42
TLAM							13	13
Total	14	0	0	0	24	48	622	708

Source: Extracted from Corona briefing slides, Lt Gen Michael Ryan, Headquarters AIRSOUTH, Naples, Italy, subject: Munitions (left-side slide no. 44), 5 December 1995, United States Air Force Historical Research Agency (AFHRA), Maxwell AFB, Ala., H-3.

Italian, or Turkish aircraft employed nonprecision munitions on area targets in which collateral-damage risks were minimal or not a concern.

Laser-Guided Bombs

Laser-guided bombs (LGB) are ballistic warheads equipped with electronic and mechanical assemblies designed to provide laser terminal guidance. One can attach such laser-guidance kits to a variety of warheads, including but not limited to general-purpose (GP) bombs, special-purpose bombs, and warheads developed and produced by other allied countries. Such a kit consists of a computer-control group and wing assembly, the former mounted at the front of the warhead and made up of a detector unit, computer section, and control unit. The wing assembly is attached both to a GP warhead and to the rear of the bomb body to provide stability and increased lift.[7] The laser-guidance system directs the bomb towards a laser "spot" reflected from the target and received by the bomb's detector. This spot may be projected by the delivery aircraft or, more commonly, by another aircraft equipped with a laser designator (referred to as "buddy designation") or by a ground unit.

- *GBU-10/10I*—a MK-84 2,000 lb GP bomb modified for laser guidance. A Paveway II variant, the GBU-10I is based on the I-2000 (BLU-109) penetration bomb, while the GBU-10 comes in both the earlier Paveway I and the Paveway II variants.[8] During the Gulf War, F-15Es and F-111s used GBU-10/10Is extensively, mainly against bridges; Scud missiles; and hardened command, control, communications, and intelligence (C³I) nodes and bunkers. During Deliberate Force only US aircraft used GBU-10/10Is, with most of the 303 bombs (46 percent of all LGBs used) dropped by F-15Es and F-16Cs from Aviano Air Base (AB), Italy. The F-16Cs' first combat use of LGBs came with their employment of the GBU-10. NATO aircraft released only 252 GBU-10s over Bosnia-Herzegovina against bridges, bunkers, and C³I nodes; F-16s jettisoned the remaining 51 in the Adriatic Sea because weather

259

obscuration in the target area prevented the aircraft from dropping them. The aircraft also had to jettison to lighten gross weight for divert fuel if the Aviano AB runway happened to close.

- *GBU-12*—a US 500 lb MK-82 GP bomb with an added GBU/Paveway I or II laser-guidance package.[9] During Desert Storm, F-111Fs, F-15Es, and A-6s employed GBU-12s, mostly against armored vehicles. During Deliberate Force both the French and the Americans dropped these bombs. Of the 125 GBU-12s expended, French Mirage 2000D/Ks dropped 10 (their first combat use of LGBs), and US aircraft dropped the remaining 115 against various soft-point targets and some artillery tubes.

- *GBU-16*—a 1,000 lb MK-83 GP bomb fitted with a Paveway II laser-guidance kit. The GBU-16 is normally associated with the US Navy, US Marine Corps, and some NATO countries; the US Air Force (USAF) does not carry a 1,000 lb GP bomb in its inventory. In Deliberate Force, Spanish, British, and US aircraft dropped a total of 215 GBU-16s. Spanish EF-18s dropped 24 of these bombs; British Harrier GR-7s expended 48, typically in flights of two accompanied by a Jaguar GR-1 as the buddy designator; and US Navy and Marine F/A-18C and D Hornets dropped the remaining 143.

- *GBU-24*—a 2,000 lb GP bomb, either an MK-84 or a BLU-109, modified with a GBU/Paveway III low-level laser-guided bomb (LLLGB) package, with improved guidance and flight-control systems. The LLLGB was designed for employment at high speed and very low altitudes to increase standoff range and reduce the launching aircraft's exposure in high-threat target areas. Although aircraft in the Gulf War employed nearly twelve hundred GBU-24s,[10] Deliberate Force aircraft released only six, all by F-15Es and primarily against bridges. Despite the F-15E aircrews' preference for employing GBU-24s, the decision to use them came late in the campaign after encountering problems with the effectiveness of GBU-10/10Is against bridges.

Laser-Guided Missile

Laser-guided missiles use guidance systems similar to those on LGBs but attached to air-to-surface missiles instead of unpowered bombs. The only laser-guided missile used during Deliberate Force was the French AS-30L. Mirage 2000/D/Ks fitted with laser pods for self-designation fired four of them.

Electro-Optical/Infrared-Sensor-Guided Munitions

- *AGM-65 Maverick*—a US-made 500 lb or 650 lb air-to-surface missile with a shaped-charge warhead designed for attacking armored vehicles or other hardened targets. Prior to launch, an EO- or IR-guided variant of the Maverick missile must acquire its target, after which the missile guides autonomously, providing tactical-standoff "launch and leave" capability at beyond-visual ranges. The USAF uses four AGM-65 variants: the EO (TV-sensor) AGM-65A and B models as well as the IR-sensor AGM-65D and larger G models.[11] The IR Mavericks can be slaved to onboard aircraft sensors, permitting more rapid target acquisition, improved target identification, and increased launch ranges. The IR sensor also allows use of the AGM-65 during darkness, against camouflaged targets, and in some adverse weather conditions. During Deliberate Force, A-10s fired all 23 of the Mavericks that were expended.[12]

- *AGM-84E standoff land-attack missile (SLAM)*—a 1,385 lb variant of the US Navy's Harpoon antiship missile designed for standoff strikes against heavily defended land targets and ships in harbor. Developed with "off-the-shelf" technology, the SLAM uses the airframe, engine, and 488 lb warhead of the Harpoon missile, the imaging IR terminal-guidance unit of the AGM-65D Maverick, the datalink capability of the AGM-62 Walleye glide bomb, and a Global Positioning System (GPS) receiver. The SLAM has EO and IR variants. In the primary mode of operation, technicians load the target location into the missile prior to launch, GPS provides midcourse guidance updates, and seeker IR video images provide terminal target acquisition.[13] This specialized PGM has a long-range standoff

261

AGM-65 Maverick

capability with pinpoint accuracy. In Deliberate Force, carrier-based US Navy F/A-18s fired 10 AGM-84Es against Bosnian Serb army (BSA) defenses around Banja Luka.

- *GBU-15 modular guided-weapon system*—a USAF glide bomb with interchangeable guidance (EO or IR), fuzing, and control systems selected according to the needs of a particular mission and fitted to either an MK-84 2,000 lb GP bomb or a BLU-109 I-2000 penetrator bomb. This

GBU-15

munition is designed for use against highly defended, hardened, high-value fixed targets by providing greater standoff range than a conventional LGB but with the same accuracy. After the aircraft releases the bomb towards the target area, it transmits datalinked TV or IR images that locate and identify the target and specific aiming point. During Deliberate Force, airlifters delivered 25 GBU-15s to Aviano AB, and USAF F-15Es dropped nine IR variants (five BLU-109 and four MK-84s) on several key air-defense targets around Banja Luka.

Cruise Missile

The BMG-109 Tomahawk land-attack missile (TLAM), the US Navy's conventionally armed cruise missile for attacking land targets, is carried aboard cruisers, destroyers, and submarines.[14] With a nominal range of six hundred nautical miles and powered by a turbofan engine following launch by a disposable rocket booster, the TLAM is a highly accurate, autonomously guided weapon that navigates using a terrain-contour-matching system. This system compares stored digital ground images with actual terrain-following radar images to determine the missile's position and make necessary course corrections. After identifying the target, the missile flies over it or initiates a vertical dive and attacks with its 1,000 lb high-explosive (TLAM-C) or cluster-munition warhead (TLAM-D). On 10 September 1995, in support of NATO air operations in northwest Bosnia, the cruiser USS *Normandy*, afloat in the Adriatic Sea, fired 13 TLAMs against integrated air defense system (IADS) targets in and around Banja Luka. Although TLAMs represented only 1.9 percent of all PGMs, their employment in support of Deliberate Force represented several firsts: the first Tomahawks used on European Command theater targets; the first used in an integrated suppression of enemy air defenses (SEAD) mission with coordination of tactical air operations; and the first used in direct support of NATO operations.[15]

Nonprecision Bombs

Nonprecision bombs fly unguided ballistic flight trajectories (free fall) after release from an aircraft. They include GP bombs with high-explosive warheads and cluster bomb units (CBU), which contain a large number of small submunitions or "bomblets." Their accuracy depends on the skill of an aircrewman who uses an onboard sighting cue to release the weapon at the proper point so that the trajectory carries it to the target or aiming point. Since the weapon falls without further guidance after release, unguided munitions are generally less accurate than guided ones. Nonprecision munitions accounted for more than 90 percent of the ordnance delivered in Desert Storm, but in Deliberate Force, NATO aircraft dropped 318 nonprecision munitions—less than half the number of PGMs (table 9.2).

General-Purpose Bombs

- *MK-82*—a US-made 500 lb GP bomb containing 192 pounds of Tritonal high-explosive filler.[16] The Dutch, French, and Italian air forces dropped 175 MK-82s during

Table 9.2

Deliberate Force's Nonprecision Bombs

Nation	GP Bombs				CBUs	Total/Nation
	MK-82	MK-83	MK-84	Total GPs		
France	71	2		73		73
Germany				0		0
Italy	10	40		50		50
Netherlands	94		42	136		136
Spain				0		0
United Kingdom		47		47		47
United States		10		10	2	12
Total	175	99	42	316	2	318

Source: Extracted from Corona briefing slides, Lt Gen Michael Ryan, Headquarters AIRSOUTH, Naples, Italy, subject: Munitions (right-side slide no. 45), 5 December 1995, AFHRA, Maxwell AFB, Ala., H-3.

Deliberate Force, accounting for 55 percent of all the unguided bombs used.

- *MK-83*—a 1,000 lb GP bomb containing 416 pounds of explosive.[17] Aircraft from Britain, Italy, the United States, and France dropped a total of 99 MK-83 iron bombs during Deliberate Force, accounting for 31 percent of all unguided bombs.

- *MK-84*—a 2,000 lb bomb, the largest used in the campaign, containing 945 pounds of explosive. F-16As of the Netherlands air force dropped 42 MK-84s during Deliberate Force, accounting for 13 percent of all unguided bombs.

Cluster Bomb Units

Cluster-munition dispensers carry a large number of small submunitions that distribute across a relatively wide area to facilitate attacks on targets such as infantry units; groups of vehicles; antiaircraft artillery (AAA) or surface-to-air missile (SAM) sites; and petroleum, oil, and lubricant facilities. The 960 lb CBU-87B/B consists of an SUU-65/B tactical-munitions dispenser plus 202 BLU-97A/B fragmentation and antiarmor submunitions.[18]

Planners decided not to use CBUs during Deliberate Force because their inaccuracy and wide dispersion pattern made them likely to cause collateral damage. However, a USAF A-10A dropped two CBU-87s during the first day of the campaign as a result of a miscommunication with the combined air operations center (CAOC). Evidently, on 30 August 1995, an A-10 (call sign Speedy 37) conducting a close air support mission requested clearance from the CAOC to drop ordnance on a BSA artillery/mortar position. Without regard to the aircraft's weapons load, CAOC gave approval to expend the ordnance, so Speedy 37 dropped all of its weapons, including a pair of CBU-87s. They scored a hit on the target but inflicted no collateral damage.

Other Munitions

In addition to guided and unguided bombs and missiles, several other types of air-to-surface munitions were used in Deliberate Force, including antiradiation missiles, rockets, and gun ammunition.

- *AGM-88 HARM*—the principal antiradiation missile used by the United States and several other allied air forces for SEAD missions. The HARM is designed to detect, home in on, and destroy radar emitters such as early warning, acquisition,

AGM-88 HARM

and tracking radars operating throughout a wide range of frequency bands. During Deliberate Force, NATO HARM-equipped aircraft included US Navy F/A-18Cs and EA-6Bs, US Marine Corps F/A-18Ds, USAF F-16 HARM Targeting System (HTS) aircraft, and Spanish EF-18s. A total of 56 HARMs were fired, 48 by US Navy and Marine aircraft, six by the F-16 HTS (their first combat use by F-16s), and the remaining two by Spain's EF-18s.

2.75-inch rocket

- *2.75-inch (70 mm) rockets*—unguided rockets carried in underwing pods and mainly used in Deliberate Force by USAF OA-10 airborne forward air controllers. These aircraft used two types in the campaign: (1) white phosphorous (WP) rockets for marking targets with smoke for incoming strikers and (2) high-explosive (HE) rockets for destroying light targets. A total of 187 WP[19] and 20 HE rockets[20] were fired during the course of the air campaign.

- *Guns*—internally mounted cannons for air combat or strafing. The A-10 and AC-130 gunships normally use their guns as primary air-to-ground weapons; only these aircraft made significant use of guns during Deliberate Force. The A-10 carries a GAU-8/A Avenger—a 30 mm, seven-barrel, Gatling-type cannon designed for attacking tanks and other

267

Loading an A-10's cannon

armored vehicles. The Avenger magazine holds up to 1,350 rounds of ammunition, normally a mix of armor-piercing incendiary and HE incendiary shells. Unfortunately, during the first day of the campaign, two A-10s experienced GAU-8 jams while strafing ground targets. An inspection revealed ammunition jammed in the gun chambers. Suspecting a bad lot of ammunition, crews replaced all of the A-10s' ammunition with new ammunition, eliminating any further incidents.[21] A-10s fired a total 10,086 rounds, strafing such targets as armored vehicles, trucks, and bunkers with remarkable precision.[22] The AC-130 Spectre gunship carries a variety of 20 mm and 40 mm rapid-fire cannons and a 105 mm M-102 howitzer that fires from the left side of the aircraft. During Deliberate Force, AC-130s attacked a variety of targets with impressive accuracy, firing 50 rounds of 40 mm and 350 rounds of 105 mm ammunition.

Nonmunition Items of Interest

The tactical air-launched decoy (TALD), an expendable US Navy and Marine unpowered-drone glide vehicle, usually is launched by an F-14 Tomcat, F/A-18 Hornet, or EA-6B Prowler to confuse enemy radars. The drone has a radar-cross-section-enhancement payload and/or an electronic-countermeasures-enhancement payload. Both enhancements create multiple false targets for threat radars while the TALD flies a wide spectrum of mission profiles, including variations in speed, range, and altitude.[23] During Deliberate Force, US Navy aircraft launched a total of 47 TALDs against the Bosnian Serb IADS.[24]

US aircraft that penetrated and operated in Bosnian airspace had to have an operable chaff-and-flare dispenser system for self-defense. Chaff bundles, dispensed manually or according to a preset program, enhance deception when aircraft penetrate a radar network and provide electronic-countermeasures self-protection when a radar-homing, air-to-air missile or SAM tracks or attacks the aircraft.[25] During Deliberate Force, Aviano-based US aircraft equipped with AN/ALE dispensers used 10,922 RR-170/A chaff cartridges.[26] The two most common US decoy flares are the MJU-7/B, used on fighters, and the MJU-10/B, used by larger aircraft such as the AC-130 or B-52.[27] During the operation, 1,591 MJU-7s and 89 MJU-10s lit the skies over Bosnia.[28]

Munitions Not Used

Although the demand for precision munitions remained high during Deliberate Force, not all PGMs in-theater or otherwise available to Allied Forces Southern Europe (AFSOUTH) were used. Most of these have ties with a particular weapons platform. For example, a hundred GBU-27 2,000 lb LGBs designed for the F-117 Nighthawk sat idle in Aviano's bomb dumps because the Italian government denied permission for F-117 basing. Similarly, USAF B-52s did not employ air-launched cruise missiles and Have Nap air-to-surface missiles. Further, the US Navy had additional PGM capability in the form of AGM-62B Walleye EO-guided bombs, AGM-65E/F laser-guided Mavericks, and AGM-123A Skipper laser-guided glide bombs but chose not to employ them.

If all the combined NATO forces had possessed PGM capability, Gen Michael Ryan, commander of Allied Air Forces Southern Europe, and his staff would not have planned to use any GP bombs or cluster munitions in the campaign. Thus, it is not surprising that many nonprecision munitions went unused. However, NATO aircraft without PGM capability had the task of striking visual-attack-area targets (those with a low probability of collateral damage) with GP bombs. Later, to ensure target destruction, a PGM mission followed up on these strikes because of the less-than-optimal accuracy of unguided bombing. The only nonprecision munition considered for use towards the end of Deliberate Force (around 13 September 1995) was the CBU-89 Gator mine for area denial and funneling of troops and equipment during BSA withdrawals. Planners decided not to employ the munition, however, because of the cease-fire and the desire to avoid noncombatant casualties, fratricide, and damage to civilian vehicles.

Finally, because of Deny Flight's air supremacy and in the absence of any challenge from Bosnian Serb MiGs, allied aircraft fired no air-to-air missiles during Deliberate Force. Similarly, although most coalition fighters carried 20 mm to 30 mm cannons, they did not use them for strafing.

Weapons Issues

The preponderant usage of PGMs in Deliberate Force indicates that accuracy played a key role in the employment of combat airpower by the combined forces—especially by US joint air forces. Precision weaponry allowed for a robust operations tempo, reduction of risks to aircrews, and degradation of BSA capability with minimal collateral damage. PGMs made the Balkans air campaign possible, allowing a relatively small force with limited objectives to have operational and strategic effects in a limited time.

Precision versus Nonprecision Weapons

Overall, the PGM to non-PGM ratio in Deliberate Force was a relatively high 2.3:1, compared to a ratio of only 1:11.5 during the Gulf War air campaign. The heavy reliance on PGMs reflects the concern of General Ryan and his staff for precision accuracy and avoidance of collateral damage, whereas in the Gulf War, collateral damage became a concern only in attacking a limited number of targets, particularly around Baghdad. Moreover, in Desert Storm the strike mix became an issue of tactical-bombing accuracy between "smart" platforms employing "dumb" bombs as opposed to dumb platforms employing smart bombs.[29] Learning from PGM use in Desert Storm, Deliberate Force planners tried to take the "dumb" out of the equation as much as possible, relying on smart platforms employing smart bombs to provide pinpoint accuracy. As mentioned above, however, some smart platforms with dumb bombs or vice versa attacked low-risk, visual-attack-area targets where collateral damage was not a concern.

Most of the allied platforms and weapons in Deliberate Force enjoyed the benefits of advanced technologies that began in the latter stages of the Vietnam War. Since the Gulf War, the number of smart aircraft that can drop and terminally guide laser and IR weapons has increased. Most notably, the F-15E, F-16C Blocks 40 and 50, F-16 HTS, F/A-18D, and F-14D can all designate their own PGMs. Although these aircraft, with their digital-electronic navigation, weapon-delivery systems, and sensors, have grown smarter, the weapons and interface with the aircraft have not kept pace. As discussed above, smart platforms interfacing with smart weapons still have their share of problems: (1) most aircraft can deliver all munitions, but only certain aircraft can provide terminal guidance; (2) dedicating PGMs to particular aircraft limits their utility; (3) retrofitting precision munitions to existing airframes causes various anomalies in software and airframe interoperability; and (4) the cost of smart technologies limits their quantity. Needless to say, these constraints tie certain aircraft to specific roles, creating difficulties in a 24-hour air-tasking cycle, as well as complicating tactical considerations for their employment.

Despite the problems of PGMs, their high probability of hitting the target, compared to the performance of nonprecision weapons, creates important results at the operational and strategic levels. Force-multiplier benefits derived from PGM usage include better probability of kill; more target damage with fewer bombs; fewer sorties and less fuel consumption; and, most importantly, enhancement of survivability by providing some standoff capability, thereby reducing the risk to aircrews and platforms.

Clearly, PGMs are the wave of the future, reflecting the principles of Joint Vision 2010. "Precision engagement is a core competency that directly links the core competencies of the Air Force to joint military operations. In 'Joint Vision 2010,' [former] Chairman of the Joint Chiefs of Staff Gen. John Shalikashvili terms precision engagement one of four operational concepts that joint forces will need to dominate an adversary in any conflict during the next century." According to Gen Ronald R. Fogleman, former Air Force chief of staff, "the essence of precision engagement is the ability to apply selective force against specific targets and achieve discrete and discriminant effects."[30] On applying this concept through the medium of air and space today and in the future, Fogleman noted that "our forces will be more precise and more effective, at day or night, in good weather or bad, whether delivering food or lethal ordnance. Technology has driven each military era's definition of precision. . . . In the 21st century, it will be possible to find, fix or track and target anything that moves on the surface of the earth. . . . This is an emerging reality that will dramatically change the conduct of warfare and the role of air and space power."[31] In reference to future global conflicts, former secretary of the Air Force Sheila E. Widnall observed that "the Air Force of the 21st century must offer options for the employment of force in measured but effective doses. To do so, the Air Force will rely on global awareness capabilities to support national decision-making and joint operations to determine military objectives and enable precise targeting. . . . Air and space forces will then apply power that is no less overwhelming because it is also discriminating."[32]

Because precision engagement will save the lives of friends, foes, and civilians by limiting collateral damage, the Air Force core competency of precision engagement, identified as such in *Global Engagement: A Vision for the 21st Century Air Force*, will remain a top priority in the next century. "It joins air and space superiority, global attack, rapid global mobility, information superiority and agile combat support as one of the fundamental capabilities that the Air Force provides the nation."[33]

If Deliberate Force indeed set a precedent for the use of PGMs in future conflicts, what about the fate of nonprecision weapons delivered by aircraft? Given a limited conflict that is anything short of another "real" war like the one with Iraq, General Ryan, Deliberate Force's combined force air component commander, answered that question by opining that "dumb bombs are dead!"[34]

Shortage of 24-Hour, All-Weather Standoff Weapons

Reiterating the concern of Gen Buster Glosson, US air component commander in the Gulf War, General Ryan expressed genuine concern for his airmen, believing that no target is worth a loss of life. Just as the obsession to negate collateral damage drove the usage of PGMs, so did concern for the survival of aircrews and aircraft against an ever present BSA threat drive the need for standoff PGM capability to ensure that strike aircraft remained outside of harm's way when they attacked their targets. Air supremacy and ingress/egress altitudes above 10,000 feet minimized much of the risk to aircrews by avoiding fire from small arms and most AAA and man-portable SAMs. However, even at medium altitudes, the threat of highly defended targets required a change in tactics for existing munitions and drove the desire for standoff weapons to avoid overflight of the target area. Tactics evolved around existing aircraft systems and weapons capability.

To avoid direct overflight, tacticians devised dynamic maneuvers with some degree of standoff to accomplish the mission with PGMs. For example, F-16s employing GBU-10s would "miniloft" (climb five to 10 degrees) at the release point, four to five nautical miles from the target, and "crank" (turn 40 degrees off the attack heading) away from the target while lasing during the bomb's time of fall. These employment tactics offered some standoff from short-range SAMs and radar-directed AAA. Aircraft could counter long-range SAM threats by popping up from terrain masking to place the release point inside the SAM's minimum engagement range. However, because aircraft in Deliberate Force operated at medium rather than low altitudes, they would find themselves in the SAM-engagement envelope unless they used electronic countermeasures or, better yet, stayed outside the SAM's range.

Generically considering SAM threats for medium-altitude ingress, some SAM systems can engage tactical aircraft at ranges of more than 40 nautical miles. The majority of precision bombs and missiles offer limited standoff capability against a sophisticated and redundant IADS. The problem with the USAF's GBU-15 modular guided-weapon system and the US Navy's AGM-84 SLAM extended-standoff capability is that only a few aircraft are capable of employing them. Also, because their cost limits the size of inventories, combat and training experience on their employment is relatively constrained. In an attempt to overcome the lack of all-weather, tactical standoff weapons, we now use strategic assets employing long-range conventional cruise missiles such as the B-52's Have Naps, air-launched cruise missiles, and AGM-130s as well as the US Navy's TLAMs. Unfortunately, these precision weapons are expensive, require long cycle times, and have small payloads.

Because of the high cost and limited numbers of cruise missiles, low-observable-technology or stealth platforms like the F-117 Nighthawk with its GBU-27s became a solution to the problem of "surgically" attacking IADS and strategic targets at medium to high altitudes. Stealth offers survivability while overflying the target(s) and employing PGMs with pinpoint accuracy. As a national asset, the F-117 requires approval from the National Command Authorities for deployment around the world, necessitating advanced planning to integrate the aircraft into an air campaign in a timely manner. As mentioned above, the Italian government thwarted the use of F-117s in Deliberate Force, so General Ryan's only alternatives were GBU-15s, SLAMs, and TLAMs.

Although we learned about the limited availability of 24-hour, all-weather standoff weapons from the Gulf War, we had to relearn the lesson nearly five years later in Deliberate Force. Fortunately, F-15Es are on-line, F-117s and B-2s are still available, and F-22s are in the near future; somewhat further out lies the possibility of the joint strike fighter. Additionally, as the twenty-first century approaches, new standoff weapons look promising. Since Desert Storm we have begun the joint development or operational test and evaluation of several new standoff weapon systems, including the joint direct-attack munition, the joint standoff weapon, the joint air-to-surface standoff missile, and the low-cost autonomous attack system. The former two are currently contracted and undergoing operational test and evaluation, while the latter two are prototypes under consideration for acquisition in the near future. This new generation of standoff-weapon technologies will have flexibility within a 24-hour air-tasking schedule; adaptability to existing platforms; true all-weather, day/night capability; autonomous control and navigation to the target after release from high, medium, or low altitudes; increased standoff; enough accuracy to minimize collateral damage; and the capability to hit both fixed and mobile targets.

These new standoff weapons will support the joint capability of precision engagement worldwide. However, like most precision weaponry, standoff munitions require effective command and control as well as precise intelligence, surveillance, and reconnaissance measures to ensure accurate employment against targets and to provide discrimination for minimizing collateral damage. In the meantime we must maintain and upgrade present aircraft, continue to use stealth assets, and use all available cruise missiles (not just TLAMs). Furthermore, cruise missiles used in an autonomous single-attack mode offer effectiveness against both critical point targets and a widely dispersed target set (i.e., a large number of aiming points)—perhaps an important consideration for future air operations. Until the new generation of weapons becomes available, combined/joint air component commanders faced with overcoming a complex IADS must seriously consider *all* available standoff weapons and plan well ahead for their employment.

Notes

1. Air Force Manual (AFM) 1-1, *Basic Aerospace Doctrine of the United States Air Force,* vol. 1, March 1992, 6.

2. Briefing slides, Lt Gen Michael Ryan, commander of Allied Air Forces Southern Europe (COMAIRSOUTH), subject: NATO Air Operations in Bosnia-Herzegovina, "Deliberate Force," October 1995, US Air Force Historical Research Agency (hereinafter AFHRA), Maxwell AFB, Ala., CAOC-13.

3. Ibid.

4. Maj Tim Reagan, USAF/SAA (Studies and Analyses Agency), "Characteristics of Deliberate Force," draft report, n.d., 4, AFHRA, SAGC-03.

5. "Evaluation of the Air War," 96-10, US Government Accounting Office/PEMD (Program Evaluation and Methodology Division) report to congressional requesters, Operation Desert Storm, July 1996, 4, AFHRA, K168.310-120. (Secret) Information extracted is unclassified.

6. AFM 1-1, vol. 2, 92.

7. Flight Manual, Technical Order 1-1M-34, *Aircrew Weapons Delivery Manual Non-Nuclear*, 31 May 1991, 1-29. (Secret) Information extracted is unclassified.

8. Ibid., 1-25. (Secret) Information extracted is unclassified.

9. The two generations of GBU-10/12 LGBs include the Paveway I with fixed wings and the Paveway II with folding wings. Paveway II variants have the following improvements over Paveway I: 30 percent greater field of view, increased detector sensitivity, reduced thermal battery delay after release, increased maximum canard deflection, and additional laser-coding options.

10. Thomas A. Keaney and Eliot A. Cohen, *Gulf War Air Power Survey*, vol. 5, *A Statistical Compendium and Chronology* (Washington, D.C.: Department of the Air Force, 1993), table 201, "Desert Shield/Storm: USAF Weapons Cost and Utilization, June 1993," 578.

11. Flight Manual, Technical Order 1-1M-34, 1-46. (Secret) Information extracted is unclassified.

12. Although only 23 Maverick shots were reported, Deny Flight logistics reports of the 7490th Composite Wing (Provisional) from 28 August to 13 September 1995 showed a decrease of 60 Maverick missiles in their munitions inventory—a difference of 37 missiles, AFHRA, AVI-05/06. The Maverick breakout from the reports is as follows: 49 AGM-65A/Bs, eight AGM-65Ds, and three AGM-65Gs. See also 7490th Composite Wing (Provisional)/DFOC (Deny Flight Operations Center), memorandum to commander, 7490th Composite Wing (Provisional), subject: Deliberate Force, 22 September 1995, for listed munition expenditures of 14 AGM-65Gs and seven AGM-65Ds for a total of 21, not 23, Mavericks shot. At the time of this writing, no record exists of how many Mavericks of what type were actually expended or returned for maintenance.

13. Keaney and Cohen, vol. 4, *Weapons, Tactics, and Training, and Space Operations* (Washington, D.C.: Government Printing Office, 1993), pt. 1, 80.

14. Science Applications International Corporation, "Tomahawk Effectiveness in the War with Iraq," 22 April 1991, 3, AFHRA, Gulf War Airpower Survey (GWAPS) Archives, NA-28.

15. Message, 111946Z Sep 95, commander, US Sixth Fleet to commander in chief, European Command, subject: Deliberate Force Post-TLAM Strike Report, 11 September 1995, 4. (Secret) Information extracted is unclassified.

16. Flight Manual, Technical Order 1-1M-34, 1-13, 1-14. (Secret) Information extracted is unclassified.

17. Ibid. (Secret) Information extracted is unclassified.

18. Ibid., 1-86. (Secret) Information extracted is unclassified.

19. This figure represents the difference between the 7490th Composite Wing (Provisional) unit logistics reports of 28 August 1995 and the unit logistics reports inventories of 13 September 1995, AFHRA, AVI-05/06.

20. Extracted from Corona briefing slides, Lt Gen Michael Ryan, Head-quarters AIRSOUTH, Naples, Italy, subject: Munitions (right-side slide no. 45), 5 December 1995, AFHRA, H-3.

21. Message, 301245Z Aug 95, 31st Fighter Wing to United States Air Forces in Europe AOS (Air Operations Support), 30 August 1995, 2.

22. Corona briefing slides.

23. Capt Jeff Hodgon, "Drones," AFHRA GWAPS Archives, TF2-64-602, 3-4. (Secret) Information extracted is unclassified.

24. Corona briefing slides.

25. Flight Manual, Technical Order 1-1M-34. (Secret) Information extracted is unclassified.

26. This figure represents the difference between the 7490th Composite Wing (Provisional) unit logistics reports of 28 August 1995 and the unit logistics reports inventories of 13 September 1995, AFHRA, AVI-05/06.

27. Flight Manual, Technical Order 1-1M-34. (Secret) Information extracted is unclassified.

28. These figures represent the difference between the 7490th Composite Wing (Provisional) unit logistics reports of 28 August 1995 and the unit logistics reports inventories of 13 September 1995, AFHRA, AVI-05/06.

29. A "smart" platform contains the digital-electronic hardware and the software required to identify a three-dimensional munitions release point in space from which a ballistic "dumb" bomb will free-fall and hit the intended impact point. A smart bomb/missile is capable of internal or external sensor guidance to the impact point; therefore, in the case of a dumb bomb, the desired release point need not be satisfied. Keaney and Cohen, vol. 4, pt. 1, pp. 85–86.

30. "Precision Engagement Reflects Joint Vision 2010," Air Force News Service, 22 January 1997; on-line, Internet, 23 January 1997, available from http://www.af.mil/news/Jan1997/n19970122_970075.html.

31. Ibid.

32. Ibid.

33. Ibid.

34. Gen Michael Ryan, interviewed by Lt Col Chris Campbell and Maj Mark McLaughlin, College of Aerospace Doctrine Research and Education, Maxwell AFB, Ala., 7 February 1996.

Chapter 10

Deliberate Force Targeting

Lt Col Richard L. Sargent

This chapter reviews the evolution of Deliberate Force target lists from conception to execution. It summarizes the history of targeting during the operation, discusses targeting options against the Bosnian Serb army (BSA), examines the desired mean point of impact (DMPI) methodology, and considers certain targeting issues.

History of Deliberate Force Targeting

In the two years prior to Deliberate Force, planners at Allied Air Forces Southern Europe (AIRSOUTH) produced numerous target sets in relation to various plans for intervention in the Bosnian conflict. The most important of these products were the Deliberate Force master target base, the Joint Target Board (JTB) approved target list, and the Deadeye and Deliberate Force target lists.

Master Target Base

With the establishment of the United Nations (UN) safe areas on 8 August 1993, North Atlantic Treaty Organization (NATO) air planners began a continuous air-planning process to cover a wide variety of actions against any Bosnian group that might attack one of these areas. For most of that period, targeting was a piecemeal process driven by functional categories connected to the safe areas. AIRSOUTH planners divided targets identified by this evolutionary process into six categories:

- *Category One*—preliminary preparation (suppression of enemy air defenses [SEAD]).
- *Category Two*—military units, positions, and equipment such as gun positions and troop concentrations in the safe area (later, zone of action [ZOA]).

279

- *Category Three*—military-unit positions and equipment not in the safe area/ZOA (e.g., logistics resupply and command and control [C^2] at the tactical and operational levels).
- *Category Four*—military infrastructure/installations that provide support outside the safe area/ZOA (e.g., ammo depots, base-supply depots, airfields, etc.).
- *Category Five*—civilian infrastructure/installations that provide support in the safe area/ZOA (e.g., armament factories, electricity stations, bridges, etc.).
- *Category Six*—command, control, and communications (C^3) infrastructure at the strategic level.[1]

AIRSOUTH designated the targets assigned to these categories as the master target base, which eventually included 444 targets. In the event of actual air operations, AIRSOUTH planners intended to draw targets out of this base, depending on the circumstances, and strike them in order of priority until the campaign ended or the subject of those attacks fell back into line. The master target base also provided the foundation for the JTB's approved target list and the Deadeye and Deliberate Force lists.

Joint Target Board Target List

Following the NATO air strikes against Udbina Airfield in November 1994, NATO and UN political leaders authorized Allied Forces Southern Europe (AFSOUTH) to develop plans for "retrospective" SEAD strikes in retaliation for attacks by Bosnian factions on interventionist aircraft. Prior to that time, the standing rules of engagement allowed only reactive strikes against air defense systems actually in the act of attacking NATO air units.[2] In December 1995 the North Atlantic Council authorized AFSOUTH to begin planning a "stand-alone" SEAD campaign in addition to planning for SEAD operations in direct support of Operation Deny Flight.[3] This stand-alone plan became Deadeye, an air campaign against the Bosnian Serb Republic's integrated air defense system (IADS). It also provided an important element of the planning that went into Deliberate Force itself.

Planning for a robust, graduated air campaign against the Bosnian Serbs, supported by Deadeye, began in earnest in the summer of 1995. On 2 June, the day of the shootdown of Basher 52, a US Air Force F-16 patrolling Bosnian airspace, Col Daniel Zoerb, director of the AIRSOUTH Deny Flight operations cell, and his planning staff briefed their targeting plan for the air campaign to Lt Gen Michael Ryan, the commander of AIRSOUTH (COMAIRSOUTH). Zoerb stated that the campaign objective was to "adversely alter BSA advantage to conduct military operations against the BiH [Bosnian army]," with a phase-one objective of "isolat[ing] leadership."[4] Zoerb advocated targeting the BSA's heavy weapons (artillery greater than 100 mm, mortars greater than 82 mm, and tanks), C^2 and C^3 networks and facilities, early warning (EW) networks, and key lines of communications (LOC), as well as isolating the leadership.

As June progressed, planners also refined AIRSOUTH's master target list for a possible air campaign in the summer of 1995, reviewed the SEAD plan, and studied the LOCs used by the BSA to move forces around the front. Meanwhile, a Pentagon planning think-tank staff called Checkmate at Headquarters US Air Force assisted in this process by providing an outside review and refinement of AIRSOUTH's plans.[5]

The JTB list evolved from these planning events in the heated atmosphere that preceded Deliberate Force. On 1 August 1995, the North Atlantic Council authorized safe-area-protection air attacks against targets throughout the wider ZOAs identified previously to guide Deadeye planning. AIRSOUTH immediately developed a target grid that identified overlapping target sets to be struck in protection of specific safe areas.[6] On 10 August 1995, at a meeting in Zagreb, Croatia, Colonel Zoerb briefed the JTB on all the targets identified for all four safe areas within the ZOAs (table 10.1).[7] The board, which consisted of General Ryan; Lt Gen Rupert Smith, commander of United Nations Protection Force (UNPROFOR); and other senior NATO air commanders, approved 155 of the 168 targets nominated by Zoerb. The JTB then forwarded this recommended list to Adm Leighton W. Smith, commander in chief of Allied Forces Southern Europe (CINCSOUTH), and Lt Gen Bernard Janvier, the UN military commander, for final approval and coordination with Gen George Joulwan, Supreme Allied Commander Europe.[8] On 14 August 1995, the JTB target list received formal approval.

Table 10.1

Safe-Area Target Sets

	Gorazde	Sarajevo	Tuzla	Bihac	Totals
C²	3	3	3	3	12
Supporting LOCs	8	11	10	5	34
Direct and Essential Support	12	17	13	8	50
Fielded Forces	*	*	*	*	*
Subtotals	23	31	26	16	96
First Priority (Deadeye)	17	17	17	21	72
Total	40	48	43	37	168

*Fielded forces (heavy weapons and troop concentrations) changed daily.

Source: Briefing, Lt Gen Michael E. Ryan, COMAIRSOUTH, to JTB, subject: NATO Air Operations to Stabilize Bosnia-Herzegovina, 10 August 1995, US Air Force Historical Research Agency (AFHRA), Maxwell AFB, Ala., NPL-02-23. (Secret) Information extracted is unclassified.

The decision of 14 August also delineated the boundaries of ZOAs covering all of Bosnia and the safe areas or total exclusion zones (TEZ) assigned to them (fig. 10.1). The northwest ZOA included Bihac and the Banja Luka airfield. The southeast ZOA included Sarajevo, Gorazde, Zepa, and Pale. The Tuzla TEZ, which NATO air planners viewed as a "swing" ZOA, encompassed SEAD targets that would be hit in the event of attacks in either of the other two ZOAs. Despite the delineation of ZOA boundaries, which mainly guided preplanned strikes, NATO planners expected to strike any air defense system that actively threatened or attacked interventionist aircraft.[9]

The ZOA targets were driven by functional categories connected to the TEZs. NATO would attack functional target categories only to the depth required to achieve the desired results—and no more (proportional response). The only exception to the ZOA targeting rule was IADS attack. Since SEAD was not connected

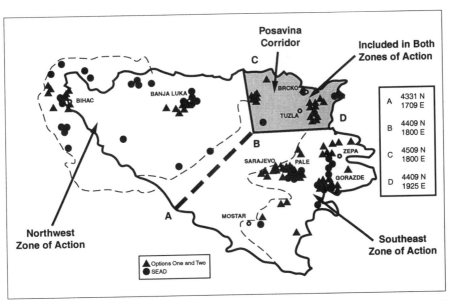

Figure 10.1. Zones of Action (From Corona briefing slides, Lt Gen Michael Ryan, Headquarters AIRSOUTH, Naples, Italy, 5 December 1995)

to the ZOAs, NATO could neutralize any threat of attack by the warring factions. In defense of the safe areas, the Military Committee Memorandum of 8 August 1993 also defined operational options for air strikes in Bosnia-Herzegovina. Given the target options, TEZs, and ZOAs, AIRSOUTH created and modified three target options encompassing the six target categories, together with priorities that would have a low-to-high range of military significance. Each of these had lateral links that one could eventually associate with achieving the military objective (fig. 10.2). More importantly, the targets were linked to a degree of risk of collateral damage and to infrastructure targets that, if destroyed, would cause undue hardship on the civilian populace.[10]

As had been the case since the summer of 1993, planners couched all of AIRSOUTH's targeting plans in the context of general options prescribed by the UN and NATO:

- *Option One*—First-Strike Phase. Air strikes would have demonstration value and limited scope and duration. Targets would represent low risk and low collateral

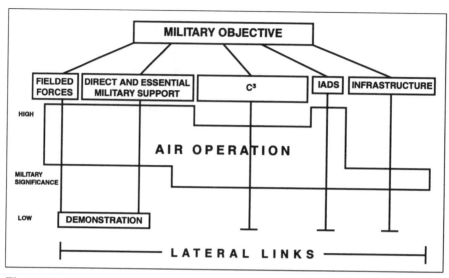

Figure 10.2. Deliberate Force Air Strike Concept (From Corona briefing slides, Lt Gen Michael Ryan, Headquarters AIRSOUTH, Naples, Italy, 5 December 1995)

damage and would include only those elements participating in a safe-area siege, such as mortar or artillery-battery positions.

- *Option Two*—Initial Follow-on Phase. Air strikes would be limited to the immediate environment of the affected TEZ. Objectives called for relieving the siege and supporting UNPROFOR. The targets would carry medium risk and medium collateral damage and would have military value (e.g., heavy weapons, supply points/ammo sites close to the area of hostilities, C^2 facilities, and EW radar/surface-to-air missile [SAM] sites).

- *Option Three*—Extended-Operations Phase. Air strikes would expand outside the immediate area under siege. The targets would have military value and could influence the sustainability of siege forces (e.g., heavy weapons, C^2 facilities, supply-point/munition sites, and EW radar and SAM sites throughout Bosnia-Herzegovina; military petroleum, oil, and lubricants; and counterair targets [aircraft and repair facilities]).[11]

Geographic proximity to a safe area determined whether a given target fell under option two or three. For example, option-two targets in the Tuzla TEZ would become option-three targets for planners working the defense of Sarajevo. Significantly, no option included infrastructure targets of the sort proposed by Colonel Zoerb in his June targeting brief.

Deadeye Target List

By mid-August 1995, as tensions mounted from the warring factions within the Balkans, AIRSOUTH continued to develop and refine air-operation and targeting plans for the Bosnia region. In anticipation of graduated air operations, two plans emerged: the Deadeye air-protection plan and Deliberate Force, an expanded air-strike plan. Developed in the early spring of 1995, Deadeye delineated AIRSOUTH's SEAD campaign to protect NATO air forces from the BSA's IADS, as mentioned above. The campaign aimed to ensure that the "BSA will no longer have an IADS for central direction of air defenses" by striking key BSA air defense communications nodes, electronic-warfare sites, C^2 facilities, missile-launch units, and missile-reconstitution capabilities.[12] AIRSOUTH extracted 36 targets from the master target list to form the foundation of Deadeye.

Deliberate Force Target List

The foundations of the Deliberate Force target list were laid in late 1994, when AIRSOUTH began planning for a wide range of offensive air operations in defense of UN safe areas and enforcement of the no-fly ban. By early August 1995, these plans comprised a body of options that an AIRSOUTH briefing referred to as "Deliberate Force." The mission of this operation entailed "execut[ing] robust NATO air operations that adversely alter the BSA's advantage in conducting successful military operations against the BiH," with the aim of getting the Bosnian Serbs to "sue for cessation of military operations, comply with UN mandates, and negotiate."[13] To achieve these objectives, AIRSOUTH extracted 87 targets from the JTB list—primarily option-two targets, consisting mainly of direct and essential support and equipment and a few supporting LOCs to isolate the BSA threat.[14]

Targeting the Bosnian Serb Army

A straightforward strategy-to-task matrix guided AIRSOUTH's process of selecting targets for the Deliberate Force list. Beginning with the basic strategic goal of degrading the BSA's military capabilities, the AIRSOUTH matrix identified the appropriate center of gravity (COG) for attack and appropriate targets whose destruction would most threaten that COG.[15] The matrix included the following principles:

- The Bosnian Serbs' COG is their historic fear of domination.
- The Bosnian Serbs' military advantage with respect to the BiH is their ability to swing more capable but less numerous forces equipped with heavy weapons to places of their need or choosing.
- Attacking the Bosnian Serbs' advantages would lead to changing the balance of power to their disadvantage.
- The Bosnian Serbs' realization of a shift in advantage would eventuate in their suing for termination of hostilities.
- The Bosnian Serbs would not come to that realization unless they are subjected to robust attack.

The next step involved determining whether the best way to degrade the ability of the BSA to swing its more capable units was through attacks on its heavy weapons, troops, or key LOCs. According to Colonel Zoerb, AIRSOUTH's preferred option called for attacking the BSA's C^2 structure, infantry, and prime LOCs all at the same time.[16] However, political considerations, particularly the presumed sensitivity of the intervening states to collateral damage, made the targeting issue more involved than a simple question of directly tearing the BSA apart.

To jump ahead of the targeting discussion somewhat, the issue of collateral damage influenced the selection and attack of Deliberate Force targets across the board. In general, AIRSOUTH planners under General Ryan's close supervision selected each target for incorporation into a target list with an eye to maximizing effect while minimizing the possibility of collateral damage. Consequently, everything from rules of engagement to aircraft, weapons, and tactics selections was driven to some degree by concerns about collateral damage. In the case of targets, AIRSOUTH planners "scrubbed" them time and again, only to see them rejected or reexamined by senior leaders. This laborious selection-and-approval process rested on detailed imagery and endless discussions of DMPIs, weapons, blast and rubble patterns, and a host of other issues that related to whether or not given target/weapon/DMPI combinations would cause collateral damage or casualties.

During the execution of Deliberate Force, these concerns carried over and were reaffirmed by several ad hoc operational rules of engagement also aimed at limiting damage: (1) targets required positive visual identification before munitions release; (2) sometimes aircraft could expend only one bomb at a time on a target; (3) aircraft had to attack certain targets during different times of the day or night to negate possible noncombatant casualties; (4) oftentimes the DMPIs were so close together that aircraft formations had to take spacing and/or loiter over the target area until the debris/smoke cleared to hit their aiming points; and (5) planners restricted attack axes for certain targets such as bridges to minimize the danger that "long" or "short" weapons would cause casualties or damage property. Before exercising these procedures, of course, AIRSOUTH planners had to settle the question of which target sets and specific targets NATO forces would hit—heavy weapons, infantry, or LOCs?

Heavy Weapons

UN resolutions required the BSA to withdraw its heavy weapons from the Sarajevo exclusion zone, defined in the summer of 1995 as an area of 20 kilometers radius from the center of Sarajevo. The UN defined heavy weapons as

1. all armored vehicles, including tanks and armored personnel carriers

2. all antiaircraft weapons (except hand-held) of caliber 12.7 mm or greater

3. all antiaircraft and antitank rocket and missile systems, whether hand-held, towed, mounted, or self-propelled

4. all surface-to-air rockets and missiles as well as their launch systems and launch vehicles

5. rocket-assisted rail-launch bombs (e.g., Krema) and their launch systems[17]

Despite its simplicity, this list presented two daunting problems for air planners. First, it included over 350 heavy weapons (tanks, artillery greater than 100 mm, and rocket launchers) and hundreds of other weapons, including mortars greater than 82 mm and other "tubes" below 100 mm. Finding and "servicing" so many weapons certainly would degrade the BSA's military capability, but the process also might take more time than the political constraints of the intervention allowed. Second, targeting those weapons might actually undermine the intervention's objective of having them moved out of the exclusion zones. As General Smith observed, "If we are asking the BSA to move these guns out of this area, then bombing those guns is not healthy, and maybe we ought not to do that. Maybe we ought to stay away from the heavy weapons. That way, they won't have the excuses—'Can't move the guns!' or 'You're destroying them!' or 'We can't move them because we are under attack.' They will use whatever excuse they can."[18]

As a result, Generals Smith and Ryan agreed that, unless the BSA fired these heavy weapons at cities or peacekeeping forces, they would not be targeted or struck. This would be the case particularly for weapons discovered on designated heavy-weapon withdrawal routes. Secondarily, NATO commanders did not want to engage Serbian heavy weapons because they felt there was no strategic need to destroy Serb military capabilities, and they saw a real danger in appearing to operate in coordination with Bosnian government and Croatian forces.[19]

Infantry

The BSA's best infantry brigades were a valid and, when they were in their barracks, an attractive target. But based on their desire to minimize casualties of any kind and despite the suggestion of some air planners, senior NATO and UN commanders elected not to target Bosnian Serb infantry or other troops unless they engaged in offensive operations against interventionist military units or the safe areas.[20]

Lines of Communications

Because the North Atlantic Council's air strike guidance of 1993 did not include infrastructure targets, LOCs were not addressed in most of the Deny Flight targeting sets except option three. However, in early August 1995, General Ryan and Colonel Zoerb briefed Admiral Smith on targeting plans that included a notional set of LOCs important to the movement and supply of BSA forces around the safe areas.[21] Specific targets on these LOCs included selected bridges and road choke points susceptible to closure by bombing. After a discussion with General Smith, who initially expressed concern about the usefulness of striking LOC targets, General Ryan agreed to coordinate strikes against such targets on a day-to-day basis. The two commanders would determine which targets to strike in order to block all routes into or out of Sarajevo, except the one designated as a heavy-weapon withdrawal route.[22] Accordingly, by early July, planners completed targeting schemes to drop key bridges and block other choke points necessary to degrade or block BSA mobility and supply operations into, out of, and among the safe areas. Recognizing the sudden ascendancy of LOC targets in importance and the coordination problems between the UN and NATO, Colonel Zoerb commented that "LOC targeting was a strange one." Despite the fact that official guidance never really specified LOCs and that no lists other than option three addressed them, the ground-force commander approved LOCs as option-two targets for a specific purpose in this case.[23]

Targeting Priorities

By mid August 1995, the Deliberate Force and Deadeye target lists were firmly established in numbers and priorities:

- *IADS (17 targets)*—EW/acquisition radars (four), SAM system (one), control reporting posts/control reporting center, communications (microwave towers, radio relays, etc.) (12).

- *fielded forces*—heavy weapons, troop concentrations, and transportation.
- C^2 *(seven)*—communications (three), command facilities and headquarters (four).
- *supporting LOCs (15)*—transportation choke points, bridges, and tunnels.
- *direct and essential military support (17)*—ammo depot and storage (one), supply depot and storage (one), supporting garrison areas (five), military logistics areas (10).[24]

Of these targets, planners had selected 36 for attack prior to the start of Deliberate Force, as well as 20 other Deadeye targets. Most were linked to the Sarajevo TEZ, and all reflected AIRSOUTH's determination to minimize the likelihood of collateral damage and casualties (table 10.2).

Table 10.2

Onset Target and DMPI Data

	Deliberate Force	Deadeye Southeast	Deadeye Northwest	Supporting LOCs	Total
Target Date (no. tasked)	21	15	5	15	56
DMPI Data (no. tasked)	261	53	17	15	346

DMPI Methodology

Since General Ryan handled the process for selecting DMPIs for each target, it was subject to frequent and sudden change. After operations began, the combined air operations center's (CAOC) guidance, apportionment, and targeting (GAT) cell nominated targets for strike. Initially, this cell consisted of General Ryan, Colonel Zoerb, two experienced air-operations officers, and two intelligence targeteers. Sitting at a table in the office of Maj Gen Hal Hornburg, CAOC director, General Ryan and the target team picked the DMPIs one by one. After a daily review of the best battle damage assessment (BDA) of the targets, the GAT team would nominate DMPIs to General Ryan on the basis of providing "militarily significant targets, meaningful targets, and the right targets from a narrow perspective of force application without being absurd."[25] The team considered collateral-damage issues when selecting targets, but it usually relied on General Ryan to make final determinations about which DMPIs posed acceptable or unacceptable risks. Upon receiving each list of nominated targets, Ryan would pass judgement and, if necessary, direct the rest of the GAT team to come up with more. Overall, most observers felt that General Ryan was notably more conservative in his approach to targeting than the rest of the team.[26]

Despite some mild initial frustration with his boss's conservatism, Colonel Zoerb, his chief planner, ultimately praised Ryan's judgement: "His sensitivity to the political and military guidance and constraints that he needed to work within were clear to him, and he applied those effectively to screen those sharp edges that I was beating."[27] His final picks then went to the master air attack plans cell for input into the daily air-tasking message.

Following up their initial DMPI selections, General Ryan and Colonel Zoerb would review BDA imagery to determine if the target DMPI(s) had been destroyed; if not, they examined the target(s) as candidates for retargeting. Ryan approached such restrike decisions with great care—so much so that he kept a personal BDA tracking notebook that was "hands off" to everyone else. He established important criteria for determining whether a target had been destroyed:

- *individual target (DMPI)*—nonfunctional, moderate to severe damage, or destroyed.
- *target complex (multiple DMPIs)*—nonfunctional or two-thirds of the individual targets (DMPIs) within that complex destroyed.[28]

Targeting Issues

Also underlying General Ryan's targeting decisions was his concern that political pressures might bring an end to the bombing campaign before it destroyed enough targets to have a significant effect on the Bosnian Serbs. According to Colonel Zoerb,

Our concern was that after the first bomb drop that everybody would lose their spine. The knock-it-off would happen at 8:00 a.m. in the morning after the first night. As soon as [Cable News Network] got there with their film and saw the destruction at some of these isolated places, they [UN/NATO] would say, "That's enough!" So, we were interested in wanting to make our initial employment as effective as we could. The IADS were nice, operating in the southeast where we could . . . suppress that piece of the IADS that we needed to suppress to do a job. We needed to get bombs on targets. We needed to get something meaningful early-on because our fear was that when they [UN/NATO] saw what bombs did, we would have to turn it off.[29]

Importantly, this concern led General Ryan to break with the classic airpower targeting tenet of thoroughly taking down an enemy's air defenses before shifting the weight of the air effort to ground attacks. Instead, he chose to strike the minimal number of the BSA's IADS targets necessary at any time to allow him to conduct the maximum number of ground strikes at the lowest risk to his aircrews. For example, he did not initially target the air defense stronghold at Banja Luka in the northwest ZOA. Instead, he focused early attacks on the air defenses and associated BSA targets in the lower-risk southeast ZOA, which included the Sarajevo area.

Targeting Heavy Weapons

Despite the importance of the BSA's heavy weapons in the exclusion zones, AIRSOUTH ultimately rejected them as a primary target set for Deliberate Force. In the first place, these weapons often proved difficult to find in the broken terrain and urban areas in which the Bosnian Serbs generally hid them.[30] That factor, in turn, likely meant that it would take longer to service those weapons than the political circumstances of the air campaign would allow. Thus, in pursuit of the quickest possible results, NATO commanders and political leaders eschewed a strategy of directly attacking BSA military capabilities in favor of a less direct strategy aimed at the C^2, logistical, and mobility underpinnings of the BSA's strength. Also, after 3 September 1995, NATO commanders decided to lay off attacks on the Serbs' heavy weapons in order to deny them an excuse for not moving them out of the exclusion zones in compliance with UN directives, mentioned above.[31]

Serb artillery

Bridges Revisited

Bridges presented their own peculiar targeting problems. Until the eve of Deliberate Force, AIRSOUTH generally relegated bridges to the option-three category, mainly because they were important economic factors in the region and because they carried a significant risk of collateral damage. This situation changed when General Smith requested attacks on some key bridges in order to channel and hinder the BSA's efforts to send reinforcements into the exclusion zones.

Accordingly, AIRSOUTH conducted numerous bridge attacks, but they generally did not produce General Smith's desired effects. The bridges were strong structures, and the tactics employed to attack them worked to minimize the danger of collateral damage and to reduce the effectiveness of individual strikes. Initial tactical restrictions placed on bridge

Bridge damage

attacks included single-bomb releases, off-axis attack runs down riverbeds to minimize the unwanted consequences of inaccurate weapons releases or bombs "going stupid," and night scheduling to reduce the likelihood of the presence of civilians when the bombs hit. Because of the durability of the targets and the various tactical constraints placed on the attacking forces, allied bombing brought down only seven of the 12 bridges targeted by AIRSOUTH by the end of the campaign.

The targeting history of Deliberate Force reveals an evolutionary as well as a centralized and flexible process. The use of a master target list from which to build individual plans worked well, giving NATO air planners the ability to generate new air plans and adjust priorities almost on demand. The division of targets into options contributed to this flexibility, both in planning and practice, as evidenced by the apparent ease with which AIRSOUTH moved bridges from option three to option two in response to the request of General Smith. In reality this building-block approach to targeting was an essential accommodation to the political and diplomatic dynamism of the Balkans conflict and the intervention. Whether AIRSOUTH's approach to targeting becomes a model for the future remains to be seen. At the time, however, it seems to have facilitated target planning nicely.

Notes

1. "Target Categories," OPLAN 40101, "Deny Flight," 3 May 1995, annex H, p. H-1, US Air Force Historical Research Agency (hereinafter AFHRA), Maxwell AFB, Ala., CAOC-01. (Confidential) Information extracted is unclassified.
2. Ibid. (Confidential) Information extracted is unclassified.
3. Ibid. (Confidential) Information extracted is unclassified.
4. Briefing, Headquarters AIRSOUTH, Naples, Italy, subject: Air Campaign Targeting, 2 June 1995. (Confidential) Information extracted is unclassified.
5. Col Daniel R. Zoerb, chief, Plans Division, Headquarters AIRSOUTH, Naples, Italy, transcript of oral history interview by Dr. Wayne Thompson and Maj Tim Reagan, 20 October 1995. (Secret) Information extracted is unclassified, AFHRA, NPL-33(T).
6. Ibid. (Secret) Information extracted is unclassified.
7. Briefing, Col Daniel R. Zoerb, chief of plans, AFSOUTH, subject: NATO Air Operations to Stabilize Bosnia-Herzegovina, 10 August 1995, AFHRA, NPL-02-23.
8. Briefing to CAOC staff, Gen Michael Ryan, CAOC, 5th Allied Tactical Air Force, Vicenza, Italy, subject: Deliberate Force, 29 August–14 September 1995, 15 October 1995, AFHRA, CAOC-13.
9. Maj Tim Reagan, "Impact of NATO Air Campaign," position paper on Royal Air Force (RAF) visit, Force Application Directorate, Air Force Studies and Analyses Agency, 21 December 1995. (Secret) Information extracted is unclassified.
10. Ibid. (Secret) Information extracted is unclassified.
11. The examples of targets cited in these options are for illustrative purposes; they do not represent a specific or all-inclusive list of targets.
12. Briefing, Headquarters AIRSOUTH, Naples, Italy, subject: Graduated Air Operations, 12 August 1995, AFHRA, NPL-02-24. (Secret) Information extracted is unclassified.
13. Ibid. (Secret) Information extracted is unclassified.
14. Briefing slide, Headquarters AIRSOUTH, Naples, Italy, subject: Target List Evolution, n.d. (Secret) Information extracted is unclassified.
15. Corona briefing, Lt Gen Michael E. Ryan, COMAIRSOUTH, subject: NATO Air Operations in Bosnia-Herzegovina: Deliberate Force, 29 August–14 September 1995, November 1995.
16. Zoerb interview. (Secret) Information extracted is unclassified.
17. Gen Rupert Smith to Gen Ratko Mladic, draft letter, subject: Withdrawal of Heavy Weapons from the Sarajevo Exclusion Zone, 3 September 1995, AFHRA, NPL 15-02-13. (Secret) Information extracted is unclassified.

18. Zoerb interview. (Secret) Information extracted is unclassified.

19. "Discussion of the Air Strategy in Bosnia," talking paper, Skunk-works, USAF/XOXS, Pentagon, Washington, D.C., 17 September 1995, 4.

20. Ibid.

21. Actually, AIRSOUTH used the term *supporting LOCs* as a caveat when talking about notional target sets. That is, once the battle began, AIRSOUTH would look at the situation and take out only those choke points that were absolutely necessary to defend the safe area.

22. Zoerb interview. (Secret) Information extracted is unclassified.

23. Ibid. (Secret) Information extracted is unclassified.

24. Corona briefing.

25. Zoerb interview. (Secret) Information extracted is unclassified.

26. Reagan position paper.

27. Zoerb interview. (Secret) Information extracted is unclassified.

28. Corona briefing.

29. Zoerb interview. (Secret) Information extracted is unclassified.

30. "Discussion of the Air Strategy in Bosnia," 4.

31. Maj Tim Reagan, "Characteristics of Deliberate Force," draft paper, Air Force Studies and Analyses Agency, n.d., 6. (Secret) Information extracted is unclassified.

Chapter 11

Deliberate Force Tactics

Lt Col Richard L. Sargent

Tactics are concerned with doing the job "right," and higher levels of strategy are concerned with doing the "right" job.

—Col Dennis M. Drew and Dr. Donald M. Snow
Making Strategy: An Introduction to National Security Processes and Problems

Strategy wins wars; tactics wins battles.

—Carl R. Oliver
Plane Talk: Aviators' and Astronauts' Own Stories

Broadly put, tactics is the art or skill of employing available forces in combat to achieve specific goals and is practiced by commanders and warriors at both the operational and tactical levels of war. At the operational level, tactics mainly involves the orchestration of forces and combat events or battles to achieve the strategic goals of theater and national commanders. That orchestration involves making decisions about the most suitable centers of gravity and targets to strike, as well as the best forces, weapons, and combat methods to make those strikes. This last set of considerations—forces, weapons, and combat methods—marks the usual interface between operational and tactical levels of air war. After operational-level commanders assign targets and allocate forces, unit-level leaders and planners usually make tactical decisions about the number of aircraft to send against specific targets, types of weapons to use, attack and weapons-release procedures, and equivalent issues of detail. In practice, both operational- and tactical-level tactics are extremely complex, time-consuming processes. Achieving success in both areas is critical to the outcome of a campaign.

This chapter describes the dynamics of the operational- and tactical-level tactics of Deliberate Force. It includes both general and specific discussions of various factors that influenced, or should have influenced, the development and execution of tactics during that campaign. It then addresses mission tactics actually utilized by North Atlantic Treaty Organization (NATO) airmen. The record of these mission tactics is an interesting and useful legacy of Deliberate Force, as is the embedded discussion of how NATO airmen developed them. Of particular note in this case, institutional boundaries between operational- and tactical-level tactics were blurred, at least in relation to general experience. During Deliberate Force Lt Gen Michael Ryan, the combined force air component commander (CFACC) and commander of Allied Air Forces Southern Europe (COMAIRSOUTH), and his staff at the combined air operations center (CAOC) often made determinations about weapons and tactics that in other conflicts would have been left to tactical planners in field units. Because this blurring of institutional boundaries reflected the complex political and diplomatic circumstances of Deliberate Force and because other peace operations also will be politically and diplomatically complex, it is one of the more salient features of the campaign for study.

Tactical Planning and Employment Factors

In many past air campaigns, operational-level commanders and planning staffs (General Ryan and his CAOC staff in Deliberate Force) focused their tactical planning on doing the "right" job. Tactical planners, in concert, usually worried about how to do the job "right," once operational planners determined what the job was. This chapter takes the position that, regardless of how operational and tactical planners in this operation divided their responsibilities, their ultimate decisions had to and did reflect the effects of certain key factors of threat and environment. Their practice of the practical art of getting the right iron on the right target at the right time depended for its success on accurate assessments and accommodation of the nature of Bosnian Serb defenses, the Bosnian climate and topography, and the characteristics of air platforms and weapons available to the interventionist coalition.

Bosnian Serb Defenses

Deny Flight operations commenced on 12 April 1993 in a high-threat environment[1] that reflected confusion over the exact status of Serbian and Bosnian Serb air defenses after the breakup of Yugoslavia. Prior to the breakup, a single air-defense operations center in Belgrade controlled four sector operations centers, each of which received data from other such centers as well as subordinate control and reporting posts; it also controlled subordinate surface-to-air missile (SAM) battalions and fighters. All of these elements provided integrated air defense system (IADS) coverage for the entire country. Following the breakup, a portion of the Yugoslavian IADS fell into Bosnian Serb hands. Parts of the system remained operational, but to what extent and with what degree of residual linkage to the national IADS remained unclear to United Nations (UN) and NATO planners.

As Operation Deny Flight progressed, NATO airmen learned more about the real capabilities of the Bosnian Serb army's (BSA) IADS. From Yugoslavia the BSA inherited a substantial array of air defense surveillance, communications, and combat equipment. BSA radar systems provided overlapping search, tracking, and targeting capabilities backed up by a tiny air force; a substantial force of large, radar-guided missiles (SAMs); man-portable air defense (MANPAD) missiles; and antiaircraft artillery (AAA) of various calibers (fig. 11.1).[2] The Bosnian Serb air arm ultimately proved to be a minor threat to NATO airmen, particularly after NATO jets shot down four of its Galeb/Jastreb strike aircraft in November 1994. Ground-based weapons posed more of a threat, evidenced by the shootdown of a British Sea Harrier on 16 April 1994 in the vicinity of Gorazde and by the shootdown of a US Air Force F-16C by a radar-guided SAM on 2 June 1995 over western Bosnia-Herzegovina. Thus, in net, at the onset of Deliberate Force on 29 August 1995, the BSA's IADS posed a formidable, though uneven, threat to NATO air forces.

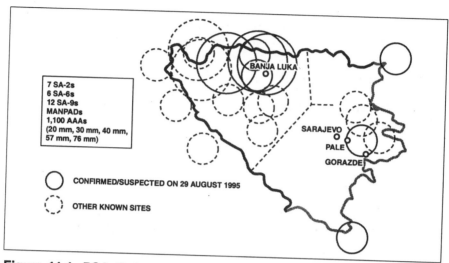

Figure 11.1. BSA Order of Battle (From Corona briefing slides, Lt Gen Michael Ryan, Headquarters AIRSOUTH, Naples, Italy, 5 December 1995)

SAMs present in the region included SA-2f Guidelines, SA-6b Gainfuls, SA-9 Gaskins (or SA-13 Gophers), and an unknown number of infrared (IR) MANPADs—SA-7b Strellas (or SA-14 Gremlins):

- *SA-2f Guideline (MOD 5 [fifth in a series of missile-system modifications])*—missile with primary mission of low- to high-altitude, medium-range air defense from fixed or semifixed sites. These missiles are best employed against targets at medium and high altitudes, but they have limited low-altitude capabilities. Their Fan Song F acquisition and tracking radars can track fighters out to medium ranges, and their electro-optical tracker can guide the missile down to a low altitude. Fighter aircraft can usually evade the old and not particularly agile "Fox" if they receive warnings of its approach. Evasion tactics include avoidance of the missile or its supporting radar systems and, if engaged by the missile, execution of mid-G orthogonal breaks into and over the missile at medium altitude.[3] During Deliberate Force, NATO jets avoided or suppressed all known SA-2 SAM sites, indicated by the apparent absence of any SA-2 launches by the BSA.

300

- *SA-6b Gainful*—a highly mobile, tracked air-defense system designed to defend against high-performance aircraft operating at low to medium altitudes. Supported by acquisition radars and a backup electro-optical tracking system, the SA-6b system can engage targets from medium altitudes to very low altitudes. An SA-6b battery can handle two targets at once with quick reaction time between initial acquisition of a target and missile launch.[4] The BSA used an SA-6b to shoot down the US Air Force F-16C on 2 June 1995, mentioned above. Despite frequent evidence of SA-6 radar activity, the Bosnian Serbs launched no missiles, probably reflecting the effectiveness of NATO's suppression of enemy air defenses (SEAD) campaign, particularly in its use of high-speed antiradiation missiles (HARM).

- *SA-9 Gaskin/SA-13 Gopher*—mobile SAM systems organic to many BSA combat units. These point-defense, highly mobile, tracked, short-range SAMs use IR seekers to acquire, track, and engage fixed-wing as well as rotary-wing aircraft. They can be effective against unaware, low-flying aircraft that transit their short engagement zones. Although these missiles were present around many potential NATO targets, they proved highly susceptible to countermeasures.

- *MANPADs*—shoulder- or tripod-launched, short-range, IR-guided missiles present throughout the Deliberate Force area of operations. The primary systems available to the BSA were the SA-7b Strella or the SA-14 Gremlin.[5] Consisting of a simple launch tube, gripstock, and thermal battery, the Strella features a very short engagement range at very low to lower-mid altitudes against slow to fast targets. If a high-performance target aircraft sees the missile, it can usually defeat it with IR countermeasures or high-speed escapes.[6] Boasting slightly better performance than the SA-7b and a better seeker head, the Gremlin can track an aircraft from any angle, unlike the SA-7b, which is a "tail chaser." As in the case of the SA-7b, high-performance aircraft can evade a detected Gremlin through high-speed maneuvering and IR countermeasures.[7] On the first day of Deliberate Force, a MANPAD shot down a French Mirage 2000C 20 nautical miles southeast of Pale, probably at an altitude at or below three thousand feet. This was the only aircraft shot down during the campaign, although on 16 April 1994 a MAN-PAD downed a Deny Flight Sea Harrier, and other such missiles damaged several NATO aircraft at different times.

- *AAA*—significant numbers of light and medium systems fielded by the BSA. Light AAA included automatic weapons from 20 mm through 60 mm characterized by automatic fire; timed and impact-fuzed, high-explosive projectiles; and vertical ranges up to four thousand meters. Medium AAA included guns larger than 60 mm characterized by single-shot, battery-controlled fire; timed and proximity-fuzed, high-explosive projectiles; and vertical ranges up to eight thousand meters. During Deliberate Force the CFACC largely avoided these weapons by restricting his aircraft to flight above 10,000 feet or, by exception, five thousand feet.

Climate and Topography

Bosnia's Mediterranean climate is characterized by long, hot summers and mild winters along the coastal region and in the extreme south, and by harsh winters (November–January) and milder summers in the interior highlands. Deliberate Force occurred during the early autumn, experiencing a typical, moderate climate for that time of year. The term *moderate*, however, belied the generally poor flying weather over Bosnia during the operation. On most days fog covered much of the land, particularly in the mornings, and tactical aircraft encountered multiple cloud layers throughout their flight regime. Often, surface visibility was between one-half to one and one-half miles. Sun angle, clouds, visibility, contrail levels, and wind influenced decisions about flight altitudes, navigation routes and checkpoints, target-area ingress and egress routes, weapons and sensor selections and employment, flight altitudes, and so forth (table 11.1).

Weather had far-ranging effects on Deliberate Force's operations and tactics. Because the rules of engagement (ROE) and special instructions (SPINS) required aircrews to identify their

Table 11.1

Obscurant Effects on Sensor Performance

Weather Element	Day Sight	Image Intensifier	Laser Designator/ Range Finder	Thermal Imagery Contrast	IR Transmission
surface wind	none	moderate	none	major	none
absolute humidity	none	moderate	moderate	minor	major
clouds/fog	major	major	major	major	extreme
rain/snow	major	major	major	moderate	extreme
dust/haze	major	major	major	moderate	major
visual smoke	major	major	major	minor	minor
Wily Pete smoke	major	major	major	moderate	major
IR smoke	major	major	major	major	extreme

Source: Adapted from Multi-Command Manual 3-1, vol. 1, *Tactical Employment Considerations,* 17 March 1995, table 3-1, "Weather Elements Which Affect IR Systems Performance"; and "Obscurant Effect Table," handout, Texas Instruments, Dallas, Texas, n.d.

assigned targets visually before releasing ordnance to avoid any chance of collateral damage, weather obscurations caused nearly 30 percent of the "no drops" by NATO aircraft over Bosnia-Herzegovina. With no alternate target on which to expend ordnance, some aircraft, like the US Air Force's F-16s and the US Navy's F/A-18s, jettisoned theirs in the Adriatic Sea. Just between the two types of aircraft, a total of 65 precision-guided munitions (PGM)—10 percent of the total expenditures of these weapons—had to be jettisoned. The F-16s jettisoned 56 GBU-10s because of safety precautions to avoid runway closure at Aviano Air Base (AB), Italy, and as a requirement for gross-weight considerations for divert fuel. F/A-18s jettisoned eight GBU-10s and one GBU-24 because of carrier-landing/arresting-cable weight limitations. Other coalition aircraft returned to their assigned bases with their weapons loads because they could not visually identify their assigned targets, primarily due to cloud coverage in the target area. Additionally, poor weather delayed attack packages on a number of days, particularly those scheduled for morning strikes.

Bosnia-Herzegovina covers an area of 19,741 square miles, most of which lies in the mountains of the Dinaric Alps. Half the region is forested, with another 25 percent arable. The coastal region supports a Mediterranean flora of palms, olives, cypress, and many vineyards. Otherwise, deciduous forest predominates, but the higher reaches of the interior contain numerous conifers. These forested conditions greatly influenced the tactics of Deliberate Force, mainly by making difficult the acquisition of tactical targets such as artillery and combat vehicles.[8] Early attempts by NATO to locate, target, and destroy SA-6 transporter-erector launchers and radars (TELAR) (platforms that house and guide the missile) and heavy weapons proved daunting in the rough terrain and poor weather that prevailed. Rugged terrain and foliation also hampered operations because foliage absorbed the energy of targeting lasers for guided weapons or because the terrain and trees prevented attacking aircraft from maintaining line-of-sight contact with their weapons.

Night operations during Deliberate Force offered NATO airmen the advantages of concealment, the disadvantages of more difficult target acquisition, and the possibility that using afterburners or dispensing countermeasures might highlight them to enemy gunners. During the operation, 260 of the over nine hundred air-strike missions were flown at night—about three-quarters by land-based US Air Force fighters and a quarter from US Navy carrier-based fighters. All but four of the attack missions on bridges were flown at night, when traffic was at a minimum, to reduce the possibility of civilian casualties. Air planners deconflicted most night missions by operating them at different altitudes and by spacing them in trail.

Weaponeering and the Joint Munitions-Effectiveness Manuals

Given the pressure from commanders to achieve maximum results from air strikes while simultaneously minimizing the likelihood of collateral damage, "weaponeering"—the matching of aircraft and weapons to achieve desired target effects—was more critical to the execution of Deliberate Force than to many other air campaigns.[9] The available guides to weaponeering decisions, the joint munitions-effectiveness manuals (JMEM), proved generally adequate to the problem of calculating the required number of weapons and aircraft sorties required to destroy a target. However, for the purposes of Deliberate Force planning, some mission planners found the JMEMs not flexible enough to encompass all the targeting criteria imposed on them by the special nature of the operation. This shortfall sprang from the complex nature of weaponeering and the conceptual underpinnings of the manuals themselves.

The weaponeering process includes several steps, the first of which entails analysis of an assigned target. Weaponeers examine the nature of the target, seeking to identify its most critical and/or vulnerable parts, and assess the desired level of destruction. Different targets have different critical and vulnerable points. For example, a bomb hit on any part of a tank likely will destroy it, while efficiently taking out a factory requires careful placement of weapons on particular parts of it. Logically, then, the next step in the weaponeering process involves identifying the particular weapons effect needed to destroy the target or its various parts. Weapons destroy things in different ways, mainly through blast, heat, or penetration by fragments or shrapnel. Their ability to do so depends upon the weight, construction, and delivery accuracy of the warheads. Accuracy, in turn, depends upon such factors as method of release, design characteristics, distance from point of release to target, weather and wind, and guidance from release to target. JMEMs describe the accuracy of weapons along with many other elements of the weaponeering process.

Perhaps the main "accuracy" message of JMEMs is the obvious one: because precision weapons have a drastically smaller circular error of probability than unguided weapons, they greatly reduce the number of weapons and sorties required to achieve a given effect on a target or aiming point. Given the demonstrably greater accuracy of PGMs, therefore, Deliberate Force weaponeers and operators utilized them to the maximum extent possible. In light of the proscription on unnecessary collateral damage, they had little choice. The accuracy of PGMs is reflected in General Ryan's declaration that any impact beyond a weapon's circular error of probability from an aiming point constituted a miss. Despite the general utility of the JMEMs, planners in the 7490th Composite Wing (Provisional) found the manuals difficult to use, particularly in making rapid

weapon and fuzing decisions driven by the fast pace and political sensitivities of the bombing campaign.

However, the 31st Fighter Wing's Intelligence Group acquired
a technological tool designed to assist in mission planning two
weeks prior to Deliberate Force. It became a great success story.
In a joint venture, Virginia Cambridge Research and the Defense
Mapping Agency developed the Power Scene Mission Planning
System, a hybrid of a mission-rehearsal system, intelligence system, and operation system. This operations and intelligence
model overlays spot satellite imagery on a terrain-elevation database, providing a three-dimensional perspective of navigation
routes, target run-ins, and threat bubbles. Remarkably, pilots
could view Bosnia-Herzegovina's database imagery in 10-, five-,
two-, and one-meter-square resolution.

Power Scene flies like an aircraft or a helicopter in either
cruise or hover mode but with very limited displays. The moving map display on a large TV screen gives the sensation of
movement as it pitches and rolls via a little joystick. The view
resembles one from a cockpit, allowing for an exceptional view
of the attack axis. Red and green bubbles display threats,
showing the maximum engagement range (or rings) of a particular SAM system. Outside the threat dome, the bubble is
red but changes to green after one enters the bubble. The
system can also provide navigation/targeting pod views (e.g.,
for a five-nautical-mile release with a 30-degree "crank" [hard
turn]). The screen can capture the flight profile on photos as
well as videotape (8 mm and VHS) for mission briefings and
target folders; thus, Power Scene enhances situational awareness prior to flying the mission.

Additionally, the system has a unique way of mensurating
target coordinates. In the hover mode, a 90-degree pitch down
with the grommet (flight-path vector marker) on the aiming
point provides coordinates in Universal Transverse Mercator
or latitude/longitude within 75 feet laterally and one hundred
to two hundred feet vertically. The ability to mensurate coordinates allows for targeting verification, an advantage that became ever apparent during Deliberate Force. On several occasions Power Scene resolved ambiguities between target
coordinates fragged by the CAOC. In one case a bridge's coordinates were fifteen hundred feet in error. The pictures and

mensurated coordinates provided by Power Scene checked the accuracy and flagged the mistake. Power Scene was a huge success with aircrews of the 7490th Wing, who cycled on and off the system 24 hours a day, seven days a week during Deliberate Force. The preview of situational awareness proved extremely valuable and greatly assisted mission planning at the unit and force levels, making Power Scene a welcomed planning and preparation tool.[10]

In the fog and friction of Deliberate Force, one of the major factors of mission preparation and execution was the unique requirements and restrictions of the tactical area of operations (TAOO)—the CFACC's area of responsibility. Theater require-ments and airspace procedures were addressed in the ROE and commander's guidance provided to the units and mission planners via SPINS. In order to prevent any unacceptable out-comes to the politico-military situation in the theater, person-nel had to follow the ROE (see chap. 14 of this volume) not only throughout mission planning but also during execution of the mission tactics.

Mission Tactics in Deliberate Force

After April 1993 Deny Flight evolved from an operation that used combat air patrols (CAP) to enforce the no-fly zones (NFZ) to a complex mission encompassing close air support (CAS) of the United Nations Protection Force (UN-PROFOR), stand-alone SEAD, offensive air operations (OAS), and associated support missions such as tactical reconnais-sance and combat search and rescue. Deny Flight's revised concept of operations (CONOPS), contained in Operations Plan (OPLAN) 40101, "Deny Flight," change four, 3 May 1995, established these combat air missions. This OPLAN was in effect during Deliberate Force.

The CONOPS, a broad flow plan that underlies the specific guidance of the SPINS, provided general guidance for estab-lishing the operational level of effort required to conduct deployment, employment, and logistics support in the Bal-kans area of responsibility. Given the politico-military con-straints in effect, the SPINS controlled and directed much of the air operations in and out of the TAOO. In light of the SPINS and tactical mission-planning factors previously mentioned (e.g., threats, targets, etc.), the general CONOPS determined the means of tactical employment (ingress/egress high, medium, or low); location of forces; ways of flowing penetrating forces in and out of the target area; and command, control, and coordination of, as well as communication with, the forces (fig. 11.2).

Deliberate Force air operations were an extension of the Deny Flight CONOPS. High-value air assets such as airborne battlefield command and control center (ABCCC) EC-130E aircraft (Bookshelf), NATO airborne early warning (NAEW) E-3A aircraft, and air-to-air refueling tankers established medium-altitude orbits over the Adriatic Sea ("feet wet"). For area deconfliction over the Adriatic, ABCCC was anchored north; NAEW was anchored south; and the tankers were stationed centrally in the "Sonny" and "Speedy" air-to-air refueling

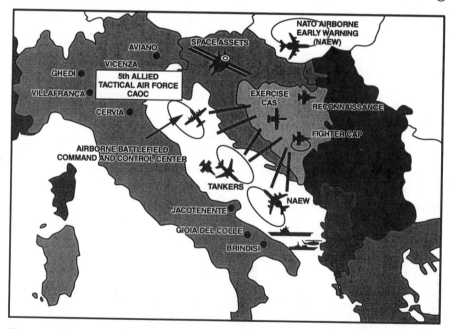

Figure 11.2. Deliberate Force Concept of Operations (From Corona briefing slides, Lt Gen Michael Ryan, Headquarters AIRSOUTH, Naples, Italy, 5 December 1995)

tracks. Land- and sea-based tactical air assets would take off, check in with the CAOC and/or ABCCC, and go feet wet to rendezvous with their assigned tankers for pre-mission refueling prior to penetrating Bosnia-Herzegovina's airspace ("feet dry").

Aircraft were procedurally rather than positively controlled to and from the area because of the identification-friend-or-foe transponder restrictions when they operated feet dry. However, when operating feet wet, the aircraft transmitted their normally assigned modes and codes. Regardless, the aircraft were primarily deconflicted in the airspace by altitudes, time, special corridors, and gates/drop points. Tactical aircraft generally flowed and operated in the medium-altitude blocks, entering between five thousand and 10,000 feet (light AAA and small-arms threats) and exiting above 10,000 feet, while rotary-wing Rapid Reaction Force helicopters always operated below three thousand feet in the TAOO.

The aircraft entered and exited the TAOO via special transit corridors that had established gates/drop points (defined by latitude/longitude coordinates), altitude blocks, and corridor widths. From flight to flight, controllers told aircraft to deviate within the limits of the special corridors to avoid being too predictable at the arrival and departure points. If operating a CAS/battlefield air interdiction (BAI) mission, strike aircraft had a tactical air control point (TACP), defined by a Bosnia-Herzegovina geographical reference and its associated coordinates. Additionally, all aircraft/aircrews were responsible for following SPINS inside the TAOO.[11]

Within the framework of the Deliberate Force CONOPS and SPINS, planners conducted and orchestrated combat air missions, including support missions, to meet and counter the threat, seize the initiative, gain the offensive, and meet tactical objectives. For example, the CONOPS for *Bouton D'or*, the air-strike plan for protecting the Sarajevo area, might include SEAD against the BSA's IADS; CAS/BAI against BSA fielded forces; and air interdiction (AI) against BSA command and control (C^2), direct and essential support, and supporting lines of communications. Thus, given the combined force mix, weapons, and targets, combat mission tactics sought to accomplish the mission accomplishment yet enhance survivability.

Combat Air Patrol

Operating in the role of offensive counterair and under close control of NAEW (call sign Magic) or another air control unit (ACU) such as a US Navy E-2C Skyhawk (call sign Cricket), CAP missions sought to detect, identify, and engage any fixed-wing or rotary-wing aircraft that violated the NFZs. The primary CAP players included the British (FMK-3), French (M2000C), Dutch (NF-16A), and Turks (TF-16). Working in the medium-block altitudes, they were routinely assigned time-on-stations in their sectored areas of responsibility to provide 24-hour force protection, all the while observing TAOO boundaries and borders of the former Republic of Yugoslavia. NAEW/ACU approved altitude variations, but Gen Hal Hornburg, CAOC director (call sign Chariot), had to approve CAP flights below 10,000 feet or into SAM rings. The NATO fighters utilized two- and four-ship roving, racetrack, or bar CAPs, usually over airfields in Bosnia-Herzegovina, and any tasked CAS/BAI support control points, always anchored feet wet over the Adriatic Sea in particular CAP stations (forward and rear/north and south), to protect high-value air assets. Although these assets supported OAS, they functioned in a defensive counterair role. Additionally, aircraft flying CAP obtained pilot in-flight reports on the weather when so requested by the CAOC; during poor weather the fighters did this every hour on the hour during daylight missions and periodically at night.

Operating in the TAOO, CAP aircraft had their orbits adjusted to prevent spillouts into internationally controlled airspace, taking care to remain well clear of the former Republic of Yugoslavia's airspace. When necessary, the fighters maneuvered to facilitate early detection and timely intercepts of unauthorized flight activity in the NFZs while informing NAEW/ACU of their intentions. After committing to an intercept, they had to abide by SPINS and air-to-air ROE.

The primary tactic of the CAP fighters was a visual identification (VID) intercept or pass to a position behind or beside the target and within weapons range. After identifying NFZ violations, the fighters reported the latitude/longitude of the contact; course, speed, and altitude; VID or unknown markings; intercept status; and time to the appropriate controlling agency. During Deliberate Force the NAEW/ACU and CAP aircraft detected 46 NFZ violations. Remarkably, no intercept engagements or employment of air-to-air weaponry occurred during that time.

Suppression of Enemy Air Defenses

Prior to Deliberate Force, SEAD missions protected friendly forces from enemy air defenses on the ground. They did so by neutralizing, degrading, or destroying ground-based electromagnetic emitters such as early warning/ground-controlled intercept; command, control, and communications systems; SAM/AAA fire-control systems; and associated surface-to-air weapons. Commanders authorized stand-alone SEAD as a separate mission when they needed continued airborne operations within the range of SAM systems and when NATO/UNPROFOR aircraft operating within the danger zone (SAM engagement ring) found themselves at risk. Because of politico-military constraints, SEAD engagements had to be proportional to the threat. By the time Deliberate Force commenced, planners had designed air operations plans Deadeye Southeast and Deadeye Northwest to neutralize, disrupt, or destroy the BSA's IADS.

In the early morning hours of 30 August 1995, Deliberate Force kicked off with a SEAD strike aimed at neutralizing the BSA's defense network in southeast Bosnia. Under Deadeye Southeast, a package of 17 aircraft—F-18C Hornets and EA-6B Prowlers from the USS *Theodore Roosevelt*—struck SAM sites, command posts, early warning radar sites, and communications nodes to the north, east, and south of Sarajevo. SEAD tactics, which included the use of AGM-88 HARMs, tactical air-launched drones, and laser-guided bombs (LGB), opened the way for follow-on air strikes by other NATO aircraft at BSA ammunition dumps around Sarajevo. After the first SEAD air strike around Sarajevo, Deliberate Force initiated a series of SEAD strikes spreading out from that city, eventually hitting early warning and communications facilities around the heavily defended Banja Luka area in northwest Bosnia. Toward the end of the air campaign, SEAD strikes used such standoff weapons as

F-18 with HARMs

Tomahawk land-attack missiles, standoff land-attack missiles (SLAM), and GBU-15s.

Daily SEAD operations generally consisted of eight to 12 assets supporting three to five strike packages of anywhere from 12 to 20 aircraft penetrating overland in Bosnia-Herzegovina. Because no NATO aircraft could operate feet dry over Bosnia-Herzegovina without SEAD support, the CAOC spread the limited SEAD assets over a coverage window that started at the arrival of the first SEAD platforms on station and closed when the last ones departed (table 11.2). During Deliberate Force the 785 SEAD sorties (including both shooter and jammer missions) averaged seven windows per day with a duration of 13.5 hours per day and an average window time of two hours.

SEAD tactics had HARM shooters (F-16 HARM Targeting System [HTS] aircraft, F-18s, and EA-6s) and jammers (EF-111s and EA-6s) getting situation updates from Magic, Bookshelf, and Rivet Joint electronic-intelligence aircraft on their

Table 11.2

SEAD Windows in Deliberate Force

Air Tasking Message Day	Dates (1995)	Window Opportunities	Time on Station (hours)	SEAD Probes
1	29–30 Aug	3	3.2	1
2	30–31 Aug	9	16.6	9
3	31 Aug–1 Sep	6	14.6	6
4	1–2 Sep	7	16.1	4
5	2–3 Sep	5	18.8	3
6	3–4 Sep	4	7.6	0
7	4–5 Sep	2	19.5	0
8	5–6 Sep	4	16.8	0
9	6–7 Sep	4	21.0	0
10	7–8 Sep	4	22.8	0
11	8–9 Sep	12	13.4	0
12	9–10 Sep	15	16.6	0
13	10–11 Sep	12	14.1	0
14	11–12 Sep	13	14.9	0
15	12–13 Sep	8	8.5	0
16	13–14 Sep	7	5.4	0
17	14–15 Sep	0	0.0	0
	Total	115	229.9	23

Source: Extracted from CAOC daily summaries, 29 August–14 September 1995. (Confidential) Information extracted is unclassified.

way into the TAOO—or a handoff situation report from the SEAD players they replaced. SEAD mission commanders were to inform NAEW/ACU on estimated time of arrival at the ingress corridor. They, in turn, would transmit the window-open time; prior to departure from the station, the SEAD commander would advise NAEW/ACU about closing the window time. As the OAS and tactical reconnaissance assets flowed into their various orbits and working areas, SEAD players adjusted their positions to electronically attack threats that came up. If the fighters penetrating Bosnia-Herzegovina overland were in several different areas, the SEAD package anchored in a central orbit could "flex" (switch) in any direction required. The key point was to allow SEAD assets to flow into the optimum location for support rather than remaining tied to one fragged location. Controllers deconflicted SEAD assets by assigning optimum employment altitudes for the particular platform systems.

All SEAD players monitored a specific frequency for requests from penetrating fighters, usually strike primary—also monitored by Magic. Any fighter requesting assistance pushed that frequency and gave his request for support directly to the SEAD package, which responded according to current ROE and in coordination with Magic and Chariot. For preplanned OAS and tactical reconnaissance missions that penetrated known SAM threat rings, direct-support SEAD packages provided optimum HARM and jamming coverage tied to that mission. All SEAD mission commanders had the responsibility to ensure that the planning and positioning of SEAD aircraft included consideration of methods to engage the desired target(s), minimize the chances of engaging unintended targets, and mitigate the impact of possible HARM ambiguities.[12]

SEAD aircraft accomplish their missions by either destructive or disruptive means, the former by shooters such as US Air Force F-16 HTS aircraft, F-117s with PGMs, or US Navy/US Marine Corps F-18s with HARMs and tactical air-launched drones, and the latter by jammers such as US Air Force EF-111s and Compass Call aircraft or US Navy EA-6Bs (which can also employ HARMs). Common to all destructive SEAD platforms is the HARM, which can be employed in one of several missile modes: range known, range unknown/self-protect, target of opportunity, or HARM-as-sensor.[13]

The success of HARM employment depends primarily on the accuracy of threat location provided by intelligence sources, ability of the pilot to achieve HARM-launch parameters, and emission-control tactics employed by the enemy. The employment range for range known is approximately twice that of range-unknown launches, given the same firing parameters. In addition, range-known launches provide an increased probability that the HARM will acquire the specific targeted radar site, especially if employed "smartly" from the F-16 HTS. This smart-shooter mode can be critical for corridor suppression and target-area-suppression tactics. Also, one can employ hunter/killer tactics by using an F-16 HTS element as the hunter, which passes target information to the killer (attacking) element.[14]

These medium-altitude tactics were employed during Deliberate Force with mixed results. After the first few days of the air campaign, the CAOC had to impose HARM-employment restrictions on preemptive shots, requiring approval from Chariot or higher to execute. While performing SEAD missions, US Navy F-18s fired a total of 33 preemptive HARMs. Additionally, aircraft could employ reactive HARMs only if aircraft were operating in Bosnia-Herzegovina or the Croatia Restricted Operating Zone (CROROZ) and one of the following conditions existed: (1) positive indication of a hostile act (e.g., confirmation of fired missiles or projectiles) or (2) dual correlation of hostile intent.[15] A total of 27 reactive HARMs were employed (what aircrews termed "magnum" shots) by EA-6s (10), F/A-18Cs (two), F/A-18Ds (four), F-16 HTS (nine), and EF-18As (two) during the course of Deliberate Force.

With regard to SEAD disruption, the primary concepts of employing jammers—Ravens, Prowlers, and Compass Call aircraft—are area-suppression operations, corridor-suppression operations, and target-area suppression. Area suppression disrupts and confuses the enemy's IADS over a relatively large area. Corridor suppression supports specific missions within a more localized area and usually employs tactics tailored for the mission package being supported. Target-area suppression suppresses enemy defenses protecting a specific high-priority target or target area.

The jammers' mission profiles or tactics include standoff jamming, close-in jamming, and direct support. In Deliberate Force, EF-111s primarily performed standoff jamming. These aircraft featured a crew of two and 10 jamming transmitters but had no armament, whereas the EA-6B featured a crew of four, eight jamming transmitters, and HARMs and surface-attack weapons. The EF-111A used the ALQ-99E platform jammer, based upon the system used by the Navy's EA-6B—the ALQ-99. Although similar, these systems differ somewhat, as does the employment of the two aircraft. Both platforms were tasked to preemptively or reactively jam the BSA's IADS over areas in Bosnia-Herzegovina and CROROZ commensurate with mission and anticipated threats. The Ravens primarily flew standoff jamming and sometimes detached direct support, whereas the

315

Prowlers flew more direct support since they were equipped with HARMs. The EF-111A retains the speed and range of the F-111 Aardvark. The EA-6B has narrower output beams than the EF-111A, thereby producing higher effective radiated power. The Raven jams off its wings, while the Prowler jams to the front of the aircraft.[16] In Deliberate Force the CAOC learned to coordinate the two aircraft to complement each other's strengths and weaknesses in a concerted effort.

Compass Call, another important SEAD asset, is an EC-130H aircraft with a computer-assisted, operator-controlled, selective-jamming system designed to support tactical air operations. During Deliberate Force, Compass Call supported offensive air operations as part of the SEAD effort, orbiting along the coast from its target area and outside lethal SAM rings. At loiter airspeeds the EC-130H could remain on station up to eight hours. Coordinating with NAEW/ACU and continually checking on each mission for threat warnings, Compass Call flew 35 SEAD support missions during Deliberate Force.

Offensive Air Operations

OAS employed air forces to execute CAS, BAI, and AI combat air missions in close coordination with UNPROFOR against targets to relieve sieges of cities and areas in Bosnia-Herzegovina, and to respond to attacks/forces that threatened the UN safe areas in Bosnia-Herzegovina. These proportional air-strike missions sought to show resolve and capability as well as discourage retaliation by the warring factions. Although limited in time and scope, OAS proved robust enough to achieve the desired effect.[17]

Close Air Support. In Deliberate Force, CAS provided 24-hour responsiveness, as required, to UNPROFOR ground units. By OPLAN 40101's definition, a CAS mission entails live air action against designated targets that require detailed coordination with friendly ground forces. The proximity of friendly forces[18] to the engaged targets necessitated positive control to integrate each mission with the fire and movement of those forces. CAS aircraft engaged targets of immediate concern to the ground commander that his forces could not engage or that proved unsuitable targets for his ground-force weapons. To be effective, CAS should fulfill the needs of the supported commander.

The signing of the NATO-UN Air/Land Coordination Document on 23 August 1995 provided General Ryan and Lt Gen Bernard Janvier, force commander of United Nations Peace Forces (FC UNPF), with an operational-level document to conduct joint air-land operations. In phase four of the air-land operations, SEAD is followed by near-simultaneous CAS, BAI, and AI missions. Air-land coordination occurred in terms of close or near-ground battles. The battles coordinated by the local commander required both a TACP to control CAS missions and deconfliction of the Rapid Reaction Force's direct and indirect fire with NATO air (the fire-support commander). The effectiveness of CAS depended upon the TACP's capability and weather conditions. The near battle coordinated by FC UNPF required coordination and communication among the fire-support coordination line, outer defensible zones, and fixed targets; the forward air controllers (airborne) (FAC-A)–controlled engagement zones; and the free-fire areas.[19]

Because of Deny Flight's CAS exercise, all OA/A-10, F/A-18D, AC-130, and certain F-16C, A-6E, or F-14 missions were FAC-A capable. CAS/BAI missions with overlapping time-on-target (TOT) could have been tasked to work with one of these FAC-A fighters. Chariot had the responsibility to ensure the deconfliction of all assigned targets within the CAS FAC boxes.[20] Aircraft engaging targets within 10 nautical miles of each other were controlled by the same TACP/FAC-A on a single frequency; however, aircraft engaging targets greater than 10 but less than 20 nautical miles of each other were controlled by TACP on separate frequencies. In this case the tasking authority made both flights aware of adjacent missions. Normally, all CAS missions occurred at or above 10,000 feet to stay above light AAA and small-arms fire and to allow reaction time to MANPADs.

The fact that NATO aircraft flew over one hundred Blue Swords—CAS requests from FC UNPF or the Rapid Reaction Force—demonstrates the responsiveness of CAS missions. After establishment of the CAS request net, such requests took over six hours for approval—eventually reduced to two hours.

CAS assets, usually A-10s, were scrambled to launch or were diverted from airborne holding orbits. The air tasking message (ATM) usually allocated one-hour alert (A-60) or three-hour alert (A-180) for requests from friendly ground units.[21]

Aircrews thought that CAS missions should have had BAI backup or vice versa to prevent ineffective missions with no drops. In retrospect, however, most of the CAS requests sought to show that airpower was responsive and ready to strike. Only four requests, two during Deny Flight and two during Deliberate Force, led to live-fire CAS missions. The Deliberate Force missions occurred on 30 August and 10 September 1995, the former involving seven A-10s, two F-16s, and one Mirage 2000, which employed Mk-82s, CBU-87s, 2.75-inch rockets, and 30 mm guns to hit 12 of 16 assigned targets, destroying four of them. Tactics varied from working a wheel (circling the targets) and maneuvering a figure eight (for the A-10s' gun employment) to restricted run-ins controlled by the FAC-A (an OA-10). A US Air Force F-16 dropped the only bomb—a laser-guided, self-designated GBU-12. On 10 September, in the last "true" CAS mission of Deliberate Force, three aircraft (an NF-16, a US Air Force F-16, and a Royal Air Force GR-7) responded to a CAS request, employing Mk-82s and a GBU-12 to destroy two bunkers and hit an artillery position.

Battlefield Air Interdiction. BAI, a NATO distinction, defined attacks that amounted to a cross between AI and CAS but did not need a FAC-A. Most strike sorties flown in Deliberate Force fell into this category. Like CAS aircraft, BAI aircraft targeted fielded forces but received target assignments primarily through the ATM and target information from the Linked Operations Intelligence Centers Europe (LOCE). Aircrews would work up preplanned strikes or raids that, unfortunately, became a nuisance because the ATM cycle constantly changed taskings and/or targets and because LOCE did not generate the necessary imagery in a timely manner. For example, aircrews would show for a three-hour alert window and prepare a flight plan for the targets, but in an hour and one-half, the ATM tasking changed, placing them on standby status awaiting a TOT. Having only 20 minutes to step time, they would receive the tasking information. With 10 minutes to coordinate, five minutes to plan, and five minutes to brief the attack, they would step to the jets to start engines. However, while in the jets with engines running, they would receive word of a one-hour postponement of the flight—and on and on, one hour to the next. These line-of-sight, inconsistent changes frustrated aircrews, who failed to see the rationale behind such target changes.

In the air, BAI aircraft maintained communications with Bookshelf or Cricket from initial check-in to mission completion. C^2 differentiation on a BAI alert versus a packaged BAI created many in-flight coordination and deconfliction difficulties. After resolving these, the aircraft would join up with their assigned tankers, feet wet, awaiting the word to enter Bosnia-Herzegovina. After receiving clearance, controllers deconflicted BAI aircraft by four quadrants (northeast, southeast, southwest, and northwest) or engagement zones (EZ). During BAI execution, aircraft not specifically tasked into an EZ were to remain clear. BAI aircraft tasked into an EZ remained outside until their assigned target-attack time or window. Any reattacks on targets inside the EZ were to be made from outside the EZ whenever practical. Prior to reattack, ABCCC resolved conflicts between reattacks outside of scheduled TOT windows and other BAI missions. On one occasion, an A-10 passed through the field of view of an F-16's forward-looking infrared radar when the F-16 was about to laze the target 10 seconds prior to impact. Despite this close call, every BAI mission had instructions to make every reasonable effort to limit collateral damage as much as possible, commensurate with the need to protect friendly forces. Thus, BAI would require a ground commander's TACP/FAC-A coordination on free-fire zones to limit collateral damage, fratricide, and casualties among refugees/noncombatants.

Because the ROE required VID of a target prior to releasing ordnance, BAI flights often cleared and identified the target area by having the flight lead do a low-altitude, high-speed pass—much like a clearing pass on a Class C conventional or tactics range—while the remainder of the flight "wheeled" overhead. Given the threat environment, the VID target pass was a "sporty" event but a necessary evil, leading some to argue in favor of generating killer scouts or "fast FACs" from CAS/BAI lines (a "push-CAS" concept).[22]

319

The killer-scout aircraft (an F-16) located targets and controlled attacks on them in a specific operating area—in this case, the EZ. The primary mission of the fast FAC, usually performed beyond the fire-support coordination line without operating as a FAC-A, entailed validating targets listed in the ATM and ensuring that no friendly forces had moved into an operating EZ or FAC box. Secondarily, this aircraft provided close control, area deconfliction, and visual lookout. If the ATM target was valid—that is, a confirmed "live" target—the fast FAC would mark the target and clear the assigned fighters to attack it under flight-lead control. In a low-threat environment, a flight of four would use curvilinear tactics from 15,000 to 25,000 feet and would sequentially attack the targets from random-attack headings. The combinations of weather, terrain, medium altitudes, C^2 delays, and fielded BSA targets (especially heavy weapons) made BAI and fast FAC very challenging missions.

Air Interdiction. During Deliberate Force, AI missions destroyed, disrupted, delayed, and funneled BSA movements throughout Bosnia. AI target sets included C^2, direct and essential support, and supporting lines of communications (bridges). Combined forces using PGMs struck most of these targets. Like BAI, AI missions employed two-ship tactics utilizing LGB delivery profiles. The tactics employed by US Air Force F-15Es and F-16s reflected the typical tactical profiles exhibited by the Navy's F-18s, Marine F/A-18s, and British GR-7s, which also expended LGBs.

The 492d Fighter Squadron's F-15E Strike Eagles from Royal Air Force Lakenheath, England, employed two-ship, medium-altitude, self-designation LGB tactics. Utilizing their inertial navigation system, LANTIRN navigation, targeting pod, and radar bit-mapping capability en route, the F-15E would update target-area features because the desired mean points of impact (DMPI) were too small to acquire visually at standoff ranges. Attacking from 20,000 feet at 0.9 Mach, the aircraft would release the LGB approximately five nautical miles from the target and check away 30–45 degrees from the attack heading. The weapon system officer (WSO) would "capture" (i.e., acquire) the target aiming point and ensure that the targeting pod was tracking the target. Just prior to the end of the LGB's time of flight (TOF), the WSO would fire the laser and self-designate his own weapon to impact. Initially, the F-15Es used a terminal-delay lazing technique (final portion of TOF), but after a few misses, possibly due to high-wind (about 75 knots!) corrections at end game, aircrews adopted a continuous lazing technique to allow the weapon to make more constant adjustments from the wind effects, thus improving their hit rates.

By far, the most difficult targets for the Strike Eagles were bridges. Although no problems existed with attack avenues and laser line of sight, they needed several trial-and-error missions to drop the bombs effectively. Despite using GBU-10Is with mixed fusing on different stations, the restrictive attack axis and laser-spot diffusion resulted in some misses on small tracks. The F-15E's weapon of choice for bridge busting is the GBU-24 Paveway III LGB, but problems with the weapon carriage precluded use of this bomb until the very end of the air campaign.

Another problem the F-15s experienced, together with poor weather, was maintaining line of sight until weapons impact while targeting bridges in deep valleys. During a bridge attack on 1 September 1995, an LGB went "stupid" (i.e., ballistic without guidance), missing the bridge, impacting the far-side embankment, and damaging a house. This incident led to restricted run-in headings and single-release ROE for a short time.

During Deliberate Force, F-15Es also expended their first GBU-15s in combat. Because of orders prohibiting penetration of SAM rings during missions in northwest Bosnia, the Strike Eagles used the GBU-15, an excellent standoff weapon, to hit targets inside those rings. Unfortunately, inexperience, lack of training, and bad weather tainted their debut with the weapon system. Of the nine GBU-15s employed during Deliberate Force, only four found their targets. Of the five misses, four failed to acquire the target, and one malfunctioned.

F-16s of the 31st Fighter Wing at Aviano AB, Italy, used similar tactics and LGB-delivery profiles but experienced their own unique problems because they were employing LGBs for the first time in combat. Although the tactics of F-16 pilots from the 555th Fighter Squadron and the 510th Fighter Squadron initially differed because they flew opposing day/night shifts, cross talk among the pilots in both squadrons led to more uniformity. Like that of the F-15E, the F-16's typical LGB delivery profile entailed two-to-four-ship, medium-altitude, delayed-lazing tactics. From a 40,000-foot slant range from the target, the F-16 released the LGB and cranked for a split/offset away from the target. After acquiring the target with help from the targeting pod, the pilot fired the laser prior to the end TOF of the weapon. The LGB would travel nearly five nautical miles before impact.

Early on in the air campaign, the F-16s experienced less-than-optimum results from their GBU-10 (2,000 lb) deliveries. Given their limited experience in employing this weapon, even the best of the pilots still missed about 50 percent of the drops. Like their counterparts in the F-15Es, F-16 pilots were not allowing enough time for their GBU-10s to acquire the laser energy and make upwind corrections. Consequently, the 31st Fighter Wing changed from GBU-10s to GBU-12s (500 lb) where weaponeering allowed. In addition, the use of GBU-12s allowed the F-16s to return to Aviano without jettisoning their bombs in the Adriatic Sea.

After consulting with the Fighter Weapons School at Nellis Air Force Base (AFB), Nevada, fighter-weapons personnel of the 31st Fighter Wing decided not to change to continuous lazing with GBU-10s, as had the F-15 pilots, because the school was teaching end-game delayed lazing. Instead, they opted to substitute weapons that might have compromised weaponeering at times because the probability of kill was less with the GBU-12s. What could they have learned from LGB employment history? For one, delayed lazing developed from high-speed, low-altitude, loft-delivery techniques—not a me-dium-altitude technique (in which low ballistic energy and premature LGB pitchovers were concerns). For another, the rule of thumb for lazing ever since the days of the F-4 Phan-tom called for continuous lazing if the weapon's TOF lasted less than 20 seconds and delayed lazing for at least half of the TOF if the latter exceeded 20 seconds. For example, if a GBU-10's TOF is 40 seconds, the WSO should fire the laser to gain range acceptance for delivery parameters, and after weapons release, the WSO should delay laze until the last 20 seconds of the TOF. Lastly, less end-game, delayed-lazing time was not the answer for F-111E/Fs and F-15Es that faced the same medium-altitude, high-wind delivery conditions in Operation Desert Storm, employing thousands of LGBs. We should not have had to relearn this lesson in Deliberate Force.

Another tactical-employment dilemma for the F-16s involved self-designating versus buddy-lazing techniques. Normally, in a high-threat scenario, F-16s prefer to employ two-ship LGB tactics by splitting the target and lazing for each other. This technique allows mutually supportive deliveries and keeps the single-seat pilot's head up after weapons release, especially in poor weather, thereby enhancing situational awareness and survivability. If buddy lazing was the preferred method of delivery, why did the F-16s end up self-designating? Unfortunately, because of night-employment conditions (spacing) and the need to employ four-ship tactics on proximity targeting of DMPIs, buddy-lazing techniques took a backseat to self-designating. With four-ship tactics, the lateral and vertical impact effects of a GBU-10 (2,000 lb bomb) at five-thousand-feet mean sea level obscure other targets. At medium altitude above the fragmentation of the weapon, the four-ship flight would have to deconflict over the target area by taking spacing (equal to the frag TOF) because the DMPI separation is less than the lateral-distance effects of the munition. Unfortunately, the CAOC did this routinely, especially with last-minute target changes.

The answer for the F-16s called for employing two-ship tactics with spacing of 10–15 nautical miles to ensure that the leader's bomb fragmentation would not interfere with the wingman's target acquisition and LGB guidance. Because of weather problems, reattack options posed other tactical problems. By the end of the air campaign, the F-16s had adopted a "shooter/cover" tactic for buddy lazing to allow at least one good laser pod on a pass. If the buddy could not capture, he would call "goalie," and the pilot on the bomb pass would designate himself—and vice versa. In hindsight the F-16s wished they could have employed more fighting-wing, buddy-lazing techniques, especially from the beginning; instead, they planned for single-ship employment, expecting good weather and low threats. However, night profiles and tight DMPI spacing complicated that game plan. The lack of a sound backup plan and slow adaptation to changing combat conditions resulted in the late implementation of better buddy-lazing tactics—a lesson learned.

With regard to one other AI tactical highlight, joint employment of the GBU-15 and SLAM in proximity (same sector) produced data-linked interference problems that surprised everyone concerned. The interference resulted in the electro-optical presentation of the GBU-15 picture, normally presented on the F-15E, intruding on the F/A-18's video screen when the Hornet was attempting to guide its SLAM. This problem trashed seven SLAMs because of command-guidance failures. The costly joint-employment lesson learned here is that in future conflicts one should write SPINS to coordinate and deconflict platforms and standoff weapons in the area, along with their respective electro-optical frequency spectrums.

Tactical Issues

Despite adverse weather, C² problems, and ROE constraints, the combined tactics used in Deliberate Force got the job done with minimal collateral damage. The successful employment of the combat air missions resulted directly from the multinational aircrews' strong leadership, mutual support, and air discipline, which remain essential to the effective employment of tactical aircraft. In retrospect several tactical issues became apparent during or by the end of the air campaign.

Adverse Weather

The aircraft of the combined forces may have been all-weather capable (i.e., able to launch and recover in bad weather), but they were not all-weather employable because they failed to accomplish mission tasking nearly a third of the time because of poor weather. Given the VID target restrictions, pilots could not drop their bombs if the aircraft's sensors could not acquire targets. Concerns about collateral damage prevented the employment of such aircraft as the F-15E with its synthetic-aperture, bit-mapping feature because of unacceptable risks involving delivery accuracy. At times this situation forced aircrews to attempt to fly through holes in the clouds to drop their bombs, only to lose sight of the target in the last few seconds. Adverse weather combined with the rugged Bosnian terrain to affect all aspects of air operations, tactics, and mission effectiveness. Because many CAS missions had no BAI backup with alternate targets, NATO aircraft "pickled" 65 LGBs in the Adriatic Sea. The dismal weather conditions created high divert fuels, which affected air-to-air refueling operations, fighter aircraft's combat loiter times, and the gross weight of weapons carriages for landing. The weather was so "doggy" that one F-16 pilot jettisoned his ordnance in the Adriatic four nights in a row! In addition, aircraft using GBU-15s could not acquire their assigned targets because of cloud obscuration.

The Gulf War was a wake-up call to war planners. During Desert Storm, weather/environmental factors affected 37 percent of the sorties flown over Iraq. But somehow the CAOC went to sleep at the wheel during Deliberate Force in terms of dealing with the weather. The ATM cycle "pushed" the weather too much, resulting in many delays, cancellations, and reschedulings, especially in the early morning and late evening. Force-mix capabilities should have been adjusted to accommodate the weather/night conditions. Although the ATM cycle usually has a 20 percent weather-attrition factor built in, perhaps that should be adjusted upwards—say, to 30 percent. The desire for robust air operations drove the schedule, regardless of weather conditions—and this sometimes replaced common sense. If the CAOC had authorized down days caused by bad weather, personnel could have regrouped and exchanged a "how goes it" with other players. Until we have the technology to permit all-weather/night-attack aircraft and precision-weapons capability within an acceptable circular error of probability, a "cookie-cutter" ATM approach, perhaps on a rotating four-to-six-hour cycle, would be considerably more advantageous than a 24-hour cycle that changes constantly. Because the weather presents challenges to all facets of air operations, war planners should act rather than react, stay informed, plan ahead, and anticipate its effect on the tempo of air operations and aircrew morale.

Single-Strike Mentality

The fight-the-way-we-train philosophy in a high-threat environment implies ingressing quickly at low altitude, with mass

325

and economy of force, moving across a target complex in minimum time, and egressing just as quickly to enhance survivability. All of the services' air-to-ground schools have incorporated this single-strike mentality, especially the Air Force's Fighter Weapons School. Massing firepower while surviving a highly defended target is affectionately known as "one pass, haul ass!"—a concept ever present on the minds of Deliberate Force strikers. After all, past European threat scenarios have us training with that mind-set. However, aircrews have come to realize—unlike the people who write the training syllabi—that in combat, elements of fog, friction, and chance (e.g., ROE, different threat conditions, poor targeting, and adverse weather) prevent them from implementing the single-strike mentality. As a result, pilots may have to perform multiple passes to accomplish mission objectives.

The early establishment of air supremacy in the Gulf War and Deliberate Force negated or minimized the threat from light AAA, small arms, and some MANPADs, so medium-altitude employment has become the way to go to war. With good intelligence, surveillance, and reconnaissance in-theater, SAM threats can be isolated and plotted to enhance avoidance and situational awareness; thus, the threat environment (high, medium, or low) changes, depending on the location of the assigned target. This rebuffs the notion of "once high-threat, always high-threat." Tactics have to be flexible enough to adapt to changing conditions of the threat locations—the battlefield as well as the TAOO.

So why not adopt a more flexible and fluid tactical response to the TAOO? The problem lies not only with peacetime training scenarios but also with the operational-level concepts of planning an air campaign. The air tasking comes down to mission commanders in strike packages of 60 to 80 aircraft that usually attack a target array in geographic proximity. The objective is to hit assigned targets with all these assets within a compressed TOT window and saturate defenses with many aircraft from different directions in the minimum amount of time. Such "gorilla" packages reflect the single-strike mentality, but in the real world—in this case the low-to-medium threat in southeast Bosnia—the situation does not demand a single-strike approach. However, large strike packages such as *Bouton D'or* employed one-pass-haul-ass tactics.

In many cases the tasking involved eight to 12 aircraft going across a single target complex within a two-to-five-minute TOT window—which works well if the fighters/bombers do not have to worry about collateral damage. But within the real politico-military constraints of Deliberate Force, the actual attack took 20 minutes because the aircraft had to VID the target, deconflict bomb impacts because of the DMPIs' proximity, and circumnavigate each other or the weather by reattacking. The massing and concentration of force packages in this type of environment is counterproductive, needlessly risks lives, and negates effective mission tactics. Although conditions warranted smart platforms and smart weapons, somehow the gorilla concept was not so smart here. Perhaps a more efficient and effective means of employment in this type of environment would entail turning the gorillas into "chimps"—specifically, a tailored, mission-specific strike package with 18 to 24 aircraft split into highly tactical chimps (two, four, or six ships) deconflicted laterally with adequate time (20–30 minutes) to hit several target areas.

The key to airpower is its inherent versatility, flexibility, and responsiveness. In future limited conflicts, with the exception of a SEAD campaign against sophisticated IADS or highly defended target complexes, we must alter the single-strike mentality of war planners to a more adaptive employment of tactical assets engaging in multiple-target attacks. The principles of mass and economy of force are important truths in employing combat forces but are not mandatory in every situation. Sometimes, maneuver and simplicity are great force multipliers. We should think in terms of chimps as well as gorillas.

Notes

1. Within surface-to-air missile (SAM)-ring radar coverage, a high-threat situation existed, characterized by a radar-intensive environment including a sophisticated surface-to-air threat (SAMs and antiaircraft artillery [AAA]) and/or an air-to-air threat. Outside the SAM-ring coverage, a low-threat environment existed, including a small-arms threat, nonradar AAA up to and including 57 mm, and some infrared (IR) man-portable air defense missiles.

2. "Electronic Warfare," OPLAN 40101, "Deny Flight," annex F, change 4, 3 May 1995, F-1, F-2. (Confidential) Information extracted is unclassified.

3. Multi-Command Manual (MCM) 3-1, vol. 2, *Threat Reference Guide and Countertactics* (U), 21 October 1994, 5-38 through -44. (Secret) Information extracted is unclassified.

4. "Combat Information," 29 June 1995, in MCM 3-1, vol. 2, 5-58 through -62. (Secret) Information extracted is unclassified.

5. MCM 3-1, vol. 2, 21 October 1994, 5-94 through -96. (Secret) Information extracted is unclassified.

6. Ibid., 5-109 through -11. (Secret) Information extracted is unclassified.

7. Ibid., 5-112, -14. (Secret) Information extracted is unclassified.

8. "Discussion of the Air Strategy in Bosnia," talking paper, Skunkworks, USAF/XOXS, Pentagon, Washington, D.C., 17 September 1995, 4.

9. Weaponeering "is the process of determining the quantity of a specific type weapon required to achieve a specified level of damage to a given target, considering target vulnerability, weapon effects, munitions delivery errors, damage criteria, probability of kill, weapon reliability, etc. When the objective of force employment is to employ lethal force against a target, targeteers use a variety of weaponeering methodologies to determine expected damage levels. These weaponeering methodologies include both nuclear and non-nuclear weaponeering techniques. Common to both methods is aimpoint selection and weapon effects analysis." Thomas A. Keaney and Eliot A. Cohen, *Gulf War Air Power Survey*, vol. 1, *Planning* (Washington, D.C.: Government Printing Office, 1993), pt. 1, fn. 9, p. 13.

10. Powerscene demonstration; and Capt Mark Hallisey and SSgt Joe Galliano, 31st Fighter Wing/IN, interviewed by author, December 1995.

11. Deny Flight SPINS 028, 26 August 1995, 2-4. (Confidential) Information extracted is unclassified.

12. Ibid., 9. (Confidential) Information extracted is unclassified.

13. Ibid., 8-17. (Confidential) Information extracted is unclassified.

14. Ibid. (Confidential) Information extracted is unclassified.

15. Ibid., 9. (Confidential) Information extracted is unclassified.

16. "Operation Desert Storm Electronic Combat Effectiveness Analysis" (Kelly AFB, Tex.: Air Force Intelligence Command, Air Force Electronic Warfare Center, January 1992), 10-14. (Secret) Information extracted is unclassified.

17. OPLAN 40101, "Deny Flight," annex D, appendix 4, change 4, 3 May 1995, D-4-1 through -2. (Secret) Information extracted is unclassified. Air Force Historical Research Agency (hereinafter AFHRA), Maxwell AFB, Ala., CAOC-01.

18. Friendly forces include NATO forces; national forces of NATO nations; UNPROFOR; Western European Union forces; and participating forces of non-NATO nations, nongovernmental organizations, and private/voluntary organizations.

19. Briefing, COMAIRSOUTH, subject: NATO/UN Air-Land Coordination, 23 August 1995, slides 1, 3.

20. Unlike the "kill-box" divisions of the Gulf War, Bosnia-Herzegovina is divided into eight FAC boxes approximately 30 nautical miles square, along with three additional areas covering the remainder of the country. Within the boxes, FAC-A and CAS/BAI aircraft operate from five thousand feet above ground level to a flight level of 20,000 feet.

21. CAS alert procedures included the following: (1) A-60 aircraft provided a two-hour response capability to the CAOC for AOCC Sarajevo requests (these aircraft were to be airborne one hour after notification of launch by the CAOC) and (2) A-180 aircraft were required on target within four hours of a CAS request from the AOCC (these aircraft were to be airborne three hours after notification, with one hour allowed for transit). Deny Flight SPINS 028, 26 August 1995, 12, AFHRA, NPL-09-02. (Confidential) Information extracted is unclassified.

22. The Marine Corps adapted the push-CAS system to ensure adequate air support to Marine ground forces. The 3d Marine Aircraft Wing began surge operations using the system on 22 February, two days before the start of the ground assault during Operation Desert Storm. The push-CAS system called for aircraft to launch according to a specific schedule but without a specific mission or target. If the aircraft were not used for a CAS mission within a specified period of time, they were handed off to the direct airborne support center for further handoff to a fast FAC for deep air support. The goals of the procedures were to maintain and continue to "push" aircraft to effective missions. Keaney and Cohen, vol. 4, *Weapons, Tactics, and Training, and Space Operations* (Washington, D.C.: Government Printing Office, 1993), pt. 1, "US Marine Corps Push CAS."

Chapter 12

Deliberate Force Combat Air Assessments

Lt Col Richard L. Sargent

Despite the politico-military constraints and sensitivities to collateral damage in the Balkans region, Deliberate Force was a successful air campaign because of very careful planning and execution that remained within the rules of engagement and combined multiroled "smart" platforms, weapons, targeting, and employment tactics. That is, the operation was a smartly run, robust air campaign—not just a "hit 'em harder with more" aerial campaign. Tying together the air campaign's platforms, weapons, targets, and tactics, this chapter graphically and statistically captures Deliberate Force by examining combat air assessments in the following areas: air operations summaries, weapon impacts, poststrike results, and tactical-employment effectiveness.

Air Operations Summaries

During Deliberate Force, aircraft from eight North Atlantic Treaty Organization (NATO) nations plus the alliance's own assets combined to fly a total of 3,535 sorties (fig. 12.1), classified as either penetrating or support (fig. 12.2). The 2,470 penetrating missions (70 percent of all sorties), which flew "feet dry" into Bosnia-Herzegovina's airspace, included close air support (CAS), battlefield air interdiction (BAI), suppression of enemy air defenses (SEAD), reconnaissance, and combat search and rescue (CSAR). The 1,065 support missions (30 percent of all sorties) included NATO airborne early warning, airborne battlefield command and control center (ABCCC), electronic intelligence/electronic support mission, air-to-air refueling, and search and rescue. The ratio of penetrating to support sorties was 2.3:1. The United States led all nations in the number of both penetrating and support sorties flown (figs. 12.3 and 12.4).

331

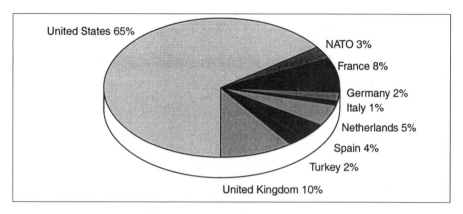

Figure 12.1. National Sortie Distribution

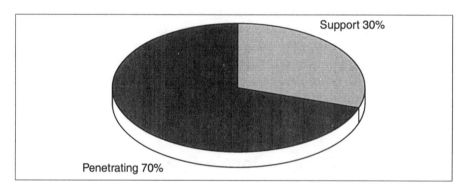

Figure 12.2. Overall Sortie Distribution

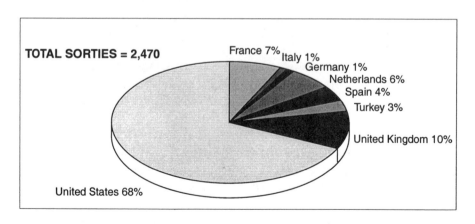

Figure 12.3. Distribution of Penetrating Sorties

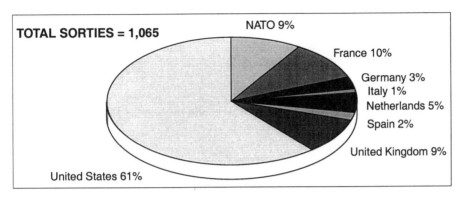

Figure 12.4. Distribution of Support Sorties

Prior to Deliberate Force, the force structure of Operation Deny Flight was divided into two tracking categories—strikers and supporters. At some undetermined time during Deliberate Force, however, the combined air operations center (CAOC)/Lt Gen Michael Ryan, combined force air component commander (CFACC), changed the strikers category to penetrators, including not only strikers but also supporters. Although *penetrators* may be a convenient term to track sorties in and out of the area of responsibility (AOR), the lumping of attackers (fighters/bombers) with supporters (passive platforms) makes for a distorted picture when one tries to examine aerospace platforms under their respective roles and missions (figs. 12.5 and 12.6, table 12.1). For instance, offensive counterair missions might have penetrated

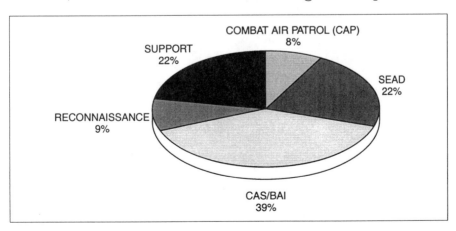

Figure 12.5. Deliberate Force Missions

333

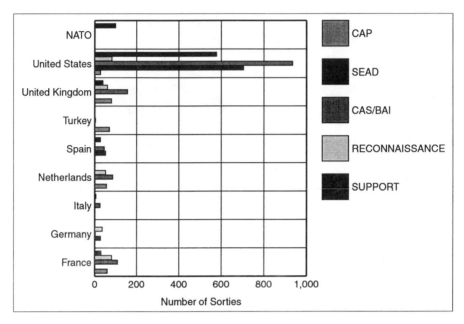

Figure 12.6. Deliberate Force Mission Apportionment

Table 12.1

Deliberate Force Mission Apportionment

Nation	CAP	SEAD	CAS/BAI	Reconnaissance	Support	Total
France	60	0	109	81	30	280
Germany	0	28	3	36	0	67
Italy	0	0	26	0	6	32
Netherlands	56	0	86	52	0	194
Spain	0	52	46	0	27	125
Turkey	70	0	4	0	0	74
United Kingdom	80	0	156	61	39	336
United States	28	705	935	82	578	2,328
NATO	0	0	0	0	99	99
Flown	294	785	1,365	312	779	3,535
Scheduled	298	858	1,173	368	788	3,485

Source: Operation Deliberate Force "Factual Review," vol. 2 of 7, annex A, appendices 2–6, AIRSOUTH, Naples, Italy, 14 October 1995, US Air Force Historical Research Agency (hereinafter AFHRA), Maxwell AFB, Ala., NPL-09. (Secret) Information extracted is unclassified.

Bosnia-Herzegovina airspace, but they were not included in the penetrating-aircraft totals.

Joint Operations

Aircraft of the US Air Force, Navy, Army, and Marine Corps flew 2,087 air-strike and air-support missions (fig. 12.7), 1,499 or 71.8 percent of which were air strikes, including SEAD, CAS, BAI, and AI feet dry over Bosnia-Herzegovina: Air Force (774 or 51.6 percent), Navy (583 or 38.9 percent), and Marine Corps (142 or 9.5 percent). The Army replaced the Marine Corps in flying support sorties (588 or 28.2 percent), including reconnaissance, air-to-air refueling, ABCCC, electronic intelligence, airborne early warning (AEW), and CSAR: Air Force (392 or 66.7 percent), Navy (165 or 28.1 percent), and the Army (31 or 5.2 percent—primarily reconnaissance flights by unmanned aerial vehicles).

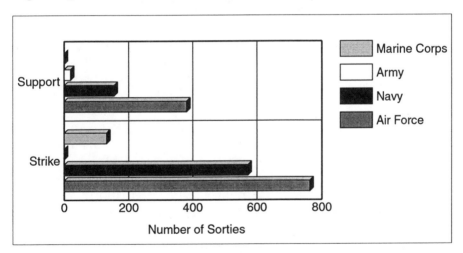

Figure 12.7. US Joint Sortie Distribution

Some people heralded Deliberate Force as a model of interservice cooperation, while others quickly pointed out that the air-strike operations were still punctuated by rivalries and misunderstandings among the services. Some of the growing pains of jointness that occurred over the 17-day US/NATO air campaign against the Bosnian Serbs included

- Navy frustration with the Air Force's centralized control of the mission tasking, especially with an air tasking message (ATM) specifying the type of ordnance to be used on particular targets.
- Rivalry over which service and aircraft should fly bombing missions because everyone wanted a piece of the action.
- Communications interoperability (getting through to the ships in the Adriatic was a big problem, especially when two carriers operated together, which put a heavy load on the limited satellite line available).
- Unfamiliarity of Marine aircrews with Air Force flight-line rules, especially entry-controlled points.
- Desire voiced by Air Force aircrews in the aftermath of Deliberate Force for augmenting the service's inventory with a 1,000 lb laser-guided bomb (LGB)—the weapon of choice with respect to joint/combined weapons interoperability.

Fortunately, none of these "cultural differences" seriously affected the air campaign. But despite more than a decade of "purple" experience, joint operations are far from seamless and need further attention prior to future conflicts.

Combined Sortie Summary

On the average, the combined forces had a daily mission-capable rate of over 90 percent in support of Deliberate Force (table 12.2), with the lowest number of sorties flown on ATM day 17 and the highest number on day 10, along with the highest number of targets tasked (27). The highest number of tasked desired mean points of impact (DMPI) (116) occurred on ATM day eight. The first cease-fire totals occurred on ATM days four through seven, numbering 737 sorties. As a minor point, one might note that the total number of penetrating sorties excludes penetrating missions flown by unmanned aerial vehicles (28) and CSAR aircraft (19).

CAOC operations, poor weather, technical (avionic) problems, or mechanical (aircraft) problems resulted in 745 ground- or air-aborted sorties (over 21 percent of the total number flown) (fig. 12.8 and table 12.3). Aborts caused by such CAOC operations as mission-scheduled line changes or

Table 12.2

Deliberate Force Sortie Summary

Date (1995)	ATM Day	Scheduled	Added	Ground Aborted	Flown	Air Aborted	Penetrated
29–30 Aug	1	124	1	3	122	0	85
30–31 Aug	2	244	24	26	242	4	170
31 Aug–1 Sep	3	237	52	16	273	23	202
1–2 Sep	4	206	5	32	179	6	118
2–3 Sep	5	272	2	91	183	8	103
3–4 Sep	6	183	11	5	189	10	122
4–5 Sep	7	185	20	19	186	3	122
5–6 Sep	8	191	84	10	265	3	176
6–7 Sep	9	193	119	25	287	43	213
7–8 Sep	10	245	103	54	294	0	232
8–9 Sep	11	226	42	11	257	17	171
9–10 Sep	12	229	13	31	211	10	145
10–11 Sep	13	223	25	26	222	1	152
11–12 Sep	14	216	48	9	255	5	180
12–13 Sep	15	162	54	6	210	0	151
13–14 Sep	16	178	44	82	140	14	81
14–15 Sep	17	171	0	151	20	1	0
Total		3,485	647	597	3,535	148	2,423

Source: Extracted from CAOC daily mission summaries, 29 August–14 September 1995, AFHRA, CAOC-15. (Confidential) Information extracted is unclassified.

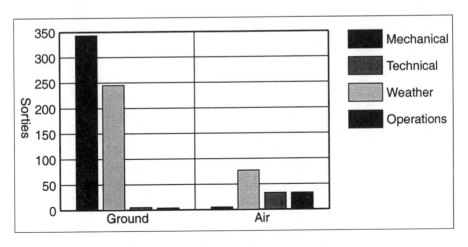

Figure 12.8. Ground- and Air-Abort Summary

ground cancellations had the greatest impact on air operations (46.7 percent), while adverse weather accounted for 43.2 percent of all aborts (affecting nearly one out of every 10 sorties).

Table 12.3

Ground- and Air-Abort Summary

	Ground	%	Air	%	Totals	%
Operations	343	57.50	5	3.40	348	46.70
Weather	245	41.00	77	52.00	322	43.20
Technical	5	0.80	33	22.30	38	5.10
Mechanical	4	0.70	33	22.30	37	5.00
Total	597	100.00	148	100.00	745	100.00
%	80.1		19.9		100	

Weapon Impacts

Deliberate Force's offensive air operations—SEAD, CAS, BAI, and AI—accounted for a total of 1,026 munition expenditures (excluding high-speed antiradiation missiles [HARM], rockets, and guns). This number included 708 (69 percent) precision munitions and 318 (31 percent) nonprecision munitions, the former including LGBs/guided-bomb units (GBU) (-10, -12, -16, -24, and AS30L), electro-optical/infrared weapons (standoff land-attack missile [SLAM], GBU-15, and AGM-65), and Tomahawk land-attack missiles (TLAM). Aircraft expended a total of 630 precision-guided munitions (PGM) primarily on three target sets: (1) air defense sites and command, control, and communications (C^3) (215); (2) ammo and supply depots/facilities (351); and (3) bridges and lines of communications (LOC) (64). Nonprecision weapons included general-purpose (GP) bombs (Mk-82, -83, and -84) and cluster-bomb unit (CBU)-87s. Aircraft expended a total of 54 GP bombs against two target sets: (1) ammo and supply depots/facilities (32) and (2) C^3 and air defense sites (22).

Ordnance expenditures by US joint forces—Air Force, Navy, and Marine Corps—for both Deliberate Force and Deadeye resulted in approximately 406 target hits (374 PGMs and 32 GP bombs). Of the 374 PGM target hits out of 618 attempts, the Air Force hit 282 of 407 (69 percent) (table 12.4), the Navy hit 65 of

166 (39 percent), and the Marines 27 of 45 (60 percent), for a joint PGM effectiveness total of approximately 60 percent (374 of 618). The hit/miss analysis of PGMs was based on a 15-foot circular error of probability. Among the standoff-weapon PGM expenditures, the GBU-15, SLAM, and TLAM results were less than ideal, the GBU-15 hitting four of nine (44 percent) with four misses due to faulty target acquisition, the SLAM hitting only two of 10 (20 percent) with seven of eight misses resulting from command-guidance failure due to GBU-15 data-link interference, and the TLAM hitting nine of 13 (69 percent). On the nonprecision side, the Air Force hit 28 of 32 GP bombs (88 percent), and the Navy four of 10 (40 percent), for a joint nonprecision hit percentage of 76 percent (32 of 42). The Marines did

Table 12.4

US Air Force Precision Munitions Analysis

Aircraft	Munition	Released	Hit	% Hit
F-15E	GBU-10 GBU-12 GBU-15	72 18 9	48 18 5	67 100 56
	Totals	99	71	72
F-16	GBU-10 GBU-12	204 81	132 58	65 72
	Totals	285	190	67
A-10	AGM-65	23	21	91
	Total	407	282	69

No. Misses	Munition	Reasons: Aircraft	Crew	Weather	Weapon
96	GBU-10	4 (4%)	26 (27%)	32 (33%)	34 (36%)
23	GBU-12	0	5 (22%)	10 (43%)	8 (35%)
4	GBU-15	0	1 (25%)	2 (50%)	1 (25%)
2	AGM-65	0	0	0	2 (100%)
Total 125		4 (3%)	32 (26%)	44 (35%)	45 (36%)

Source: Briefing slides, Col Chuck Wald, commander, 7490th Composite Wing (Provisional), Aviano AB, Italy, subject: Operation Deliberate Force Update, 15 September 1995 (unclassified), AFHRA, AVI-04.

not expend any "dumb" (unguided) bombs. Thus, the joint combined-munition (precision/nonprecision) hit percentage was 61.5 percent (406 of 660).

Poststrike Results

The most basic possible targets of airpower are will and capability. Will is the determination of an actor to resist influence; Clausewitz's trinity of the leadership, the people, and the military represent [sic] the will of the nation. Will is the ultimate target—not capability. . . . Capability is the ability to resist influence. Will can be indirectly targeted by destroying capability. If a leader believes he cannot effect his military strategy (offense or defense) because his military capability is being destroyed, he will often cede to enemy influence, especially when his enemy's demands are limited.

—Skunkworks, "Discussion of the
Air Strategy in Bosnia"

As an instrument of United Nations (UN)/NATO policy and objectives in Bosnia, a major part of the air strategy involved the application of airpower to degrade the combat capability of the Bosnian Serbs, which would jeopardize their ability to sustain combat operations. Because of the manner in which alliance forces would employ airpower, the Bosnian Serbs would be hard pressed to make additional territorial gains and might be unable to defend currently held territories. As a result, the possibility of a successful Croatian or Muslim ground offensive would increase. Thus, the Bosnian Serbs would be more likely to negotiate in good faith.[1]

By the time of the second call for a cease-fire during Deliberate Force at 2200Z on 14 September 1995, the air strategy had paid off. The will of the Bosnian Serbs ceded to the efficacy of the bombing: the Bosnian Serb army (BSA) ceased hostilities, complied with requirements to withdraw heavy weapons from the total-exclusion zones, and began negotiations for a peaceful settlement. The demonstrated resolve of airpower in carrying out an effective targeting plan, along with some limited NATO ground-force artillery efforts, led to the degradation of the Bosnian Serbs' military capability.

With respect to air-strike missions, the combined air campaign destroyed nearly 87 percent of the target sets within the range of military significance that had lateral links to the overall military objective (fig. 12.9). BSA target sets included direct and essential military support, C³, integrated air defense systems (IADS), infrastructure (supporting LOCs), and fielded forces (table 12.5). Aircraft attacked a total of 357 individual targets or DMPIs, 290 of which (81 percent) met damage criteria, while 67 (19 percent) did not. During two days of CAS missions, 30 August and 10 September 1995, alliance aircraft attacked 19 targets in the BSA's fielded forces: seven artillery tubes, five bunkers, three antiaircraft artillery sites, three mortar sites, and one small warehouse. Overall, an impressive two out of three individual targets were totally destroyed.

Fixed targets and their respective aiming points (DMPIs) for the Sarajevo zone of action (ZOA) and for Deadeye Northwest and Southeast (tables 12.6 and 12.7) met damage criteria when two-thirds of the DMPIs had been destroyed. Mission reports, ground reports, cockpit videos, tactical reconnaissance, national imagery, and signal intelligence verified the bomb damage assessments (BDA). By the time Deliberate Force came to a close, 308 of the 346 DMPIs had been attacked, and 305 of them met

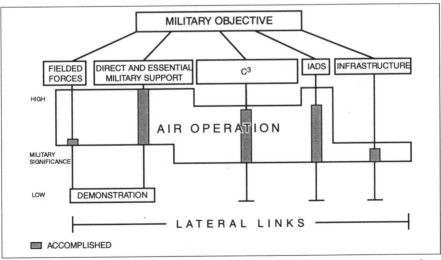

Figure 12.9. Poststrike Results (From Corona briefing slide no. 49, Lt Gen Michael Ryan, Headquarters AIRSOUTH, Naples, Italy, 5 December 1995)

Table 12.5

Individual Targets Attacked/Destroyed

Target Categories	Targets Attacked	Did Not Meet Damage Criteria		Met Damage Criteria	
		No Damage	Light Damage	Moderate to Severe Damage	Destroyed
C³	9	0	1	0	8
Infrastructure (Supporting LOCs)	13	1	3	0	9
Direct and Essential	246	7	40	42	157
Fielded Forces	19	4	unknown	9	6
IADS	70	1	10	7	52
Total	357	13 (4%)	54 (15%)	58 (16%)	232 (65%)

Source: Corona briefing slides, Lt Gen Michael Ryan, Headquarters AIRSOUTH, Naples, Italy, 5 December 1995.

BDA criteria, obviating the need for reattack—thus, only 41 required return visits (fig. 12.10).[2]

By the end of Operation Deliberate Force on 14 September 1995, only seven Sarajevo ZOA targets and one Deadeye target remained, as well as 32 Sarajevo DMPIs and 11 Deadeye DMPIs (figs. 12.11 and 12.12). The remaining option-two targets could

Table 12.6

Sarajevo ZOA Targets

	Total Fixed Targets	Total Aiming Points	Damage Criteria Met	Targets Remaining
Command and Control	4	9	4 of 4	0
Supporting LOCs	15	15	9 of 15	6 of 15
Direct and Essential	17	258	16 of 17	1 of 17
Ammo Storage Area	10	190	10 of 10	0
Total	46	472	39 of 46	7 of 32

Source: Corona briefing slides, Lt Gen Michael Ryan, Headquarters AIRSOUTH, Naples, Italy, 5 December 1995.

Table 12.7

Deadeye Targets

	Total Fixed Targets	Total Aiming Points	Damage Criteria Met	Targets Remaining
Command and Control	3	14	3 of 3	0
Early Warning	4	24	4 of 4	0
Radio Relay	12	38	11 of 12	1 of 12
Surface-to-Air Missiles	1	1	1 of 1	0
Total	20	77	19 of 20	1 of 12

have lasted another two or three days before planners would have had to nominate option-three targets, which carried moderate to high risks for collateral damage. Fortunately, bad weather and the second cease-fire abated an otherwise difficult near-term targeting situation.

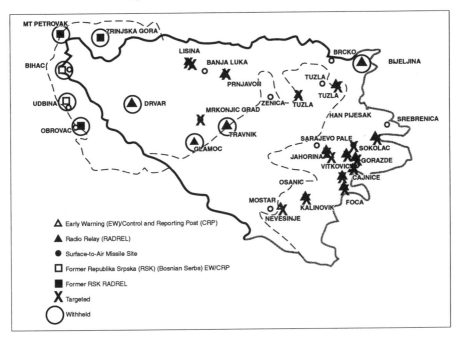

Figure 12.10. Deadeye Results (From Corona briefing slide no. 22, Lt Gen Michael Ryan, Headquarters AIRSOUTH, Naples, Italy, 5 December 1995)

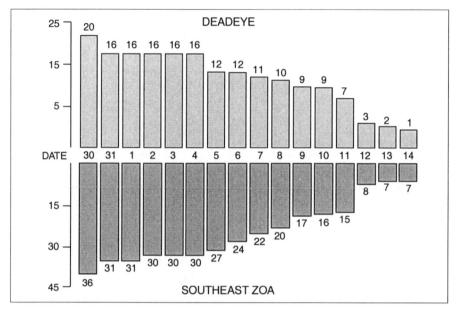

Figure 12.11. Targets Remaining (From Corona briefing slide no. 46, Lt Gen Michael Ryan, Headquarters AIRSOUTH, Naples, Italy, 5 December 1995)

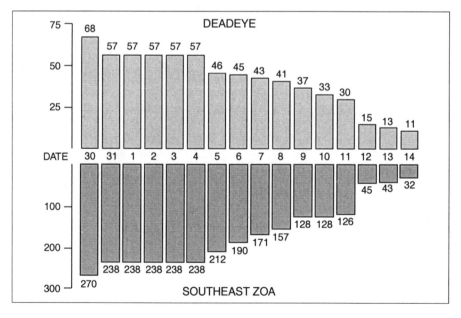

Figure 12.12. DMPIs Remaining (From Corona briefing slide no. 47, Lt Gen Michael Ryan, Headquarters AIRSOUTH, Naples, Italy, 5 December 1995)

Tactical-Employment Effectiveness

According to Air Force Manual (AFM) 1-1, *Basic Aerospace Doctrine of the United States Air Force,* Deliberate Force was a medium-intensity, combined air operation that employed conventional smart weapons with limited resources to achieve limited, lower-level objectives in a situation in which nuclear, chemical, or biological warfare was not an issue.[3] By Gulf War standards, the intensity of the Balkans air campaign was very modest. In two-fifths the time, Deliberate Force involved only one-fourth the assets, one-twenty-fifth the sorties, and less than one-hundredth the bomb tonnage compared to Operation Desert Storm. Nevertheless, the two operations were both successful coalition air campaigns, aided by an intricate combination of weapon systems, support systems, and tactics. Thus, Deliberate Force provides a "snapshot" opportunity for reviewing the performance of the multinational air show of weapons and tactics used in achieving General Ryan's tactical objective of leveling the playing field in Bosnia-Herzegovina.

Although the CFACC usually works at the operational level of war, the politico-military environment and constraints of Deliberate Force drove General Ryan to focus his attention at all levels, leading to his tight control of the air campaign and orchestration of the combined NATO forces to accomplish mission objectives within the Balkans AOR. This entailed effective conception, organization, and conduct of the major air operations that guided successful tactical events against Bosnian Serb ground forces. Here, the focus is on those tactical missions that applied combat power as military leverage to alter the advantages gained by the BSA from violating UN resolutions.

Combat Air Patrol/Offensive Counterair

All told, the multinationals flew 294 CAP sorties, providing continuous air cover and protection 88 percent of the time over the course of the campaign. Remarkably, during the 17 days of the operation, the only CAP gaps (on-station losses) amounted to 39 hours and 45 minutes. Eighty-eight percent of the gap time stemmed from aborts or cancellations because of poor weather; the rest air-aborted for mechanical reasons

345

and one for lack of an available tanker. NATO airborne early warning/air control unit and CAP aircraft detected 46 no-fly-zone violations during the course of the air campaign. No intercept engagements or employment of air-to-air weaponry occurred. Overall, the multinational air patrols accomplished their assigned mission—to deny the warring factions the capability to fight in the air and to protect the United Nations Protection Force from air attacks.

Suppression of Enemy Air Defenses

During Deliberate Force, SEAD assets (both shooters and jammers) flew 785 sorties, providing 115 SEAD window opportunities (e.g., SEAD protection) for ingressing and egressing aircraft flying feet dry over Bosnia-Herzegovina. The window (on-station protection) totaled 229 hours and 39 minutes—an average of 13.5 hours per day and a typical window time of two hours.[4] Conducting 23 probe attacks, SEAD aircraft employed 65 AGM-88 HARMs, the United States firing 63 of them—36 preemptive and 27 reactive. Spain's EF-18 Hornets fired only two.[5] The United States flew 89 percent of the SEAD missions with the remainder split between Spain (7 percent) and Germany (4 percent). Among the 705 US SEAD sorties, the Navy flew 56 percent (395), the Air Force 35 percent (244), and the Marine Corps 9 percent (66).[6] During the Deadeye campaigns, not one multinational aircraft was lost to the BSA's radar-guided surface-to-air missiles or antiaircraft artillery.

Offensive Air Operations

US joint forces accounted for nearly half the strike platforms used in Deliberate Force and flew 68.5 percent of the air strikes, outflying the allies 2.2:1. The Air Force flew the majority of the strikes (44.5 percent), with F-16s flying the most strike missions (25 percent) of all platforms. The Fighting Falcon outflew its closest competitor—the Hornet—nearly 2:1. The Royal Air Force flew 36.3 percent of the strike sorties not flown by the United States, followed by the French air force (25 percent) and the Dutch air force (20 percent). The GR-7 Harrier II and the NF-16A led all allied aircraft in total strike sorties. The following statistics suggest the effectiveness of the tactical employment of strike aircraft during Deliberate Force:

- Average number of PGMs per destroyed DMPI—2.8

- Average number of GP bombs per destroyed DMPI—6.6

- Average number of attack sorties per destroyed DMPI—1.5

- Combined precision bombing (GBU/LGB) per destroyed DMPI—3.7

- Precision munitions (other than GBU/LGB) per destroyed DMPI—3.9

- Total combined precision weapons (all PGM) per DMPI (hit effectiveness)—2.9

- Total combined bombing (all types) per DMPI (hit effectiveness)—3.5 (nearly half that of the Gulf War)

Support missions flown in Deliberate Force also proved quite effective.

Air-to-Air Refueling

Multinational tankers provided more than sufficient air-refueling capability for fighter missions 24 hours a day over the Adriatic Sea. The only tanker problems involved an inflexibility in changing track altitudes to get clear of clouds to enhance visual rejoins, as well as a lack of entry/exit gates to the tanker tracks to accommodate a vast number of aircraft needing fuel before and after missions.

Reconnaissance

Using infrared, electronic, radar, or optical sensors, reconnaissance assets flew 312 sorties, which amounted to nearly half (48.2 percent) of all intelligence, surveillance, and reconnaissance (ISR) sorties and less than a third (28.6 percent) of all Deliberate Force support sorties. Tactical-reconnaissance assets averaged 18 sorties and approximately 35 target requests per day—nearly two targets per sortie.[7]

Electronic Intelligence, Electronic Warfare/Electronic Support Measures

By the end of Deliberate Force, airborne intelligence, including Compass Call aircraft, accounted for 169 (26.1 percent) of the ISR sorties and 15.5 percent of the campaign's support sorties. Not surprisingly, the United States led all NATO nations with 155 sorties (92 percent), with the United Kingdom and France each flying seven of the remaining 14 sorties. The US Navy provided 89 electronic warfare/electronic support measures sorties (57.4 percent) versus the Air Force's 66 (42.6 percent).

Airborne Early Warning

By the end of Deliberate Force, NATO E-3A/D airborne warning and control system aircraft and US Navy E-2C Hawkeyes had provided continuous surveillance coverage over the Balkans AOR, flying a total of 165 missions[8] that accounted for 25.7 percent of the ISR sorties and 15.2 percent of the campaign sorties. Of the total airborne early warning sorties, the E-3A/D Sentries flew 99 (60 percent), the US Navy's Hawkeyes flew 61 (37 percent), and the French air force's E-3F flew five (3 percent).[9]

By obtaining needed combat information, ISR platforms played a key role in the planning, execution, and combat-assessment phases of Deliberate Force. Overall, ISR sorties accounted for 647 (59.3 percent) of the total support sorties and 18.3 percent of the total campaign sorties.

Airborne Battlefield Command and Control Center

Four EC-130Es, which had deployed to the 7490th Composite Wing (Provisional) at Aviano Air Base, Italy, flew a total of 32 sorties, providing around-the-clock command and control with limited gaps in coverage. Although ABCCC aircraft accounted for only 3 percent of Deliberate Force's support sorties, this highly dependable aircraft enhanced 24-hour air operations by averaging two sorties per day, each flight covering a 12-hour window with refueling. Although one sortie was aborted and relaunched later on ATM day one, the only other time an ABCCC did not get airborne occurred on the last day of the campaign because of extremely bad weather conditions at Aviano and within the Balkans AOR.[10]

Combat Search and Rescue

Four US HC-130Ps assigned to the joint special operations task force based at Brindisi, Italy, worked in concert with MH-53Js during CSAR missions. The rescue Hercules flew a total of nine CSAR sorties in a coordinated effort with the Pave Low III helicopters, but both were unable to locate and recover the aircrew of Ebro 33, a French Mirage 2000 hit by a man-portable, infrared surface-to-air missile.[11] In his Corona briefing, General Ryan said that CSAR was broken and needed fixing.

Thus, Deliberate Force players performed a variety of missions while fulfilling various air roles in support of the CFAAC's air campaign. General Ryan controlled the combat environment with air supremacy assets, applied firepower through offensive air strikes, multiplied combat effectiveness with specialized supporters and high-value air assets, and sustained forces through allied bases. No one role stood alone during Deliberate Force; rather, roles and missions were interdependently applied in a concerted effort throughout the planning and execution of this air campaign.

Deliberate Force was NATO's first sustained air-strike operation and the first to use more precision than nonprecision munitions. Its multinational force consisted of over five thousand personnel from 15 nations and over four hundred aircraft (nearly 260 land-based) from eight nations, bedding down at 18 air bases in five countries as well as on as many as four aircraft carriers in the Adriatic Sea at any one time. The combined NATO forces flew a total of 3,535 sorties, averaging more than 207 sorties per day over the 17-day air campaign. Of the total sorties, 2,470 flights penetrated airspace over Bosnia-Herzegovina while another 1,065 provided support outside that country's airspace. Over a third (36 percent) of the penetrating sorties were of the fighter/attack variety that released 1,026 bombs and missiles (excluding HARMs, rockets, and guns), of which 708 (69 percent) were precision munitions and the remaining 318 (31 percent) were nonprecision. Eleven of the 17 days of the air campaign saw combined air strikes hitting 48 target complexes, including 338 individual DMPIs within those complexes. Precision bombing effectively limited collateral damage and allowed Deliberate Force to accomplish its objectives: protecting the safe areas from threats or attacks, removing heavy weapons from the total-exclusion zones, opening the Sarajevo airport, and providing unhindered road access to Sarajevo. In short, Deliberate Force was not only a determined force but also a decisive force. The air campaign met its objectives by persuading the warring factions to cease hostilities and agree to conditions set out in the UN-brokered framework agreement, the latter eventually leading to the Dayton Peace Accords, which contributed to the overall peace process in the Balkans.

Notes

1. "Discussion of the Air Strategy in Bosnia," talking paper, Skunk-works, USAF/XOXS, Pentagon, Washington, D.C., 17 September 1995, 3, United States Air Force Historical Research Agency (hereinafter AFHRA), Maxwell AFB, Ala., Misc-01.

2. Extracted from "Target and DMPI Summary Statistics," BDA track sheet, crisis action team cell, CAOC, C-5, 5th Allied Tactical Air Force, Vicenza, Italy, 29 September 1995, AFHRA, CAOC-19. (Secret) Information extracted is unclassified.

3. Air Force Manual (AFM) 1-1, *Basic Aerospace Doctrine of the United States Air Force,* vol. 1, March 1992, 2.

4. Extracted from CAOC daily mission summaries, 29 August–14 September 1995. (Confidential) Information extracted is unclassified.

5. Briefing slide (munitions summary), Col Chuck Wald, commander, 31st Fighter Wing, Aviano AB, Italy, subject: 7490th Lessons Learned, 14 October 1995 (unclassified), AFHRA, AVI-77.

6. Ibid.

7. Extracted from CAOC daily mission summaries, 29 August–14 September 1995. (Confidential) Information extracted is unclassified.

8. A total of 166 airborne early warning sorties were logged. A Navy ES-3A flew the extra sortie on ATM day 12 as a backfill to the E-2C when the Navy carriers were swapping out in the Adriatic Sea.

9. Extracted from CAOC daily mission summaries, 29 August–14 September 1995. (Confidential) Information extracted is unclassified.

10. Ibid.

11. Ibid.

Chapter 13

Aspects of Leading and Following:
The Human Factors of Deliberate Force

Lt Col John C. Orndorff

The military art is deeply concerned with the performance of the human group under stress.

—Gen Sir John W. Hackett

Operation Deliberate Force presents an interesting and instructive view of the relationships among the nature of war, leadership style, and victory. A notable aspect of this air campaign was the strong and comprehensive leadership exercised by Lt Gen Michael Ryan, commander of Air Forces Southern Europe (AIRSOUTH), from his combined air operations center (CAOC) with regard to strategy making, operational planning, and even tactical actions. In his cognizance of and direct involvement with such a full range of campaign details, General Ryan exhibited a style of leadership more reminiscent of Napoléon Bonaparte's personalized "great captainship" than the generalship model given the modern world through the groundbreaking reforms of the Prussian military leaders of the nineteenth century, ending with Helmuth von Moltke (the elder).

Although great captains up to and including Napoléon embraced every detail of war, the Prussian staff system accommodated the industrialization and democratization of Western warfare that began during Napoléon's reign by distributing and compartmentalizing information processing and decision making in ways that allowed a group of ordinary men to embrace and control somewhat the expanding scope and duration of modern war. Given the fact that industrial war became the norm, at least in the West, after Napoléon exhausted himself trying to fight in the old way, the Moltkian staff system became the accepted mechanism for controlling military forces.

Thus, General Ryan's apparent reversion to a highly centralized and personal direction of such a broad range of military

351

activities during Deliberate Force raises intriguing questions. First, why did he adopt the leadership style of Napoléon in a Moltkian age, and, second, did this apparent reversion help or undermine the campaign? Answering these questions begins with clarification of the differences between the Napoleonic and Moltkian styles of leadership.

The Napoleonic Model

Napoléon, as had countless military leaders before him, commanded in a style appropriate to the demands of preindustrialized war. Such wars were characterized by small armies of rarely more than 80,000 soldiers and battles that were simultaneously conducted on battlefields of a few miles breadth at most. Often, these battles proved crucially decisive to the outcome of a given campaign and even to the political destiny of a state. One individual could manage and command such battles, assuming he had the experience and genius to miss few details, anticipate events at least better than his counterpart in the opposing army, and exploit the rudimentary command and control (C^2) systems (visual signals and messengers, mainly) of the time. Thus, the style of leadership called Napoleonic in this study was appropriate to a military environment in which individual tactical engagements were often strategically important and in which the available C^2 systems adequately embraced the scale and duration of combat.

Napoléon was the master of this particular environment, his chief characteristic being his detailed planning and instructions to his troops. He was "his own commander in chief" and took little council of anyone.[1] "Napoleon made all the key decisions; he developed his own estimates and usually dictated to his subordinates. . . . He never used [his staff] for anything but for collecting the information he demanded and communicating his instructions."[2] The latter were so detailed regarding where to go and what to do that Martin van Creveld referred to him as "the most competent human being who ever lived."[3] Through his ability to visualize how he wanted the battle to take place and his capability to maintain control over his forces, Napoléon had the flexibility to respond appropriately to each situation. As history bears out, his generalship proved effective as long as the scope of battle remained within his ability to react quickly and maintain control.

Unfortunately for Napoléon, the industrialization and democratization of war, which began in the late eighteenth century, created military forces that, by the latter years of his reign, outstripped the ability of even the greatest individual to maintain continual and detailed control. Innovations that began in the mid-seventeenth century with the beginnings of steam power led to an acceleration in the efficiency and precision of manufacturing and the introduction of interchangeable machined parts.[4] These innovations made the production of cannons, muskets, and supplies to equip large armies both easier and cheaper. The expansion of republican and democratic ideals as well as political philosophies during this same period created large armies to absorb all this new materiel. Epitomized by the experience of France under Napoléon, these industrial and political developments created huge armies, in relation to those of the previous age, populated by enthusiastic citizen-soldiers or quasi-citizen-soldiers fired by national or ideological loyalties rather than fickle mercenary obedience to a sovereign or aristocrat. These armies (France's numbered at least a million at Napoléon's zenith) were spread across vast areas in independent field corps and garrisons. Clearly, the time had come for a new method of exercising military command.

The Prussian or Moltkian Model

In the half century following the Napoleonic Wars, which ended in 1815, a series of Prussian military reformers developed a philosophy and methodology of command that sought to "institutionalize" Napoléon's genius and control of armies on a scale suitable to the steadily expanding military forces and conflict boundaries of the age.[5] By professionally educating officers in formal schools and rotating them between field and staff positions, the Prussians anchored their command system on a corps of military professionals who could both advise senior field commanders on matters of strategy and who could themselves undertake the smaller details of supplying and conducting warfare formerly handled, albeit haphazardly, by the great captains of the past. Informed by their commander's objectives, these officers were trained to take the initiative in accomplishing their subordinate missions and staff assignments, more or less independently, guided only by broad directives from their superiors. The Prussians called this system of senior commanders issuing broad orders to subordinate officers responsible for and capable of acting with independent initiative *Auftragstaktik* (mission tactics).[6]

Although this system of distributed responsibility and subordinate initiative denied commanders the close, detailed control of all facets of military affairs exercised by Napoléon, it did provide modern mass armies with adequate control in general and with flexibility in the face of changing circumstances. Moreover, commanders supported by such a system were able to orchestrate their campaigns by providing general guidance to skilled subordinates rather than by attempting, probably with disastrous results, to exercise detailed control over individual battles. This pattern of centralized guidance and decentralized execution by subordinates became the pattern for modern military systems.[7] Its main strength, von Moltke reasoned, was that in the uncertainties of war, it protected senior commanders from suffering the consequences of decisions made obsolete by a changing environment by allowing subordinates to react and make decisions of their own.[8] In essence, this system, which the United States also adopted in the latter nineteenth century, allowed the commanders of great armies to focus on strategy while their subordinates handled the details of operational planning and tactical engagements.

Leadership Requirements of Deliberate Force

At first examination the operational conditions surrounding Deliberate Force were hardly different from the main themes of industrial-age war, which the decentralized or Moltkian model of command and leadership proved so effective in controlling. On the NATO side at least, military forces were fully equipped with cutting-edge technology. Corresponding to these advanced systems, NATO boasted competent and motivated staff and operational personnel at all levels, especially within the key CAOC and wing staffs. Moreover, in a military sense anyway, individual engagements were not likely to have a profound strategic or operational impact since they involved small packages of aircraft striking point targets.

Yet, Deliberate Force also manifested some operational and political similarities of pre-Napoleonic warfare. First, for the allies the political objectives of the air campaign—bringing peace to a historically troubled region—were limited. Second, in a way reminiscent of warfare in the Western Age of Enlightenment, the Balkans conflict was important in the abstract to NATO governmental leaders because it affected the stability of Europe and NATO but garnered little popular interest from the domestic populations of these governments, particularly that of the United States. Third, as a consequence of its limited scope and duration, the command, control, communications, and intelligence (C³I) requirements for directing the campaign fell well within capabilities available to the allies. Further, because General Ryan, the key air commander involved, assumed that each tactical engagement could have profound strategic political importance, he imposed close control over the tactical as well as strategic direction of the campaign.

General Ryan's Leadership and Its Effects

At the beginning of Deliberate Force, the three senior officers in the CAOC included Maj Gen Hal M. Hornburg, the director; Brig Gen David Sawyer, his deputy; and Col Douglas Richardson, chief of operations. These officers had led the CAOC during the preceding months of Operation Deny Flight. However, General Ryan, the senior air commander, moved to the CAOC from his headquarters in Naples at the outset of Deliberate Force to exercise personal control over tactical-level decisions, such as the selection of targets and aiming points, and to approve sortie launches. The move gave Ryan—who brought along his closest staff officers—close, direct control over the air campaign. In a sense the CAOC provided General Ryan with what Napoléon also would have sought at the beginning of a battle—a prominent point for overseeing and controlling events.

General Ryan's move to the CAOC had an immediate effect on the duties of Maj Gen Michael Short, his principal deputy and AIRSOUTH vice commander. In this instance, General Short worked hard to provide details of the campaign to Adm Leighton Smith, commander in chief of Allied Forces Southern Europe, who constantly demanded campaign updates. However, Short had problems obtaining timely information from the CAOC; in some cases when he did obtain needed details of the campaign's status, the data was overcome by other events due to the high tempo of the operation. In other instances, by the time Short had obtained the information, Admiral Smith had gotten the data directly from the CAOC and moved on to other things. Thus, by the end of Deliberate Force, General Short noted he was about three cycles of information behind Admiral Smith's requests. With the advantage of hindsight, one can see that General Short should have positioned a contact in the CAOC to feed him information when he needed it.[9] This experience points out one particular difficulty attendant upon an operational commander's move to tactical-level headquarters.

As several people reported, General Ryan's direction of the campaign from the CAOC at first glance appeared to constitute micromanagement, reminiscent of Vietnam.[10] However, considering the politically sensitive background of Deliberate Force (e.g., ethnic and national sensitivities, a concern for civilian casualties and collateral damage, etc.), as well as the joint and combined character of the CAOC, Ryan felt he had to keep a close hold on operations, including the selection of targets and personal management of battle damage assessment (BDA).[11] By centralizing control of the target list and the selection of desired mean points of impact (DMPI—i.e., aiming points), Ryan could shape the campaign as he believed appropriate, particularly in light of the operation's political sensitivity. For example, he especially wished to prevent the type of collateral damage that might occur with a misdirected bomb, resulting in media coverage of civilian targets accidentally hit by the allies or sparking a Bosnian Serb attack on United Nations (UN) troops. Above all else, General Ryan wanted to remain personally responsible for all major decisions in the campaign—primarily to take appropriate blame should anything go wrong or come under question.[12]

Although neither understood nor appreciated by members of the CAOC at the time, General Ryan's physical presence at the CAOC allowed him to buffer the center's staff, especially its senior officers, from direct and possibly distracting interaction with more senior commanders interested in the campaign—particularly Gen George A. Joulwan, Supreme Allied Commander Europe, and Admiral Smith.[13] Directly in contact with events, a very senior commander such as Ryan could provide Smith and others with the real-time, informal summaries and details of the campaign they requested without burdening CAOC personnel with providing formal answers to the same question for their less senior commanders to take to the senior commanders. In that sense, Ryan's presence actually instilled the CAOC with a more relaxed and free operating atmosphere. Whether or not these actions added to the efficiency of the CAOC remains a matter of personal opinion, depending on whom one asks.

Some CAOC members complained of several drawbacks to General Ryan's constant and dominating presence in detailed staff processes. For example, although Ryan's inner circle—consisting mainly of his small coterie from AIRSOUTH—was generally aware of current iterations to air tasking messages (ATM) and other planning documents and actions, people outside that circle in some cases did not know about changes that the general had made—even though they depended upon those changes as they planned their own parts of the campaign.[14] Predictably, other CAOC members felt that Ryan's centralization of so many detailed decisions tended to slow the planning process, leading to numerous complaints about late target lists and last-minute changes to ATMs. Still, for the reasons already given, General Ryan believed that his presence—as well as that of familiar and trusted staff officers and noncommissioned officers—at the CAOC was essential.[15]

Col Daniel "Doc" Zoerb, director of the Deny Flight air operations cell and a key member of General Ryan's inner circle, agreed with the general on this matter. If one can liken Ryan to Napoléon as regards direct leadership style and broad cognizance of events and planning details, then Doc Zoerb was Ryan's Marshal Louis-Alexandre Berthier, the brilliant chief of

357

staff who transcribed and transmitted Napoléon's orders to everyone else.[16] Colonel Zoerb understood the political and military situation surrounding the campaign, at least from General Ryan's perspective, better than anyone other than the general himself. Like his immediate superior, he noted that since Deliberate Force was more about peacemaking than making war, "every bomb dropped had to be helpful."[17] Familiar with working closely with General Ryan, Zoerb developed most of the plans for the operation from his commander's detailed decisions. More than a mere transcriber of orders, however, Zoerb played such a major role in key targeting decisions and strategy deliberations that one officer called him the "Dave Deptula of Deliberate Force," thus linking him to another officer who played a pivotal role in planning the coalition air offensive against Iraq in 1991.[18] Zoerb's ability to plan and communicate General Ryan's directions was perhaps vital to the success of Deliberate Force; thus, the colonel's enthusiasm for his boss's close leadership is hardly surprising.

The combined nature of the CAOC staff has also produced differing perceptions about the impact of leadership. A number of US and non-US officers felt that CAOC leaders appropriately included all officers in the organization's staff functions. Indeed, General Hornburg noted that he made efforts before the start of Deliberate Force to get the allies more involved in the CAOC by asking NATO—unsuccessfully—for a colonel to serve as chief of plans. In his opinion, until Deny Flight actually heated up into Deliberate Force, most NATO countries had little interest in sending senior officers to 5th Allied Tactical Air Force (5 ATAF) and the CAOC.[19] Moreover, Lt Col Bernd Jansen, liaison officer (LNO) for the German air force at the CAOC during the operation, noted that commanders made efforts to ensure participation by all allies—even to the extent of sacrificing operational effectiveness.[20] Col Arjen Koopmans, LNO for the Netherlands air force, was also satisfied with the allies' role in Deliberate Force, noting that all nations participated as planned. He added that the United States performed the greatest number of missions because of its unique capabilities. In this case he did not feel that he and his air force in any way had been left out of the operation.[21]

However, countervailing perceptions existed regarding the degree to which non-US officers participated in the CAOC's planning and control processes. Wing Commander Andy Batchelor of the Royal Air Force (RAF), assigned to the CAOC BDA cell, mentioned that US officers seemed to feel that the CAOC staff operated as a bifurcated "US and NATO" entity rather than a truly combined "NATO" entity with a fully integrated international staff. Several American officers who worked at the CAOC also reported that some of the European allied officers felt left out and that the United States had taken over the operation.[22] An interesting indication of the actual "Americanization" of the CAOC staff was the fact that it had no US LNO since, according to General Hornburg, it was unnecessary in an organization whose senior leaders were all Americans. In retrospect, therefore, it seems reasonable to say that, for several reasons, the CAOC did not function as a fully integrated, combined staff at the start of Deliberate Force and that the press of events permitted only a minimal increase in non-US participation before the operation ended.

General Ryan's tight control of targets, DMPIs, and BDA also caused concern for a number of individuals in the CAOC and at the units. This tight control served Ryan's desire to remain personally answerable for anything that might go wrong and to reduce the chance of collateral damage. However, it also resulted in a frequently changing target list and delayed mission-release decisions that caused people in the CAOC and the fighter squadrons to wonder what was going on. Speaking of his and Ryan's efforts to mitigate such unintentional confusion, General Hornburg stated that "I know we jerked around the guys in the field, but we tried not to."[23] He also noted that he and his commander tried to avoid changes to the target list by issuing them late, after most of the changes had been made. In spite of their efforts, the targets still changed several times. Thus, aircrews in particular felt that they were at the end of a whip.

Lieutenant Commander Michael "Gator" Dunn, of the CAOC crisis-action team (CAT) cell, said that receiving late target lists made it difficult for his office to process the ATM in a timely manner. At Aviano, some pilots became frustrated—not with receiving the targets late but with the constantly changing nature of the target list. Several noted that their targets changed as they prepared to launch, compounding the difficulty of that process. Capt Todd Gentry of the 510th Fighter Squadron described this instability as the most frustrating part of the operation.[24] It probably did not help that few, if any, people in the field knew that delays and changes to the target list arose from General Ryan's careful efforts to avoid collateral damage and to reduce the number of perturbations in mission planning they actually did experience.

The views of senior commanders and unit-level officers diverged on the matter of force protection as well. General Ryan held back from wholesale attacks on Serbian surface-to-air missile (SAM) sites to minimize both the risk to his crews and to avoid unnecessary Serbian casualties and collateral damage. Understandably, a number of pilots felt that they should have been allowed to destroy SAM sites at will to remove them as threats to coalition aircraft, and they expressed frustration at not being able to do so. Ryan preferred to have his aircrews fly outside the SAM rings and thus avoid the danger, if possible. Even though Ryan's policy accepted the continued threat of the Serbian defenses, most pilots agreed that he did his best to keep them out of danger.[25]

General Ryan's decision to keep BDA on close hold became a particularly sensitive leadership-related issue within the CAOC and at the units. Wing Commander Batchelor said he was surprised at the importance of BDA to Ryan and his restrictive instructions for disseminating it. The latter forbade the wholesale and unfiltered passing of BDA from the CAOC, even to field units launching missions. Explaining this policy, Colonel Zoerb said that his commander had three reasons for jealously guarding BDA: (1) Ryan did not want his judgment second-guessed, (2) he did not want outside organizations making assessments of BDA, and (3) he did not want to be held to his first assessment, should it change. Wing Commander Batchelor agreed with Zoerb's assessment, but he still questioned a close hold of BDA from field units.[26]

Generally, personnel at Aviano shared Batchelor's concerns. Charged with assessing the ongoing status of 31st Fighter Wing targets and accomplishments, Capt Mark Hallisey and Capt Pete Ornell from the 31st Wing's intelligence flight found the close hold of BDA one of the most frustrating aspects of Deliberate Force. Given his responsibilities, Captain Ornell found the CAOC's frequent response of "you guys don't need to know this" to his requests for target and strike imagery particularly galling.[27] Captain Hallisey conceded that he understood General Ryan's reason for not wanting some pilot standing in front of Cable News Network (CNN) saying, "Look what I did," yet he believed that pilots and tactical-level planners needed to know how they were doing. Although he could not release actual BDA information, Hallisey reported that Wing Commander Batchelor alleviated the friction between the CAOC and the 31st Wing somewhat by commenting on the wing's BDA assessment. Hallisey would fax his assessment to Batchelor, who, after reviewing the data, would say something to the effect that "you're 99 percent correct in your assessment."[28]

Pilots flying combat missions also doubted the wisdom of General Ryan's close hold of BDA. Capt Scott MacQueen of the 510th Fighter Squadron said that sometimes he and his fellow pilots had no idea of the real situation on the ground due to the lack of BDA.[29] Not knowing the situation on the ground had specific meaning for Captain Hallisey: although the ATM might direct a particular flight to hit DMPIs three and four at a particular target, the pilots might see those DMPIs as the first and second aiming points since they had no prestrike BDA photos showing that previous strikes had obliterated original DMPIs one and two. Fortunately, after Hallisey explained this problem to the CAOC planners, they released more BDA to the wing.[30] Nevertheless, BDA remained a sore issue among field personnel well after the operation had ended.

Subordinate Leadership and Followership in the CAOC

The leadership of General Hornburg and General Sawyer nicely complemented that of their commander, General Ryan, and proved critical to the successful operation of the CAOC, even though their leadership styles differed somewhat. During a postoperation interview, Hornburg indicated that he probably would have taken a more decentralized approach to planning than did Ryan. For example, he would have allowed his staff to present him with DMPIs for his approval, although he also pointed out that he was not sure whether the targeteers would have selected the DMPIs as carefully as did Ryan. Hornburg also stated that he would have spent more time with the non-US LNOs to let them know what they were doing, largely in response to their complaints about being left out.[31] Similarly, Capt Patricia Mauldin, the CAOC squadron section commander, described Sawyer as an "altogether different leader" than his two superiors—more personable and more willing to "get in and ask questions of people as well as let people know what was going on."[32] Despite these leadership differences, observers in the CAOC generally saw that Hornburg and Sawyer provided very strong leadership in implementing the campaign as Ryan directed.[33]

Many of these CAOC staff members also saw that the three general officers had more or less subconsciously divided responsibilities among themselves in ways that matched their duties and leadership styles. General Ryan planned and ran the air war. General Hornburg "flew cover" for his boss by attending meetings, hosting visiting dignitaries, and overseeing the CAOC staff's execution of the campaign. General Sawyer ran the CAOC night shift and spent more time with "the troops."[34] To imply, however, that these officers kept "shifts" is somewhat misleading since all of them spent over 16 hours per day in or around the CAOC. Hornburg saw things a little differently. He agreed that a division of labor existed among the CAOC senior commanders, particularly to the extent that he and Sawyer made sure that one of them was always available at the CAOC. Other than that, he remembered no formal agreement concerning who would take a particular role.[35]

Although General Sawyer made efforts to keep people informed about the status of the operation, complaints arose that the word was not getting out within the CAOC. As noted earlier, part of the problem lay in General Ryan's tendency to focus the flow of information on himself and his inner circle, which included only Hornburg, Sawyer, Zoerb, and two or three other individuals. Thus, the inner circle knew the status of events, but other members of the CAOC staff often did not. This failure in communication got to the point that some cells worked with outdated iterations of the ATM and other planning elements.[36]

Despite these problems with the flow of information within the CAOC, one found no general problem with morale or motivation among the assigned personnel. For instance, key cell directors such as Colonel Richardson made up the shortfall with their own efforts to keep people informed and motivated. Several CAOC members cited Richardson not only for carrying out General Hornburg's instructions but also for keeping people up to speed[37]—just one example of the informal leadership efforts by subordinate CAOC officers that enhanced the overall operation.

Gen Sir John Hackett, in his book *The Profession of Arms,* stated that "there must be a requirement to be led for the leader to emerge and discharge leadership."[38] Beyond Colonel Richardson, several people in the CAOC emerged to fill the requirement for intermediate leadership. Lieutenant Commander Dunn, for example, drew praise as "the person who made things happen." Wing Commander Batchelor mentioned him as one of the best examples of middle-management leadership within the CAOC—someone "quite outstanding," knowledgeable, professional, firm, and tactful. Batchelor also noted that "Lieutenant Commander Dunn was very focused and knew how to get others to work as well" and that, although some superior officers seemed to flounder from the inadequate information flow, Dunn quickly and tirelessly kept a handle on situations and did effective staff work.[39]

Lt Col John Gibbons also stood out as a strong leader within the CAOC. Lieutenant Commander Dunn mentioned Gibbons as a key player in accomplishing the mission in Deliberate Force. Despite constantly changing target lists, Gibbons could match aircraft, munitions, and targets on the spot.[40] Maj Keith Kiger, who augmented the CAOC from Sixteenth Air Force, described Gibbons as a special asset during the operation, noting that, as a permanent assignee to 5 ATAF, he knew how to get things done during the long hours, days on end, that he spent on the job.[41]

Many such people successfully met the leadership challenge of Deliberate Force. However, key leaders in the CAOC probably spent most of their time worrying about the technical demands of their positions as opposed to leadership issues.

From General Ryan's attention to detail in the selection of targets and DMPIs to Lieutenant Commander Dunn's rigorous targeteering, most CAOC officers appear to have been more concerned about getting the job done than acting as leaders in the traditional sense. However, this does not imply that they neglected their leadership responsibilities. The focus and styles of General Ryan and his subordinates seem to have been appropriate, given the generally high quality of the CAOC staff, the intensity of the campaign and operations within the CAOC, and the technological ability to exercise control in a more centralized manner.[42] Indeed, once they became engaged in the actual campaign, the professionalism of most or all of the CAOC members seems to have sustained them in their duties without the need for any formal motivation.

Personnel management, however, did suffer from the technical focus of the CAOC leadership in ways that could have undermined the organization's efficiency had the operation gone on longer. Based on the dictum of Air Force Manual (AFM) 1-1, *Basic Aerospace Doctrine of the United States Air Force,* that "man, not his machines, sets the ultimate limits on battle performance . . . [and] commanders' effectiveness depends in large part on their understanding of the human limitations of their subordinates," CAOC leaders probably should have paid more attention to leadership issues such as the distribution of work, length of the workday, and personnel augmentation.[43]

Most CAOC staffers interviewed for this study indicated that personnel were stretched as far as they could go. During the first few days of the operation, Maj Dave Goldfein, General Ryan's aide, noted that he and his boss, as well as others in the CAOC, worked "20-to-30-hour days,"[44] recognizing that few people could maintain such a pace for very long. In fact, Chaplain, Lt Col Bobby Edwards noted that the level of work in the CAOC was so intense during Deliberate Force that people would have to go out of the building to their cars to catch a little sleep because they had neither a break area nor time to go home. Still, he remarked that all personnel remained very professional, working closely together and taking pride in what they were doing.[45] Importantly, both General Hornburg and subordinate members of the CAOC staff acknowledged that these man-breaking workloads were not distributed evenly.

For some people, the recruitment of 120 augmentees to the CAOC during Deliberate Force reinforced the perception that the workload was not well balanced. MSgt Steve Wells, the CAOC first sergeant, said he felt that the personnel system was mismanaged during the initial spin-up period in the first days of the campaign. According to him, colonels in the CAOC on temporary duty (TDY) would contact their home bases outside of normal personnel channels to request people, who would then unexpectedly arrive saying, "They called and said for me to show up."[46] Many of these late arrivers had little to do during the operation, while others were overworked. This decision by the CAOC's American leaders to go outside normal NATO channels to augment the staff complicated the situation even further. But Captain Mauldin noted that, had these entrepreneurial colonels gone through normal NATO channels to find help, they would have waited for three to six months to get needed people.[47] Nevertheless, the sudden influx of augmentees created confusion among many of the personnel in the CAOC—too many people arrived too quickly for the busy individuals already there to train them for their new jobs. At times, some people wondered whether anyone was in control of the personnel situation.[48]

Leadership and Followership at Aviano

The outstanding leadership and followership characteristic of the CAOC staff was also evident within the 31st Fighter Wing and 7490th Wing (Provisional) at Aviano Air Base (AB) as well. Interviews revealed a strong sense of pride and motivation to accomplish the mission at all levels of both units. Col Charles Wald, the 7490th commander, said that General Ryan told him the wing belonged to him (Wald) and that he should do what he needed to do. Wald added that he had total access to Ryan and that he received whatever he needed to accomplish his mission.[49] Col David Moody, 31st Fighter Wing vice commander, also praised General Ryan's leadership, saying that the wing implemented whatever higher headquarters directed and that the campaign went very smoothly. He mentioned that when a wing commander has the time and peace of mind to fly with his wing, as did Wald, it's a sign that things are good.[50] Other Aviano personnel indicated that Colonel Wald did an excellent job leading the wing. According to Captain MacQueen, Wald was a take-charge kind of leader who let people know what to do and then let them do it. Rather than micromanage, the wing leadership let people do their jobs. Pilots such as MacQueen stated that they "had the right people at the right place at the right time."[51]

Lt Col Gary West, the 510th Fighter Squadron commander, also had praise for the wing leadership but from a somewhat different perspective, describing Colonel Wald as an "in-your-face kind of guy."[52] He went on to state that Wald spent so much time in the squadron at first that he (West) felt he should be able to fly more because "a wing commander [ran] the squadron." However, once the 31st Wing's Deny Flight operations center was up and running, West said that Wald spent more time there. Overall, personnel at the 31st Fighter Wing agreed that they enjoyed good leadership which allowed them to do their jobs.[53] This assessment seems to underscore West's own effectiveness as a leader and a follower, in that his squadron seemed unaware of his frustrations over what he may have perceived as Wald's micromanagement.

As far as his own leadership was concerned, Lieutenant Colonel West said his most important responsibility was to get everyone involved in the campaign,[54] a sentiment echoed by other members of his squadron. Captain MacQueen praised West, saying, "It was good having a squadron commander with combat experience." He felt that West, a veteran of Desert Storm, knew how to fight a war, manage a squadron, and keep everyone involved. He pointed out that West led by example, telling the flight leads how to take care of their people and how to detect indications of emotional stress in their pilots.[55] Many other squadron members expressed the same opinions about West's leadership.[56]

Not only did participants appreciate their leadership but also the personnel at Aviano expressed satisfaction with the joint and combined nature of the campaign. Although some reports indicated the presence of friction between the Air Force and other services, aircrews at Aviano believed that interaction with the Marine Corps and Navy went smoothly.

Colonel Wald mentioned that he treated the Navy and Marine TDY crews like any other squadron in the wing family, adding that Aviano took pains to take care of the TDY folks.[57] Captain MacQueen declared that the marines and Navy personnel "always did well and were never late." He also commented that after communication was established with NATO allies flying in combined packages with the Aviano crews, missions ran very smoothly with them as well.[58] Pilots also seemed satisfied with the joint and combined nature of the operation, although Aviano personnel drew their motivation and enthusiasm from the Deliberate Force mission itself.

From the CAOC to the Aviano flight line, American participants across the board in Deliberate Force ascribed much of their motivation to knowing they were doing an important job. In the CAOC, people worked hours on end in an intense and stressful environment because they knew that their actions would affect the lives of both aircrews and countless civilians on the ground. Although everyone agreed on the importance of leadership, people found satisfaction in their jobs and their own sense of professionalism, as well as excitement in doing what they were trained to do. Captain MacQueen compared his unit's role in Deliberate Force to an athlete's getting to do what he trained for.[59] Similarly, Lieutenant Colonel West noted that "a real warrior never wants to kill anybody, but when there's a war going on, there's no other place he'd want to be,"[60] while Capt Tim Stretch commented that "everyone was leaning forward in the straps."[61]

Impact of the Presence of Dependents at Aviano

The presence of American dependents at Aviano, the main combat base, during the campaign was a unique aspect of the operation. People who had combat experience in Desert Storm preferred to have their families with them,[62] while those for whom Deliberate Force was their first combat thought they should have been elsewhere.[63]

Many members of the 510th Fighter Squadron appreciated the support and psychological boost provided by the squadron suppers prepared each night by the spouses,[64] but younger pilots favored not having the wives around. Captain Gentry, for instance, found it distracting to have his wife at Aviano. Specifically, he was concerned for her safety since burglars targeted the easily identifiable American homes in the Aviano area. Further, he feared that terrorists could easily determine where US families lived and attack them.[65] Captain Mac-Queen, who shared this fear, felt that combat units should operate from isolated locations without family distractions.[66] Although he did not know of any pilots who took their frustrations out on their families, he thought it prudent to remind aircrewmen not to take their work home with them.

Lieutenant Colonel West, however, enjoyed having his family with him, pointing out that his wife did not worry as much about him since, unlike the situation in Desert Storm, she saw him every day during Deliberate Force. Also, West's sons were very interested in his activities during the operation, usually asking "Did you drop?" when he returned from flying a mission. West thought that other crewmen who had flown in Desert Storm shared his appreciation of his family's presence.[67]

Generally, the spouses of aircrewmen flying combat missions agreed that they preferred to remain with their husbands. Reinforcing her husband's evaluation, Colette West confirmed the anxiety she felt during Desert Storm, when she had no information about what her husband was doing, except what she heard on CNN. Addressing other sources of stress, she commented that saying good-bye in the mornings during Deliberate Force was no different than at other times, since, as the wife of a pilot, she knew that something might go wrong. Moreover, she said it was important to kiss her husband good-bye and tell him she loved him.[68]

Vickie Jo Ryder, wife of Lt Col Edward Ryder, also preferred being with her husband. She said that some of the newer spouses seemed concerned at first, but all the wives eventually handled the stress of being around ongoing combat operations very well. She noted that the best thing she could do for her husband was provide a stable home for him. Other than that, because the spouses wanted to help the effort in any way they could, they began preparing meals for the squadron, as mentioned above. She felt that it was important for the wives to stick together and respond to each other's needs.[69]

In addition to supporting their husbands during Deliberate Force, some spouses were directly involved in support operations. TSgt Janelle Bearden, US Air Force Reserve (USAFR), wife of Capt Bryan Bearden, and Capt Tami Turner, USAFR, wife of Col James Turner, both served with intelligence during the operation—Bearden in the 31st Wing and Turner in Sixteenth Air Force. They, too, tried not to think about the possibility of their husbands not returning. Bearden remarked that she tried to stay totally focused on accomplishing the mission and supporting the pilots. In this respect she said she did not think of her husband any differently than she thought of any other pilot flying in Deliberate Force.[70]

Turner agreed that while she was at work during Deliberate Force, she focused on the job at hand. However, she did mention that she was in the air operations center when Capt Scott O'Grady was shot down in June 1995 and wondered whether her husband was flying then. In this sense she worried about her husband but maintained that she would rather remain with him in a situation like this. She went on to mention that because of crew rest, her husband had more time off during the campaign than during normal operations. In Deliberate Force he would have 12 hours off for crew rest—more free time than he normally had. According to Turner, enlisted families probably shouldered the greatest burden, considering they had no crew rest, endured long commutes to work, and experienced greater financial stress.[71]

Although most wives preferred to be with their husbands during a combat operation, they did concede that their attitude might have changed had the wing suffered losses. However, in the case of families assigned to the 8th Fighter-Bomber Wing at Itazuke AB, Japan, during the Korean War in 1950, wives wanted to stay with their husbands during combat even though the wing experienced casualties. Although the wives took the first casualties very hard, one wife whose husband died maintained she still would have wanted to stay at Itazuke because of the Air Force community's support and understanding.[72] Like the pilots in Aviano, though, those in Japan preferred not having their families with them during wartime.[73]

Still, in both instances spouses supported themselves and the war fighters in ways that would be difficult to duplicate.

Specific Circumstances and Leadership Evaluation

In addition to the presence of families at Aviano, Operation Deliberate Force manifested elements of preindustrial and industrial-age warfare. Political considerations, the technological capabilities of communications, and the scope of the campaign moved senior leaders to adopt, more or less subconsciously, a leadership style more akin to the great captaincy of Napoléon than to the less centralized, Prussian-derived system formalized under von Moltke. The degree of centralization reached the point that, in the words of Captain MacQueen, "it completely took the judgment out of the cockpit."[74]

This implies no criticism of the leadership style employed in Deliberate Force. Although the highly professional followers in the CAOC and at Aviano clearly would have been more comfortable with a less centralized, delegating style of leadership, they were quite capable of functioning under General Ryan's centralized approach. Given the intensity and confusion reported in the CAOC and, at times, at the wing level, the professional qualities of his followers allowed Ryan to command as he did. Less mature and professional personnel probably could not have endured the stress and performed their duties so well in the face of such an unprecedented—for them—leadership style.

Time also shaped General Ryan's leadership style during the operation. After the window of opportunity opened to begin bombing Bosnian Serb positions, he faced the possibility that it would quickly close. Ryan felt that he could not take the chance that collateral damage reported by the ubiquitous press might terminate the campaign before it accomplished its military objectives. Thus, he consciously took on the most sensitive elements of Deliberate Force—targets and mission releases—as a personal responsibility. The element of time influenced leadership decisions in other ways as well. Lieutenant Colonel West, for one, didn't know how long the campaign would last, so he decided to have everyone fly on the first night so no one would be left out. He maintained that this aspect of his leadership was the most important thing he did or could have done during the operation.[75]

Considerations for Future Commanders

Because a number of factors influenced General Ryan's leadership style in this campaign, one must examine the context of the campaign to benefit from the lessons of Deliberate Force, a relatively short air campaign conducted in a limited theater of operations with easily managed resources. Although not all weapon and support systems were fully functional when the operation began, the CAOC was available and ideally suited for C² of the campaign. As Major Goldfein observed, Ryan could pick DMPIs the way he did because of the restricted scale and scope of the campaign—which was not the same as Desert Storm. Ryan had the time to pay close attention to what was going on—something he couldn't have done had the campaign gone on any longer.[76] Further, as we have seen, leaders must not take the development of subordinate personnel for granted—another reason that context is of critical importance in the consideration of the leadership style.

The issue of centralized control—and, to some degree, decentralized execution—also warrants consideration. In the case of Deliberate Force, such control proved an irritant to aircrews. However, the ability of US pilots to think and execute independently has always been a great strength. AFM 1-1 notes the risk in placing too much control in one place, which can become a problem during a loss of communications.[77] By exercising too much centralized control, a commander risks losing opportunities that only subordinates can seize at the tactical level.

One final consideration for future campaigns has to do with the presence of dependents in the theater of operations. General Hackett noted that being in the military during peacetime is in many ways more difficult than during wartime because of the attention one must pay to families, welfare, education, barracks maintenance, and so forth. In war, such concerns go by the wayside.[78] However, to some degree we see the complexities of both peacetime and wartime mixed in Deliberate Force, creating an added burden, according to some of the younger pilots. Although the presence of family members provided a psychological boost, of even more concern was the potential disaster associated with their becoming casualties.

Even though spouses preferred remaining with their pilot husbands, what would have happened had we suffered losses, as in the Korean conflict? Would wives who were also military members have been expected to continue with their duties after learning their spouse was missing or dead? In this case an adversary could reasonably expect that some shootdowns would affect US operations more than others. Furthermore, as Captain Gentry feared, what would have happened if terrorists had targeted the families of aircrews? Fortunately, none of these problems arose during Deliberate Force, but they warrant further study.

From the CAOC staff to the wives of aircrew members, the people involved in Deliberate Force proved themselves extremely competent and dedicated. By employing a style of leadership perhaps more centralized than the industrial-age norm, General Ryan correctly read the environment and understood the requirements for the type of campaign he directed. Like the change in warfare that dictated the shift from Napoléon's generalship to von Moltke's general staff, Deliberate Force required a reversion to something similar to that of the great captain. This seems to indicate that, at the present time, one should evaluate each campaign on its own merits and select a method of command accordingly. That is not to say this will remain the best approach. The real challenge for future commanders lies in understanding when this style of leadership is called for and when it is not.

The key, then, to understanding the impact of leadership in Deliberate Force resides in the context of the campaign as General Ryan saw it. First, he understood that the limited objectives of NATO and the UN were highly sensitive. Second, the use of extreme force could leave one vulnerable to domestic and international criticism, particularly if any collateral damage occurred. Third, because time was short, Ryan selected every target for maximum effect in order to achieve objectives. Finally, abundant resources enabled the servicing of virtually all the targets available to him, at least politically, by 12 September.

Given this context, General Ryan's leadership style proved natural and effective, particularly so in light of the available equipment and personnel. Using C^2 capabilities that he and Gen Joseph W. Ashy, his predecessor as AIRSOUTH commander, built up over a period of years, Ryan placed command attention on critical decisions that would lead to achieving the campaign's objectives. Furthermore, as mentioned above, he exploited the leadership and followership of the uniquely capable subordinates under his command. Thus, in the context of environment and capabilities, General Ryan's leadership was indeed what Deliberate Force needed at the time. Still, one must acknowledge the existence of drawbacks to this style of leadership although some elements did not emerge because of the short duration of the campaign.

These drawbacks had to do with personnel issues and the unusual demands of the situation. First, close attention to tactical details of the campaign tended to rob other important areas, such as manning and morale, although the enthusiasm and professionalism of subordinates mitigated its impact. Second, the intensity of the campaign pushed key participants to near exhaustion, while others remained virtually idle—a situation that could have undermined later decisions. Third, unusual demands (e.g., BDA dissemination and channelization of the information flow to and from General Ryan) tended to frustrate junior and senior staff alike. In the final analysis, however, criticism of General Ryan's style of leadership is inappropriate.

General Ryan's direction of Deliberate Force was appropriate for several reasons. Under the circumstances, his close direction made sense, fit him in terms of ability to manage the situation, and made a major contribution to the success of the campaign. Thus, the issue here is not to make too much of the Napoleonic and Moltkian styles of leadership but to acknowledge the existence of the two options and understand that the highly centralized style of a great captain may have a new viability in modern operations other than war, particularly those whose tactical details have such latent or actual strategic importance. Indeed, future commanders, regardless of their training or proclivities, may have little choice other than replicating some of General Ryan's arrangements and focus. In so doing, however, they should be fully aware of the Napoleonic style's circumstantial suitability, advantages, and drawbacks.

Notes

1. Martin van Creveld, *Command in War* (Cambridge, Mass.: Harvard University Press, 1985), 65.

2. Albert Sidney Britt III, *The Wars of Napoleon,* The West Point Military Series (Wayne, N.J.: Avery Publishing Group, Inc., 1985), xvi.

3. Van Creveld, 64.

4. Col Owen E. Jensen, "Information Warfare: Principles of Third-Wave War," *Airpower Journal* 8, no. 4 (Winter 1994): 36.

5. T. N. Dupuy, *A Genius for War: The German Army and General Staff, 1807–1945* (Fairfax, Va.: Hero Books, 1984), 18.

6. Ibid., 304, 116.

7. Ibid.

8. Antulio J. Echevarria II, "Moltke and the German Military Tradition: His Theories and Legacies," *Parameters* 24, no. 1 (Spring 1996): 97.

9. Maj Gen Michael Short, vice commander, AIRSOUTH, interviewed by Lt Col Robert Owen, Naples, Italy, 4 December 1995.

10. Lt Comdr Michael "Gator" Dunn, CAOC crisis-action cell, telephone interview with author, 3 January 1996; and Capt Scott MacQueen, 510th Fighter Squadron, interviewed by Lt Col Bradley Davis and author, Aviano Air Base (AB), Italy, 20 February 1996. Interestingly, General Ryan related that during a visit with his father—commander in chief of Pacific Air Forces—when Ryan was serving in Vietnam, he (the younger Ryan) mentioned that it seemed someone was trying to get him and his brother (who was also in Vietnam) killed with the type of missions they were flying. Ryan's father replied, "That's me." Gen Michael Ryan, interviewed by Maj Tim Reagan and Dr. Wayne Thompson, 18 October 1995.

11. Maj Michael Holmes, European Command (EUCOM) Operations Division, interviewed by Lt Col Bradley Davis and author, Stuttgart-Vaihingen, Germany, 16 February 1996.

12. Ryan interview. General Ryan himself stated that Deliberate Force was very different from Operation Rolling Thunder in Vietnam because the former was a very specific operation for a very specific result—stop the Bosnian Serbs from shelling Sarajevo. Regarding his tight control over the campaign, he stated that "you can not delegate the selection [of targets]. [The] commander must ask all of the detailed questions. There will be no time in the future when he will have the option to say, 'I delegated that responsibility.' . . . The commander must be accountable for all actions taken by his forces. This is particularly notable, given our use of [precision-guided munition] strikes from the air." Gen Michael Ryan, interviewed by authors of the Air University Balkans Air Campaign Study at Air Command and Staff College, Maxwell Air Force Base (AFB), Ala., 7 February 1996.

13. Maj Gen Hal Hornburg, CAOC director, meeting with authors of the Air University Balkans Air Campaign Study at the Air Force Wargaming Institute, Maxwell AFB, Ala., 12 March 1996.

14. Col Charles Wald, commander, 7490th Wing (Provisional), said that the chaotic nature of the CAOC was due to the nature of airpower—specifically, flexibility and change. At the CAOC, things would change daily. Interviewed by Maj Tim Reagan and Dr. Wayne Thompson, Aviano AB, Italy, 6 October 1995.

15. Ryan interview, 18 October 1995.

16. See J. F. C. Fuller, *The Conduct of War* (London: Methuen, 1961), 53.

17. Col Daniel "Doc" Zoerb, director, Decisive Endeavor air operations cell, interviewed by Lt Col Chris Campbell, Headquarters AIRSOUTH, Naples, Italy, 7 February 1996.

18. Holmes interview. Deptula was Gen Buster Glosson's chief planner in Desert Storm and is widely recognized for his work on the air campaign. See Richard P. Hallion, *Storm over Iraq: Air Power and the Gulf War* (Washington, D.C.: Smithsonian Institution Press, 1992), 153, 209.

19. Hornburg meeting; and Maj Gen Hal Hornburg, interviewed by Dr. Wayne Thompson and Maj Tim Reagan, Vicenza, Italy, 16 October 1995. Royal Air Force wing commander Andy Batchelor, who ran BDA during the operation, said people felt that this was a US and NATO operation and that he had corrected others who remarked that "this is a NATO operation." When asked what could have been done to make it a more combined operation, he suggested that having a division chief from another NATO country might have helped. Interviewed by author, Ramstein AB, Germany, 14 February 1996.

20. Lt Col Bernd Jansen, German air force, Air Branch action officer, AFSOUTH, noted that sometimes commanders did not use the optimum aircraft/weapons mix to ensure that all the nations got a part of the operation. Interviewed by Lt Col Christopher Campbell, Sarajevo, 9 February 1996.

21. Col Arjen Koopmans, Netherlands air force, interviewed by Lt Col Bradley Davis and author, Vicenza AB, Italy, 21 February 1996. The observations of Colonel Koopmans were confirmed by other NATO officers as well. Maj Marc Anthony of the Belgian air force stated that he worked in the C-5 plans and projects cell during the operation and did not feel excluded at all. Interviewed by Lt Col Christopher Campbell, Heidelberg, Germany, 13 February 1996.

22. Maj Michael Holmes related that just prior to Deliberate Force, he went to the Dutch officers to have them review a plan, and they responded by asking, "Are all the Americans sick?" They then lectured him about this being the first time he had consulted them since their arrival. He went on to add that NATO officers felt they were not included, while US officers felt the Europeans were never around. Holmes interview. Lieutenant Commander Dunn said much the same thing. Dunn interview.

23. Hornburg interview.

24. Capt Todd Gentry, 510th Fighter Squadron, interviewed by Lt Col Bradley Davis and author, Aviano AB, Italy, 20 February 1996; and Mac-Queen interview.

25. Lt Col Gary West, commander, 510th Fighter Squadron, interviewed by Lt Col Bradley Davis and author, Aviano AB, Italy, 20 February 1996. At one point the 510th was tasked to use an eight-ship formation to make a reconnaissance pass over the target to make sure there was no collateral damage, return, drop a single bomb, make another pass to drop a second bomb, and then make a final reconnaissance pass. Commander West said the order didn't make sense to him because it put his people in too much danger. He called the CAOC for clarification and was told that General Ryan, who was now asleep, had made the decision and that they would not wake him. In this instance, West felt he did not receive a good answer.

26. Batchelor interview; and Col Daniel Zoerb, memorandum to Lt Col Robert C. Owen, director, Air University Balkans Air Campaign Study, subject: Deliberate Force BDA Process, 25 March 1996.

27. Capt Pete Ornell, 31st Fighter Wing, interviewed by Lt Col Bradley Davis and author, Aviano AB, Italy, 20 February 1996.

28. Capt Mark Hallisey, 31st Fighter Wing, interviewed by Lt Col Bradley Davis and author, Aviano AB, Italy, 22 February 1996.

29. MacQueen interview.

30. Hallisey interview.

31. Hornburg meeting.

32. Capt Patricia Mauldin, CAOC, interviewed by author, Ramstein AB, Germany, 14 February 1996; MSgt Steve Wells, CAOC, telephone interview with author, 24 January 1996; and Chaplain, Lt Col Bobby O. Edwards, telephone interview with author, 29 January 1996.

33. Mauldin interview.

34. This observation is based on discussions with the first sergeant, squadron section commander, and chaplain. While General Ryan and General Hornburg were consumed with duties relating to the campaign, General Sawyer talked to people about their work and the air campaign.

35. Hornburg meeting; and Col Douglas Richardson, chief of operations, CAOC, interviewed by Maj Ron Reed and Maj Mark Conversino, Vicenza, Italy, 16 January 1996. Richardson noted the tremendous stress during Deliberate Force on general officers, who worked 15-to-18-hour days and got phone calls all night. General Hornburg also noted that he would sometimes sleep for two hours, get a phone call, and then return to the CAOC.

36. Lieutenant Commander Dunn noted that no one in the CAOC seemed to have the "big picture" and that he had a hard time finding people to push information to him. Dunn interview. Maj Michael Holmes also mentioned that getting information down to the "worker bees" was a problem in the CAOC during his stay there just prior to Deliberate Force. Holmes interview. Wing Commander Batchelor mentioned that he was not particularly impressed with the leadership other than General Ryan. According to him, majors and lieutenant colonels, who ran here and there

typing up notes or working on the computer, were doing work better left to lieutenants and captains. He thought that the CAOC was disorderly. Batchelor interview.

37. Mauldin interview. Captain Mauldin went on to note that Colonel Richardson was deeply involved in the details, wanting to know everything that was going on and then ensuring that his people were equipped to do their jobs.

38. Gen Sir John Hackett, *The Profession of Arms* (New York: Macmillan Publishing Co., 1983), 218.

39. Batchelor interview; and Col Steven Teske, CAOC chief of plans, interviewed by Lt Col Christopher Campbell, Lt Col Bradley Davis, and author, Ramstein AB, Germany, 14 February 1996. Major Holmes also mentioned that Dunn was an especially good officer, saying that he did everything, including putting the plan together and monitoring it. The fact that he had a strong operational background and familiarity with joint force air component commander issues helped him on the job. To him, Dunn was "essential to the execution of the campaign." Holmes interview.

40. Dunn interview.

41. Maj Keith Kiger, CAOC crisis-action team cell, interviewed by Lt Col Bradley Davis and author, Headquarters Sixteenth Air Force, Aviano AB, Italy, 21 February 1996. Major Holmes also said that Colonel Gibbons was good at putting the daily schedule together and could do it in his head. Holmes interview. Colonel Teske also mentioned that Gibbons was a strong leader. Teske interview.

42. General Hornburg mentioned that he wished he could have spent more time with the NATO liaison officers as well as other personnel so as to keep them informed. There was just no time for anything other than focusing on the job at hand. Hornburg meeting. Colonel Teske said that if it had been possible, General Ryan would have been out front leading the attack—like Alexander the Great. As in ancient times, once the orders were given and the battle joined, the focus shifted to the technical side of fighting the battle. By leading the charge, Ryan focused on technical duties. Teske interview.

43. Air Force Manual (AFM) 1-1, *Basic Aerospace Doctrine of the United States Air Force*, vol. 2, March 1992, 19–20.

44. Maj Dave Goldfein, interviewed by author, Air Force Wargaming Institute, Maxwell AFB, Ala., 7 February 1996.

45. Edwards interview.

46. Wells interview.

47. Mauldin interview.

48. Ibid.

49. Wald interview.

50. Col David Moody, vice commander, 31st Fighter Wing, interviewed by Maj Ron Reed and Maj Mark Conversino, Aviano AB, Italy, 18 January 1996. Wald flew with his wing on 30 August 1995.

51. MacQueen interview. Other wing personnel were just as complimentary of the leadership at this level.

52. West interview.

53. Ibid.

54. Ibid. Colonel Wald also said that he did not want anyone left out. Wald interview.

55. MacQueen interview.

56. Capt Tim Stretch, 510th Fighter Squadron, interviewed by Lt Col Bradley Davis and author, Aviano AB, Italy, 20 February 1996. Stretch said that Colonel West kept the "big picture" in mind, constantly watched out for his people, and made sure everyone kept a level head. Captain Gentry also noted that West, a war veteran, was professional, fatherlike, and an excellent leader. Gentry interview.

57. Wald interview.

58. MacQueen interview. Captain Gentry and Captain Stretch also indicated in their interviews that the joint and combined nature of the operation was no problem. However, Jon R. Anderson reported the services' frustration regarding ordnance, missions, and Air Force flight-line rules. Interestingly, as far as the aircrews were concerned, the campaign ran very smoothly. "Rivalries on US Side Emerged during Airstrikes," *Air Force Times,* 9 October 1995, 6.

59. MacQueen interview.

60. West interview.

61. Stretch interview.

62. West interview.

63. MacQueen interview.

64. Ibid.; Stretch interview; Gentry interview; and West interview. Captains Stretch and MacQueen, both single, stated that they survived on those meals!

65. Gentry interview.

66. MacQueen interview.

67. West interview. Colonel Wald also thought that having families there was a good idea. He noted that it was probably harder on the families in terms of anxiety and at times a distraction for the aircrews, but in the balance it was probably better having them there, especially since the families could see what the pilots were going through. Wald interview.

68. Colette West, interviewed by Lt Col Bradley Davis and author, Aviano AB, Italy, 22 February 1996.

69. Vickie Jo Ryder, interviewed by Lt Col Bradley Davis and author, Aviano AB, Italy, 22 February 1996. In an article, Charles R. Figley listed several things one could do to deal with stress while a spouse was engaged in a conflict. These included increasing contact with others, avoiding worry by channeling energy, maintaining contact with the spouse [easy to do in a situation like Deliberate Force], and focusing on healthy habits. Interestingly, Deliberate Force spouses did just these things to cope with stress. "Coping with Stressors on the Home Front," *Journal of Social Issues* 49, no. 4 (Winter 1993): 61.

70. Janelle Bearden, interviewed by Lt Col Bradley Davis and author, Aviano AB, Italy, 22 February 1996.

71. Tami Turner, interviewed by Lt Col Bradley Davis and author, Aviano AB, Italy, 22 February 1996. An article in *Airman* magazine reported on the stresses experienced by families at Aviano during Deny Flight. As was the case with some of the people interviewed for this study, the article pointed out that life at Aviano is stressful to begin with, mentioning problems with housing, facilities, and long commutes. The article also noted that although families could not have a normal life, they still felt they could have a happy one: "I think about what could happen, but I refuse to let it preoccupy my thoughts." TSgt Timothy P. Barela, "Calm before the Storm," *Airman,* October 1995, 3–9.

72. Larry Keighly, "The Wives Wait Out the War," *Saturday Evening Post,* 30 September 1950, 116. See also Robert Frank Futrell, *The United States Air Force in Korea, 1950–1953* (Washington, D.C.: Office of Air Force History, 1983), 1–37.

73. Keighly, 116.

74. MacQueen interview.

75. West interview.

76. Goldfein interview.

77. AFM 1-1, vol. 2, 115.

78. Hackett, 215–16.

Chapter 14

Chariots of Fire:
Rules of Engagement in
Operation Deliberate Force

Lt Col Ronald M. Reed

The title of this chapter doesn't refer to an Academy-Award-winning Hollywood movie dealing with a race to victory. Rather, it refers to the effective, albeit highly centralized and restricted, rules of engagement (ROE) that applied to military air operations during the North Atlantic Treaty Organization's (NATO) Operation Deny Flight from 1992 to 1995 and its suboperation, Deliberate Force, in August and September 1995. Maj Gen Hal Hornburg, code name Chariot, director of the combined air operations center (CAOC) at Vicenza, Italy, was the lowest-level commander who had the authority to approve weapons release during these two operations.[1] Unless a superior commander authorized such a release, NATO aircraft struck nothing in the tactical area of operations without Chariot's approval. This fact, combined with some unique provisions for close control and coordination with United Nations (UN) forces (the "dual-key" phenomenon, discussed later), meant that ROE had to be restrictive enough to satisfy the political and operational sensitivities of both NATO and UN political and military authorities. At the same time, ROE needed to be flexible enough to provide for force protection as well as the accomplishment of assigned military objectives. The Deny Flight/Deliberate Force ROE, which successfully walked this tightrope of competing influences, offers some insight into appropriate ROE for coalition peace operations of the future.

Before discussing the implementation of ROE in Deliberate Force, one must provide a framework for analyzing these rules. This chapter does so by examining the general nature of ROE, particularly its function and importance in military operations; by presenting several historical examples that illustrate certain issues which have affected military operations; by addressing the actual ROE for air operations in Deliberate Force and following the evolution of ROE from the beginning of NATO air operations in Bosnia in 1992 until the conclusion of Deliberate Force in September 1995; by identifying several key issues that highlight the more problematic situations faced by military planners and operators in the Balkans; and by discussing implications for the future development of ROE.

Nature and Definition of ROE

Abraham Lincoln said that "force is all-conquering, but its victories are short-lived."[2] This assertion illustrates the concept that unbridled force may help achieve short-term, tactical-level success, but without some strategic direction or guidance, the chance of realizing overall objectives is diminished. Carl von Clausewitz recognized this fact in his discussion of the relationship of policy and war: "At the highest level the art of war turns into policy—but a policy conducted by fighting battles rather than by sending diplomatic notes. . . . The assertion that a major military development, or the plan for one, should be a matter for *purely military* opinion is unacceptable and can be damaging" (emphasis in original).[3] The contemporary mechanisms that interconnect the political-policy sphere of influence with the military-strategic sphere of influence and that ensure compliance with national and international legal constraints are rules of engagement.

By delineating the circumstances and limitations under which one may use military force, ROE provides the method to ensure relevancy and congruency between the means (military force) and the ends (political/diplomatic objective) one seeks, while always ensuring compliance with international law and the law of armed conflict. These political/diplomatic, military, and legal influences converge to form the basis for ROE. Capt J. Ashley Roach, a judge advocate in the US Navy, notes that ROE results from a composite of these three factors (fig. 14.1).[4] The relative influences of each of these factors will vary according to the circumstances; therefore, the diameters of the circles, as well as the degree of convergence, differ according

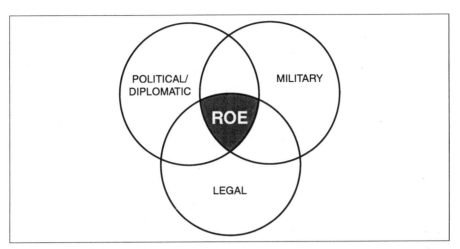

Figure 14.1. ROE Influences (Adapted from Capt J. Ashley Roach, "Rules of Engagement," *Naval War College Review* 36, no. 1 [January–February 1983]: 46–48)

to the situation.[5] The political/diplomatic circle represents the assurance that military operations are conducted in accordance with national policy. According to Roach, ROE should be flexible enough to accommodate changing circumstances and should be designed to allow military courses of action that advance political intentions with little chance for undesired escalation or reaction.[6]

The military circle takes into consideration the practical, operational considerations for a particular military situation. ROE represents the upper bounds on the freedom of the commander to use military force toward successful mission accomplishment.[7] ROE provides guidance to the commander in balancing the enemy threat (and the concurrent needs for self-defense) with the need to avoid conflict escalation. According to ROE expert D. P. O'Connell, "the conduct of operations in tension situations always involves a nice balance of threat and counter-threat on the part of both sides, and the main purpose of rules of engagement is to prevent that balance [from] being disturbed by thrusting the apparent necessity of self-defense too obviously upon one player rather than upon the other."[8] O'Connell would consider a "tension situation" to be a confrontation between two or more military forces in which both the threat of the use of force and the desire to avoid escalation are present. The military circle, therefore, represents this balance of threat, capability, and intent that one must consider when developing appropriate ROE.

The legal circle represents the combined domestic and international legal considerations that one must adhere to in any military operation. The laws of war provide the absolute limit on the use of force in any conflict scenario. Domestic laws and regulations also provide restrictions on the employment of force (such as restrictions on the use of certain weapons, including approval requirements of the National Command Authorities [NCA] for use of nuclear weapons or chemical and riot-control agents). Although obligations of US and international law always influence and limit ROE, the rules normally operate well within the boundaries of the law.[9]

Commanders often limit the use of force by making decisions that are more restrictive than legal or ROE constraints. For example, W. Hays Parks cites the freedom-of-navigation exercise conducted against Libya's claim over the Gulf of Sidra in 1981.[10] Even though both international law and ROE in effect at the time allowed the use of force in self-defense against demonstrated hostile intent, the commander issued orders that US forces not fire unless first fired upon. In this case two Libyan Su-22 Fitters engaged two Navy F-14s on a head-to-head intercept, clearly demonstrating hostile intent. The F-14s withheld fire until the Su-22s fired air-to-air missiles. In response, the Navy fighters quickly evaded the oncoming missiles and then downed both Fitters. This example shows the distinction among a commander's rights under the law, his or her authority under ROE, and the exercise of his or her discretion.[11]

The legal circle also represents ROE's raison d'être: the inherent right to self-defense, which is the foundation for US Standing Rules of Engagement (SROE). When considering ROE, one normally first thinks of the need to restrict the use of force and provide guidance to commanders on the constraints within which they must operate. In reality, however, written SROE does not exist today because of a need to restrict military operations politically; rather, SROE resulted from incidents involving the USS *Stark* and the US Marine

Corps barracks in Beirut, Lebanon, as well as the need to ensure that commanders understand the right and obligation to protect themselves and their forces.[12] The commander's principal task in any military operation is to take all necessary and reasonable actions to protect his or her forces from attack or from threat of imminent attack. The legal standard for the use of armed force in self-defense remains the same whether protecting the individual, the unit, the aircraft, or the nation: a situation must require the use of force (necessity) and the amount of force must correspond to the situation giving rise to the necessity (proportionality).[13]

Necessity arises not only when an armed attack occurs (hostile act), but also when one confronts the threat of imminent attack (hostile intent). In other words, a commander need not absorb the first shot before returning fire. The often perceived requirement to fire only if first fired upon is legally false—an important concept in today's world of high-speed and high-lethality weaponry. Waiting to be fired upon can have disastrous results. Nevertheless, several nations view the issue of hostile intent in a different light, especially in military peace operations. At a recent legal conference in the Netherlands, Canadian and British representatives indicated that they do not follow ROE based on hostile intent in any peacekeeping operation, even to the point of suffering casualties before using military force.[14] In their opinion the need to maintain impartiality and to avoid becoming a party to the conflict carries a higher priority than the right of self-defense. They view casualties incurred as a result of this inhibition on the use of force as the cost of doing business. As discussed later, international law does not require this restriction, and it is inconsistent with US SROE.

Joint Publication (Pub) 1-02, *Department of Defense Dictionary of Military and Associated Terms,* defines ROE as "directives issued by competent military authority which delineate the circumstances and limitations under which United States forces will initiate and/or continue engagement with other forces encountered."[15] Although this definition adequately defines ROE at the strategic/operational level, one can more practically define ROE at the operational and tactical levels as the commander's rules for what can be shot and when.[16]

Several issues relating to the US definition of ROE become apparent immediately. Under the current US SROE, "competent military authority" refers to the NCA.[17] Although combatant commanders may augment SROE to reflect unique political and military policies, threats, and missions specific to their areas of responsibility, one must submit any changes resulting in different rules governing the use of force to the NCA for approval.[18] Obviously, political policy makers use SROE as a mechanism to ensure that military commanders completely understand when and how to use force to support policy objectives. Therefore, policy makers have the final authority on ROE for use of force in any given situation.

Next, "delineating the circumstances" under which one may use military force relates to the fact that situations often drive ROE. The amount of force one can use in a given situation depends upon a variety of political, military, and legal factors that meld to create the contextual environment for that engagement. The situation may have geographic implications. For example, during the Rolling Thunder campaign in Vietnam, air commanders could not attack targets within a 30-mile radius from the center of Hanoi, a 10-mile radius from the center of Haiphong, and within 30 miles of China.[19] Another type of geographical implication is the exclusion zone. In the Balkans conflict, the entire area of Bosnia-Herzegovina represented a no-fly zone (NFZ); ROE provided for engagement of any unauthorized aircraft operating within that zone.[20] Similarly, ROE also applied to other geographic zones in the Balkans.[21]

Another aspect of the situational nature of ROE relates to the type of conflict. ROE for peacekeeping differs from ROE for peace enforcement or limited war. Peacekeeping generally involves the most restrictive ROE due to the need to maintain strict impartiality on the part of the peacekeeping force. Because of the need to restrict the use of force, ROE for peacekeeping operations typically limits it to self-defense only. Peace enforcement and limited war, however, presuppose the use of force as a coercive mechanism to change the behavior of a particular party. ROE for these operations often is less restrictive and authorizes the use of force in a wider range of situations.

Adam Roberts notes that "peacekeeping is, notoriously, a very different type of activity from more belligerent or coercive use of force, and the differences cause serious problems. The three principles on which peacekeeping operations have traditionally been based (impartiality, consent of host states, and avoidance of use of force) are different from the principles on which other uses of force have been based. Further, the dispersion of forces and their lightly armed character, mean that they are intensely vulnerable to reprisals in the event force is used on their behalf."[22] This problem, discussed later, played a significant role in the development of ROE for NATO military operations in the Balkans. The inherent incompatibility between the UN's role in providing peacekeepers on the ground and NATO's role in providing peace enforcers in the air became obvious during Deny Flight, which occurred prior to the execution of Deliberate Force in August 1995.

Additionally, "delineating the circumstances" refers to the basic purpose of any ROE: the inherent right to self-defense. According to the introduction to the US SROE, the purpose of these rules is to "implement the inherent right of self defense and provide guidance for the application of force for mission accomplishment."[23] Further, "these rules do not limit a commander's inherent authority and obligation to use all necessary means available and to take all appropriate action in self-defense of the commander's unit and other U.S. forces in the vicinity."[24] The concept of self-defense in SROE covers situations involving both hostile act and hostile intent. As mentioned above, SROE defines the elements of self-defense as (1) necessity (a hostile act occurs or a force or terrorist unit exhibits hostile intent) and (2) proportionality (the force used must be reasonable in intensity, duration, and magnitude, based on all facts known to the commander at the time, to decisively counter the hostile act or hostile intent and to ensure the continued safety of US forces).[25]

SROE's provisions apply not only to individual self-defense but also to "national, collective, and unit" self-defense. National self-defense is defined as "the act of defending the United States, U.S. forces and in certain circumstances, U.S. citizens and their property, U.S. commercial assets, and other designated non-U.S. forces, foreign nationals, and their property, from a hostile act or hostile intent."[26] Collective self-defense, a subset of national self-defense, authorizes the NCA to provide for the defense of designated non-US forces, personnel, and their property. Unit self-defense entails the act of defending a particular unit of US forces, including elements or personnel thereof, and other US forces in the vicinity against hostile act or hostile intent.[27] In essence, US forces have the authority and obligation under SROE to use all necessary means available and to take all appropriate action to defend themselves, their unit, other US forces in the vicinity, and (with NCA approval) non-US forces against hostile act or hostile intent.

The precise meaning of "all necessary means" depends upon the unique circumstances of a particular situation. SROE provides guidelines for self-defense: "(1) Attempt to Control without the Use of Force; (2) Use Proportional Force to Control the Situation; and (3) Attack to Disable or Destroy,"[28] each of which focuses on military necessity and proportionality. Normally, the use of force in a self-defense scenario is a measure of last resort. When time and circumstances permit, one should warn a hostile force and give it a chance to withdraw or cease threatening actions. When one must use force, the nature, duration, and scope of the engagement should not exceed whatever is needed to "decisively counter the hostile act or hostile intent and to ensure the continued safety of U.S. forces or other protected personnel or property."[29] Any attacks in the name of self-defense to destroy or disable a hostile force are allowed only when they must be used to prevent or terminate a hostile act or hostile intent. When a force ceases to pose an imminent threat, one must terminate any engagement of that force. Thus, the provisions for self-defense permit no retaliatory strikes. If a hostile force remains an imminent threat, however, US forces may pursue and engage it under the concept of immediate pursuit of hostile foreign forces.[30] The discussion of self-defense in SROE assumes the commitment of a hostile act or the existence of the threat of force by a foreign or terrorist unit.

Although it is generally easy to identify and define a hostile act on the ground and in the air, the elements that constitute hostile intent vis-à-vis aerial ROE are not easily delineated. For example, at what point does an enemy aircraft or surface-to-air weapon provide sufficient indications of hostile intent to warrant the use of force in self-defense? Normally, maneuvering into weapons-release position or illuminating friendly aircraft with fire-control radar indicates hostile intent. The presence of other factors, however, such as defensive maneuvering capabilities of the friendly aircraft or stealthy characteristics, might negate the threat.

To give adequate guidance on what is and is not allowed, one might be tempted to define and legislate every conceivable type of threat that a pilot could encounter. However, not only is it impossible to predict every eventuality, but also the more detailed ROE becomes, the more such rules restrict the flexibility and judgment of the person best able to correctly assess the threat—the pilot in the air. This difficulty illustrates one of the most troublesome dilemmas in drafting effective ROE—the desire for clear, unequivocal guidance as to what pilots may or may not do and for maximum latitude in exercising their judgment and discretion.[31]

During the stages leading up to Deliberate Force, the US Navy on several occasions requested more specific ROE regarding air-to-air and air-to-ground threats of hostile intent. General Hornburg, sensitive to the need for flexibility and judgment, responded by stating, "You guys are professional pilots; I'm not going to give you a cookbook, and I'm not going to tie your hands."[32] This guidance is consistent with the conclusions of Parks: "In preparing ROE for a particular situation, threat, or operation, less always is better than more, in order to allow the individual in the 'hot seat' maximum latitude in making decisions when being confronted with a threat."[33] As mentioned later in this chapter, even though ROE for Deliberate Force extensively restricted the employment of military force, the rules never infringed upon the judgment of the pilot to respond to an immediate and unavoidable threat.

Ultimately, ROE bridges the gap between the policy maker and the military commander. The primary consideration for the policy maker is ensuring control over the use of military force so it best serves national or alliance objectives. The primary consideration for military commanders is ensuring that they can defend their forces and employ them to accomplish the assigned mission in the most effective manner. According to a RAND study by Bradd C. Hayes, these two considerations provide both the foundation and dilemma for people who draft

ROE—a dilemma of action versus reaction.[34] To maintain close political control and avoid the escalation of hostilities, ROE in peacetime (including peacekeeping operations) tends to be more restrictive. However, as Hayes correctly points out, the political price for reaction and hesitancy can prove unacceptably high—witness the incidents involving the USS *Stark* and the Marine barracks in Beirut.[35] Conversely, preemptive self-defense can also have high political costs—witness the shoot-down of the Iranian commercial airliner by the USS *Vincennes*.[36]

Because one must often sacrifice military objectives to achieve political objectives,[37] writers of ROE must develop and evaluate these rules within the context of both the political and military considerations of a particular operation. According to Clausewitz, "war is not merely an act of policy, but a true political instrument, a continuation of political intercourse carried on with other means. . . . The political object is the goal, war is the means of reaching it, and means can never be considered in isolation from their purpose."[38] Consistent with the description of the nature and purpose of rules of engagement, several historical examples illustrate their influence and impact on past military operations in ways that build on the framework used here to analyze ROE in Deliberate Force.

Background/Historical Examples

The bombing of the US Marine barracks in Beirut, the attack on the USS *Stark,* and the shootdown of the civilian Iranian airliner by the USS *Vincennes* illustrate several important matters pertaining to the impact of ROE on military operations. Each of these incidents provides insight into how ROE can affect military operations and suggests issues one should consider when drafting ROE.

The bombing of the Marine barracks in 1983, which cost 241 soldiers, sailors, and marines their lives, shows how interpretation of ROE can have disastrous results. Because the commander of the 24th Marine Amphibious Unit considered his mission to maintain "presence" in a peace operation, he did not want his troops to look or act like an occupation force.[39] Although the Marines initially faced a permissive environment in Beirut, it became increasingly hostile the longer US forces remained.[40] Neither the immediate commander nor the chain of command noticed this shift in the threat environment, and this lack of sensitivity led to ROE, in effect at the time of the incident, that did not require the sentries on duty to have a round in the chamber of their weapons or a magazine inserted into their weapons.[41]

At about 0621 on 23 October 1983, a heavy truck loaded with explosives entered the parking lot at Beirut International Airport, made a right-hand turn, crashed through a concertina-wire barrier, drove past two sentries and through an open gate, traveled about 450 feet, and passed three large drainage pipes before ramming into the building that housed the battalion landing team. The truck immediately detonated, destroying the building and killing 220 marines, 18 sailors, and three soldiers. The Department of Defense (DOD) Commission Report indicated that during the few seconds it took the truck to ram into the team's building, the sentries could take no action to stop the truck because their weapons were unloaded.[42] Even though written ROE specifically stated that the marines could defend themselves against both hostile acts *and* demonstrated hostile intent, the commander's interpretation (or misinterpretation) of the mission and the threat environment resulted in an overly restrictive application of the rules. Having the sentries put their bullets in their pockets violated the first rule of any ROE—the inherent right of self-defense.

The crew of the USS *Stark* found itself operating in the Persian Gulf in support of reflagging operations for Kuwaiti oil tankers. On 17 May 1987, an Iraqi F-1 Mirage launched two Exocet missiles at the *Stark*. The United States accepted Iraq's apology, which claimed that the attack—responsible for the deaths of 37 sailors and the wounding of 21 others—was unintentional.[43] A Navy study chaired by Rear Adm Grant Sharp concluded that "the rules of engagement that were in existence on May 17, 1987 were sufficient to enable *Stark* to properly warn the Iraqi aircraft, in a timely manner, of the presence of a US warship and if the warning was not heeded, the rules of engagement were sufficient to enable *Stark* to defend herself against hostile intent and imminent danger without absorbing the first hit."[44] The study determined that the commander of the

Stark failed to appreciate the obvious change in the threat environment in the central Persian Gulf. It also concluded that the commander/watch team improperly understood the use of fire-control radar to illuminate a threatening aircraft as a measure short of deadly force—an act that could have secured the ship's safety.[45] Like the Beirut bombing, this incident illustrates the potential pitfalls of commanding officers failing to ensure the inherent right to self-defense under ROE in a "noncombat" environment with a dynamic threat.

In both of the previous examples, the problem did not arise so much from overly restrictive ROE as from a lack of sensitivity on the part of the commanders to a changing threat environment. Both examples illustrate the tendency in noncombat situations and peace operations to be overly controlling and to curtail reaction to the threat. An effective ROE, therefore, should be highly flexible so that one can meet changes in the threat environment with an effective response. At the same time, both examples illustrate that no matter how robustly one writes ROE, nothing can compensate for the poor judgment of a commanding officer, who must ultimately decide how to react and employ forces in any given situation. The underuse or overuse of force in any scenario may negatively affect mission accomplishment. The "genius" of the commander, as Clausewitz would say, determines the effectiveness of the use of military force in any military operation.

In contrast to the Beirut and the *Stark* incidents, the one involving the USS *Vincennes* shows how aggressive, preemptive self-defense can be militarily and politically costly. In this case misinterpretation of the threat caused a US Navy Aegis cruiser to shoot down an Iranian civilian airliner. Regardless of whether the blame lies with an overaggressive, triggerhappy commander or with human and/or mechanical error during a confused naval battle, this tragic mistake resulted in the death of 290 civilians aboard the airliner.

Although the official investigation of the *Vincennes* incident absolved the captain and crew from fault, several questions arose after completion of the investigation.[46] Nearly four years after the incident, *Newsweek* ran an article that described the story of "a naval fiasco, of an overeager captain, panicked crewmen, and the cover-up that followed."[47] In response, the director of the Oceans Law and Policy Department at the Naval War College drafted a memorandum refuting many of *Newsweek*'s claims.[48] Despite differences in interpretation, everyone agrees upon certain matters of fact.

On the morning of 3 July 1988, the USS *Vincennes* was on duty in the Persian Gulf, assisting in escort operations for reflagged Kuwaiti oil tankers. Responding to notification by the USS *Montgomery* that approximately 13 Iranian gunboats might be preparing to attack a merchant ship, the *Vincennes* proceeded north to investigate. After one of the Iranian vessels fired upon a helicopter performing routine morning patrol from the *Vincennes*, the latter became involved in a surface engagement with the gunboats. During this time an Iranian civilian airliner took off from Bandar Abbas (a joint military/civilian airfield in Iran) on a flight path that would take the airliner over the area of the naval engagement. Misidentifying the airliner as an Iranian F-14, the *Vincennes* issued 11 warnings that it should remain clear of the area and then fired two SM-2 missiles, shooting it down. Approximately three minutes and 45 seconds elapsed from initial identification of the aircraft as possibly hostile until shootdown.[49]

The previously mentioned RAND study of naval ROE noted that the rules in the Persian Gulf applicable during the *Vincennes* incident had been changed after incidents involving the USS *Stark* and USS *Samuel B. Roberts* (the latter had struck a mine in the Gulf approximately one month before the *Vincennes* arrived) to encourage anticipatory self-defense.[50] This study, however, did not blame "hair-trigger" ROE for the shootdown of the Iranian airliner. Rather, it concluded that the hostile environment and ongoing sea battle played a prominent role in the decision and that ROE probably did not significantly affect the decision to use force to deal with the presumed threat.[51]

The official DOD report concluded that, under ROE, the primary responsibility of the commanding officer is defense of the ship from attack or from threat of imminent attack.[52] Based on information he believed to be true at the time, the captain of the *Vincennes* shot down the Iranian airliner in self-defense—a clear case of the "damned if you do, damned if you don't" dilemma faced by military commanders operating in noncombat environments euphemistically called "operations other than war." The best a commander can hope for is ROE flexible enough to be relevant to a changing threat environment, information and communications to appreciate when those changes take place, and experience and judgment to make the correct decision when faced with a threat that might require forcible response.

The Beirut, *Stark,* and *Vincennes* incidents all illustrate the importance not only of having effective and flexible ROE but also of the judgment of the commander in every conflict. Of course the commander's—or, for that matter, the pilot's—judgment depends on the real-time information available at the point of decision. The fog and friction of war often inhibit or distort the flow of accurate and timely information. ROE, therefore, must provide guidance consistent with the political and military realities of the conflict to bridge the gap between military means and political ends in an uncertain environment. The rest of this essay uses this test of consistency and relevance to explore and evaluate the evolution and execution of ROE in Operation Deliberate Force.

Evolution of ROE in Operation Deliberate Force

The rules of engagement for Deliberate Force arose from various changes and additions in NATO military operational tasking in the Balkans brought about by numerous United Nations Security Council resolutions (UNSCR) relating to Bosnia-Herzegovina. Consequently, any full analysis of ROE for Deliberate Force must begin with an examination of the genesis and evolution of ROE from the inception of NATO air operations in Operation Sky Monitor, through Deny Flight, and culminating in the air strike operations conducted in August and September of 1995. To truly comprehend ROE requires an understanding of the complex political and military environment that faced the military planners and operators during the entire period of operations. The changing character of this political and military environment, in turn, caused ROE to evolve from a policy of not using force in the simple monitoring of the UN-declared NFZ to a robust use of force in the air strike campaign executed in August and September of 1995. The changing environment shaped the intent and purpose of formal ROE and reflected the impact of multinational/multialliance influences on its formulation.

A flow of contributions and guidance provided the framework for ROE development in Deny Flight/Deliberate Force (fig. 14.2). The UNSCRs served as the legal basis under the UN Charter and international law for use of military force by nations and/or regional organizations or arrangements in support of specific provisions outlined in the resolutions. In response to a UNSCR, a regional organization (in this case, NATO's North Atlantic Council [NAC]) issues to forces under its control a mandate authorizing the use of military force, the latter limited by the UNSCR and further restricted by any NATO concerns. The mandate is translated into a military operations plan (OPLAN), which includes an annex detailing ROE to be used in the NATO military operation. For Deliberate Force the commander in chief of Allied Forces Southern Europe (CINCSOUTH) promulgated OPLAN 40101, "Operation Deny Flight," and the supporting ROE annex.[53] An operations order (OPORD) contains the next level of ROE—in this case, OPORD 45101.5, "Deny Flight," issued by the commander of 5th Allied Tactical Air Force (COM5ATAF).[54] One should note that each subordinate level of ROE can be *no less* restrictive than the combined ROE for each of the higher levels. Subordinate ROE, however, can be *more* restrictive as long as the rules remain congruent with the intent of superior commanders and overall political objectives. Special instructions (SPINS) provide additional ROE guidance. For Deliberate Force, COM5ATAF and the CAOC director issued periodic SPINS that included a section on "ROE and Commander's Guidance" (SPINS 028 was in effect during Deliberate Force).[55] Lastly, each air tasking message (ATM), which provides daily, specific information on targets selected for attack, may contain information regarding special ROE for that particular attack. To fully examine ROE for Deliberate Force, one must therefore follow the rules' evolution through each of these steps, beginning with NATO's first involvement in October 1992.

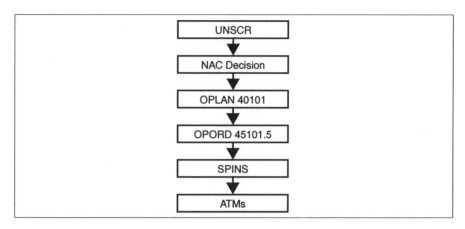

Figure 14.2. Development of ROE

On 16 October 1992, NATO forces began Operation Sky Monitor in response to UNSCR 781, which requested member states to assist the United Nations Protection Force (UNPROFOR) in monitoring the ban on military flights in the airspace of Bosnia-Herzegovina.[56] Although the resolution created an NFZ, it did not authorize the engagement of unauthorized flights. Rather, it called upon member states to "nationally or through regional agencies or arrangements" [read NATO] provide technical monitoring and other capabilities to monitor compliance with the NFZ.[57] Accordingly, ROE for Sky Monitor limited the use of force to self-defense, with no provisions for engagement of aircraft based solely upon their violation of the NFZ.[58] The rules that applied during this period of operations derived from Supreme Allied Commander Europe (SACEUR) Support Plan 10001D, "NATO Europe Integrated Air Defense,"[59] which attempted to balance the desire to limit the possibility of provocation and escalation with the sovereign right to take action in self-defense.[60] Under this ROE, one could engage aircraft only for self-protection. For all other situations, including the protection of other friendly forces, pilots had to request specific approval.[61] The restriction on the defense of friendly forces is clearly contrary to the previously discussed US SROE notion of collective and unit self-defense.[62] However, it illustrates the type of ROE expected in an observation/peacekeeping military operation in which any use of force is extremely circumspect.

NATO airborne early warning (NAEW) aircraft already involved in Operation Sharp Guard (the naval monitoring and subsequent embargo operations in the Adriatic) carried out the monitoring of the NFZ. The addition of an NAEW orbit established over Hungary with the support of the Hungarian and Austrian governments in late October 1992 enhanced the monitoring of the NFZ. The UN noted that more than five hundred flights violated the NFZ from 16 October 1992 to 12 April 1993.[63]

The numerous violations of the NFZ ban resulted in the enactment of UNSCR 816, adopted on 31 March 1993, which provided an extension of the NFZ ban to include all fixed-wing and rotary-wing aircraft in the airspace of the Republic of Bosnia-Herzegovina. It also included provisions for member states, subject to close coordination with UN secretary-general Willy Claes and UNPROFOR, to take "all necessary measures" to ensure compliance with the NFZ ban on flights.[64] The resolution led to an NAC decision on 8 April 1993 to enforce the NFZ with NATO military aircraft. This decision resulted in the development and implementation of OPLAN 40101, which began at noon Greenwich mean time (GMT) on 12 April 1993 with aircraft from France, the Netherlands, and the United States.[65]

Annex E to OPLAN 40101 contained ROE applicable to the enforcement of the NFZ. The planners who wrote the ROE—vigorously supervised by UN, NATO, and individual national authorities[66]—attempted to include the maximum amount of military flexibility within the politically charged planning environment. Since the NAC approved all ROE, any one of the 16 sovereign NATO member nations had veto power over the rules. The military feared that this "lowest common denominator" approach would produce ineffective, "watered down" ROE.[67] Fortunately, this fear was never realized, and the resulting ROE provided, for the most part, robust rules for self-defense and mission accomplishment. A five- or six-man team that comprised a small "Black Hole" type of planning group led by Lt Gen Joseph Ashy, commander of Allied Air Forces Southern Europe (COMAIRSOUTH), tightly controlled the whole planning process for ROE at Headquarters Allied Forces Southern Europe (AFSOUTH).[68]

Within the first two weeks of operations, a significant problem arose with enforcement of the NFZ. ROE provided for
termination of *all* air use by the parties within Bosnia, making
no distinction between fixed- and rotary-wing aircraft. In fact,
the UNSCR specifically addressed the ban of all unauthorized
fixed-wing *and* rotary-wing aircraft within Bosnian airspace.
Unfortunately, the engagement of helicopters proved problematic. Ultimately, COMAIRSOUTH issued guidance (endorsed
by the UN and NATO) that defined away the problem by determining that helicopters had no military significance.[69] The
thinking was that the risks for accidentally shooting down a UN
helicopter or some other helicopter transporting civilians or
casualties were so great that they outweighed the military significance of rotary-wing aircraft. The memory of the shootdown
of the US Army Blackhawk helicopter in Iraq by US Air Force
F-15s in April 1993 had some bearing on this conclusion.[70]

Even though COMAIRSOUTH decided not to engage helicopters, the written ROE remained unchanged. During NATO's
monitoring and reporting of helicopter flights, the authority
remained in place to engage helicopters under certain circumstances.[71] This situation illustrates the point that writing, in-
terpreting, and implementing ROE are not always coextensive,
highlighting the importance of judgment on the part of on-scene
commanders. Since "legislating" the military significance of any
particular item is impossible, a responsible commander—such
as COMAIRSOUTH—must ensure the interpretation and execution of ROE in accordance with the overall concept of operations
and political sensitivity associated with a given situation.

The next significant change in air operations occurred as a
result of UNSCR 836,[72] which responded to threats against the
previously created "safe areas" of Sarajevo, Bihac, Srebrenica,
Gorazde, Tuzla, and Zepa.[73] It did so by authorizing the use of airpower to support the UNPROFOR mandate of deterring attacks
against the safe areas and responding in self-defense to any
attack, incursion, or deliberate obstruction in or around those
areas that affected the freedom of movement of UNPROFOR
or protected humanitarian convoys. At a meeting on 10 June
1993, NATO foreign ministers agreed that NATO would provide
protective airpower in case of attacks against UNPROFOR in
Bosnia-Herzegovina in accordance with the request for UN

member-state assistance.[74] A report by the UN secretary-general on 14 June 1993 asked NATO to "prepare plans for provisions of the necessary air support capacity, *in close coordination with me and my Special Representative for the former Yugoslavia*" (emphasis added).[75] UNSCR 836 and the request of the UN secretary-general led to the deployment of close air support (CAS) aircraft to the Southern Region and NATO's air cover for UNPROFOR.[76] The specific requirement for "close coordination" with the UN resulted in the infamous dual-key process.

In addition to the deployment of CAS aircraft, NATO decided to make immediate preparations for stronger measures, including air strikes, against the people responsible for the strangulation of Sarajevo and other areas in Bosnia-Herzegovina, as well as those responsible for wide-scale interference with humanitarian assistance. At an NAC meeting on 2–3 August 1993, NATO military authorities had the task of drawing up, in close coordination with UNPROFOR, operational options for air strikes, including appropriate command and control (C^2) and decision-making arrangements for their implementation. On 9 August 1993, they produced a memorandum listing operational options for air strikes approved by NAC.[77] Out of this memorandum flowed several crucial ideas and themes that ultimately affected both ROE and air operations executed during Deliberate Force. These included C^2 coordination between UN and NATO (the dual key), proportionality of force used in air strikes, sensitivity to collateral damage, military necessity, phased approach to expanded air strikes, and breakout of target categories into option-one, -two, and -three targets. OPLAN 40101, change two, annex E, "Rules of Engagement" reflects these issues and themes.[78]

The breakout of potential targets into three categories had its basis in the concepts of proportionality, military necessity, and gradual application of force.[79] The NAC memorandum's discussion on the use of force articulated these concepts.[80] The discussion on air strike options noted that the selection of targets needed to take into consideration proportionality as well as the importance of showing resolve and capability; the selection should also discourage retaliation.[81] The concept of operations entailed a phased approach in which the first phase commenced with an initial use of airpower, limited in time and scope but robust enough to achieve the desired effect. Thereafter, if required and when authorized by the appropriate political authority, NATO would conduct air strikes in phases that focused first on the immediate environs of Sarajevo or other areas. These strikes would have the specific purpose of assisting relief of the siege, facilitating the delivery of humanitarian assistance, and supporting UNPROFOR in the performance of its mandate. NATO might have to employ subsequent phases to expand operations to encompass targets that influenced the sustainability of the siege forces.[82] Planners, therefore, needed to group and prioritize targets to show target type and geographic locality to assure congruence with political and legal mandates.

As a result of these considerations, NAC decision MCM-KAD-084-93 established option-one, -two, and -three target sets to meet these requirements. Option-one targets encompassed the first-strike phase and included not only militarily significant targets but also those—such as specific artillery batteries participating in a siege—that visibly impeded or prevented the implementation of UNSCRs.[83] Option-two targets covered the initial follow-on phase and included direct and essential support items such as artillery/heavy weapons, supply points and munitions sites, C^2 facilities, and early warning radar and surface-to-air missile (SAM) sites.[84] Option-three targets covered the expanded operations phase and included targets of strategic value outside the immediate areas under siege. Many of the same types of targets discussed in option two but not located in the immediate area of the siege fell into option three, as well as items such as military-related petroleum, oil, and lubricants and anything that would tend to degrade overall military capability throughout Bosnia-Herzegovina. By breaking out the potential targets into separate option sets, military and political authorities could control the escalation of violence by authorizing attacks in a phased and gradual approach. For each of the target options, one fact remained constant—no matter the option chosen, no attack could occur without close coordination with the UN through UNPROFOR.

The issue regarding C^2 coordination between the UN and NATO resulted in what has come to be known as the dual-key process. From the very beginning of Deny Flight, an ongoing dialogue had occurred regarding what the term *close coordination* meant and who controlled the use of military force within Bosnia-Herzegovina.[85] As noted above, the requirement to coordinate closely with the UN before initiating CAS or air strikes came from the language in the UNSCR and the report of the UN secretary-general. In practice, the dual-key process required approval of the appropriate level of authority in the NATO *and* UN chains of command (fig. 14.3) before execution of any weapons release.

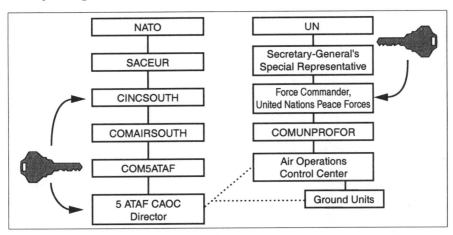

Figure 14.3. NATO and UN Chains of Command

The NATO chain of command proceeded directly from SACEUR through CINCSOUTH to COMAIRSOUTH to COM5ATAF and finally to the CAOC director. The approval authority for CAS support on the NATO side was delegated all the way down to COM5ATAF and the CAOC director.[86] On the UN side, however, the approval authority proved somewhat problematic. The UN secretary-general himself held approval authority for the first use of CAS. Thus, if a UNPROFOR ground unit came under attack, a tactical air control party (TACP) or forward air controller (FAC) assigned to the unit would initiate a "Blue Sword" CAS request. The request would go through the air operations control center to Sarajevo for evaluation by the UNPROFOR commander and, if approved, to the force commander of United Nations Peace Forces (FC UNPF) in Zagreb, where a crisis-action team cell would also evaluate the request. It then went to Yasushi Akashi, the UN secretary-general's special representative (SGSR) to the former Yugoslavia and, finally, to New York for approval by the UN secretary-general himself.

The first attempted request for CAS by a UNPROFOR ground unit provides an example of the difficulties associated with the dual-key approach. On 12 March 1994, a French TACP in the Bihac area called for CAS to stop a Serbian 40-millimeter antiaircraft artillery (AAA) attack on UNPROFOR troops. Even though an AC-130 was in the area and had the offending artillery piece in its sights, approval from the UN side of the dual key was not forthcoming. Due to problems in locating Akashi, the request was not approved until six hours after the TACP's request. In the meantime, the AC-130 left the area and came back two or three times. Unfortunately, when the approval finally came through, the TACP and the AC-130 could no longer positively identify the target, so the former called off the CAS request.[87]

The dual-key process also caused some initial confusion regarding the distinction between receiving approval to drop weapons and actual clearance to do so. OPLAN 40101, change two, provided ROE conditions required for weapons release.[88] Concerns for collateral damage and the imperative to avoid fratricide resulted in ROE that not only required approval from both UN and NATO channels but also required positive identification and clearance from the FAC. Because there was no requirement to ask the FAC whether he had received prior approval through the UN chain of command, the pilot could assume that if the FAC gave clearance for attack, the latter had requisite approval from the UN to do so. After receiving Chariot's approval, the pilot could attack a positively identified target if the FAC gave clearance to do so.

For the entire period leading up to Deliberate Force, UN-PROFOR ground personnel received approval for CAS a total of three times. The first use of CAS occurred on 10 April 1994 in response to a request made by UNPROFOR military observers in Gorazde. After approval by the SGSR, two US Air Force F-16Cs dropped bombs under the control of a UN FAC. Approval from the UN chain of command took less than two hours.[89] The next day, UNPROFOR again requested air protection for UN personnel in Gorazde. Two US Marine Corps F/A-18A aircraft, also under the control of a UN FAC, bombed and strafed targets. The last CAS request came in July 1995 during the siege of Srebrenica by the Bosnian Serb army (BSA).[90] Often, in lieu of an approved CAS mission, NATO aircraft would engage in "air presence" demonstrations, conspicuously showing themselves to the offending ground forces by flying over the area at high speed with afterburners to scare the enemy into stopping the attack. Even though the aircraft released no weapons in these passes, the demonstrations often proved effective in temporarily halting attacks on UNPROFOR positions.[91]

The ineffectiveness of the dual-key process came under intense fire after the fall of the Srebrenica and Zepa safe areas in July 1995. Even though NATO aircraft were available and present during the Bosnian Serb siege of Srebrenica, the UN did not turn its key until nearly three days after the attack had begun. By this time CAS could not save the safe area. A report presented by the Dutch Ministry of Defense in December 1995 blamed the UN's misinterpretation of Bosnian Serb objectives and the UN command structure for withholding NATO airpower to deter the BSA attack.[92] The report stated that despite repeated requests for CAS from the Dutch peacekeepers on the ground in Srebrenica—with NATO CAS aircraft on airborne alert over the Adriatic—the UN approved only one last-minute CAS mission,[93] which helped the peacekeepers regroup north of Srebrenica but did not stop the BSA from taking the town. As a consequence of this incident, Secretary-General Claes transferred the UN key from Akashi to Gen Bernard Janvier, the FC UNPF. At this point, decisions about how and when to use military force fell to the UN and NATO military commanders.[94]

The close coordination and consultation procedures also applied to the use of air strikes in response to violations of the UNSCRs. Because UNPROFOR, a lightly armed UN peacekeeping force, could protect neither itself nor the safe areas from BSA attacks, NATO airpower became both a mechanism for providing force protection (i.e., CAS) for UN personnel and a threat to deter the BSA.[95] In February 1994 NAC decided to establish a 20-kilometer (km) exclusion zone around Sarajevo, declaring that 10 days after 2400 GMT on 10 February 1994, heavy weapons not removed from this zone or turned over to UN control would be subject to NATO air strikes.[96] NAC authorized CINCSOUTH, in close coordination with the UN, to launch air strikes against artillery or mortar positions in or around Sarajevo (including areas outside the exclusion zone) that UNPROFOR considered responsible for attacks against civilian targets in that city.[97] Because the threat of airpower proved successful in forcing effective compliance with the NATO ultimatums, the air strikes were not required. Ultimately, NAC established exclusion zones around each of the remaining safe areas. The threat of using air strikes against a limited exclusion zone or a specific piece of military hardware influenced military operations throughout Deny Flight and Deliberate Force.

After Krajina Serbs fired on the Bihac safe area from Croatian territory and in light of the history of problems experienced by UN forces in the Krajina area dating back to September 1993, UNSCR 908 extended CAS support to the territory of the Republic of Croatia on 31 March 1994. Later that year UNSCR 958 extended the mandate under UNSCR 836 for CAS and air strikes to the Republic of Croatia.[98] Change four to OPLAN 40101 reflected these UNSCRs, both of which prompted subsequent NAC mandates.[99] The resolutions and mandates tended to react in a limited and proportional manner to the nature of the situation in Bosnia and Croatia. Each time the UN responded to an act of Serbian aggression, it raised the ante—but never in a proactive or preventive manner.

Throughout the remainder of Deny Flight, NATO conducted limited air strikes in accordance with the provisions of UNSCR 836 and 958. One such strike occurred in response to attacks by Bosnian Serb aircraft flying out of Udbina airfield in Serb-held Croatia. Although NATO carried out the attack of Udbina under UNSCR 958, the UN—not wanting to kill anyone—prohibited strikes against aircraft on the ground.[100] Although NATO complied with this restriction, it refused to conduct the air strike without hitting the enemy air defense system that protected the airfield. Although the UN had the same reservations about killing people who operated the integrated air defense system (IADS) equipment, NATO prevailed in the discussion by pointing out that it would conduct suppression of enemy air defenses (SEAD) strikes strictly to defend the attacking aircrews.[101] This reluctance by the UN to cause any kind of casualty (whether military or civilian) carried through to the execution of Deliberate Force.

In addition to CAS and air strikes, air-to-air engagements also took place prior to Deliberate Force. On 28 February 1994, the engagement and shootdown of four fixed-wing Galeb/Jastreb aircraft in the airspace of Bosnia-Herzegovina demonstrated ROE's air-to-air procedures. After NAEW aircraft detected unknown aircraft south of Banja Luka on the morning of the 28th, two NATO aircraft (US Air Force F-16s) intercepted and identified six Galeb/Jastreb aircraft in the area. In accordance with this phase of ROE, the NAEW aircraft issued two warnings to land or exit the NFZ, ignored by the Galeb/Jastreb pilots. Indeed, during the warnings, the violating aircraft dropped bombs in Bosnia-Herzegovina. Following the ROE and after receiving Chariot's approval, the NATO fighters engaged the planes and shot down three of them. A second pair of NATO fighters (also US Air Force F-16s) arrived and shot down a fourth violator. The two remaining enemy aircraft left the airspace of Bosnia-Herzegovina.[102]

This incident illustrates the phased and stepped nature of ROE developed for Deny Flight. The political and military sensitivity of operations in the Balkans required flexible ROE able to control the use of force as the threat warranted and able to avoid the escalation of hostilities. ROE drafted for OPLAN 40101, after the enactment of UNSCR 836 and the resulting NATO Military Committee Memorandum MCM-KAD-084-93, contained basically the same provisions existing at the time NATO executed Deliberate Force. Planners linked ROE to a phased approach to operations that depended upon the situation at hand.

Each of the ROE phases reflects several of the elements noted earlier in reference to MCM-KAD-084-93. The concepts of proportionality, military necessity, and collateral damage dominated the thought process surrounding the development and execution of ROE for air strike options. The single most defining element of every planning and execution decision was the overriding need to avoid collateral damage and escalatory force. Thus, by focusing on the concepts of proportionality, military necessity, and collateral damage, NATO planners hoped to keep military options congruent with political objectives. The degree to which NATO adhered to these principles is likely the ultimate reason for the success of the mission and the initiation of the peace process in Dayton, Ohio.

After the fall of Srebrenica and Zepa, ROE remained basically unchanged and ready for the upcoming execution of Deliberate Force. The fall of these two safe areas precipitated the discussions and decisions that led to the planning and ultimate execution of this operation.

Implementation of ROE in Operation Deliberate Force

After the fall of the Srebrenica and Zepa safe areas in July 1995, initial discussions by NATO and UN officials dealt with an appropriate response to the Bosnian Serbs should they make any moves toward taking Gorazde (later extended to include Sarajevo, Tuzla, and Bihac). The NATO London Conference on 21 July 1995 decided that "an attack on Gorazde will be met by substantial and decisive airpower."[103] NAC decisions of 25 July and 1 August specified meeting further Bosnian Serb action with a firm and rapid response aimed at deterring attacks on safe areas and employing, if necessary, the timely and effective use of airpower until attacks on or threats to these areas had ceased.[104] The conference may have been a way to finesse the UN and avoid a confrontation in the UN Security Council, where the Russians probably would have vetoed any increased use of force over the Bosnian Serbs.[105] By creating an NAC decision that "interpreted" already existing UNSCR mandates, the conference avoided the possibility of a problem with the UN Security Council.

The NAC decision established "trigger" events that would initiate graduated air operations as determined by the common judgment of NATO and UN military commanders: "(1) Any concentration of forces and/or heavy weapons, and the conduct of other military preparations which, in the common judgment of the NATO and UN Military Commanders, presented a direct threat to the remaining UN Safe Areas or (2) Direct attacks (e.g., ground, artillery or aircraft) on the designated safe-areas."[106] The trigger events applied equally to each of the safe areas. Adm Leighton Smith, CINCSOUTH, pointed out that confirming the first trigger would have been difficult for each of the safe areas because the BSA already had a high concentration of forces and heavy weapons located there. Ultimately, it would have come down to the difficult matter of gauging the intent of the BSA (although NATO did have several indicators for doing so).[107]

In accordance with the London agreement, once the UN and NATO military commanders agreed that a trigger event had occurred, NATO authorized the attack of targets associated with option two from MCM-KAD-084-93, including concentrations of forces. The NATO/UN military commanders could continue the air strikes as long as they thought they were needed to defend a safe area and a wider geographic area (zone of action [ZOA]). The strikes also could target any concentrations of troops deemed to pose a serious threat to the UN safe area.[108] The NAC decision assigned execution authority for air actions to Lt Gen Michael Ryan, COMAIRSOUTH.[109]

Because of the negative experience with the dual-key process and the perceived inability of the UN political structure to make timely decisions, NAC stressed the importance of the UN's transferring execution authority for air actions to its military commanders.[110] In apparent agreement with this request, the UN secretary-general transferred the key from Akashi to General Janvier, as mentioned above. This action showed the UN's trust and confidence in the ability of military leaders to ensure that any military use of force would comply with UN mandates and policy guidance without the need for direct political oversight. Although never executed, the NAC decision also included provisions to authorize expanded operations against option three or elements thereof if any of the warring factions continued offensive operations against the safe areas in spite of air strikes under option two.[111]

Lastly, the NAC decision addressed the use of SEAD aircraft against the BSA's IADS.[112] NATO would attack enemy IADS if and when air strikes in support of a safe area commenced and would continue to attack only for the duration of that operation. One can consider attacks on enemy IADS a form of preemptive self-defense since IADS posed a threat to friendly air forces operating in proximity. This policy proved troublesome for many UN political leaders who viewed attacks on anything not directly located in or around the safe area exclusion zone as verging on option three.

The NAC decision generated a memorandum of understanding (MOU) between General Janvier and Admiral Smith, providing UN interpretation of the NAC decisions discussed above.[113] This MOU covered the phasing of operations, operation considerations (including ZOAs, IADS, and air-land coordination), targeting arrangements (including targeting boards and approved target lists), and conditions for initiation (trigger events). The memorandum led to discussions between General Janvier and Admiral Smith regarding the types of targets that could be struck and the ZOAs that would apply if a trigger event occurred.

Initially, the UN wanted the ZOA limited in order to closely relate to the attacked or threatened safe area; it also felt that NATO should direct air strikes only toward those forces that committed the trigger offense. According to Admiral Smith, General Janvier thought that the ZOA should extend the current exclusion zone to 25 km rather than 20 km. Admiral Smith and NATO, however, thought ZOAs should apply to a much wider geographic area as long as one could establish a connection to the threatened safe area and the target.[114] After some debate, the UN proposed two ZOAs dividing Bosnia-Herzegovina in half with overlap in the area around Tuzla (fig. 14.4).[115] Accordingly, should a trigger event occur in Sarajevo or Gorazde, planners would activate the southeast ZOA, and aircraft would strike targets associated with that zone. Alternatively, if Bihac were the location for the trigger event, air strikes would focus on the northwest ZOA. If Tuzla were attacked or threatened, either one or both ZOAs could be activated.

Regardless of the location of the trigger event, NATO could strike IADS wherever it affected friendly air operations. Consequently, NATO developed Deadeye Southeast and Deadeye Northwest as two IADS target sets, both of which were tied to the self-defense needs of the aircrews operating in the tactical area of operations rather than to ZOAs.[116] For all other targets,

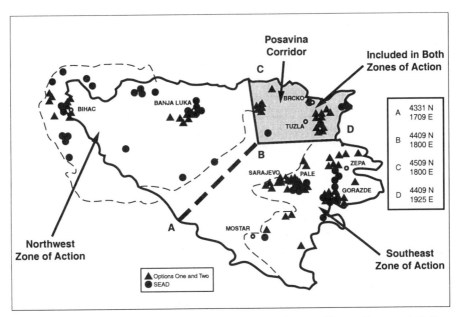

Figure 14.4. Zones of Action for Deliberate Force (From Corona briefing slides, Lt Gen Michael Ryan, Headquarters AIRSOUTH, Naples, Italy, 5 December 1995, United States Air Force Historical Research Agency, Maxwell AFB, Ala., H-3)

the ability to target was based upon location of the trigger event and the active ZOA.

Targeting for Deliberate Force did not amount to an all-out strategic bombing campaign designed to destroy the Serbs' industrial infrastructure and capability to wage war. Rather, NATO limited the targets and used force in a graduated manner to compel the behavior of the Bosnian Serbs. General types of targets for Deliberate Force included IADS (early warning radar/acquisition radar/SAM sites/communications, etc.), fielded forces (heavy weapons/troop concentrations), C^2 (headquarters/command facilities/communications), direct and essential support (ammo/supply depot and storage/supporting garrison areas/logistics areas), and lines of communications (transportation choke points and bridges).[117] In selecting specific targets within these categories, the Joint Targeting Board (UN and NATO) worked hard to find easily hit targets with limited potential for collateral damage.

In addition to the normal concerns about collateral damage, General Janvier remained extremely sensitive to casualties (including BSA casualties). When the general reviewed one of the initial target lists, he demanded that a target labeled "barracks" be removed because he wanted to avoid killing people.[118] Admiral Smith had failed to explain to General Janvier the distinction between targets and desired mean point of impact (DMPI). Targets could involve a number of individual DMPIs within a target complex. The fact that planners describe a target as a barracks does not mean that aircraft would strike a barracks building. In fact, the same barracks complex might include a very lucrative ammunition storage area with a different DMPI than that of the barracks. Understanding General Janvier's concern, Admiral Smith merely redefined the DMPIs selected for attack, and General Janvier agreed to the targets.[119]

The trigger event for Deliberate Force was the shelling of a Sarajevo marketplace, presumably by the BSA. When Admiral Smith saw the results of the shelling on Cable News Network (CNN), he called the NATO liaison to the FC UNPF and told him to tell General Janvier that if the UN determined that BSA had fired the shell, then NATO requested air strike options according to the MOU.[120] Once Lt Gen Rupert Smith, commander of UNPROFOR (who was sitting in for the vacationing General Janvier), confirmed BSA responsibility, the UN and NATO turned their keys, and Operation Deliberate Force began. General Janvier later concurred with this decision.

During Deliberate Force several issues relating to the interpretation and execution of ROE arose, the most prominent being the degree to which concerns over collateral damage drove the planning and execution of air strikes. The most telling indication of the concern over collateral damage was the fact that General Ryan personally selected every DMPI because he felt that the political sensitivity of the operation demanded strict accountability on the part of the air commander. He believed that every bomb dropped or missile launched not only had a tactical-level effect but a possible strategic effect. Accordingly, Ryan directed his staff to evaluate all proposed targets and DMPIs for their military significance and their potential for high, medium, or low assessments of collateral damage. For example, intelligence personnel described the Pale army supply depot as a key BSA supply but with high potential for collateral damage.[121] Similarly, they assessed the Pale ammo depot south as having medium potential for collateral damage and the Jahorina radio communication (RADCOM) station as having low potential.[122] These examples illustrate the spectrum of collateral-damage probabilities for various targets. Based upon the importance of each target and its potential for collateral damage, General Ryan selected the specific DMPIs for attack.

In addition to the actual selection of DMPIs, the concern for collateral damage often drove weapons selection and tactics for weapons release. Clearly, precision-guided munitions (PGM) were the weapons of choice. Of the more than one thousand munitions dropped during Deliberate Force, nearly 70 percent were precision munitions.[123] Of all munitions dropped by US aircraft, more than 98 percent were precision munitions.[124] Although ROE did not specifically require PGMs, it did state that "target planning and weapons delivery will include considerations to minimize collateral damage."[125]

At one point during the operation, an aircraft bombed a bridge, using the standard profile of attacking along the length of the span, and released two PGMs on the designated DMPI. Unfortunately, the second PGM went long and destroyed a farmhouse located next to the end of the bridge.[126] As a result, ROE underwent modification via the ATM/SPINS to require a much more restrictive approach for attacking bridges.[127] Aircrews would now have to make a dry pass over the targeted bridge, attack on an axis perpendicular to the bridge rather than along its length, and release only one bomb per pass.

When first notified of this change in ROE, the commanders and aircrews at Aviano Air Base (AB) became very concerned, feeling that it placed pilots at increased risk. Despite Aviano's initial refusal to fly the mission as directed, pilots eventually flew the mission successfully.[128] Upon hearing the concerns of the aircrews over the dry-pass ROE, General Ryan and General Hornburg decided to rescind the ROE restriction in the ATM of 12 September 1995, the next day.[129] This incident illustrates the difficulty commanders faced in reconciling the competing

411

demands of force protection and minimization of collateral damage—a balance that shifted as operations progressed.

Every section of ROE included a statement concerning the need to minimize collateral damage. These included sections dealing with the engagement of air-to-air and surface-to-air systems ("take into account the need to minimize collateral damage");[130] with CAS ("limit collateral damage to the minimum that is militarily feasible");[131] and with SEAD ("no unacceptable collateral damage").[132] Clearly, concerns about collateral damage represented the defining issue for Deliberate Force.

Thirty-five hundred sorties and more than one thousand dropped munitions produced only two confirmed instances of any significant collateral damage (the farmhouse incident mentioned above and an accidental strike on a water-treatment plant).[133] When questioned by a CNN journalist about reports of significant amounts of collateral damage, Admiral Smith pointed out that if such damage had indeed occurred, CNN would be filming the damage instead of interviewing him.[134] The careful selection of DMPIs by General Ryan, combined with careful attacks by NATO aircrews, resulted in one of the most precise operations ever conducted.

Concern for minimizing collateral damage also resulted in one of the more controversial ROE issues in Deliberate Force—the "dual correlation" requirement for reactive SEAD strikes. SPINS required all SEAD mission commanders to see that planning and positioning of SEAD aircraft included consideration of methods to ensure engagement of the desired target, minimize chances of engaging unintended targets, and mitigate the impact of possible high-speed antiradiation missile (HARM) ambiguities.[135] Due to these concerns, aircraft detecting a possible SAM engagement were directed to depart the immediate threat area, using an appropriate defensive profile and countermeasures as required. Only in extreme situations (e.g., experiencing a threat without reasonable means of escape) were aircrews authorized to use any measure for self-defense.[136] Preemptive HARM strikes were not authorized without Chariot's approval, and pilots could employ reactive HARM strikes in Bosnia-Herzegovina or Croatia only if one of the following conditions existed:

A. Positive indication of a hostile act (confirmed missile or projectiles fired), or

B. Dual correlation of positive indications of hostile intent, further defined as aircraft illuminated by surface-to-air (SAM)/anti-air artillery (AAA) fire control radar and/or any air defense system radar directly related to these SAM/AAA systems.

C. Other instances of demonstrated hostile intent, including other instances by systems other than those described in para B of this section, when approved by Chariot.[137]

Although the dual-correlation requirement infringed upon the inherent right to self-defense, it did reduce the likelihood that reactive and preemptive SEAD operations would cause otherwise avoidable collateral damage. Dual-correlation ROE was restrictive, but leadership preferred to err on the conservative side.[138] Even though NATO had a limited number of SEAD aircraft, the chance of HARM ambiguity represented too great a risk for fratricide or collateral damage to allow more extensive use of lethal SEAD by aircraft without dual-correlation capability.[139]

Dual correlation potentially reduced collateral damage; however, it definitely imposed tactical handicaps on NATO fliers. US Navy aircrews, for example, were not pleased by the restriction the policy placed on their use of preemptive HARMs.[140] Most SEAD aircraft had no problems with dual correlation since both the aircraft and the weapon they carried, typically a HARM, had separate internal capabilities to achieve correlation. However, for other less capable aircraft, ROE required that unless an off-board platform provided the second correlation, the aircraft would have to depart the immediate threat area.

The section of ROE dealing with combat search and rescue (CSAR) also caused some concern. NATO ROE authorizing search and rescue (SAR) aircraft and naval vessels to use "*self-defense* force as necessary" (emphasis added)[141] to ensure the recovery of survivors was inconsistent with US ROE for CSAR, which provided for a greater degree of force in recovering survivors by allowing "*minimum* force as necessary" (emphasis added).[142] Since US ROE applied to Operation Provide Promise (the humanitarian airlift operation into Bosnia) missions and NATO ROE applied to Deny Flight and Deliberate

Force missions, special operations forces designated to go into the same threat area to recover survivors could theoretically be authorized a different level of force, depending upon what the aircraft was doing when it was shot down. For example, if a special-ops helicopter gunship were approaching the location of the survivor of a downed aircraft, the helicopter—under NATO ROE—could not fire upon an enemy truck with armed personnel unless it committed a hostile act or demonstrated hostile intent toward the helicopter (reactive). Under US ROE, however, the helicopter could use the minimum force necessary to prevent the enemy truck from capturing the pilot or interfering with the pickup (preemptive).

The difference between the levels of force authorized in the two ROEs resulted, in part, from the fact that NATO doctrine does not address the "combat" part of CSAR. Understandably, SAR—without the combat perspective—relates to issues of self-defense. CSAR, a more robust form of SAR that is unique to the US military, seeks to recover survivors within a hostile threat environment.

The Navy's Sixth Fleet made several requests to use US rather than NATO ROE for CSAR operations. In a NATO conference that addressed the issue of US versus NATO ROE, NATO members agreed that US ROE would apply to any US forces engaged in a CSAR mission.[143] However, no one made changes to the written ROE in OPLAN 40101. During Deliberate Force the actual ROE for a CSAR mission proved "very sketchy," especially considering the political sensitivity of the operation.[144] The Navy continued to press for more specific ROE and urged the adoption of US SROE. According to Maj Dan Bush, legal advisor to the CAOC during Deliberate Force, Generals Ryan and Hornburg decided that because Deliberate Force was a NATO operation, NATO ROE—in accordance with OPLAN 40101—would apply to everyone involved. Anyone not using NATO ROE would fail to appear on the ATM schedule.[145] Fortunately, ROE for CSAR was not put to the test during Deliberate Force.

Targeting and execution differed from ROE in the context of casualties. Commanders for Deliberate Force repeatedly stressed that "stuff" (things) rather than people were the targets for this operation.[146] Although the Bosnian Serbs' lack of personnel, compared to the Bosnian Muslim and Croatian forces, constituted a potential center of gravity, planners decided not to target them. In essence, NATO strategy sought to wage aggressive peace rather than war. Since one of the key strengths of the BSA was its armor and heavy weapons, NATO planned to take away as much of that strength as quickly as possible.

NATO's desire to minimize the loss of civilian and military life constrained tactics and target selection in other ways. In the parlance of the CAOC staff, structures associated with "soft pudgies" (people) were not intentionally targeted.[147] If they were, aircraft often hit them at night, when people were less likely to be around. For the same reason, General Ryan decided to move attacks on bridges, originally scheduled for the daytime, to night.[148]

At the same time ROE and military commanders restricted targeting options and execution to minimize collateral damage, commanders continually stressed the importance of force protection. Admiral Smith's three priorities for Deliberate Force, in order of precedence, were (1) force protection, (2) minimization of collateral damage, and (3) effective strikes on targets.[149] Specifically designed to ensure the safety of NATO forces, ROE maximized force protection by limiting the exposure of NATO aircraft to threatening situations and by allowing aircraft to use force in self-defense against both hostile acts and demonstrated hostile intent. ROE limited the exposure of NATO aircraft to threats by prohibiting operation over land in Bosnia or Croatia without SEAD protection and by prohibiting non-SEAD aircraft from operating within known SAM threat rings.[150] If an aircraft were engaged or threatened with demonstrated hostile intent without a reasonable means of escape (as determined by the pilot at the time), aircrews could use any measure for self-defense,[151] the latter defined in OPLAN 40101 as "action taken in consonance with international law to protect oneself, or other Friendly Force in the vicinity."[152]

This definition closely tracks the definition of self-defense found in US SROE discussed earlier in this chapter. ROE therefore proved robust enough to authorize the use of force to protect NATO forces from any attack or demonstration of hostile intent. ROE that provided the authority to act and the flexibility to use sound judgment in determining when and how to use force in self-defense alleviated concerns about force protection. The lessons of the USS *Stark* and the Marine barracks in Beirut were not forgotten.

The combined concerns of force protection, collateral damage, and overall success of the mission resulted in very restricted operations. Aircraft could strike only assigned DMPIs—no targets of opportunity.[153] SPINS contained specific reference to these constraints: "For fixed sites, aircrews will attack ATM specified DMPIs only, even if these DMPIs have previously been hit."[154] In fact, the ATM reinforced the ROE: "The only valid target DMPIs are those assigned via the ATM process or directly assigned, real time, by the CAOC battle staff director. . . . Target DMPIs assigned via the ATM are only valid for the period of that ATM."[155]

This tight control resulted in what officials at Aviano AB termed the effective but inefficient use of airpower. From the tactical perspective, constant changes in targets as well as interference in weapons and tactics proved frustrating. From the strategic perspective, however, NATO air planners felt they could accept a little inefficiency, particularly if that was the price of avoiding an incident such as the one that occurred in the Al Firdos bunker during Operation Desert Storm. To ensure effectiveness, leadership gave supreme importance to the minimization of collateral damage and ordered the development and implementation of ROE to translate these concerns into meaningful guidance for the effective prosecution of Deliberate Force.

Implications for the Future

Having explored ROE for Operation Deliberate Force, one becomes aware of several implications for the use of airpower in future peace operations. First, and perhaps the most obvious, is the degree to which the military restricted its own operations in Deliberate Force. The restrictions placed on targeting remind one of those used in Vietnam. Unlike the political restrictions placed on military operations in Vietnam, however, in Deliberate Force the military's own restraint limited operations. We may, therefore, be witnessing a 180-degree shift in the relationship between political and military influences

416

in ROE. Rather than politicians tying the hands of the military, the military may now be tying its own hands.[156] The Air Force Studies and Analysis Division came to a similar conclusion in its report on Deliberate Force: "There was nothing in the upper levels of DELIBERATE FORCE's command and control structure to compare with President Lyndon Johnson's sometimes weekly sessions picking targets for the Rolling Thunder campaign over North Vietnam in the 1960s. To an impressive degree, guided bombs had permitted Air Force officers to internalize the kind of restraint Johnson wished to impose upon them. In DELIBERATE FORCE, it was General Ryan himself who exercised most of the restraint."[157]

This internalization of restraint by the military leadership is due in many respects to the "years of inculcation in the law of armed conflict."[158] NATO political authorities trusted the ability of their military leadership to take general guidance and plan and execute military operations consistent with that guidance. One can attribute part of this trust to the perception that US and NATO military forces understand and comply with the laws of war. Since Vietnam, US forces have consistently shown that they conduct military operations in an extremely professional manner and exercise the utmost restraint in using force to achieve an objective. The tight control that General Ryan placed over military operations likely will reinforce the perception that, in many respects, the military is a self-regulating instrument of power. In the future this demonstration of restraint may allow the NCA to feel confident that, given mission-type orders, the military will plan and execute operations consistent with political objectives and in compliance with the laws of armed conflict. The commander on the scene, cognizant of the political objectives and sensitive to the unique threat conditions facing forces in the area of operations, is in the best position to draft effective ROE. The latitude given by political authorities and the degree to which the military controls its operations are key factors in the development of acceptable and effective ROE.

A related issue is the importance of congruence of context, objectives, and means in conflicts such as Deliberate Force. A complete divergence of objectives and means occurred between NATO and UN forces during Deny Flight. On the one

417

hand, UN forces, who sought to keep a peace that did not exist, operated under very restrictive, self-defensive ROE and had limited military capability. Despite operating as the UN Protection Force, they could not even protect themselves. On the other hand, NATO forces, present under peace-enforcement provisions, sought to deter or compel behavior through the use of military force. NATO ROE, therefore, provided for a much more robust use of force to achieve the desired objectives.

Differences in ROE on when and how the UN and NATO could use military force doomed the dual-key process from the start. NATO always viewed the use of force in terms of compelling the Bosnian Serbs to do or not do something. But the UN viewed force in the much more limited context of self-defense. Only after Srebrenica and Zepa fell and the UN decided to pull back its forces to allow NATO to conduct air strikes, did congruence occur among the situation in Bosnia, the political objectives, and the use of military force to obtain those objectives. Clearly, ROE for a peace operation should relate not to its title (peacekeeping, peace enforcement, etc.) but to the reality of the situation on the ground. If no peace agreement exists and fighting continues, then one should write ROE to provide for the compellent use of military force until the factions agree to a truce. If a UNSCR proves insufficient to warrant the more aggressive type of ROE, then one should deploy no military forces until the adoption of such a resolution.

The ROE concept of categories of target options, designed to keep the level of force to the minimum amount necessary, was an excellent method of ensuring maximum control over escalation. However, the use of target-option categories can be harmful if one exhausts the target list without having achieved the political objectives. At that point one either escalates the level of force to the next target-option category or the use of force loses credibility. Such was the case in Deliberate Force: negotiators had great concerns that NATO would run out of option-two targets before convincing the Bosnian Serbs to accept a truce and join peace talks. An interview with Ambassador Christopher Hill revealed that the US State Department and Ambassador Richard Holbrooke harbored exactly these concerns.[159]

The fact that officials at the State Department had concerns about the execution of the air operation highlights the need for a State Department liaison to the air operations center in any operation in which one uses airpower as a coercive tool to achieve diplomatic leverage. Future operations similar to Deliberate Force probably will use airpower to provide an environment conducive to diplomatic negotiations. To ensure complete congruence between the desires and concerns of the negotiation team and the execution of the air operation, the liaison should coordinate these concerns with military personnel who plan and execute the air operations. Such a person would not necessarily exercise political oversight but act as a conduit to ensure connectivity among diplomatic negotiators, military commanders, and planners.

The last major implication of the implementation of ROE in Deliberate Force is the high percentage of precision weapons used in the operation. To reiterate, nearly 70 percent of all munitions used and more than 98 percent of munitions dropped by the United States were precision weapons. Concerns over the minimization of collateral damage led to this unprecedented reliance on PGMs. The issue for ROE is whether the use of PGMs has minimized the chance for collateral damage to the point that one expects zero collateral damage and legally requires it for future operations.

The law of armed conflict does not require that one conduct military operations so as to eliminate the possibility of collateral damage. Arguments that the existence of PGMs have increased the standard of care required to conduct military operations to this point or that one cannot use "dumb bombs" because they are indiscriminate remain legally untenable. The law of armed conflict requires that the application of force be in accordance with the tests of military necessity, humanity, and proportionality.[160] Military necessity involves the right to use any degree or means of force not forbidden by international law to achieve a military objective. Humanity, related to necessity, entails the infliction of suffering, injury, or destruction not actually necessary for accomplishing legitimate military purposes. Proportionality provides the link between the concepts of military necessity and humanity by balancing the degree of likely damage to noncombatants with the military

419

value of the proposed target.[161] The general immunity of non-combatants from attack does not prohibit operations that may cause collateral damage (including death, injury, or destruction of property). International law requires only that the military balance the value of the proposed target with the likelihood and degree of collateral damage. Therefore, although PGMs may actually increase the numbers of targets that one could justifiably strike by lowering to tolerable levels the collateral damage coincident to striking them, international law includes nothing that requires their use against any target of military value. Thus, judge advocates should assist in the drafting of ROE to ensure that no one misinterprets the requirements of international law and that no one places restrictions based upon erroneous applications of the law on planning and executing air operations.

The *expectation* of zero collateral damage, however, is another matter. The more the military uses PGMs and shows, through the international press media, guided bomb units hitting the crosshairs overlaying targets of all kinds, the more the public will expect such precision in the future. As discussed earlier, such expectations create political pressures that have just as much impact on ROE and military operations as do legal obligations. The reality of the situation is that guided bombs sometimes miss. In fact, US Air Force analysis of PGMs after Deliberate Force revealed that nearly one-third missed their individual aiming points on targets (because of human error, weather problems, and weapon problems equally).[162] The careful DMPI selection process and the professional weapons-employment tactics by aircrews kept the amount of collateral damage low. Unfortunately, military leadership sometimes overstates its case to show the effectiveness of operations, as did Secretary of Defense William Perry after the conclusion of Deliberate Force: "From Aviano and from the decks of carriers in the Adriatic, we launched one of the most effective air campaigns that we've ever had. It was over one thousand sorties. Every target that had been designated was destroyed, and there was zero collateral damage. This was a rare instance where by combination of exclusive use of precision guided ammunitions and very strict rules of engagement, we conducted this massive campaign with no damage, no damage to civilians, no collateral damage of any kind."[163]

Although the air operations in Deliberate Force achieved a high degree of success in minimizing collateral damage, one cannot say that no collateral damage of any kind occurred. Such overstatement may create unrealistic and potentially dangerous expectations for future air operations. Political and military leaders need to be sensitive to the fact that the military can minimize but never eliminate collateral damage. General Hornburg stressed that this was the mind-set of personnel at the CAOC.[164] Regardless of political pressures to minimize collateral damage in the future, one should base ROE on reality rather than abstract ideals and therefore refrain from writing rules of engagement under the constraints of zero collateral damage. Minimizing collateral damage instead of achieving zero collateral damage should become the political standard for ROE.

In conclusion, ROE drafted and implemented in Deliberate Force effectively balanced the competing interests of force protection, minimization of collateral damage, and mission accomplishment. The CAOC military leaders' close control over operations proved appropriate, considering the political and military realities of the situation in Bosnia-Herzegovina. Although the circumstances in Bosnia are unlikely to be repeated, many lessons relating to the evolution and implementation of ROE will remain applicable to future uses of airpower in support of peace operations. As long as we evaluate these lessons from the perspective of the context in which they arose, Operation Deliberate Force offers an example of the value of well-conceived and masterfully implemented rules of engagement.

Notes

1. Commander in chief, Allied Forces Southern Europe (CINCSOUTH) Operations Plan (OPLAN) 40101, "Operation Deny Flight," change four, 3 May 1995. (NATO Confidential) Information extracted is unclassified. (Operation Deliberate Force was a subset of Operation Deny Flight. The OPLAN for the latter contained ROE that applied during Deliberate Force.)

2. *Correct Quotes,* version 1.0; CD-ROM (Novato, Calif.: Wordstar International, Inc., 1994).

3. Carl von Clausewitz, *On War*, trans. and ed. Michael Howard and Peter Paret (Princeton, N.J.: Princeton University Press, 1989), 607.

4. Captain Roach uses four circles in his diagram, dividing the political and diplomatic influences into two circles. Since these issues are usually very closely related, I have combined them into one circle. Each of the circles comprises a multitude of individual factors that fall under the umbrella of that particular generic factor. Capt J. Ashley Roach, "Rules of Engagement," *Naval War College Review* 36, no. 1 (January–February 1983): 46–48. The three-circle approach is consistent with current doctrine as expressed in the *Joint Commander's Handbook for Peace Operations* (Fort Monroe, Va.: Joint Warfighting Center, 28 February 1995), 74.

5. Roach, 46.

6. Ibid., 47.

7. Ibid., 48.

8. D. P. O'Connell, *The Influence of Law on Sea Power* (Annapolis: Naval Institute Press, 1975), 180.

9. W. Hays Parks, "Righting the Rules of Engagement," *US Naval Institute Proceedings* 115, no. 5 (May 1989): 87.

10. Ibid., 88.

11. Ibid.

12. Col Philip Johnson, chief, International and Operations Law, Headquarters United States Air Force (USAF)/JAI, interviewed by author, Pentagon, Washington, D.C., 20 December 1995.

13. Roach, 50.

14. Johnson interview.

15. Joint Publication 1-02, *Department of Defense Dictionary of Military and Associated Terms*, 23 March 1994, 329.

16. Scott R. Morris, ed., *Operational Law Handbook* (Charlottesville, Va.: US Army Judge Advocate General's School, 1998), 8-1.

17. Chairman of the Joint Chiefs of Staff Instruction (CJCSI) 3121.01, *Standing Rules of Engagement for US Forces*, 1 October 1994, par. 6.

18. Ibid., par. 6a.

19. Mark Clodfelter, *The Limits of Airpower: The American Bombing of North Vietnam* (New York: Free Press, 1989), 119.

20. Col Roberto Corsini, "The Balkan War: What Role for Airpower?" *Airpower Journal* 9, no. 4 (Winter 1995): 55.

21. These include the 20 km exclusion zone for heavy weapons around each UN-designated safe area, the Croatian restricted-operating zones, and the zones of action related to trigger events for Deliberate Force, discussed later in this chapter.

22. Adam Roberts, "From San Francisco to Sarajevo: The UN and the Use of Force," *Survival: The IISS Quarterly* 37, no. 4 (Winter 1995–1996): 14.

23. CJCSI 3121.01, par. 1a.

24. Ibid., enclosure A, par. 2a. To emphasize this passage, the writers placed it in all-capital letters and boldface.

25. Ibid., enclosure A, par. 5d.

26. Ibid., enclosure A, par. 5b.

27. Ibid., enclosure A, par. 5c.

28. Ibid., enclosure A, par. 8.

29. Ibid.

30. Ibid., enclosure A, par. 8b.

31. Parks, 84.

32. Maj Dan Bush, USAF, interviewed by author, Department of State, Washington, D.C., 18 December 1995. Major Bush was the legal advisor to the CAOC, Vicenza, Italy, from June 1995 until October 1995.

33. Parks, 93.

34. Bradd C. Hayes, *Naval Rules of Engagement: Management Tools for Crisis,* RAND Note N-2963-CC (Santa Monica, Calif.: RAND, July 1989), 21.

35. Both the *Stark* and Beirut Marine barracks incidents, as well as the *Vincennes* incident, receive more extensive analysis later in this chapter.

36. Hayes, 21.

37. Ibid., 24.

38. Clausewitz, 87.

39. Martha Lynn Craver and Rick Maze, "Reports Criticize Military for Beirut Security," *Air Force Times,* 2 January 1984, 4.

40. *Report of the DOD Commission on Beirut International Airport Terrorist Act, October 23, 1983* (Washington, D.C.: Commission on Beirut International Airport Terrorist Act, 20 December 1983), 47.

41. Ibid., 89. The commander explained that he decided not to permit insertion of magazines in weapons on interior posts to preclude accidental discharge and possible injury to innocent civilians.

42. Ibid., 94.

43. Richard C. Gross, "Lessons Learned the Hard Way: The USS *Stark,*" *Defense Science & Electronics* 6, no. 12 (December 1987): 9.

44. Ibid., 10.

45. Ibid.

46. Rear Adm William M. Fogarty, "Investigation Report: Formal Investigation into the Circumstances Surrounding the Downing of Iran Air Flight 655 on 3 July 1988" (U) (Washington, D.C.: Department of Defense, 28 July 1988).

47. John Barry and Richard Charles, "Sea of Lies," *Newsweek,* 13 July 1992, 29–39.

48. Richard J. Grunawalt, director, Oceans Law and Policy, Naval War College, memorandum to dean, Center for Naval Warfare Studies, subject: USS *Vincennes* (CG 49) and the Shootdown of Iranian Airbus Flight 655, 18 September 1995.

49. Fogarty, 7.

50. Hayes, 54. The RAND study noted that the definitions of *hostile act* and *hostile intent* were revised and that one should now consider all aircraft and ships potentially hostile. All neutral and friendly shipping became eligible for US assistance.

51. Ibid., 55.

52. Fogarty, 13.

53. CINCSOUTH OPLAN 40101, change four. (NATO Confidential) Information extracted is unclassified.

54. COM5ATAF OPORD 45101.5, "Deny Flight," 30 September 1993. (NATO Confidential) Information extracted is unclassified.

55. COM5ATAF SPINS 028, 241530Z August 1995. (NATO Confidential) Information extracted is unclassified.

56. UNSCR 781, 9 October 1992. This resolution established the NFZ in the airspace of Bosnia-Herzegovina in order to ensure the safety of the delivery of humanitarian assistance and as a decisive step for the cessation of hostilities in Bosnia-Herzegovina. The ban of military flights did not apply to UNPROFOR flights or others in support of UN operations, including humanitarian assistance. The UNSCR did not authorize enforcement of the ban but requested that UNPROFOR and member states monitor compliance with the NFZ.

57. Ibid.

58. Operation Deny Flight fact sheet; on-line, Internet, 25 February 1999, available from http://chinfo.navy.mil/navpalib/intl/bosnia/denyflt.txt.

59. SACEUR Support Plan 10001D, "NATO Europe Integrated Air Defense." (NATO Confidential) Information extracted is unclassified.

60. Ibid. (NATO Confidential) Information extracted is unclassified. COM5ATAF OPORD 45101.5, par. 4, incorporates the restrictions of the NATO Europe Integrated Air Defense ROE.

61. SACEUR Support Plan 10001D. (NATO Confidential) Information extracted is unclassified.

62. CJCSI 3121.01, A-4. These provisions discuss the inherent right to use all necessary means available and to take all appropriate action to defend one's self, one's unit, and other friendly forces, including personnel and their property.

63. Deny Flight fact sheet.

64. UNSCR 816, 31 March 1993. This resolution, which provides the legal basis to engage violators of the NFZ, specifically indicates that it acts under chapter seven of the United Nations Charter, which provides for peace-enforcement powers through a general system of collective security.

65. Deny Flight fact sheet.

66. Lt Col Lowell R. Boyd Jr., tape-recorded interview by Lt Col Robert Owen, Headquarters AIRSOUTH, Naples, Italy, 6 December 1995, United States Air Force Historical Research Agency (AFHRA), Maxwell Air Force Base (AFB), Ala.

67. Ibid.

68. Ibid. At that time, General Ashy was COMAIRSOUTH, and Lieutenant Colonel Corzine worked on the planning staff. The term *Black Hole* came from the nickname of the location where a small cadre of personnel planned the air operation against Iraq. Personnel in the Black Hole produced all of the daily taskings for air strikes.

69. Lt Gen Michael Ryan, presentation at the School of Advanced Airpower Studies, Maxwell AFB, Ala., 8 February 1996.

70. Boyd interview.

71. COM5ATAF SPINS 028, par. 3D(2)(B)1. (NATO Confidential) Information extracted is unclassified.

72. UNSCR 836, 4 June 1993. This resolution provided the basis for NATO CAS support of UN ground forces as well as the authority to respond to attacks, incursions, or obstruction of freedom of movement in or around the safe areas. In essence the seeds for Operation Deliberate Force were planted with the enactment of this UNSCR.

73. UNSCR 819, 16 April 1993; and UNSCR 824, 6 May 1993. These resolutions created the listed safe areas within Bosnia-Herzegovina.

74. Deny Flight fact sheet.

75. S/25939, *Report of the Secretary-General Pursuant to Security Council Resolution 836 (1993)* (New York: United Nations, 14 June 1993), par. 4.

76. North Atlantic Military Committee, memorandum to UN secretary-general, subject: MCM-KAD-084-93, "Operational Options for Air Strikes in Bosnia-Herzegovina," 8 August 1993. (NATO Secret) Information extracted is unclassified. This memorandum led to the deployment of CAS aircraft to the Southern Region and served as the basis for providing CAS support.

77. Ibid. (NATO Secret) Information extracted is unclassified.

78. CINCSOUTH OPLAN 40101, change two, 13 August 1993. (NATO Confidential) Information extracted is unclassified.

79. MCM-KAD-084-93, enclosure, par. 2. (NATO Secret) Information extracted is unclassified.

80. Ibid., par. 5. (NATO Secret) Information extracted is unclassified.

81. Ibid., par. 9b. (NATO Secret) Information extracted is unclassified.

82. Ibid. (NATO Secret) Information extracted is unclassified.

83. Ibid., par. 9b(1). (NATO Secret) Information extracted is unclassified.

84. Ibid., par. 9b(2). (NATO Secret) Information extracted is unclassified.

85. Lt Col Chris "Red" Campbell, interviewed by author, Maxwell AFB, Ala., 22 March 1996. Stationed in Zagreb during this time, Campbell indicated that a lack of understanding existed between NATO and the UN as to who was really in charge with respect to the enforcement of the UNSCRs, specifically concerning the use of airpower in the tactical area of operations. UN personnel generally took the position that they controlled the trigger mechanism for use of force and that every action had to be coordinated with them before execution. The issue of whether ROE allowed air-to-air engagement without the coordination and/or approval of the UN was hotly debated.

86. CINCSOUTH OPLAN 40101, change two, E-1. (NATO Confidential) Information extracted is unclassified.

87. Boyd interview.

88. CINCSOUTH OPLAN 40101, change two, phase three, step four, subpar. (6). (NATO Confidential) Information extracted is unclassified.

89. Boyd interview.

90. Deny Flight fact sheet.

91. Boyd interview.

92. Joris Janssen Lok, "The Netherlands: Learning the Lessons of Srebrenica," *Jane's Defence Weekly* 25, no. 5 (31 January 1996): 35.

93. Ibid.

94. Adm Leighton Smith, CINCSOUTH, "Operation Deliberate Force," videotaped lecture presented at the Air War College, Maxwell AFB, Ala., 9 November 1995, AFHRA.

95. Ibid.

96. Deny Flight fact sheet.

97. Ibid.

98. UNSCR 958, 19 November 1994. This resolution extended the provisions of UNSCR 836 to Croatia and was the basis for establishing restricted operating zones there.

99. CINCSOUTH OPLAN 40101, change four. (NATO Confidential) Information extracted is unclassified.

100. Smith lecture.

101. Ibid.

102. Deny Flight fact sheet.

103. Operation Deliberate Force fact sheet, AFSOUTH/PIO, Naples, Italy, 6 November 1995; on-line, Internet, 4 March 1996, available from gopher://marvin.stc.nato.int:70/00/yugo/df0611.

104. NATO NAC Notice C-N(95)65, 26 July 1995, AFHRA, CAOC-06 (NATO Secret) Information extracted is unclassified; and MCM-KAD-057-95, "NATO Air Operations to Stabilize Bosnia-Herzegovina beyond Gorazde," 31 July 1995, AFHRA, CAOC-06-03 (NATO Secret) Information extracted is unclassified.

105. Lt Gen Michael Ryan, lecture, School of Advanced Airpower Studies, Maxwell AFB, Ala., 7 February 1996.

106. MCM-KAD-057-95, annex A-1. (NATO Secret) Information extracted is unclassified.

107. Smith lecture.

108. MCM-KAD-057-95, annex A-2. (NATO Secret) Information extracted is unclassified.

109. Ibid., annex A-3. (NATO Secret) Information extracted is unclassified.

110. Ibid., annex A-4. (NATO Secret) Information extracted is unclassified.

111. Ibid. (NATO Secret) Information extracted is unclassified.

112. Ibid., annex A-6. (NATO Secret) Information extracted is unclassified.

113. CINCSOUTH, memorandum of understanding with FC UNPF, subject: UN Interpretations of NAC Decisions, 10 August 1995. (NATO Secret) Information extracted is unclassified.

114. Smith lecture.

115. From Corona briefing slides, Lt Gen Michael Ryan, Headquarters AIRSOUTH, Naples, Italy, 5 December 1995, AFHRA, H-3.

116. Ibid.

117. CINCSOUTH, memorandum of understanding, par. 14. (NATO Secret) Information extracted is unclassified.

118. Smith lecture.

119. Ibid.

120. Ibid.

121. Target description, Pale army supply depot, target no. C0006, Aviano AB, Italy, AFHRA, AVI-43. (NATO Secret) Information extracted is unclassified.

122. Target description, Pale ammo depot south, target no. C001, Aviano AB, Italy (NATO Secret) Information extracted is unclassified; and target description, Jahorina RADCOM station, target no. D087, Aviano AB, Italy (NATO Secret) Information extracted is unclassified.

123. Operation Deliberate Force fact sheet. Of the 1,026 munitions dropped, 708 were precision (including laser-guided bomb/guided bomb unit [GBU] -10, -12, -16, and -24; AS30L; standoff land-attack missile; GBU-15; Maverick; and Tomahawk land-attack missile), and 318 were non-precision (MK-82, MK-83, MK-84, and cluster-bomb unit [CBU]-87).

124. Ryan interview.

125. COM5ATAF OPORD 45101.5, change one to annex E, par. 6a(3), 6 July 1994. (NATO Confidential) Information extracted is unclassified.

126. Maj Gen Hal M. Hornburg, videotaped interview by Lt Col Robert Owen and author, 12 March 1996, Maxwell AFB, Ala., AFHRA.

127. CAOC air tasking message, 11 September 1995, MSGID/AIRTASK/ HQ 5ATAF/11/SEP//PERID/110300Z/TO: 120259Z//. (NATO Secret) Information extracted is unclassified.

128. Lt Col Gary West, commander, 510th Fighter Squadron, recorded interview with Lt Col Bradley Davis and Maj John Orndorff, Aviano AB, Italy, 20 February 1996.

129. CAOC air tasking message, 12 September 1995, MSGID/AIRTASK/ HQ 5ATAF/12/SEP//PERID/120300Z/TO: 130259Z//. (NATO Secret) Information extracted is unclassified.

130. CINCSOUTH OPLAN 40101, change four, annex E, par. 5a(6). (NATO Confidential) Information extracted is unclassified.

131. Ibid., annex E, par. 5d(4). (NATO Confidential) Information extracted is unclassified.

132. Ibid., annex E, par. 6a(1)(d). (NATO Confidential) Information extracted is unclassified.

133. Hornburg interview.

134. Smith lecture.

135. COM5ATAF/CAOC Deny Flight SPINS 028, 241530Z August 1995, par. 3D(2)(D)1 (NATO Confidential) Information extracted is unclassified; and Capt Ken Calise, US Navy, C-5 and battle-staff director, CAOC, Vicenza, Italy, interviewed by Maj Mark Conversino and author, 16 January 1996.

136. COM5ATAF/CAOC Deny Flight SPINS 028, par. 3D(3). (NATO Confidential) Information extracted is unclassified.

137. Ibid., par. 3D(2)(D)4. (NATO Confidential) Information extracted is unclassified.

138. Calise interview.

139. Ibid.

140. Bush interview; and Maj Keith Kiger, Sixteenth Air Force, Weapons and Tactics, interviewed by Maj Mark Conversino and author, Aviano AB, Italy, 19 January 1996.

141. CINCSOUTH OPLAN 40101, change four, annex E, par. 5a(8). (NATO Confidential) Information extracted is unclassified.

142. Maj Steve Irwin, CAOC legal advisor, tape-recorded interview with author, Aviano AB, Italy, 18 January 1996.

143. Ibid.

144. Bush interview.

145. Ibid.

146. Hornburg interview.

147. Kiger interview.

148. Calise interview.

149. Smith lecture.

150. COM5ATAF/CAOC SPINS 028. (NATO Confidential) Information extracted is unclassified.

151. Ibid. (NATO Confidential) Information extracted is unclassified.

152. CINCSOUTH OPLAN 40101, change four, appendix one to annex E, par. 11. (NATO Confidential) Information extracted is unclassified. Note the changes in the definition of *friendly forces* that occurred from change two to change four of the OPLAN.

153. Ryan interview.

154. COM5ATAF/CAOC SPINS 028, par. 3D(2)(C)2. (NATO Confidential) Information extracted is unclassified.

155. CAOC air tasking message, 8 September 1995, MSGID/AIRTASK/HQ 5ATAF/8/SEP//PERID/80300Z/TO: 90259//. (NATO Secret) Information extracted is unclassified.

156. Congress, Senate, *Senator Thurmond of South Carolina Speaking in Reference to the Rules of Engagement for the Vietnam War,* 94th Cong., 1st sess., *Congressional Record,* 6 June 1975, vol. 121, pt. 14, 17558. Senator Thurmond states that "the public would not approve of it. They would not approve of sending their men into battle with their hands behind their backs to fight that way, to make gun fodder, so to speak, out of them. The parents would not approve of it; the country did not approve of it."

157. Dr. Wayne Thompson and Maj Tim Reagan, "Deliberate Force: A Distinctive Campaign," Washington, D.C., December 1995. (Secret) Information extracted is unclassified

158. Lt Col John G. Humphries, "Operations Law and the Rules of Engagement in Operations Desert Shield and Desert Storm," *Airpower Journal* 6, no. 3 (Fall 1992): 38. Humphries discusses the importance of the trust between the NCA and the military that developed partly due to the

military's intensive efforts after Vietnam to train and inculcate the ideas associated with the law of armed conflict.

159. US Ambassador Christopher Hill, interviewed by Lt Col Robert Owen, 27 February 1996.

160. Air Force Pamphlet (AFP) 110-31, *International Law: The Conduct of Armed Conflict and Air Operations,* 1976, pars. 1-5, 1-6, 5-3, 6-2.

161. Ibid.

162. Ryan interview.

163. William J. Perry, secretary of defense, DOD news briefing, speech to the Adjutants General Association of the United States, 7 February 1996.

164. Hornburg interview.

Chapter 15

Roads Not Taken: Theoretical Approaches to Operation Deliberate Force

Lt Col Robert D. Pollock

They want war too mechanical, too measured; I would make it brisk, bold, impetuous, perhaps even audacious.

—Baron Henri Jomini

Historians violate the adage "never second-guess success" at some peril, particularly in the case of the highly successful application of airpower during Operation Deliberate Force. From most perspectives, the planners and executors of Deliberate Force seem to have assessed the diplomatic and political goals of the operation correctly and to have worked an exquisite match of military operations to those goals. Still, at least from the perspective of theoretical opportunities, looking again at the strategy and operational execution of this important air campaign has some value. Indirectly, Gen David Sawyer, deputy commander of the North Atlantic Treaty Organization's (NATO) combined air operations center (CAOC), which directed Deliberate Force, suggested the value of such a second look by pointing out that the campaign might not have been necessary at all had key political and military leaders understood air strategy more completely. In Sawyer's opinion, a more forceful use of airpower in the earlier phases of Operation Deny Flight, of which Deliberate Force was a phase, might have obviated the need for the later bombing campaign. Moreover, General Sawyer felt that a fundamental difference of view among many United Nations (UN) and NATO leaders and American air commanders delayed NATO's and the UN's approval of Deliberate Force in its ultimate form. Most NATO and UN leaders expected a "direct" campaign that targeted the actual guns and mortars which their political leaders wanted silenced, while American air commanders wanted an "indirect" campaign that targeted more easily

431

located things, such as bridges and supply bunkers, to coerce the Serbians to stop shelling the UN safe areas.[1]

General Sawyer's comments, although intended to illustrate the coordination required to win approval of a coalition military plan, also point out the likely existence of other ways to conceive, plan, and execute Deliberate Force. The tension between direct and indirect air strategy illustrates this point, but it does not encompass all possible approaches. Other recently articulated air theories, for example, might have suggested using different concepts or target lists to win the political and diplomatic goals of Deliberate Force. Such theories include the so-called five-ring theory of Col John Warden III, the effects-based concept emanating from the faculty of Air Command and Staff College (ACSC) at Maxwell Air Force Base (AFB), Alabama, and the denial strategy of Dr. Robert A. Pape Jr.

Whether these approaches to air warfare would have enjoyed more success than the one actually used in the Balkans, of course, lies beyond the scope of responsible historical analysis. But laying out their differences has value, both to illustrate and exercise their theoretical construction and to better understand the circumstances under which one strategic approach might prove more useful than another. Thus, one of the overriding questions to consider here is, What were the most important theoretical models available for planning this air campaign? And the other is, Were they suitable to its military, diplomatic, and political environment? This chapter seeks to answer those questions by briefly describing the campaign as planned and executed, examining the three prevailing strategic concepts in general, and describing what the campaign would have been like had planners used these other approaches in the Balkans during August and September of 1995.

Context and Operational Restrictions

Before proceeding, one must briefly review the contextual and operational-art elements that affected the actual planning of the campaign,[2] especially the political and military objectives of the operation as well as restrictions imposed on the campaign. These elements capture the constraints of Deliberate

Force and provide the notional framework for evaluating viable, alternative strategies for action.

All theoretical approaches to air campaign planning are founded upon strategic and military objectives provided by decision makers. NATO resolutions clearly articulated the strategic objectives: (1) assure freedom of access to the cities in Bosnia-Herzegovina and (2) remove the heavy weapons from around Sarajevo. Based on these clear objectives, Gen Michael Ryan, commander of Allied Air Forces Southern Europe, and the CAOC distilled the following military objective: "Take away what the Bosnian Serbs held dear and drive them to military parity with the Bosnian Croats and Muslims."[3] To meet this objective, CAOC planners designed a campaign that identified the Bosnian Serb military advantages: command, control, communications, computers, and intelligence (C^4I); weapon-storage infrastructure; direct and essential support; firepower; and mobility. By having NATO forces attack these elements, General Ryan and his staff believed that the UN would achieve its military objective. The resulting campaign plan relied on having the Bosnian Serbs understand and recognize the loss of their military advantages and their hold on the region's balance of power. If they wanted this surgical reduction halted, they had to ensure freedom of access to the cities and remove their weapons from around Sarajevo.[4]

Restrictions on the planning for Deliberate Force, including methods for selecting and approving targets and the desire to reduce or even eliminate collateral damage, became limiting factors in developing potential courses by the CAOC planning staff. Deliberate Force targets were approved for planning through the Joint Targeting Board process established by the UN and NATO to permit joint validation of targets and linkage to mission objectives mandated by the UN and NATO.[5]

Due to heightened worldwide political tensions and media attention on Bosnia, General Ryan personally chose and approved each target and placed certain restraints on delivery means and methods (read tactics) involving its associated desired mean point of impact (DMPI), the actual point at which pilots would aim their weapons.[6] He considered himself *the* campaign planner and would not delegate the approval processes because of political implications, feeling that he should be held accountable. Ryan clearly stated his rationale for assuming such expansive duties: "If we had committed one atrocity from the air, NATO would forever be blamed for crimes, and the military threat would be lessened."[7]

Essentially the same planning staff, CAOC, and rules of engagement in place for Deny Flight also applied to Deliberate Force.[8] General Ryan took the reins for overall campaign planning and target selection, and the rest of the staff supported him.[9] According to Maj Gen Hal Hornburg, director of the CAOC, air campaign planning started with a desired military end state of halting the Bosnian Serb army (BSA) shelling of UN safe areas. The planners used this end state to determine what they wanted the campaign to do.[10] Planning began in February 1995 for Operation Deadeye (the suppression-of-enemy-air-defenses portion of what became Deliberate Force) at the CAOC.[11] General Ryan expanded Deadeye's scope, transforming it into the plan that eventually became Deliberate Force.[12]

Carl von Clausewitz wrote that "war is a continuation of policy by other means,"[13] which usually implies that militaries will receive political direction during the planning and execution of operations. Deliberate Force, however, lacked formal national and international political guidance throughout the planning process. CAOC planners and General Ryan designed a campaign that primarily targeted perceived centers of gravity (COG) in the BSA as well as some potential COGs in the Bosnian and Croatian armies.[14] Planners identified these COGs and their associated targets by category, putting antiaircraft weapons and heavy-artillery positions at the top of the list, followed by the BSA communications system, military infrastructure, and military stores.[15]

Because of his deeply held concern over unnecessary and unacceptable collateral damage,[16] General Ryan placed specific restraints on weapons delivery, aircraft approach patterns, number of passes permitted, and number of weapons released on a single pass.[17] These constraints met with some resistance from theater airmen, but the latter managed to achieve the desired effects, inflict little ancillary damage, and leave the world's perception of the use of airpower untainted. NATO forces conducted Operation Deliberate Force as a day-and-night air campaign from 31 August 1995 to 14 September

1995 (halting temporarily for diplomatic negotiations) and continued it until 21 September 1995, when the Bosnian Serb government and military agreed to withdraw heavy weapons from the mountains surrounding Sarajevo and to enter into peace talks with the Bosnian Croats and Muslims.[18]

The Five-Ring Approach

To achieve strategic objectives, Colonel Warden, author of *The Air Campaign: Planning for Combat*, and conceptual architect of the strategic air campaign against Iraq in 1991, emphasizes the precise application of airpower to cause systemic paralysis in an opponent's psychological and physical abilities to resist. Warden's planning approach assumes that the fundamental object of warfare is to convince the enemy leadership to do what it otherwise would not do.[19] In his view, air warfare can exert such an influence by attacking key target systems he refers to as rings. Warden argues that one can describe all physical things, from nation-states to military organizations to individual soldiers in terms of five such rings, each, in turn, a fractal of the same five rings (fig. 15.1).

Leadership controls, directs, and sets objectives for any given system. Warden's model provides a framework for a systematic analysis of leadership to identify its key elements, vulnerabilities,

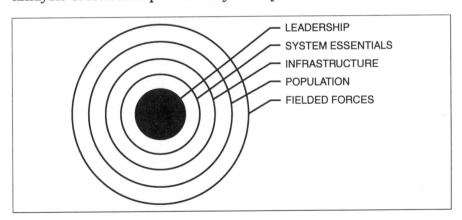

Figure 15.1. Warden's Five Rings (Adapted from Richard P. Hallion, *Storm over Iraq: Air Power and the Gulf War* [Washington, D.C.: Smithsonian Institution Press, 1992], 152)

435

and interrelationships. A systems approach yields links and nodes that one can exploit to influence the enemy.[20]

System essentials are facilities or processes required by the system to function—for example, electricity, petroleum, food, water, and information. Degrading critical system essentials places considerable strain on the system and influences its leadership, thus helping to achieve strategic objectives.[21]

Traditionally, one often thinks of *infrastructure* as the enemy state's transportation network, but this is not always the case. Anything required to support system functions fits into this category, including the electrical net, political-party headquarters, religious centers, supermarkets, industry, ports, railroads, highways, bridges, telecommunication networks, and so forth. By its nature, the infrastructure ring has significantly more redundancy than do the system-essentials and leadership rings, thus making it harder to affect with a given weight of attack.[22]

Population is a critical category in Warden's approach. By analyzing and influencing the social, cultural, and political makeup of a given population, one can identify critical nodes and potential COGs that can directly affect the system's leadership.[23]

Warden views direct attacks on *fielded forces* as the least effective use of airpower. He feels that this form of attack is useful only as a means of affecting an opponent's inner rings; instead, one should strike directly at potentially more lucrative and decisive targets in the other rings.[24]

Warden's approach assumes that (1) the military planner links military strategy to the task and links military objectives to political objectives and (2) the outer rings protect inner ones, especially the all-important leadership ring. For Warden, combat effectiveness—consisting of two equal elements, the physical and the moral (or psychological)—is the key to military execution. Thus, one can represent his model as an equation: combat effectiveness = physical x moral. By selecting physical targets to bring combat effectiveness to zero, the moral aspects will then suffer. The reverse is also true.

Warden's approach also reflects his idea that systems and rings are fractal in nature (i.e., characteristics of lower subsystems are similar to those of higher systems, though on a lesser scale). For example, part of a nation's infrastructure consists of a road system that, in turn, consists of national, state or provincial, county, and local road nets, each with its own unique set of five rings. Understanding a given system as a layered congeries of fractals reveals, in Warden's opinion, common threads or patterns that, if effectively attacked, can produce cascading effects which can paralyze an entire system with a minimum of force. To use the infrastructure example, by knocking out a critical juncture of a local or regional road system, the effects of the new bottleneck could ripple throughout the entire transportation system, depending largely on that system's ability to work around or compensate for the damage.

Utility of Warden's Approach

For air planners, Warden's model offers advantages and potential disadvantages, one of the former including its explicitly holistic picturing of enemies, rings, systems, and subsystems. This view provides a good starting point for detailed campaign planning and helps planners categorize the elements of a potential adversary's system so they can project a means of upsetting it in a way that will achieve military objectives. Planners' knowledge of the adversary's weaknesses and their personal intuition are key influences that translate the five-rings model into a campaign plan.

A key disadvantage of Warden's approach is its tendency to assume that other nation-states respond to US attacks in the same way the United States would respond to a similar attack. Further, given the complexity and robustness of enemy systems, this strategic approach does not inherently consider that enemies can react and rapidly adjust to damage from air attacks in unexpected ways. This too is left to the intuition of the campaign planner. Thus, if unimaginatively applied, Warden's theory seems to promise greater certitude regarding the strategic effects of air attack than living, reactive enemies will actually allow.

Given these advantages and limitations, using the five-ring approach is most appropriate when one knows a good deal about the enemy or during crisis-action planning—when time is of the essence. Because of its inherent simplicity, one can apply the approach to any number of situations. However, a

437

five-ring analysis requires continual updating, revising, and maintaining during both peace and war.

Warden's approach is most useful in determining COGs at the strategic, operational, and tactical levels of the adversary's systems. Establishing firm linkages to UN objectives, developing an effective strategy, and determining an effective means of targeting these COGs require the planner to go beyond the five-ring model for guidance. That is, Warden's approach does not provide an appropriate vehicle for understanding how the broader concerns of grand strategy, national strategy, and operational strategy are linked to form an effective campaign plan designed to achieve national objectives and the desired end state.

Applying Warden's Approach to Deliberate Force

Warden has long believed that any campaign worth the expenditure of our most precious assets—military men, women, and equipment—is worth considerable advanced research and detailed planning.[25] This research must first provide the political objective for the campaign and the desired political and military end state to the crisis. From these he would derive the military objectives for a campaign.

Given the context of July 1995, the political objectives would call for a halt to the shelling of UN-mandated safe areas. One can extrapolate the political end state from the national security strategy of the United States: a peaceful resolution to the ethnic crisis and a democratically elected, multiethnic government for Bosnia-Herzegovina, free to exercise all instruments of power within its internationally recognized borders. Having determined these political objectives and the end state, one could derive the military objective: neutralizing military threats to this vision and driving the opposing sides to a mutually acceptable, peaceful resolution.

The next logical step would entail identifying the COGs. Since Colonel Warden contends that one can represent militaries and nations as systems, this research would focus on finding systematic points that could lead the BSA and the Bosnian Serb government to reconsider their shelling of UN safe areas and adopt a peaceful solution to the crisis.

In *The Air Campaign: Planning for Combat,* Warden makes a strong case that the first objective of any air campaign is to achieve air superiority, whether total, temporary, or even localized. Thus, one would logically design a campaign that began with a strong parallel attack against enemy air defenses throughout the zones in which the air campaign would operate.

This analysis would identify (to Warden's way of thinking) leadership as the BSA's principal COG—specifically, the ability of President Radovan Karadzic and Gen Ratko Mladic to lead their forces. Disrupting the communications that these men needed to lead and control their forces and population would cause a breakdown in the adversary's system. The analysis would also identify the BSA's inherent strength—its heavy weaponry and copious supplies—as the secondary, supporting COG. Denying these elements would eliminate the BSA's strength, place it on par with the Bosnian and Croatian forces, and thus put it in an untenable situation likely to lead to overtures for peace.

Thus, a campaign based on Warden's five-ring approach would strike enemy air defenses at *zero hour* and conduct an immediate, parallel, precision air attack against all military C⁴I and military-stores targets in and around the Bosnian Serb capital of Pale. By showing might and conviction and by eliminating all local support, this attack would directly influence Karadzic's civilian leadership, leaving him isolated, incommunicado, unsupported, psychologically shaken, and more willing to reconsider his position. At *zero plus 10 minutes,* NATO aircraft armed with precision-guided munitions (PGM) would strike known heavy-weapons sites around Sarajevo to eliminate the Serbs' ability to retaliate against civilian and military targets in Sarajevo. Elimination of these targets would probably require follow-on strikes. News of the strikes on Pale and the weapons around Sarajevo would have filtered to the field commanders by *zero plus one hour.* Using stealthy aircraft as the vanguard, coalition air forces would conduct parallel strikes against outlying BSA C⁴I targets and military-supply cassernes known to contain large stockpiles of ammunition, arms, and heavy weapons. This attack would deny the BSA long-term sustainment and again influence its leadership to accept our will. At *zero plus six hours and onward,* follow-on operations would continue the reduction in BSA sustainability and command and control (C^2). Thus, initial strikes would show coalition capability and might, while follow-on strikes would show the will to carry on until UN mandates are upheld—perhaps even until parties agree to a negotiated peace.

The Effects-Based Approach

Air Command and Staff College's effects-based approach proposes that campaign planning is an integrated process that begins with strategic objectives and develops an entire campaign which carries through to a clearly articulated and defined end state.[26] The approach stresses that campaign planning is a top-down process in a world accustomed to bottom-up operations, stressing the synergistic power behind a coordinated economic, political, and military campaign. The process forms a loop that constantly evaluates strategic and military objectives and campaign planners' intended results against desired economic, political, and military end states. In linking strategic objectives and military objectives, planners need to evaluate six contextual elements. In turn, translating strategic objectives into successful military campaigns through COG analysis and translating to a practical master attack plan require the innovative application of six elements of operational art (fig. 15.2).

In effects-based planning, one cannot consider these contextual and operational-art elements in isolation since they are interlinked in a matrix of relationships. Additionally, each of the elements contains two dimensions—the US perspective and an enemy perspective—each of which one must understand both in and of itself and from the other perspective. Thus, Sun Tzu's dictum "know the enemy and know yourself; in a hundred battles you will never be in peril" remains a key ingredient of planning.[27]

After ascertaining the political end state, one then determines the military objective of the campaign plan. This may be easier said than done for several reasons: (1) strategic objectives, defined by political leadership, may be vague and unclear to military planners, (2) political problems may create

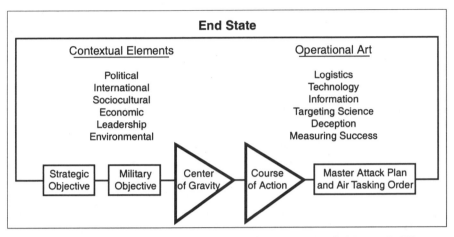

Figure 15.2. The Campaign-Planning Model (From Lt Col Larry A. Weaver and Maj Robert D. Pollock, "Campaign Planning for the 21st Century: An Effected-Based Approach to the Planning Process," in *War Theory*, vol. 3 [Maxwell AFB, Ala.: Air Command and Staff College, September 1998], 28)

strategic objectives that do not have a clear political, economic, and military end state to plan against, and (3) military objectives must align with strategic objectives, or the entire campaign process breaks down or becomes irrelevant. These problems, if not overcome, may confuse and disrupt the planning process and lead to military failure.[28]

To address these three obstacles, we need to recognize that the form of government that created these objectives exerts an influence on them. The creation of clear strategic objectives can become a difficult process in a democratic/parliamentary government because of the problems presented by politics and consensus building. These factors cloud the issue of clear objectives in the military's planning process.

The ACSC model's six contextual elements—which affect potential military operations but usually remain beyond the influence of the military planner and commander—aid military planners in deriving military objectives from the strategic objectives provided them. The commander must build upon these political, international, sociocultural, environmental, leadership, and economic foundations. Each element can have either positive or negative effects on the commander's ability to execute his or her mission. A clear understanding of the contextual elements of campaign planning allows the crucial and time-consuming process of COG identification to begin.

The operational-art elements of effects-based campaign planning tell the planner what is possible and when success has occurred. The idea is to maximize operational strengths and apply them against an adversary's weaknesses. These elements—logistics (including personnel and training),[29] technology (including the military technical revolution),[30] information (quickly obtaining the right data at the right time to exploit an enemy's vulnerabilities),[31] targeting science and its related concept of targeting for effect (identifying effects beforehand, whether strategic, operational, or psychological),[32] deception,[33] and measuring success—become the link between an abstract plan and concrete targeting in the master attack plan and air tasking order.

An effective element will advance the accomplishment of the strategic objective. Targeting science categorizes effects in a number of ways. For example, most effects are either intended or unintended. Often, the unintended effect of a course of action causes a planner the most problems during a campaign. Key issues for campaign planners become how to accurately predict the effects of actions taken, how to anticipate unwanted effects, how to select the military option that best achieves the desired effects, and how to assess the effectiveness of cumulative actions. Air-warfare planners face thinking and reactive enemies; therefore, they must anticipate likely enemy courses of action and the potential effects of those actions on friendly operations.

Targeting for effect is a two-way street. One must assess one's own vulnerabilities, anticipate likely enemy actions, and understand potential effects of enemy actions on one's own objectives. Although it is impossible to avoid an unintended effect entirely, planners must recognize the thinking and reacting powers of an adversary and consider the many ways the adversary could interpret their proposed actions. For intended effects, planners can consider three ways that the proposed action might alter the campaign equation: strategic, operational, or psychological.[34] Any action taken can produce all three effects simultaneously, and the course of action proposed by campaign planners will constantly change the equilibrium of these three effects.

In contrast to traditional approaches, targeting for effect links anticipated physical damage to the broader strategic, operational, and psychological effects anticipated from the attack. It matches the desired physical and psychological effects with the appropriate application of force that will achieve these effects. A feedback mechanism helps planners recognize the effectiveness of their course of action. This strategy considers the effectiveness of given attacks in terms of their net influence upon strategic objectives. Targeting science, then, combines traditional targeteering with targeting for effect.

For example, in Deliberate Force, targeting science matched the desired operational effect (selective destruction of heavy weapons and related storage sites) with carefully selected desired mean points of impact and specific weapon platforms delivering precision weapons (F-16s attacking a surface-to-air battery's acquisition-and-tracking radar with high-speed anti-radiation missiles). All of these actions were designed to achieve the strategic effect of halting heavy-weapon fire into UN safe havens. Reconnaissance indicators revealed operational effects, and diplomacy revealed strategic effects. Thus, targeting for effect recognizes that the core objective of target planning entails affecting, changing, modifying, or impeding an enemy activity—not just maximizing the physical destruction of targets for a given number of sorties and weapons.

Measuring success—an ongoing element best defined as knowing when one is done—requires planners to know their enemy and assess whether they are achieving the desired effects (developed in targeting science). Planners need to compare actual and predicted results and provide feedback into the ongoing campaign process.[35] Measures-of-merit analysis and effect-cause-effect models[36] provide planners an analytical tool for evaluating how well the military accomplishes its objectives.

Effects-based planning produces one major output: a plan for operations, whether a concept of operations or a master air-attack plan, both of which convert ideas into targets and sorties. These documents must concur with the desired end state. The entire process is useful only if leaders at all levels know what end state they seek. The question becomes, What do we want the world to look like politically, militarily, and economically at the end of the war? The answer must be specific in terms of political structure, military capacity, and the economy. For the planner, the end state reintroduces the issue of the strategic objective. If they match, the nation has achieved its war aims.

Utility of the Effects-Based Model

For a campaign planner, the effects-based approach has several key advantages over Warden's five-ring approach, the most important of which is its all-encompassing construction. The effects-based model starts with a defined statement of the desired end state for an operation and cycles the planner through key steps needed to design a campaign plan that acknowledges the needed synergy among the political, military, and economic instruments of power. Unlike Warden's approach, which leaves much to the planners' intuition, the effects-based approach gives this intuition a boost, providing planners with a series of memory-jogging contextual and operational-art elements to consider while refining the military objectives, selecting the COGs, and establishing viable courses of action. The last significant advantage of the effects-based approach is the concept of targeting for effect and all the military benefits derived from a logical application of military might against a designated COG directly linked to achieving objectives and the desired end state.

Some limitations of the effects-based approach include the giant size of the planning task associated with its application. Campaign planners not well versed in the interrelationship of military, economic, and political power may find this approach frustrating. Also, planners with limited data available on an adversary *must* tailor the approach to use it effectively.

Given these advantages and limitations, *the effects-based approach is most appropriate during deliberate planning, when one can spend time on researching a potential adversary, or in crisis-action planning, when one already knows much about the enemy.* Because of its thoroughness, one can apply the approach to any number of analysis situations. As with any analysis, the effects-based approach requires continual updating, revising, and maintaining during both peace and war.

One most appropriately would use effects-based theory to design an overall joint, operational-level campaign plan. It would prove equally useful in designing service- or functional-component campaigns that link political objectives with national strategy and operational strategy to form a campaign plan designed to achieve national objectives and the desired end state.

Applying the Effects-Based Approach to Deliberate Force

As mentioned previously, the effects-based approach calls for the synergistic employment of all instruments of national power (political, economic, informational, and military) in order to achieve the stated national objectives, and the political objectives and desired end state must serve as the foundation of the campaign plan. Since Warden's approach is a subset of the effects-based approach, one would derive the same objectives and COGs. That is, the political objective of Deliberate Force would entail bringing about a halt to the shelling of UN-mandated safe areas, and the political end state would include a peaceful resolution to the ethnic crisis and a democratically elected, multiethnic government in Bosnia-Herzegovina, free to exercise all instruments of power within its internationally recognized borders. Again, one could state that the military objective would call for neutralizing the military threats to this vision and driving the opposing sides to a mutually acceptable, peaceful resolution. The COG would be the BSA—specifically, the ability of President Karadzic and General Mladic to lead their forces, dependent upon effective communication with their troops and the population. The secondary, supporting COG would be the BSA's inherent strength—its heavy weaponry and copious supplies. Preventing the BSA from using them would eliminate its strength and place it on an even playing field with the Bosnian and Croatian forces—a situation likely to facilitate the peace process.

Planners would have designed the campaign much as NATO forces actually prosecuted it. As with the Warden model, the effects-based plan would call for immediate strikes against

445

enemy air defenses. However, in this case, strikes would range across all BSA-held territory. The remaining target sets would be similar to Warden's (supply points, depots, C⁴I nodes, etc.), adding some power stations serving the political center at Pale and the military center at Banja Luka. Planners might target other limited military/civilian infrastructure targets (such as bridges and television/radio stations) for mild damage on the second and third days in order to drive home to the BSA the coalition's determination and will. Coalition forces would strike in parallel, applying maximum effort on the first night/day throughout territory held by the Bosnian Serbs. Diplomatic efforts (backed by air operations specifically aimed at *military* targets around Sarajevo and Pale) would continue throughout the effort until the Bosnian Serbs withdrew their heavy weapons from the heights around Sarajevo. Initial air strikes would show coalition capability and might, while follow-on strikes would demonstrate the will to carry on until the Serbs agreed to UN mandates and a peaceful solution.

Coercive Airpower: Denial Theory

As an assistant professor at the School for Advanced Airpower Studies, Dr. Robert A. Pape Jr. developed an effects-based theory of operational campaigning that focused on coercing the adversary through the employment of airpower. Specifically, Pape's theory focuses on *denying an adversary's strategic and military goals by destroying his fielded military forces.* Pape's steadfast concentration on the destruction of the adversary's military to achieve strategic objectives stands in stark contrast to both the five-ring and effects-based approaches. Military personnel find his inherently purist military approach very attractive, compared to ACSC's more complex and fusionist effects-based theory.[37]

To Pape the most effective way to defeat enemies lies in confounding their strategies by doing the most harm to their military forces and the least harm to their civilians.[38] His preferred instruments of coercion include aerial-delivered, conventional, precision weapons. The coercer must nullify the enemy's military strategy and undermine his confidence that he can achieve his goals. "According to the Denial theory, the real key to coercion lies in exploiting military vulnerability as the means of driving down the enemy's probability of achieving his desired benefit."[39] Quick, hard attacks against an enemy's military deny that enemy the ability to apply his military strategy of choice. When the enemy realizes that he has no effective means to strike back, he is more willing to accept the coercer's goals. Put another way, "in conventional disputes, the success of coercion is likely to be a function of military vulnerability and will be largely unaffected by civilian vulnerability. If hitting military targets in the victim's homeland dramatically impairs his confidence of battlefield success, then he is likely to change his behavior."[40]

Dr. Pape assumes that a nation's leaders are rational actors who continually calculate the risks and benefits of their actions and respond accordingly. To Pape "coercion is all about altering an opposing state's resolve," and denial—with its rapid elimination of military capability—is the best way to alter that state's resolve.[41] Theoretically, the systematic targeting (and destruction) of an adversary's military assets will make his remaining assets even more vulnerable, thereby convincing the adversary to yield. Failure to yield will result in military defeat and a total denial of all benefits from the enterprise in which he is engaged. By denying the adversary the ability to respond militarily, the denial strategist makes the adversary's planned military strategy ineffective and the expected costs of his countervailing military action prohibitive and not worth the effort.[42] Maj Mark Sullivan notes that the

> *Denial* theory argues that in conventional conflicts the most effective means of coercion is reducing the victim's expected benefits . . . below expected costs . . . in his decision calculus. First, specific benefits . . . may be targeted as a means to reduce expected benefits, but Pape maintains that states are incapable of manipulating opponents' perceived benefits. "The assailant cannot gain coercive leverage by attempting to alter the target's basic interests; it can only hope to persuade the target to ignore or stop acting on these interests." The value of the benefits is relatively static during conflicts and belligerents can do little to change their opponent's perception of the attractiveness of these benefits. . . . Perceived benefits are relatively constant during conflicts.[43]

Utility of the Coercive-Denial Model

Some advantages of the coercive-denial approach include its focus on denying an enemy any net benefit from his military actions. Campaign planners using Pape's approach can rapidly concentrate on destroying the adversary's military will and coercing him to accept a desired position or take a desired action. Planners need not consider any actions by the adversary in the political or economic arena because these have no relevance to the approach. Coercive denial maximizes on-the-job military knowledge and intuition by permitting planners with limited data on an adversary to mirror-image possible responses to the coercion. With some knowledge of the adversary, planners can make fairly accurate predictions of the enemy's response to an action. Pape's approach also permits concentration of forces and application of mass against a single target set.

A limitation to the Pape approach is its singular focus and dependence on denying adversaries effective military responses to the Pape-strategist's actions. As long as friendly forces deny an adversary weapons of mass destruction (which he might use as a weapon of last choice or as a threat) and as long as he has no ally or coalition willing to intervene on his behalf, the approach remains viable.

Given these advantages and limitations, *the coercive-denial approach is most appropriate during crisis-action planning, when time is of the essence, and in designing an operational-level campaign plan that rapidly emasculates an adversary's military might and forces the adversary's leadership to capitulate rather than face continued destruction.* Because of its narrow scope, limited target sets, and concentration on military targets, one can apply Pape's approach to any number of situations. As with any analysis, it requires continual updating, revising, and maintaining during both peace and war.

Applying the Coercive-Denial Approach to Deliberate Force

Dr. Pape's approach relies heavily on prohibiting the opposition unrestricted access to its military forces; it requires no data beyond the military objective and a knowledge of what part of the enemy's military is most important—and therefore most likely to cause a change of will if denied him. Although Pape does not explicitly call this vital point a COG, his coercive theory does in fact seek to deny a COG.

A key feature of this approach is the need for the Bosnian Serb leaders to recognize and acknowledge the military hopelessness of their situation. Hence, the campaign plan would attempt to leave clear lines of communications open among Pale, Banja Luka, and the forces in the field. In this regard the coercive-denial theory varies significantly from Warden's theory, the effects-based theory, and the approach chosen by the CAOC and General Ryan. Conventional wisdom strongly advocates blinding, deafening, and muting the communications and control networks of one's opponent, thus denying him centralized control of his forces. The Pape approach requires that these C^2 networks be degraded but left standing (and working) so that the enemy can understand what is happening to his forces and react. At this point the campaign planner must knowingly add the risk of a quickly reacting enemy to the plan. Of course, the quick reaction that the planner wants from the enemy is an acknowledgment of his reduced capability and subsequent capitulation. The campaign would also seek to deny the BSA's COG by destroying heavy weapons and supply depots.

Deliberate Force appears to have closely followed Pape's coercive-denial approach in its design and execution. Had Pape himself designed the campaign, no doubt it would have strongly resembled the actual prosecution. Target sets would have been similar, if not identical, with the exception of requiring less damage to C^2 networks for the reasons mentioned above. Further, Pape's timing of the air campaign would have been far more deliberate and much slower, allowing the Bosnian Serbs to assimilate damage reports from within. As the campaign went on, preplanned pauses (unilateral cease-fires) would have allowed diplomats time to entreat the enemy. Through this slower, more deliberate process of coercion, the Bosnian Serbs eventually would have been driven to withdraw their remaining heavy weapons from around Sarajevo and adopt the UN mandates.

449

Conclusion

Assessing alternate approaches to any past campaign can verge on second-guessing the people who actually prosecuted the battle—certainly not the intent of this chapter. Instead, it examined viable options that could have produced other, perhaps equally viable, courses of action. It is up to the planning staff to decide which of these approaches to use.

A review of the Deliberate Force campaign as designed shows that planners employed elements of the five-ring model to identify the key Bosnian Serb COGs and elements of the effects-based approach to achieve end-state-based military objectives. In its operational approach, Deliberate Force executed a coercive-denial air campaign to achieve its objectives. Thus, the CAOC's planning staff employed all three of the current theories discussed above, although it did so subconsciously and by happenstance. The bottom line for our Air Force is to understand the robust and viable options available for planning air campaigns and the planning conditions under which they are best applied to the problem of taking down an enemy. We have the ability to vary our planning patterns—and we should, since applying a variety of campaign styles allows us to orchestrate unpredictable and synergistic air campaigns that will dispatch our enemies with surprise, speed, and might.

Notes

1. Quoted by Col Douglas Richardson, director of operations, CAOC, interviewed by Lt Col Robert Ċ. Owen and Richard L. Sargent, 7 December 1995.

2. Contextual and operational-art elements are key to ACSC's air-campaigning framework. See Lt Col Larry A. Weaver and the author, "Campaign Planning for the 21st Century: An Effected-Based Approach to the Planning Process," in *War Theory* (Maxwell AFB, Ala.: Air Command and Staff College, September 1998), 3:27–33.

3. Gen Michael Ryan, interviewed by authors of the Air University Balkans Air Campaign Study at Air Command and Staff College, Maxwell AFB, Ala., 7 February 1996.

4. Ibid.

5. Briefing, Allied Forces Southern Europe (AFSOUTH) Public Affairs, October 1995.

6. Maj Gen Hal Hornburg, CAOC director, interviewed by Lt Col Robert Owen et al., Air Force Wargaming Institute, Maxwell AFB, Ala., 14 March 1996.

7. Ryan interview. General Ryan went on to say that "henceforth, the air commander will be—must be—applying the overarching air strategy at the tactical level. You cannot delegate the selection. The commander must ask all of the detailed questions. There will be no time in the future when he will have the option to say, 'I delegated that responsibility.' The commander must be accountable for all actions taken by his forces. This is particularly notable, given our use of [precision-guided munition] strikes from the air."

8. Lt Col Thomas D. Entwistle, interviewed by Lt Col Robert C. Owen, Washington, D.C., 1 December 1995.

9. Ryan interview.

10. Maj Gen Hal M. Hornburg, presentation to Joint Doctrine Air Campaign Course students, College of Aerospace Doctrine Research and Education, Maxwell AFB, Ala., 14 March 1996.

11. Hornburg interview.

12. Ryan interview.

13. Carl von Clausewitz, On War, ed. and trans. Michael Howard and Peter Paret (Princeton, N.J.: Princeton University Press, 1976), 87.

14. Hornburg interview.

15. Ryan interview.

16. Ibid.

17. Hornburg interview.

18. AFSOUTH briefing.

19. John A. Warden III, "Air Theory for the Twenty-first Century," in Challenge and Response: Anticipating US Military Security Concerns, ed. Karl P. Magyar et al. (Maxwell AFB, Ala.: Air University Press, 1994), 319.

20. ACSC Teaching Plan, "SS525: Leadership as a Center of Gravity" (Maxwell AFB, Ala.: Air Command and Staff College, 6 October 1995).

21. See Col John A. Warden III, "The Enemy as a System," Airpower Journal 9, no. 1 (Spring 1995): 40–55.

22. Ibid.

23. ACSC Teaching Plan, "SS526: Population as a Center of Gravity" (Maxwell AFB, Ala.: Air Command and Staff College, 24 October 1995).

24. Warden, "Enemy." In this case Colonel Warden follows in the footsteps of Giulio Douhet, Hugh Trenchard, John Slessor, and Billy Mitchell, all of whom thought that airpower could be used more effectively against targets other than fielded forces.

25. Briefing, John A. Warden III to ACSC course directors, subject: ACSC Curriculum Goals for Academic Year 1996, 2 May 1995.

26. For an expanded discussion of the effects-based model, see Weaver and the author.

27. Sun Tzu, The Art of War, trans. Samuel B. Griffith (New York: Oxford University Press, 1971), 84.

28. See Col Dennis M. Drew and Dr. Donald M. Snow, *Making Strategy: An Introduction to National Security Processes and Problems* (Maxwell AFB, Ala.: Air University Press, August 1988), 23.

29. Weaver and the author. Logistics serves as the glue of armies and societies. In *Brute Force: Allied Strategy and Tactics in the Second World War* (New York: Viking, 1990), John Ellis argues that the United States won the war because its ability to generate war materiel overwhelmed the enemy. In addition to the traditional notions of equipment, ships, weapons, and spares, logistics also includes the personnel to use the materiel, training, transportation, communications, and more. This element of operational art also considers the factories, laboratories, workers, farmers, and scientists in the equation. Planning requires that one also examine the opposition's logistics system for vulnerabilities.

30. Weaver and the author. Technology is not just technological advancement but the military application of technology. It includes the trained individual who can employ the new technology using new tactics, as well as new organizations that exploit this new technology.

31. Ibid. Information and its subset—intelligence—are not new problems. However, growth in the amount of data available makes it critical that operators ask the right questions and that intelligence officers learn to tailor their answers for the intended user. Systematic analysis of our enemy will identify vulnerabilities to exploit. The military planner must quickly obtain the right data at the right time to exploit these vulnerabilities. We must train our minds to make the best use of the information provided. Risk will always be part and parcel of the planner's and the commander's lives. Information can help reduce the risk.

32. Ibid. Targeting science is the heart of operational art. For years the US Air Force concentrated on targeteering—the selection and matching of the target and the servicing weapon, as well as timing. ACSC emphasizes that this is but one element of the larger concept of targeting science. The question today is not how much damage one can inflict but how well one achieves the desired effect by servicing a target.

33. Ibid.

34. One may define *strategic effect* as the consequence of an action felt throughout the entire system. Achieving such effects will impact a nation's ability to efficiently and effectively apply the political, military, economic, and informational instruments of power. For example, strategic effect can range from impairing a nation's ability to function normally, through paralyzing key political and economic systems, to rendering the nation unable to provide the most basic services. It seeks to create systemwide paralysis. Typically, the closer one targets to the center ring, the greater the strategic effect. One may define *operational effect* as the consequence of an action that impairs one's ability to use a specific instrument of power (political, military, economic, and informational) in a given region. Operational effects typically focus on impairing the ability to apply military power within a theater of operations. For example, operational effects might range from

reducing an enemy's military capability, through increasing attrition, to annihilating his forces in an area. Operational effect may also result in the diversion of military forces from the main effort. *Psychological effect* is the consequence of an action that negatively impacts the enemy's state of mind or positively impacts the mental state of friendly forces or allies. For example, psychological effects can range from achieving surprise and confusion in the mind of the enemy leadership, commanders, population, and/or troops; through dissuading the enemy from resisting; to inspiring friendly leadership, commanders, population, and/or troops to hold out against great odds.

35. This assessment should examine one's effectiveness in hitting certain targets. This includes the appropriateness of one's choice of COGs and the entire COG-selection process, from the establishment of military objectives, to the selection of COGs, to the prioritization of COG targets. One's assessment should then analyze the actual effects, their causes, and gaps in the logic chain. Most importantly, it should assess the validity of the measures and indicators one uses and the validity of one's assumptions.

36. See ACSC Teaching Plan, "Measuring Success" (Maxwell AFB, Ala.: Air Command and Staff College, 9 February 1996) for additional details on the effect-cause-effect scenario.

37. *Purist* and *fusionist* are terms that describe how military members view their profession. A purist concentrates on the military means available to meet an objective, while the fusionist looks at all applicable instruments of power (military, political, and economic) and recommends the approach to apply them synergistically to achieve the desired objective.

38. Robert A. Pape, "Coercion and Military Strategy: Why Denial Works and Punishment Doesn't," *Journal of Strategic Studies* 15, no. 4 (December 1992): 465.

39. Maj Mark P. Sullivan, *The Mechanism for Strategic Coercion:* Denial *or* Second-Order Change? (Maxwell AFB, Ala.: Air University Press, April 1995), 18.

40. Pape, 424. This concept dovetails nicely with the effects of PGMs. Mary FitzGerald comments on the Russian view that PGMs used against key command, control, communications, and intelligence systems have the same effects as a nuclear weapon. If used against a nuclear-capable enemy, PGMs could force an escalation to nuclear war. "Russian Views on Future War" (paper presented at Air University, Maxwell AFB, Ala., March 1995).

41. Robert A. Pape, "Coercive Air Power" (PhD diss., University of Chicago, December 1988), 57.

42. Sullivan, 11.

43. Ibid., 17. See also Robert A. Pape, "Coercive Airpower in the Vietnam War," *International Security* 15, no. 2 (Fall 1990): 110. In order to analyze the denial effect empirically, Pape uses territory as the primary benefit over which nations struggle.

Chapter 16

Summary

*Col Robert C. Owen**

This chapter summarizes and suggests implications of the final report of the Balkans Air Campaign Study (BACS).[1] The former deputy commander in chief of United States European Command, Gen James Jamerson, and the former commander of Air University, Lt Gen Jay W. Kelley, chartered this study in October 1995. The purpose was to "capture" the planning, execution, and results of Operation Deliberate Force, the North Atlantic Treaty Organization (NATO) air campaign conducted against the Bosnian Serbs between 30 August and 14 September 1995, as part of a broader international intervention into the Bosnian conflict. The specific charters were to explore broadly the salient events and implications of this brief but unique air campaign and to gather a comprehensive documentary and oral archive to support later in-depth research. The generals' intention was that the team would lay out a "mile-wide-and-foot-deep" baseline study of Deliberate Force, one aimed more at identifying and delineating issues than at putting them to rest.

The BACS team adopted a core research question that highlighted the study's focus on the planning and execution of an air campaign: "How and with what considerations did the planners and executors of Deliberate Force link military operations with the strategic, political, and diplomatic goals they were charged to attain?" To be useful to a potentially broad audience, the answer to this question required a survey of the geopolitical, sociological, diplomatic, technological, and operational factors influencing this particular air campaign. Thus the general organization of the study and the chapters of its report were divided into sections that primarily dealt with (1) the

---

*An earlier version of this essay appeared in the Summer and Fall 1997 issues of *Airpower Journal.*

455

Gen James Jamerson   **Lt Gen Jay W. Kelley**

political and institutional context of Deliberate Force planning, (2) the actual planning of the campaign, (3) its execution, and (4) the implications of those experiences. To the extent that these chapters had a unifying theme, it was an effort to determine to what extent the planners and executors of Deliberate Force were cognizant of and/or wielded influence over the forces that shaped the form, execution, and effects of the air campaign. In other words, to what extent were they in charge of events, and to what extent were events in charge of them? The answer to that question and others raised—and to various extents answered by the BACS team—carries significant implications for the theories and doctrines of airpower strategy and planning.

Political and Institutional Context

In an ideal world, military planners base their work on concise and clear articulations of the political and diplomatic goals set by their political leaders. If they are to organize forces, develop strategies, select intermediate objectives, and execute operations, they need to know those goals and the degree and the nature of the force they can employ in their attainment. Although the truth of this concept likely would be transparent to any military thinker, most would also agree that the inherent complexity, chaos, and obscurations of wars and conflicts often make the clear and lasting articulations of specific political and diplomatic goals difficult. In the practical world, as a consequence, military planners usually base their work on expressions of goals that are sometimes clear, sometimes obscure, and sometimes unknowable or only assumed. This mix of the knowable and the unknowable was particularly evident in the planning context of Deliberate Force. In the origins and nature of the conflict and in the multicoalition structure of the outside intervention into it, there lay a complex and changing web of objectives, commitments, and restraints that shaped military planning, even though the planners involved perceived some of its strands only imperfectly or had no knowledge of them.

In general terms the Bosnian conflict was a by-product of the economic and political decline of the Yugoslav Federation during the 1980s. The net effect of this prolonged crisis on Yugoslavian national and provincial politics was the breakup of the country. The republics of Slovenia and Croatia left in the summer of 1991, while Bosnia and Macedonia pulled out in the winter of 1991–92. Left behind in a rump state referred to as "the former Yugoslavia" were Serbia, Vojvodina, Montenegro, and Kosovo—all under the domination of Serbia and its president, Slobodan Milosevic. The breakup was not peaceful. The Yugoslavian People's Army (JNA) fought a 10-day war in June and July 1991 to keep Slovenia in the federation, and it fought a much longer and bitterer war to quash the Croatian secession between August 1991 and January 1992. In cooperation with the JNA, Serbian minority groups in Croatia and Bosnia fought to hold those provinces in the federation and under the pale of Milosevic or, failing that, to carve out their own ethnic enclaves (Krajinas) for ultimate unification with "greater Serbia." All of these conflicts were characterized by an appalling viciousness on all sides, including massacres of civilians and captured soldiers, mass robbery and rape, and scorched-earth conquests—all encapsulated in a new international term: *ethnic cleansing.* Dismay and disgust at that violence and its implications for regional stability prompted outside states and international organizations to intervene in the Balkans crisis in general and in Bosnia in particular.

From the perspective of the intervening states and the later planners of Deliberate Force, knowing that the Bosnian conflict sprang from the collapse of the Yugoslavian Federation provided little foundation for strategic planning. Crudely put, a political breakup, in and of itself, provides few targets against which air strategists may ply their trade. Building air strategy in the case of Bosnia required more detailed understanding of the conflict, beginning with a clear description of its sustaining causes. *Sustaining causes* is a term useful in this discussion to designate the forces and mechanisms that "move" a conflict from its root cause to its ultimate form. These causes drive the evolution of a conflict, sustain it, and characterize its key features, such as objectives, scope, intensity, and political dynamics. In the present discussion, the sustaining causes of the Bosnian conflict are the things that led the country's people and leaders to take the course that they did in response to the uncertainties and fears engendered by the collapse of the existing federal political system. They had choices, after all. To resecure its future, the collective Bosnian polity could have chosen to continue the peaceful coexistence of its people in a unitary state, to divide into a Swiss-like confederation of cantons, or to select some other option to gross interethnic violence. Instead, Bosnians went for each other's throats, arguably at the instigation of elements of the Serb community. Explanations as to why they did so vary, but most identify some combination of three underlying forces as the predominant cause of their choice: (1) ethnic tension, (2) inflammation of ethnic tension by national and provincial politicians in pursuit of personal power and other political ends, and (3) a military imbalance grossly in favor of one Bosnian ethnic group—namely the Serbs.[2]

Ethnic tension may have been historically endemic to Bosnian politics, but interethnic violence was episodic. In their ancient roots in the barbarian invasions of the Roman Empire, the people of Bosnia were all South Slavs. In the latter twentieth century, they still looked like each other, and they spoke dialects of the same root language. But, as was the case for the South Slavs of the Balkans region in general, centuries of the divide-and-rule policies of their Ottoman and Hapsburg overlords, internal migration, differing religious experiences, and wars had divided Bosnians into distinct—though geographically intermixed—communities of faith and, to a lesser degree, culture. Proportionally in 1991 the three largest ethnic groups in Bosnia were the Muslim Serbs (referred to in the report as Moslems),[3] Orthodox Christian Serbs, and Catholic Croats, who comprised 44 percent, 31 percent, and 18 percent of the population, respectively. Nevertheless, following the creation of Yugoslavia after World War I, these communities generally lived in peace and increasingly intermarried, particularly when times were good and the federal government was strong. But when times were tough and the central government weakened, as was the case during World War II and during the economic and political crisis of the 1980s, ethnic loyalties regained preeminent importance for enough Bosnians to orient political competition and widespread violence along communal—rather than ideological, economic, or class—lines.

The fact that ethnic chauvinism emerged as a predominant theme of Bosnian politics in the latter 1980s was to some degree the consequence of the manipulations of federal and provincial politicians. Indeed, the chronology of the Bosnian conflict has its tangible beginnings in the demagoguery of Milosevic. Maneuvering for power, in 1987 he began using his position as president of the Yugoslavian League of Communists as a platform to whip up the ethnic pride and paranoia of the Serb community of Serbia. Milosevic's rhetoric also helped stir up Serbian groups living in the Krajina of southwestern Croatia and in a number of smaller Krajinas in Bosnia. By mid-1990 Croatian Serbs were committing acts of defiance and limited violence against the Croatian government. When Croatia declared its independence from Yugoslavia in June 1991, Croatian Serbs cooperated with the JNA in an open war to crush the independence movement or at least to establish Serbian control over the Krajina. This war ended in January 1992 with the establishment of a tense truce in the Krajina and creation of a United Nations Protection Force (UNPROFOR) to supervise it. By that time, elements of the Bosnian Serb community, under the general if sometimes very loose leadership of Radovan Karadzic, were preparing to resist a similar declaration of independence by Bosnia. In the early months of 1991, the majority of Croats and Muslims, under the leadership of President Alija Izetbegovic, had voted for independence. Preempting that vote, Karadzic established an independent Serbian Republic. Bosnia formally withdrew from Yugoslavia in March 1992, and heavy fighting followed immediately after. Forces of the Serb Republic, with overt assistance from the JNA, advanced to expand its borders, while the relatively weak Bosnian army fought to preserve the territorial integrity and authority of its newly independent state. Within a few weeks, Serbs controlled almost two-thirds of the territory of Bosnia.

The boldness and success of the Bosnian Serbs' military offensive were consequences to some degree of their great military advantage over the Moslem and Croat factions. During 1991 a number of Serb military and paramilitary units formed in Bosnia and prepared to fight. The JNA, which remained present in the country until after independence, greatly helped their preparations. Before and as it withdrew, the JNA opened arsenals to Serb military units and released sympathetic personnel to join it. Meanwhile the Bosnian government did little to arm itself. In reality, President Izetbegovic had little opportunity to do otherwise. The only significant local source of arms was the JNA, and it gave willingly only to Serbs. Moreover, the United Nations (UN) in September 1991 had imposed an arms embargo that made it difficult and expensive for the Bosnian government to import arms and materiel from the outside. Thus when the country fractionated, the Bosnian Serbs had the will and overwhelming military power—particularly in a vast preponderance of aircraft and heavy field weapons—to advance around the northern and eastern parts of Bosnia. There they carved out an ethnic state with direct connections to Serbia proper and to the Serbian Krajina of Croatia. In a matter of weeks, then, the Bosnian government found itself surrounded by unfriendly and mutually supporting Serbian enclaves and states.

By that time the direct international intervention that eventually would have a crescendo in Deliberate Force was under way. Concerned with the growing violence and the possibility of intervention by Yugoslavia, several European states and the United States recognized Bosnia in April 1992, and on 20 May the UN Security Council recommended Bosnia for admission to the General Assembly. On 29 June the Security Council resolved to provide peacekeeping forces to protect the flow of humanitarian relief supplies into Sarajevo Airport, under the protection of UNPROFOR, whose charter was extended to include peace operations in Bosnia. NATO airpower became involved in the region at about the same time in the form of airborne warning and control system aircraft flying in support of Sharp Guard, a NATO and Western European Union operation to enforce the regional arms embargo and economic sanctions against the former Yugoslavia. Direct cooperation between the UN and NATO began on 16 October, when by prearrangement the UN issued United Nations Security Council Resolution (UNSCR) 781, banning all military flight operations over Bosnia, and NATO activated Operation Sky Watch to observe and report violations of that ban. After observing hundreds of no-fly violations over the next several months, particularly by combat aircraft of the Bosnian Serb faction, the UN and NATO again cooperated to toughen the no-fly ban. On 31 March 1993, the UN issued UNSCR 816, banning *all* flights not authorized by the UN and authorizing member states to take all necessary actions to enforce that ban. Simultaneously, NATO replaced Sky Watch with Operation Deny Flight to signify the new element of force. Over subsequent months NATO and the UN added other missions to Deny Flight, including close air support (CAS) to protect UN personnel under attack, offensive air support (OAS) to punish factions violating UNSCRs, and suppression of enemy air defenses (SEAD) to protect NATO aircraft flying the other missions. To coordinate planning and, particularly, the targets identified for attack in these missions, NATO's North Atlantic Council (NAC) also activated at the start of Deny Flight a joint target coordination board composed of senior NATO and UN tactical commanders concerned with the use of airpower in the region and its consequences. These developments and the planning that went into them constituted an incremental, evolutionary process that laid the foundations of Deliberate Force, which technically was but a phase of Deny Flight.

Intervention air planning evolved for nearly three years, roughly from the early fall of 1992 to the end of August 1995.

An important reason for that prolongation was the difficulty experienced by NATO, the UN, and the international community as a whole in reaching consensus on what the conflict was about. Observable events made it obvious that the principal sustaining elements of the Bosnian war were ethnic tensions, political manipulation of those tensions, and the imbalance of military power. But which sustaining element or elements exerted the most influence on its shape, scope, and virulence? In his research for the first chapter of this book, Prof. Karl Mueller identifies two distinct schools of thought on this issue, particularly among interventionist governments. One school emphasized ethnic conflict. Somehow, in this view, Slavs were predisposed culturally to slice each other's throats. Bosnia was just a case in point—a place where collapse of the Yugoslav federal system's restraints merely unfettered the long-restrained-but-never-forgotten ethnic hatreds in a perennially unstable and violent region. At the beginning of the Bosnian conflict, Mueller argues, this was the official view of most European interventionist governments—importantly, Britain and France—which provided most of the peacekeeping troops for Bosnia. The second school emphasized the political manipulations of Serbian political leaders such as Milosevic and Karadzic. Whatever the inherent instabilities of the region, this school of thought held that the current round of fighting had been sparked and sustained by the venal racism of irresponsible demagogues. This view of the conflict, which reflected the predominant, official position of the United States after the spring of 1993, thus held that violence in the region was episodic—not perennial.

For air planners these two views of the sustaining elements of the Bosnian war were directly significant because each implied a different strategy of intervention. If the war were the consequence of endemic cultural forces, then it had no culprits. All sides were equally guilty and equally innocent—victims of forces beyond their control. If that were the case, then the proper role of an intervention was that of a neutral mediator. To the extent that one used force in such an intervention, one should do so only to protect the innocent, separate the warring factions, and encourage communications and confidence between them. In current US military usage, then, the view

462

that conflict was perennial to Bosnia led to a *peacemaking* strategy aimed at ameliorating suffering and facilitating a cease-fire and political settlement as soon as possible. In contrast, if the war were the consequence of political manipulation, then it had culprits—the politicians exploiting the situation to sustain war for their own interests and those of their constituents. If that were the case, then coercion was also a legitimate role of military intervention, along with relief and confidence building. Assuming that one could identify the risk-benefit calculi of the political culprits, then one might be able to identify military targets that, if attacked or threatened, would shift the balance of their calculations toward peace. One could also use intervention military force to remediate the consequences of war crimes and territorial conquest by the war's aggressors. In that case an immediate cessation of fighting might not be appropriate if it denied the interventionists the time required to set, or help set, things "right." In current US military usage, then, the view that conflict in Bosnia was episodic and opportunistic led in part to a strategy of *peace enforcement* aimed at coercing the appropriate warlords to accept peace and redress wrongs.

These two views of the causes of the war also had indirect significance for air planners because their contrariety undermined the ability of NATO and the UN as corporate organizations to develop consensus between themselves and among their members on what exactly to do about Bosnia. Consensus was a necessary prelude to action because both organizations are voluntary associations of sovereign states. Once stated, this seems an obvious truth. But in the heat of events, military planners sometimes forget that, compared to the hierarchical order of military organizations, these international organizations operate on a basis akin to institutionalized anarchy. No matter how orderly and cooperative the internal processes of these organizations, their member states are not subordinate to them or the majority will of the other members. Even small states can block corporate actions simply by withholding their support from them. As a consequence, most of the senior diplomats interviewed for the BACS pointed out, explicitly or implicitly, that no general plans or policies for Bosnia, including those related to the use of airpower, had any hope of success unless they were endorsed by all the principal states in the intervention—particularly those in the Security Council and NATO. According to Robert Hunter, the US ambassador throughout Deny Flight, building such consensus support for increasingly robust use of airpower over Bosnia was a difficult and months-long diplomatic process—but an absolute precursor to action.[4] Little wonder that Mueller describes the debate over the sustaining causes of the war as "one of the major obstacles to Western efforts to deal with the crisis."

The slow pace of policy development had one advantage for NATO airmen, including those who eventually put together Deliberate Force: it gave them time to overcome the institutional and doctrinal impediments they faced in planning and executing sustained air operations over Bosnia. In the second chapter of this book, Lt Col Bradley Davis describes the organizational structure NATO had in place during Deny Flight. The Bosnian region fell under the purview of NATO's 5th Allied Tactical Air Force (5 ATAF), with headquarters at the Italian air force's Dal Molin Air Base (AB), Vicenza, Italy. The Italian general commanding 5 ATAF, who at the time of Deliberate Force was Maj Gen Andrea Fornasiero, reported to the commander of Allied Air Forces Southern Command (AIRSOUTH). From December 1992 the AIRSOUTH commander was Lt Gen Joseph Ashy until his replacement by Lt Gen Michael E. Ryan in September 1994. These two United States Air Force officers, in turn, reported to United States Navy admirals commanding Allied Forces Southern Europe (AFSOUTH), headquartered in Naples, Italy. The commander in chief of AFSOUTH (CINCSOUTH) at the beginning of Deny Flight was Adm Jeremy Boorda until his replacement by Adm Leighton W. Smith Jr. To complete the chain of command, AFSOUTH reported to the Supreme Allied Commander Europe (SACEUR), also an American four-star commander. SACEUR took his general guidance from the ambassadors sitting on the NAC.

The problem, Davis assesses, was that neither 5 ATAF nor AFSOUTH was organized, manned, or equipped to handle the scale and complexity of an operation like Deny Flight, let alone Deliberate Force. In late 1992, 5 ATAF was charged to oversee and control indirectly the air defense of Italy. Accordingly it had modest communications connections with air defense centers and radar sites throughout Italy. But the 5 ATAF headquarters was small, and its control center was equipped with obsolescent equipment. It possessed none of the state-of-the-art automated air-planning and information downlink systems that had proven so successful in the 1990–91 Persian Gulf War. Similarly, AIRSOUTH was a small planning headquarters, charged with doing air planning for AFSOUTH and overseeing the activities of 5 ATAF and two other ATAFs based in Greece and Turkey. Neither AIRSOUTH nor AFSOUTH had crisis-planning cells to deal with the rapid onset and fast-paced political and military evolution of something like Deny Flight.[5] Overall, the established strengths and equipment of the two headquarters fell far short of the likely demands of continual observation and no-fly enforcement operations over Bosnia.

NATO's formal doctrinal foundations for peace operations over Bosnia were also uneven. Since most key commanders and staff planners were Americans, Lt Col Robert Pollock examines in his chapter the formal body of theories that might have been relevant to planning Deliberate Force and available to AIRSOUTH planners. He explores three theoretical constructs available in open literature at the time: Robert Pape's denial strategy, John Warden's five-ring paradigm, and the Air Command and Staff College's "systems" approach to air targeting. Despite their markedly different theoretical propositions and planning approaches, Pollock finds that these three theories generally produced target sets similar to one another and to the targets actually bombed during Deliberate Force. The differences among them were marginal issues of timing and focus. For all the potentially useful guidance and reassurance these three concepts could have offered, however, neither Pollock nor other members of the BACS team uncovered oral evidence that AIRSOUTH planners had any working knowledge of them.

In his examination of written NATO doctrines, Col Maris McCrabb determines that Deny Flight planners also found little guidance in their manuals and publications. That guidance was particularly spotty for operations other than war (OOTW), of which peace operations are a subset. Summarizing his findings, McCrabb notes that "NATO . . . air planning doctrine . . . focuses on coalition considerations but remains largely silent on OOTW, while US joint doctrine features greater emphasis on the unique aspects of OOTW but does not fully consider coalition considerations. An additional issue that bedevils both sets of doctrine is the role of airpower in either OOTW or conventional war." These doctrinal shortfalls were glaring in relation to the unique and unprecedented relationship of NATO, primarily a regional military alliance, acting in military support of the UN, primarily a global political organization. Notably, established doctrines were largely silent on how airmen could reconcile, in their plans and target lists, the conflicting objectives and restraints that likely would crop up between two powerful organizations in a peacemaking situation in which at least one combatant did not want to make peace. Thus, addressing one of the principal corollary research questions of the BACS, McCrabb concludes that "the question . . . of whether these planners consulted the existing body of doctrine or just 'winged it' is largely moot—they had almost nothing to which they could refer."

This virtual absence of guidance for conducting multicoalition peace operations was understandable, given the unprecedented nature of the UN-NATO relationship. But it was an important void in the context of NATO air planning because the overall focus of UN strategy and the operational focus of NATO air commanders began to diverge almost at the start of Deny Flight. Under Sky Watch the strategic focus of the intervention and NATO flyers was on peacemaking—observe and report, but don't engage. But the decision to activate Deny Flight added peace enforcement as a potential feature of intervention strategy. Though they never challenged the UN's overall commitment to maintaining its position as a neutral peacemaker, General Ashy and other senior NATO commanders immediately recognized that their operational focus would be on peace enforcement.[6] Moreover, since the Bosnian Serbs possessed far and away the largest air arm in Bosnia, Deny Flight clearly was aimed predominantly at them.[7] That focus sharpened in the spring and summer of 1993, when CAS and OAS missions were added to the Deny Flight menu; the UN designated certain cities under the control of the Bosnian government as safe areas and committed itself to protect them. With those developments NATO was flying in great part to restrict both the Serb faction's employment of a key military advantage and its ability to assail cities held by its enemies. That hardly was an act of peacemaking impartiality, and its contrast with the overall UN mission became a source of frustration for NATO airmen and of strategic debate, particularly within NAC.

Given all these elements of their planning context, NATO airmen seem to have received their planning and operational responsibilities for Deny Flight under unenviable circumstances. The conflict they were engaging was complicated enough in its origins and convoluted regional politics. But their task was complicated further by the presence of at least two broad interpretations of the conflict at play among their direct and indirect political leaders, and each one of those interpretations spoke to a different approach to the use of airpower. In their formal chain of command, the American flag officers in charge of Deny Flight worked for NAC, which was acting in support of the UN Security Council. At the beginning of Deny Flight, most of the member governments of both organizations were determined to restrict the intervention to peacemaking operations and, consequently, to avoid any military operations that would appear to favor one Bosnian faction over the other. Yet in their informal chain of command, these officers were American, and by mid-1993 their government was on record in support of the use of airpower to halt or punish Serb aggression—a position with which AFSOUTH leaders were inclined to agree. Compounding this strategic issue, AFSOUTH was neither materially nor doctrinally ready for Deny Flight. Consequently, while the strategic debate rolled on and the Bosnian crisis unfolded, these airmen would have to build up their conceptual understanding of the conflict as well as the command infrastructure and force structure required to plan and execute operations. To put it mildly, they faced a great challenge.

Planning

To study the planning of Deliberate Force is to study Deny Flight. Until just a few weeks before the actual execution of the campaign, there existed no plan or plan annex called *Deliberate Force*. When the term did appear in text, it seems to have done so first in the title of an AIRSOUTH briefing given in early August 1995—"Air Operations in Bosnia-Herzegovina—Deliberate Force."[8] But the briefing did not delineate the theaterwide bombing campaign that Deliberate Force became. It mainly listed the various contingency air plans thus far developed by AIRSOUTH to execute various aspects of the Deny Flight mission. As a menu of specialized plans to enforce UNSCRs, protect specific safe areas, and suppress Bosnian Serb air defenses, this briefing offered NATO air commanders a foundation for responding to a future crisis, but it did not propose a specific action for a specific crisis. Accordingly, a few weeks later when the operation since recognized as Deliberate Force began, one saw the activation and rapid modification of several plans originally developed under the aegis of Deny Flight. Despite its obvious differences in focus and intensity from the main body of Deny Flight, therefore, one can understand Deliberate Force only as an evolutionary outgrowth of the preparations and planning that went into the more prolonged operation. Col Chris Campbell and Lieutenant Colonel Davis detail various aspects of this planning effort in their chapters, which form the foundation for much of what follows here.

Deliberate planning for Deny Flight began almost from the inception of Operation Sky Watch in mid-October 1992. By mid-November after observing continued no-fly violations by all Bosnian factions but particularly by Serb combat aircraft, the UN and NATO began developing the details of a more robust enforcement plan. Air planners at Supreme Headquarters Allied Powers Europe (SHAPE), Mons, Belgium, began developing organizational, operational, and force-structure concepts for such a plan. Among other issues, they suggested that it would be necessary, in accordance with standard NATO practice, to establish a stand-alone combined air operations center (CAOC) to control expanded air operations over the region.[9]

This suggestion raised an issue of whether such a CAOC, if established, should be an expansion of the 5 ATAF command and control center at Vicenza or a new and separate creation. Responding to a NATO request to look into the issue, Gen Robert

C. Oaks, commander of United States Air Forces Europe (USAFE), dispatched Maj Gen James E. "Bear" Chambers, his Seventeenth Air Force commander, to visit and assess 5 ATAF's suitability for taking on the expanded responsibilities of the anticipated operation. An experienced air commander who knew airpower as well as the region and who was already running USAFE's part of the Provide Promise humanitarian airlift into Sarajevo, Chambers was a logical choice for the task. By December, planning to increase AIRSOUTH's ability to impose a no-fly enforcement regime over Bosnia was proceeding along several tracks.

General Ashy received command of AIRSOUTH at just that time. Literally on the day that he took over, Ashy sat down with Admiral Boorda and did "some serious planning for an air operation in the Balkans . . . to police a no-fly zone."[10] One of his first concerns was to settle the CAOC organizational issue. Holding General Chambers in high regard and wanting to utilize his familiarity with operations at Vicenza, Ashy elected to set up a stand-alone CAOC under Chambers's direction.[11] On paper this CAOC was to be a subordinate extension of the existing 5 ATAF command center, but in practice General Chambers would report directly to AIRSOUTH. Ashy chose this arrangement over expanding the 5 ATAF facility because he believed it would give him tighter control over what he anticipated was going to be a fast-paced and politically hypersensitive situation. Ashy also considered either bringing the CAOC down to Naples or moving his own headquarters up to Vicenza, to place both the planning and execution staff functions of the forthcoming operation in one place. After some thought he decided to accept the physical division of his staff in order to preserve other advantages. Leaving the CAOC in Vicenza had the advantage of preserving at least the form of the existing NATO command structure by keeping the Italian commander of 5 ATAF in the formal chain of command. Keeping his own planning headquarters in Naples would facilitate the daily, face-to-face contact with Admiral Boorda that Ashy felt he needed to do his job.[12]

The next order of business was to enhance the staff, planning, and communications capabilities of AIRSOUTH and the CAOC to match the likely demands of Deny Flight. Finding the

CAOC operating with "ancient" equipment, Ashy and his staff pressed to bring up-to-date communications and intelligence data terminals into the CAOC and to connect the center to AIRSOUTH and to the NATO field units and squadrons that had begun deploying to bases around Italy. As part of this process, the CAOC received analysts and terminals for NATO's Linked Operations-Intelligence Centers Europe system. AIRSOUTH's intelligence capabilities were strengthened further by the transfer of intelligence personnel from Headquarters Sixteenth Air Force at Aviano AB, Italy, to Naples.[13] Recognizing that the permanently authorized strengths of the AIRSOUTH and CAOC staffs were still too small for the task at hand, Ashy also began to augment them on a rotating basis with personnel coming in on 30-to-90-day assignments. These temporary-duty (TDY) personnel soon comprised the overwhelming majority of the CAOC staff and a significant portion of the AIRSOUTH force.

Meanwhile, AIRSOUTH planners began to lay the documentary foundations for Deny Flight and possible combat operations. The focus of their work was CINCSOUTH Operations Plan (OPLAN) 40101, "Deny Flight," the overall guide for NATO air operations in support of UN peace operations in Bosnia. Much of this document and its iterations remains classified and, consequently, outside the scope of this chapter (see Colonel Campbell's chapter on the air campaign plan for more information). But it is appropriate to say here that OPLAN 40101 started out as a skeletal document laying out rules of engagement (ROE) and the CINC's concept of operations, and then evolved into a more thorough document that laid out the situation appraisals, strategy choices, coordination procedures, logistics issues, ROE, and so on that CINCAFSOUTH believed were pertinent to the new, complex operation before his command. Since Deny Flight was primarily an air operation, a few members of the AIRSOUTH staff or other parts of AFSOUTH did most of the work on 40101, with the close involvement of General Ashy and his subordinates.[14]

The first two versions of OPLAN 40101 came out in rapid succession, reflecting the quick expansion of the Deny Flight mission in the first half of 1993. The first version, approved by NAC on 8 April, mainly described how AIRSOUTH would intercept, inspect, and engage aircraft violating the no-fly mandate.

The second version came out on 13 August with provisions reflecting the UN's and NAC's addition of CAS and OAS to the menu of possible NATO air missions.

The addition of CAS and OAS to the OPLAN necessitated that AIRSOUTH create a target list and get NAC's approval, the latter obtained through an NAC decision statement issued on 8 August, just days before the release of the second iteration of OPLAN 40101. This decision statement spelled out three targeting options for offensive air strikes. Option one provided for CAS strikes of limited duration and scope against military forces and weapon systems directly violating UN resolutions or attacking UN peace forces or other personnel. Option-two targets were mechanisms for lifting sieges. Their focus remained on military forces and supporting elements, but their scope expanded to include targets throughout the immediate environs of a besieged safe area. Option-three targets marked out a broader campaign against targets outside the immediate area of a siege.[15] Over the coming months, AF-SOUTH produced many variations of its target lists, but the essential categorization of these targets into three options remained a predominant, perhaps universal, theme in all of them.

By the time all these organizational and planning events had taken place, the inherent tension between the UN's peacekeeping focus and the peace-enforcement character of Deny Flight was affecting operations profoundly. The establishment and, more to the point, the interpretation of ROE for the operation provided an early indication of that tension. In his chapter on ROE, Lt Col Ron Reed explains that these rules are a natural bellwether of problems in a military operation. Their function is to link objectives, strategy, operations, and international law to establish the methods and limits of force usable in a conflict. To be viable, coalition ROE must reflect the views of all members and the realities of the situation. If either of those conditions is not met, then disputes will quickly rise over and around them. In the case of Bosnia, NATO officially endorsed the UN's strategic vision. So in the absence of overt conflict, General Ashy and his staff worked out and got UN and NAC approval for an initial set of ROE by February 1993.[16] The real tension came from what proved to be the UN's greater reluctance, at least compared to the inclination of involved air

471

commanders, actually to act on ROE. "NATO," Colonel Reed concludes in his study, "always viewed the use of force in terms of compelling the Bosnian Serbs. . . . But the UN viewed force in the much more limited context of self-defense." Indeed, despite many opportunities to do so, the UN did not release a CAS attack in defense of peacekeeping forces on the ground until 12 March 1994.[17]

The fact that UN political leaders exercised such close control of air operations was another manifestation of the internal peacekeeper/peace-enforcer posture of the intervention. In June 1993 NATO and the UN adopted a so-called dual-key procedure for releasing CAS and OAS strikes. Drawing metaphorically on the procedural requirement for two individuals to "turn keys" to release or launch nuclear weapons, the arrangement required appropriate officials in both the UN and NATO to turn their keys before any NATO aircraft could release weapons against an air or ground target. For NATO any military commander, from the CAOC director up, could authorize CAS strikes in response to a UN request. CINCAFSOUTH retained release authority for offensive air strikes. For the UN the decision thresholds were raised one organizational level. Secretary-General Boutros Boutros-Ghali authorized his special representative, Ambassador Yasushi Akashi, to release CAS strikes, while retaining for himself the authority to release offensive air strikes.[18] Thus the dual-key arrangement was an overt effort to counterbalance UN and NATO control over air operations. As such, it indicated at least a corporate presumption among the member states of each organization that some possibility of misunderstanding or irresponsibility existed in the way one organization or the other might interpret the standing ROE and the immediate circumstances of a proposed strike.

A question arises here: If the corporate membership of both organizations feared the possibility of an irresponsible or ill-advised use of airpower, who did they think would do it? To a large extent, the evidence available to the BACS suggests that the main concern centered around the "Americanization" of the intervention's air option. Since the summer of 1993, and with greater fervor after the following winter, US political leaders were the most outspoken advocates of the punitive use of airpower in the Balkans. From the beginning of Deny Flight,

NATO airpower in the Balkans was under the control of American flag officers, albeit ones serving as NATO commanders. Moreover, most of the alliance's offensive air strength resided in a powerful American composite wing based at Aviano AB in northeastern Italy. Several European states, particularly those with lightly armed peacekeeping forces committed on the ground, had fears (ill grounded or not) that these circumstances could lead to a unilateral, American use of the air weapon in a manner that might escalate the level of violence in the region or the intervention's role in it. Thus, according to Ambassador Hunter, several members of NAC proposed the dual-key procedure to both NATO and the UN in an effort to set up an arrangement that most people believed would preclude any offensive air action.[19] US ambassador Richard Holbrooke shared Hunter's assessment.[20] Part of the dual-key arrangement was about controlling a powerful and politically sensitive "weapon" in the coalition's arsenal, and part of it was about controlling the holders of that weapon.

If ROE and the dual-key arrangement reflected the tension between and within the UN and NATO over the proper strategy of intervention in Bosnia, they also helped to increase those tensions on many occasions. This particularly was the case whenever the two organizations actually prepared to use airpower against the Bosnian Serbs. In the press of events, NATO air commanders and American diplomats generally found themselves pushing for aggressive and strong air strikes while most other intervention partners and leaders of the UN called for caution and restraint.

The air strike against Udbina Airfield on 21 November 1994 highlighted this tension. NATO and the UN ordered the strike to punish recent violations of the no-fly ban by Bosnian Serb and Krajina Serb aircraft, some of which were based at the airfield in the Serb-controlled Krajina region of Croatia. General Ryan, who had taken over AIRSOUTH only weeks before, anticipated an active defense of the field and requested a comprehensive "takedown" of it, to include strikes against the offending aircraft themselves, the runway and taxiways, and the air defense systems and weapons in the area. Echoing his air commander's approach, Admiral Smith said the proper goal of the attack was "to make a parking lot out of Udbina

Airfield."[21] Intending to show restraint and to limit Serb casualties, however, Secretary-General Boutros-Ghali approved attacks only against Udbina's runway and taxiways—not against aircraft and local air defense systems, which presumably would be manned during the attack. Among other considerations, the secretary-general hoped to avoid provoking the Bosnian Serbs into taking UN hostages, as they had done once already in retaliation for a NATO CAS strike near Gorazde the previous April. Viewing the UN's restrictions as rendering the proposed air strikes largely ineffective and increasing the risks to their aircrews, Smith and Ryan pressured the secretary-general and Ambassador Akashi to put aircraft and defense systems back on the target list. The UN leaders finally agreed to preapprove attacks against defense systems of immediate threat to NATO aircraft only. They continued to bar attacks against Serb aircraft.[22] NATO jets struck several antiaircraft artillery sites and a surface-to-air site in the immediate vicinity of the airfield, but otherwise they struck only the runways.[23] It was a less-than-convincing demonstration of NATO airpower or resolve—one that left American air commanders and some diplomats very frustrated.[24]

The gulf between the views of NATO air commanders and the UN on the proper use and aggressiveness of airpower continued to widen after Udbina. The UN's reluctance to employ the weapon came out clearly after the attack, when Ambassador Akashi pointedly drew a line between the UN and the peace-enforcement action just performed by NATO jets. He wrote to Karadzic that NATO aircraft remained under UN control but would act only in defense of UNSCRs and UNPROFOR. Despite the implications of the air attacks on the Serbs, he reported that NATO aircraft were "neither the enemy nor the ally of any combatant."[25] NATO commanders increasingly became frustrated with the UN's long decision process in relation to releasing air strikes. This frustration reached a peak in the summer of 1995, Admiral Smith recalled, when UN peacekeepers "protecting" the city of Srebrenica called desperately for CAS. NATO jets were ready for attack within minutes, but the UN refused to turn its key for two days, by which time the fall of the city to the Serbs was assured.[26] Reflecting the views of many American leaders involved in Bosnia, Ambassador

Holbrooke declared the dual-key arrangement an "unmitigated disaster" that placed the UN and NATO in a stressful and improper relationship of overlapping responsibility and friction.[27]

The political sensitivity of the airpower issue also influenced Deny Flight planning activities. Throughout the operation Generals Ashy and Ryan took pains to ensure that their planning efforts and operations did not undermine the confidence of NATO and UN political leaders in the professionalism and self-control of their command. To that end, all iterations of OPLAN 40101, ending with change four in May 1995, carefully tied anticipated AIRSOUTH operations to the protection of UN forces and the enforcement of specific UNSCRs, whether they were air-to-air, SEAD, CAS, or OAS missions. The OPLAN also admonished NATO airmen to ensure that their strikes, when authorized at all, were "proportional" (i.e., that they avoided unnecessary casualties and collateral damage).[28] Also, the three target options listed in AIRSOUTH attack plans offered reassurance that NATO forces were a flexible instrument and tightly under control. According to Ambassador Hunter, the implicit reassurances of these provisions were essential underpinnings of his efforts to garner and maintain support among NAC members for more robust air operations.[29]

From the inception of Deny Flight, Generals Ashy and Ryan had asked NATO to send non-US colonels and general officers on a permanent basis to fill key command and staff billets at AIRSOUTH and the CAOC. Despite their continued requests, on the eve of Deliberate Force, all major staff positions at the CAOC and most at AIRSOUTH were filled by US Air Force colonels.[30] Most of their subordinates at the CAOC were American junior officers and sergeants. This was an anomalous situation in the NATO command structure, in which commanders and their deputies usually are of different nationalities, as are commanders at succeeding levels of organization. The essentially American manning of the CAOC and the air command structure may have been as much a product of the unease some NAC member states felt about the air weapon as it was a cause of that unease. Several BACS researchers heard secondary reports that the situation at the CAOC grated the non-US officers there, but the team's letters asking such individuals directly about their perceptions and attitudes were not answered. Significantly, however, Ambassador Hunter never heard complaints voiced by the national representatives on the NAC, where such complaints would have necessitated corrective action. In his opinion the willingness of NATO political leaders to accept the arrangement may well have reflected both their unwillingness to have their nationals too closely associated with what might become a politically explosive employment of airpower and their recognition that US Air Force personnel were best trained and equipped to handle the anticipated air operations.[31] The BACS team found no documentary support for Hunter's perception, but most senior air commanders shared it, according to the interviews. Further, one cannot escape the fact that other NATO states did not send officers to fill key command positions.

NATO's ambivalence about the potential use of combat airpower in Bosnia also seems to have undermined whatever willingness UN leaders had to allow NATO to use air more freely in defense of their resolutions. As in the case of the use of any military force, a halfhearted or incomplete air operation would be indecisive, politically and diplomatically vulnerable to global criticism, susceptible to breaking up what support existed in the UN and NATO for continued intervention, and, as a consequence of all other effects, more likely to stir up the Bosnian hornet's nest than calm it. Thus, Ambassador Hunter reported, a large measure of Secretary-General Boutros-Ghali's unwillingness to authorize CAS operations in defense of UN troops, let alone to consider a robust OAS campaign against Serb targets throughout the area, was due to his belief—through the spring of 1995—that NATO did not have the political cohesion or commitment to carry such operations to a successful conclusion. The secretary-general made it clear to Hunter that he would never approve such operations unless he was convinced the UN would stick them out for their full course. Most of Hunter's diplomatic efforts in NAC during 1994 and 1995, therefore, focused on building such cohesion and commitment among the other member governments. Until enough or all of them decided to back a robust air operation, he did not expect the UN to release NATO jets to pound the Bosnian Serbs.[32]

Consensus support for offensive air strikes to protect the safe areas began to build among NATO member states in the spring and early summer of 1995, as a result of several considerations and events. In general, three years of brazen Serbian defiance of UN resolutions and the laws of war probably had worn the patience of most of the governments intervening in Bosnia and had infused the intervention with a sense of desperation. By mid-May 1995 the international press reported that, as a result of the seemingly unstoppable fighting, "the nearly 40,000 UN peacekeepers in the region are descending into a state of ever more irrelevance and danger," that Ambassador Akashi had "become a comic figure," and that there was a "willingness to declare the Contact Group [see below] dead."[33] To punish the Bosnian Serbs for violating the Sarajevo safe area, NATO jets struck Serb ammunition depots around the city of Pale on 24 May 1995. The Serbs responded by taking 370 UN peacekeepers hostage and chaining some of them to potential targets, thereby paralyzing the intervention. This humiliation, as it played out, led Secretary of Defense William Perry to declare that "the credibility of the international community was at stake."[34] It also moved most interventionist governments nearer to the standing US position that only a robust air campaign would force the Serbs to obey UN resolutions.

Support for forceful action grew through June and into mid-July in the face of continued Serb attacks on the safe areas of Zepa, Gorazde, and Srebrenica, and with the shootdown of a US F-16 by the Bosnian Serbs.[35] Finally, after the UN rejected an AFSOUTH request of 20 June for air strikes to punish Serb violations of the no-fly edict, after Srebrenica fell to brutal assault on 11 July, and with Zepa apparently next on the list for Serbian conquest, the foreign ministers of 16 intervening states met at London during 21–25 July, largely at the prodding of Secretary of State Warren Christopher. The purpose of the meeting was to prepare the way for and lay out the form of a more forceful intervention in the Bosnian conflict. The weapon of necessity, as every diplomat probably understood at that time, would have to be NATO airpower.

By the time the foreign ministers gathered at London, NATO air planners had amassed a comprehensive set of plans for dealing with specific aspects of the Bosnian conflict, along with a clear idea of how they wanted to apply those plans. All of these plans were subelements of the basic OPLAN 40101, though most had been initiated after General Ryan took over AIRSOUTH in October 1994. Standing out among these plans was Operation Deadeye, the SEAD plan initiated by General Ryan following the strikes on Udbina Airfield. Deadeye's purpose was to protect NATO aircraft from Bosnian Serb air defenses as they flew in protection of the safe areas or on other missions. A salient feature of the operation, one that set it apart from the geographic restrictions placed on CAS and OAS strikes, was its provision for comprehensive attacks against integrated air defense system (IADS) targets throughout Bosnia, if necessary. In early 1995, as the plan evolved in detail, it incorporated a division of Bosnia into southeast and northwest zones of action (ZOA), based on the Sarajevo and Banja Luka areas, respectively. As described by Col Daniel R. Zoerb, director of the AIRSOUTH Deny Flight operations cell, Maj Keith Kiger of his staff proposed these ZOAs "to facilitate deconfliction of planned simultaneous fighter attacks on the IADS," but they did not imply any restrictions on the overall freedom of NATO airmen to attack elements of the IADS throughout Bosnia to defend themselves. If his aircraft flew in defense of a city in either ZOA, General Ryan expected to launch attacks against air defenses throughout the embattled country.[36]

On an ongoing basis, AIRSOUTH planners also created plans to protect specific safe areas and updated them as necessary. Following the Pale bombings at the end of May 1995, General Ryan's planners developed a briefing called "NATO Air Operations in Bosnia-Herzegovina," which mainly listed and described the various attack options available—but not Deadeye. During July and early August, this briefing expanded to include a concept of operations suggesting that ground-attack plans to defend Bosnian cities also be based on the ZOA boundaries laid out for Deadeye. Under existing arrangements, NATO aircraft striking in defense of a safe area were limited to hitting targets within the 20- or 30-kilometer exclusion zone around it. AFSOUTH planners called for the freedom to strike a broader array of targets throughout the ZOA that included the besieged city. Thus by the time the London conference convened, NATO air planners in AFSOUTH were thinking in terms of broad-ranging ground attacks supported by a theaterwide SEAD campaign in defense of Bosnian cities, rather than the halting and piecemeal applications that had characterized the use of airpower to that point.

From the American perspective, London began as an effort to issue a powerful threat of air strikes against the Serbs for what Secretary Christopher called their "outrageous aggression."[37] At the end of the conference's first day, Christopher asserted that the ministers had agreed that "an attack against Gorazde will be met by decisive and substantial air power."[38] Moreover he announced that "existing command-and-control arrangements for the use of NATO air power will be adjusted to ensure that responsiveness and unity are achieved." By this he meant that the United States expected the UN's role in tactical decision making to diminish, perhaps by ending the dual-key procedure.[39] Last, Christopher asserted that the gathered ministers agreed that "the taking of hostages will no longer be allowed to prevent implementation of our policies." All this, he stated, reflected a general belief that "so long as the Bosnian Serb aggression continues, any political process [for peace] is doomed to failure."[40] In sum, Christopher was forecasting an intervention strategy in which airpower would force the Serbs to halt their attacks on Bosnian cities, thereby opening the way to productive peace negotiations.

In contrast to Secretary Christopher's confident predictions, however, other events at the London conference indicated that the gathered ministers were not all fully behind the American proposal to unleash a determined air assault on the Bosnian Serbs. British foreign secretary Malcolm Rifkind announced that "although there was strong support for airpower, there were also reservations . . . [and] it would be used only if it was felt necessary."[41] In a similar vein of caution, the French delegation reconfirmed a demand that ground reinforcements precede any bombing operations, particularly regarding the endangered city of Gorazde.[42] As a consequence of these reservations, the conference's declaration actually extended the threat of air strikes only in protection of Gorazde, a limitation that prompted the Bosnian prime minister, Haris Silajdzic, to declare it a "green light" to attacks everywhere else. Publically at least, Bosnian Serb leaders also were not intimidated by the London conference's threats, as evidenced by the Bosnian Serb army's (BSA) continued attacks on UN-protected cities.[43]

Meanwhile at NATO headquarters, Ambassador Hunter, Secretary-General Willy Claes, and other leaders were orchestrating events in NAC to give some credence to the London conference's threat of decisive air action. Following an NAC meeting on 25 July, the day the conference ended, Claes announced that NAC had approved "the necessary planning to ensure that NATO air power would be used in a timely and effective way should the Bosnian Serbs threaten or attack Gorazde." The secretary-general also indicated that planning would begin to protect the other safe areas, and he warned that "such operations, once they are launched will not lightly be discontinued."[44] Not included in Secretary-General Claes's press release were the operational details settled by NAC. These included adoption of the so-called trigger events that would start the bombing. NAC also approved AFSOUTH's plan to defend each Bosnian city by striking Serb targets throughout the ZOA that included the city.[45] Finally, NATO sent three air commanders to Bosnia to convince the Bosnian Serb military commander, Gen Ratko Mladic, of the alliance's determination to carry out its threats.[46]

All of these events were welcome news for General Ryan and Admiral Smith. They were particularly pleased by NAC's clearance to strike throughout a given ZOA in defense of a city within it. Had they been held to hitting only targets in the military exclusion zones surrounding the safe areas, they believed that their sorties would be expended against hard-to-find-and-attack tactical targets, such as artillery pieces and armored vehicles. The two commanders anticipated that air attacks against those kinds of "direct" targets would be slow to inflict enough "pain" on the Serbs to force them to comply with UN demands. Consequently they welcomed the opportunity to plan against a wider range of "indirect" targets, such as bridges, command facilities, supply dumps, and so on, that they also knew would be easier to find and destroy. Moreover, Ryan and Smith anticipated that, sortie-per-sortie, such a campaign would inflict more coercive pain on the Serbs and at less cost in blood and time than one focused on direct targets.[47] Ryan and Smith believed that blood and time would be their greatest concern because they anticipated that public support for the campaign would quickly dwindle, particularly if NATO bombs began to kill civilians—or even Bosnian Serb soldiers.[48]

In addition to broadening AFSOUTH's planning leeway, NAC's actions on 25 July also opened the way for UN leaders to drop their resistance to a heavy campaign of offensive air strikes. As public and strong statements of intent to punish Serb attacks on the safe areas, NAC's decisions went a long way toward showing the UN secretary-general that most, if not all, NATO member states had found the commitment and domestic political stamina to initiate and stay with an air campaign long enough to have an effect on Serbian actions and policy. In response, the secretary-general on that same day transferred the UN keys for approving offensive air strikes and CAS from his hands and those of Ambassador Akashi, respectively, to those of Gen Bernard Janvier, force commander of United Nations Peace Forces (UNPF, previously known as UN-PROFOR).[49] The power to launch strikes against the Serbs now lay in the hands of military commanders on the scene.

As Colonel Campbell describes in his chapter, General Ryan responded to these rapid shifts in the political and diplomatic environment of the intervention by accelerating the ongoing air-planning effort. His staff continued to refine individual safe-area plans and Deadeye. Exploiting the freedom to plan attacks across a ZOA, AIRSOUTH staffers also produced a plan called Vulcan, which postulated wide-ranging strikes in the southeastern ZOA to protect Sarajevo. Another new briefing titled "Graduated Air Operations" proposed a stepwise escalation of attacks across a ZOA to force the Serbs to back away from one or more safe areas. By 3 August these planning actions had reached a point that Admiral Smith and General Ryan could brief Secretary-General Claes and Gen George Joulwan, SACEUR, on how they intended to apply offensive air strikes in the Balkans. With the endorsements of these leaders in hand, Admiral Smith signed a memorandum on 10 August with General Janvier and British lieutenant general Rupert Smith, his deputy in Sarajevo, that clarified the "over arching purpose," "phasing," "assumptions," and so on to guide the looming air campaign.[50] At the same time, AIRSOUTH worked out further air-ground coordination arrangements and target lists with UN ground commanders and with British major general

David Pennyfather, chief of staff of the NATO Rapid Reaction Force (RRF), which had been deploying into Sarajevo for several weeks.[51] By the third week of August, then, at least General Ryan had the plans in place to fight on behalf of the UN.

As the summer passed, General Ryan took advantage of the relaxed diplomatic restraints on planning large-scale offensive operations by expanding the CAOC's manning and equipment as quickly as possible. Guided and underpinned, in part, by the recommendations of a Pentagon study team that assessed the CAOC's readiness for expanded air operations in late July, Ryan drew heavily on US manpower and equipment to expand the CAOC's capabilities.[52] Several hundred TDY augmentees began flowing in from US bases everywhere, along with a flood of state-of-the-art communications, intelligence, and automated planning systems. Perhaps most importantly, elements of a US Air Force Contingency Theater Air Planning System (CTAPS) began to arrive, which, when fully assembled and operating, would vastly enhance the CAOC's ability to plan, monitor, and control high-intensity air operations in near real time.

Taken together, these actions pretty much completed the effective "Americanization" of the CAOC, but that was a price Ryan and Lt Gen Hal Hornburg, director of the CAOC, felt ready to pay in the rush to get ready. For months, politics had restrained their ability to prepare for an enlarged air war, and now politics had suddenly presented them with the likelihood of just such a war—much faster than they could adjust their forces to accommodate.[53] Nevertheless, despite the fact that the vast majority of their CAOC personnel had been in Italy for less than a few weeks or even days, and despite the piles of unopened CTAPS equipment boxes lying around, Admiral Smith, General Ryan, General Hornburg, and Brig Gen David Sawyer—deputy director of the CAOC and deputy commander of 5 ATAF—were ready for a fight by the third week of August—about a week before they found themselves in the middle of one.

Operations

Given the protracted political and military run up to it, the actual start of Deliberate Force was almost anticlimactic. The specific trigger event for the campaign was the explosion of a mortar bomb in Sarajevo's Mrkale marketplace that killed 37 people on the morning of 28 August 1995. In the normal course of events for the unfortunate city, a mortar explosion was unremarkable, but this one caused exceptional and immediately televised bloodshed. Its timing made an interventionist response virtually certain. Since General Janvier was in Paris, Admiral Smith contacted General Smith, Janvier's deputy in Sarajevo, as soon as he heard the news. The two commanders agreed that, while UN investigators worked to assign certain blame for the attack, Admiral Smith would begin preparing for bombing operations, if required. At 0200 on the 29th, General Smith called Admiral Smith to report that he was now certain that Bosnian Serb forces had fired the shell and that he was turning his key. The UN general, however, asked Admiral Smith to delay launching attacks for 24 hours to give peacekeeping units in Bosnia time to pull into positions they could defend, should the Serbs launch retaliatory attacks against them. Also, General Janvier had to approve the final list of targets for the initial strikes. After a number of conversations with Admiral Smith during the day, Janvier finally did approve 10 of 13 initial targets proposed by Generals Ryan and Smith and already tentatively approved by Admiral Smith.[54]

Meanwhile, General Ryan and his staff at the CAOC worked feverishly to ready the assigned NATO air forces for battle. In fact, Ryan had come to the CAOC on the morning of the 29th to lead a preplanned exercise—the Vulcan protection plan for Sarajevo. With an actual crisis at hand, the general canceled Vulcan and focused his staff on activating and modifying as necessary the operational plans and unit reinforcements that comprised what amounted to the Deliberate Force plan. While waiting for orders to start operations and approval of the initial target list by General Janvier and Admiral Smith, the AIRSOUTH commander concentrated on alerting his units, refining the air tasking message that would guide their operations for the first day of bombing, and bringing additional air and support forces into the theater as required. The delay in starting operations proved useful, in that it provided time to flow additional US Air Force, Navy, and Marine aircraft into

Aviano and to swing the carrier *Theodore Roosevelt* into the Adriatic in time to launch aircraft for the first strikes. Ryan also reaffirmed to his staff that he intended to ensure that the weapons and tactics utilized by NATO would be selected and flown to accomplish the required levels of destruction at minimum risk of unplanned or collateral damage to military and civilian people and property. Ryan and Admiral Smith fully agreed that the diplomatic sensitivities of the campaign made collateral damage an issue of pivotal strategic importance. Ryan believed that a stray bomb causing civilian casualties would take the interventionists off the moral high ground, marshal world opinion against the air campaign, and probably bring it to a halt before it had its intended effects.[55]

Ryan's command was ready for operations by the end of the 29th. After waiting out the 24-hour delay to allow UN peacekeepers time to hunker down in their defensive positions, the first NATO jets went "feet dry" over the Bosnian coast at 0140 on the 30th, laden with bombs to make the first strike.

The physical and temporal dimensions of the ensuing campaign were fairly compact, particularly when compared to the scale and scope of a major air campaign, such as Operation Desert Storm during the Gulf War of 1990–91. Compared to the vast reaches of Southwest Asia, NATO air attacks in Deliberate Force occurred in a triangular area only about 150 nautical miles wide on its northern base and stretching about 150 miles to the south. The weight of the NATO attack also was relatively limited. Desert Storm lasted 43 days, but during the 22 calendar days of Deliberate Force, NATO aircraft and a single US Navy ship firing a volley of Tomahawk land attack missiles (TLAM) actually released weapons against the Serbs on just 12 days. Two days into the campaign, NATO military commanders halted offensive air operations against the Serbs for four days to encourage negotiations. When useful negotiations failed to materialize, they resumed bombing on the morning of 5 September and continued through 13 September. When notified by General Smith on 14 September that General Mladic and President Karadzic of the Serb Republic had accepted the UN's terms, CINCSOUTH and General Janvier jointly suspended offensive operations at 2200. They declared the campaign closed on 20 September.

The total air forces involved included about 220 fighter aircraft and 70 support aircraft from three US services, Great Britain, Italy, Germany, Holland, Greece, Turkey, Spain, and France—all directly assigned to AIRSOUTH and based mainly in Italy—and a steady stream of airlift aircraft bringing forward units and supplies. On days when strikes were flown, AIRSOUTH-assigned forces launched an average of four or five air-to-ground "packages" involving perhaps 60 or 70 bomb-dropping sorties and another one hundred to 150 other sorties to provide combat air patrol, defense suppression, tanker, reconnaissance, and surveillance support to the "shooters." In total, Deliberate Force included 3,535 aircraft sorties, of which 2,470 went feet dry over the Balkans region to deliver 1,026 weapons against 48 targets, including 338 individual desired mean points of impact (DMPI).[56] These figures equated to just about a busy day's sortie count for coalition air forces during the Gulf War—and only a tiny fraction of the 227,340 weapons those air forces released against the Iraqis in the 43 days of Desert Storm.

For all of the brevity, limited scale, and operational one-sidedness of Deliberate Force, the various researchers of the BACS all discovered that the execution phase of the operation offered many insights into the application and usefulness of airpower in a complex regional conflict. This summary includes only those discoveries that seem to have the broadest importance to the general community of airpower thinkers. Some of these discoveries stem from the operational context of the conflict—others from the continued, even increased, political and diplomatic complexity of Deliberate Force in its execution phase.

From the inception of its study, the BACS team anticipated that leadership would be a broadly interesting area of inquiry. Reports from the field and subsequent interviews highlighted the exceptionally close control exercised by General Ryan over Deliberate Force's tactical events. Reflecting his and Admiral Smith's conviction that "every bomb was a political bomb," General Ryan personally oversaw the selection of every DMPI in every target. He also personally scrutinized every selection or "weaponeering" decision made for the actual weapons to be used against DMPIs, and he examined or directed many tactical decisions about such things as the strikes' launch times, the specific composition of attack formations, and the selection of bomb-run routes. In his words, Ryan felt obliged to exercise such close control to minimize the risk of error and, if mistakes were made, to ensure that they would be attributable to him—and him alone.[57] That is, Ryan consciously chose this approach to leadership, which he considered appropriate to the circumstances as he saw them.

Placing General Ryan's acute attention to tactical details in a broader historical context, Lt Col Chris Orndorff points out in his chapter that Ryan's actions had much in common with the great captaincy of field commanders in the period up to and including the Napoleonic era. Great captains and great captaincy, Ordorff explains, were epitomized by Napoléon—the master practitioner of an art of command characterized by close attention to the logistical and tactical details of armies, as well as the master of strategic guidance. Great captains practiced this broad range of intervention because it was vital to their success and because they had the means to do so. Because armies were small, individual tactical events assumed great importance, and contemporary communications allowed a single commander to monitor and control such details in a timely manner.

But as the industrial revolution progressed through the nineteenth century, the size of armies and the scope of their operations vastly increased. Great captaincy, at least to the extent that it involved close oversight of logistical and tactical details, became impractical in wars between large industrial states. In response, the Prussians led the world in developing a military system based on centralized strategic command, generalized planning by trained staff officers, and decentralized execution of operations and logistical support by standardized units in accordance with the guidance of the first two groups. Among the many features of this system was a division of labor that had senior commanders thinking strategically and eschewing close management of tactical details. These cultural arrangements, coupled with a sophisticated approach to military training and education, were, in the summation of one historian, an effort by the Prussians to institutionalize a system whereby ordinary men could replicate the military genius of a great captain, such as Napoléon, on a sustained basis and on an industrial scale.[58] Given that perspective, Orndorff suggests that General Ryan's close supervision of Deliberate Force's tactical details merits close examination of the conditions that made it apparently successful in an age when the staff system seems to have otherwise supplanted great captaincy in war.

In net, Colonel Orndorff's conclusions echo the opinion of everyone interviewed for the BACS that General Ryan's exceptional involvement in the tactical details of Deliberate Force reflected both his prerogatives as commander and an appropriate response to the political and military circumstances of the operation. Such was the case, Orndorff believes, because the circumstances of Deliberate Force conformed in important ways to circumstances that gave rise to preindustrial command practices. Tactical events, namely the destruction of specific targets and the possibility of suffering NATO casualties, potentially carried profound strategic implications. The NATO air forces involved were small in relation to the capacities of the command, control, communications, and intelligence systems available to find targets, monitor and direct forces, and maintain command linkages. Drawing on the analogy of an earlier commander standing on a hill, Orndorff suggests that General Ryan had the sensory and cognitive capability to embrace the air battle comprehensively, assess the tactical and strategic flow of events, and direct all of his forces in a timely manner. In the words of one senior US Air Force leader, therefore, General Ryan not only could exercise close tactical control over his forces but also was obliged to do so.[59]

Colonel Orndorff and other members of the team did identify some potential drawbacks of General Ryan's great captaincy. Most notably it focused a tremendous amount of work on the general and a few members of his staff. Individuals working closely to Ryan in the CAOC, such as Colonel Zoerb, AIRSOUTH director of plans; Steven R. Teske, CAOC director of plans; and Col Douglas J. Richardson, CAOC director of operations, worked 18-hour days throughout the campaign.[60] By their own accounts, after two weeks they were very tired. At the same time, other members of the CAOC staff were underutilized, as the small group of officers working around

487

Ryan absorbed some of their corporate tactical responsibilities, at least in their culminating steps.

Meanwhile some of the higher responsibilities that might have fallen on Ryan in his capacity as the senior operational commander devolved on Maj Gen Michael Short, his chief of staff in Naples. Acting as the rear-echelon commander of AIRSOUTH, General Short became responsible for, among many things, aspects of the public affairs, logistical, political, and military coordination functions of Deliberate Force. In retrospect, although he believed that this division of labor made good sense under the circumstances, General Short felt that he and General Ryan had not fully anticipated all of the staff and communications requirements needed to keep Ryan up-to-date on operations and other issues. As a consequence, General Short sometimes found it difficult to prepare timely answers to higher-level inquiries about operations or General Ryan's plans.[61] Together with the effect of General Ryan's centralized leadership style on the CAOC's division of labor, General Short's experience indicates a need for airmen to anticipate that leadership style is an important choice—one that can shape staff processes and morale significantly.

Lt Col Mark Conversino's chapter on Deliberate Force operations focuses primarily on the activities of the 31st Fighter Wing at Aviano AB.[62] In net, his research reveals that the wing's great success in the campaign reflected the professionalism and skills of its personnel, ranging from its commander to individual junior technicians working on the flight line. From July 1995 the 31st Wing formed the core of the 7490th Wing (Provisional), an organization established to embrace the numerous US Air Force fighter and support squadrons and US Navy and Marine air units brought to Aviano for Deny Flight. These units made Aviano a busy place.

At its peak strength, the 7490th Wing included about one hundred aircraft, all crowded onto a base with only one runway and designed normally to handle a wing of about 75 fighters. The crowded conditions of the base made the choreography of maintaining, servicing, and moving aircraft about the field so tight and difficult that many of the people working there began calling it the "USS *Aviano*," alluding to the conditions normally prevailing on the deck of an aircraft carrier.

Moreover, Col Charles F. Wald, commander of the 7490th, and his staff were responsible for tactical coordination with other NATO squadrons scattered around Italy. Time pressures and limited communications channels made this task daunting. Had the 31st Wing's permanently and temporarily assigned personnel not performed at such a high level across the board, Deliberate Force in reasonable probability would have fallen flat on its face.

At the same time, Colonel Conversino's chapter identifies several sources of psychological stress at Aviano that, over a more protracted campaign, might have undermined the provisional wing's high performance and morale. The presence of families was one potential source of stress. Because Aviano was the 31st Wing's permanent base, the families of many of the wing's personnel lived in the vicinity. During Deliberate Force, these families could be both a source of emotional strength for combat aircrews and a potential source of worry and distraction. On the one hand, spouses brought meals and moral support to the units. On the other hand, they and their children were *there*, complete with their school problems, broken cars, anxieties, and so on. Although morale generally stayed high at Aviano, one must realize that the campaign lasted only two weeks and that the wing took no casualties. Many of the individuals and some commanders interviewed by Conversino and other BACS members expressed concern at what would have happened to the emotional tenor of the base community and to the concentration of the combat aircrewmen had the campaign gone on longer, with casualties or with the materialization of terrorist threats against families. During operations, one squadron commander even considered evacuating dependents if Deliberate Force dragged on.[63]

Another source of stress stemmed from the unfamiliar nature of the Deliberate Force mission. Actually, at the level of tactical operations, the operational tempo, tactics, and threats of the campaign were much like those that 31st Wing airmen would have expected to face in a high-intensity conflict. Daily flights as elements of "gorillas" of attack, defense suppression, electronic warfare, escort, and tanker aircraft—potentially in the face of radar-directed antiaircraft defenses—look pretty much the same tactically, regardless of the "limited" or "conventional" nature of a conflict at the operational and strategic levels. But these conflicts do differ at the operational and strategic levels, and therein lay a source of confusion and tension between the field units and the CAOC.

Airmen in the field found themselves fighting a tactically conventional campaign at potentially substantial risk from enemy action. The CAOC made plans and issued orders that reflected the operational- and strategic-level constraints and restraints inherent in the air campaign's identity as the military arm of a limited peace operation. The difference between these perspectives was manifested in the confusion and frustration felt by some interviewed airmen over such things as ROE, outside "interference" with their detailed tactical plans and decisions, apparent restrictions on the flow of intelligence information to the field, and so on. Since these things came to the field via the CAOC, a number of the BACS interviewees expressed a sense that they were fighting one war and that the CAOC was fighting another one, with the CAOC's version of the war tending to put the flyers at greater and unnecessary risk.[64]

Colonel Conversino also identifies several logistical problems that might have undermined the power of the air campaign had it gone on longer. Under the US Air Force's "lean logistics" concept, air bases normally do not have large stocks of supplies and spare parts on hand. The concept assumes that modern logistics techniques can move supplies and parts from homeland depots quickly enough to meet demands and thereby reduce the size of the warehouse and maintenance operations a base has to maintain to sustain operations. At Aviano, one manifestation of lean logistics was that the base experienced shortages in several areas of supply as soon as operations began. One of the more critical shortages involved aircraft tow vehicles ("bobtails") and their tires. Compounding the problem, the "war" began on a Wednesday, meaning that stateside depots, which stayed on a peacetime schedule, were closed for the weekend—just as urgent requests for supplies began to flow in from Aviano. Quick calls to supervisors opened up the depots, but some supply problems, such as bobtail tires, remained unsolved during Deliberate Force operations.

Complementing Colonel Conversino's broad review of Deliberate Force operations, Lt Col Rick Sargent's chapters shift the focus of BACS to a more microscopic assessment of the weapons, tactics, and targeting aspects of the air campaign. After a detailed discussion of the types of manned and unmanned aircraft employed during the operation, Sargent describes the precision-guided munitions (PGM) used and their fundamental importance to the conduct and outcome of Deliberate Force. Because NATO air commanders were concerned with getting the fastest possible results from their operations while minimizing collateral damage and casualties, Sargent argues that "precision guided munitions became the overwhelming weapons of choice during air strike operations." Of the 1,026 bombs and missiles expended during Deliberate Force, 708 were PGMs.

Most of Colonel Sargent's detailed discussion of specific weapons and employment tactics remains classified. In general, however, his work demonstrates that PGM employment has become a complex science. Numerous types of PGMs are now available, each with distinct characteristics of target acquisition, range, terminal effects, and cost. Tacticians and weaponeers must know and understand those characteristics to be able to make suitable decisions about employing PGMs within the boundaries of time, targets, and ROE. The criticality of those decisions will only increase for many likely conflicts, for, as Sargent quotes General Ryan, "Dumb bombs are dead." Unguided weapons likely will retain their utility in many circumstances, but in cases in which time and tolerance for unwanted effects are in short supply, they are becoming unnecessarily risky to use.

Sargent's research and that of other members of the BACS team also highlighted the need for air planners and weaponeers to recognize that PGMs not only differ in their technical characteristics and effects, but also may differ in their political and emotional effects. The case in point here was the employment of 13 TLAMs on 10 September. General Ryan requested and Admiral Smith approved the use of these long-range, ship-launched missiles mainly on the military grounds that they were the best weapons available to take out key Bosnian Serb air defense systems in the Banja Luka area without risk to NATO aircrews. As it turned out, however, these missiles were more than just another weapon in the context of Bosnia. TLAMs represented the high-end of PGM technology. Their sudden use in Bosnia signaled to many people that NATO was initiating a significant escalation of the conflict, although such was not the intent of the military commanders. Additionally, many NAC members were upset by the fact that they had not been consulted beforehand on the use of these advanced weapons.[65] At the same time, Admiral Smith reports that he subsequently learned from an American diplomat in contact with the Bosnian Serbs that the TLAMs "scared the sh— out of the Serbs." According to Smith the use of the missiles showed the Serbs that NATO was serious and that they "did not have a clue where we could go next."[66] Clearly the term *weaponeering* must carry a broad meaning for senior commanders and technicians involved in the process.

In a similar vein to Colonel Sargent's effort, Maj Mark McLaughlin's chapter examines the nature of NATO combat assessment during the air campaign. Beginning at the theoretical level, McLaughlin writes that combat assessment is the process by which air commanders determine how they are doing in relation to attaining their objectives. Through a three-step process of battle damage assessment (BDA), munitions effectiveness assessment, and reattack recommendations, commanders learn if their attacks and weapons are bringing the enemy closer to defeat at the best possible rate. Effective combat assessment, therefore, remains a vital tool for evaluating and refining tactics and operational concepts.

At the practical level, McLaughlin writes that, while the CAOC's combat-assessment process worked well, problems existed—particularly in the area of BDA. Notable even before Deliberate Force were the near absence of NATO BDA doctrine and the uneven experience and training levels of the various national personnel doing BDA in the CAOC. The different NATO air forces had different standards and methods for assessing damage. For the sake of standardization, CAOC BDA managers attempted to train their subordinates in US doctrine and procedures. But the rapid turnover of their staffs, engendered by the practice of manning the CAOC mainly with TDY personnel, undermined that process. The net effect of these problems, according to McLaughlin, was a somewhat sluggish pace in the flow and assessment of BDA data into, within, and out of the CAOC. In turn, the potentially negative effects of the slow pace of BDA, at least in terms of avoiding conflicting public assessments of how the bombing campaign was going, were minimized by the compactness of the air campaign and its target list, by General Ryan's decision to make all definitive BDA determinations himself, and by Admiral Smith's close hold on the outflow of combat-assessment information to the press and even to NATO member governments. Whether or not the flow of the combat-assessment process was painfully slow, neither commander intended to or had to make judgments under the pressure of public scrutiny and perhaps counter-vailing analysis.

In another chapter Major McLaughlin offers a succinct as-sessment of the effectiveness of Deliberate Force. Recognizing that the perspectives of Bosnian Serb leaders had to be the foundation for assessing the campaign, McLaughlin proposes that "one should judge NATO air operations in light of their direct impact as well as the concurrent victories by Croatian and Muslim (federation) ground forces, American-sponsored diplomatic initiatives, and Serbia's political pressure on its Bosnian Serb cousins." Following this prescription, McLaugh-lin illustrates the effects of the bombing on the psyche and calculations of the Serb leaders through the accounts of vari-ous diplomats who dealt with them. Noting the campaign's progression through active bombing, pause, and more bomb-ing, McLaughlin traces a steady deterioration in the will of President Milosevic, President Karadzic, and General Mladic to resist NATO and UN demands. Croatian and Muslim (federa-tion) ground offensives going on at the same time served to increase pressure on the Serb leaders even further.

In rapid shuttle diplomacy, Ambassador Holbrooke ex-ploited these pressures to coax and bully the Serbs into mak-ing concessions. A major barrier to progress went down on 8 September, when regional leaders met with Holbrooke at Ge-neva and agreed that the future Federation of Bosnia would include Croats and Muslims and a separate and coequal Serb Republic. The agreement also allowed the two entities to "es-tablish parallel special relations with neighboring countries," and it recognized that the federation and the Serb Republic would control 51 percent and 49 percent of Bosnia's territory, respectively—a division of land long established in the Contact Group's proposals.[67] Thus the Bosnian Serbs had in hand what they most wanted—autonomy. Under continuing pressure from ground and air attacks, they found it easier to accept UN demands, and on 14 September Holbrooke and Milosevic successfully pressured Karadzic and Mladic to end their active military pressure on Sarajevo.

Diplomacy

Deliberate Force was about diplomacy—getting the Bosnian Serbs to end their sieges of the safe areas and to enter into productive negotiations for peace. Consequently several BACS researchers, Major McLaughlin particularly, examined the interconnections between Deliberate Force and the ongoing diplomatic process.[68] In general they found that these interconnections were difficult to "package" and describe in a manner distinct and separate from other events and forces influencing the course of diplomacy. Despite its brevity and limited military scope, Deliberate Force turned out to be a complex diplomatic event influenced by military operations other than the air campaign—and by the conduct of diplomatic activities in several venues. A useful and defensible description of the relationship between airpower and diplomacy in this case, therefore, requires a clear understanding of these other operations and activities.

One of the more immediate effects of the bombing campaign was that it underscored and, to some degree, mandated a temporary shift of the intervention's diplomatic lead from the UN to the so-called Contact Group. Formed in the summer of 1994, the Contact Group represented the foreign ministries of the United States, Great Britain, France, Germany, and Russia. The group's sole purpose was to provide an alternative mechanism to the UN for negotiating a peace settlement in the region. Since it had none of the UN's humanitarian and peacekeeping responsibilities to divert its attention or weaken its freedom to negotiate forcefully, the group's relationship with the Bosnian Serbs was more overtly confrontational than the UN's. This suited Ambassador Holbrooke, the US representative to the group, just fine. As the assistant secretary of state for European and Canadian affairs, he had been involved closely with Balkans diplomacy for some time and was an outspoken proponent of aggressive action against the Serbs.[69] Upon hearing of the Mrkale shelling, for example, he suggested publicly that the proper response might be a bombing campaign against the Serbs of up to six months.[70] Holbrooke's opinion was important because by the summer of 1995, he was the de facto lead agent of the Contact Group, and it was his small team of American diplomats and military officers that conducted face-to-face shuttle negotiations with the Serbs and other belligerent leaders during the bombing campaign. These negotiations took the Holbrooke team to Yugoslavia at the start of the bombing, to Brussels and NAC during the pause, to Geneva for a major face-to-face meeting of the factional leaders on 8 September, to the United States, back to Belgrade on the 13th, and to a host of other points in between.

The irony of Holbrooke's call for robust bombing was that the UN and NATO could not and did not initiate Deliberate Force to influence the peace process. Officially and publicly, NATO initiated the campaign to protect the safe areas. But as Ambassador Hunter pointed out, it would have been naive to think that the air attacks would not undermine the Serbs' military power and coerce them diplomatically. Nevertheless, Hunter believed, the bombing had to be "represented" merely as an effort to protect the safe areas. The consensus within NAC for air action rested solely on support for the UNSCRs. There was no overt, general commitment to bomb the Bosnian Serbs into talking.[71]

Also during the time of Deliberate Force, the intervention conducted two military operations of consequence to the course of diplomacy. UN peacekeeping forces remained in the region though their role was mainly passive during the period of offensive air operations. In the weeks prior to the start of bombing, the UN had quietly drawn its scattered peacekeeping units in from the field and concentrated them in more defensible positions. This process rushed to conclusion in the final hours before bombing actually began. During the bombing, these forces mainly held their positions or conducted limited patrol operations, but they did not go on the offensive. At the same time, elements of NATO's Rapid Reaction Force took an active though limited role in the intervention's offensive. The

RRF deployed into the Sarajevo area, beginning in mid-June. During the first two days of Deliberate Force, its artillery units shelled Bosnian Serb military forces in the Sarajevo area. These bombardments certainly had some effect on Serb military capabilities, and they probably had some effect on their diplomatic calculations. Given the lack of emphasis placed on them by the diplomats interviewed by the BACS teams, however, the effects of these activities on diplomatic events probably were limited, at least in relation to the effects of the air campaign and military operations of regional anti-Serb forces. At the same time, the passive value of the peacekeeping forces to prevent the Serbs from more or less walking into and taking the remaining safe areas or taking intervention peacekeepers hostage certainly must have been a factor in their military calculations, though one not explored in depth by the BACS.

All diplomats and senior military commanders interviewed by the BACS attributed great military and diplomatic importance to Croatian and Bosnian offensive operations against local Serb forces, which had begun before Deliberate Force and which continued parallel to and after the operation. These offensives began in the spring of 1995, and they marked the end of the overwhelming military advantages of Serbian forces. In May the Croatian army began a successful offensive to reestablish government control of western Slavonia. In late July the Croatian army launched a major offensive—Operation Storm—to retake the Krajina and to relieve the Serbian siege of the so-called Bihac Pocket—a small area under Bosnian control. In a few days, a Croatian force of nearly one hundred thousand well-equipped troops penetrated the Krajina at dozens of places and captured Knin—a vital center of Croatian Serb power. Over the next several weeks, the Croatians systematically cleared the Krajina of Serb resistance, moving generally from west to east.[72] At the same time, forces of the Bosnian Federation launched a series of operations against the Bosnian Serbs. Under pressure from the United States and other intervening governments, the Bosnian Croat and Muslim factions had reestablished the federation in March 1994 and, since that time, had worked to improve the combat capabilities of their army. By the summer of 1995, the Bosnian army was ready to go on the offensive, and—as the

Croats swept around the northern borders of Serb-held Bosnia—it struck west and north to push the Serbs back from the center of the country. Caught between a hammer and an anvil, the Serbs retreated precipitously, and by mid-September the Croatian government controlled its territory—and the portion of Bosnia under Serb control had shrunk from 70 percent to about 51 percent.

The existence of a powerful ground offensive in parallel to Deliberate Force complicates any determination of the air campaign's distinct influence on diplomacy. Undoubtedly the Bosnian Croat offensives drastically altered the military prospects not only of the Serb factions in the two countries but also those of the Serbian leaders of the former Yugoslavia. Even before the Croatians launched their Krajina offensive, Slobodan Milosevic offered to act as a peace broker between the Bosnian Serbs and the intervention. At the time, some observers attributed Milosevic's move to his concerns over the growing strength of non-Serb military forces and over the worsening economic condition of his country, brought on by UN sanctions.[73] In this light Norman Cigar, a long-time analyst of the Balkans region, argues that the Serbian military reverses on the ground were more important than the air operations of Deliberate Force in getting the Serbs to accept UN demands. Ground operations, Cigar argues, confirmed for the Serbs that they were losing control of the military situation and thus had a profound impact on their diplomatic calculations. In his view the air campaign had minimal direct effect on the Serbs' military capabilities and consequently had little impact on their diplomacy.[74]

Senior diplomatic and military leaders interviewed by the BACS, as well as some analysts, generally saw a more synergistic relationship between air, ground, and diplomatic operations in terms of their effects on the calculations of the Serbs. Although most of them emphasized that the simultaneity of the two campaigns was unplanned, they also recognized that their conjunction was important to the ultimate outcome of negotiations.[75] Just as the Bosnian Serbs were facing their greatest military challenge on the ground, the air campaign drastically undermined their ability to command, supply, and move their forces. The combination of effects placed them in a much more immediate danger of military collapse than would have been the case with separate land or air offensives. The Bosnian Federation offensive also established a division of territory between it and the Serb faction that almost exactly equalled the 51/49 percent split called for in intervention peace plans and reconfirmed at the Geneva peace talks on 8 September 1995. Ambassador Holbrooke maintained that this event greatly eased the subsequent peace negotiations at Dayton, Ohio, since it placed the Serbs in the position of merely acknowledging an existing division of territory rather than giving up hard-won territory that they previously had refused to relinquish.[76]

Moreover, every diplomat and senior commander interviewed believed that the air campaign distinctly affected the moral resistance of the Serb leaders and, consequently, the pace of negotiations. Prior to the bombing, Ambassador Christopher Hill observed that President Milosevic "always had a rather cocky view of the negotiations, sort of like he's doing us a favor," but after the bombing began, "we found him . . . totally engaged . . . [with an] attitude of let's talk seriously."[77] Not surprisingly, Holbrooke and Ambassador Hunter perceived that Serb diplomats relaxed somewhat when the bombing paused on 1 September. When the bombing resumed on 5 September, Holbrooke perceived that Serbian diplomatic resistance weakened rapidly, to the verge of collapse.[78] This effect was clear at the meeting between Holbrooke's negotiating team and the Serbs on 13–14 September. At the meeting Holbrooke found Mladic "in a rush" to end the bombing[79]—so much so that the meeting had hardly begun when Milosevic produced President Karadzic and his military commander, General Mladic, to participate directly in the talks. Mladic, who had the figurative noose of an indicted war criminal around his neck, arrived at the meeting looking "like he'd been through a bombing campaign."[80] After six hours of negotiations, the Serbs unilaterally signed an agreement to cease their attacks on and remove their heavy weapons from Sarajevo, without a quid pro quo from Holbrooke or the UN of stopping the bombing. Ambassador Hill attributed this capitulation to the threat of further bombing.[81] Interestingly, as he left the meeting, Karadzic plaintively asked Holbrooke, "We are ready for peace. Why did you bomb us?"[82]

NAC's NATO diplomats also recognized the importance and value of the bombing campaign. Their collective decision to authorize air operations in the first place was clear evidence of their expectation that the potential benefits outweighed the risks. Ambassador Hunter learned the depth of his compatriot's commitment to the bombing operations at the very beginning of the bombing pause. On the same afternoon of the pause, Secretary-General Claes called a meeting of NAC to confirm that the members remained willing to let operations resume when the commanders deemed necessary. For his part Hunter anticipated some resistance to allowing the campaign to restart. To his surprise all members favored resuming the bombing if the Serbs failed to show evidence of complying with UN demands. Having gotten over the question of restarting the campaign with unexpected ease, Hunter recalled that the real debate—one that consumed "about an hour-and-a-half" of the council's time—was over whether to give the Serbs 48 hours or 72 hours to comply.[83] Having taken the international and domestic political risks of initiating Deliberate Force, the members of NAC were determined to see it through.

Ambassadors Holbrooke and Hunter offered two distinct but interrelated explanations for the profound and immediate influence of the bombing on Serbian diplomatic resistance. Ambassador Holbrooke's explanation was to the point. Serb leaders, he felt, were "thugs and murderers" who responded well to force.[84] Ambassador Hunter painted a more calculating picture of the Serbian leaders. In his view they understood in the late summer of 1995 that their sole remaining diplomatic advantage in the Bosnian conflict lay in their ability to manipulate the internal divisions within and among the NATO and UN member states. The Serbs knew, Hunter believed, that neither organization could take decisive action against them unless consensus existed in the NAC and at least in the UN Security Council. For that reason they should have taken NAC's endorsement of the London agreement and the UN secretary-general's transfer of the air-strike keys to his military commander as disturbing omens. Based on past experience, however, the Serbs also had reason to hope that neither organization was really serious and would back off after a few halfhearted air strikes. The bombing pause probably rekindled that hope. NAC's debate of 2 September, which Hunter believed the Serbs were privy to, and the resumption of the bombing itself shattered that hope.[85] The action offered hard evidence that the UN's and NAC's expressions of unanimity and commitment were real.

Thus, even more than the ongoing advances of the Bosnian Federation forces and the initial start of the bombing, the knowledgeable participants interviewed by the BACS team all agreed that resumption of the bombing became the pivotal moment of the campaign. In Ambassador Hill's estimate, the bombing "was really the signal the Bosnian Serbs needed to get to understand that they had to reach a peace agreement."[86] Hunter believed that the decision and the act of resuming the attack clearly signaled to the Serbs that the UN and NATO were committed to winning a decision and that their opportunities for military success and diplomatic maneuver were running out.

An interesting feature of Deliberate Force, given the close connection between air operations and diplomacy, was that the direct operational commander, General Ryan, and the principal negotiator, Ambassador Holbrooke, never spoke to one another during the operation. Holbrooke spoke frequently during the campaign with UN commanders and on several occasions with Admiral Smith and General Joulwan, SACEUR. He even conferred with NAC during the bombing pause but never spoke with the individual who made immediate decisions about the sequence, pace, weapons, and other tactical characteristics of the air attacks. General Ryan, for his part, thus never spoke to the individual most directly responsible for exploiting the diplomatic effects of his operations. What they knew of one another's perceptions, priorities, and intentions, they derived indirectly from information flowing up and down their respective chains of command.

From a legalistic perspective, the lack of contact between Holbrooke and Ryan was proper and politically necessary. First, as a US State Department representative and the leader of the Contact Group, Holbrooke had no formal place in either the UN or the NATO chain of command. Properly, any contact between him and Ryan should have moved up through State Department channels over to the secretary of defense or to

NAC and then down through those chains of command to Ryan, who acted both as the commander of Sixteenth Air Force and as a NATO air commander. Given the circumstances, the NATO chain of command was really the operative one. Second, any direct contact with the air commander possibly would have established the perception that the bombing supported Holbrooke's diplomacy—something that neither the UN nor NATO wanted to happen. Ambassador Hunter suggested that members of NAC wouldn't have wanted any direct contact between Ryan and Holbrooke "other than to keep one another vaguely informed—that is, to exchange information." All political decisions related to the air campaign, he said, had to be made at NAC. Hunter believed that any "tactical" cooperation between the general and the diplomat would have been a "very big mistake"; had Ryan adjusted his operations in response to information passed to him by "any negotiator," NAC would have "had his head"—especially if something went wrong.[87]

During Deliberate Force, consequently, Admiral Smith wanted no direct contact between his air commander and Holbrooke. The admiral himself avoided operational or targeting discussions with Holbrooke or his military deputy, US Army lieutenant general Wes Clark, because he "did not want either of them to even think they had an avenue by which they could influence me."[88] Fully aware of his exclusion from the NATO and UN command channels, Ambassador Holbrooke never based his pre–Deliberate Force negotiating plans on a bombing campaign, even though he believed that one would facilitate their successful outcome greatly.[89]

Unavoidable as it was under the circumstances, the lack of contact between Holbrooke and Ryan appears to have allowed disconnects in their understanding of key issues. Those disconnects, in turn, appear to have influenced the way the two individuals pursued their missions. For example, General Ryan's concern over collateral damage probably exceeded that of at least the US diplomats involved. Although the general was concerned that a significant collateral-damage event, particularly one causing the deaths of civilians, might rob the air campaign of its political support before it had decisive effect, the US diplomats involved generally believed that the air campaign had enough political support to carry it through perhaps even

501

a serious incident of collateral damage.[90] As regards the climate of opinion in NAC, Ambassador Hunter pointed out that the member states had invested too much domestic political capital in starting bombing operations to bring them to a halt by the unintended death of civilians and soldiers.[91] No one advocated casual slaughter, but the net focus of the intervention's diplomatic community remained on getting results from what may have been NATO's last bolt in Bosnia, rather than on preventing or reacting to incidents of collateral damage.

Whether closing this disconnect between NATO air leaders, mainly Ryan and Admiral Smith, and their diplomatic counterparts, mainly Holbrooke and Hunter, would have changed the flow of events is, of course, speculative. Even had they known that the diplomats were not poised to end the air campaign at the first incident of significant collateral damage (whatever "significant" meant in this case), Smith and Ryan certainly would not have reduced their efforts to minimize collateral damage and casualties. For military, legal, and moral reasons, neither leader had any intention of doing more harm to the Bosnian Serbs than their mission to protect the safe areas required. Likely, Admiral Smith still would have expected Ryan to make every DMPI, weapon, and other decision with the intent of getting maximum effect at minimum collateral cost. Knowing that the diplomats were not as sensitive to collateral damage as they thought, however, might have given the military commanders a sense that they had more time to conduct their operations. That, in turn, might have let them slow the pace of the bombing—something that might have been desirable, even if just to reduce the wear and tear imposed by the actual pace of operations on everyone from General Ryan to the personnel in the flying units in the field. Indeed, at one point during the bombing, some CAOC staffers briefly discussed slowing the pace of the campaign in the interest of safety. People, including the aircrews, were beginning to show signs of fatigue. But they rejected the idea in short order, believing that the diplomatic vulnerability of the operation required maximum effort to ensure that it had a decisive effect before political reasons shut it down.[92]

A disconnect also existed between Ryan's and Holbrooke's understandings of the dynamics of the bombing campaign and its possible duration. With his jets focusing their attacks almost exclusively on the targets covered in options one and two of OPLAN 40101, around 10 September General Ryan passed the word to his commanders that he would run out of such approved targets in a couple of days at the present pace of operations. For their part, Ryan and his planners did not necessarily equate running out of currently approved targets with ending the campaign automatically. Several available targeting options could have permitted a continuation of the bombing. These options included (1) hitting or rehitting undestroyed DMPIs among the targets already approved, (2) adding and/or approving new option-one and -two targets to the list, or (3) hitting option-three targets. In fact AIRSOUTH planners were already looking at new option-one and -two targets, and General Joulwan had already raised the option-three issue with NAC, with a negative response.[93] Nevertheless, in the second week of September, AFSOUTH had several options for usefully extending the air campaign, should that be politically or militarily required.

That was not the information that got to Ambassador Holbrooke and his boss, Secretary of State Christopher, however. Based on his conversations with Admiral Smith and a report to the National Security Council on 11 September by Adm William Owens, vice chairman of the Joint Chiefs of Staff, Ambassador Holbrooke recalls that he and the secretary understood unequivocally that running out the existing target list meant the end of bombing operations. Because that news had such drastic implications for his negotiations, Holbrooke relates, he immediately asked Admiral Owens to see if there was some way to extend the campaign.[94] Interestingly, General Ryan later could not recall ever hearing about the ambassador's interest in stretching things out.[95]

Whatever the causes of the informational disconnect between Ryan and Holbrooke, it had an immediate effect on American and, it follows, Contact Group diplomacy. After the meeting of the National Security Council, Holbrooke relates, Secretary Christopher directed him to return immediately to Belgrade to resume negotiations with President Milosevic. The two statesmen had planned to wait a week longer before reengaging the Serbians, in the hope that the continued bombing would further soften their obstinate resistance to meeting both the UN's and the Contact Group's demands. In other words, Holbrooke was determined to get the Serbs to halt their attacks on the safe areas *and* to begin making territorial concessions necessary to give reality to the just completed Geneva Agreement. But with the end of offensive air operations apparently imminent, Christopher adjusted his diplomatic plan, and Holbrooke immediately left for Serbia to get what he could from the Serbs before the bombing ended.[96] Fortunately, although it was already becoming public knowledge that NATO was running out of option-two targets and was unlikely to shift to option three, the Serbs were beaten and ready to accept at least the UN's demands.[97] Consequently, Holbrooke got little for the Contact Group other than promises to participate in some sort of peace conference, but he did get a commitment from the Serbs to lift the sieges and pull their heavy weapons out of the Sarajevo exclusion zone. Attributing his partial success to the need to get a settlement before the Serbs became aware of the impending halt to the bombing, Holbrooke later related, "I would have been . . . willing to continue the negotiations if Smith or Joulwan had said, 'Boy, we have a lot of great targets left out there!' "[98]

Again, arguing that closing the disconnect between Ryan and Holbrooke on this issue might have reshaped the air campaign—even had it been possible to do so—remains a matter of speculation. After all, Ryan was still functioning as a NATO commander and Holbrooke was not in his chain of command; furthermore, for reasons of political sensitivity, he was not even free to discuss operations openly with the air commander. In actual practice, however, the operational and political boundaries between the UN and NAC, on the one hand, and the United States and the Contact Group, on the other, were not as sharp as the formal diplomatic arrangements suggested. To be sure, the bombing was under way to secure the safe areas and protect peacekeepers, but most leaders involved understood that the coalition was not likely to obtain those objectives unless the Serbs were humbled militarily and agreed to serious negotiations over the political and territorial proposals of the Contact Group. Similarly, although the UN officially had the political lead in terms of sanctioning and benefiting from the bombing, Ambassador Holbrooke exercised the practical diplomatic lead during Deliberate Force.

It was he, in fact, who extracted concessions from the Serbian leaders on 14 September that allowed the UN and NATO to announce success and turn off their keys. He was, therefore, acting as a de facto diplomat for the other international organizations, even if none could say so.

Thus, while the political-military arrangements existing around Deliberate Force made good *formal* sense at the time, their artificiality, in terms of what was going on operationally, clearly influenced the course of diplomacy and air operations in ways that arguably were undesirable. In point of fact, the indirectness of the flow of information between Ryan and Holbrooke created a situation whereby the commanders pressed their operations to get their full diplomatic effect before the *diplomats* arbitrarily cut off the bombing, even as the diplomats scrambled to get what diplomatic effect they could before the *commanders* arbitrarily cut off the bombing. The irony of the situation is notable.

Even after it ended, Deliberate Force—or at least its memory—remained an active factor in the shape and pace of subsequent negotiations for Bosnian peace. Formal talks were taken up in November at Wright-Patterson Air Force Base (AFB), near Dayton, Ohio. Holbrooke considered it a fortuitous choice of venue. Arriving Serb diplomats walked from their airplanes past operational combat aircraft parked on the ramp nearby. Ambassador Hill arranged to hold the welcoming banquet on the floor of the United States Air Force Museum, where the Serbs literally sat surrounded by "an awesome display of airpower," including some of the very aircraft and weapons recently used against them.[99] According to their American escort officer, the Serbs remained tight-lipped about their impressions of the event.[100] But one cannot doubt the importance that key interventionist diplomats attached to keeping airpower before the Serbian diplomats.

Observations and Implications

During the course of their research, the BACS team members observed and described a number of things about Deliberate Force that carry important implications for the planners of future air campaigns. Once again, this chapter only summarizes those implications that some—though not necessarily all—of the team members felt had value beyond the specific circumstances of Deliberate Force. For all its uniqueness, Deliberate Force offers broadly useful implications because one can describe its key characteristics with some precision. For the NATO airmen involved, it was a strategically limited, tactically intense, high-technology, coalition air campaign conducted under tight restraints of time and permissible collateral damage; further, it was aimed at coercing political and military compliance from a regional opponent who had no airpower. To the extent that military planners will plan future air campaigns in the context of some or all of these characteristics, they should first understand what the Deliberate Force experience suggests theoretically about how things might work under similar circumstances.

As a first observation, *the determined and robust character of Deliberate Force was essential to its near-term success.* The campaign's objectives were limited, but to achieve them, NATO airmen had to be free to make their plans and execute their operations within the full limits of appropriate boundaries of political objectives and the laws of war—all of which should have been, and generally were, encapsulated in ROE. A half-hearted, overly restrained, or incomplete air campaign likely would have been disastrous to NATO and UN credibility—and it certainly would have prolonged the war. As RAND researcher Stephen Hosmer concludes, a weak air campaign probably would have "adversely conditioned" the Bosnian Serbs and other factions to believe that both bombing and the interventionists were indecisive and, therefore, that they should fight on. "To reap the psychological benefits of airpower," Hosmer writes, "it is also important to avoid adverse conditioning. The enemy must not see your air attacks as weak or impotent. The hesitant . . . bombing campaign against North Vietnam in 1965 is a prime example of adverse conditioning. The hesitant use of NATO airpower in the former Yugoslavia prior to mid-1995 is another example of adverse conditioning."[101] In parallel, Ambassador Holbrooke felt that the actual targets struck during Deliberate Force were less important to the effect on Bosnian Serb leaders than the fact that the NATO campaign was sustained, effective, and selective.[102]

As a second observation, *precision-guided munitions made Deliberate Force possible.* Given the campaign's restraints of time, forces available, and its political sensitivities, NATO could not have undertaken it without a relatively abundant supply of PGMs and air platforms to deliver them. Precision weapons gave NATO airmen the ability to conceive and execute a major air campaign that was quick, potent, and unlikely to kill people or destroy property to an extent that would cause world opinion to rise against and terminate the operation. The BACS team found no substantiated estimates of the number of people killed by Deliberate Force.[103] The simple fact that Bosnian Serb leaders made no effort to exploit collateral damage politically indicates that they had little to exploit. Had NATO and UN leaders expected enough collateral damage to give the Serbs a political lever, they probably would not have approved the initiation of Deliberate Force, or if such damage had begun, they probably could not have sustained the operation politically for long. Indeed, as Ambassador Hunter recalled, trust in the implied promise of NATO airmen to execute the air campaign quickly and with minimal collateral damage permitted members of NAC to approve its initiation in the first place.[104] Had those diplomats doubted that promise, therefore, Deliberate Force never would have happened, and if NATO airmen had failed to deliver on either part of their promise, the campaign almost certainly would have come to a quick end.

The third observation follows from the first two: *NATO's primary reliance on air-delivered precision weapons during Deliberate Force shielded the international intervention in Bosnia from "mission creep."* Had NATO chosen to conduct a joint air and ground offensive against the Serbs or to rely on nonprecision aerial weapons in the bombing campaign, Deliberate Force certainly would have involved greater casualties on both sides. Instead of a series of just over one thousand carefully placed explosions and a few seconds of aircraft cannon fire, Deliberate Force likely would have involved protracted operations by tens of thousands of troops, systematic air and artillery barrages in support of their advance across the land, and thousands more explosions of not so precisely placed bombs and artillery shells. Put another way, in any form but an independent air campaign, Deliberate Force would have given

507

the Serb faction a vastly greater opportunity to fight back and inflict casualties on NATO and UN forces. Reasonably, the Serbs would have fought back, at least long enough to see if killing some number of interventionist troops would break the will of their political leaders. The problem with such casualties, however, is that they could have reshaped the political, normative, and emotional nature of the campaign against the Serbs. Televised reports of rows of dead Bosnian Serb soldiers, shelled towns, lines of refugees, and NATO body bags likely would have reshaped every participant's view of the conflict, and there would have been more time for those changed views to have political effect. Of course there is no way to tell if a protracted air-land campaign or nonprecision-bombing campaign would have changed NATO's "disciplinary" peace-enforcement mission into "real war" missions of retreat, conquest, or retribution. The very uncertainty of the direction in which the interventionist mission would have crept underscores the value of airpower's characteristics of precision, control, and security in this particular peace operation.

The fourth observation is that *contacts between military leaders and some key diplomats do not seem to have kept up with the pace of events just before and during Deliberate Force.* Because of limitations of the interview information the BACS team collected, the width of the gap in the diplomatic and military discourse is not clear, but it is clear from the evidence collected that the gap existed and that it shaped political and military events to some degree. Perhaps most significantly, Ambassador Holbrooke and General Ryan made plans and took actions in ignorance of one another's positions in key areas such as preventing collateral damage and extending the air campaign. Reflecting on the possible diplomatic consequences of the disconnect between him and Ryan over the practicality of the campaign, Holbrooke writes, "I regret greatly that . . . I did not have direct contact with Ryan; it might have allowed us to follow a different, and perhaps tougher, strategy."[105] Moreover, although the bureaucratic distance between these individuals may have been understandable under the circumstances of this operation, it may not have needed to extend to an absolute proscription of contact between them. Speaking from his perspective as a member of NAC, Ambassador

Hunter, for one, indicated that a passage of factual information between the commander and the diplomat probably should have happened. At the same time, it is clear from the context of Hunter's statement that he still thought that any such contact between Ryan and Holbrooke should have avoided giving the impression that they were actually coordinating their efforts.[106]

In contrast to the reflections of the diplomats, Admiral Smith and General Ryan remained convinced, nearly two years after the fact, that any direct contact between Holbrooke and AIRSOUTH would have been improper and diplomatically risky. Both commanders believed that such contact would have violated the established military chain of command and the proper interface between the diplomatic and military leadership. In Admiral Smith's view, had he allowed Holbrooke and Ryan to talk, he would have placed the whole operation at risk diplomatically, and he would have undermined his boss, General Joulwan.[107] In separate comments, General Ryan echoed that position, maintaining that to "even hint" at direct coordination between him and Holbrooke was "ludicrous." Since part of Holbrooke's sanction to negotiate in the Balkans came from the UN and since NATO was likewise operating at the behest of the UN, Ryan argued that the proper level of coordination between the diplomat and soldier should have and could have occurred only at the "strategic level." Thus Ryan suggests that the real area of inquiry in this issue may lie in the possible inadequacy of the information flow between the NAC and UN leaders.[108]

The operative point remains, however, that Ryan's and Holbrooke's activities were intertwined during the bombing, regardless of the bureaucratic and diplomatic arrangements and fictions maintained, and that those arrangements did not adequately support their requirements for information. The implication for future architects of politically charged, fast-paced military interventions is that they must pay close attention to keeping the formal and informal communications channels and boundaries between soldiers and diplomats current, coordinated, and flexible. It also will be important to make sure that the right soldiers and diplomats are talking to each other at the right time, within limits and on topics appropriate to the circumstances. This may mean that they remain linked cleanly and traditionally at the tops of their respective chains of command. But it also may be that in the close-coupled political-military environments of future peace operations, for example, some linkages at subordinate levels will be appropriate. This observation certainly does not justify diplomats mucking about with tactics or soldiers hijacking diplomacy. Nor does it bow to generalized beliefs that diplomats and soldiers operate in separate realms. In reality, war is about diplomacy, and diplomacy's final sanction is war. Diplomats and soldiers will always be in each other's "mess kits." The real issue is how both groups can anticipate and educate themselves and one another on the appropriate boundaries and rules of their relationship under given circumstances. The political-military experience of Deliberate Force should prove to be an interesting case study in that educational process.

Fifth, and in a similar vein, *although the focus and style of General Ryan's leadership was mandated by and appropriate to the immediate task of keeping the air campaign politically viable, they also created stresses within AIRSOUTH staff elements that may have become problems, had the campaign continued much longer.* Given the necessity of ensuring that the targets, weapons, and tactics of every attack sortie were selected and controlled to minimize the possibility of collateral damage, General Ryan's decision to centralize such decisions (i.e., make them himself) made sense. But making all those decisions day-to-day locked the general into 18-hour workdays with minimal time and energy to consider other responsibilities that fall to a senior component commander. Part of this load fell to General Short, Ryan's chief of staff, who stayed in Naples to oversee AIRSOUTH's administrative, logistics, personnel, and public-relations tasks and to maintain day-to-day liaison with Admiral Smith. Short was up to the task, but he did comment to the team that at times he lacked the continual contact with the CAOC that he needed to fulfill his liaison and press responsibilities in a timely manner. From the CAOC itself, several staffers commented that Ryan's centralization of technical decisions of targeting and weaponeering created a division within the CAOC staff. On one side of this division, they felt, was a small group of a half-dozen officers who also worked unsustainably long days to help the general make his tactical decisions. On the other side was the bulk of the several-hundred-strong CAOC staff who did little more than gather and distribute data and who tended to feel under-utilized in comparison to General Ryan's arguably overworked inner core.

Obviously, one can make too much of this issue, particularly since the BACS was not chartered and equipped to collect the comprehensive sociological and organizational data necessary to credibly describe the real effects of Ryan's or anyone else's leadership. But the patchy evidence collected by the team does suggest that future air commanders and their subordinates should be aware that the stylistic—as well as the substantive—elements of leadership will have far-reaching effects on the work, morale, and endurance of their staffs. Further, it suggests a potentially valuable line of inquiry for future research.

Sixth, *despite the relative smallness of their force structure, NATO commanders chose to conduct operations for operational- and strategic-level effects rather than tactical ones.* In US force-planning terms, AFSOUTH conducted Deliberate Force with about a two-fighter-wing-equivalent combat force and an appropriate support slice of reconnaissance, surveillance, electronic warfare, SEAD, lift, and other aircraft. AIRSOUTH commanders had the option of conducting their attacks for primarily tactical effects by concentrating on the Serbian materiel targets encompassed in option one. Instead they elected to focus their attacks on option-two targets to achieve broader and quicker operational and strategic results—namely, by destroying the mobility and command infrastructure of the BSA and thereby coercing its leaders to accede to UN demands. In other words the NATO air force was not the giant fielded for Desert Storm, but it still had a strategic option. This is an important point for US air planners pondering the problems of conducting air war in secondary theaters, where they perhaps will be allocated relatively small forces to accomplish big jobs in a hurry. It is also important for the planners and commanders of smaller air forces. The possession of a strategic or lead-force option depends less on the size of an air force than on the military-political circumstances, doctrine, materiel, and

511

available targeting options. It follows then that the leaders and budget masters of air forces of even moderate size should not reject the strategic- and operational-level options of air warfare out of hand. If their anticipated employment opportunities suggest the utility of strategic attack, broad-ranging interdiction operations, or other asymmetric ways of bringing airpower to bear against their enemies, then they should step up to making the appropriate investments in air vehicles, munitions, support infrastructure, command and control systems, and so on.

Seventh, and at a more tactical level, *for NATO airmen, the operational features of this limited conflict differed little from those of major war.* They attacked the Bosnian Serbs in 1995 with the aircraft, tactics, weapons, and operational tempos they would have employed against the Warsaw Pact seven years before, at the close of the cold war. That observation suggests several things about the flexibility of airpower. It implies that airpower's role in the sphere of low intensity conflict continues to expand as new strategies, weapons, and sensor systems improve the ability of airmen to find and destroy important targets of all types under varying conditions. To the extent that a given low intensity conflict or operation other than war requires military surveillance and attacks (and most do), the Deliberate Force experience suggests that airpower is becoming an ever more equal partner with ground power. Moreover, the fact that ordinary air tactical units flew in Deliberate Force speaks to the relative ease with which one may shift such units between conflicts, as compared to ground forces. Ground units often require months of training to prepare for the differing tactical tasks of various types of conflicts. Training a battalion for peace operations, therefore, can reduce its capabilities and availability for conventional war. That is less often and less extensively the case for air units. Squadrons preparing for strike operations in Korea, for example, would not find strike operations over Bosnia much different in concept and basic technique; of course, they might find some adjustment for local conditions of geography and weather. Once again, one should not overstate this point. For example, airmen involved in Deny Flight report that some of their specific battle skills, such as flying high-performance air-combat maneuvers, degraded in the course of patrolling the skies over Bosnia for months on end. Moreover, the relative flexibility of surface forces, as compared to that of air forces, becomes a variable factor as one begins to look at specific missions and tasks—and at different branches, such as infantry and artillery.

This summary of the BACS now turns to a final observation about the decisiveness of Deliberate Force's contribution to ending the conflict in Bosnia. In general, airpower was *a* decisive factor in ending the 1992–95 Bosnian conflict, but one must understand its specific contribution in relation to the state of the conflict and to other events unfolding in the region. Like all struggles the Bosnian conflict was going to end someday. Either exhaustion or the victory of one side or the other would bring it to a close. Creation of the Bosnian Federation in March 1994 and the sudden successes of its forces in the spring and summer of 1995—in concert with those of Croatia—suggested that military dominance and victory were slipping, perhaps permanently, from the grasp of the Bosnian Serbs. Norman Cigar convincingly argues that some Bosnian Serbs and certainly Slobodan Milosevic realized that at the time.[109] Moreover, for domestic political reasons of his own, Milosevic needed the fighting to stop and, accordingly, tried to position himself as a peace broker in July.[110]

Nevertheless, the long-term outcome of the conflict and its likely length still were not in sight at the end of August 1995. No one had solid reasons to think that the bloodshed in Bosnia would not continue for at least another campaign season or longer. Significantly, the Serbs were still advancing against the safe areas in eastern Bosnia, even as they gave up ground in the western areas. But people in the outside world had seen enough of the butchery and mindless inhumanity in Bosnia. To put it bluntly, they wanted the war to end or at least get off Cable News Network. At the London conference in July, the interventionists announced that they intended to mitigate or, if possible, end the horror—by using airpower.

And that's what Deliberate Force did. It did what three years of factional ground fighting, peacekeeping, and international diplomacy had yet to achieve. Almost at the instant of its application, airpower stopped the attacks on the safe areas and made further large-scale fighting over Bosnian territory largely pointless. In so doing, it drastically altered the military situation on the ground, and it gave the UN and NATO control of the pace and content of the peace process.

The period of peace that came to Bosnia in the fall of 1995 probably emerged in the following way: First, Bosnian Federation and Croatian ground advances in the spring and summer of 1995 gave the Serbs a long-term signal that their opportunities for further military gains were coming to an end. American diplomats interviewed by the BACS team suggested that the federation advance also had the fortunate consequence of bringing the distribution of land under federation and Serbian control almost exactly to the 51/49 percent split called for at the time in UN and Contact Group peace plans.[111] This development probably influenced the peace calculations of several Serb leaders, but the diplomats generally agreed that its greatest value may have been to facilitate the final settlement at the Dayton peace talks in the following November. Second, the Deliberate Force air campaign "broke" the Serbs and was the proximal cause of the cessation of large-scale fighting in Bosnia and of the Serb agreement to participate in future peace talks according to a timetable set by the intervention. Third, the provision for a federal government in the peace plan made acquiescence to UN and Contact Group demands more palatable for the Serbs. Since the federation potentially offered them one of their dearest objectives—a degree of political autonomy—it seems reasonable to think that it lowered their willingness to fight on in the face of simultaneous NATO air attacks and ground offensives by their regional enemies.

This last point requires further research once it becomes possible to interview Bosnian Serb leaders on their views of the linkage between Deliberate Force and their political decisions. As one should expect in any conflict, then, the interventionist coalitions achieved their aim of stopping the fighting in Bosnia by blending diplomacy and military force, by plan and by happenstance, into a combination that simultaneously coerced the Bosnian Serbs and made it easier for them to give in to UN and Contact Group demands.

Deliberate Force ultimately impressed the BACS team as the creation of doctrinally and operationally sophisticated diplomats, air leaders, and planners. As they had done in the general case of Deny Flight, NATO airmen crafted and executed the bombing campaign against the Bosnian Serbs in an optimal manner that accommodated the conflicting political, diplomatic, operational, and technological limitations and constraints of their situation. At the same time, many of the key forces and events that shaped the context and success of Deliberate Force were, in fact, beyond the control or even the cognizance of the senior planners involved. As in most, if not all, military operations, the outcome of Deliberate Force was the product of good planning, courage, and luck. Certainly, the campaign plan was not perfect in its conception and execution. Where possible the BACS team tried to identify and describe its more important imperfections, all the while keeping in mind that hindsight does not guarantee a clear vision of what was or was not the best way to do something. In the main, however, the various team members tended to be more impressed by the success of the campaign than with possible errors of planning and execution.

The conclusion of this report, then, is that airpower delivered what it promised in Deliberate Force. It was a decisive element in bringing a new period of peace to Bosnia—quickly, cleanly, and at minimal cost in blood and treasure to the intervening states and, indeed, to the Bosnian Serbs. For the United States, if its national security strategy of global engagement is to last very long, its military forces will have to provide similar successes at similarly low costs—perhaps many times. It is useful to know, therefore, that in the case of Bosnia in mid-1995, airpower not only was the lead arm of American involvement in the region but also was almost certainly the only politically viable offensive arm available for use by the United States and any of its partners to end in a controllable way an ugly war of indeterminate cause and uncertain future.

Notes

1. For all official documents, interviews, and studies, see the BACS file at the United States Air Force Historical Research Agency (hereinafter AFHRA), Maxwell Air Force Base (AFB), Ala.

2. Some important analysts of this conflict would add a fourth sustaining cause: the misguided intervention of outside states and organizations in the conflict. In their view, the collapse of Yugoslavia created a constitutional crisis delineated by those who wanted to preserve a multiethnic federal

state where individual rights and economic opportunities were protected by law, and those who sought security and opportunity in the creation of ethnic-based nation-states carved out of the existing republics of the federation. In this view, individual European states, notably Germany, strengthened the nationalist position and assured the breakup of Yugoslavia by recognizing the independence of Slovenia and Croatia. Similarly, war became inevitable in Bosnia when the United States successfully pressured the UN and the European Community into recognizing its independence in March and April 1992. This is an important argument that relates directly to the effects of Deliberate Force. But the gross effect of the intervention on Bosnian politics was not a strategy consideration for NATO air planners. They were not asked if they should intervene—they were simply given the parameters of their part of the intervention and told to do it. Thus this particular issue is not included in the list of sustaining causes in this study of air planning, though it no doubt is a critical consideration—particularly at the level of grand strategy. For the details of this case, see Susan L. Woodward, *Balkan Tragedy: Chaos and Dissolution after the Cold War* (Washington, D.C.: Brookings Institution, 1995); and Christopher Bennett, *Yugoslavia's Bloody Collapse: Causes, Course and Consequences* (New York: New York University Press, 1995).

3. Terminology for describing the Moslem-Serb community is a problem. Some analysts use *Bosniaks,* apparently to give them a nonreligious label, like *Serbs* and *Croats.* The problem with that term is that it implies a closer link between the Moslem community and the cause of preserving the multi-ethnic unity and territorial integrity of Bosnia than it does for Serbs and Croats. With many individual exceptions, such may have been the case at the start of the Bosnian conflict, but in the pressure cooker of war, Moslem leaders adopted increasingly "ethnic" political objectives and rhetoric. So this chapter refers to Moslems as such, when appropriate, and refers to the national government or cause as *Bosnian.*

4. Robert A. Hunter, tape-recorded interview by author, 23 July 1996, side A, index 50.

5. Lt Col Lowell R. Boyd, AIRSOUTH planner, Headquarters AIRSOUTH, Naples, Italy, transcript of interview by author, 6 December 1995.

6. Gen Joseph W. Ashy, commander, US Space Command, transcript of interview by author, 29 April 1996, 10; and Adm Leighton Smith, "NATO Operations in Bosnia-Herzegovina: Deliberate Force, 29 August–14 September 1995," presentation to Air War College, Maxwell AFB, Ala., 9 November 1995, AFHRA, videotape, index 1046, BACS file Misc-19.

7. Publicly, however, NATO commanders never wavered from their commitment to support UN peacekeeping. Even with the Deliberate Force bombing under way, Admiral Smith stated, "I do not consider myself to be taking sides." Bruce W. Nelan, "More Talking, More Bombing," *Time Magazine,* 18 September 1995, 76.

8. Briefing, "NATO Air Operations in Bosnia-Herzegovina—Deliberate Force" (U), c. 1 August 1995. (NATO Secret) Information extracted is unclassified.

9. Col Larry Bickel, discussion with author, Ramstein AB, Germany, 24 August 1996. At the time of this discussion, Bickel was assigned to Headquarters United States Air Forces Europe (USAFE), but in the fall of 1992, he served at SHAPE as a Balkans-region air planner. He (probably along with others) suggested the initialism *CAOC*, in conformity with NATO terminology and practice.

10. Ashy interview, 4.

11. Ibid., 6.

12. Ibid., 25–57.

13. Ibid., 28–32; and Boyd interview, 12–13.

14. Boyd interview, 6. Throughout the period under discussion, Colonel Boyd acted as one of General Ashy's principal planners, and he was particularly responsible for ROE development. Boyd also mentions that Maj Richard Corzine was involved in AFSOUTH ROE development in the early phases of Deny Flight.

15. Memorandum for the NATO secretary-general, NAC Decision Statement, MCM-KAD-084-93, subject: Operational Options for Air Strikes in Bosnia-Herzegovina, 8 August 1993.

16. Ashy interview, 36.

17. In the course of its research, the BACS team realized that not all participants understood the boundaries of the dual-key arrangement in the same way. Some interviewees implicitly or explicitly extended its coverage to include the release of attacks against aircraft violating the no-fly edict. In reality the dual key applied only to air-to-ground attacks. What seems fair to say, however, is that the dual key reflected a pervasive caution in the UN and NATO over the use of any military force that, in turn, made leaders in both organizations cautious about enforcing the no-fly edict as well. As it was, therefore, NATO leaders did not release an attack on violating aircraft until 28 February 1994, when alliance jets downed four Bosnian Serb aircraft in the act of dropping bombs on facilities controlled by the Bosnian government. Importantly, the CAOC director released this attack without coordination with the UN.

18. Smith presentation, index 865–900.

19. Hunter interview, side A, index 350–450.

20. Ambassador Richard Holbrooke, tape-recorded interview by Maj Mark McLaughlin and Dr. Karl Mueller, 24 May 1996, side A, index 584. BACS researchers also heard statements that the dual-key setup may have been a way of giving the French an indirect veto over NATO air operations. With lightly armed peacekeeping forces on the ground, the French had reason to be concerned over any action that might prompt attacks on them. Without a chair on the NAC, however, the French had no direct say in the use of NATO airpower. But through its permanent seat on the UN Security Council, the French government could influence those operations through the UN key. The BACS team uncovered no documentary or direct oral evidence that French concerns influenced NATO's decision to propose the

dual-key setup, but the idea seems plausible. Clearly, this is an attractive area for further research.

21. Smith presentation, index 1280.

22. Ibid., index 1270–1330.

23. Maj Scott G. Walker, Maxwell AFB, Ala., interviewed by author, 28 February 1997. Walker was the deputy mission commander of the Udbina air attack. See also "NATO Jets Knock Out Base for Serb Planes," *The Stars and Stripes,* 22 November 1994, 1–2.

24. Holbrooke interview, side A, index 567.

25. Yasushi Akashi to Radovan Karadzic, letter, 10 December 1994.

26. Smith presentation, index 1080–1105.

27. Holbrooke interview, side A, index 029–040.

28. Headquarters Allied Forces Southern Europe, CINSOUTH OPLAN 40101, "Deny Flight," change four, 3 May 1993. (Secret) Information extracted is unclassified.

29. Hunter interview, side B, index 035; and idem, tape 2, side A, index 2835.

30. Briefing, Lt Gen Hal Hornburg to BACS team, Air Force Wargaming Institute, Maxwell AFB, Ala., 14 March 1996. General Hornburg was deputy commander of 5 ATAF and director of the CAOC at the time of Deliberate Force.

31. Hunter interview, tape 2, side A, index 949.

32. Ibid., side A, index 1157–1559.

33. James L. Graff, "A Good Season for War," *Time Magazine,* 15 May 1995.

34. Quoted in "Pity the Peacekeepers," *Time Magazine,* 5 June 1995, 39.

35. In November 1995 Adm Leighton Smith reported that the brutality of the Serbian conquest of Srebrenica was the decisive event in bringing the foreign ministers to London. By 14 July, he later reported, he and General Janvier recognized that the "Serbs could walk in and take Zepa," so the focus thereafter and at London was on protecting Gorazde. Smith presentation, index 1570; and Adm Leighton Smith, "Further Comments on 2nd Draft of BACS," fax transmission, 2 August 1997, 1.

36. Admiral Smith reports that he took the ZOA concept to General Joulwan—his commander—and then to NAC in the period after the fall of Srebrenica and after the London conference. With NAC approval in early August and after some discussion, he convinced General Janvier to sign a memorandum of understanding in support of the concept. This took some doing, Smith reported, because the peacekeeping focus of the UN commanders limited their understanding of the utility of air strikes to punishment of only the forces actually violating UNSCRs. Eventually, Smith said, he convinced Janvier that attacks against the "second echelon" of the Serb forces actually would be the better way to secure the safe areas. For this account see Smith's presentation, index 1700–2100. For details of the actual plans developed, see Colonel Campbell's chapter on planning, much of which, unfortunately, remains classified at this writing.

37. For impressions and reportage on the conference, see Michael Evans's two articles in the *London Times* of 22 July 1995: "Muted Threat

Falls Short of Summit Hopes" and "American Deal Sours over Dinner." See also text of Secretary Christopher's speech of 22 July: "The International Conference on Bosnia: Now We Must Act," *U.S. Department of State Dispatch*, 24 July 1995, 583–84.

38. Christopher, 583.

39. This reflects Michael Evans's view in "American Deal Sours."

40. Christopher, 584.

41. Quoted in Evans, "Muted Threat."

42. Evans, "American Deal Sours."

43. Evans, "Muted Threat."

44. NATO, "Press Statement by the Secretary General Following North Atlantic Meeting on 25 July 1995," Brussels, 26 July 1995.

45. Gen George Joulwan, SACEUR, tape-recorded interview by Jerry McGinn, SHAPE, Casteau, Belgium, 24 July 1996, side A, index 832–1128.

46. Gen James L. Jamerson, deputy commander in chief, US European Command, interviewed by author, 23 July 1996. General Jamerson was one of the officers sent, as was Air Marshal William Wratten, CINC of the Royal Air Force's Strike Command.

47. Smith presentation, index 1950–2065.

48. Lt Gen Michael Ryan, Headquarters AIRSOUTH, Naples, Italy, interviewed by Maj Tim Reagan, Air Force Studies and Analysis Agency, and Dr. Wayne Thompson, Center for Air Force History, 18 October 1995.

49. Boutros Boutros-Ghali, UN secretary-general, to Willy Claes, NATO secretary-general, letter, 26 July 1995.

50. Adm Leighton W. Smith Jr., CINCSOUTH, memorandum of understanding with Gen Bernard Janvier, force commander, UNPF, subject: NAC Decisions of 25 July and the Direction of the UN Secretary-General, 10 August 1995.

51. AIRSOUTH, Operation Deliberate Force fact sheet, n.d., 2.

52. For the study, see Col John R. Baker, deputy director of current operations, Headquarters US Air Force, "Report of Assistance Visit to Operation Deny Flight Combined Air Operations Center (CAOC), Vicenza, Italy, 24–30 July 1995."

53. CAOC organization charts exist in several documents collected by the BACS team. For example, see "USAFE's Response to the Balkans Crisis: A Brief History of Operations Provide Promise and Deny Flight," August 1995, AFRHA, BACS file CAOC-24, folder B-1b(2)-3.

54. See Rick Atkinson's "Air Assault Sets Stage for Broader Role," *Washington Post*, 15 November 1995, for an early published account of these events, which Admiral Smith expanded upon in his presentation to Air War College on 9 November 1995. See also Smith, "Further Comments," 2.

55. General Ryan has made these points numerous times, as he did during an interview with the author and Colonel Sargent at Naples. See the author's "Synopsis of Interview of General Michael Ryan, COMAIRSOUTH, AFSOUTH HQ, Naples IT, 1030–1200, Tuesday, 5 Dec 1995," AFHRA, BACS files.

56. AIRSOUTH fact sheet, 2–8.

57. Gen Michael Ryan, Headquarters AIRSOUTH, Naples, Italy, interviewed by author and Richard Sargent, 5 December 1995.

58. For this argument, see Col Trevor N. Dupuy, *A Genius for War: The German Army and General Staff, 1807–1945* (Englewood Cliffs, N.J.: Prentice-Hall, 1977).

59. Maj Gen Charles D. Link, assistant deputy chief of staff, plans and operations, Headquarters USAF, discussion with author on the progress of the BACS study, 28 February 1996.

60. Richardson was both outspoken in his praise of the leadership of Generals Ryan and Hornburg, and in his amazement at how they sustained their workloads. See Col Douglas J. Richardson, transcript of oral history interview by Maj Mark Conversino, Vicenza, Italy, 16 January 1996, AFHRA.

61. Maj Gen Michael C. Short, chief of staff, AIRSOUTH, interviewed by author, Naples, Italy, 4 December 1995.

62. The focus on Aviano was a product of the research time and resources available to the BACS team. Certainly US naval forces and air units of the other participating countries also have stories to tell. Because the BACS had little time to reach out to those forces, the author decided early on to focus the team on Aviano and rely on the US Navy and the other countries to report on their experiences and lessons learned from Deliberate Force.

63. See Colonel Conversino's chapter.

64. Maj Gen Hal Hornburg, director, CAOC, interviewed by author et al., USAF Wargaming Institute, Maxwell AFB, Ala., 14 March 1996; and Conversino.

65. Hunter interview, side A, index 1042–1100.

66. Smith, "Further Comments."

67. For details, see President William Clinton's press statement, "Establishing a Basis for Peace in Bosnia-Herzegovina," *U.S. Department of State Dispatch,* 11 September 1995, 679; and Nelan, 76–77.

68. See Major McLaughlin's chapter on political-military connections in Deliberate Force.

69. For an early expression of Holbrooke's position, see Robert J. Guttman, "Richard Holbrooke," *Europe,* December 1994–January 1995, 12.

70. Steven Greenhouse, "U.S. Officials Say Bosnian Serbs Face NATO Attack If Talks Stall," *New York Times,* 28 August 1995.

71. Hunter interview, side B, index 1114–1300.

72. Kevin Fedarko, "The Guns of August," *Time,* 14 August 1995, 44–46.

73. Karsten Prager, "Message from Serbia," *Time,* 17 July 1995, 24–25.

74. Norman Cigar, "How Wars End: War Termination and Serbian Decisionmaking in the Case of Bosnia," *South East European Monitor,* January 1996, passim.

75. Holbrooke said the relationship between the bombing and diplomacy was an "accident." Negotiations were already under way when the bombing began in response to the Mrkale mortar attack. The conjunction of events "just happened." Holbrooke interview, side A, index 064–080. See also "Silence of the Guns," *Time Magazine,* 25 September 1995, 41, for a journalistic discussion of

the military dilemma presented to the Bosnian Serbs by the conjunction of the bombing and the land war.

76. Holbrooke interview, side B, index 1534. See also Bruce W. Nelan, "Not-So-Rapid Response," *Time,* 19 June 1995, 30.

77. Christopher Hill, transcript of interview by author and Maj Mark McLaughlin, 27 February 1996, 4–5, AFHRA, BACS files.

78. Holbrooke interview, side A, index 001–028, 135–40.

79. Richard Holbrooke, "Annals of Diplomacy: The Road to Sarajevo," *The New Yorker,* 21 and 28 October 1996, 100.

80. Hill interview, 9.

81. Holbrooke interview, side A, index 300–360; and Hill interview, 9–10.

82. Holbrooke, "Annals of Diplomacy," 104.

83. Hunter interview, side A, index 2045–2120, 2245–3100.

84. Holbrooke interview, side A, index 400–413; and idem, "Annals of Diplomacy," 104.

85. Hunter interview, side A, index 2045–2310.

86. Hill interview, 19.

87. Hunter interview, tape 2, side A, index 030–150.

88. Smith, "Further Comments."

89. Holbrooke interview, side A, index 051–058.

90. Ibid., index 369–400, 484–500; and Hunter interview, tape 2, side A, index 800. The BACS team did not attempt to interview the domestic leaders of the NAC member states to determine if they also were prepared to ride out the political repercussions of a major collateral-damage incident.

91. Hunter interview, side A, index 1550–1595, 1800–1815, 2830–3000.

92. Col Douglas Richardson, director of operations, CAOC, said that this deliberation took place as an informal "hallway discussion" between him and "several" other senior CAOC leaders, perhaps including Generals Sawyer and Hornburg. Interviewed by author and Richard L. Sargent, 7 December 1995.

93. Admiral Smith reports that all of these options had drawbacks. As regards adding new option-one and -two targets to the list or revisiting targets, Smith advised his commanders that there were not many left on the existing list that would have enough effect to risk aircrews. Consistent with the opinion of Ambassador Hunter and his own feedback from General Joulwan, Smith did not believe that any political support existed for striking option-three targets. See Smith, "Further Comments"; and Hunter interview, side B, index 1026–1112.

94. Richard Holbrooke, "Comments to 2nd Draft of BACS," 11 July 1997, 2.

95. Gen Michael E. Ryan, discussion during interim briefing of BACS by the author, USAFE/XO conference room, Ramstein AB, Germany, 24 August 1996.

96. Holbrooke, "Comments," 2.

97. As an example of the permeability of NATO security on this issue, *Time Magazine* published an article, clearly written before the results of the 13–14 September meeting were known, noting explicitly that "the allies will run out of so-called Option 2 targets—as early as next week" and that a

decision to move to option three presented NATO with "a problem." See Nelan, "More Talking, More Fighting."

98. Holbrooke interview, side A, index 306–57; and Hill interview, 8.

99. Holbrooke interview, side A, index 104; and Hill interview, 17.

100. Capt Dave Miller, telephone interview by author, 21 March 1996, synopsis in AFHRA, BACS files. The other two liaison officers interviewed were Maj Keith Yockey, who escorted the Croatians, and Maj Mark Dipadua, who escorted the Bosnian Croats and Muslims during the Dayton talks.

101. Stephen T. Hosmer, *Psychological Effects of U.S. Air Operations in Four Wars, 1941–1991: Lessons for U.S. Commanders* (Santa Monica, Calif.: RAND, 1996), 198.

102. Holbrooke interview, side A, index 078.

103. At the time of this writing, the number of casualties caused by Deliberate Force remains uncertain. The BACS team received an unsolicited videotape—"US/NATO Bomb Serb Civilians, 9/95"—that purported to show that civilian casualties and collateral damage were widespread and intentional. The origins of the tape, on file in the BACS archive at AFHRA, are unclear, as is its usefulness as an indicator either of the truth or of general Bosnian Serb perceptions of the intent and impact of the air campaign. Ambassador Christopher Hill recounted to his BACS interviewers that President Milosevic told him that his investigation indicated that about 25 people died as a result of the bombing. Hill interview, 16. This estimate conforms in magnitude with the findings of an investigation conducted by the Red Cross shortly after the bombing, which identified 27 civilian deaths and damage to civilian property as probably caused by the bombing. From the Red Cross's account, it appears that all of these deaths and damages were collateral consequences of attacks on other targets of military significance, including bridges, cantonment areas, a water reservoir, and a former Bosnian Serb field headquarters. International Committee of the Red Cross, "ICRC Report on Certain Aspects of the Conduct of Hostilities and the Consequences from a Humanitarian Point of View of NATO Air Strikes," November 1994, AFHRA, BACS files. What seems reasonable to say, then, is that the 1,026 weapons released during Deliberate Force killed fewer than 30 people.

104. Hunter interview, tape 2, side A, index 2835–2900.

105. Holbrooke, "Comments," 2. One should note that Holbrooke was responding to my initial analysis of this issue, so his assessment rises or falls on the credibility and accuracy of my information and case. I would remain responsible for any error that someone might later prove or attribute to his position.

106. Hunter interview, tape 2, side A, index 113–75.

107. Smith, "Further Comments."

108. Gen Michael E. Ryan, "Further Comments on 2nd Draft of BACS," E-mail message, 20 August 1997.

109. Cigar, passim.

110. Ibid.

111. Hill interview, 19.

Contributors

Col Christopher M. Campbell is director of academics at the NATO School (Supreme Headquarters Allied Powers Europe) at Oberammergau, Germany. He previously served as an instructor in the Joint Doctrine Air Campaign Planning Course and as director of the Information Warfare Division for the College of Aerospace Doctrine Research and Education at Maxwell AFB, Alabama; as deputy chief air liaison element to Headquarters Allied Land Forces Central Europe, in Heidelberg, Germany; as a staff member on the United Nations Protection Force, Zagreb, Croatia; and as chief, War Plans Branch, Headquarters 4th Allied Tactical Air Force, Heidelberg, Germany. He also has held a number of positions in the F-15A community. A command pilot with over twenty-four hundred flight hours, primarily in the F-15A/C and F-4D/E, Colonel Campbell holds a BS in international relations from the United States Air Force Academy and an MBA in management from Golden Gate University. His military education includes Squadron Officer School, Air Command and Staff College, Armed Forces Staff College, and Air War College.

Lt Col Mark J. Conversino is commander of the 93d Maintenance Squadron, 93d Logistics Group, 93d Air Control Wing at Robins AFB, Georgia. He has served as a flight-line maintenance officer; an avionics maintenance supervisor; an assistant professor of history at the United States Air Force Academy; a maintenance operations officer at Fairchild AFB near Spokane, Washington; director of maintenance at Riyadh Air Base, Saudi Arabia; and professor of airpower theory and employment, School of Advanced Airpower Studies, Maxwell AFB, Alabama. Colonel Conversino, who holds a bachelor's degree in history from Eastern Kentucky University as well as a master's degree in US history and a PhD in US political history from Indiana University, is the author of the book *Fighting with the Soviets: The Failure of Operation FRANTIC, 1944–1945* and numerous articles on airpower and defense-related issues.

Lt Col Bradley S. Davis is the senior arms-control policy advisor, Verification and Compliance Division, Arms Control and Disarmament Agency, Washington, D.C. A career missileer and strategic-policy analyst, he has held a variety of positions at operational Minuteman missile wings; Headquarters Strategic Air Command; Headquarters United States Air Force; and recently as Academic Department chairman at Air Command and Staff College, Maxwell AFB, Alabama. He has written extensively on strategic nuclear and conventional arms control and on chemical and biological weapons of mass destruction. He is also coeditor of three textbooks on national security matters published by Macmillan and Air University Press. Colonel Davis holds a BA in history from UCLA and an MS in organizational behavior and human-resource management from Chapman University.

Col Maris "Buster" McCrabb, USAF, Retired, taught economic warfare and campaign planning at Air University's Joint Doctrine Air Campaign Course, Air Command and Staff College, and School of Advanced Airpower Studies, Maxwell AFB, Alabama, from 1992 to 1996. A fighter pilot and Fighter Weapons School graduate, he flew F-4s and F-16s in the United States, United Kingdom, Philippines, and Spain. He saw combat and served as the campaign planner for the 7440th Composite Wing (Provisional), Joint Task Force Proven Force during the Persian Gulf War. One of the Air Force's leading experts on campaign planning, he has published extensively on the subject. Since retiring as chief of the Force Development and Experimentation Division in the Aerospace Command and Control Agency, where he was responsible for the vision, doctrine, education, training, readiness, and new technology to support all Air Force command and control, he has worked for Logicon Advanced Technology, where he is chief of the Advanced Concept Development Division. Colonel McCrabb holds a BA from Bowling Green State University, an MS and MPA from Troy State University, and a DPA from the University of Alabama.

Maj Mark C. McLaughlin is an intelligence officer and chief of the Subcontinent Division at the Joint Intelligence Center Pacific, Pearl Harbor, Hawaii. When he worked on the Balkans

Air Campaign Study, he was chief of Research and Presentations within the College of Aerospace Doctrine Research and Education at Maxwell AFB, Alabama. During his 16-year military career, he has held assignments at the unit, major-command, and Air Staff levels, and served as a communications-electronics officer and a ground launched cruise missile launch-control officer. Major McLaughlin and his wife, Karen, have a son, Matthew.

Dr. Karl Mueller is assistant professor of comparative military studies at the School of Advanced Airpower Studies, Maxwell AFB, Alabama, where he teaches international relations, defense policy, and strategic airpower theory and application. He previously taught at the University of Michigan and Kalamazoo College. He has written articles on a variety of national security topics, including alliance politics, nuclear strategy, deterrence theory, economic sanctions, coercive airpower, and the implications of space weaponization. He is completing a book about the deterrence strategies of European small and middle powers from the 1930s through the cold war. Dr. Mueller received his BA in political science from the University of Chicago and his PhD in politics from Princeton University.

Lt Col John C. "Chris" Orndorff is the chief of Requirements for Headquarters Air Force Office of Special Investigations (AFOSI), Andrews AFB, Maryland. He has served as an instructor at Squadron Officer School and Air Command and Staff College, Maxwell AFB, Alabama; as an AFOSI special agent and detachment commander; and as an administrative officer. He has published articles in *Airpower Journal, TIG Brief, Intercom, Global Reliance,* and *Command.* Colonel Orndorff holds a BA in religion and an MA in humanities from Western Kentucky University.

Col Robert C. Owen (see "About the Editor," p. xv).

Lt Col Robert D. Pollock is deputy program manager for wing/unit command and control (C²) systems, Combat Air Forces C² Systems Program Office, Electronic Systems Center,

Hanscom AFB, Massachusetts. He is responsible for managing the research, development, test, and evaluation as well as supportability of a 31-program portfolio with annual budgets in excess of $60 million annually. He has over 15 years of acquisition experience in fighters, bombers, transports, weapons, missiles, and C² systems. A former director of war theory at Air Command and Staff College, Maxwell AFB, Alabama, Colonel Pollock has published several papers on air campaigning.

Lt Col Ronald M. Reed is staff judge advocate at Pope AFB, North Carolina. He has previously served as an international and operations law attorney with the Office of the Staff Judge Advocate at United States Pacific Command, Camp H. M. Smith, Hawaii; as a deployed staff judge advocate during Operation Desert Storm; and as an instructor at the Air Force Judge Advocate General's School. Colonel Reed received a BS in chemistry from the University of Notre Dame, a JD from De Paul University, and a Master of Airpower Art and Science from the School of Advanced Airpower Studies, Maxwell AFB, Alabama.

Lt Col Richard L. "Hollywood" Sargent is a combat historian at the United States Air Force Historical Research Agency, Maxwell AFB, Alabama. A master weapon systems officer (WSO) with over twenty-three hundred hours of fighter time, he is a graduate of the USAF Fighter Weapons School at Nellis AFB, Nevada. He has written articles on combat air operations in the Gulf War and World War II and is currently working on a monograph dealing with weapons and tactics used in the Balkans air operations. Colonel Sargent holds a BS in business from Florida State University and an MBA from Troy State University.

Index

93, 100–103, 105, 107–8, 110–11,
113–17, 123–24, 126, 134–35, 138,
145, 149, 157, 161, 179–80, 183,
189–91, 193–96, 201, 236, 243,
269–70, 281, 285–86, 289, 291–92,
298–99, 301, 335, 340, 345, 356,
370, 403–4, 406, 409, 414, 418, 433,
435, 438–39, 446, 449–50, 455,
459–61, 466, 468, 472–74, 476–81,
483, 491–97, 500, 502, 506–8,
512–15
Bouton D'or, 136, 309, 327
Boutros-Ghali, Boutros, 39, 41, 56, 92,
472, 474, 476
Brindisi, Italy, 149, 216, 236, 349
British army, 92
Broz, Josip. *See* Tito
Brussels, Belgium, 25, 495
Bulatovic, Momir, 12
Bulgaria, 3
Bush, Dan, 414

Cable News Network (CNN), 159, 292,
361, 368, 410, 412
Calise, Ken, 136, 161, 165
campaign objectives, 350, 506
Carrington, Peter, 12, 15
Carter, Jimmy, 23
casualties, 248, 257, 270, 287–88, 290,
304, 319, 356, 502
cease-fire, 270, 336, 340, 343, 463
center of gravity (COG), 57, 69–70,
72–73, 101, 107, 109, 114, 117,
122–23, 286, 297, 415, 434, 436,
438–40, 442, 444–45, 449–50
Central Intelligence Agency, 182
centralized control, 80, 371
Cervia, Italy, 208, 218, 224
chaff, 213–14, 236, 269
Chambers, James E., 93–94, 469
Chariot (code name), 132, 136, 154,
161–62, 381, 402, 405, 412–13
Checkmate, 55, 98, 102, 281
Chetniks, 3
China, 138
Chirac, Jacques, 25–26
Christopher, Warren, 477, 479, 503–4
Churkin, Vitaly, 21
circular error of probability, 305, 325,
339
Claes, Willy, 41, 56–57, 59, 92, 138–39,
146–47, 397, 403, 480–81, 499
Clark, Wes, 501

Clausewitz, Carl von, 162, 382, 390,
392, 434
Clinton, Bill, 21, 26
close air support (CAS), 19, 21, 24, 41,
56, 59, 75, 79, 97, 100–103, 105–6,
114, 124, 137–38, 144–46, 154–58,
163, 167, 206, 209, 213–14, 216–18,
233, 248–49, 266, 307, 309–10,
316–19, 325, 331, 335, 338, 341,
399, 401–5, 412, 461, 466, 471–72,
474–76, 478, 481
close control, 472, 485–87
coercive-denial model, 448–49
cold war, 4–6, 76–78, 119, 121, 512
collateral damage, 58, 87, 99–100, 106,
109, 111, 115, 125, 136, 144,
150–51, 159–61, 166, 168, 242, 248,
257, 259, 265–66, 270–73, 275,
283–84, 286–87, 290–91, 293, 303–5,
319, 324, 327, 331, 343, 350, 356,
359–60, 370, 372, 399, 402, 405–6,
409–13, 415–16, 419–21, 433–34,
475, 484, 491, 501–2, 506–8, 510
combat air patrol (CAP), 111, 146,
157–58, 206–10, 217–19, 246–47,
307, 310–11, 345–46, 485
combat search and rescue (CSAR), 24,
137, 148–49, 158, 216, 219, 236–37,
307, 331, 335–36, 349, 413–14
combined air operations center (CAOC),
19, 46–52, 54–58, 77, 79–80, 91,
94–95, 97–98, 100–103, 105–6,
109–13, 115, 118–19, 122–25, 132,
134–39, 144–49, 152, 154–63,
165–67, 179–86, 192, 227–29, 235,
238, 243, 246, 266, 290, 298, 306,
309–10, 312, 315–16, 323, 325, 333,
336, 351, 355–65, 367, 370–72, 381,
395, 401, 414–16, 421, 431, 433–34,
449–50, 468–70, 472, 475, 482–83,
487–88, 490, 492, 502, 510–11
combined force air component
commander (CFACC), 87, 91, 94, 98,
109, 113, 124, 178, 200, 222,
246–47, 273, 298, 302, 307, 333,
345, 349
Cominform, 4
command and control (C^2), 37, 46–48,
52, 59, 68–69, 80, 94, 97, 99, 101,
110–11, 117–19, 132–34, 137, 155,
162–63, 167, 235, 275, 280–81,
284–86, 290, 292, 309, 319–20, 324,

531